Creative
Teaching
_in_
Early Childhood
Education

Creative Teaching in Early Childhood Education

A Sourcebook for Canadian Educators and Librarians

Bonnie Mack Flemming
Darlene Softley Hamilton

Donald K. McKay
The School of Early Childhood Education
Ryerson Polytechnic Institute

Songs and Parodies
JoAnne Deal Hicks

With contributions by
Julie Creighton, Canadian Toy Testing Council
Joanne Graham, Librarian, Boys and Girls House, Toronto Public Library
Adele Kostiak, Deputy Chief Librarian, Vaughan Public Library

Harcourt Brace Jovanovich

TORONTO   ORLANDO   SAN DIEGO   LONDON   SYDNEY

Edited by JOYCE M. WILSON, WILSON EDITORIAL SERVICES
Cover and interior design by JACK STEINER GRAPHIC DESIGN
Typeset by COMPUSCREEN TYPESETTING LIMITED
Printed and bound by THE ALGER PRESS

Canadian Cataloguing in Publication Data

Main entry under title:

Creative teaching in early childhood education

ISBN 0-7747-3095-1

1. Education, Preschool—1965-   . 2. Education, Preschool—Activity programs. 3. Teaching—Aids and devices. 4. Creative activities and seat work.   I. Flemming, Bonnie Mack.

LB1140.2.C73 1988   372'.21   C88-093341-0

Printed and bound in Canada
5   92

Acknowledgments and Copyrights

The authors and Harcourt Brace Jovanovich, Canada, thank the individuals and publishers listed below for granting permission to reproduce materials in this book. Every effort has been made to trace the ownership of each selection and to fully acknowledge its use. If any errors remain, they will be corrected in subsequent editions on notification of the publisher. Many of the selections are traditional, with the author unknown.

Textual Material

Thea Cannon, for "The Digger," from *Finger Plays and How to Use Them.* © 1952 by the Standard Publishing Company.

Ebony Jr., for material from "Kwanza Feast," by Sharon Bell Mathis (December 1973); "Gifts of Love," by Norma R. Poinsett and "Candy Maker's Kitchen: Sweet Potato Candy," by Shirley A. Searey (December 1974); and "The Seven Lessons of Kwanza," by Karama Fufuka (December 1975). Permission to adapt granted by *Ebony Jr.*

Lutheran Church in America, for "Guess What?" "Guess Who?" "Hide and Seek," "Hot Potato," "Skip-Stoop," "Together, Together," "Who Am I?" and "The Farmer Plants His Seed," from *The Bible for Three-Year-Olds* (1952); "Picture Card Guess," from *Three-Year-Olds and Jesus* (1954); "Little Friend, Little Friend" and "Look and See," from *Friends of Jesus* (1960); "Bobby Plants His Seed," from *Three-Year-Olds in Summer* (1951); "Match-'Em," "Name It," and "Scramble," from *My Storybook of Jesus* (1956); all by

Darlene Hamilton, published by the Muhlenberg Press, Philadelphia. Used by permission of the Lutheran Church in America.

Oxford University Press, for "Sun, Sun" by Robert Heidbreder, from *Don't Eat Spiders*. © 1985. Oxford University Press, Toronto. Used by permission.

Standard Publishing Company, for "The Digger," by Thea Cannon, and "The Clock" and "The Turkey," by Louise M. Oglevee, from *Finger Plays and How to Use Them*. © 1952. The Standard Publishing Company, Cincinnati, Ohio. Used by permission.

Illustrations

Text illustrations and diagrams drawn by Ric Chin, Marilyn Grastorf, Elsie Halvorsen, Ed Malsberg, Steve Saxe, Bert Schneider, Vladimir Yevtikhiev.

A special thanks to David Mottram (age 5) and Susie Mottram (age 6) for the art on the cover and the part opening pages.

Photo Credits

Greg Beaumont: Pages 10, 14, 15, 16, 17, 25, 26, 30, 33, 37, 46, 52, 55, 56, 69, 73, 117, 144, 169, 203, 237, 239, 274, 323, 349, 381, 467, 540, 542, 559.
Darlene Hamilton: Pages 282, 293.
Donald K. McKay: Pages 61, 131, 385, 412, 465.
J. R. Nollendorfs: Pages 62, 63, 64, 65, 66, 67, 391, 393, 476, 483, 513, 554, 565.
David von Riesen: Pages 60, 521.

To all educators of young children. Your respect for and dedication to children encourages the joy and sense of wonder of childhood.

Preface to the American Edition

Resources for Creative Teaching in Early Childhood Education combines a quick reference for basic information about a great many subjects and a practical, scannable format. It is perforated and three-hole punched so that it can be used in a loose-leaf binder. This affords ease in handling and versatility in sequencing the sections, and allows for inserting additional ideas to tailor the book to each teacher's group and situation. A section of the book describes games, dramatic play props, music and art accessories, and playground equipment that can be inexpensively made by the teacher. Commercial games, records, and their manufacturers, as well as a concise bibliography, are also included. The book deals with a variety of subjects presented as guides and grouped under the general headings Self-Concept, Families, Family Celebrations Throughout the Year, Seasons, Animals, Transportation, and My World. For the most effective use of the book, it is essential that a teacher become familiar with the Guide Outline, p. 1, and Basic Resources for the Teacher, pp. 7–101.

Because it is an accessible reference, this book provides the teacher-aide, the substitute, student, or veteran teacher with the means to fully develop individual and group responses to various learning opportunities. A unique feature of the book is that it integrates curriculum ideas and learning opportunities for a given subject into every part of a day's program. Consequently, children can learn a concept through experiences in many different well-equipped and well-planned environments under the supervision of their teacher.

Another important factor necessary for optimum learning opportunities is a child's own feeling of worth and competence. We feel this positive self-image is fostered when the teacher accepts a child as he or she is, and allows children to grow in creativity and to express their identities without stereotyping by sex, race, religion, economic status, or level of development. We recommend that teachers honestly assess their learning centres, classroom equipment, and teaching program and behaviour to minimize prejudice of any kind. It is our belief that *Resources for Creative Teaching in Early Childhood Education* will provide the basis for teachers to develop in the classroom a world of understanding for living and learning.

Preface to the Canadian Edition

The Canadian edition, *Creative Teaching in Early Childhood Education*, was inspired by Harcourt Brace Jovanovich, Canada, who recognized the need for a Canadian, updated version of this successful American text. The goals of the project were to produce a text for Canadian educators and librarians that would include extensive, readily available resources featuring Canadian content, that would recognize the comprehensive and excellent resources produced in Canada for use by and with young children, and that would bring up to date the material in the original American edition of the book.

The resulting text includes many changes. All resource lists have been updated to ensure that the material cited is currently available. Book lists include titles by publishers from every province in Canada. At the time of printing, every book listed is in print. The Learning, Language, and Readiness Materials Centre lists focus on providing descriptions of ideal materials, rather than listing specific products. It is hoped that this change will help educators find materials in their setting or locality that are readily available. When specific products are suggested, it is to give the educator an example of the type of resource that is useful for the themes under discussion.

Although the thematic approach of the original text has been preserved, the Canadian edition places greater emphasis on cognitive developmental theories. New material in the text also recognizes the multicultural nature of Canadian society. Other modifications to the text reflect current societal attitudes. Throughout the new edition attempts have been made to avoid duplication of theme. For example, elements of the original chapter on food have been introduced into one chapter on taste in Part I, and the chapters formerly entitled Rail Transportation and Road Transportation have been consolidated under the new heading Ground and Road Transportation.

Some highlights of the changes in the book are as follows: Part Two, Families, has been rewritten to reflect contemporary family lifestyles. Materials are presented that are suitable for use with all children, and that respect a variety of family constellations, principles of employment equity, and Canadian approaches to human rights. Part Three, Family Celebrations Throughout the Year, is structured around the calendar. Holidays and celebrations that are likely to be observed by children across the country are identified. Only major celebrations are featured, but it is hoped that the description of these holidays will provide the readers of the book with models for developing other celebrations. Part Four, Seasons, includes activities and ideas that match Canadian weather patterns. In this part and in Part Five, Animals, material has been introduced to meet the needs of educators working in rural and small town settings. Part Five contains additional material on animals that reflects the developmental level of younger children. Parts Six and Seven, Transportation and My World, have been revised extensively so that advances in technology and scientific knowledge are reflected in the text. These chapters have also been revised to match the developmental interests of young children.

In addition, the book now contains detailed tables of contents for each of its seven parts to assist the reader in locating material quickly and easily.

Finally, the Basic Resources section has been fully updated. This section is the key to the text, and all readers are encouraged to read it and the Guide Outline before sampling other parts of the book.

Note to Educators

This book has been prepared to meet the needs of the many educators working in day-care centres, nursery schools, kindergartens, and parent–child programs across the country. In addition to providing you with many specific activities and resources, it is designed to demonstrate current approaches to the education of young children. The curriculum strategies in this book are designed to allow maximum flexibility in planning, so that your program will meet the developmental needs of all the children with whom you work. The book is intended as a reference that you can consult whenever you are planning activities for children.

Note to Librarians

This book will be a useful resource for the many librarians who are running varied and excellent programs for young children across the country. In addition to providing you with many specific activities and resources, this book demonstrates current approaches to working with young children. We hope that you will be able to benefit from our models in developing your own programs and in meeting the developmental needs of all the children with whom you work. The book may also be useful to librarians in selecting titles for their collections.

The users of *Creative Teaching in Early Childhood Education* can contribute to the improvement of the book in subsequent editions by sending their comments and suggestions to Donald McKay in care of the publisher. Such letters are invaluable, and we will look forward to receiving them.

Acknowledgments

This Canadian edition, *Creative Teaching in Early Childhood Education*, has been developed from the original U.S. edition prepared by Bonnie Mack Flemming, Darlene Softley Hamilton, and JoAnne Deal Hicks. We are greatly indebted to these authors, for the original book contained such fine material that it was always a pleasure to work from their text. The many people who contributed to the original edition are acknowledged in that book.

The Canadian project was inspired, shaped, and guided by Heather McWhinney of Harcourt Brace Jovanovich, Canada. Without Heather's enthusiasm, energy, and support, this edition would never have been completed. We are also indebted to our editor, Joyce Wilson, who worked so effectively to improve the organization and readability of our manuscript. Special thanks go to my colleague and friend Gary Woodill, who suggested and encouraged my involvement in this edition. Julie Creighton, Joanne Graham, and Adele Kostiak's contributions to the early drafts of the book were invaluable. Thanks are insufficient for all the work they have put into this project. The co-operation and support of colleagues at Ryerson Polytechnical Institute is appreciated. Special thanks are due to Margaret McKay, John McKay, the Denis family, and Jim Laughlin for believing in my ability and tolerating the temperamental author.

Donald McKay

Contents

PART *1* **Self-Concept**

PART *2* **Families**

PART 3 Family Celebrations Throughout the Year

PART 4 Seasons

PART 5 Animals

PART 6 Transportation

PART 7 My World

Guide
Outline

The order of the parts of the guide does not imply any prearranged teaching sequence. A logical grouping of subjects under headings such as "Family Celebrations," "Seasons," "Animals," "Transportation," has been made for easier reference.

Basic Understandings

Concepts children can grasp from the subject are written as statements. Choose the simplest statements for the children with the least experience and the statements with more detailed information for the children with previous experience. Some statements contain more than one concept and may be simplified as needed.

Additional Facts the Teacher Should Know

1. Carefully researched information about the subject
2. Precautions about the subject or activities
3. Care and maintenance of materials, equipment, plants, or animals

Methods Most Adaptable for Introducing this Subject to Children

A conversation, story, picture, special event, shared item, visitor, or trip may be the stepping-stone to the subject. Your choice will depend on:

1. Your children's previous experiences
2. Your children's most recent interests
3. The season, the weather, staff skills, and community resources

Vocabulary

1. Create a basic list of new words to be discovered while exploring the subject
2. Add familiar words within your group's previous experiences

Learning Centres

Discovery Centre

First-hand experiences to help the children grasp the basic concepts include:

1. Physics and chemistry experiments, including cooking
2. Exploring nature—plants, animals, and the five senses
3. Exploring our world—sun, water, air, soil, rocks
4. Books and magazines with pictures that show discovery concepts to the children

Dramatic Play Centres

Suggestions are included here for encouraging children to play out learning experiences related to this subject in the sections on Home-living centre, Block-building centre, and other Dramatic Play Centres (see "Basic Resources," p. 14). Select ideas considering your own equipment, space, budget, community resources, and the creative interest and ability of your staff.

Learning, Language, and Readiness Materials Centre

Included here are manipulative, language, and cognitive materials related to learning new concepts and to making thinking judgments such as colours, shapes, numbers, spatial relationships, and classifications. These materials are divided into two sections:

1. *Commercially made games and materials.* Listed are types of manipulative and cognitive materials that are available commercially and criteria for choosing them. As suppliers vary so widely across the country, it was decided to include criteria for choice and examples that meet the criteria, rather than listing specific equipment and manufacturers. Most of these items are included in educational catalogues and many are sold in good independent toy stores.
2. *Teacher-made games and materials.* Suggestions are included for teacher-made cognitive materials. Variations of learning games are described in the "Basic Resources," p. 50.

Art Centre

It is assumed that basic art media are offered on a daily basis in your art centre (see "Basic Resources," p. 27). Variations of the basic media and special activities related to each subject are included. Asterisks serve as a guide to the selection of experiences for your group:

- • Youngest and least skilled
- •• More skilled
- ••• For the most experienced child

Experiences are grouped as follows:

1. Creative art experiences, which include painting, crayoning, molding and sculpturing, cutting and pasting, collage, printing, mixed media
2. Other experiences in the art centre using art media include creating objects or materials to be used for games, as dramatic play props, as gifts, or for teaching skills

Book Centre

Books here are to be explored by children individually or read to one or two children by a teacher or aide (see "Basic Resources," p. 54). Listed alphabetically by author, the books are coded by text length, type of illustration, concept level, and the age and experience of children.

- • Assumes no previous exposure; brief text and simple illustrations
- •• Assumes some previous exposure; longer text and simple illustrations
- ••• Assumes much previous exposure; longer text and more detailed illustrations
- •••• More informative text and excellent illustrations (often photographs); read or read-tell; use primarily in the discovery centre or as a basis for a language or cognitive experience

Planning for Group Time

The following suggestions may be used when children are gathered in small groups of three to seven, or larger groups when everyone is involved. Your group size will vary with the interest and maturity of the children, the number of children enrolled, and the size of your staff.

Music

1. Original songs will be listed by title and page number.
2. Parodies are included to supplement your music library program.
3. Copyrighted songs from Core Library music books, pp. 76–77, are listed by title and page number for easy reference.
4. Records are listed by artist, title, and recording company.
5. Rhythms and singing games are listed in the same manner as songs.

Fingerplays and Poems

1. Original or traditional fingerplays and poems are written out with actions.
2. Copyrighted material from Core Library books, p. 76, is listed by title and page number for easy reference.

Stories

(To read, read–tell, or tell to a group)
This section gives suggestions for how one or two books from the book centre list may be used for storytelling. For suggestions on storytelling see "Basic Resources," pp. 48–49.

Games

Games in this section can be played successfully with children in a small or large group at a together time. Some of these games may have been listed under teacher-made games (for an explanation, see the section on "Learning Games," pp. 50–59. *Flannelboard ideas*, when used, will be noted in the appropriate sections depending on their use: to illustrate a song, to illustrate a story, fingerplay, poem, or game, or when used with an individual child. For instructions on how to make and use flannelboards, see "Basic Resources," pp. 45–48.

Routine Times

Suggestions are made for capitalizing on teachable moments during routine times. Appropriate activities for learning concepts related to a subject are listed to use during snack time, meal time, toileting, resting, dressing, transitions, or in transit (busing or walking).

Large Muscle Activities

These suggestions will primarily be used outdoors (see playgrounds, p. 60). When the weather is unsuitable, use a basement, gym, or other large space indoors (see p. 68). Circle games, direction games, and problem-solving games described in the "Basic Resources," pp. 54–59, will be included as appropriate.

Extended Experiences

Suggestions are noted for utilizing trips, visitors, films, and other special experiences to extend children's knowledge of a subject (see "Basic Resources," pp. 70–72).

Teacher Resources

Pictures and Displays

Ways are suggested for creating your own bulletin boards or displays. Ideas are given for rearranging the room to best use the materials suggested.

Books and Periodicals

These are primarily teacher references, but some of the resources may be materials for older children which the teacher or librarian could adapt for use with young children. See the discussion on developmentally appropriate material on pp. 2–3.

Films and Videos

This section lists material that can be used in support of your program.

Community Resources and Organizations

This section lists people, places, groups, associations, and things in your community that may assist you in planning your program.

Government Agencies

This section lists various government agencies that supply materials that will assist you in program planning.

Basic Resources for the Teacher

Contents

Basic Resources for the Teacher

Good Curriculum Planning

1. Begin with a basic knowledge of how young children grow, develop, and learn.
2. Recognize that children learn best
   a. when they have a good self-image and are accepted as they are by both adults and other children.
   b. if given repeated opportunities to discover, explore, be challenged, and problem-solve through direct experiences.
   c. when given diverse choices that can lead to independence, self-confidence, self-control, and a sense of responsibility.
   d. through a rich environment that considers their total development and each one's individual needs and interests.
   e. when supervised by adult facilitators who protect and ensure each child's rights without sacrificing any individual child's right to the freedom to learn.
3. Provide and allow for a balance of activities:
   a. Structured/unstructured
   b. Informative/creative
   c. Active/quiet
   d. Indoor/outdoor
   e. Observing/participating
   f. Alone/together
4. Capitalize on the individual strengths of the staff and the assets offered by parents and community.
5. Recognize weaknesses of each member of the staff and plan for individual personal growth. Constantly search for new ideas and for ways of improving teaching skills by encouraging the staff to:
   a. Read—refer to Core Library for suggested resources.
   b. Visit other centres.
   c. Share ideas and problems with other early childhood educators.
   d. Attend workshops.
   e. Invite resource people from the community.
   f. Involve parents as teachers and planners.
   g. Join a professional organization such as the Canadian Association for Young Children or the Council for Exceptional Children.

Short and Long Range Planning with Staff

All planning should be based on the developmental needs of the children in your centre. It is critical that the strengths and needs of the children be the main criteria for deciding if an aspect of the program is appropriate. Your child or human development text is a major support for program planning. A number of resources that describe programs based on developmental needs are listed on p. 74, as are a few human development texts.

1. Block out a general program by the year/month/week/day:
   a. Choose subject guides as aids, considering the need for repetition and the particular interests, needs, and experience of your group.
   b. Study your overall plan to determine the equipment and materials most necessary for carrying out your projected plans.
   c. Familiarize yourself with this Basic Resources section for ways your staff can augment your budget and extend the educational opportunities offered.
   d. Expand your resources by purchasing some of the recommended Core Library books on music, songs, fingerplays, and poems, pp. 76–77.
   e. Make a plan for starting or supplementing your art, music, science, fingerplay, and other idea files. Encourage input by all members of the staff and the parents.
   f. At appointed intervals evaluate your daily plans, noting recommendations for the future. Modify and adapt the plans for use again with another group at another time.
   g. Organize the teacher storage space and maintain it by periodic reorganization. Repair and replace or duplicate items most needed and used.
2. Make a detailed program plan for the week:
   a. Consider every learning centre in the classroom and each time segment of the day.
   b. Make special plans for individual children; be selective in choice of materials and ideas you will present by considering each child's need, abilities, and interests.
   c. Build on previous experience of the children. Cross references in this book will help you plan related experiences.
   d. Gather materials needed.
   e. Try out recipes, patterns, ideas, or experiments in advance, especially foods, arts, and science.
   f. Be flexible—be ready to change plans, expand or substitute, as moments of readiness are identified.
   g. Anticipate the need for alternative plans. Consider change of weather, shortage of staff, personal crises, and limitations of plant space because of multiple uses of a facility.
   h. Consider and plan for special needs requiring more staff, special equipment, materials, visitors, trips, and safety supervision.
   i. Define and assign specific responsibilities to staff members. Outline ways in which volunteers may be enlisted to assist. Encourage substitutes (volunteers and parents) to attend staff planning meetings for better continuity.
   j. Each staff member should be encouraged to accept a learning centre, a routine time, or a program activity for which she or he is totally responsible.
3. Make your plans unique:
   a. Be selective—choose only those basic understandings and curriculum ideas that meet the needs of your children as reflected by their ability, previous experience, opportunity, ethnic culture, geographic environment, and economic situation.
   b. Choose ideas for development that best fit your teaching philosophy, style, and skills, and about which you can be most enthusiastic.
   c. Adapt to the potential and the limits of your type of program, length of school day, total physical environment, and community resources.

NOTE: This resource is not all inclusive; you should continue to add your own ideas. It is unlikely, and inappropriate, that you will use all the materials and activities suggested under any one subject with any one child or group.

Learning Centres

Learning centres are areas in a school or a classroom that define a special focus or that afford a specific opportunity not otherwise possible. Centres often planned for young children may include a discovery centre; dramatic play centres including a home-living centre, a block-building centre, and other dramatic play centres; a learning, language, and readiness materials centre; an art centre; a book centre; a music centre; and a centre for large muscle activities. Space for sleeping, resting, and eating, apart from the above or in a multiple use of the above, may also be provided as needed.

These centres divide a school or a classroom in such a way as to allow children to make choices, to move freely and independently, and to grow in areas of need. They also give opportunities for a large number of children to learn individually or in smaller groups so that the teacher can take advantage of moments of readiness, keen interest, and desire. In a more structured grouping, these activities might not otherwise be possible.

The child can be invited into the mainstream of learning in the least coercive way. The shy child may choose to enter a quiet corner and pursue learning in his or her own way, while another child, who seeks and needs companionship, can join a co-operative play group such as dramatic play or a group playing a learning game that requires several participants. A child with a keen interest and/or an ability in art or science may wish to begin the day in an area where he or she feels more confident, comfortable, and eager.

Learning centres tend to invite a child to come and see, come and do, come and learn. A wise staff is alert to the responsibility to invite, guide, and encourage children to explore all the centres and ultimately learn in several. The staff should offer enough opportunities to learn concepts so that, whether a child selects one centre or another, the end result will be the learning necessary for that particular child's growth. By helping each child find that there are alternative ways of learning the same thing, the child will discover what is the best way for him or her to learn.

Room arrangements, materials and equipment, staff, and concepts to be learned will all influence the organization of a good learning environment for young children. By setting up a series of centres within this environment, you can provide opportunities

1. for children to make choices.
2. for children to discover and learn through direct experience.
3. for children to gain self-confidence and competence as a result of learning skills.
4. to help children enlarge their vocabularies and to help them develop skills in communicating their ideas through the creative use of language, materials, and equipment.
5. for imaginative dramatic play through role playing.
6. for children to learn to think and to problem-solve by using a variety of materials.
7. for children to develop physical and motor skills—co-ordination and manipulation—as they use the equipment.
8. for children to develop socially as they learn to relate to others.
9. for children to share and to be responsible to others as members of a group.
10. for children to use and care for materials and equipment.
11. for children to complete tasks and to plan group projects.
12. for children to discover and expand their learning of specific information relating to a subject.

Some considerations in planning for centres

1. Space (floor, table, display, and storage)
2. Light, ventilation, heat
3. Exits, entrances, and traffic patterns
4. The number of children, their interests, abilities, and needs
5. Availability of enough sturdy, safe, multipurpose equipment and materials

6. Size of budget for additions to basic equipment, supplementing with homemade and donated or recycled materials
7. Number of staff (permanent and volunteer)
8. Length of school day, program services offered, size and form of the physical plant
9. Availability of an extended classroom space such as a gym, park, or outdoor yard

Remember, providing a rich environment is not enough. Adults must be facilitators, participants, and supervisors interacting with the children, other staff members, and the environment (see pp. 100–101 for specific suggestions).

Arrange centres in such a manner as to allow easy supervision (viewing) by staff from strategic spots without limiting the children's use of materials. There are times when a teacher may need to supervise several centres alone, such as the beginning or the end of each day. Therefore, at times, some centres may need to be closed or "off limits." If so, make the alternatives challenging, interesting, and exciting.

Discovery Centre

Guidelines for teaching science in the discovery centre

1. Encourage each child to observe keenly:
   a. What do you see?
   b. What is it like?
2. Invite each child to think by posing such questions as:
   a. Why do you suppose?
   b. What do you think?
   c. What might happen if?
   d. How can we find out?

Science corner of the discovery centre. A table in the science corner will allow children to take information books or science materials, such as the ear of Indian corn, from the supply shelf for closer scrutiny. Note the box used for storage.

3. Help each child to look for explanations.
4. Encourage each child to grow and know. Invite and listen to his or her questions. Help the child to discover misconceptions.
5. Give each child a variety of experiences. Provide a well-balanced program using:
    a. Living things—plants, animals—to illustrate growth and life
    b. Matter and energy—heat, wind, electricity, sound, motors, fire, magnetism, cooking
    c. The earth and its elements—rocks, soil, sand, metals, water, air
    d. Regions beyond the earth—sun, moon, stars, outer space
6. Give each child an opportunity to discover. Provide the necessary equipment and materials that will make experimentation and discovery possible (see lists below).
7. Repeat experiences; relate to what else the child is doing and learning; give opportunities for progressive learning.
8. Use a variety of media: real specimens, models, filmstrips, pictures, resource persons, and trips that allow for direct observation and experimentation.
9. Develop in the child a respect for all living things.
10. Give cautions regarding safety in the use of equipment.

NOTE: You don't need elaborate equipment. Observe nature: water, shadows, sun, sky, earth. You can do many things with only a magnifying glass, measuring cup, and a ruler.

Discovery centre equipment

A quiet centre should be planned where discoveries and exploration of materials can be made by individuals and small groups of children. A closet or ample cupboard space to store equipment is needed. The centre should be furnished with shelves, a variety of containers, small tables, nooks, and a few comfortable chairs or cushions. Items that will be referred to in the book include:

METRIC AND IMPERIAL MEASURING DEVICES

mass/weight—balance pans; bathroom, kitchen, and spring scales
area/length—measuring tape, ruler, metric stick
fluid volume—litre, quart, pint, measuring cup, and measuring spoons
temperature—centigrade and Fahrenheit thermometer

SPECIMENS

rocks, minerals, fossils, gems	seashells	coconut shells
halite (salt in original form)	sponges	corn, wheat, other seeds
wool (raw, carded, spun, dyed)	driftwood	bird nests, eggs
cotton ball, thread, cloth	feathers	butterflies, moths
silkworms (preserved), cocoons	animals	flowers, growing plants
leaves (pressed in wax paper)	insects	

DISCOVERY AIDS

magnifying glasses (tripod and hand)	electric clock	switch box
magnets (horseshoe and bar)	colour paddles	binoculars
simple machines or tools (pulleys	globe	telescope
with rope and chains, wheels,	tuning fork	flashlight
wedges, screws, levers, springs)	mirrors	microscope
dry-cell battery	prisms	stethoscope
animal cages (with exercise wheel	ant farm	telephone
or chambers and tunnels to allow	compass	terrarium
small animals to exercise)	cheesecloth	vivarium
vases, pots, bowls	rubber tubing	aquarium

Storage

One key to taking advantage of a spontaneous interest in science or to responding to that teachable moment is *accessibility* of resources. Science trays, such as illustrated on p. 15, allow for stacking and compact storage. Fruit shipping cartons with rope handles are easily transported. Cover top half of carton with a large plastic bag to keep it airtight; the other half (bottom) can be used as another tray. Label the side for quick identification of items sought. Other suitable storage boxes for smaller items include see-through unbreakable plastic boxes and shoe boxes, available from most department stores. These sometimes are colour-coded, which may help you with your storing by categories.

ITEMS FOR TRAY STORAGE

shapes—circle, square, triangle, star, ellipse, oval or egg shape, rectangle, octagon
leather and fur—sheepskin, suede, cowhide, etc; good sources are gloves, purses, shoes, and scraps from leather shops

Science opportunities are everywhere—what can children discover?

1 Under or beside a rock or a log?

slugs	insects	damp soil
snails	worms	mushrooms, toadstools
toads	lizards, snakes	moss
turtles	small animals	

2 On a sidewalk?

footprints	grass or weeds in cracks	sections to count
wet leaves/leaf prints	ice, snow, puddle of water	a game marked with
ants	crevices	chalk
		worms after rain

3 On, in, or under a tree or a bush?

nuts	crevices	small animals
fruit	holes	toadstools
birds	knots	protection from rain for
insects	branches	people and animals
flowers	twigs	designs and shapes made
pinecones	sap	by shadows and
bark	nests	formation of branches

4 In or near a pond or a lake?

cattails	fish	turtles
water lilies	minnows	crayfish
swans	insects	mud
ducks	leaves, seeds	rocks, stones
snakes	algae	place for birds, animals
skunks	twigs	to find water for
elephant's-ear plant	grass, moss	drinking and bathing
reflection of yourself	frogs, tadpoles	

colour—include prisms, coloured glasses, colour paddles and paint, carpet and upholstery samples in primary and secondary colours (see colour guide, p. 525)

wood—include crosscuts of a tree and a limb, wood shavings, shingles, sawdust, plywood, samples of various colours and grains of wood, bark, toys and utility items made of wood

tree, flower, fruit, and vegetable seeds —place in closed, clear, unbreakable containers (pill bottles)

nest and broken (bird) eggshells—have donor help you label the type of bird by location of nest; include a picture of the bird with its nest or a birdhouse

plumbing equipment—include faucets, elbows, T's, adapters, long and short lengths of pipe; check with plumbing companies for supplies

lock box—padlock, chain lock, cupboard latch

NOTE: See also the specimens listed on the previous page for many more items that can be stored in trays.

---

5 At the beach?

sand	driftwood	crabs
seagulls	seaweed	clams
water	insects and bugs	
seashells	fish	

6 In a pile of soil?

insects	worms	different colours of soil
seeds	rocks, pebbles	gravel, sand

7 In a garden or on a lawn?

turtles	birds	grasses
dandelion and other seeds	bunnies	feathers
anthill	bird feeder and a birdbath	worms
four-leaf clovers	kitchen garden	insects
colours	flowers	slugs

8 In the centre, school, or library?

conservation	how colours are made
how foods are made	how sound is produced
gravity	texture
weight	how light works

Exploring and discovery experiences. The child on the left is filling and measuring cornmeal, which is a good substitute for sand. Measuring spoons and cups are excellent additions to this discovery activity (see mathematics guide, p. 551). The child on the right is discovering rock and mineral specimens hidden in a box of fine sand. Other possibilities for hidden treasures are shells and driftwood pictured under the tripod magnifying glass. Children will also enjoy using these treasures to create designs in their miniature sandbox.

> **NOTE:**   the sandbox is contained in a second box to minimize spilling, and the cornmeal in a tight-lidded container for storage.

Dramatic Play Centres

Home-living centre

1. Set up in an accessible, contained area. If adjacent to the block-building centre or special dramatic play centres, it will allow interaction and co-operative play.
2. Arrange to duplicate (simulate) a real home. Set the scene by posting pictures and putting out accessories to develop interest and related play.
3. Keep orderly—clothes clean and mended and equipment repaired. Orderliness invites constructive use.
4. Equipment should be sturdy enough for group use, large enough for a child to use by himself or herself.

5. Post rules and suggestions for guiding or modifying behaviour such as:
   a. Mops stay on the floor, brooms are for sweeping.
   b. It is easier to walk when the floors are clear.
   c. Food should stay on the table, in the cupboards, or in the pans on the stove.
   d. Dolls, doll clothes, dishes should be kept off the floor (except for picnics).
   e. If the family is too large, invite a child or several children to participate in another activity or encourage them to build another house, sharing the furniture.
   f. Help a child to join the group by asking if the family could use a grandmother or an uncle.
   g. All members of the family should help to keep the house clean and neat.
6. Avoid or monitor the use of shared accessories that might pose a health hazard, for example, combs, wigs, pacifiers, teething rings, or silverware.
7. Rotate (remove or add) special items to renew interest in the centre and encourage an expanded use of basic equipment.
8. Support the children's right to reflect a nonsexist viewpoint toward dramatic play roles chosen by themselves or others in dramatic play.

Home-living dramatic play centre. Individual servings of food have been cut from magazines and TV-dinner cartons, glued to corrugated cardboard, and laminated with clear contact. Eggs are of unbreakable plastic or lathed out of wood and painted white. The plastic fruit has been filled with sawdust and glue and allowed to harden, which makes it more durable. The flower vase is made of two particle-board roll-ends glued together to hold a bouquet of artificial flowers. Roll-ends are available from small print shops, newspaper printers, and from doctors' offices.

Block-building centre. Children are constructing a building using hollow cardboard blocks and plastic and rubber tools. Note their resourceful use of a lunch box as a tool kit. The hard hat in foreground is an authentic prop; the one on child's head is available commercially.

Block-building centre

NOTE: Low-pile carpeting reduces the noise level.

1. Allow enough space away from the classroom traffic ways.
2. Arrange blocks according to shape and size so they are accessible on the shelves.
3. Provide sufficient accessory toys to expand and develop broader use of blocks as interest development demands. Remove those not needed.
4. Station teachers near the centre so they can assist with supervision.
5. Chalked boundaries on the floor will prove helpful in insuring property rights.
6. Label buildings for children so they will become interested in language.
7. To prevent hoarding, limit the number of blocks accumulated by one child before construction begins.
8. Pick up or help pile stray blocks that may otherwise bother the construction and/or movement of other children. Keep area clean, orderly, and all equipment in good repair.
9. Expand interests with the use of books, excursions, pictures, and other aids.

10. Post rules and suggestions for guiding or modifying behaviour, such as:
    a. We build with blocks.
    b. We need an open path to the block shelves. Invite children to build away from the shelves.
    c. Put blocks that are alike together when picking them up. Remember that teachers and others can help in the clean-up task.
    d. Build no higher than your chin. (This rule keeps child visible and gives child a measurement for safety.)
    e. Encourage children to build with blocks *before* using accessories. It will encourage more constructive and creative uses of both.

    NOTE: An exception might be a new, shy, or insecure child who may wish to hold an accessory while observing or before joining play.

Dramatic play props

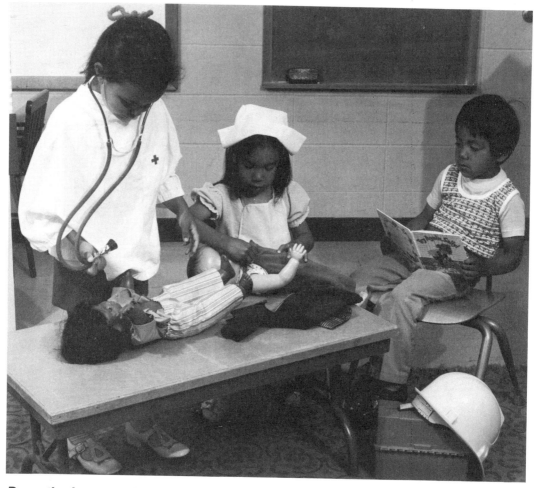

Dramatic play props. A man's shirt worn backwards can be a doctor's shirt, as above, or a male nurse's outfit. Male nurses do not wear caps, they wear a pin. The pin can be made from two small pieces of press-on or iron-on red tape. See p. 21 for suggestions on altering helper shirts, and p. 22 for the apron pattern (worn by the seated girl in this photo).

Collect dramatic play props

▷ **Letter carrier**

hat (see p. 468)
stamps
mailbag
mailbox
letters
packages
money
rubber stamps
cash drawer

▷ **Railway worker (engineer, brakeman, conductor, porter, dispatcher)**

lunch bucket
overalls
ticket punch
coloured tickets
lantern (without glass)
hat (see p. 22)
watch
pillows
luggage
trays
chef's hat
neckerchief

▷ **Ranch hand**

hat
chaps
rope
bolero
stickhorse
neckerchief

▷ **Grocery clerk**

apron
vendor's hat (see p. 23)
baskets
play money
cash register
food cartons, boxes
pad and pencil
shopping bags
shelves
plastic or papier-mâché fruits and vegetables

▷ **Pilot/flight attendant**

cap
airplane
steering wheel (see p. 467)
serving trays
travel folders
packing-box cockpit
walking-board
wing

▷ Baker

hat (see p. 23)
pans
apron
rolling pin
wooden spoons
plastic bowls
cookie cutters

▷ Fisherman

net
cardboard for oars
poles with string,
    spools
paper, cardboard,
    or plastic fish
box for boat
styrofoam packing
    worms

▷ Circus performers/ workers

tickets
crepe paper to
    decorate
    wheels
black hat for
    ringmaster
crazy hats,
    costumes, and
    ruffled collars
    for clowns
cardboard cartons
    cut to resemble
    cages with
    bars
stands for animals
    to perform on
white hats for
    popcorn
    vendors (see p.
    23)

▷ Painter

cap
paintbrushes
bucket and water

▷ Sanitary engineer

sacks
garbage cans
wagons

▷ Firefighter

hose
wagon
ladder
rubber or
    cardboard
    hatchet
hat (see p. 468)

▷ Service station attendant

oil can
cap
flashlight
rubber hose
    lengths
rope (short
    lengths)
sponge and
    bucket
rubber or soft
    plastic tools
cash register
credit cards
play money

▷ Police officer

hat
badge
tickets
licence
traffic signs
handcuffs
keys to jail
pencil and pad

▷ Doctor, nurse, nursing attendant

nurse's cap
tape, cotton
pad and pencil
two telephones
kit or bag
thermometer
    container
sunglasses
    (without
    lenses)
unbreakable
    supplies (pill
    bottles)
bandages (strips
    of sheeting)
stethoscope
baby scale
tape measure or
    height chart

Adapt dramatic play props

▷ **Save accessories**

length of hose (protect nozzle or
 remove; a bicycle handle grip
 makes a good nozzle)
empty oil cans
empty food containers
paper punch or empty stapler
buckets and brushes
pads and pencils
rubber stamp with handle

▷ **Make your own**

temporary props of paper or
 cardboard: hat bands, money,
 signs
fishing poles, smokestacks, and oars
 can be made of empty upholstery
 rollers
enlist aid of volunteers to sew simple
 cloth hats such as bakers' hats,
 engineers' caps, scarves, stoles,
 shortened skirts with elastic
 waistbands, white bib aprons
 using elastic instead of ties (see
 patterns, p. 22)

▷ **Build equipment**

mount laundry, fat, or flour barrels
 for tunnel or airplane (add wings)
 (see illustration, p. 65)
use empty cartons, tote boxes, pop
 cartons, tile boxes, desk cartons,
 large florist cartons
use discarded tires for swings,
 climbers, or tunnels
mount a wheel for a multiple-use
 vehicle

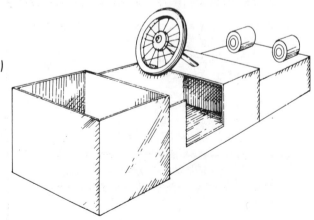

▷ Alter helper shirts

cut off sleeves

reverse collars

adjust neck buttons and sew on a
large button

helper shirts that are often available:
letter carrier; work shirt; white or
pastel shirts for doctors, orderlies,
nursing attendants; lab or
pharmacist coats; nurses' outfits
(see illustration, p. 17)

grocery or ice cream aprons can be
made with elastic neck straps and
an elastic waist in back (see
pattern, p. 22)

▷ Collect real helper hats

discontinued or damaged letter
carrier's cap

paint cap (free at a paint dealer)

sailor's hat

nurse's cap

construction hard hat

old felt or straw hat

bright coloured woman's hat, turban,
scarf

service station attendant's hat, cap

chef, firefighter, or police officer's hat

Patterns for dramatic play props

NOTE: Seam allowance measurements included
for all patterns.

Mail bag

Cuff open edge of large paper sack with a
strip of cardboard folding top edge of sack
twice over cardboard for durability. Staple
ends of strap on inside of sack as shown in
diagram.

NOTE: Strap must be attached to opposite
side.

Train engineer's cap

Take overlapping tucks at points A-AB-B, C-CD-D, E-EF-F, and so on, and then gather remaining shape into headband. Attach bill at one of the short sides and line with dark upholstery or plastic for sturdiness.

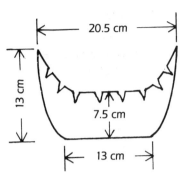

Cut two 5 cm x 58 cm bands with 2 cm slashes on inside edge of bill (finished bill 5.5 cm deep)

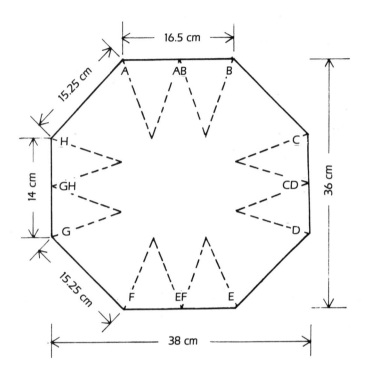

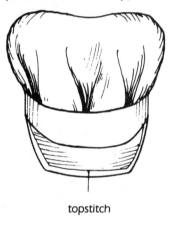

topstitch

Grocer's apron

Use 28 cm elastic for neck and 18 cm elastic for waist. Bottom hem is indicated by dotted lines. Attach elastic at neck and waist. Allow for other hems when cutting; measurements are finished size.

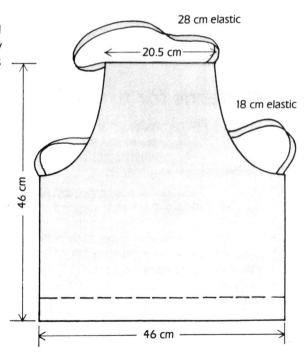

Baker's hat

Gather a circle 53 cm in diameter onto a double band about 46 cm long and 2.5 cm wide. When circle is completely gathered into headband, insert a 5 cm long piece of wide elastic as shown above. Allow for adjustment to various head sizes.

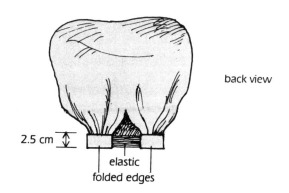

back view

2.5 cm

elastic
folded edges

Food vendor's hat

Sew two of part A pieces together around curve between points **abcd** leaving straight edges at **bd** open. Sew other two part A pieces in same manner, turn inside out to form lining for first crown. Cut two of part B, open both pieces out flat. Sew together (one on top of other), bind top edges with bias tape, and leave straight edges open. Insert straight open edges of brim into open ends of both crown and lining at circumference of **bd** (headband). Top stitch, tuck in raw edges.

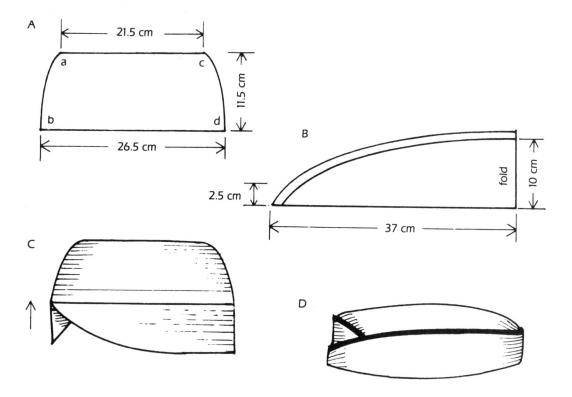

Cardboard and cartons

The common box or carton can offer an endless number of possibilities for temporary equipment. Students in a Headstart Supplementary Training Program (U.S.) once pooled their ideas and listed 100 uses for cartons in an early childhood education centre. Here are a few of those ideas.

Home-living centre

1. *Stoves:* Make from sturdy rectangular boxes about 60 to 80 cm high. Paint circles for burners. Attach wooden beads or knobs on the front of the carton for heat selector dials. Secure them with plastic-coated wire and a disc of plastic on *both* sides of the cardboard to prevent tearing. Cut a three-sided opening for a door and use masking tape to reinforce the fold instead of a hinge. Insert an inverted box inside for an oven floor. To make a latch, hook a yarn loop on a button that has been secured with plastic discs on both sides of the cardboard.
2. *A doll's bed:* Make from a shallow box of appropriate size. Turn the top flaps to the inside of the carton and secure by stapling, sewing, or tying the flaps down. Use a pillow for a mattress and cover it with sheets or a blanket.
3. *Tote box:* Make as for bed except add rope loops for handles. Paint it for greater durability and attractiveness.
4. *Partition or room divider:* Use three sides of a large desk, stereo, or cupboard carton to make a three-way play screen. Cut an opening for a door or window in one section. Can be painted or wallpapered.
5. *As a mailbox:* Paint rectangular cardboard boxes red to resemble mailboxes.
6. *Shelves and a cupboard:* Set cartons inside other cartons.
7. *To make a desk or dressing table:* Invert a carton, open-end down. Cut open one side for kneehole space. Cut like a T and fold back to reinforce opening. It can also be used as a fireplace.
8. *For a television:* Cut a hole in the bottom of a carton to form a frame then turn the carton on its side.
9. *To make a table:* Turn a carton upside down; reinforce it; then leave two sides open.

Block-building centre

1. *Suitbox:* Make cardboard highway sections to use with proportional blocks and cars. Use proportional double longs, Y and X shapes, arches and curves as guides and make your cardboard road segments double size for two-lane traffic. Line a median strip on each. Let children lay out these cardboard roadways and save the blocks for buildings along the highway.
2. *Tabletop play board:* Use a double section of a mattress, stereo, or pool-table carton. Hinge in the centre with masking tape so that it can be stored. Paint overall surface green except where you wish to leave roadways or cement areas. Paint an irregularly shaped oval lake in the centre of one section (see p. 190 for illustration). VARIATION: Make a cloverleaf roadway or a subdivision pattern of streets. Leave grass space for constructing houses or public buildings.
3. *Cardboard planks:* These make convenient space holders for windows in hollow-block buildings or shelves. Double sheets of corrugated cardboard are more durable than single-thickness sections. Make 28 cm by 84 cm.
4. *Rectangular carton:* Use for transportation vehicles (train, car, boat, wagon). Glue cloth or upholstery to the bottom of the box so it will pull smoothly and not scratch the floor. Attach rope pulls or use rope to link cartons together.

5. *Zoo cage:* See zoo animals guide, p. 416.
6. *Tile boxes:* Use for hollow blocks. Reinforce inside by inserting two slotted pieces of strong corrugated cardboard that have been formed into an X-shaped partition. Tape the lids shut and paint. They will then be sturdy enough for long use.

Learning, Language, and Readiness Materials Centre

This centre needs good lighting, easy access to shelves, and groups of tables arranged in a manner for individual or group use. Sometimes placing a table against a dividing wall allows a child more room for activity without having to disturb or compete with another child across the table for space. Other times, centre materials can be shared more easily when children's chairs are placed around the end of a table or by using a round table.

In some centres you may choose to hinge narrow tables to a wall; these can then be lifted up and braced for extended table space when needed, and used for displaying pictures when collapsed. These hinged tables allow for additional floor space when lifted.

This centre, when adjacent to the book centre, allows for the easy transition from one to another for language development experiences that may be offered in either space. (See p. 52 for preparing the book centre.)

Directions game. *Children above are playing "Directions," the learning game described on page 57. Additional props may be added to develop vocabulary and understanding of such parts of speech as the following adverbs: by, beside, behind, above, beneath, under. For example, with farm animals, a barn, a fence, and a trough might be used. "Susan, can you place the cow **behind** the fence? Michelle, can you place the lamb **inside** the barn in **front** of Chris?" VARIATION: This game may be played using any animals in the animal guides. With animals from woods or zoo you might want to use props such as fences, cages, trees, bushes, rocks, or hollow logs.*

Language arts both in this centre and the book centre should include opportunities for:

1. *Listening:* Help the child discover and know that thoughts can be expressed aloud.
2. *Thinking:* Give opportunities for problem solving.
3. *Speaking:* Encourage the children to talk about what they are doing, will do, and can do in sharing times; to name objects; to role play in the dramatic play centres; to talk into a telephone. Accept what the children have to say as important. Listen to the children's expressed thoughts and ideas. Use fingerplays and learning games to build vocabulary and to learn nouns, adjectives, prepositions, and adverbs.
4. *Writing:* Help children discover that words and thoughts can be written down, such as labelling objects in the centre; using signs, song charts with words, and words lettered on bulletin boards with pictures; or lettering children's thoughts about their pictures.
5. *Reading:* Read to children. Show children that words and pictures are symbols for thoughts expressed. Relate words to pictures or objects helping children to realize the need for, and excitement of, reading signs, books, and other matter in their world. Let children see their thoughts when you have written them down, encouraging them to want to write for themselves.

Art centre: Left: Preparing geometric shapes for spatterpainting with a screen. **Centre:** Using a vegetable brush for spatterpainting with a screen. **Right:** Fingerpainting on a formica square.

Art Centre

An art centre is best placed in an area with a washable floor, near a sink. It should have ample storage space and be out of traffic patterns. No one but the child can create the picture or idea that is in his or her mind. The creations will reflect *experience*. The *process* is more important than the *product*. Art media experiences can release emotions to allow for creation. A child often expresses feelings as well as ideas through art. When working with children in the art centre:

1. Introduce a variety of media.
2. Be prepared.
3. Provide choices.
4. Offer support.
5. It is better to ask, "Would you tell me about it?" than, "What is it?"
6. Let children explore.
7. Provide space for drying finished products.
8. Supervise.
9. Compare only against child's previous effort.
10. Offer large sheets of paper, long-handled brushes, thick chalk, and pencils.

Favourite recipes for art materials

Non-hardening no-cook play dough

454 mL/2 cups cups self-rising flour
30 mL/2 T alum
30 mL/2 T salt
30 mL/2 T cooking oil
227 mL/1 cup, plus 2 T boiling water

Mix and knead.

Salt paint

75 mL/⅓ cup salt
1.25 mL/¼ tsp food colouring

Spread in pan to dry before putting in shakers.

Cooked play dough

227 mL/1 cup flour
113 mL/½ cup salt
227 mL/1 cup water
15 mL/1 T vegetable oil
10 mL/2 tsp cream of tartar

Heat until ingredients form ball, add food colouring.

Potter's clay

113 mL/½ cup flour
113 mL/½ cup cornstarch
227 mL/1 cup salt dissolved in 350 ml/3¾ cups of boiling water

Blend flour and cornstarch with enough water to make paste. Boil water and salt. Add to cornstarch mix and cook until clear. Cool overnight then add 1360 to 1820 mL (6 to 8 cups) of flour and knead until you have the right consistency

NOTE: Keep a metal salt shaker full of flour handy for the children to keep their clay from sticking.

Iridescent soap bubbles

227 mL/1 cup water (hard or soft)
30 mL/2 T liquid detergent
15 mL/1 T glycerine
2.5 mL/½ tsp sugar

Mix all ingredients.

Fingerpaint

150 mL/⅔ cup elastic dry starch
227 mL/1 cup cold water
680 mL/3 cups boiling water
227 mL/1 cup Ivory soap flakes
oil of cloves, a few drops (preservative)
calcimine pigment or vegetable colouring

Dissolve elastic starch in cold water. Smooth lumps and add boiling water. Stir constantly. Thicken, but do not boil more than one minute. Add rest of ingredients (hot or cold). Use on glazed paper, newsprint, or wrapping paper.

Sugar flour paste

227 mL/1 cup flour
227 mL/1 cup sugar
0.95 L/1 qt water (half cold/half hot)
15 mL/1 T powdered alum
0.15 mL/3 drops oil of cloves

Mix flour and sugar together. Slowly stir in 227 mL/1 cup of water. Bring remainder to boil and add the mixture to it, stirring constantly. Continue to cook and stir (½ hr in a double boiler) until fairly clear. Remove from heat and add oil of cloves. Makes almost 1L of paste. Paste keeps a long time. Keep moist by adding small piece of wet sponge to top of small jar of paste.

Bookbinder's paste

5 mL/1 tsp flour
10 mL/2 tsp cornstarch
1.25 mL/¼ tsp alum (powdered)
75 mL/⅓ cup water

Mix dry ingredients. Add water slowly, stirring out lumps. Cook in a double boiler over low heat, stirring constantly. Remove from heat when paste begins to thicken; it will thicken more as it cools. Keep covered. Thin with water when necessary.

Sand paint

113 mL/½ cup sand (washed, dried, and sifted)
15 mL/1 T powdered paint

Shake onto surface brushed with watered glue

NOTE: Empty plastic vitamin or soap bubble bottles make excellent containers.

Soap paint

340 mL/1½ cups soap flakes
227 mL/1 cup hot or warm water

Whip with an eggbeater until stiff.

Sally's play dough recipe (Sally Wysong)

Below is a play dough recipe similar to the commercial type and more durable. Keep in a plastic bag or closed container when not being used.

227 mL/1 cup flour
227 mL/1 cup water
15 mL/1 T oil
15 mL/1 T alum
113 mL/½ cup salt
30 mL/2 T vanilla
food colouring for desired intensity

Mix all dry ingredients. Add oil and water. Cook over medium heat, stirring constantly until it reaches the consistency of mashed potatoes. Remove from heat and add vanilla and colour. Divide into balls and work in colour by kneading.

Creative art tips

1. A candy box or cheese box with holes cut in its lid to hold small cans or jars makes an excellent paint-holder rack that resists tipping.
2. Rubber foam with holes makes an excellent chalk holder.
3. Old broken crayons may be shaved, and shavings spread between two thicknesses of wax paper and ironed with a warm iron. Be careful not to put colours too close together.
4. Sponge pieces may be obtained from upholstery shops and cut into various geometric shapes for sponge printing.
5. Woven baskets or solid-coloured margarine tubs make good crayon holders.
6. For table use, buy white glue by the gallon and pour into small detergent bottles or squeeze bottles.

   ★ **CAUTION:**   Clear spout after each use and insert round toothpick for a stopper.

7. Discarded toothbrushes may be used for spatterpainting.
8. To make a spiral book for the children, use turkey or chicken rings available through hatcheries. Use grocery bags for pages. Remove end and slit at seam.
9. Discarded toothbrushes with a hole in one end may be cut off to about 7.6 cm in length and filed to make a blunt needle for sewing open-mesh vegetable bags. Thread bright yarn through the hole end of the toothbrush and tie a button at the other end of the yarn to prevent the end from sliding through mesh when weaving.
10. When children are cutting paper, tape a cuffed paper bag to the edge of the table for scraps.
11. A printing shop is an excellent source for small scraps of coloured paper and cardboard.
12. Mark the storage box for creative art supplies on the end or top with a picture to identify its contents. Clear plastic boxes may also be used.
13. Place a piece of wet sponge inside the lid of a jar of paste to keep the paste moist between uses.
14. Crisp collage paper is a free discard from department stores; ask clerks to save lingerie and blouse inserts.

Creative art media

1. *Brayers:* These can be made of wooden or plastic spools and the top half of a coat hanger that has been cut and bent to form a tong-like handle. In each end of the spool, insert one of the prongs (ends). For a smooth brayer, attach a piece of sponge or upholstery fabric. Use without covering to make plaid lines or stripes (see photo, p. 30).

Arts and crafts materials for the art centre: Clockwise from lower left: Plastic-spool brayer; loose-weave fabric on cardboard for needle weaving; crayons sorted by colour; rolling pin with textured fabric; bent vegetable brush for spatterpainting; roll-on deodorant tubes filled with paint; sponge shapes for printing; shaker and squeeze bottles for sandpainting; crayon shavings for wax pictures; colour cones, cups, and caps; corrugated cardboard for stamp printing; chalk stored in a section of upholstery foam; clothespin and sponge; Q-Tip and yarn for paint daubers; plastic screen for weaving.

2. *Cardboard overlays:* These allow children to glue or paste layers of geometric-shaped cardboard scraps on a surface. Children may choose to paint on top of the overlay. A print can be taken from the painted surface using a monoprint technique (see nos. 9, 10 below).

3. *Sewing:* Styrofoam meat and pastry trays make good contrasting forms for sewing on yarn. For the youngest children, punch holes with a nail or an ice pick at random over the tray and allow children to select the hole they need for sewing. Use a threaded bobby pin for a needle. Tape prongs shut with cellophane tape. With supervision older children can use blunt tapestry needles. Bright coloured rug yarn is great.

4. *Weaving cards:* Different shapes of notched cardboard can be wrapped with yarn then later woven with another colour. When ready to weave, the best needle for young children is made by dipping the end of yarn in glue or wax. Let dry before using. A cellophane-taped end also works well.

5. *Crayon sandpaper prints:* Allow children to draw pictures with crayons on sandpaper. Place a plain piece of white paper over the crayoning and press with a warm iron. The result is a stippled-effect painting on the paper and a vivid blurred print on the sandpaper. Use discarded sandpaper belts from a free source.

6. *Colour cones:* Melt down old broken pieces of small crayons. (Scrape surfaces of light colours before melting to keep pure colour, and melt crayons in sequence—light to dark —so you can use the same can.) Be sure to watch pans set in hot water. (This is a teacher-only process.) When slightly cool, pour into paper cones. Children love the result. Cone crayons can be gripped like a handle (point up), grasped by the base, or rubbed on the side for a fast sweep of colour.

    NOTE: This crayon is easier for a disabled child to grasp and move. VARIATIONS:

    a. *Colour cups:* Pour 2.54 cm or more of the hot crayon wax into muffin tins. These use less wax than the colour cones. To remove, dip muffin tin quickly in and out of a pan of hot water.
    b. *Colour caps:* Spoon hot crayon wax into pop-bottle caps. Leave wax in lids and use for counting, collage material, or colour games.
    c. *Homemade crayon chubbies:* Pour melted crayon wax into large, wide, or tall plastic pill bottles. When hardened, dip or roll in very hot water to remove.

7. *Imagination paper:* Glue one scrap or shape of coloured paper to a larger piece of paper. Prepare as many sheets of paper as necessary for each of the children in your group to have their own. Let children choose the piece that makes them think of a beginning for their individual picture. Using crayons and their imagination, children can complete their pictures by adding to the basic scrap or lines. VARIATION: As a starter, use a felt-tip marker to make wavy, straight, zigzag, or dotted lines.

8. *Wire sculpture:* Cast-off plastic-coated telephone or electric wires make excellent material for wire sculptures. Offer different lengths, colours, and thicknesses.

9. *Clay boards/monoprint surfaces:* May be made by cutting formica or linoleum scraps into squares or rectangles for use with clay, play dough, or fingerpaint.

10. *Monoprinting:* Children fingerpaint directly on a surface (see photo, p. 26); then they wash and dry their hands and place a dry piece of newsprint over the painting. As it is lifted off a reverse print is revealed.

11. *Displaying children's work:* Provide a space for each child. Let the child display what he or she feels is his or her best picture. Each child deserves recognition, but the work should be measured against a previous effort for optimum growth. Avoid displaying a dozen of one kind of picture together.

Book Centre

Select books for young children with care. The following list provides some guidelines for choosing books.

1. The story and illustrations should be captivating and imaginative. Select books with one to three characters in a story for youngest children.
2. Attractive pictures with vivid colours and interesting detail appeal to children.
3. The plot should not be too complex.
4. Look for use of repetitious catch phrases, humour, surprise, action, rhyme, direct conversation, and a reasonable, satisfying conclusion.
5. Books should be sturdily bound and easy for children to handle.

Setting up a book centre

This is another centre that requires good lighting, some privacy, and quiet. It should be located away from the mainstream of more active work and play. By placing this centre adjacent to the science area, books are within easy reach for reference, and the aquarium, terrarium, or plants will give a homey touch to this comfortable spot for looking at or reading picture books.

Change the books that are in the centre frequently. Have a special display for the books that relate to your current theme and also leave out a selection of the children's favourites. When you are going to change the books, invite the children to help you choose which ones to take out of storage. When going to the public library, take the children along to help you select the books. It is useful and enjoyable to talk to the children about their particular choices. Take advantage of the public library programs and reading.

When adjacent to the home-living centre, this area may become an extended study or library. Some equipment that will aid in the use of books include:

1. A circular table with chairs, and space in the centre for a few selected books
2. Two or three child-size rocking chairs
3. A few casually placed small beanbag chairs or a large one to share
4. A stack of upholstery or carpet squares or cushions for sit-upons
5. A small area rug with pad (so it will not slip if area is not carpeted)
6. Mobiles that are more visible from a beanbag or rocking-chair position
7. A bulletin board with informational pictures relating to special books on display
8. Taped background music or a record player with musical selections or story records available.
9. An overstuffed couch or chair (plastic or washable fabric is best), with legs removed so it is low enough to get on and off easily
10. Murals, framed art pictures, or nature scenes
11. A flannelboard (see pp. 46–48) with figures for acting out stories
12. Puppets and a puppet theatre or TV box for dramatic play and story presentations
13. Headsets for listening to pre-recorded stories; tape recorders for recording tapes of children's stories; VCRs for screening recorded stories

Planning for Group Time

A part of every well-planned program for young children includes directed learning experiences in a group. These directed learning experiences are possible when children are gathered into organized small or large groups for a specific activity with one teacher. Several types of groups might include:

1. A small group, when three to five children are focusing on a special need or interest and interacting with an adult. This type of grouping may occur spontaneously in an existing learning centre or elsewhere anytime during the day.
2. A larger group, such as a "together time," when all the children or a group of six to twelve (or more) may be gathered for a longer period of directed learning with a lead teacher (other teachers may assist). Experiences in this larger group often include the use of music, fingerplays, stories, games, poetry, and rhythms.
3. Outdoor (or indoors in inclement weather) groups, when children may be organized into a more structured group for large muscle activities, such as circle games, exercises, or practising a motor skill.
4. Routine time groups, when all the children may be eating, resting, moving in or out of doors at one time.
5. Those when trips or excursions necessitate children's being in a more controlled grouping.

   NOTE: See special suggestions under the Planning for Group Time sections in each part of the guide.

Music accessories. Left photo: Homemade circular sheer skirts with panty hose elastic bands and commercially made tutus. **Right photo:** An embroidery-hoop tambourine. For making these and other homemade rhythm and music activity accessories see instructions on pp. 36–38.

Music Centre

Provide a centre for the exploration and creative use of music and musical equipment and accessories.

1. Let children listen to records (vocal and instrumental) for music appreciation and to increase their vocabulary.
2. Make rhythm band instruments available for exploring to encourage awareness and sensitivity to sound.
3. Record children's original songs on tape and play them back.
4. Encourage children to sing songs for their own enjoyment.
5. Plan opportunities for rhythmic movement. It will encourage dramatic expression and promote growth in motor control.
6. Encourage self-expression through music. Invite musicians to come and play for the children.

Music in the child's world

Music is a part of every child's environment, whether it be in the form of the song of a bird, a whistler on the street, a TV commercial, the rhythm of raindrops, a woodpecker pecking, footsteps in the hall, the staccato crack of lightning, the rumble of thunder, songs sung, or music played on instruments. By inviting children to explore instruments, to listen to nature, to participate in singing, we offer them the opportunity and experience to naturally express their feelings or ideas through music. Listen for the children's creative interpretations and encourage the spontaneous responses of your children when they are exploring sound. Tape segments of original songs or chants (with or without their instrumental accompaniment). If one of the teachers can play back on a piano or other instrument an original composition of a child, the other children will be encouraged in their musical expression and will be delighted at the recognition of their creative effort.

Listed below are several suggestions of relative sounds or emotions that may be suggested by the use of instruments as you plan music with your children:

1. *Triangle:* Raindrops, night sounds, birds, flowers, sunset, water, waterfalls, tiptoeing, dawn, snow, splashing, falling leaves, quiet, tears
2. *Drum:* Thunder, Native dances, marching bands, heavy footsteps, anger, hammering
3. *Tambourine and maracas:* Dancing, the word *suddenly*, fluttering, eerie Halloween sounds
4. *Bell:* Fire alarms, school or church bells, clock alarms, buoys, fire trucks
5. *Cymbals:* Garbage can lids, pan lids when cooking
6. *Finger cymbals:* Seeds, dawn, very small flowers, first raindrops
7. *Sand block:* Feet shuffling, rustling sounds, shredding, sanding, wood in the woodshop, squirrels in the leaves, trash rattling
8. *Rhythm sticks, claves, tone blocks, or wood blocks:* Clocks ticking, hoofbeats, running, pecking, raindrops, footsteps, hammering, ascending or descending stairs

When choosing instruments for the use of young children it is important to consider the following:

1. How sturdy is the instrument? Will it last for a long time?
2. Do the notes played by the children sound in tune? Many instruments made for children as toys are not in tune.
3. Does the instrument encourage the child to create musical sounds or does it encourage noise?

(For further details please refer to the publication, *Move, Sing, Listen, Play* by Donna Wood, on p. 77.)

Teacher's song for music

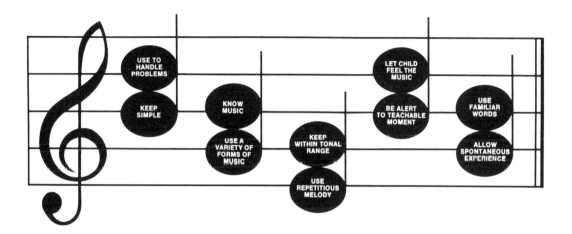

VERSE 1: Be interested in the rhythm of children's bodies. Rattles, scarves, flags, jingle bracelets, hoops with bells sewn on them, maracas, and tapping sticks will all invite movement.

VERSE 2: A spoken idea, a chanting rhyme and rhythm, the rhythm of a hammer or a swing, a picture, or a scarf may also stimulate movement.

VERSE 3: Use music outside, especially rhythms. Try a guitar, records, or tape recordings. You need fewer limits to sound or movements as the freedom of space outdoors minimizes both. Dance can go on continuously.

VERSE 4: The presence of an adult in a music area will act as a magnet.

VERSE 5: Counting songs, melodies that teach information, as well as transition singing games are several other ways to use music.

The choice of songs for children is very important, because children's voices and language abilities are still developing. The song lists do not have asterisks to indicate the developmental level for which individual songs are appropriate. The choice of song is determined by many factors, but the children's experience in music is a critical one. As a result, a given song could be equally suitable for a group of four-year-olds or a group of two-year-olds. When choosing songs, carefully consider the amount and type of musical experience the children have had and the following criteria:

1. Is the song within the children's range? It should be approximately one octave starting at the B below middle C.
2. Is the key appropriate for the mood of the song? A minor key is good for a sad song.
3. Can the children manage the rhythmic pattern? A simple and repeated rhythmic pattern is best for young children.
4. Do the words match the music? If the song is about birds flying high in the sky or low to their nest, does the music go high and low with the words?

(For more detail please refer to Donna Wood's book, *Move, Sing, Listen, Play,* on p. 77.)

Teaching songs to children

1. Before introducing a new song, you may wish to use it first as background music or as a segment for rhythms or accompaniment for a rhythm band if it has a strong rhythmic beat.
2. Since children learn by repetition, sing a new song to the children first. Children will soon master a short segment (one verse or just the refrain).
3. Invite children to join you, if they wish, as you sing the song again and again.
4. Use prompters such as pictures, flannelboard figures, or hand actions to help the children remember the words.

    NOTE: If you have an overhead projector, you might show selected pictures or illustrations as the children sing.

5. Use a simple accompaniment with a guitar, autoharp, or recorder. If you play the piano, use a few basic chord variations or a one-hand accompaniment since the melody should be recognizable. Elaborate accompaniment is not recommended.
6. Make certain all the teachers on your staff are familiar with the new song.

    NOTE: To aid volunteers or substitutes, post the words of the song on a wall above the lead teacher's head. This will serve as a teleprompter and aid regular staff.

7. Use the new song often until the children know it.
8. Teach one song at a time.
9. Give the children opportunities to sing songs at other times during the day. Allow and encourage them to sing at play by taping their original songs or by echoing their chants when they sing.

Music accessories

1. *Dance costumes:* Ask dancing schools to put up a request for discarded dance costumes or tutus to use for dress-up. Remove crotch and seam hems on costumes to allow children to pull them on over their clothes.

    NOTE: Commercial tutu bands are ideal because they fit all young children without alterations (see photo, p. 33).

2. *Drapery sheer skirts:* Ask seamstresses in drapery shops to save colourful cut-off lengths of sheer curtains. It usually takes two scraps of a width of sheer material to make a full skirt. Alternate colour with white or a complementary tint or shade. Make a casing at the top to allow for gathering with elastic. Discarded pantyhose makes an excellent source of soft, sturdy elastic and is the right circumference for a young child. Use the selvage edges of the fabric as bottom hem. French-seam the side seams so the material will not fray.

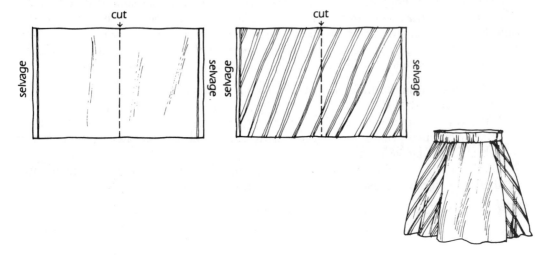

3. *Scarf lengths:* Gather sheer drapery scraps roughly 15 cm wide and 60 cm long at one end. Hem the other end and sides. Attach a yarn ball or a loop of discarded pantyhose elastic. The ball can be held in hand but does not need a tight grip so children's muscles are relaxed. The wristlet of soft elastic allows free movement of the wrist, fingers, and hand. When the wristlet is attached to shoulder straps or belts it can simulate wings or tails, as the children may choose.

4. *Ankle bells:* Make a 15 to 20 cm circle of elastic (from discarded panty hose). Bind two or three Christmas bells together (loosely enough so bells can jangle) with a piece of plastic-coated wire from the telephone company or an electrical shop. Then sew wire on wristlet or ankle band. This wire keeps the metal bells from cutting the thread that attaches them to the fabric. Tennis wrist bands with bells sewn on also work well.

5. *Tambourines:* Encircle an embroidery hoop on the outside edge with plastic-covered wire threaded through four large sleigh bells. Cover wire hoop with a continuous blanket stitch of rug yarn using a 10 m ball of yarn. Begin between bells, make tassel when yarn meets, and attach it. Spacing opposite tassle allows surface for tapping against other wrist or hand.

6. *Flags:* Make a casing on one side of a chiffon scarf large enough and tight enough to slide over a length of cut-off hard-core upholstery pole (18 to 20 cm). Scarf can then be removed easily for laundering. Upholstery pole is sturdier and safer than doweling.

7. *Jingle paddles:* Lace large Christmas jingle bells (available in variety stores year-round) with heavy wire through drilled holes in a discarded wooden paddle. Lightweight paddles are usually available in variety stores with a small rubber ball attached by a rubber string to the paddle.

8. *Music and rhythms:* Use a taped sequence of appropriate music, marking the beginnings of different types or sections of music segments on the tape. Great when you cannot play the piano or afford a large collection of records. Leaves the teacher free to watch and supervize the children. It also allows the segment to be a predetermined, reasonable length.

Homemade music and rhythm band instruments. Clockwise from top: Paddles used as bell and lid tambourines; sand blocks with drawer-pull handles; plastic bottle with stones inside for shaker; embroidery-hoop tambourine; stick bell; homemade tone block; scarf attached to elastic loop; metal cymbals; telephone-wire tambourine; baton and director's cap; scarf taped to cardboard tube; drawer-pull wood blocks.

9. *Gymnastic ribbons:* Ribbons similar to those used by gymnasts can be made by cutting 2 m wide pieces of felt into 5 mm by 2 m strips. Children can use their imagination to move with these in time to a variety of music.

Using your piano

How many times have you wished you could play the piano at least well enough to play simple melodies or rhythms for your children? We recognize that no crash course in music or piano will equal the preparation a musician receives through study and practice, but we encourage you to use some simple piano melodies with care. Only use the piano when you are comfortable enough to pay more attention to the children than the piano. Don't use the piano for performance. It is to be used to expand the children's musical horizons.

Try the graphic instructions given below. We hope they will assist you to improvise background music on the piano to accompany children's movements for walking, running, jumping, galloping, hopping, skipping, or swaying. Suggestions are also included for tonal representations of train whistles, fire engines, clocks, raindrops, wind, and bells. The shaded sections under each heading are more difficult variations and will require using both hands and more frequent changes of the notes played. Select the version you can master most easily.

Black keys may be sharps (♯) or flats (♭)

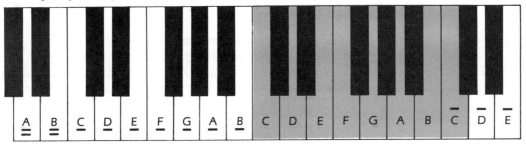

Middle C

Code

1. *Letters* identify the keys on the piano keyboard (see illustration). Shaded keys are the C-major scale, which has no sharps or flats.
2. *Lines* printed above or below these letters refer to their distance from middle C:

   $\overline{C}$ = one octave *above* middle C $\overline{\overline{C}}$ = two octaves *above* middle C

   $\underline{C}$ = one octave *below* middle C $\underline{\underline{C}}$ = two octaves *below* middle C

3. *Octave* is the distance between any one key on the piano and the next key above or below bearing the same name: E, $\overline{E}$, $\underline{F}$ $\underline{\underline{F}}$ $\overline{G}$, $\overline{\overline{G}}$.
4. *Numerals* correspond to the fingers and thumb used with either hand.
   L.H. = left-hand fingering 1-2-3-4-5 from thumb to little finger, moving *left*.
   R.H. = right-hand fingering 1-2-3-4-5 from thumb to little finger, moving *right*.

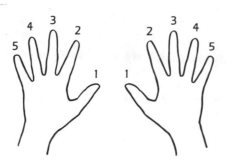

5. *Chord* (in this book) is any two or three notes played simultaneously such as CE. If the letters are grouped together, they will designate a chord: CEG, R.H. (1-3-5). If the letters are separated by dashes, they indicate single notes played in succession: C-E-G, R.H. (1-3-5).

6. *Sharp* (♯) is the black key *above* a white key of that letter (except for E♯ or B♯, when it is the adjacent white key above). Sharps raise the tone one-half step.

7. *Flat* (♭) is the black key *below* a white key of that letter (except for F♭ and C♭, when it is the adjacent white key below). Flats lower the tone one-half step.

8. *Rhythm* is the regular recurrence of grouped strong and weak beats. The terms *long* and *short* will be assigned to notes to suggest a time pattern. Accents will be identified, pauses noted, or familiar rhythmic patterns to be imitated will be cited.

9. Please read each instruction carefully, then experiment at your piano.

Walking

Using your right thumb (1) and middle finger (3), repeat any two notes alternately. Think of the left–right, left–right cadence as you strike each note. Step up the pace for a brisk walk and slow down the tempo for a leisurely stroll (C-E, C-E). Or begin with finger (4) (R.H.) on F and proceed down the scale to C and up again, using fingers 4-3-2-1, 1-2-3-4 (repeat over and over). F-E-D-C-C-D-E—F-E-D-C-C. Note that C and F are repeated when reversing the order sequence.

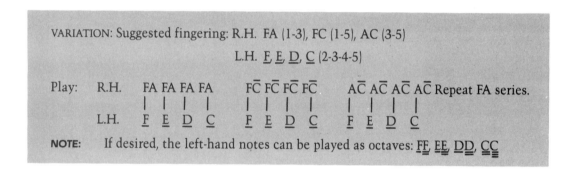

Running

Play any key on the middle of the keyboard with your right forefinger (2), and then the adjacent key to the right with the middle finger (3). Repeat the separate keys rapidly: C-D-C-D-C-D-C-D or play the following notes rapidly, C-D-E-F-G-F-E-D. Then repeat. Use fingers 1-2-3-4-5-4-3-2 (R.H.). End final sequence with C.

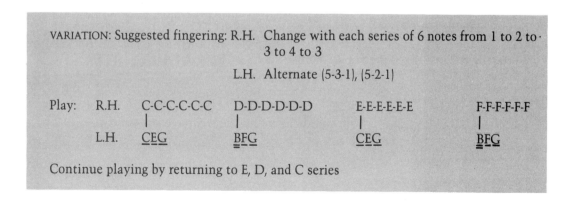

Galloping

With the right hand, play three consecutive notes on the keyboard using adjacent fingers and accenting the first note of each series of three: C-D-E, C-D-E (accenting the Cs as when saying GAL-lop-ing). Or play E-G-C̄, E-G-C̄, E-G-C̄ accenting E and using (1-2-5) fingering.

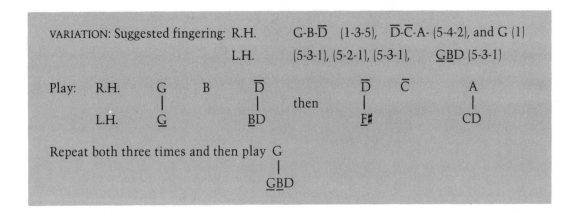

Hopping

Think of as many animals as you can that move by hopping in a steady manner. Play G-B, G-B with your right hand using fingers 1-3. Repeat. Or play C-E-G-E-C, pause and repeat. Use fingers 1-3-5-3-1 for this rhythm exercise. Quickly release each finger from the piano keys as the children hop-hop-hop across the room.

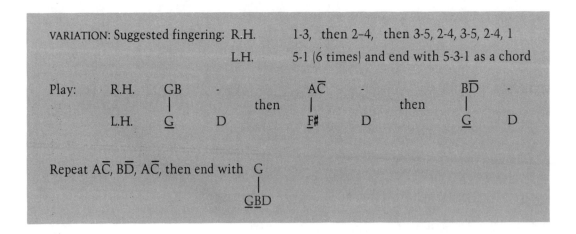

Jumping

More deliberate pace than hopping: Use alternate chords of C̲E̲G̲ and C̲F̲A̲ played with the left hand on the lower keyboard. Suggested finger is (L.H.) 5-3-1, then 5-2-1. Accent the thud of each jump by striking the second chord harder, such as C̲E̲G̲ ...**CFA**, C̲E̲G̲ ...**CFA**.

Swaying

Play alternately two chords (one high and then one low) very slowly and gently.

Play:	R.H.	(1-2-5)	E̅G̿C̿		E̅G̿C̿		repeat
	L.H.	(5-3-1)		C̲E̲G̲		C̲E̲G̲	repeat

Leaping

Play C and then C̄ (accenting C̄). Use a rhythmic pattern of short–long, short–long. Suggested fingering is (R.H.) 1-5.

| VARIATION: Suggested fingering: | R.H. | 1-5-3-2 |
| | L.H. | 5-2-1 and 5-3-1 |

Play: R.H.   C - C̄ - A - G   Play this three times, then A—F   R.H. (3 - 1)

L.H.   CFA   CEG   FF   L.H. (1 - 5)

Bending and stretching

For bending, slowly play C̄-G-E-C-G̲-E̲-C̲

(R.H.) (5-3-2-1-3-2-1)

For stretching, slowly play C̲-E̲-G̲-C-E-G-C̄

(L.H.) (5-3-2-1-3-2-1)

VARIATION: Suggested fingering: R.H.   5-2-1

L.H.   1-3-5

Play: *Alternating* right and left hands,   C̄-G-E   C-G̲-E   C̲-G̲-E̲   C̲ to bend
(R.H.)   (L.H.)   (R.H.)   (L.H.)

Reverse the sequence for stretching

Skipping

Using a rhythmic pattern of long, short, long, short, long with the right hand play C-C, E-E, G-G, E-E, C-C, E-E, G-G, E-E, C-C, and so on. Suggested fingering is 1-1, 3-3, 5-5, 3-3, 1-1.

VARIATION: Suggested fingering: R.H. 1-3, 2-4, 3-5, 4-2, 3-1, 2-1, 2, 2

L.H. 5-3-1 and 5-2-1

Play: R.H.   C - E   D - F   E - G   F - D   E - C   D - B̲   C   C

L.H.   CEG   B̲FG   CEG   B̲FG   CEG   B̲FG   CEG   CEG

Or you may break the chords in the left hand as follows:

L.H.   C - EG   B̲ - FG   C - EG   B̲ - FG   C - EG   B̲ - FG   CEG   CEG

(Right hand remains the same)

Fire Alarm

Play simultaneously both notes in the octave chord CC̄ four times in a series and then pause. Play: CC̄ CC̄ CC̄ CC̄ (pause) CC̄ CC̄ CC̄ CC̄. Use 1-5 (R.H.) or alternate rapidly the notes in the above sequence (left to right) C-C̄, C-C̄, C-C̄, C-C̄.

Clocks

Play alternately middle C and the higher C̄ (R.H. 1-5). Strike the notes to make an appropriate beat.

> VARIATION: Vary the intensity and length of the interval between strikes depending upon the size of clock or watch you are duplicating: try TICK-TOCK: F̱ - C̲ (L.H. 1-4), tick-tock: F-C̄ (R.H. 2-5), tick-tick-tick-tick: C̄-C̄-C̄-C̄- (R.H. 5) or C̲-C̲-C̲-C̲ (R.H. 1).

Train engine

Play with the right hand down the scale G to C and then back up to G (5-4-3-2-1-2-3-4-5). Repeat the sequence to simulate the sound of a train engine. You may wish to play the same notes with each hand separately or with the left hand only. Increase in speed and volume as the train begins to move.

> VARIATION: Begin with two long toots on the whistle, which means "go ahead," playing the chord F♯C̄. Have the train pull out of the station slowly. Gradually pick up speed. Three short toots on the whistle means "stop" at the next station. Begin to slow the train down. One long toot means the train is approaching the station. Slow down even further and stop.

Bells

Play C (L.H. 4) then: C̄-B-A-G (R.H. 4-3-2-1) then: F-E-D-C (L.H. 1-2-3-4). Repeat same sequence holding the pedal down.

> VARIATION: Suggested fingering: R.H.   1-2-5 (repeat for all chords)
>
>   L.H.   1-2-3-4
>
> Play: R.H.   EGC̄   DFB   CEA   BDG
> | then | then | then |
>   L.H.   C̄   B   A   G
>
> Use the right pedal for a gong effect
>   You may wish to play the chords in both hands simultaneously in different octaves or to play the right hand alone

Raindrops

Use the black keys and play F♯ C♯ A♯ D♯ (R.H. 3-1-5-2) or C̄♯ F̄♯ D̄♯ Ā♯ (R.H. 1-3-2-5). Repeat quickly using a desired rhythm. You may wish to change hands on the keyboard as you play:

(R.H.)	(3) F♯		(5) A♯		(3) F̄♯		(5) Ā♯	
(L.H.)		(2) C♯		(1) D♯		(2) C̄♯		(1) D̄♯

Use the right pedal for a gong effect.

Or play (R.H.) C̄-Ḡ-Ā-D̿ (1-2-3-5) as separate notes for a raindrop sequence (drip–drop–drip–splash!)

Repeat quickly three shorts and then a long. For a drip–drop, drip–drop sequence use C̿-C̄ C̿-C̄ C̿-C̄ C̿-C̄ (5-1-5-1), repeat, or for a pitter-patter: C̿-C̄ C̄-C̄ C̄-C̄ C̄-C̄ (5-5, 1-1), repeat.

Heavy wind

Begin softly and gradually play the following chords louder, then diminish to become softer again. Repeat. Use the right pedal to slur the notes.
Suggested fingering is 1-3-5.

Play: R.H.   C̄EG   D̄♭FA♭   D̄F♯A   E♭ḠB♭   ĒG♯B.   Reverse the sequence as often as desired.

Light breeze

Suggested fingering is 1-2-3-4-5 (thumb on C̄ and progressing to the right to Ḡ). To make a bigger gust of wind use lower keys C-D-E-F-G (L.H. 5-4-3-2-1).

Playing your piano

Now, are you ready to try some simple improvising on your own? Chording is the secret. Play one or more of the following five chords: CEG, CFA, CEG, BFG, CEG one after the other, much like a chord sentence. These same chords may be used as accompaniment to any simple melody in the key of C (no sharps or flats) played with the other hand. These basic chords may be played anywhere on the keyboard and at whatever point in the song you choose. You do not always have to play them in sequence.

(R.H.) 1-3-5, 1-3-5, 1-3-5, 1-4-5, 1-3-5
(L.H.) 5-3-1, 5-2-1, 5-3-1, 5-2-1, 5-3-1

Usually you may play each chord whenever one of the notes within that chord is played in the melody with the opposite hand. You will find that some very simple melodies may be accompanied by the use of a single chord, while more complicated tunes may require the use of two or more of the suggested chords. Experiment and select what sounds best together. Another chord sentence, similar to the one given above, that can be used for skipping might be CEG, DFG, CEG, BDG, CEG.

(R.H.) 1-3-5, 2-4-5, 1-3-5, 1-2-5, 1-3-5
(L.H.) 5-3-1, 4-2-1, 5-3-1, 5-3-1, 5-3-1.

Try breaking these same chords and playing them in segments as C-EG, D-FG, C-EG, B-DG, C-EG or as single notes C-E-G, D-F-G, C-E-G, B-D-G, C-E-G.

Variations to the series of notes given above to use with the key of C: If you wish to play chords to accompany a tune using any flats or sharps, use the following guide, remembering the suggestions noted for the key of C.

Key of D (2 sharps)	DF♯A	DGB	DF♯A	C♯GA	DF♯A
Key of E (4 sharps)	EG♯B	EAC̅♯	EG♯B	D♯AB	EG♯B
Key of F (1 flat)	FAC̅	FB♭D̅	FAC̅	EB♭C̅	FAC̅
Key of G (1 sharp)	GBD̅	GC̅E̅	GBD̅	F♯C̅D̅	GBD̅
Key of A (3 sharps)	AC♯E	ADF♯	AC♯E	G♯DE	AC♯E
Key of B (2 flats)	B♭DF	B♭E♭G	B♭DF	AE♭F	B♭DF
Key of E (3 flats)	E♭GB♭	E♭A♭C̅	E♭GB♭	DA♭B♭	E♭GB♭

NOTE: It is helpful to know that almost all songs end on the note that is the key for the song. Sometimes a song starts (the first note) on the note that is the key; however, sometimes when the song begins in the middle of a measure the first note is not the key note.

Fingerplays and Action Songs

Originally these rhyme games were written using only the fingers and hands to act out the words. They were used primarily by parents to help teach their youngest children body parts, numbers, and shapes. Some of them date back nearly 2000 years.

In the nineteenth century, Friedrich Froebel, the man who developed the kindergarten in Germany, took adult games and songs and adapted them for children for educational purposes. He used them to integrate meanings and the emotional satisfaction of sensing relationships among parts.

Today, the best fingerplays and action songs use the *whole body* (large and small muscles) for total participation.

Value of fingerplays and action songs

1. Increase manual dexterity and muscular control.
2. Develop an understanding of rhythms of speech, music, and life's activities.
3. Encourage understanding of concepts of size, shape, and place or direction.
4. Build vocabulary and aid in language development.
5. Allow for self expression, encouraging a child's own response in his or her use of body and speech for interpreting concepts.
6. Help teach number concepts, especially one to ten.
7. Provide relaxation (a legitimate opportunity to move and wiggle).
8. Assist the child in learning to follow directions.
9. Teach order and sequence.
10. Increase attention span.
11. Develop listening skills.
12. Give an opportunity to have fun.

Suggestions for teaching fingerplays and action songs

1. Demonstrate appropriate actions as you say or sing the words to the group.
2. Replay finger game encouraging the children to imitate only the action.
3. Do fingerplay again allowing those who wish to participate with both action and words.

4. Keep actions and movement slow enough so that children do not have trouble keeping up.
5. Repeat fingerplays often enough for children to become familiar with them.
6. Introduce variations or a new approach to an old favourite.
7. Be enthusiastic, use those songs that you enjoy.
8. Repeat old favourites. (Children enjoy repetition.)
9. Occasionally send parents the words and music to fingerplays currently being used so that they can use them at home.
10. You may wish to make a fingerplay card file for yourself to use as a prompter during group time, although it is better to memorize the fingerplays you use.
11. When learning a new fingerplay or song, letter a large sign as a teleprompter and post on an adjacent wall at eye level for the staff and volunteers.

★ **CAUTION:** Select one or two fingerplays for each subject, making certain they teach *best* the concept to be learned. As with books, poems, and songs, watch for the difficulty of vocabulary, the length of verse, the concept to be learned, and the maturity level of your group. Use the simplest fingerplays with the youngest or the least mature group; increase the complexity as the group shows readiness.

Flannelboards

A flannelboard is a felt or flannel-surfaced board (can be cardboard) used as a visual teaching aid. It supports, vertically, illustrative materials that have been backed with a texture that will adhere to its surface (see illustrations, pp. 46–48).

Value of a flannelboard

1. It provides for an attractive focus of attention.
2. It helps to sustain interest by providing an element of surprise or continuing suspense as materials are added to the screen.
3. It can be inexpensively made from a variety of available materials.
4. It can be a versatile and a flexible medium if made in various sizes and forms.
5. A flannelboard allows teachers to expand understanding through both visual and auditory means.
6. Its use (as far as what can be done on a surface) is limited only by the creativity and resourcefulness of the teacher.
7. Flannelboard props can act as a teleprompter to children as to the sequence in a game, story, song, fingerplay, or poem.
8. It can encourage children to participate verbally, thus building their vocabulary and language skills.

Using a flannelboard

1. Select a story, game, song, poem, fingerplay, or concept to be introduced.
2. Decide on subjects or pictures to best highlight sequences of events or steps in learning.
3. Gather or prepare prop materials.
4. Arrange parts in sequence, or number backs of pieces.
5. Rehearse or test out before presenting to group.
6. Consider visibility for all who are to view presentation.
7. Eliminate prop or illustrative materials that seem contrived.

NOTE: Manipulating prop materials should not distract you or your listeners *or* detract from the story.

Singing games.
These children are using individual flannelboards (flannel is stapled to a one-foot square of heavy cardboard). As children (or teacher) sing, the child holds up the appropriate felt cut-out when his or her fruit (or animal or object) is mentioned in the song. These children are responding to the verses of a song about fruits. This idea may be adapted for use with any song, fingerplay, or action story in which a series of objects or things is mentioned.

8. Evaluate after use to improve your next presentation.
9. Let children participate or use flannelboard materials on their own (see photo above).
10. Store flannelboard in a file where it will be readily available for spontaneous use.

Types of flannelboards and their construction

Easel flannelboard

You can make exchangeable sections, using the same base, for a painting easel or for a flannelboard. Staple, glue, or tape felt or heavy flannel to wallpaper book covers. Enamel or spray paint wallpaper book covers to make a painting easel that is washable. One book makes a double easel. Edges of carton used for base should be covered with masking tape before they are painted. Slash carton notches diagonally at the angle desired for easel. An inverted carton wedged inside the box will brace the easel and provide shelf space to store extra boxes of flannelgraph props. Use spring clothespin to hold paper.

Pocket apron flannelboard

Pocket is handy for holding flannelgraph figures. Arms are free to place cutouts on flannel-board. To make a 5 cm pocket, allow 10 cm of extra material to fold back. Make the board *your* trunk length (chin to lap) when seated. Staple, glue, or tape flannel or felt to heavy cardboard. Use braided yarn for a soft strap (see photo, p. 554).

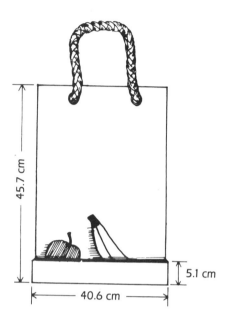

Triangle tent/tabletop flannelboard

Construct from masonite as freestanding flannelboard above, or cut out bottom of a square cardboard carton, slit the side at one corner, and overlap as shown to form a triangle. Measurements may vary with box used.

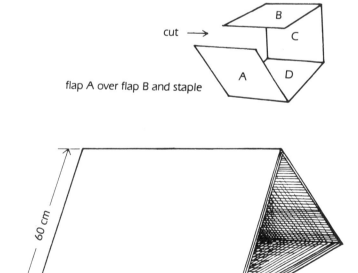

Freestanding flannelboard

A triangle-shaped flannelboard can be braced so that it will not tip over. Lace the edges together with plastic or leather strips threaded through holes drilled in flannel-covered masonite. This flannelboard can be placed upright on a floor or tent-like on a tabletop. It can simultaneously accommodate three children using different materials.

Flannelboard tips

Magnetize your flannelboard by inserting a piece of wire screen between backing and flannel or making one side metal. Cookie sheets or metal stove protectors make good magnetic boards. Flannel, felt, sandpaper, flocked paper, and pellon may all be used as cutouts or backings to cutouts on the flannelboard. Colouring books of food and

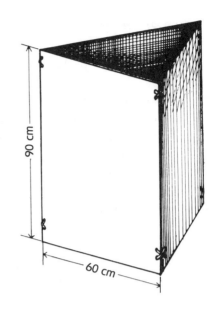

animals are excellent sources of outlines for the teacher to duplicate. Colouring books are not recommended for children's use.

Some Do's and Don't's for Storytelling to Young Children

When you select a story

1. Before choosing a book, refer to checklist on p. 32. *Don't* use any book for a group-time story without scanning and evaluating it.
2. Adapt it for your group. Shorten, expand, or change wording for age level, time allotted to tell story, and the occasion. Emphasize the incidents that appeal to children (sound, humour, action). Remember that for very young children three minutes is a long time. *Don't* memorize word by word and recite the story. Leave out unimportant details. Optimum delivery will be jeopardized if you concentrate on a recitation. Quote only author's choice of words that cannot be improved.
3. Evaluate and edit it. If a phrase, paragraph, or picture needs to be omitted because of insensitivity to an ethnic group, to handicapped people, or to people's economic status, paper-clip pages or write in the word change. *Don't* discard a book because of one offensive illustration or paragraph. Modify the picture or the text.

As you prepare the story

1. Know it. If you need prompters, clip and mark key pages where you want to read a section or be reminded of a sequence of subjects. Be sure you understand the story as a whole and the relationship of every character to the main plot so that you can better set the scene. Tell the story slowly; pause for emphasis; speed up for excitement or urgency; vary volume of voice to suggest emotion or change of character. Speak distinctly. *Don't* tack on facts you have forgotten after the sequence is past. *Don't* forget punch line. *Don't* read too rapidly or mumble.
2. Rehearse the story before you tell it to the group. This will allow eye contact with the children. Practise telling it aloud in front of a mirror. Tape record the story for a revealing self-criticism. *Don't* extemporize unless you are an experienced and very talented teacher. Your extemporaneous rendition will only tend to insulate the child against a later encounter with the story told by someone who has planned their presentation.

3. Locate the test props. Make sure they mesh with the story's flow. Manipulation of puppets or flannelboard materials should not distract you or your listeners from the story. *Don't* take too long a pause locating the next character or finding missing figures.

Before you begin the story

Get comfortable. Make certain the children can see and hear and are not crowded. Consider personalities and individual needs of the children. Sit where the children will be least distracted by surroundings. Be flexible. Regroup children if necessary. *Don't* allow children to sit too close to each other. *Don't* let yourself be driven by a time schedule.

When you tell the story

Make characters come alive. Use direct conversation. Involve yourself, empathize with the feelings of the main characters. Use gestures, facial expressions, vary your voice, and pace your delivery for emphasis. Maintain eye contact. *Don't* tell the story using vague characters in an obscure setting. *Don't* make your delivery monotonous by using the same pattern of inflection regardless of the story line.

During and after the story

Listen for children's responses and comments. Let them think, ponder, show pleasure or displeasure. Allow the story to state its message or entertain the children. Allow children to identify with the story from their own experience. Answer children's questions but *don't* editorialize, moralize, or interpret.

Extended Experiences with Books

1. Use flannelboard.
2. Use background music.
3. Use puppets.
4. Use props and pictures.
5. Use tape recorder for individual listening.
6. Let children dramatize.
7. Talk about the story.
8. Tell part of a story and let the children make up a new ending.

When and How to Use Poetry

1. Instead of reading a story at grouptime, substitute a poem.
2. For a plus experience, use it to supplement another activity in the classroom.
3. Use poetry to encourage active participation (fingerplays and action rhymes).
4. Read poems with background mood music.
5. Use poetry as a chant with a large muscle activity.
6. Record a child's chant or verse recited while playing.
7. Share a child's poem with the whole group.
8. Make a file of poems. Place a key illustration in the corner of each card for quick identification. Illustrate one side of the card to show the children, as you share the poem, what is printed on the back of the card.
9. Hang illustrated poems on the walls at appropriate spots in the various centres for easy reference while teaching.

Learning Games

Value of games

Games offer an excellent vehicle for learning while having fun. With games a child can

1. increase his or her vocabulary by learning to identify objects, pictures, and materials.
2. develop her or his sense of sight and hearing.
3. learn to discriminate and classify.
4. learn to follow directions and take turns.
5. discover cause and effect.
6. gain experience and social skills with other children and adults.

Uses of games

Games without props can be used at anytime, and are especially useful to assist in the transition from one activity to another

1. while children are *assembling* for a story group, singing time, or a snack time.
2. while children are *waiting* for something to be prepared.
3. while children are slowly *dispersing* to go home and are leaving at different times.
4. while a child or children *wait* for others to finish lunch, to finish their nap, to go outside or to another room.
5. while *riding* to and from nursery school or the daycare centre in a carpool or on a bus.
6. while children are removing or putting on outdoor clothes.
7. when the teacher is *diverting* silly or unacceptable types of conversation or behaviour.
8. when preparing for a specific activity, such as an introduction of a new idea in art or science, or following a story.
9. during group time as a tool to teach a concept.

NOTE: Games with props can be planned for the whole group, with a small group, or with an individual child during a free choice time. These games extend the opportunities for learning because of the sensory properties of the props used.

Suggestions for teaching games

1. Young children learn best in a small group because it eliminates long waiting periods and offers more person-to-person opportunities.
2. Remember that young children's attention spans for any concentrated effort last about one minute more than their age. By varying the pace and activity you may, however, keep children in an organized group for longer periods, such as group time, stories, songs, and games.
3. In the games, introduce only one or two concepts at a time.
4. Keep games simple, making sure instructions are clear. Try to demonstrate as much as possible.
5. Ensure each child's opportunity to participate and succeed.
6. Watch for restlessness. Stop when interest wanes.
7. Rather than insist that every child participate in a game, appeal through a special interest or past experience to encourage each to want and ask to play.

   NOTE: Some young children may appear never to enjoy a group participation game but will learn the song or game by observing and will frequently use it at home. Sometimes unwillingness to follow rules is an indication that the game has gone on too long or is too structured. Perhaps those who wish to continue could do so and the others might be given an alternative activity.

8. Relays and winner games are not recommended at this age level. Children should be encouraged to compete only against their own past performances. They need many opportunities to succeed and to feel good about themselves. Too many failures can defeat this purpose. Avoid games that require waiting or inactivity by the children.

Identification games

★ CAUTION:　　When introducing the materials to be used, always identify an object as being real or just a picture, model, or toy.

Name it

A series of three or more objects is placed in a row. Identify each of them. Have children name them from left to right. Rearrange or scramble them and let children name the objects in their new order.

NOTE:　　Excellent for vocabulary building and for observation, or for developing interest, if you select items relating to the interest theme.

I see something, what do you see?

This game and its variations are excellent to play while on a walk, a sightseeing excursion, or a ride in a car. The leader simply states what he or she sees and asks the children to respond with what they see. VARIATION: Use other senses.

Look and see

Select three or more familiar objects or models. Ask the children to close or cover their eyes. Hide one of the objects behind your back or under a cover. Then say to the participating children, "Look and see." Let the children guess which object is missing by noting what remains. As their skill develops, add or remove more than one object at a time. Children will enjoy hiding an object from the other children. When a child guesses successfully, let that child hide the next object. Flannelboard figures may also be used.

★ CAUTION:　　Make certain every child gets an opportunity to hide an object. If you do not select the child to be "it," suggest that a child who is eligible for a second turn choose one who has not had a turn to be next.

Sniff and smell

Place several seasonings or spices that have a distinctive odour familiar to the children in small unbreakable containers. Film containers with punched lids are excellent. A circle of nylon cloth glued as an inner lid will prevent spills but still allow sniffing through punctured holes. Include items such as cinnamon, onion salt, coffee, cocoa, talcum, and dry mustard. VARIATION: Make a double set of the sniff and smell cans. Children can match cans with the same contents by their odour. Teacher may double-check when children have completed the matching task. You may wish to code the bottom for your convenience. Tape over the lid holes to preserve the odour while they are stored.

★ CAUTION:　　Breakable plastic bottles can be used only with careful supervision, which limits their use for exploring. Plastic is extremely dangerous when broken, especially if a piece is swallowed.

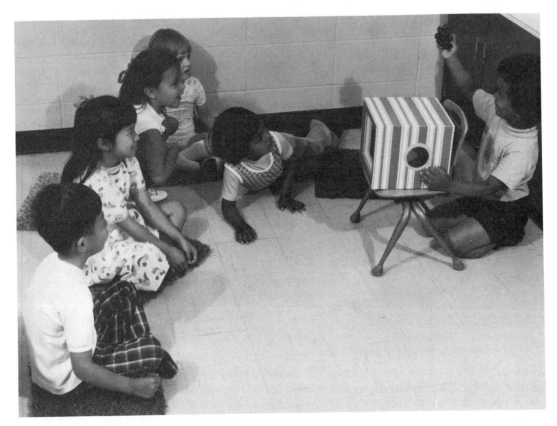

Identification games. Children are playing "Reach and feel" in a "feel it box." The child has guessed that the object he was feeling in the box was grapes.

Reach and feel

Set out a series of objects with different textures and shapes. Identify them (children may assist). Discuss how the objects are alike and how they are different. Let the children touch, feel, and hold the objects before you begin the game. Then place the objects inside a cloth bag or paper sack. Let the children reach inside the bag and identify by feeling one of the objects inside the bag before removing it to verify their guess. VARIATION: Let the children guess by feeling through a hole or holes of a "feel it box" (see photo, above). Leave the opposite side of the box open for the children in the group to watch as one child guesses. Children can clap if the child guesses correctly or shake their heads or call out "Guess again!" if the child's guess is wrong. If objects are different enough, the children can be encouraged to guess by feeling a single object through the cloth bag. Keep the bag securely closed.

Listen and hear

Identify objects and drop or manipulate them to produce their characteristic sounds so children can see and hear. Have the children close their eyes and cover them with their hands. You may choose to produce the sound from behind a screen. Let the children recall the sound heard and identify it. VARIATION: You may tape record and play back other familiar sounds for children to guess.

★ CAUTION: Children resist blindfolds and they are not sanitary. Alternatives are closing eyes and covering them with hands, using a screen, having children turn their heads, or using a sleep mask (available in drug stores and travel shops) with a fresh tissue covering for each child.

Chew, lick, and taste

Have toothpicks or coffee stirrers and small paper cups into which foods may be distributed and sampled. This will avoid children dipping into the main source. Identify the foods as the children taste them. Talk about differences in flavours and textures.

★ CAUTION: Be aware of allergic reactions or restricted foods for individuals in your group.

Can you remember?

Show a group of children a tray of objects related to a special interest. Help identify the objects by name. Remove the tray, or cover it, and ask them to recall what was on the tray. Display five items at first, increasing the number as the children become more skillful.

Language games

Guess who? Who am I?

Begin by saying, "I see somebody who is wearing a red ribbon. Guess who it is?" Eventually include each child. Continue to add clues if children cannot identify the person from the first clue. When they make a mistake say, "Guess again" and restate the statement as a fact: "Mary is wearing a blue ribbon and she has blonde hair, doesn't she?" (Re-establish facts in order to unlearn mistakes.) VARIATION: Describe a community helper, storybook character, or animal.

Guess what? What am I? What can I do?

Begin by describing something in the form of a question: "What is sometimes soft, always round, and bounces when you drop it?" Answer: a ball. Descriptions can also include sounds and uses.

What did you hear?

Encourage the children to duplicate (or describe) the sounds of animals in the nature centre, sounds of eating, sounds of well-known vehicles. Let them also try to duplicate a clapping rhythm or imitate a rhythm beaten on a rhythm stick or a drum.

Listening

Choose one child to be the listener. Child should be seated on the floor or on a chair in front of the group with face turned away from the group. Point to another child in the group who will become the mystery voice. She or he can say, "Hi," or any other greeting. Let the first child guess who the mystery voice is. If the child cannot guess correctly, let the speaker say something else. You may wish to use two telephones while playing the game.

Who's missing?

Select a child who is to be "it." Ask the child to hide his or her eyes. Select another child in the group to hide in a designated place. When the child is safely hidden ask the child who is "it" to look and guess "Who is missing?" You may give hints or rename all the children who are present that day.

Let's tell a story

Teacher may show children a picture and ask one of them to make up a story by telling what *is* happening, what *did* happen, or what *will* happen?

News time

Encourage each child to prepare something to tell or show the group. Encourage more telling and less showing as traditional "show and tell" often ends up as a time for showing off how many expensive toys a child has rather than a time for encouraging language development. Be ready to ask questions that will assist the children to talk, as some children become shy in front of a group.

Problem-solving games

How many?

Ask any question that demands problem solving. Choose those that allow for a variety of possible answers. For example: "How many ways can you think of to get to school?" "How can you get from one side of the room to the other without walking?"

How can I? How can you?

Ask a child a question on how to solve a simple problem: "How could I (you) play the record player if it were on a high table and I (you) were too short to reach it?"

Which?

Similar to game above. Often your first question, "Which?" is followed by the second question, "Why?" Select questions about things that involve a judgment or opinion.

NOTE: See also "grouping" and "sorting" in the next section. After the child has told you which," ask, "Why?" Objects and pictures: "Which one do you wear on your feet?" "Which one do you use to brush your teeth?" "Which animal would make a good pet?"

Why? or If?

Preface questions with the word "why?" or "if?" "Why do cows live in the country?" Let's think, "What is it that cows eat?" Is there much grass in the city?"

Sequence or Which comes first?

Present pictures depicting the *before* and *after* of an event to see if the child can identify the sequence. Then move on to a story sequence or series of three or four pictures. Ask the child to re-order and give reasons for choices. Some pictures might be reversible: clean/dirty, chicken/egg.

Classification games

Match-them

"Match-them" is a matching game similar to the commercial games called, "Perception Plaques" and "Match-Ems." Show and identify several sets of identical picture cards, squares, objects, or flannelgraph figures for children. Scramble the items. Let the children find

Grouping and sorting by association. *The girl on the left is matching the animal with the food it eats. The cutout pictures are laminated with clear coating and glued to abstract felt shapes. When the picture is mounted on felt, the child or teacher can use it on a flannelboard for other learning games. The girl standing is grouping selected objects by colour into circles of similarly coloured yarn.*

matching pairs. The teacher may hold the item to be matched or the children may be given half of a match and take their turn to draw a match from the centre of the table. If children make mistakes, call their attention to the differences. Praise their success. To vary, place draw cards facedown on the table.

Alike, different, and the same

Show children several items that are identical. Then introduce something different but similar, such as all alike except one is smaller, larger, a different colour, or belongs to a different group. Begin with obvious differences and later progress to the more difficult as the child is ready. You may use real objects, pictures, or models.

Grouping and sorting by association

Encourage children to sort and group real objects, pictures, or miniature objects into trays, boxes, or circles of yarn. Sort by content (as furniture into various rooms), by rhyme (as a goat, coat, boat, note), by type (as hat-clothes, apple-fruit), by use (as saddle with horse, cup with saucer). Begin with simple, obvious groupings like all red, all dogs, and then progress to finer differentiations such as farm animals, pets, zoo animals.

Classification games. The girl at left is playing the "ring it" game. She is placing coloured rings around objects of a similar colour. The girl at right is counting "how many?" as she plays a conservation game.

Lotto

There are many commercial lotto games available. You may also make your own lotto cards using cards and large gummed seals or cutouts. Any game played with cards divided into four, six, or nine squares with corresponding cards that are drawn to cover the squares can be considered a lotto-like game. The first child to cover all the spaces or a row on his or her card completes the game.

NOTE: For very young children, continue the game until all the children's cards are complete. Those who finish first may help the other children find the missing cards.

Ring it

Cut out the centres of plastic lids 6 to 8 cm in diameter. Wrap each remaining circlet with bright coloured yarn until a coloured ring is formed. Encourage children to use this ring to circle a matching colour in any picture or on a game. This game is self-correcting.

Direction games

Follow the leader

Select a child to be the leader. Children all follow the leader doing as he or she does. It is an excellent game for a rainy day. Make alternate suggestions if a child cannot think of an idea. VARIATION: Set up a maze to allow children to crawl under a table, step up and over a chair, walk around a pole. You may also make it more complex by having the children follow actions of the leader (changing arm, head, leg positions) as they follow.

Directions

Fill a small, shallow carton with a number of items familiar to the children. Select a child or call for a volunteer. Give a direction to move an object to a certain place. Clap if the child succeeds. If not, assist the child with, "What was it you were going to put where?"

Together, together

This game is similar to "follow the leader" but can be played sitting down. The teacher says, "Together, together, let's all (do something) together." This game may be used to direct a group to another activity.

Sally says/Sam says

This game is similar to "together, together." Instead of using a simple instruction to do something, you preface it with, "Sally says do _____." When the leader omits the statement, "Sally says," the children are instructed to stay as they were. With older children, another type of limitation might be to say, "All those wearing white may go to the table."

NOTE: The name used does not matter. Children enjoy alliteration.

Counting games

How many?

Set out a number of familiar objects. One to five for the younger children, one to ten for older children. Then ask: "How many _____ are there?" Select kind, colour, or any other set of objects within a grouping.

Circle games

Save these games for the most mature group or modify without a formal circle formation.
Play traditional action songs, such as:
"Farmer in the Dell"
"Round and Round in the Village"
"Hokey Pokey"
"This Is the Way"
"Sally Go Round the Stars"
"Did You Ever See a Lassie?" (Laddie)
"Looby Loo"
"Mulberry Bush"
"Pop! Goes the Weasel"
"Skip to My Lou"/"Fly Little Bluebird"

"Fly Little Bluebird"

(tune: "Skip to My Lou")

Fly little bluebird, through my window	Hop little bluebird, in my garden
Fly little bluebird, through my window	Hop little bluebird, in my garden
Fly little bluebird, through my window	Hop little bluebird, in my garden
Um diddle um dum dey.	Um diddle um dum dey.

Children form a circle holding hands with arms raised in Verse 1 to make windows. One child is selected to be the bluebird. After child finishes hopping in the garden (inside the circle), teacher may select successor.

Friend, friend from over the way

The children choose a friend who will come to visit to begin the game. Then they say together:

> "Friend, friend from over the way,
> Please come over now and play" (CHILD KNOCKS ON THE TABLE OR DOOR)

Children say:

> "Come in **John** from over the way, (USE CHILD'S NAME)
> What would you like to play today?"

The child chooses what he or she would like to play. Everyone pantomimes or acts out the action.

Musical stars or skip squat

Set on the floor enough paper stars for all the children. Play a short interlude of music. Explain to the children that when the music stops they are to stand on a star or on designated spots. Have one less star than there are children to add excitement and an element of chance. VARIATIONS: Blue puddles, brown rocks, snowflakes.

★ CAUTION: Never eliminate more than one star during the entire game. Make no emphasis on the last one down and assist each to safely land on a star sometimes. Then there is never anyone out of the game; instead the child left without a star rejoins the group again as soon as the music begins.

"Sally Go Round the Stars"

Sally go round the stars,	F F F F G A
Sally go round the moon,	B♭ B♭ B♭ B♭ A G
Sally go round the chimney pots,	F F F F G A A A
On a Sunday afternoon. Whoops!	A A G G A G F A C F (chord)

Children make a circle with hands joined and slide to left as they sing. They drop each other's hands and with hands raised over heads, jump into the air and clap hands when they sing, "Whoops!"

Hot potato

Tie up a small towel, clean cloth, or nylon stocking so it is soft, light, and somewhat like a ball. Pretend it is a "hot potato." The children sit in a circle with their feet outspread and touching the feet of the child on either side. As the ball is tossed to them, they quickly toss it to someone else. Since cloth does not bounce and is soft, this is safer than a regular ball or beanbag.

Beanbag toss

Select a target such as a wastebasket, carton, or innertube. (A clown face can be painted on a cardboard box with a hole for a mouth or nose.) Allow the children to toss or throw a beanbag into the container. Encourage success by offering toss (underhand flip) or throw (forceful thrust) opportunities side by side.

Singing games using action songs

There are many action songs that invite a child to respond to music. A child may even choose to sing along as he or she moves to the music. These songs will be suggested in each part of the guide under the sections "Large Muscle Activities" or "Rhythms and Singing Games."

Participation records

Some singing games and songs that describe a specific series of responses are recorded and can be used as accompaniment games if you are not a singer or do not have anyone to play the piano, guitar, or autoharp.

Routine Times

Parts of the program that vary little from day to day are considered routine and become a framework for the daily program. They give the children the security that comes with knowing what will happen next. Most often, arrival, health inspection, snack time, toileting, meal times, nap time, group movement, and dismissal times are considered the routine times of the school day.

If not planned for as an integral part of the total program of the day, these times may become boring and humdrum. A matter-of-fact acceptance of routine by the staff will assist children to accept the routine for their basic physical comforts and needs. There is no need for bribes, cajoling, threats, punishment, or excessive praise.

Accidents involving elimination should be handled in a matter-of-fact way.

Remember that the children's ability to accept and function within the school routines will vary considerably.

1. Some are a member of a group for the first time (an only child).
2. School routines are often quite different from home routines.
3. The school or centre may have different values, rules, and limits from those of the child's home.
4. Some children are more flexible and willing to imitate, while others, who are more independent, may resist and need time and assistance to adjust.
5. Physical needs and skills will also vary with the child's age, sex, past experience, and development.

Flexibility is a valuable trait for children in today's world. The extreme conformist has as much trouble as the rebel. Therefore it is helpful if the children can become more flexible with regard to routines by:

1. Giving the children a few minutes notice before making a necessary change in program
2. Encouraging everyone to help so that they can all be ready sooner to participate in the next experience
3. Giving reasons for routine tasks required
4. Assisting children to recognize the benefits from group experience as well as individual achievement

When planning for routine times refer to the suggestions noted in each part of the guide and take advantage of opportunities for learning and variations that will make these times more pleasant. See also the sections on Uses of Games and Fingerplays and Action Songs, pp. 50 and 44 respectively. Plan for a happy balance between the work activity and the rest, with opportunities for refreshments and toileting at necessary intervals.

Large Muscle Activities

Opportunities for the development of motor skills through large muscle activities should be a part of every daily program for very young children. Plans should include experiences both indoors and outdoors with specific plans for your group and those assessed as necessary for individual children in the group. Children attending an all-day program will have a greater need for these types of activities as they have less chance in the remaining portion of the day to do them in their home environment. Days of inclement weather, especially rainy days, will increase the need to implement routine opportunities for these experiences indoors.

Outdoor Large Muscle Activities Centre

Consider your playground an extension of your classroom

1. Provide adequate space for the size and age of your group. Enclose your play area with hedge, fence, or walls; include a gate with a lock to provide for safety from street traffic

Playground sandpit. The abstract-shaped sand pit in the centre of this playground is surrounded by a wide paved area that allows traffic to flow to simple and complex play units. Note climbing-tree log and sawhorses in left foreground. Cement ship in left background has multiple uses.

and easier supervision of the children by the staff. When there are no local required licensing standards, define boundaries by using ropes or sidewalks or other natural boundaries.

2. If limited by size of outdoor yard space available, consider scheduling playground use at different intervals during the day with fewer children in the yard at one time.

3. Augment and allow for alternative space by the use of adjacent parks, gymnasiums, or other play space.

4. Use space wisely, planning and evaluating the potential of every nook and corner, purchasing and making multipurpose equipment. Make certain that no less than one-third of the playground space is uncovered.

5. Build a storage unit for keeping extra equipment or accessories and for items needed for seasonal activities. If built with a flat roof and a sturdy guardrail and deck on the upper level, it can be used for a play area. Add ladders, stairs, or an incline from one level to the other.

6. Plan for your playground's accessibility to the classroom, toilet, and cloakrooms. Use large doors and a ramp for easier mobility.

7. Consider the climate and the need for protection from harsh inclement weather. Build sheltering walls and windbreaks, plan for drainage, and landscaping vegetation to provide shade and to prevent soil erosion. Plan to utilize the play yard all year.

8. Arrange for open areas, equipped areas, and secluded areas with space for individuals and for groups.

9. When weather permits, move some of your learning centres to the outdoor play area.

Outdoors in winter. Although you may be prevented from using the outdoor play area in excessively cold or inclement weather, many winter days will allow for a full range of outdoor activities. See Large Muscle Activities in the "Winter" chapter.

Designing your play area

1. *Digging space:* Use a sandbox or enclosed sandpile to provide an area of dirt for mud play, construction, and/or gardening. Remember, sand needs to be covered when not in use so that it is not used as a litter box by animals.

2. *Shade:* Use a variety of trees, shrubs, and vines of different sizes, colours, and growing cycles. Consider the use of canopies, covered patios, or terraces, as well as temporary shelters such as tents, hung blankets, or beach umbrellas.

3. *Pathways:* Construct a wide curved pathway that may circle around or return to a larger paved area, allowing for group play and preventing traffic jams. When possible, include a slope and hill for variation. Hard surfaces could be blacktop or concrete. Spread cedar filings near play equipment to allow for drainage and to cushion children's falls. When paving surfaces, consider drainage to avoid standing water. Stepping-stones make interesting detours to smaller play areas.

4. *Active play areas:* Include low-branched trees, a large cylindrical cement tunnel under a mound of dirt, tree trunks or logs relocated in a bed of sand or wood chips, cubbies to crawl inside, bushes, climbers, self-pumping swings, or pieces of climbing equipment made from telephone poles or tree logs cut into varying lengths and set perpendicularly in cement to form a series of stumps of varying heights. Consider need for social interaction and co-operative play.

5. *Quiet play areas:* Allow for areas of grass and have mushroom seats, a blanket, a shallow pool, or a single swing away from other equipment. Consider need for solitary play space.

Uneven tree stumps in the playground. *Children are walking and climbing on tree stumps secured in cement and surrounded by sand and dirt. Note varied height of stumps, which also serve to define an area.*

6. *Discovery area:* Provide places to explore and discover including space for animal cages, bird feeders, birdhouses and birdbaths, bushes and plants for insects and small animals. Have an automatic weather gauge, weathervane, and thermometer, as well as space for flowers and trees, and areas where children can enjoy the snow, leaves, seeds, and water.

7. *Surfaces and terrain:* Provide for a variety of levels and surfaces (see photos in this section).

Plan for a variety of play equipment

1. Budget for the repair, replacement, and maintenance of existing equipment as well as for the addition of new equipment each year.

2. Contact members of the community for the possible acquisition of an old boat to be used for dramatic play. Be alert to hinges or apertures in which a child's hand, head, or foot might be caught. Paint with a wood or metal preservative to avoid weathering or rusting.

3. Build your own multiple use equipment, such as a playhouse/storage shed with stairs, railing around roof, or a cubby underneath (see p. 67 for a picture of climbing platforms).

4. Recycle discarded items into valuable, durable play equipment (see following pages).

5. Include play equipment that offers simple and complex challenges and meets the needs and abilities of your group. Add accessories to make them more versatile.

6. If you have a square play yard, which is one of the more difficult to use, locate a sandpile, one major piece of equipment for multiple use or a large surface area for dramatic play in the centre of the playground (see photos, pp. 60 and 67.) The outside corners can be smaller play areas.

Conversation swing. *Children are using this conversation swing in a variety of ways. While the swing invites sociability, it also allows children to individualize it for their own dramatic play and self-expression.*

Tire walls. This is a sturdy, safe, economical, and versatile piece of climbing equipment. Tires are bolted together. Holes are drilled into tires to drain water.

Obstacle course

Plan an obstacle course in the shape of a broken circle, square, rectangle, octagon, or U-shape that will allow the children to begin again once they have completed one cycle. This encourages a continual flow of participants, incurs less traffic confusion, and discourages haphazard sampling by children who may not wish to attempt a more difficult task. Vary skill opportunities by changing the obstacle course as group or individual needs are identified. Provide for a broad variety of motor experiences that will allow children to balance, climb, slide, jump, tumble, push and pull, and swing.

Tires

1. Tractor tires can be made into sandpile enclosures if placed on a sand-based, tiled or bricked area that will allow drainage. Cover when not in use.
2. Tires can be used as jumping circles. Tires slit on the worn tread line into two halves form canals for sailing boats.
3. One or more large tires can be stood upright and buried in the ground (up to the centre opening) to form an archway or tunnel.
4. Large innertubes can be covered with laced canvas to form a small trampoline.
5. A series of three tires of varying circumference can be hung on three cables horizontally one above the other with space between each seat to allow for an interesting swing.

6. A series of seven or more tires can be bolted together like a flat bed mosaic and hung by cables from four poles to form a conversation swing (see photo, p. 63).
7. A series of twelve tires can be bolted together standing on end one above the other in rows of three each and cabled to two posts for a climbing tire wall (see p. 64). Remember to drill drain holes in each tire so that rain water will not accumulate.

Telephone cable spools

1. Paint and use telephone cable spools as tables near the sandpile or a shady tree.
2. Smaller cable spools on wheels can be used for platforms to do tricks on if children wish to be performing like clowns or animals.

Laundry or fat barrels

1. Cut out both ends of a barrel and mount it on a platform to make a tunnel. Use with cleated planks for a ramp in an obstacle course.
2. Cut out one end (top) and a large hole on one side of the barrel and use it to toss in balls. The hole on one side allows the child to retrieve the ball without help. It also can suggest the more difficult feat of throwing a small ball or beanbag into the side hole.
3. Leave both ends of the barrel in and cut out a door on one side to form a cozy nook for a private place.
4. Cut out a cockpit-type hole on one side of the barrel for the child to crawl in when using the barrel as a spaceship. Wings and propellers may be attached if you wish to make an airplane.
5. Peepholes at various spots may be cut in the side of a barrel for other dramatic play, such as a puppet theatre, window counter, or small playhouse.

Cartons or packing crates

While not very durable, cartons can afford a variety of pleasant play experiences if children are allowed to explore freely.

Laundry barrel. This is placed on a wooden base to form a tunnel. Separate parts make storage easier. The barrel can also be used for skill games that involve throwing balls into a container.

Climbing devices.
Children are climbing a tree specially cultivated to allow easy access to low branches.

Duffel bag or one trouser leg

Both can be stuffed with a pillow or foam rubber and used as a punching bag. Attach a spring or a canvas strap to the bag and hang it from a hook.

Tree trunks, logs, and stumps

1. A solid tree trunk with many notched sturdy branches, stripped of bark and treated for weathering, makes an interesting climbing apparatus.
2. A tree that has been topped and the smaller branches removed makes another interesting climbing piece when laid on its side in sand or dirt.
3. Tree stumps or crosscuts of a telephone pole embedded in sand or cement can also be used for sitting or climbing on.
4. Screwing a plywood circle to a stump makes a low table.
5. Railroad ties used as boundaries also make steps or balance boards.

Concrete sewer pipe

1. Use as a tunnel; or it can be attached to other equipment in a grouping. (See photo, p. 67, and note the other learning opportunities when pipe is painted with symbols, signs, and numerals.)
2. Makes a good base for creating both a tunnel and a small hill on a playground. To maintain the hillside on the overhead mound, turf and seed the dirt.

Playground equipment. The play area above combines concrete sewer pipes with tree trunks, platforms of various heights, a tree, a tire, and a conversation swing. This creates a multi-use play structure for climbing, crawling, jumping, and hiding. Painted concrete sewer pipes offer additional opportunities to conceptualize numerals and directions.

Enclosure walls, fences, and stair rails

1. Paint murals or learning concepts on walls in play areas or hallways (see photo, p. 565).
2. Suspend easels on fences for outdoor artists. If you dismiss your children from the play yard, use clothespins to clip take-home pictures to the fence.
3. Hang planters (can be large oil cans) on a stair rail outside to discourage sliding or climbing on it and to provide an opportunity to discover and explore while moving from one area to another.
4. If your view is desirable, plan your enclosures to allow the children to take full advantage of their surroundings.

Tips for supervising the playground

1. Stand (or sit) facing the children you are supervising. Position yourself near equipment where safety is a consideration.
2. Try to equalize the number of children being supervised by one teacher.
3. Remind children to bend knees when jumping and crawling.
4. Allow creative use of materials but with consideration for children's safety and for care of materials and equipment.
5. Encourage children to grasp bars when climbing or swinging with a monkey grip (thumb under, fingers over).
6. Limit turns on equipment in great demand by using a timer or counting number of turns. Encourage one-way traffic on obstacle courses to avoid collisions.

Indoor Large Muscle Activities Centre

To individualize your program for motor development you will need to provide for large muscle activity space both indoors and outdoors. This type of indoor space will also be needed when inclement weather will not allow the children to go outside. Those rainy days need not become days dreaded by either the children or the teacher if alternative plans have been made. Below are some suggestions for creating an indoor large muscle activity centre.

Designing your play area

1. Use centre space areas (part of the regular classroom) for large muscle activities. Provide additional opportunities by equipping a large muscle activity centre with one or more of the following:
   a. Tumbling mat
   b. Punching bag
   c. Climbing gym or ladder box
   d. Rocking horse or boat

2. Use converted classroom space. Move furniture out of the way or close off an area such as the block centre and utilize that floor space to set up portable large muscle play equipment. Select a seldom-used doorway for hanging climbing ropes, a rope ladder, or a swing. Other portable equipment might include:
   a. Balance beam or walking board
   b. Ladders, sawhorses, planks
   c. Swing, climbing rope, rope ladder, bar (doorway equipment)
   d. Laundry or fat barrel (see p. 65)
   e. Tunnel
   f. An indoor-outdoor climber (e.g., Quadro climber)

3. Take advantage of indoor alternative space available when weather does not permit children to go to the playground. This might include a wide hallway, a gymnasium, or an adjacent room.

   ★ CAUTION: Consider the need for clear trafficways in hall areas and emergency exits when using these spaces. A single exit or narrow passageway should not be blocked with a swing, bar, or other equipment.

4. Plan for large muscle games and group exercises. See p. 57 and each part of the guide for specific suggestions.

5. Provide for an expanded use of music and rhythm activities. Use participation records, and see the music section, pp. 39–41, for specific suggestions for rhythms.

6. Plan skill games with equipment, such as:
   a. Horseshoes
   b. Balls (nylon, sponge, rubber)
   c. Skill-toss games
   d. Wadded balls for indoor snowball fights (crumple tissue or newspaper for balls)
   e. Feathers, blown to keep in midair
   f. Bubbles or balloons (blow and catch them)
   g. Bleach bottle scoops for catching balls
   h. Many suggestions found in nos. 1 and 2 could also be used here depending on space

Skill games. Left: Children are blowing feathers to keep them floating in mid-air. **Below:** Large-muscle rainy day activities include colour candles for jumping games.

Extended Experiences

Trips and Excursions

To go or not to go? That is the question

1. Weigh whether the excursion is the best way to introduce children to this discovery and learning experience.
2. Is each child secure enough with the group and at the centre to leave to go on a trip?
3. Is this trip best taken at this age?
4. Exactly what can the children learn, see, do on this trip?
5. Will your group be welcomed? Will young children be accepted?
6. When did you take your last trip? Remember, once a week is too often.

Have you made reservations?

1. Make contacts. Call ahead regarding a visit or excursion.
2. Set time and date (make reservations for appointed day and time).
3. Don't forget to confirm the reservation the day you go.
4. Make suggestions to the person conducting the tour as to what the children will be interested in, might understand, and what their attention span is.

Are you and the children prepared?

1. Scout the area before you go. Are you knowledgeable about destination? Have you defined what is to be explored?
2. Enlist extra help: parents, volunteers, drivers.
3. Plan for extra and special means of transportation.
4. Plan with staff. Define individual teaching responsibilities. Discuss elements of concern, such as crossing a busy street.
5. Accidents may happen. Take a survival kit for assurance.
6. Make certain to include snacks and drinks, and to make provisions for toileting.
7. Watch the clock. Children have built-in timers for their needs, such as rest, eating, toileting.
8. If distance is great, you may want to stop en route for rest and/or a snack break.
9. A walk in the rain might be fun, but what about a downpour?
10. You can always cancel, but have an excellent alternate plan ready.
11. Alert parents as to need for special clothing, funds for tickets, a bag lunch, boots, mittens, swimsuits. Get written permission slips and inform parents of specific plans (destination, date, time).

Keep a travel log

1. Take photos, make a recorded tape segment (sounds of a zoo), take notes for a next trip.
2. Learn from your mistakes and build on what was positive.
3. Note signs of learning; sometimes they are not immediately evident.

Are you a good tour leader?

1. Prepare the children by introducing the idea and letting them help plan the trip.
2. When plans are definite, share them with the children, but not too far ahead.
3. Brief your travellers regarding rules. Modify and make your own to meet your specific group needs.
4. Use travel time for learning as well as helping the children to pass the time.

Follow up with follow through

1. Be prepared for an energetic response when you get back to your centre by:
   a. Having appropriate dramatic play props and dress-ups ready for use
   b. Having selected books available in book centre before and after the trip
   c. Collecting poems, games, and songs that might be used when appropriate interest is shown
   d. Planning art activities considering the thrust of the trip
2. Provide for instant replay. Listen enroute for children's initial responses.
3. Allow chances for verbalization of children's experiences in group time and small groups.
4. Treasures and souvenirs may be shared in "show and tell."

Evaluate the trip

1. Give children time to react and respond to the experience. Then evaluate the trip with your staff.
2. Would you do it again? What would you do differently?

Planning for Visitors

Select the visitor

1. Choose someone who likes and is interested in young children.
2. Request educational officers from community resources or people who have very young children of their own. When invited on their day off, working parents can be more flexible about time.
3. Select members of both sexes and of different cultural groups.
4. Choose someone most knowledgeable or skilled in the resource you need. Remember grandparents, students, and retired citizens.

Interview the visitor

1. Interview the visitor by telephone or in person. Set a specific date and time that best suits both of your schedules and plans.
2. Visit the persons at their place of work. They may then suggest other items or subjects you might want to include.

Brief the visitor

1. List questions the children might ask or need to know.
2. Suggest items to wear or share (within children's experience).
3. Give cautions about safety in regard to tools (or other items) to be shared.
4. Describe the setting the visitor will be in with children.
5. Offer a few tips on ways to deal with behaviour that may occur.

Preplan for the visit

1. Set the scene. Give children opportunities to discover related information from other activities before the visitor arrives.
2. Preplan some follow-through experiences for the children after the visit. Purchase or obtain equipment necessary for these experiences.
3. Encourage children to help prepare an invitation and later thank-you notes of appreciation to a visitor.

Using Films and Filmstrips

1. Preview a film or filmstrip. Double check that extension cords and extra bulbs are handy.
2. Select a film much as you would a book—for content, pictures, length, age level, appropriateness to interest development, and authenticity.
3. Reserve film or filmstrip, projector, and screen.
4. Edit films or, if a filmstrip, the story line to meet your needs. Make a note of sections you wish to roll past.
5. Select a room that can be darkened. Leave a small light on for children who may be frightened by darkness.
6. Mark floor for placement of screen and projector after you have focused the picture. Choose a clear wall for projection if no screen is available.
7. Have a table for the projector handy so it can be placed on the marked space.
8. If the children are seated on the floor, shoot the picture so they can all see but not so high that they must sit with their necks in an uncomfortable position.
9. While viewing the film, listen and watch for children's responses (verbal, facial, and body language). When you can, encourage children to answer their own questions, if they are able, by redirecting the question with another question. If they cannot, answer them yourself or help children to discover the answers. You may wish to rerun the filmstrip.

Planning a Party for Parents and Friends

1. Make certain every child can have one parent, family member, or friend attend the party.
2. If you plan to let parents observe children in a group-time experience, select things to do that children enjoy: play games, sing songs, and tell or read a story just as you usually do. Make certain there is no focus on any one child! Keep it simple and unrehearsed, and follow the usual routine if possible.
3. Have parents seated behind the children or on the side of the room so children will be less aware they are being observed (ideally, let parents and children sit together and both participate).
4. There should be no pressure on performance.
5. The group should be only those children who are normally in the room together.
6. Hold the party during regular school hours.
7. Plan a parents' party for a time of the year when the calendar is not likely to be so filled with events, when the weather is usually good, and when most parents and children can attend. (In the fall, children beginning school may be coming down with the usual childhood communicable diseases—measles, chickenpox, mumps.) You may wish to invite parents, family members, or friends for only one small group of your whole class at a time. Invite these different small groups of parents over a series of succeeding days.

Teacher Resources

Pictures, Displays, and Special Room Arrangements

1. Create your own. Start or add to a picture file. Have parents, staff, and volunteers help in the collection. Besides clipping magazines, watch for good picture sources in your community. Seasonal or topical posters in grocery stores, drugstores, department stores, travel agencies, or the post office may be available for the asking.
2. Talk to store managers about discarded cardboard shelf displays. These have many uses with little change except a coat of paint.

3. Make your own cardboard display boards or scrapbooks. (Use chicken-wire rings for spiral hinges.) Pegholed fibreboard is another possibility for a sturdy surface to which pictures can be taped.
4. Screw butterfly-wing clips to the wooden frame of a blackboard to hold a section of plasterboard. This will instantly transform a blackboard into a bulletin board.
5. Make a kiosk for displaying science or art items. Use the flat surfaces to show pictures and the niches to display treasures for examination or exploration (see photo below).

Mounting pictures

1. Whenever possible mount teaching pictures using a uniform size for easier filing.
2. File smaller pictures in see-through envelopes for use with games, bulletin boards, or pasting.
3. Label pictures on the back or place in alphabetized folders.
4. If you mount pictures in colour, dramatize the most important subject or object by repeating its colour in the border. Always leave a wider margin at the bottom of a mat than the other three sides, which may have equal margins. Occasionally use an abstract or odd shape behind picture to mount it more attractively. Use pinking shears or tear edges for other variations.
5. Try to get a complete figure of an animal, person, or object in the picture. If mounted and displayed with other pictures choose those of appropriate sizes (relative to each other) so children will not be confused by the misproportions.

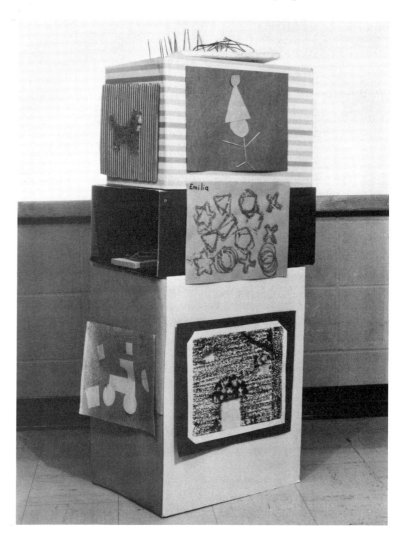

Mounting pictures. A kiosk is used to display children's art in the round. Children have chosen their best work to display. The kiosk is made by bolting cartons together. Sections may be covered with a variety of materials, such as cloth, wallpaper, or plastic, or they may be painted.

Displaying or posting teaching pictures

1. Use thumbtacks at the edge, *not* through the picture. If you use tape, remove it after each hanging before you return the picture to the file.
2. Save some duplicate pictures for expanded use. Look for sequence pictures.
3. Use walls, hallways, stairwells as display places for children's art pieces. Change displays often. Invite a local artist to paint a mural or child-scaled wall design (see photo, p. 565).
4. Don't forget the ceiling of the resting area. Hang mobiles or pictures to suggest relaxation or pleasant memories, such as nature scenes, children holding pets, parents hugging children.
5. Use bulletin boards at an entrance for parents' notices and messages, in the group-time area for focus of theme or interest development or for reference, or inside an entrance door for children to discover as they arrive.
6. Make a bulletin board attractive by using twisted crepe paper strips, abstract shapes of complementary colours (if you doubt your own judgment look at fabrics or paintings for shades or tints used together). Cut out coloured or black letters for bolder messages. Use coloured yarn or string to circle related pictures.

NOTE: Suggestions are made in each guide for specific uses of pictures in games, language development, and other activities.

Core Library

The following titles can be obtained through bookstores or from the publishers. Titles that are no longer in print can be found at the public library.

General books about child development

Elkind, David. *The Hurried Child.* Reading, MA: Addison-Wesley, 1981.
Evans, Richard. *Piaget: The Man and His Ideas.* New York: Dutton, 1973.
Ginsberg, H., and S. Opper. *Piaget's Theory of Intellectual Development.* New York: Prentice-Hall, 1979.
Irwin, D.M., and M.M. Bushnell. *Observational Strategies for Child Study.* New York: Holt, Rinehart and Winston, 1980.
Kagan, Jerome. *The Nature of the Child.* New York: Basic Books, 1984.
Katz, Lillian. *Current Topics in Early Childhood Education.* All Volumes. Norwood, NJ: Ablex Publishing.
Piaget, Jean. *The Child's Conception of Number.* New York: Norton, 1965. (If you are fluent in French the original *La Genese du Nombre chez l'Enfant.* Geneva: 1941, is much clearer.)
_____. *The Child's Conception of the World.* Totowa, NJ: Littlefield, 1975.
_____. *The Grasp of Consciousness.* Cambridge, MA: Harvard University Press, 1976.
Turner, J.S., and D.B. Helms. *Lifespan Development.* New York: Holt, Rinehart and Winston, 1983.

General curriculum resources

Baratta-Lorton, Mary. *Workjobs.* Don Mills, Ont.: Addison-Wesley, 1972.
Coombs, Ernie, and Shelley Tanaka. *Mr. Dressup's Book of Things to Make and Do.* Toronto: CBC Enterprises, 1985.
Daniels, Betty Ternice. *The Prairie Kid's Cookbook.* Cochin, Sask. Prairetopian Enterprises, 1983.
Debelak, M., et al. *Creating Innovative Classroom Materials for Teaching Young Children.* San Diego: Harcourt Brace Jovanovich, 1981.

Deiner, P.L. *Resources for Teaching Young Children with Special Needs.* Toronto: Harcourt Brace Jovanovich, Canada, 1983.

Indenbaum, Valerie, and Marcia Shapiro. *The Everything Book.* Livonia, MI: Partner Press, 1985.

Linton, Marilyn. *The Maple Syrup Book.* Toronto: Kids Can Press, 1983.

MacDonald, Kate. *Anne of Green Gables Cookbook.* Don Mills, Ont.: Oxford University Press, 1985.

Mendelson, Susan. *Let Me In the Kitchen.* Vancouver: Douglas & McIntyre, 1982.

Owl's Summer Fun. Toronto: Greey de Pencier Books, 1982.

Owl's Winter Fun. Toronto: Greey de Pencier Books, 1980.

Rockwell, R.E., et al. *Hug a Tree and Other Things to Do Outdoors With Children.* Mt. Rainier, MD: Gryphon, 1983.

Walker, Lois, and Hub Walker. *Crafts for Kids: The Puppcorn Way.* Toronto: Deneau Publishers, 1982.

Children's literature

Butler, D. *Babies Need Books.* Markham, Ont.: Penguin Books, 1980.

Casearli, A. *Good Books to Grow On.* New York: Warner Books, 1985.

Charlton, J., ed. *Children's Choices of Canadian Books.* Ottawa: Citizen's Committee on Children, 1978–1985.

Ciancids, P.J. *Picture Books for Children* (2nd ed.). Chicago: American Library Association, 1981.

Egoff, S., et al., eds. *Only Connect.* Toronto: Oxford University Press, 1980.

Gillwapie, J.T. *Best Books for Children.* New York: Bowker, 1981.

Landsberg, Michelle. *Michelle Landsberg's Guide to Children's Books.* Markham, Ont.: Penguin Books, 1985.

Growing With Books: Children's Literature in the Formative Years and Beyond. Toronto: Ontario Ministry of Education.

Russell, William. *Classics to Read Aloud to Your Children.* New York: Crown Publishers, 1984.

Saltman, J. *Modern Canadian Children's Books.* Toronto: Oxford University Press, 1987.

Stott, Jon C. *Children's Literature from A to Z.* New York: McGraw-Hill, 1984.

—————. *Children's Literature in Canada: A Guide to Authors and Illustrators.* Toronto: Harcourt Brace Jovanovich, Canada, 1988.

Alphabet books

Good programs for young children encourage and enhance the development of language and communication. All of the activities in this text encourage the appropriate use of language, but they do not deal directly with children's interest in letters and words. Letters and words should be a theme that runs through your program planning at all times. All activities involve communication and should encourage language development.

- Blades, Ann. *By the Sea: An Alphabet Book.* Toronto: Kids Can Press, 1986.
- Cleaver, Elizabeth. *A B C.* Toronto: Oxford University Press, 1982.
- • Harrison, Ted. *A Northern Alphabet.* Montreal: Tundra Books, 1982.
- • • Mastin, Colleayn. *Canadian Wild Animals A-Z.* Sandhill Books, 1986.
- • Moak, Allan. *A Big City A B C.* Montreal: Tundra Books, 1984.
- • Morgan, Nichola. *The Great B.C. Alphabet Book.* Markham, Ont.: Fitzhenry & Whiteside, 1985.
- Pare, Roger. *The Annick ABC Activity Set.* Willowdale, Ont.: Annick Press, 1985.
- • Poulin, Stephan. *Ah! Belle Cité/A Beautiful City ABC.* Montreal: Tundra Books, 1985.

Language games, fingerplays, and poetry

Brown, Marc. *Finger Rhymes*. New York: Dutton, 1980.

_____. *Hand Rhymes*. New York: Dutton, 1985.

Chenfeld, Mimi, B. *Creative Activities for Young Children*. San Diego: Harcourt Brace Jovanovich, Publishers, 1983.

Cole, Joanna. *A New Treasury of Children's Poetry*. New York: Doubleday, 1984.

Debelak, M., J. Herr, and M. Jacobson. *Creating Innovative Classroom Materials for Teaching Young Children*. San Diego: Harcourt Brace Jovanovich, Publishers, 1981.

Downie, Mary Alice. *The New Wind Has Wings*. Toronto: Oxford University Press, 1984.

Fowke, Edith. *Sally Go Round the Sun*. Toronto: McClelland and Stewart, 1969.

Glazer, Tom. *Eye Winker, Tom Tinker, Chin Chopper*. Garden City, NY: Doubleday, 1973. Fingerplays with piano.

Gravson, Marion F. *Let's Do Fingerplays*. New York: David McKay, 1962.

Heidbreder, Robert. *Don't Eat Spiders*. Toronto: Oxford University Press, 1985.

King, Karen, and Ian Beck. *Oranges and Lemons*. Toronto: Oxford University Press, 1985.

Lee, Dennis. *Alligator Pie*. Toronto: Macmillan of Canada, 1974.

_____. *Jelly Belly*. Toronto: Macmillan of Canada, 1983.

_____. *Lizzy's Lion*. Don Mills, Ont.: Stoddart, 1984.

Prelutsky, Jack. *Read Aloud Rhymes*. New York: Knopf, 1986.

Silverstein, Shel. *Where the Sidewalk Ends*. New York: Harper and Row Junior Books, 1974.

Simmie, Lois. *An Armadillo is Not a Pillow*, Saskatoon, Sask.: Western Producer Prairie Books, 1986.

_____. *Auntie's Knitting a Baby*. Saskatoon, Sask.: Western Producer Prairie Books, 1984.

Sneyd, Lola. *The Asphalt Octopus: A Child's World in Poetry*. Toronto: Simon & Pierre, 1982.

_____. *The Concrete Giraffe*. Toronto: Simon & Pierre, 1984.

Souster, Raymond. *Flight of the Roller Coaster*. Ottawa: Oberon Press, 1985.

Stacey, Ann. *The Enchanted Bear and Other Poems*. Winnipeg: The Prairie Publishing Co., 1986.

Williams, Sarah. *Round and Round the Garden*. Toronto: Oxford University Press, 1983.

Wynne-Jones, Tim. *Mischief City*. Vancouver: Douglas & McIntyre, 1986.

Art books

Cherry, Clare. *Creative Art for the Developing Child*. Belmont, CA: DS Lake Publishers, 1972.

McDonald, Pauline, and Doris V. Brown. *Creative Art for Home and School*. Alhambra, CA.: Borden Publishing, 1961.

Music books

Birkenshaw, Lois, and David Walden. *The Goat With the Bright Red Socks*. Toronto Board of Education, 1978.

Blay, Edgar. *The Best Singing Games for Children of All Ages*. New York: Sterling, 1957.

Burton, Leon, and William Hughes. *MusicPlay*. Don Mills, Ont.: Addison-Wesley, 1979.

_____. *Treasury of Songs for Children*. Scarborough, NY: Songs Music Inc., 1964.

Glazer, Tom. *Do Your Ears Hang Low?* New York: Doubleday, 1980.

_____. *Eye Winker, Tom Tinker, Chin Chopper*. New York: Doubleday 1973.

Gordon, Shelley. *Songs to Sing and Sing Again*. Toronto: S. Gordon, 25 Belsize Dr. Toronto, M4S 1L3, 1984.

Haines, J.E., and L.L. Gerber. *Leading Young Children to Music*. Toronto: Merrill Publishing, 1984.

Hart, Jane. *Singing Bee!* New York: Lothrop, Lee and Shepard, 1982.

Magadini, Peter. *Music We Can See and Hear.* Oakville, Ont.: Frederick Harris, 1982.
Murray, Helen. *Stepping Along in Music Land.* Books I and II. London, Ont.: Middlesex Printing Co., 1983.
Nelson, Esther. *Musical Games for Children of all Ages.* New York: Sterling, 1976.
Nye, Vernice. *Music for Young Children.* Dubuque, IA: W.C. Brown, 1979.
Pugmire, M.C.W. *Experiences in Music for Young Children.* Albany, NY: Delmar, 1977.
Raffi. *The Baby Beluga Book.* Toronto: McClelland and Stewart, 1986.
Sharon, Lois and Bram. *Elephant Jam.* Toronto: McGraw-Hill Ryerson, 1980.
Wayman, Joe. *The Colours of My Rainbow.* Carthage IL: Good Apple Inc., 1978.
Warner, L., and P. Berry. *Tunes for Tots.* Carthage, IL: Good Apple Inc., 1982.
————. *More Piggyback Songs.* Everett, WA: Warren Pub., 1984.
————. *Piggyback Songs.* Everett, WA: Warren Pub., 1983.
Wood, Donna. *Move, Sing, Listen, Play.* Toronto: Gordon V. Thompson Music, 1982.

Guides for taking trips

Clarke, Sheila, Marilyn Linton, and Jeanne Scargall. *Toronto Is for Kids.* Toronto: Greey de Pencier Books, 1976.
Murray, Kristen, and Allan Shute. *Kidmonton.* Edmonton: Tree Frog Press, 1978.
Small, Cecile. *Saskatchewan: 2 Kids and a Camera.* Saskatoon Sask.: Turner Warwick, 1982.
Stein, Sherry, and Howard Shapiro. *Kidding Around Montreal.* Don Mills, Ont.: Collier Macmillan Canada, 1976.
Wood, Daniel, and Betty Campbell. *Kids! Kids! Kids! and Vancouver.* Vancouver: Fforbez Enterprises Ltd. 1978.
————. *Kids! Kids! Kids! and Vancouver Island.* Vancouver: Fforbez Enterprises Ltd., 1977.

Special Canadian resources

Anderson, Karen, and Gary Woodill. *Community Resources for Canadian Families.* Orillia, Ont.: Ptarmigan, Pub., 1985.
Burnaby, B. *Language in Education Among Canadian Native Peoples.* Toronto: OISE Press, 1982.
Dawe, Tom. *Land Wash Days (Nfld.).* St. John's: Newfoundland Book Publishers, 1980.
Marsh, James, ed. *The Canadian Encyclopedia.* Edmonton: Hurtig Publishers, 1985.
Mock, K. *Multicultural Preschool Education: A Resource Manual for Supervisors and Volunteers.* Toronto: Ontario Ministry of Citizenship and Culture, 1985.
Publications List, Secretary of State. Ottawa: Multiculturalism Directorate, Government of Canada 1980.
Sawyer, Don, and Howard Green. *The NESA Activities Handbook for Native and Multicultural Classrooms.* Vancouver: The Tillacum Library, 1984.
Smallwood, J. *The Encyclopedia of Newfoundland and Labrador.* St. John's: Newfoundland Book Publishers, 1981.
Woodill, Gary, and Karen Anderson. *Canadian Resources for Children with Special Needs.* Orillia, Ont.: Ptarmigan, Pub., 1985.

The Children's Book Centre

A very special Canadian resource is the Children's Book Centre, a national, nonprofit organization, which was established in 1976 to promote the reading and writing of Canadian children's books. It serves parents, teachers, librarians, booksellers, publishers, students, writers, illustrators—in fact anyone who cares about children and the books they read. The Children's Book Centre is a national organization that regardless of where you live, can provide you with information about Canadian children's books. And further, it offers:

▷ a reference library, open to the public
▷ a quarterly newsletter to keep you up to date on the latest books, personalities, developments, and great ideas for introducing books to children
▷ print and audio–visual materials on authors, illustrators, book production, and publishing
▷ workshops on writing for children
▷ staff presentations on all aspects of Canadian children's literature
▷ an annual national Children's Book Festival to salute Canadian books with author and illustrator presentations, special kits, and celebrations from coast to coast

The Centre has its national office in Toronto and regional offices across the country:

The Children's Book Centre
229 College St
5th Floor
Toronto, Ont
M5T 1R4
(416)597-1331

The Children's Book Centre
9421-144th St
Edmonton, Alta
T5R 0R8
(403)452-6754
     424-7764

The Children's Book Centre
3142 Eastview
Saskatoon, Sask
S7J 3J4
(306)477-1308

The Children's Book Centre
881 Kilkenny Dr
Winnipeg, Man
R3T 3Z4
(204)261-4630
     945-6457

The Children's Book Centre
6069 Coburg Rd
Halifax, NS
B3H 1Z1
(902)423-7626
     423-0962

Additional resources for children's books are:

B.C. Association of Learning Materials and Educational Representatives
c/o Ren Speer 1-2336 South Grandview Highway
P.O. Box 66019, Station F
Vancouver, B.C.
V5N 5L4
(604)872-3042

Canadian Society of Children's Authors, Illustrators and Performers
P.O. Box 280 Station L
Toronto, Ont.
M6E 4Z2
(416)651-3759

Commercial Sources for Learning Materials

Toys

The following resource list is taken, with the permission of the Canadian Toy Testing Council, from the *Toy Report* 1987, published by the Consumer's Association of Canada.

NOTE: Retail outlets are not included in this list.

Acme Ruler Co Ltd
P.O. Box 239
Mount Forest, Ont
N0G 2L0
(519)323-3100

Amay Industries Ltd
2345 Lapierre St
LaSalle, Que
H8N 1B7
(514)367-2628

Ambt
Represented by:
Pierre Belvedere Inc

American Plastic Toys
Represented by:
Chieftain Products Inc

Amloid
Represented by:
Ritvik Toys Inc

Amram's Division of Russ
315 Attwell Dr
Rexdale, Ont
M9W 5K9
(416)675-1040

Amtoy
Represented by:
Charan Toy Company Inc

Anthes Universal Ltd
341 Heart Lake Rd S
Brampton, Ont
L6W 3K8
(416)451-0200

Aqua Toys Ab
Represented by:
Pierre Belvedere Inc

Arco
Represented by:
Mattel Canada Inc

Avril
Represented by:
Irwin Toy Ltd

Axlon
Represented by:
Ganz Bros. Toys Ltd

Bambina
Represented by:
Laurentide Appliances Ltd

Bambola
Represented by:
Maison Joseph Battat Ltd

Battat Ltd Maison Joseph
8440 Darnley Rd
Montreal, Que
H4T 1M4
(514)341-6000

Bernard Young & Co Ltd
356 Eastern Ave
Toronto, Ont
M4M 1B8
(416)469-1193

Berol Canada Inc
105 Rene Philippe St
Ville Lemoyne, Que
J4R 2J9
(514)861-6311

Binkley Toys
Box 6064, Station F
Hamilton, Ont
L9C 5S2
(416)575-9654

Binney & Smith (Canada) Ltd
P.O. Box 120
15 Mary St W
Lindsay, Ont
K9V 4R8
(705)324-6105

Birkenhead
Represented by:
Bernard Young & Co Ltd

Bluebird
Represented by:
Maison Joseph Battat Ltd

Bô-Jeux Inc
8711 Place Ray Lawson
Ville d'Anjou, Que
H1J 1H8
(514)355-4444

Borgfeldt Toys (Canada) Ltd
3440 Pharmacy Ave
Scarborough, Ont
M1W 2P8
(416)497-2004

Brigitta's Import Inc
131 Citation Rd
Concord, Ont
L4K 2R3
(416)669-1570

Brio Scanditoy Inc
4995 Timberlea Blvd
Unit 2
Mississauga, Ont
L4W 2S2
(416)629-2740

Britains
Represented by:
WG Distributors

Buddy L
Represented by:
Grand Toys Ltd

Buffao-Eastcantra Inc
1300 Pomba
St-Laurent, Que
H4R 2A1
(514)333-8550

Burago Diecast
Represented by:
Borgfeldt Toys (Canada) Ltd

Cambridge Recreation Products
543 Conestoga Blvd
Cambridge, Ont
N1R 6T4
(519)623-9680

Canada Games Co Ltd
61 Wildcat Rd
Downsview, Ont
M3J 2P5
(416)661-6203

Candu Toy Co Ltd
400 Esna Pk Dr
Unit 21
L3R 3K2
(416)475-8864

Candym Enterprises Ltd
44 East Beaver Creek
Unit 16
Richmond Hill, Ont
L4B 1G8
(416)764-3000

Capsela
Represented by:
Irwin Toy Ltd

Caran d'Ache
Represented by:
Pierre Belvedere Inc

Carters
Represented by:
Dennison Manufacturing Canada Ltd

Charan Toy Co Inc
1087 Alness St
Toronto, Ont
M3J 2J1
(416)663-9830

Chicco
Represented by:
Candu Toy Co Ltd

Chieftain Products Inc
265 Champagne Dr
Downsview, Ont
M3J 2C6
(416)636-4100

Clowny Canada
50 Ronson Dr
Suite 122
Rexdale, Ont
M9W 1B3
(416)247-6139

Coleco (Canada) Ltd
4000 St Ambroise
Montreal, Que
H4C 2C8
(514)934-4100

Colourforms
Represented by:
Canada Games Co Ltd

Combi Riding Toys
Represented by:
Irwin Toy Ltd

Commonwealth
Represented by:
Irwin Toy Ltd

Consumers Distributing
Check local listings for the store in your area

Corolle Dolls
Represented by:
Pierre Belvedere Inc

W.E. Coutts Company
2 Hallcrown Pl
Willowdale, Ont
M2J 1P6
(416)492-1300

Craft House Corporation
Represented by:
Chieftain Products Inc

Crayola
Represented by:
Binney & Smith (Canada) Ltd

Creata International Inc
Represented by:
Irwin Toy Ltd

Creative Toys
Represented by:
Daylin Sales & Marketing Ltd

DMA Industries Inc
4135 Griffith St
St-Laurent, Que
(514)738-6922

R. Dakin & Co Canada Ltd
4500 Sheppard Ave E
Unit 21
Scarborough, Ont
M1S 3R6
(416)293-6786

Daylin Sales & Marketing Ltd
2300 South Sheridan Way
Mississauga, Ont
L5J 2M4
(416)823-9190

Dennison Manufacturing Canada Inc
200 Base Line Rd E
Bowmanville, Ont
L1C 1A2
(416)623-6311

Diana Doll's Wear Ltd
197 Barton St
Stoney Creek, Ont
L8E 2K3
(416)662-4281

Diset
Represented by:
Pierre Belvedere Inc

Dixon Ticonderoga Inc
531 Davis Dr
Newmarket, Ont
L3Y 2P1
(416)386-4529

Dominion Skate Co Ltd
45 Railroad St
Brampton, Ont
L6X 1G4
(416)453-9860

Durham Industries
Represented by:
View-Master Ideal (Canada) Inc

Easton Court Manufacturing & Marketing
16-50 Paxman Rd
Etobicoke, Ont
M9C 1B7
(416)622-9166

Eatons
Check local listings for the store in your area

Educo Services
207-80 Chippewa Rd
Sherwood Park, Alta
T8A 3Y1
(403)467-9772

Eff-N-Tee Sales and Marketing
201 Snidercroft Rd
Unit 1
Concord, Ont
L4K 2J9
(416)669-6322

Empire of Carolina
Represented by:
Irwin Toy Ltd

Eole 2 Inc
30 Est rue St-Paul
Montreal, Que
H2Y 1G3
(514)861-4655

ERTI Canada
1262 Don Mills Rd
Don Mills, Ont
M3B 2W7
(416)339-4000

Exclusive Ideas Inc
P.O. Box 820
Suite J.J.6
800 Niagara St N
Welland, Ont
L3B 5Y5
(416)735-0181

Faber-Castell Canada Inc
77 Brown's Line
Toronto, Ont
M8W 4X5
(416)259-5051

Family Pastimes
R.R. 4
Perth, Ont
K7H 3C6
(613)267-4819

Famosa
Represented by;
Bô-Jeux Inc

Fischerform
Represented by:
Lundby of Sweden (Canada) Inc

Fischertechnik
Represented by:
Grand Toys Ltd

Fisher-Price Canada
5300 Tomken Rd
Mississauga, Ont
L4W 1P2
(416)624-6600

Galoob Toy Canada
5800 Ambler Dr
Suite 106
Mississauga, Ont
L9W 4J4
(416)624-9557

Galt Toys
1147 Bellamy Rd
Unit 6
Scarborough, Ont
M1H 1H6
1-800-268-4011

Ganz Bros. Toys Ltd
One Pearce Rd
Woodbridge, Ont
L4L 3T2
(416)851-6661

Gayla-Haugh Kites Ltd
25 Rutherford Rd S
Brampton, Ont
L6W 3J3
(416)356-3964

General Plastics
Represented by:
Louise Kool & Galt Ltd

Gil Toys
Represented by:
DMA Industries Inc

Grand Toys Ltd
1710 Trans Canada Highway
Dorval, Que
H9P 1H7
(514)685-2180

Grazioli Giochi
Represented by:
Bô-Jeux Inc

Grumbacher (Canada) Inc
460 Finchdene Sq
Scarborough, Ont
M1X 1C4
(416)299-7000

Gund Inc
Represented by:
Candym Enterprises Ltd

Gunther
Represented by:
Maison Joseph Battat Ltd

H-G Industries, H-G Toys
Represented by:
Charan Toy Company Inc

HP Plast, HP Toys
Represented by:
Maison Joseph Battat Ltd

H.K. Video Technology Canada Ltd
250-10991 Shellbridge Way
Richmond, BC
(604)273-5131

Handicraft
Represented by:
Chieftain Products Inc

Harbutt's
Represented by:
Canada Games Co Ltd

Hasbro Canada Inc
2350 de la Province
Longueuil, Que
J4G 1G2
(514)670-9820

Henry Ltd
1 Head St
Dundas, Ont
L9H 3H5
(416)628-2231

Heros
Represented by:
Brigitta's Import Inc

High Game Enterprises
Represented by:
Waddington Sanders

Hilroy Division of Abitibi-Price Inc
250 Bowie Ave
Toronto, Ont
M6E 2R9
(416)782-4411

Horn Abbot Ltd
Represented by:
Chieftain Products Inc

Hudson's Bay Co Ltd
Check local listings for the store in your area

IPL Inc
140 Commerciale
St-Damien, Que
G0R 2Y0
(418)789-2880

Ideal
Represented by;
View-Master Ideal (Canada) Ltd

Ikea Canada
3200 Sweden Way
Richmond, BC
V6V 2A5
(604)273-2051

Ikecho
Represented by:
Maison Joseph Battat Ltd

Illco
Represented by:
Consumers Distributing

Illfelder
Represented by:
Grand Toys Ltd

IMCO
Represented by:
Consumers Distributing

Irwin Toy Ltd
43 Hanna Ave
Toronto, Ont
M6K 1X6
(416)626-6600

Jofrika
Represented by:
Maison Joseph Battat Ltd

John Adams
Represented by:
Steppe Enterprises

Jouets Eco
Represented by:
Brigitta's Import Inc

Jumbo
Represented by:
Maison Joseph Battat Ltd

Kawada
Represented by:
Maison Joseph Battat Ltd

Kenner
Represented by:
Kenner Parker

Kenner Parker
7883 Keele St
Concord, Ont
L4K 1B7
(416)669-1210

Kiddicraft
Represented by:
Bô-Jeux Inc

L.J.N. Toys
Represented by:
Grand Toys Ltd

Lakeside
Represented by:
Irwin Toy Ltd

Lanard
Represented by:
Consumers Distributing

Lanco Inc
Various representatives

Lasy of North America Ltd
108 Lake Erie Place SE
Calgary, Alta
T2J 2L4
(403)271-7657

Laurentide Appliances Ltd
160 Bates Rd
Montreal, Que
H3S 1A3
(514)731-3348

Lauri Puzzles
Representative unknown

Lego Division
Samsonite
753 Ontario St
Stratford, Ont
N5A 3J9
(519)271-5040

Lena
Represented by:
Brigitta's Import Inc

The Little Tikes Co
589 Massey Rd
Guelph, Ont
N1K 1G3

Louise Kool & Galt Ltd
1147 Bellamy Rd
Unit 6
Scarborough, Ont
M1H 1H6
(416)439-4332

Lundby of Sweden (Canada) Inc
1515 Matheson Blvd
Unit C-2
Mississauga, Ont
L4W 2P5
(416)625-5160

Maison Joseph Battat Ltd
8440 Darnley Rd
Montreal, Que
H4T 1M4
(514)341-6000

Majorette (Canada) Inc
7650 Kimbel St
Unit 16
Mississauga, Ont
L5S 1L2
(416)673-2511

Matchbox
Represented by:
Irwin Toy Ltd

Mattel Canada Inc
800 Islington Ave
Toronto, Ont
M8Z 4N7
(416)252-5192

Maxigames
4 Simcoe Rd
Kettleby, Ont
L0G 1J0

Meccano
Representative unknown

Micki Gemla—Sweden
Represented by:
Bô-Jeux Inc

Mighty Star Ltd
2250 de Maisonneuve Blvd E
Montreal, Que
H2K 2E5
(514)527-8715

Milton Bradley
Represented by:
Hasbro Canada Inc

Mona
Represented by:
Maison Joseph Battat Ltd

Montrose Industries Inc.
P.O. Box 1444
Place d'Armes
Montreal, Que
H2Y 3K8
(514)875-5530

Nasta Industries
Represented by:
Hasbro Canada Inc

Nathan, Fernand
Represented by:
Bô-Jeux Inc

Noma
375 Kennedy Rd
Scarborough, Ont
M1K 2A3
(416)267-4614

Norca Industries Ltd
19151 Cruickshank Ave
Baie d'Urfé, Que
H9X 3N9
(514)457-2840

Ohio Art
Represented by:
Irwin Toy Ltd

Optex Corporation/Tasco
52 Lesmill Rd
Don Mills, Ont
M3B 2T5
(416)449-6470

Page
Represented by:
Anthes Universal Ltd

Panosh Place
Represented by:
Charan Toy Company Inc

Parker
Represented by:
Kenner Parker

Pastime
Represented by:
Pax Mfg Co Ltd

Pax Mfg Co Ltd
50 Carroll St
Toronto, Ont
M4M 3G3
(416)461-0439

Pedigree
Represented by:
Irwin Toy Ltd

Pentalic Corporation
Represented by:
M. Grumbacher (Canada) Inc

Petite
Represented by:
WG Distributors

Pierre Belvedere Inc
105 Rue St-Paul est
Montreal, Que
H2Y 1G7
(514)866-2817

Played Games
Represented by:
Russell Mfg Co Inc

Playgroup
Represented by:
Thinkway Toys

Playmates Toys Inc
5430 Timberlea Blvd
Mississauga, Ont
L4W 2T7
(416)629-2274

Playmobil Canada Inc
6155 Tomken Rd
Mississauga, Ont
L5T 1X3
(416)677-6202

Playskool
Represented by:
Hasbro Canada Inc

Playtime
Represented by:
Consumers Distributing

Playtoy Industries
29 Ingram Dr
Toronto, Ont
M6M 2L7
1-800-268-1408

Prang
Represented by:
Dixon Inc

Precision
Represented by:
Victoria Precision Inc

Presto Magix
Representative unknown

Preston Manufacturing Ltd
185 King St E
Cambridge, Ont
N3H 4S1
(519)653-7143

Processed Plastics
Division of Grand Toys Ltd

Quercetti
Represented by:
Pierre Belvedere Inc

Radio Shack Canada
Box 34000
Barrie, Ont
L4M 4W5
(705)728-6242

Radio Steel and Mfg Co
representative unknown

Ravensburger
Represented by:
Pierre Belvedere Inc

Reeves
Represented by:
Anthes Universal Ltd

Reich Brothers Inc
5745 Pare St
Montreal, Que
H4P 1S1
(514)739-2336

Reliable Toy Co Ltd
258 Carlaw Ave
Toronto, Ont
M4M 2S2
(416)462-1771

Revell
Represented by:
WG Distributors

Ritvik Toys Inc
760 Lepine Ave
Dorval, Que
H9P 1G2
(514)631-2790

Rose Art
Represented by:
DMA Industries Inc

Roylco Ltd
650 Colby Dr
Waterloo, Ont
N2V 1A1
(519)885-0451

Russ
Represented by:
Amram's

Sandford's
Represented by:
Eff-N-Tee Sales and Marketing

Sargent Art
Represented by:
Waddington Sanders

Scholaquip
Represented by:
Steppe Enterprises Ltd

Sheaffer Pen Textron
Division of Textron Canada Ltd
520 Huron Rd
Goderich, Ont
N7A 3Z1
(519)524-7341

Shelcore
Represented by:
Irwin Toy Ltd

Simex
Represented by:
Brigitta's Import Inc

Simplex
Represented by:
Maison Joseph Battat Ltd

Spear's
Represented by:
Borgfeldt Toys (Canada) Ltd

Spectra Star Kites
Represented by:
Touch the Sky Inc

Springbok Puzzles
Represented by:
W.E. Coutts Co

Staedtler-Mars Ltd
6 Mars Rd
Rexdale, Ontario
M9V 2K1
(416)749-3966

Steppe Enterprises Ltd
61 Sherbrooke St
Winnipeg, Man
R3C 2B2
(204)284-4720

Steven Mfg Co
Representative unknown

Tamiya
Represented by:
Borgfeldt Toys (Canada) Ltd

Tasco
Represented by:
Optex Corporation

Tente
Representative unknown

Testor Canada
206 Milvan Dr
Weston, Ont
M9L 1Z9
(416)742-1626

Texas Instruments Inc
280 Centre St E
Richmond Hill, Ont
L4C 1B1
(416)884-9181

Thinkway Toys
3761 Victoria Pk Ave
Units 3 and 4
M1W 3S2
(416)492-3388

Tilco International Inc
260 St-Michel
St-Jean-sur-Richelieu, Que
J3B 1T4
(514)348-3895

Tofa
Represented by:
Maison Joseph Battat Ltd

Tomy
Represented by:
Coleco (Canada) Ltd

Tonka Corporation Canada Ltd
7630 Airport Rd
Mississauga, Ont
L4T 2H6
(416)677-1861

Torpedo Inc
3677 Levis St
Lac-Megantic, Que
G6B 2H7
(819)583-5513

Touch the Sky Inc
836 Yonge St
Toronto, Ont
M4W 2H1
(416)964-8624

Toyco Recreation Products Inc
350 Louvain W
Suite 133
Montreal, Que
H2N 2E8
(514)383-6844

Tuff Tuff
Represented by:
Maison Joseph Battat Ltd

Tupperware Home Parties
Check local listings for the number
in your area

Tyco
Represented by:
Irwin Toy Ltd

Uneeda Dolls
Represented by:
Candu Toy Co Ltd

Uniset
Represented by:
Pierre Belvedere Inc

Viceroy Rubber & Plastics Ltd
1655 Dupont St
Toronto, Ont
M6P 3T1
(416)762-1111

Victoria Precision Inc
2901 Rouen St
Montreal, Que
H2K 1N9
(514)524-1143

Victory
Represented by:
Borgfeldt Toys (Canada) Ltd

View-Master Ideal (Canada) Inc
755 The Queensway E
Units 11-12
Mississauga, Ont
L4Y 4C5
1-800-268-2873

Viking Plastic
Represented by:
Pierre Belvedere Inc

V-Tech Educational Electronics
Represented by:
H.K. Video Technology (Canada) Ltd

Vuillard
Represented by:
Brigitta's Import Inc

Vulli
Represented by:
Irwin Toy Ltd

WG Distributors
200 Sheldon Dr
Cambridge, Ont
N1R 5X2
(519)623-3590

Waddington Sanders Ltd
202 Sparks Ave
North York, Ont
M2H 3G2
(416)497-4014

Waddingtons
Represented by:
Waddington Sanders

Weber Costello of Canada Ltd
6800 Rexwood Rd
Mississauga, Ont
L4V 1L8
(416)677-4970

Weible
Represented by:
Brigitta's Import Inc

Wham-O
Represented by:
Irwin Toy Ltd

Whitman Golden Ltd
200 Sheldon Dr
Cambridge, Ont
N1R 5X2
(519)623-3590

Wintergreen Communications Ltd
124 Connie Cres, #1
Concord, Ont
L4K 1L7
(416)669-2815

Wis-Ton Toy Mfg Co Ltd
48 Abell St
Toronto, Ont
M6J 3H2
(416)537-1925

Wooden Toy Co
39 Wellington St E
Oshawa, Ont
L1H 3Y1
(416)576-3311

Worlds of Wonder
Represented by:
Charan Toy Co Inc

Children's bookstores

The following list was provided by the Children's Book Centre. This list does not cover every source for children's books, but it does provide a list of many useful sources. Most good bookstores stock children's books and will order books for you.

Alberta

Aspen Books
10624 Whyte Ave
Edmonton, Alta
T6E 2A7
(403)433-7352

Audrey's Books
10702 Jasper Ave
Edmonton, Alta
T5J 3J5
(403)423-3487

Dormouse
49 Elizabeth St
P.O. Box 765
Okotoks, Alta
T0L 1T0
(403)938-7417

Greenwood's Small World
8123-10th St
Edmonton, Alta
T5E 4E4
(403)439-5600

New Leaf Bookshop
22 Deer Valley Shopping Centre
1221 Canyon Meadows Dr SE
Calgary, Alta
T2J 6G2
(403)278-3382

Play and Learn
Sundridge Mall
2525-36th St NE
Calgary, Alta
T1J 5T4
(403)280-3828

Play and Learn
Parent–Teacher Store
3372 Parsons Rd
Edmonton, Alta
T6N 1B5
(403)463-4733

Play and Learn
311-5th St S
Lethbridge, Alta
T1J 2B4
(403)320-9949

Sandcastle Books and Toys for Children
814-16th Ave SW
Calgary, Alta
T2R 0S9
(403)278-0812

Sandpiper Books
1587-7th St
Calgary, Alta
T2R 1N5
(403)228-0272

Storybook Store
718 Edmonton Trail NE
Calgary, Alta
T2E 3J4
(403)230-7074

Treehouse Books
1829 Ranchlands Blvd NW
Calgary, Alta
T2J 0N3
(403)278-0553

Village Bookshop Volume 11
10228-140th St
Edmonton, Alta
T5N 2L4
(403)454-7781

Village Children's Bookshop
10212-140th St
Edmonton, Alta
T6N 2J4
(403)452-3791

British Columbia

Adrian Books
255 Bernard Ave
Kelowna, BC
V1Y 6N2
(604)763-4443

Bookstore on Bastion Street
76 Bastion St
Nanaimo, BC
V9R 3A1
(604)753-3011

Bookworks
1-2543 Montrose St
Abbotsford, BC
V2S 3T4
(604)853-4625

Borogrove Book Shop
10 Centennial Square
Victoria, BC
V8W 1P7
(604)386-8736

Duthie Books Ltd
919 Robson St
Vancouver, BC
V6Z 1A5
(604)684-4496

Hager Books
2176 West 41st Ave
Vancouver, BC
V6M 1Z1
(604)263-9412

Karen's Bookworld for Children
8693-120th St
Delta, BC
V4C 6R4
(604)594-0110

Muffy Two: A Place for Children
33779 Essendene Ave
Abbotsford, BC
V2S 2H1
(604)859-1103

Page 11 Bookstore
410-11th Ave
Campbell River, BC
V9W 4G3
(604)286-6476

Real Mother Goose
3636-4th Ave W
Vancouver, BC
V6R 1P1
(604)734-0522

Talisman Books
241 Alexander St
Box 1347
Salmon Arm, BC
V0E 2T0
(604)832-8444

Through the Looking Glass
305 Baker St
Nelson, BC
V1L 4H6
(604)352-3913

Vancouver Kidsbooks
2868 W 4th Ave
Vancouver, BC
V6K 1R2
(604)738-5335

Vancouver Kidsbooks
1496 Cartwright St
Vancouver, BC
V6H 3R7
(604)685-5741

Manitoba

Growing Minds
269 Edmonton St
Winnipeg, Man
R3C 1S1
(203)943-1437

Toad Hall Toys
54 Arthur St
Winnipeg, Man
R3B 1G7
(204)956-2195

Newfoundland

Granny Bates' Bookstore
2 Bates' Hill
St. John's, Nfld
A1C 4B4
(709)739-9233

Readmore Bookstore
Village Mall
430 Topsail Rd
St. John's Nfld
A1C 9C6
(709)364-2073

Nova Scotia

A Choice for Children Bookstore
P.O. Box 745
Sydney, NS
B1P 6H7
(902)727-2339

A Pair of Trindles
Old Red Store
Historic Properties
Lower Water St
P.O. Box, Station M
Halifax, NS
B3J 1SP
(902)423-7528

Book Room
1664 Granville St
P.O. Box 272
Halifax, NS
B3J 2N7
(902)423-8271

Box of Delights Bookshop
Box 899, Main St
Wolfville, NS
B0P 1X0
(902)752-3712

R. and C. Sagors Bookstore
686 King St
Bridgewater, NS
B4V 1B4
(902)543-4204

Rainbows
121 George St
New Glasgow, NS
B2H 5K7
(902)752-3712

Woozles
1533 Birmingham St
Halifax, NS
B3J 2J3
(902)423-7626

Northwest Territories

Yellowknife Book Cellar
Lower Scotia Mall
Box 1256
Franklin Ave
Yellowknife, NWT
X1A 2N2
(403)902-2220

Ontario

A Different Drummer Books
513 Locust St
Burlington, Ont
L7S 1V3
(416)639-0925

Albert Britnell Book Shop
765 Yonge St
Toronto, Ont
M4W 2G6
(416)924-3321

Bookcraft
183 Main St S
P.O.Box 1051
Mount Forest, Ont
N0G 2L0
(519)323-2421

Bookery of Ottawa
541 Sussex Dr
Ottawa, Ont
K1N 6Z6
(613)238-1428

Books for Children
347 King St E
Kingston, Ont
K7L 3B5
(613)542-5551

Bookshelf Cafe
41 Quebec St
Guelph, Ont
N1H 2T1
(416)821-3311

Children's Book Shop
1544 Regent St S
Sudbury, Ont
P3E 3Z6
(715)522-3191

Children's Book Store
604 Markham St
Toronto, Ont
M6G 2L8
(416)535-7011

Children's Loft
The Book Cellar
144 St. James St S
Hamilton, Ont
L8P 3A2
(416)525-7172

Creative Child
47A Colborne St
Toronto, Ont
M5E 1E3
(416)368-1931

Gulliver's Quality Children's Books
953 Pinewood Rd
North Bay, Ont
P1B 4P2
(705)474-7335

Lindsay's Books for Children
101 Bloor St W
Toronto, Ont
M5S 1P8
(416)968-2174

Little Crow's Book Room
239 Huron St
Collingwood, Ont
L9Y 3Z5
(705)445-1900

London Children's Book Shop
225 Queen's Ave
London, Ont
N6A 1J8
(519)432-1275

Longhouse Book Shop
626 Yonge St
Toronto, Ont
M4Y 1Z8
(416)921-9995

Maple and the Butterfly
8 Spring St
P.O. Box 91
St. Jacobs, Ont
N0B 2N0
(519)664-2671

Oxford Book Shop
740 Richmond St
London, Ont
N6A 1L6
(519)438-8336

Oxford Book Shop
Eaton Square
Wellington St
London, Ont
N6A 3N7
(519)438-2161

Oxford Book Shop
Festival Square
10 Downie St
Stratford, Ont
N5A 7K4
(519)273-3567

Pick of the Crop Books
245 Lakeshore Rd E
Oakville, Ont
L6J 1H9
(416)844-5363

Robert Holmes Ltd
248 Dundas St
London, Ont
N6A 1H3
(519)438-4151

Science City Jr.
Science City Science Book Stores
50 Bloor St W
Toronto, Ont
M4H 1H2
(416)968-2627

Shirley Leishman Books
Lower Concourse
Westgate Shopping Centre
Ottawa, Ont
K1Z 7L3
(613)722-8313

Stories
177 Woolwich St
Guelph, Ont
N1H 3V4
(519)823-5691

Story Tree
502 Eglinton Ave W
Toronto, Ont
M5N 1A5
(416)488-2223

Storytale Lane
399 Roncesvalles Ave
Toronto, Ont
M5R 2N1
(416)532-1350

Sweet Thursday Bookshop
30 St. Paul St
Thunder Bay, Ont
P7A 4S5
(807)344-2866

Tiddley Pom
43 Colborne St
Toronto, Ont
M5E 1E3
(416)366-0290

Toy Circus
2036 Queen St E
Toronto, Ont
M4L 1J1
(416)699-4971

Toy Shop
62 Cumberland Ave
Toronto, Ont
M4W 1J5
(416)961-4870

Willoughby's Book Store
3441 Yonge Street
Toronto, Ont
M4N 2N1
(416)489-5889

Words Worth Books
88 King Street S
Waterloo, Ont
N2J 1P5
(519)884-2665

Quebec

Books and Things
900 rue Principale
Box 214
Morin Heights, Quebec
J0R 1H0
(514)226-2201

Saskatchewan

Country Bookstore
P.O. Box 69
Brownlee, Sask
S0H 0M0
(306)759-2302

Challis Book and Toy Shops
No. 5 Territorial Mall
P.O. Box 1056
North Battleford, Sask
S9A 3E6
(306)445-7244

Play and Learn
Golden Mile Plaza
3806 Albert St
Regina, Sask
S4S 6B4
(306)525-0341

Play and Learn
5 Grosvenor Park Shopping Centre
Saskatoon, Sask
S7H 0T8
(306)373-5105

Rocking Horse Books
Broadway Park Centre
Yorkton, Sask
S3N 0P3
(306)782-5600

Children's Corner Bookstore
2335-11th Ave
Regina, Sask
S4P 0K2
(306)522-5828

Bookworm's Den
38 Grosvenor Park Shopping Centre
Saskatoon, Sask
S7H 0T8
(306)373-3411

Saskatoon Book Store
148-2nd Ave N
Saskatoon, Sask
S7H 2P2
(306)664-2572

Canadian publishers

The following is a list of Canadian publishers and distributors of children's books. Contact them for their catalogues and seek out local publishers to find books that may be especially suitable for your region.

Annick Press Ltd
15 Patricia Ave
Willowdale, Ont
M2M 1H9
(416)221-4802

Black Moss
P.O. Box 143, Station A
Windsor, Ont
N9A 6K1
(519)252-2551

Breakwater Books Ltd
277 Duckworth St
P.O. Box 2188
St. John's, Nfld
A1C 6E6
(709)722-6680

Camden House Publishing
7 Queen Victoria Rd
Camden East, Ont
K0K 1J0
(613)378-6661

Canadian Children's Annual
The John Street Press
26 John St E
Waterloo, Ont
N2J 1E7

Canadian Stage and Arts Publications
52 Avenue Rd
Toronto, Ont
M5R 2G2
(416)971-9516

CBC Enterprises
Canadian Broadcasting Corporation
P.O. Box 500, Station A
Toronto, Ont
M5W 1E6
(416)975-3528/3490

Collier Macmillan Canada Inc
1200 Eglinton Ave E
Suite 200
Don Mills, Ont
M3C 3N1
(416)449-6030

Coteau Books/Thunder Creek Co-op
2337 McIntyre St
Regina, Sask
S4P 2S3
(306)352-5346

Crabtree Publishing Co Ltd
120 Carlton St
Suite 309
Toronto, Ont
M5A 4K2
(416)967-5106

D.C. Heath Canada Ltd
100 Adelaide St W
Suite 1600
Toronto, Ont
M5H 1S9
(416)362-6483/7597/7598

Douglas & McIntyre
1615 Venables St
Vancouver, BC
V5L 2H1
(604)254-7191

Dundurn Press Ltd
1558 Queen St E
Toronto, Ont
M4L 1E8
(416)461-1881

Fifth House Ltd
406 Clarence Ave S
Saskatoon, Sask
S7H 2C7
(306)242-4936

Firefly Books Ltd.
3520 Pharmacy Ave
Unit 1C
Scarborough, Ont
M1W 2T8
(416)499-8412

Fitzhenry & Whiteside Ltd
195 Allstate Parkway
Markham, Ont
L3R 4T8
(416)477-0030

Franklin Watts of Canada
20 Torbay Rd
Markham, Ont
L3R 1G6
(416)474-0333

Frederick Harris Music Co
529 Speers Rd
Oakville, Ont
L6K 2G4
(416)845-3487

Gage Educational Publishing Co
164 Commander Blvd
Agincourt, Ont
M1S 3C7
(416)293-8141

General Publishing
30 Lesmill Rd
Don Mills, Ont
M3B 2T6
(416)445-3333

General Store Publishing House Inc
1 Main St
Burnstown, Ont
K0J 1G0
(613)432-7697

Greey de Pencier Books
56 The Esplanade
Suite 306
Toronto, Ont
M5E 1A7
(416)868-6001

Grolier Ltd
20 Torbay Rd
Markham, Ont
L3R 1G6
(416)474-0333

Grosvenor House Press Inc
111 Queen St E
Suite 375
Toronto, Ont
M5C 1S2
(416)364-5510

Groundwood Books Ltd
26 Lennox St
3rd Floor
Toronto, Ont
M6G 1J4
(416)537-2501

Harbour Publishing Co Ltd
P.O. Box 219
Madeira Park, BC
V0N 2H0
(604) 883-2730

Harcourt Brace Jovanovich, Canada
55 Horner Ave
Toronto, Ont
M8Z 4X6
(416)255-4491

Hayes Publishing
3312 Mainway
Burlington, Ont
L7M 1A7
(416)335-0393

Highway Book Shop
Cobalt, Ont
P0J 1C0
(705)679-8375

Hurtig Publishers Ltd
10560 105th St
Edmonton, Alta
T5H 2W7
(403)426-2359

Hyperion Press Ltd
300 Wales Ave
Winnipeg, Man
R2M 2S9
(204)256-9204

Irwin Publishing Inc
180 West Beaver Creek Rd
Richmond Hill, Ont
L4B 1B4
(416)731-3838

James Lorimer & Co, Publishers
35 Britain Street
Toronto, Ont
M5A 1R7
(416)362-4762

Jesperson Press
26A Flavin St
St. John's, Nfld
A1C 3R9
(709)753-0633

Kids Can Press
585 1/2 Bloor St W
Toronto, Ont
M6G 1K5
(416)534-6389

Lester & Orpen Dennys Ltd, Publishers
78 Sullivan St
Toronto, Ont
M5T 1C1
(416)593-9602

Macmillan of Canada
29 Birch Ave
Toronto, Ont
M4V 1E2
(416)963-8830

McClelland and Stewart
481 University Ave
Toronto, Ont
M5G 2E9
(416)598-1114

McGraw-Hill Ryerson Ltd
330 Progress Ave
Scarborough, Ont
M1P 2Z5
(416)293-1911

Methuen Publications
150 Laird Dr
Toronto, Ont
M4G 3V7
(416)425-9200

NC Press Ltd
260 Richmond St W
Suite 401
Toronto, Ont
M5V 1W5
(416)593-6284

Nimbus Publishing Ltd
P.O. Box 9301, Station A
Halifax, NS
B3K 5N5
(902)455-4286

Oxford University Press
70 Wynford Dr
Don Mills, Ont
M3C 1J9
(416)441-2941

Pemmican Publications Inc
504 Main St
Room 411
Winnipeg, Man
R3B 1B8
(204)942-0926

Penguin Books Canada Ltd
2801 John St
Markham, Ont
L3R 1B4
(416)475-1571

Penumbra Press
P.O. Box 248
Kapuskasing, Ont
P5N 2Y4
(705)335-2988

Playwrights Union of Canada
8 York St
6th Floor
Toronto, Ont
M5J 1R2
(416)947-0201

Porcépic Books
235-560 Johnson St
Victoria, BC
V8W 3C6
(604)381-5502

Porcupine's Quill Inc
68 Main St
Erin, Ont
N0B 1T0
(519)833-9158

Quill and Quire
56 The Esplanade
Toronto, Ont
M5E 1A7
(416)364-3333

Ragweed Press Inc
149 Kent St
P.O. Box 2023
Charlottetown, PEI
C1A 7N7
(902)566-5750

Red Deer College Press
56th Avenue & 32nd
Red Deer, Alta
T4N 5H5
(403)342-3300

Royal Ontario Museum
Publication Services
100 Queen's Pk
Toronto, Ont
M5S 2C6
(416)586-5581

Scholastic-TAB Publications Ltd
123 Newkirk Rd
Richmond Hill, Ont
L4C 3G5
(416)883-5300

Simon & Pierre Publishing Co Ltd
P.O. Box 280, Adelaide St Stn
Toronto, Ont
M5C 2J4
(416)363-6767

Stoddart Publishing Co Ltd
34 Lesmill Rd
Don Mills, Ont
M3B 2T6
(416)445-3333

Theytus Books
P.O. Box 218
Penticton, BC
V2A 6K3
(604)493-7181

Three Trees Press
85 King St E
Suite 304
Toronto, Ont
M5C 1G3
(416)534-4456

Tree Frog Press Ltd
10144 89th St
Edmonton, Alta
T5H 1P7
(403)429-1947

Tundra Books Inc/Les Livres Toundra Inc
1434 St-Catherine St W
Suite 308
Montreal, Que
H3G 1R4
(514)932-5434

Western Producer Prairie Books
2310 Millar Ave, P.O. Box 2500
Saskatoon, Sask
S7K 2C4
(306)665-3548

William Collins Sons & Co Canada Ltd
100 Lesmill Rd
Don Mills, Ont
M3B 2T5
(416)445-8221

Women's Press
229 College St
Suite 204
Toronto, Ont
M5T 1R4
(416)598-0082

The Young Naturalist Foundation
56 The Esplanade
Suite 304
Toronto, Ont
M5E 1A7
(416)364-3333

Commercial Sources for Records and Cassettes

A & M Records of Canada Ltd
939 Warden Ave
Scarborough, Ont
M1L 4C5
(416)752-7191

Berandol Music Ltd
110-A Sackville St
Toronto, Ont
M5A 3E5
(416)869-1872

Capitol Records—EMI of Canada Ltd
3109 American Dr
Mississauga, Ont
L4V 1B2
(416)677-5050

Elephant Records
24 Ryerson Ave
Toronto, Ont
M5T 2P3
(416)364-3387

Kids' Records
68 Broadview Ave
Suite 303
Toronto, Ont
M4M 2E6
(416)461-0268

Troubadour Records Ltd
6043 Yonge St
Willowdale, Ont
M2M 3W2
(416)222-2592

Commercial Sources for Audio-Visual Producers and Suppliers

Addison-Wesley Publishers
26 Prince Andrew Place
P.O. Box 580
Don Mills, Ont
M3C 2T8
(416)447-5101

Art Gallery of Ontario
317 Dundas St W
Toronto, Ont
M5T 1G4
(416)977-0414

Bell & Howell Ltd
230 Barmac Dr
Weston, Ont
M9L 2X5
(416)746-2200

CBC Enterprises
P.O. Box 500
Station A
Toronto, Ont
M5W 1E6
(416)975-3528/3490

Copp Clark Pitman Ltd
495 Wellington St W
Toronto, Ont
M5V 1E9
(416)593-9911

Dominie Press Ltd
1361 Huntingwood Dr
Unit 7
Agincourt, Ont
M1S 3J1
(416)291-5857/1101

Gage Educational Publishing Co
164 Commander Blvd
Agincourt, Ont
M1S 3C7
(416)293-8141

The Learning Tree Ltd
3269 American Dr
Mississauga, Ont
L4V 1V4
(416)673-2644

McGraw-Hill Ryerson Ltd
330 Progress Ave
Scarborough, Ont
M1P 2Z5
(416)293-1911

TV Ontario
P.O. Box 200
Station Q
Toronto, Ont
M4T 2T1
(416)484-2618

Commercial Sources for Learning Materials in the United States

ABC School Supply, Inc
437 Armour Circle NE
Box 13084
Atlanta, GA 30324

Childcraft Education Corp
20 Kilmer Rd
Edison, NJ 08817

Constructive Playthings
1040 E 85th St
Kansas City, MO 64131

Creative Playthings
A Division of CBS Inc
Princeton, NJ 08540

David C. Cook Publishing Co
850 N Grove Ave
Elgin, IL 60120

Instructo Corp
Subsidiary of McGraw-Hill Inc
Cedar Hollow and Mathews Rd
Paoli, PA 19301

Judy Instructional Aids
The Judy Co
250 James St
Morristown, NJ 07960

Lakeshore Equipment Co
PO Box 2116
1144 Montague Ave
San Leandro, CA 94577

Playskool Inc
Milton Bradley Co
Springfield, MA 01100

Russell Mfg Co Inc
1150 Main St
Leicester, MA 01524

Scholastic Early Childhood Center
904 Sylvan Ave
Englewood Cliffs, NJ 07632

Superior Toy & Mfg Co Inc
3417 N Halsted St
Chicago, IL 60657

Tara Toy Corp
Hauppauge, NY 11788

Thomas Y. Crowell Co
666 Fifth Ave
New York, NY 10019

Totsy Mfg Co Ltd
PO Box 509
Holyoke, MA 01040

UNICEF
331 E 38th St
New York, NY 10016

Windsor Toy Inc
140 Grand St
Carlstadt, NJ 07072

Notes for Guiding Behaviour

Suggestions for guiding behaviour

1. Know everything you can about each child.
2. Decide what you want each child to learn.
3. Plan the children's environment.
4. Establish positive, friendly relationships with each child.
5. Encourage each child in his or her growth and development of a good self-image.

Ways to build trust

1. Like the child. Take him or her seriously. Assure the child that you like and care about him or her.
2. Talk to the child at her or his level. Bend down, put your arm around the child's shoulder, hold hands gently, or kneel down beside the child. Eye contact is very important.
3. Be positive not harsh; gentle not weak; pleasant, calm, firm, sincere, and matter-of-fact. Be consistent about your expectations and guidance; it develops dependability.
4. Speak softly, slowly, patiently, be friendly but firm.
5. Make a suggestion rather than give a command. Save commands for emergencies.
6. Listen to child's explanation of how he or she feels. Accept his or her right to feelings.
7. Encourage child to share success, give praise, show understanding, help and learn through discovery and failure.
8. Set an example, expect co-operation, make self–co-operation possible.
9. Offer choice only when legitimate. Offer compromises or alternatives if needed.

Remember, if I know each child, I can

1. regroup
2. protect each child's rights
3. divert
4. allow a child the opportunity to resolve his or her own problem
5. offer a compromise when rights are unknown
6. show a child how
7. ask a child a question
8. overlook certain behaviour (always considering safety)
9. be flexible
10. make allowances for age-phase behaviour
11. give a child a chance to rebel (within reason)
12. stop certain behaviour (when safety is a factor)
13. offer duplicate materials or equipment rather than expect a child to share arbitrarily

I can prevent difficulties by

1. preparing for a variety of activities, using materials and equipment in good repair that offer opportunities for every child to succeed
2. defining areas, arranging rooms attractively, and rotating activities and materials to invite challenge
3. planning for total supervision for each space with defined roles for all teachers (remembering to consider each one's abilities and special interests)
4. giving guidance and support when needed, allowing for discovery, exploration, and creativity

If I plan I can

1. allow time to complete tasks
2. substitute when alternatives are needed
3. arrange equipment, space, and program to avoid accidents, overstimulation, or cross-traffic
4. set reasonable limits for safety
5. effect smooth transitions for individuals (and group) by allowing for individual differences and experiences
6. use the proximity of an adult to help modify behaviour

PART

1

Self-Concept

★★

Part One: Self-Concept

Contents

I'm Me, I'm Special

★★★★★★★★★★★★★★★★★★★★★★★

Basic Understandings

(concepts children can grasp from this subject)

▷ I'm me, I'm special. *There is no one else just like me.*
▷ I had a special name given to me when I was born. It is on my birth certificate.
▷ No one has a voice just like mine; no one has fingerprints just like mine.
▷ I am like others in some ways; I am different from others in some ways.
▷ I can do some things easily; I can do some things well.
▷ Some things are hard to do; some things I cannot do well yet.
▷ I can do many things now that I could not do when I was a baby.
▷ As I get older, I will be able to do more things than I can do now.
▷ I do not have to be good at everything; I can make mistakes.
▷ I have feelings; at different times I may be glad, sad, angry, tired, or have other feelings.
▷ I can learn some good ways to show my feelings.
▷ If I know I am special, I know others can be special in their way too.
▷ Others need to know that I think they are special. Sometimes I need to know them better to know how special they are (in what ways they are special).
▷ No one can know what I think or how I feel unless I tell them or show them.
▷ When I share my own ideas or do things in my own way I am being creative.
▷ My thoughts and ideas are important. Other people have good ideas, too.
▷ I am likeable (loveable) to someone. I can learn to like (love) others.
▷ I have a right to share the materials, equipment, and the attention of the teacher and to be safe and protected in school.
▷ Some children are special because they have extra special needs: braces, glasses, crutches, hearing aids, a wheelchair, speech therapy.
▷ Each year I have a special day called my birthday. (See the chapter "Mathematics in My Everyday World" for experiences related to birthday celebrations.)

Some things about me are very special

▷ My family is very special.
▷ My friends are very special. I may not have the same friends as another child.
▷ I have special thoughts. I can dream, wonder, wish and enjoy just looking at things or watching others.
▷ Sometimes I keep my thoughts to myself and sometimes I tell others my thoughts.
▷ I have special places, special toys, special treasures, and special pets that are mine.

▷ I can have special quiet times just for me; I don't always have to be busy with activities.
▷ I have a wonderful body. It has many parts: eyes, ears, nose, mouth, feet, hands, hair, skin, fingers, toes.
▷ I can do many things with my body—I can see, touch, taste, smell, hear, talk, move, think, and learn.

I am a member of a family and a community

▷ I am someone's son/daughter (grandson/granddaughter).
▷ I may also be someone's brother/sister/cousin/nephew/niece.
▷ I can be a part of a group (my family, my class, my neighbourhood).
▷ Someday I may choose to become a wife/husband and a father/mother.
▷ Someday I may become an aunt/uncle, grandfather/grandmother, or cousin to someone.
▷ A friend is someone who likes me just as I am.
▷ A neighbour is someone who lives close to where I live.
▷ I need to help my family (group) by caring for and sharing the things we own, helping in plans, sharing my ideas, and doing what I am asked to do or need to do.
▷ I live in Canada. I may have been born in another country. I may have relatives in another country.

My family is special

▷ My family is made up of _____, _____, _____.
▷ Adults in my family can be helpful because they know many things that I do not know.
▷ My family has certain beliefs and special ways of living and doing things. (See "Living in Families" and "Families at Work," on p. 185 and p. 199.)
▷ My family celebrates days that are important to us: birthdays, Mother's Day, Father's Day, Valentine's Day, anniversaries, and graduations. (See "Family Celebrations" and "Seasons" on p. 213 and p. 313.)
▷ My family and I may have different customs, beliefs, and celebrations than other families. (See "Family Celebrations" and "Seasons.")
▷ My family and I may speak a different language from others near us.
▷ Adoption is one way a child can become a member of a family.
▷ I may be part of two families. (Many children share time between two homes.)

I live in a special place

▷ I live with my family:
  in a home _____ (what kind?)
  in a city _____ (name)
  in a _____ (village, town, municipality, city, or county)
  in a _____ (province or territory)
  in the world (on the planet Earth)

I can change by growing

▷ I can get bigger (taller and heavier) until I am a grownup.
▷ I can get fatter or slimmer if I eat more than I need or less than I need.
▷ I need food, exercise, and rest to help me grow.
▷ Each year I have a birthday and become one year older until I die (stop living).

I can change by learning

▷ When I think, remember, and decide, things can be better.
▷ I can learn about my body and make it work for me and for others.

▷ I can learn to do many things. If I try over and over again I should be able to learn to do something very well.

▷ I can learn by doing and discovering when I use my mind to think, eyes to see, ears to listen, fingers to feel, tongue to taste, and nose to smell.

▷ I can learn to do things for myself.

▷ I can help to keep myself clean and healthy.

▷ I can be thoughtful of others in what I do and what I say.

▷ I can learn to follow directions; I can learn to follow rules.

▷ I can learn to take care of, or help, other people.

▷ I can learn to take care of other things in my world: plants, animals, parks, streams, sidewalks, and so on.

▷ I can learn how to use things the right way and how to care for them properly.

I can change by pretending

▷ I can play that I am someone else when I pretend and when I do things like that person does.

▷ I may wear a costume to make myself look like someone other than myself.

▷ I may wear a wig to change the colour of my hair and to change the way it is fixed.

I can change by dressing differently

▷ I can get a haircut or change the way I wear my hair so that I look different.

▷ I can wear various kinds of clothes and look different.

▷ I can get cleaned up or get dirty, and I may look different.

▷ I may wear glasses if I need them.

▷ I may wear a cast if I break an arm or a leg, but . . . I am still me!

I can change by getting sick/well

▷ If I skin or bruise myself, I look different until the injury heals.

▷ If I break a bone, I may look different until it mends.

▷ When I get a fever or feel sick, I do not look the same as when I am well.

▷ When I am tired I look different than when I am rested; sometimes I become cross and unhappy.

▷ Doctors, nurses, my family, and my teachers help me to keep healthy and help me grow.

I can change by acting differently

▷ I can learn better ways to show my feelings: talk when I am angry, tell someone when I need help.

▷ I can let others know how I feel. I can listen to others and find out how they feel and what they think.

▷ I can work and play by myself; I can learn to work and play with others.

▷ I can feel good about myself when I do my share of work at home and at school.

▷ Sometimes I help my friends and share things. Because we are different, we sometimes argue, disagree, or even fight.

▷ I can learn good manners; I can learn to be polite.

▷ I can show others I like (love) them.

▷ Sometimes I am not proud of what I have done. I feel happier if I am allowed to help make things better by fixing what I have spoiled, cleaning up if I have made a mess, or being more thoughtful or friendly the next time.

▷ People like me better if I am friendly. I am still me, I like myself, and I am proud to be me.

▷ I can make some things better by
   1. learning to do things as well as I can, and helping when I can.
   2. understanding that others have problems, too.
   3. preventing accidents that may cause problems or make people unhappy.
   4. asking for help from adults to learn what I can do and to become what I would like to become.

Some things I cannot change

▷ I cannot change my height or skin colour.
▷ I may not like some things about myself that I cannot change, such as having to use crutches, take special medicine, wear glasses, eat special foods, or use a hearing aid; but any of these things are a part of me that I will learn to accept.
▷ I cannot change my family or where I live.
▷ I cannot solve problems that make my parents or guardians drink, take drugs, argue, or fight.
▷ I cannot provide food, clothes, or a place to sleep for myself.
▷ I cannot keep my parents or guardians from getting a divorce, going to jail, or leaving me; but I can tell someone else who could help me if my parents hurt me or leave me alone.
▷ Some things I cannot change until I am older because they are the problems or responsibilities of grownups.
▷ Sometimes I am not proud of what I have done. I can be more thoughtful or friendly the next time.
▷ Until I am older I can make things better by
   1. telling my parents or guardians I love them, if I do.
   2. avoiding accidents that may cause problems or make people unhappy.
   3. learning to do things as well as I can, and helping when I can.
   4. learning to do what I am asked.
   5. knowing (realizing) that others have disabilities and problems too.
   6. asking for help from adults to do what I can do and to become what I would like to become.
   7. staying with others in another place when people at home are unable to care for me or when it is not a pleasant or a happy place to be.

Additional Facts the Teacher Should Know

1. A good feeling about one's self is often considered a prerequisite to learning, or a beginning point toward achieving whatever one is capable of becoming. Each child is "special" (unique) and deserves to be accepted at whatever level of development he or she has attained physically, mentally, socially, and emotionally. Many early childhood classes have children enrolled whose first language is neither English nor French and whose cultural heritage may be different from the majority of children in the class or the majority of teachers in the centre. Also, many classes are integrating, and contain children who are developmentally delayed, physically disabled, hearing-impaired, emotionally disturbed, or delayed in language development.

   a. Teachers should familiarize themselves with each child and his or her family or living group. Background information gathered from a pre-enrollment interview, completed information forms, and a home visit prior to the opening of school should provide a good beginning of understanding. The staff should operate on the basis that the parents or guardians are the primary educators of the child and that they will all have to work together throughout the year for the benefit of the child.

b. Traditional family structures have changed. It is important for teachers to put aside their judgments and accept the cultures and lifestyles of all children as well as helping them feel good about themselves, their families, and their life style. Teachers should help children to share their knowledge, skills, and cultures with one another on a level that even young children can comprehend. (See "Families" and "Family Celebrations" sections.)

c. All children should be assessed individually to determine their present skills and concepts, and a plan should be devised for supplementing their education regardless of their handicap or cultural background. Individual record files are important to keep, but you should not stereotype a child with an identified behaviour or learning problem as being hopeless because a previous teacher recorded a lack of success. A year of maturation or a change in staff can make a great deal of difference. If a child is not making progress, assess your teaching methods instead of assuming the child is "unteachable."

d. Parents or guardians must become partners in the education of their children if real progress is to be made. The staff should try to make the parents or guardians feel welcome in the classroom. They need to share the plans they have for the particular child and should keep the parents informed as to the child's progress throughout the year by the use of conferences and written reports.

e. A rich and varied environment will help develop competence and the ability to function independently in the world. The children should be encouraged to do what they can for themselves, but they should be helped with tasks that are too difficult before frustration sets in. Provide materials and directed learning experiences that are appropriate to the age, ability, and competencies of each child in order to capitalize on their readiness, minimize frustration, and structure success.

f. At times you may wish to group children with similar needs together, such as at story time, some cognitive learning sessions, and some art experiences. At other times you should group so that children with fewer skills or knowledge are able to learn from those with more skills and knowledge.

g. Positive rather than negative guidance builds a positive self-image. The staff should be constantly alert for praiseworthy actions by the children in order to reinforce them with their warm approval. Artificial or unwarranted praise should not be given as children can detect insincerity. Staff members should accept the child's feelings as important. Then they can help each one work through negative feelings to a greater understanding. Teachers should respect the dignity of each child. If corrective action is needed, it should be done quietly, firmly, and in such a manner as to avoid shaming a child in front of peers. By your manner, the child will discover that you are still friends and that it is the behaviour of which you disapprove, not the child. Young children easily confuse discipline with personal rejection.

h. Children should be encouraged to share their ideas and to respect those of others. Self-concept should be an ongoing theme throughout the daily program year, not merely an aid toward getting acquainted.

i. It is now the law in most provinces that you must report child abuse, when you have knowledge of it. It is critical that any suspected abuse should be reported to the appropriate community authorities as quickly as possible. Remember that your first responsibility is to the child. In instances of abuse the teacher is of utmost importance in giving the child security and emotional support. Many colleges, universities, government departments, and community agencies offer short courses on reporting and preventing child abuse.

j. Stress professionalism at all times. As staff, you will be in possession of privileged information about children and their families. Never discuss this information with others who are not professionally involved. If you wish to share a positive or humorous incident it can be done without using names. Be sure to share all these incidents with the child's family, too.

2. Cultural awareness is important to each child's self-image. Canada has provided a haven for refugees. Although the English and French cultures dominate our educational traditions, there is now a need to incorporate children's cultural heritages into our curricula. There are a number of organizations that provide teaching resources to assist you with planning heritage programs.

Unfortunately, space does not permit us to discuss each cultural group that resides in Canada. In our research, we soon discovered we could not generalize about any one ethnic group, as there appear to be many subgroups. Also, each cultural group has members who may be termed liberals, moderates, or conservatives. All these groups are seeking to preserve and practise their individual beliefs with differing emphasis on traditions. Further modification occurs as each succeeding generation adapts the cultural traditions to suit themselves and the ever-changing times in which they live. All these factors make it difficult to describe a single set of values or a uniform method of celebrating a special event.

In view of this, we wish to share some guidelines for becoming more sensitive and more culturally aware.

a. Every teacher should recognize and accept the fact that each child and each family has a cultural heritage and unique way of life. The individual family's mode of living has been shaped not only by its culture, but by its religious beliefs, education, economic circumstances, geographic location, experiences, and interpersonal relationships. Teachers should recognize that families from minority cultures are not necessarily "deficient" or "deprived." To deny or downgrade a family's culture or life style may damage a child's self-image and result in an individual with "no culture" because he or she is not happily a member of either a minority group or the mainstream group.

b. A disabled child or one of a different culture in your class should be more a matter for celebration rather than concern. The enlightened staff has the perfect opportunity to demonstrate its teaching skills and to enrich the lives of those in the class in a manner that would not be possible without that child or children.

c. The staff should not make generalizations about various ethnic groups or types of disabilities as "unteachable." They should educate themselves to a knowledgeable level about each culture, as needed, so that they can help every child develop his or her potential to the fullest. Staff meetings and in-service training should be planned to increase cultural understanding and improve teaching skills. Capitalize on opportunities to meet and make friends with others from another culture. You will be less likely to make quick judgments and broad generalizations. Ask questions, read (see "Books and Periodicals," p. 127), and discuss. Avoid isolating yourself from life and the world as it really is by being concerned only with your small segment of it. "Different" can mean "unique and special" rather than "strange and threatening." It can be an exciting and rewarding adventure.

d. Staff attitudes toward those with disabilities or cultural differences will influence the attitudes of the other children. Examine your attitudes, prejudices, and behaviour toward others who are "different" as honestly as you can. Try to be understanding. Ask yourself how things might look from the parents' or child's point of view. How might they feel? Why?

e. Call everyone by their preferred name. Never give a child a nickname or attempt to simplify their name. Similarly, adults in the class should be called by their preferred name and title. Children can easily understand diversity in names and titles.

f. Most Canadians, regardless of culture, wear street clothes in style in this country. When children wear culturally different clothes for religious or other reasons, it is important to respect this and teach other children to respect it as well.

g. Keep in mind that children will have various mores and customs they have been taught by their families or within their cultural community. For example, some children may feel severely admonished or disciplined when embarrassed or shamed and therefore may wish to stand aside and observe until they feel comfortable enough to join an activity. Furthermore, there are children who have been taught that to show respect for adults they must hold back and wait for the adult to speak. They may also have been taught to lower their eyes when they are speaking to an adult. Do not assume that any of these behaviours are signs of disrespect or negative feelings from the children.

h. Many black Canadians have emigrated from Caribbean countries. Do not assume that curriculum materials prepared for black Americans will be relevant for children from the Caribbean, as the traditions are quite different. Parents and local cultural associations will help you assess the suitability of materials.

i. When non-English speaking children are enrolled, a competent, trained staff member who is able to communicate with these children should be available on a full-time basis. This person may speak a pure form of the language but must be willing to accept the various dialects of the families as authentic forms of communication. A child's first language should be respected and used, as necessary, while a second language is being taught. Neither language is right or wrong, each is unique. If the first language escapes a negative label, the child will learn to use each in its appropriate place and will become truly bilingual.

j. Each culture has many individuals who have made outstanding contributions to Canada; and each culture has traditional foods, dances, songs, games, art objects, ceremonial dress, and celebrations that can be appreciated by most young children. We have included some of these in the parts of the guide on the Seasons and Family Celebrations. We realize this is only a beginning, and that there are many local celebrations and customs that can, and should, be included in your program. Enlist the help of local resource people and of parents as you plan your program. Every family has skills, hobbies, household articles, toys, picture books, instruments, and art objects that can be shared in some meaningful way with encouragement from an imaginative and understanding staff.

k. When children from other cultures are sharing with their classmates, avoid embarrassing them or making them feel uncomfortable. Do not expect very young children to teach the others, but allow them to share when they are ready to do so. They are anxious to be part of the group and not to be isolated. They cannot be expected to know all the history of their ancestry any more than any other child of their age. It might be wise to ask yourself, "What could I share about my heritage as a child?" Why then expect a member of another culture to be more informed or aware?

l. Be alert to prejudice being shown by children or their parents in car pools, on playgrounds, or at parent meetings. Give assistance and be supportive whenever possible. Focus on ways to deal with misunderstanding or ignorance. Whenever you can, disprove stereotypes or misconceptions and help others to do the same.
  ▷ Note contributions of Canadians from every ethnic group.
  ▷ Focus on the need for equal opportunities for education and career training.

m. Try not to make misrepresentations of a culture by careless use of a phrase, a story, a song, or a joke. Guard against subtle ridicule of a group's or a class's self-image by using a garbled imitation of the language, dress, customs, gestures, or mannerisms. In a quote, always use actual words and correct pronunciation.

n. Being informed will help you to take advantage of the teachable moment. If an illustration in a storybook or painting is inaccurate, you will be able to discuss why. Offer a photograph or illustration that will portray the same object or individual more accurately.

o. Many new multicultural materials are now available. Some are very good and will be helpful; others are reactionary or inaccurate. Be selective. Good multicultural materials should meet these criteria:
  ▷ accurate content

▷ cultural relevancy and significance to the child

▷ if portraying the present, accurate in its representations of current attitudes and customs

▷ if portraying the past, historically accurate

▷ easily understood and interrelated with the curriculum and reflecting multicultural aspects

p. Avoid gender stereotyping.

▷ Teach children nonsexist language by example, i.e. use proper but comfortable nonsexist English: instead of firemen, say fire*fighters*. Use he and she only when referring to particular people, otherwise use a specific noun or the third-person plural.

▷ Try to avoid dividing children into groups by sex. Use some other attribute or counting games to set up groups. Group children using a variety of factors, such as by colour of shoes, simple counting games, etc.

▷ Don't judge children's sex-role attitudes, as they may be expressing a strongly held view from their own families. Instead, offer them alternative opinions.

Space does not permit a detailed list of terms to avoid and common misconceptions. By giving you such a list we might actually be doing you a disservice in that awareness begins with your discovery and no one else can instantly sensitize you. We hope that you will be challenged to make your teaching of young children one that is truly a "small world" of living and learning, and one that will have meaning for all the families you are privileged to work with.

Methods Most Adaptable for Introducing this Subject to Children

1. Introduce children and teachers to each other when they enter school. Encourage children to call each other by their first names.

2. Names of children should be placed near coat hooks (or in cubbies) with a special picture to help children identify their things. (Names should be lettered clearly on art work in the upper left-hand corner for left to right orientation.)

3. A Child may bring a special possession from home to share with the group.

4. Daily health inspection provides opportunity for learning about body parts and general health care.

5. Ask parents to write their child's name with a waterproof marker on a couple of old shirts or have felt names put on at a T-shirt shop. The children can wear these shirts until the teachers learn their names. Name tags can also be made of colourful fabric that can be pinned to the children's clothes. Be sure that the names are printed in both upper and lower case letters, for example, Julie *not* JULIE. Use permanent markers or fabric crayons to print the names on the cloth.

6. Take pictures of the children and post them with their names on each. The children will enjoy seeing their pictures, and visitors and student teachers in the class will have a quick reference to help them call the children by name.

7. Tape record the children's voices, songs or a conversation. Play it back and have the children guess who is speaking. Have a simple tape recorder with earphones available in a quiet area so that children may tape and listen to their own voices.

8. Have full length and hand mirrors available for children to use to help them develop a sense of body image.

9. Ask the children for their ideas when planning activities or when solving problems. Only do this when you will be able to follow up and use the children's ideas.

10. Encourage the children to talk about their family activities.

11. Play a game or sing a song that includes everyone's name.

Vocabulary

learn	hers	region	haircut
easy	ours	county	care for
hard	you	province	doctor
play	yours	territory	dentist
work	theirs	apartment	nurse
help	them	home	hairdresser
share	avenue	friend	barber
like/love	street	cavity	examination
feelings	country	sick	neighbourhood
I	city	well	names of family members
me	house	healthy	names of classmates
mine	farm	checkup	names of ethnic groups
myself	village	shots	colours of skin, hair, eyes
we	field	wash	names of body parts
us	port	clean	names for body actions
they	town	brush	names for celebrations
his	municipality	dirty	

Learning Centres

Discovery Centre

1. Introduce a full-length mirror or small metal hand mirrors to use to explore individual characteristics, such as eyes, skin, clothing, and hair.
2. Use a magnifying glass to explore skin, fingers, and hair.
3. Use a tape recorder to identify voice characteristics and to allow children to listen to themselves.
4. Weigh and measure children at the beginning of and regularly during the year to be aware of individual growth changes. Compare growth against the child's own previous record, not another's.
5. Take Polaroid camera pictures of the children to use in the classroom or as gifts for the parents.
6. Make hand or footprints. Compare and note differences. Notice that no two are alike. Only you can make that print. Comment about the use of footprints for identification of newborn infants, if this is done in your area.
7. Make a silhouette of each child using a flashlight to throw a shadow and tracing around the shadow. This is generally done by the teacher. Children can identify silhouettes.
8. Use a Dymo labelling machine to print each child's name. The children may then use them to label special things.
9. With older children who live within a kilometre radius of the school or in a small town, post a map of the district or region or hand draw a simplified version. Put a map pin on the street where each child lives. Around the map put pictures of the children and/or their houses with the addresses printed underneath. Run yarn from the map pin to the picture. Add a picture of the school and other places the children visit throughout the year. Talk about who lives the closest (farthest) from the school, the fire station, the grocery store, and so on.

10. Prepare a display of various materials used for identification: ID cards from a university, plant, armed forces; birth certificates, ID bracelets, name labels in clothing, name tags, library cards, licence plates, a driver's licence, credit cards, an office name plate, monograms, personalized clothing, jewellery, pencils. Choose those most appropriate to your group. Allow children to examine these and help identify the ones they know. Discuss their uses.

Dramatic Play Centres

Home-living centre

1. Offer a wide variety of men's and women's dress-up clothes and a full-length mirror. Invite those interested to select a suitable style or colour. This will help children with awareness of self, encourage them to enact home experiences, and to understand various roles of family members. (See the home-living centre in the "Living in Families" guide, p. 188.)
2. The addition of boy and girl dolls, dolls showing different ethnic groups with authentic features, brother and sister dolls, and drink-wet dolls gives children many concept possibilities about the self.

   ★ CAUTION: Avoid commercial dolls where only skin colour is changed. (See commercially made games.)

Block-building centre

1. Label with a sign any buildings made by the children, such as "Pete's Garage."
2. Take a Polaroid snapshot of a child's block building. Pin up on an adjacent wall and share with parents.
3. Add wooden, rubber, or flexible plastic people. Make an open-top play house with unit blocks.

Other dramatic play centres

1. Set up a variety of dramatic play centres that represent sites within your community. These could include a doctor's office, a dairy, a grocery store, a feed store, a marine supply store, a fire hall, etc. For example, a shoe store could include shoe boxes, various old shoes, a ruler for measuring feet, money, and a cash register. Encourage all children to experiment with various roles in the centres. For instance, encourage both girls and boys to work in the firehouse, to be doctors, to be nurses, to be store clerks, to be captains of fishing boats, to be hairstylists, etc.

   ★ CAUTION: Use only plastic or washable hats and wigs for sanitary reasons.

2. A variety of puppets representing people of various ages, sexes, and races will offer children the opportunity to act out their feelings about themselves and others. Animal puppets can be fun, but they are not appropriate when used in place of puppets which represent people. Encourage children to use animal puppets as animals, not people.
3. Make and send seasonally appropriate cards. This can be built into a trip to the post office and gives children a sense of a part of their community as well as showing them a way to be kind to other people.

Learning, Language, and Readiness Materials Centre

Commercially made games and materials

(See "Basic Resources," pp. 79, 100, for manufacturers' addresses.)
1. *Puzzles:* Those that show children and adults of a wide variety of races and cultures. Be sure to have puzzles with knobs for the use of younger children.

2. *Construction and manipulative toys:* Dolls, animals and dressing boards that help children develop skills in buttoning, lacing, zipping, etc. Be sure the toys can be placed so that the children are practising the skills in the same position as they would be if they are dressing themselves; for example, "Sam the Snake for Dressing Skills" (Toy Magic).

3. *Dolls and puppets:* Choose dolls and puppets that reflect a variety of races and cultures; for example multiracial dolls from Louise Kool.

4. *Flannelboards and flannelboard aids:* There are a large number of flannelboard kits that are aids to the development of body awareness and cultural awareness; for example, "Flannelgraph Body Parts" set (Instructo).

Teacher-made games and materials

NOTE: For a detailed description of "Learning Games," see pp. 50–59.

1. Name it: Use Polaroid pictures of the children.
2. Name it, look and see, reach and feel: Play it with
   a. a nail file, comb, toothbrush, or hand mirror.
   b. things we wear on our hands, such as rings, gloves, and mittens.
   c. headwear such as a scarf, hat, helmet, bathing cap, or beret.
   d. footgear such as boots, rubbers, slippers, sandals, and shoes.
   e. brushes that help us keep clean such as nailbrushes, toothbrushes, bath brushes, hairbrushes, shoe brushes, and clothes brushes.
   f. dolls or pictures to represent family members.
   g. a stethoscope, dentist's mirror, thermometer, or eye chart.

A learning centre. By their choice of different art activities, these children reflect their individuality. Each represents a particular racial background; each chooses to use different skills; one is left-handed; each is totally absorbed in his or her activity. Yet all are sharing the same table with one another.

3. Match-them: Use pairs of socks, pairs of mittens, or pairs of shoes.

4. Alike, different, and the same: Use items in no. 3.

5. Grouping and sorting by association: Things we wear on our head, feet, and hands.

6. Which?
   a. Have a pair of shoes for a man, woman, child, and baby. Ask which pair is worn by a baby? A man? A woman? A child? Ask which is heaviest? Lightest? Biggest? Smallest? Has the highest heel? Is brown? and so on.
   b. Use pictures of hands doing things, such as handshaking, waving good-bye, clapping, praying, holding something, and washing.
   c. Use pictures of children doing things, such as getting a haircut, putting on shoes, brushing teeth, getting a checkup, or running, swimming, climbing, and swinging.

7. Guess who? I'm thinking of someone, who is wearing . . . describe child.

8. Listening: See Identification Games in "Basic Resources," p. 51.

9. Who's missing? See Identification Games in "Basic Resources."

10. How can I? or How can you? See Problem-Solving Games in "Basic Resources," p. 54.

11. Find your name: Prepare a name card with each child's first name (you may add last name later in year). Call each child's name and ask him or her to find his or her card. Clap when the child chooses correctly.

12. Can you remember? See Identification Games in "Basic Resources."

13. Let's tell a story: See Language Games in "Basic Resources," p. 53.

14. Boy or girl faces: Make flannel faces with interchangeable parts for eyes, nose, mouth, depicting various feelings and skin tones. Use *natural* skin tones, not pink and white.

15. Paper dolls mounted on flannel representing family members to use with identification games or story telling. Provide a variety of clothes so the children may dress the dolls as they wish. Pattern books are a good source of multi-ethnic figures.

16. Make your own self-help frames or learning vests. Include zippers, buttons, lacings, snaps, and hooks for openings. Some may be made on pockets.

Art Centre

••• 1. Paint and draw pictures of self, family, and friends (teacher must be sure to accept child's picture, not prod for more finished work that may be developmentally beyond the child).

••• 2. In late part of year or with older children, have them lie on the floor and trace around them on wrapping paper. Children can *paint* the figure to correspond with the clothing they are wearing. Teacher can cut out figures after they are painted and display them on classroom walls. Have different skin tone paints mixed for children to choose or allow children to mix colours to match what they need.

• 3. Fingerpaint activity can end with each child making a handprint on a separate piece of paper. This helps use up excess fingerpaint before they go to wash and also gives them a concept of their own hand size. They can make fingerprints on paper and will notice that each person's are different. The teacher can use stamp pad ink for this as well as fingerpaint. VARIATION: Footprints can also be made.

• 4. Handprints made of clay dough or plaster of paris can be used as gifts for parents.

••• 5. Clay people can be made by older children. Natural clay soil in some areas is excellent and can be baked in a kiln if desired. The lump method of pulling features out of a ball of clay is more successful for baking. Pieces pulled out are less likely to break off than those put on as appendages.

• 6. A class mural can be made by putting a roll of newsprint on the floor and having each child add to the group effort by choosing the medium he or she prefers; for example, paints, crayons, chalk, or charcoal. If some children choose to work with dough or clay, their creations can be displayed in a kiosk (see p. 73) or on a low shelf below the mural.

• 7. "Imagination" paper: (see p. 31 for description of materials needed and method for introducing) offer a variety of paper in all shapes, sizes, and colours. (Print scraps are excellent.) Circles, ovals, triangles, and long narrow strips make interesting pictures.

•• 8. Finish the picture; paste small irregular shapes of coloured paper to a piece of paper. Let the children choose one that suggests an idea to them. Curved or wavy lines, dots and squares may also be penned on with a magic marker.

••• 9. For special occasions, have the children plan how the class will be decorated. Use a group time for planning and then provide the children with the materials they need in the art centre. Use another group time to complete the decorating.

Creative Art Media

••• 1. Papier-mâché puppets: Make family puppets using papier-mâché. When dry, paint using skin-tone paints. Collage and fabric scraps can be used for clothes.

••• 2. Sack puppets: Paint sacks with skin tones using paints or crayons. Put on facial features with paint, crayons, yarn, or collage trims.

> NOTE: Throughout the year display *each* child's creative efforts frequently. Let each child select which one he or she would like to have displayed. Group a variety of media together focusing on individuality and avoiding unfair comparisons and competition. Change frequently. Use hallways, stairwalls, bulletin boards, and classroom walls for flatwork and kiosks or low shelves for sculpture and other three-dimensional pieces.

Book Centre

••• Alderson, Sue Ann. *Bonnie McSmithers You're Driving Me Dithers.* Edmonton: Tree Frog Press, 1974.

• Aliki, Diogenes. *A Weed Is a Flower.* Englewood Cliffs, NJ: Prentice-Hall, 1965. (Read-Tell)

•• _____. *Jack and Jake.* New York: Greenwillow Press, 1986.

• _____. *My Hands.* New York: Thomas Y. Crowell, 1962.

••• Anglund, Joan. *A Friend Is Someone Who Likes You.* New York: Harcourt Brace Jovanovich, 1966.

••• _____. *Love Is a Special Way of Feeling.* New York: Harcourt Brace Jovanovich, 1960.

•••• _____. *What Colour Is Love?* New York: Harcourt Brace Jovanovich, 1958.

• Asch, Frank. *I Can Blink.* Toronto: Kids Can Press, 1985.

• _____. *I Can Roar.* Toronto: Kids Can Press, 1985.

•• Bourgeois, Paulette. *Franklin in the Dark.* Toronto: Kids Can Press, 1986. (Also available in French from Scholastic-TAB Publications Canada.)

• Brenner, Barbara. *Bodies.* New York: E.P. Dutton, 1973.

• _____. *Faces.* New York: E.P. Dutton, 1970.

• Brown, Margaret Wise. *The Important Book.* New York: Harper & Row, 1949.

•• Caines, Jeanette. *Abby.* New York: Harper & Row, 1973.

••• Carle, Eric. *Do You Want to Be My Friend?* New York: Harper & Row, 1986,

•• _____. *The Very Hungry Caterpillar.* New York: G.P. Putnam's Sons, 1981.

••• Chislett, Gail. *Pardon Me Mom.* Willowdale, Ont: Annick Press, 1986.

••• _____. *The Rude Visitors.* Willowdale, Ont: Annick Press, 1984.

••• Cohen, Miriam. *Jim Meets the Thing.* New York: Greenwillow Press, 1981.

••• _____. *No Good in Art.* New York: Greenwillow Press, 1980.

•• de Paolo, Tomie. *Andy (That's My Name).* Englewood Cliffs, NJ: Prentice-Hall, 1973.

•• Dickson, Barry. *Afraid of the Dark.* Toronto: James Lorimer, 1986.

••• Downie, Mary Alice. *Judy Greenteeth.* Toronto: Kids Can Press, 1984.

••• Dumas, Jacqueline. *And I'm Never Coming Back.* Willowdale, Ont; Annick Press, 1986.

•• Etherington, Frank. *When I Grow Up Bigger Than Five.* Willowdale, Ont: Annick Press, 1986.

- • Ets, Marie H. *Just Me*. New York: Viking Press, 1965.
- • • • Feelings, Muriel. *Jambo Means Hello: Swahili Alphabet Book*. New York: Dial Press, 1974.
- • • • Fernandes, Eugenie. *A Difficult Day*. Toronto: Kids Can Press, 1986.
- • Flack, Marjorie. *Ask Mr. Bear*. New York: Macmillan, 1971.
- • • • _____ . *The Story About Ping*. New York: Viking Press, 1970.
- • Freeman, Don. *Dandelion*. New York: Viking Press, 1964.
- • • Fujikawa, Gyo. *A Child's Book of Poems*. New York: Grosset & Dunlap, 1972.
- • • • _____ . *Let's Play*. New York: G.P. Putnam's Sons (Zokeisha Publications), 1974.
- • • _____ . *Puppies, Pussy Cats and Other Friends*. New York: G.P. Putnam's Sons (Zokeisha Publications), 1975.
- • • • Gill, Gail. *There's an Alligator Under My Bed*. Toronto: Three Trees Press, 1984.
- • • • Gilman, Phoebe. *Jillian Jigs*. Richmond Hill, Ont: Scholastic-TAB Publications, 1985.
- • • • Green, Carrolle. *The Too Busy Day*. Willowdale, Ont: Annick Press, 1985.
- • • • • Greene, Carol. *The Insignificant Elephant*. San Diego: Harcourt Brace Jovanovich, 1985.
- • • • Hutchins, Hazel. *Leanna Builds a Genie Trap*. Willowdale, Ont: Annick Press, 1986.
- • • • Jensen, Virginia. *Sara and the Door*. Don Mills, Ont: Addison-Wesley, 1977.
- • • • Joose, Barbara. *Spiders in the Fruit Cellar*. New York: Knopf, 1983.
- • • • Keats, Ezra Jack. *Goggles*. New York: Macmillan, 1969.
- • • • _____ . *Jeannie's Hat*. New York: Harper & Row, 1966.
- • • • _____ . *Peter's Chair*. New York: Harper & Row, 1967.
- • • • • _____ . *Whistle for Willie*. New York: Viking Press, 1964.
- • • • Kellog, Steven. *Much Bigger than Martin*. New York: Dial Press, 1973.
- • • • Klein, Norma. *Girls Can Be Anything*. New York: E.P. Dutton, 1973.
- • • • Krasilovsky, Phyllis. *The Girl Who Was a Cowboy*. Garden City, NY: Doubleday, 1965.
- • • • Lasker, Joe. *He's My Brother*. Chicago: Albert Whitman, 1974.
- • • • • Leaf, Munro. *Who Cares? I Do*. Philadelphia: J.B. Lippincott, 1971.
- • • • • MacEwan, Gwendolyn. *The Chocolate Moose*. Toronto: New Canada Publications, 1981. (Read-Tell)
- • Martin Jr., Bill, and John Archambault. *Here Are My Hands*. Markham, Ont: Fitzhenry & Whiteside, 1987.
- • • • Morgan, Allen. *Daddy-Care*. Willowdale, Ont: Annick Press, 1986.
- • • • Munsch, Robert. *David's Father*. Willowdale, Ont: Annick Press, 1983.
- • • • _____ . *50 Below Zero*. Willowdale, Ont: Annick Press, 1986.
- • • _____ . *Thomas's Snowsuit*. Willowdale, Ont: Annick Press, 1985.
- • • Munsil, Janet. *Dinner at Aunt Rosie's*. Willowdale, Ont: Annick Press, 1984.
- • • • Newman, Marjorie. *School Concert*. Markham, Ont: Penguin Books (Hamish Hamilton Books), 1986.
- • O'Brien, Anne Sibley. *Don't Say No*. Markham, Ont: Fitzhenry & Whiteside, 1986.
- • _____ . *I Don't Want to Go*. Markham, Ont: Fitzhenry & Whiteside, 1986.
- • _____ . *It Hurts!* Markham, Ont: Fitzhenry & Whiteside, 1986.
- • _____ . *It's Hard to Wait*. Markham, Ont: Fitzhenry & Whiteside, 1986.
- • • • Plantos, Ted. *Heather Hits Her First Home Run*. Windsor, Ont: Black Moss, 1986.
- • • Price, Matthew. *Do You See What I See?* Toronto: Kids Can Press, 1985.
- • Scarry, Richard. *Nicky Goes to the Doctor*. New York: Western Publishing, 1972.
- • • Scott, Ann Herbert. *On Mother's Lap*. New York: McGraw-Hill, 1972.
- • • • _____ . *Sam*. New York: McGraw-Hill, 1967.
- • • • Selfton, Catherine. *Flying Sam*. Markham, Ont: Penguin Books (Hamish Hamilton Books), 1986.
- • • Slobodkin, L. *Excuse Me! Certainly!* New York: Vanguard Press, 1959.
- • • • _____ . *Magic Michael*. New York: Macmillan, 1973.
- • • • Staunton, Ted. *Puddleman*. Toronto: Kids Can Press, 1983.
- • • • _____ . *Simon's Surprise*. Toronto: Kids Can Press, 1986.
- • • • • _____ . *Taking Care of Crumley*. Toronto: Kids Can Press, 1984.
- • • • Stein, Sarah B. *Making Babies*. New York: Walker and Company, 1974.
- • Stinson, Kathy. *Big or Little*. Willowdale, Ont: Annick Press, 1983.

- _____ . *The Bare Naked Book.* Willowdale, Ont: Annick Press, 1986.
- •••• Strauss, Joyce. *How Does It Feel . . .?* New York: Human Sciences Press, 1979.
- ••• Stren, Patti. *There's a Rainbow in My Closet.* New York; Harper & Row, 1979.
- ••• Szendak, M. *Where the Wild Things Are.* New York: Harper & Row, 1963.
- •••• Viorst, Judith. *Alexander and the Terrible Horrible No Good Very Bad Day.* New York: Atheneum, 1972.
- •• von Konigslow, Andrea Wayne. *That's My Baby.* Willowdale, Ont: Annick Press, 1986.
- ••• Weiss, Nicki. *Maude and Sally.* New York: Greenwillow Press, 1983.
- •• Wells, Rosemary. *Noisy Nora.* New York: Dial Press, 1973.
- ••• Williams, Vera. *Something Special for Me.* New York: Greenwillow Press, 1983.
- •• Zander, Hans. *My Blue Chair.* Willowdale, Ont: Annick Press, 1985.
- •• Zion, Gene. *Harry, the Dirty Dog.* Markham, Ont: Fitzhenry & Whiteside, 1956.

Planning for Group Time

NOTE: All music, fingerplays, poems, stories, and games listed here may be used at other times during the session as appropriate. See Core Library, "Basic Resources," p. 95 for publishers and addresses. See p. 99 for record company addresses. In parodies, hyphenated words match music notes of the tune used.

Music

Songs

GUESS WHAT I SEE?

(tune: "I'm a Little Teapot," first 2 lines)
Adaptation by JoAnne Deal Hicks

Children take turns holding the mirror and tell others what they want sung.

VERSE 1:
Looking in a mir-ror, guess what I see?

A _____ , _____ face that belongs to me!
(happy,
sad,
silly
etc.)
(brown, white, pink, tan,
black if suggested by child
following a discussion
on skin colour)

VERSE 2:
Looking in a mir-ror, guess what I see?

_____ , _____ eyes that belong to me!
(big, light, bright,
round, dark)

(blue, brown, green,
black, gray)

VERSE 3:

Looking in a mir-ror, guess what I see?

_____, _____ hair that belongs to me!
(curly, long,
straight, short)
blonde, black,
red, brown)

VERSE 4:

When I stand in sunshine, guess what I see?

A _____ black shadow that belongs to me!
(long, short,
depends on time of day)

VERSE 5:

When I look in wa-ter, guess what I see?

A wig-gling face that belongs to me!

NOTE: Be sensitive to children's need to choose the descriptive words they like best to be sung for self-
          concept.

MY SPECIAL FRIEND (a parody)

(tune: "Hi Ho—Hi Ho," the work song from Snow White)
Adaptation by JoAnne Deal Hicks

My spe-cial friend, my ver-y spe-cial friend,
He (she) likes to run and play with me, I love my very-y spe-cial friend.
He (she) has a ver-y spe-cial drum, (TEACHER SHOWS CHILDREN A TOM-TOM)
And has some silver jewel-lery, too.
I love my friend!

My spe-cial friend, my ver-y spe-cial friend,
He (she) likes to run and play with me, I love my ver-y spe-cial friend.
He (she) has a lit-tle wood-en bowl, (TEACHER SHOWS BOWL AND CHOPSTICKS)
And has a spe-cial way to eat. (PRETEND TO EAT WITH CHOPSTICKS)
I love my friend!

My spe-cial friend, my ver-y spe-cial friend,
He (she) likes to run and play with me, I love my ver-y spe-cial friend.
He (she) has a differ-ent way to speak,
A differ-ent lan-guage all his (her) own.
I love my friend!

My spe-cial friend, my ver-y spe-cial friend,
He (she) likes to run and play with me, I love my ver-y spe-cial friend.
He (she) has a ver-y spe-cial name,
A spe-cial voice, a spe-cial face.
I love my friend!

NOTE: The parody above includes Indian, Asian, non-English-speaking children.

WILL YOU BE A FRIEND OF MINE?
(tune: "Merrily We Roll Along")

Will you be a friend of mine,
Friend of mine, friend of mine,
Will you be a friend of mine,
And play a game with me?
(**or** And send a val-en-tine?)

Yes, I'll be a friend of yours,
Friend of yours, friend of yours,
Yes, I'll be a friend of yours
And play a game with you!
(**or** And send a val-en-tine!)

From *Sally Go Round the Sun*, Fowke
"If You're Happy," p. 44
"Head and Shoulders," p. 46
"It Doesn't Really Matter," p. 46
"Foot and Finger Plays,: pp. 100–106 (good for body image)

From *Songs to Sing and Sing Again*, Gordon
(See index for songs in languages other than English.)
"Here Is What I Can Do," p. 36
"One Finger, One Thumb," p. 44

From *The Goat With the Bright Red Socks*, Birkenshaw and Walden
"This Is Me," p. 2
"These Are My Eyes, Eyes, Eyes," p. 3
"I Feel Glad," p. 7
"I Can Count," p. 8
"Theleftrightfrontbackupanddown Dance," p. 13
"Rig a Jig Jig," pp. 14–15
"What Makes House a Home?" p. 20

From *The Baby Beluga Book*, Raffi
"To Everyone in All the World," p. 21
"Over in the Meadow," p. 28

From *What Shall We Do and Allee Galloo*, Winn
"Come On and Join in the Game," p. 4
"This Is What I Can Do," p. 10
"Who's That Knocking at My Door," p. 84

Rhythms and singing games

1. Body exercise songs—touch body parts as you sing. With the older children you may add other verses using other parts of the body.

   (tune: "Oats, Peas, Beans")
   Heads and shoulders, knees and toes
   Heads and shoulders, knees and toes
   Heads and shoulders, knees and toes
   Let's point to them together.

   (tune: "Mulberry Bush")
   My head, my shoulders, my knees, my toes
   My head, my shoulders, my knees, my toes
   My head, my shoulders, my knees, my toes
   Then we stand together.

   GOOD GROOMING

   (tune: "Mulberry Bush")

   "This is the way we wash our face . . ."
   "This is the way we put on our clothes . . ."
   "This is the way we brush our teeth . . ."

2. Rhythms in names: When children have had some rhythm experience beat out a rhythm pattern chanting the children's names to it; for example, 1-2-3 for Tom-my Smith and 1-2-3-4 for Pedro Gar-za. Later in the year, beat out the rhythm and have children guess each person's name in the class that would fit the pattern.
3. The twist: Encourage children to respond to rhythmic music in their own individual way. When space is limited, provide each with a small piece of carpet a foot square. Place on a smooth floor, nap side down. Each child may move, twist, sway anyway he or she chooses as long as his or her feet remain on the square or carpet. Children become quite skillful as they twist on the carpet. Use music with a fast beat.

From *Fingers, Feet, and Fun*, Evans
"Five Little Fingers," p. 24
"One, Two, Three, Four, Five," p. 30
"Peter Hammers," p. 40
"There Was a Little Girl," p. 42
"Growing," p. 46
"My Mirror," p. 82
"Hide and Seek," p. 83
"Me," p. 85

From *The New Wind Has Wings*, Downie
"Laughter," p. 10
"O Earth, Turn," p. 19

From *Hand Rhymes*, Brown
"My Book," p. 5
"Five Little Babies," p. 6

From *Finger Plays and Action Rhymes*, Jacobs
"Good Morning," p. 7
"A Big Boy," p. 41

NOTE: Any rhythm activity record you have that features development of large muscles could be used. Also any songs featuring self-concepts in record collections you already own should be used.

Records and cassettes

Sandy Tobias Oppenheim. *If Snowflakes Fell in Flavours.* (Berandol Records)
"Let's Play the Statue Game"
"I Am Sick"
"I Feel Grouchy"
"My Wish Song"

Sharon, Lois, and Bram. *Smorgasbord.* (Elephant Records)
"Peanut Butter"
"'A' You're Adorable"

Fingerplays and Poems

TEN LITTLE FINGERS

I have ten little fingers (HOLD UP BOTH HANDS)
And they all belong to ME (POINT TO SELF)
I can make them do things
Would you like to see? (POINT TO CHILD)
I can shut them up tight (MAKE FIST)
I can open them up wide (OPEN FINGERS)
I can clap them together and make them hide (CLAP, THEN HIDE)
I can jump them up high, I can jump them down low (OVER HEAD AND DOWN)
And fold them together and hold them just so (FOLD IN LAP)

THIS LITTLE HAND

This little hand is a good little hand (HOLD UP ONE HAND)
This little hand is his brother. (HOLD UP OTHER HAND)
Together, they wash and they wash and they wash (WASHING HANDS)
One hand washes the other.

WHERE ARE YOUR _____?

Where are your eyes? Show me your eyes—baby's eyes can see.
Where are your eyes? Show me your eyes—shut them quietly.

Where is your nose? Show me your nose—baby's nose can blow.
Where is your nose? Show me your nose—wiggle it just so.

Where is your mouth? Show me your mouth—it can open wide.
Where is your mouth? Show me your mouth—how many teeth inside?

Stories

(To read, read–tell, or tell. See Book Centre on p. 119 for complete list.)
The choice of stories in the self-concept area is easy because of the wealth of material that is available. It is important to choose stories that are relevant to the current interests and concerns of the children.

A book such as Chislett's *The Rude Visitors* would be a good choice if the children are concerned with manners and being considerate of other people.

Anglund's *A Friend Is Someone Who Likes You* is an excellent story to read when children are going through a stage of having a new "best friend" every day.

Games

(See Learning Games, pp. 50–59, and teacher-made games in this part of the guide for directions.)
1. *Identification games:* Guess who? Who's missing? Listen, and Look and see
2. *Circle games:* Looby loo; Hokey pokey; Farmer in the dell; Did you ever see a lassie?; Friend, friend from over the way
3. *Direction games:* Together, together; Sally says; Follow the leader; Directions

Routine Times

1. All routines: Explain to new children the reasons for inspection, resting, eating, hand washing, and teeth brushing. Throughout the year continue to teach the value of these routines.
2. Greeting children: Always try to welcome each child individually upon arrival. Special attention should be given to those who have been absent.
3. Inspection: Talk about keeping clean, keeping healthy, and help children to learn their body parts. Watch for healing of bruises and scrapes.
4. Children can take turns telling each other's names at snack or mealtime.
5. Children may find their place identified by a name card or place card. You might use this for snack time, meal time, or any activity time.
6. Throughout the year serve foods at snack or meal times that are enjoyed by various ethnic groups in Canada and around the world.
7. Hand washing: Talk about the importance of washing hands after toileting and before eating.
8. When toileting, use correct biological terms for body parts and bodily functions; for example, genitals, penis, anus, rectum, navel, urinate, eliminate, bowel movement, and feces.

Large Muscle Activities

1. Note special progress and praise accomplishments in any skill, games, or exercises, such as using the balance beam, walking boards, and slide, or pumping in a swing, or running, hopping, climbing, crawling, and skipping with older children.
2. Encourage the children to try new feats. Compare their progress only against their *own* former efforts.
3. Use gym mats to do somersaults and other tumbling exercises.
4. Playing in the snow offers many children the opportunity to learn more about their bodies. Activities such as making snow angels and building snow houses use large muscles and improve co-ordination. Building snowpeople is also useful for co-ordination and large muscle development as well as encouraging co-operation.

Extended Experiences

NOTE: See p. 71 regarding visitors.

1. Invite a community police officer to come and show the children about fingerprinting.

    ★ CAUTION: Be sure you have facilities planned so that the children can wash their fingers off after being fingerprinted. You should contact the police officer ahead of time in order to discuss what you think your children will be able to understand.

2. Invite a doctor or dentist, through the local public health nurse, to perform any required checkups in the school if adequate space can be provided for the examinations.
3. Invite a dental hygienist to talk to the children about taking care of their teeth and demonstrate the correct method of brushing.
4. Invite a nurse to talk to the children about good health habits and to assist you in weighing and measuring the children. Record height and weight on a measuring chart. Leave the chart up or save it until the late spring or summer and measure again. Compare the results.
5. Invite a physical education teacher or dance instructor to assist the children in learning exercises or simple dance movements.

6. Arrange to visit children's parents at work to give children a sense of their community and an understanding of the diversity in their families.
7. Select suitable filmstrips.
8. A private place could be used by an individual child when
    a. Listening to records or story tapes
    b. Looking at books
    c. Exploring cognitive or manipulative materials
    d. Thinking or resting
    This space can be created
    a. On a raised platform—add carpet or pillows
    b. In a closet—take off the door, provide a light, and a pillow or beanbag chair
    c. In a fibre barrel with top and one side cut away—add a round pillow
    d. In a quiet corner made by partitioning it off with shelves or screen—add carpet, overstuffed chairs with legs removed, or beanbag chairs

Teacher Resources

Pictures and Displays

▷ Pictures of each child can be taken with a Polaroid or other camera, and displayed with their names beneath.

▷ Children's art work should also be displayed throughout the year with everyone having his or her work selected frequently (see the Art Centre, p. 118).

▷ Display a group of pictures portraying children involved in various activities, illustrating many skills, such as dressing, brushing teeth, climbing a tree, riding a tricycle, and so on.

Books and Periodicals

Ames, L.B., et al. *Don't Push your Preschooler.* New York: Harper & Row, 1980.

_____ . *Your Two Year Old: Terrible or Tender.* New York: Dell, 1980.

_____ . *Your Three Year Old: Friend or Enemy.* New York: Dell, 1980.

_____ . *Your Four Year Old: Wild and Wonderful.* New York: Dell, 1980.

Anderson, Eugene. *Self-Esteem for Tots to Teens.* Deephaven, MN: Meadowbrook, 1984.

Berne, Patricia. *Building Self-Esteem in Children.* New York: Continuum, 1981.

Cooper, Terry Touf, and Marilyn Ratner. *Many Hands Cooking: An International Cookbook for Boys and Girls.* New York: Thomas Y. Crowell, 1974.

Harrison, Barbara G. *Unlearning the Lie: Sexism in School.* New York: Liveright Publishing, 1973.

Klagsburn, Francine. *Free to Be . . . You and Me.* New York: McGraw-Hill, 1974.

Lorin, M.J. *The Parents Book of Physical Fitness for Children.* New York: Atheneum, 1978.

Oppenheim, Joanne. *Kids and Play.* New York: Ballantine Books, 1978.

Prudden, Suzy. *Exercise Program for Young Children.* New York: Workman, 1983.

Films and Videos

The National Film Board has an excellent and constantly growing collection of audio visual material that can enhance your curriculum planning in this area, as well as being useful for staff education. Your local public library can assist you in obtaining this material.

Community Resources and Organizations

▷ Parents of children in your classroom or friends of another culture or foreign students at a nearby college
▷ Pediatrician and nurse
▷ Dentist and dental hygienist
▷ Speech and hearing clinic
▷ Mental health clinic
▷ Department of Public Health
▷ Child development department of early childhood department in the local college or university
▷ Various cultural organizations in your community
▷ The Canadian Mental Health Association
▷ Provincial and territorial mental health associations

Government Agencies

▷ The federal government's multicultural agency is an invaluable resource
▷ Provincial and territorial ministries concerned with multiculturalism
▷ Provincial, territorial, and federal ministries concerned with health, welfare, and social services

2 Sight

★★★★★★★★★★★★★★★★★★★★★★

Basic Understandings

(concepts children can grasp from this subject)

- ▷ We see with our eyes.
- ▷ We learn things by using our eyes.
- ▷ We need light to help us to see; if it is completely dark, we cannot see.
- ▷ Some animals, such as cats, can see in the dark.
- ▷ We need to take good care of our eyes so that we can see.
- ▷ Some people need glasses to help them to see.
- ▷ Some people cannot see at all; they are blind (see other chapters on senses).
- ▷ Our eyes take pictures somewhat like a camera does.
- ▷ Our eyes help tell us the colour of things.
- ▷ Our eyes help tell us the size of things.
- ▷ Our eyes help tell us the shape of things.
- ▷ Things that are far away look smaller than when we are close to them.
- ▷ The coloured part of the eye is called the iris. The colour of eyes may be different.
- ▷ The black circle of the eye, called the pupil, is really an opening to let in light so that we can see.
- ▷ If the sun is too bright, our eyes may not keep out enough light. We can protect our eyes when we are out in bright sun by wearing a peaked cap or a sun visor.

    NOTE: Some doctors suggest that sunglasses, especially children's cheap sunglasses, weaken children's eyes and should be discouraged.

- ▷ Eyebrows and eyelashes help protect the eyes from dust particles.
- ▷ If something gets in one of our eyes, our eyes shed tears to help wash it out.

Additional Facts the Teacher Should Know

1. The optic nerve relays the image viewed by the retina to the brain. Nerve fibres from the retina run through the optic nerve. It is the nerve cells in the retina that make sight possible.
2. The *iris* of the eye is the coloured part of the eye. The *pupil* is actually an opening in the iris. The lens of the eye is located behind the pupil. The *retina* is the inner layer of the eyeball. Light enters the eye via the pupil and passes through the colourless liquid contained in the eyeball cavity. The muscles of the eye focus the lens of the eye.

3. Some people are nearsighted; some are farsighted. A concave lens in glasses corrects nearsightedness, a convex lens corrects farsightedness.

4. Some children have visual difficulties, such as seeing reverse images, colour blindness, nearsightedness, farsightedness, and strabismus (crossed-eyes). Squinting, holding objects or books close to the eyes, bumping into objects, tripping, or persistently erring in colour identification may indicate vision problems. Ask parent(s) to refer such children to an eye doctor for further examination and testing.

NOTE: Other chapters related to this subject are "Colour in My World," on pp. 525–536 and "Day and Night," pp. 499–507. This is an excellent area for introducing children to basic eye care and safety. See the teacher resources for sources of information in this area or consult with your centre's public health nurse.

Methods Most Adaptable for Introducing this Subject to Children

1. Place eyeglasses, binoculars, microscope, magnifying glasses, kaleidoscope, and View Masters on a table. Talk about why some people need or use these.

2. In a group setting, ask children to put their hands over their eyes, then ask, "Can you see?"

3. If children are willing, put a sleepmask over their eyes, ask, "How could you walk around if you couldn't see?" "What do you think would happen?"

   ★ CAUTION: Wrap the mask with fresh tissue for each child using it.

4. If you have a doll with broken eyes, show it to the children and say, "If a doll gets an eye pushed out, we can fix the eye, but children cannot get new eyes, so they need to take very good care of the ones they have."

5. Use the story and/or the record of Muffin, the little dog who couldn't see for a while because he got a cinder in his eye. "What if we cannot see?"

Vocabulary

glasses	eyelash(es)	vision	frames
spectacles	look	blind	nosepiece
contact lenses	see	iris	magnifying glass
eye(s)	sight	pupil	microscope
eyebrow(s)	sighted	lens	telescope
sunglasses	sun visors	tears	
monocle			

Magnified objects. A giant magnifier leaves a child's hands free to move objects under viewer. A dark piece of paper under a light object, or the reverse, will make viewing easier.

Learning Centres

Discovery Centre

1. Go for an observation walk. This can be a general or a specific walk, such as "Look for bugs," or "Look for leaves." Take some binoculars, a magnifying glass, and a sack for the treasures you may find.
2. Look at the objects through a magnifying glass. Have a supply of interesting specimens, such as rocks, shells, or insects. Decide which are shiny, which are dull coloured. Use a magnifier to look at a telephone book. Invite the children to choose or bring in objects that they wish to observe under the magnifier.
3. Have a visual theme for a treasure hunt, in which children look for objects in the room with particular visual attributes; for example all red objects, all round objects, etc.
4. Use cooking activities to see the difference in appearance *before* and *after*. Suggested for this:

Jell-o	pancakes	scrambled eggs
gingerbread	pudding	waffles
bacon	cupcakes	

Popcorn: This one illustrates the five senses. You can *see* it pop if you have a popper with a glass or plastic lid; you can *hear* it popping; you can *smell* it; you can *taste* it; and you can *feel* the shapes of the kernels. Sing the "Popcorn" song, p. 135.

★ CAUTION: Be sure to have all the required utensils and ingredients available before you start.

5. Have a table for the children to bring their special finds for the week. Ask the children to bring objects with special visual attributes: '

6. Look at an object far away. Talk about how little it looks. Walk closer to it and see how much bigger it looks.

7. When you see an airplane in the sky, talk about how little it looks and how big it really is when you are close to it. Compare pictures of both instances.

8. Have an eye chart for children. Talk about the reasons some people need glasses. Recall magnifying-glass exploration.

9. If adults in the group, parents or children wear glasses or contact lenses, ask them to show the group what they look like and how they fit.

10. Have a peep box with a small light in it. Let children look in when it is dark and when the light is on.

11. Talk about some objects that are round, big, or blue. For example, "Look at this ball. What colour is it? What shape is it? What size is it? How did you know it was round, big, and blue? Did you hear it? Did you taste it? Did you feel it? No, you saw it with your eyes."

12. Display different things that help us to see when it is dark such as a lamp, a candle, a lantern, a flashlight, or a kerosene lamp.

13. Observe or "make" a rainbow—for directions see the chapter, "Colour in My World," p. 528.

14. Make a display of things people read, such as books, magazines, Braille books, newspapers, pamphlets, and posters.

   NOTE: Choose illustrated items if possible.

15. Display items we need to read or see to help us; for example, something dirty or clean, a thermometer, a clock, a television, a filmstrip, a recipe book, travel signs, street and house numbers, maps, timetables, tour brochures, a telephone book, a picture dictionary.

16. Take pictures of the children and have them developed at a one-hour photo shop, if possible, to demonstrate the use of a camera. (If you have access to a Polaroid camera, use it.) Allow older children to take their own pictures. Remember to keep track of which child shot which picture.

17. Have a special colour day, on which everyone is asked to wear a specific colour and all the activities revolve around that colour. For example, on green day, green, blue and yellow paints would be provided at the easel; green vegetables would be served at lunch along with green pasta, etc. [Source: Indenbaum, Valerie, and Marcia Shapiro. *The Everything Book*. Livonia, MI: Partner Press, 1985.]

18. Rent a video camera and monitor at a local retail outlet to record and view a special event in the centre. Be sure to rent a camera that will work in normal lighting conditions.

Dramatic Play Centres

Home-living centre

1. Have a flashlight available to look for things in dark places.
2. Have a discarded or toy camera available to take "pretend" pictures of the dolls.
3. Set out sunglass frames with the lenses removed.
4. Provide unbreakable hand and wall mirrors.
5. Place a magnifying glass and a telephone book by the toy telephone.

Block-building centre

1. Set out road signs and traffic signals for use with road building.
2. Display pictures of people driving at night. Talk about the use of headlights at night and during the day (if you are in a province or territory that has a daytime headlight law.)

Other dramatic play centres

1. Eye doctor: Set out an eye chart, doctor's coat, flashlight, mirror, and frames of glasses.
2. Set up a shop to sell eyeglasses, frames for glasses and sunglasses. Remove lenses.
3. Make a television movie (see the "Art Centre" which follows) and let children pretend to run a theatre (picture show) or a drive-in movie.
4. Play library (after a visit to a library); collect picture books, set out reading tables, and put up bookshelves. Provide the librarian with a desk or a counter, stamp and stamp pads, cards, and a telephone. Paste pocket cards in the books.

Learning, Language, and Readiness Materials Centre

Commercially made games and materials

(See "Basic Resources," pp. 79, 100, for manufacturers' addresses.)

1. *Puzzles:* Colourful and visually stimulating puzzles. Be sure to have some puzzles with knobs for younger children.
2. *Construction and manipulative toys:* Coloured peg boards. Peg boards with illuminated pegs such as Hasbro's *Lite Brite*, available in most toy stores. Inexpensive binoculars. Plastic magnifying glasses of different sizes. Magnifying glasses on stands, available in most science stores. Microscopes, such as the *Micro Explorer Set* from Fisher Price.
3. *Outdoor Toys:* Prisms for observing the colours in sunlight. (Suitable for older children.)

NOTE: Be sure to remind the children not to look directly at the sun.

Teacher-made games and materials

NOTE: For a detailed description of "Learning Games," see pp. 50–59.

1. Look and see: Use several objects of different colours or shapes
2. I see something, what do you see?
3. Who's missing?
4. Guess who?
5. Match-them
6. Grouping and sorting by association: Sort by size, shape, and colour
7. Alike, different, and the same
8. Sequences from workjobs (see "Teacher Resources," p. 139) is a fun teacher-made game for exploring sight

Art Centre

- 1. Easel painting: Let the children mix colours; add black or white.
- 2. Paint with tempera on clear cellophane and then put it up against a window to let light shine through.
- 3. Paint with tempera on aluminum foil or styrofoam trays.
- 4. Drip painting: Use two parts salt, one part flour, to three parts water. Add powdered tempera for desired colour. Drip from a brush onto paper.
- 5. Spatter painting: Place small items found on the observation walk on a piece of paper and spatter paint over them. This may include small stones, leaves, small branches, twigs, pine cones, seeds.
- 6. Mural painting: Put large lengths of paper on the wall or the floor and let the children paint or colour what they saw on the walk.
- 7. Make a collage using different shapes and colours of paper, yarn, ribbon, or items found on the nature walk.

••• 8. Encourage the older children to make pictures about a pet. Together, write a story and glue a series of pictures on a long strip of shelving paper. Thread through slots in a carton to make a movie screen.

NOTE: See the chapter on "Colour in My World" for many other suggestions. When possible take easels, clay dough, and carpentry workbench outdoors. If weather does not permit that, place easels near the discovery centre where live pets and plants may be observed while young artists are at work.

Book Centre

••• Aliki Diogenes. *My Five Senses.* New York: Thomas Y. Crowell, 1962.
•• Anglund, Joan Walsh. *What Colour Is Love?* New York: Harcourt Brace Jovanovich, 1966.
•• Asch, Frank. *Bear Shadow.* New York: Prentice-Hall, 1985.
••• Brown, Margaret. *Walk With Your Eyes.* Danbury, CT: Watts, 1979.
• Chermayeff, Ivan. *Tomato and Other Colours.* Englewood Cliffs, NJ: Prentice-Hall, 1981.
•• Domanska, Janina. *What Do You See?* New York: Macmillan, 1974.
•• Emberly, Ed. *Green Says Go.* New York: Little Brown, 1968.
• Fisher, Leonard Everett. *Look Around! A Book About Shapes.* Markham, Ont.: Penguin Books, 1986.
• Gay, Zhena. *Look!* New York: Viking Press, 1952.
•• Ginsberg, Mirra. *The Sun's Asleep Behind the Hill.* New York: Greenwillow Press, 1982.
• Hoban, Tana. *Circles, Triangles and Squares.* New York: Macmillan, 1974.
• _____ . *Is It Larger? Is It Smaller?* New York: Greenwillow Press, 1985.
• _____ . *Is It Red? Is It Yellow? Is It Blue?* New York: Greenwillow Press, 1978.
• _____ . *Look Again.* New York: Macmillan, 1971.
• _____ . *Take Another Look.* New York: Greenwillow Press, 1981.
•• Jonas, Ann. *Round Trip.* New York: Greenwillow Press, 1983.
•• Lionni, Leo. *Little Blue and Little Yellow.* New York: Pantheon Books, 1969.
• Livermore, Elaine. *Find the Cat.* Boston: Houghton Mifflin, 1973.
•• MacLachlan, Patricia. *Through Grandpa's Eyes.* New York: Harper & Row, 1980.
•• Newth, Phillip. *Roly Goes Exploring.* New York: Collins, 1981.
•• Parramon, J.M., and J.J. Puig. *Sight.* New York: Barron, 1985.
•• Pluckrose, Henry. *Seeing.* Danbury, CT: Watts, 1986.
•• Polland, Barbara Kay. *The Sensible Book: A Celebration of Your Five Senses.* Millbrae, CA: Celestial Arts Publishing, 1974.
•• Raskin, Ellen. *Spectacles.* New York: Macmillan, 1972.
•• Reuter, Margaret. *My Mother Is Blind.* Chicago: Childrens Press, 1974.
••• Shaw, Charles, G. *It Looked Like Spilt Milk.* New York: Harper & Row, 1947.
•• Shulevitz, Uri. *Dawn.* New York: Farrar Strauss, & Giroux, 1974.
•• Stinson, Kathy. *Fun with Colours.* Burlington, Ont: Hayes Publishing, 1986.
•• _____ . *Red Is Best.* Willowdale, Ont: Annick Press, 1982.
•• Wolff, Ashley. *Only the Cat Saw.* New York: Dodd Mead, 1985.
• Zolotow, Charlotte. *One Step, Two.* (Rev. Edition) New York: Lothrop, Lee & Shepard, 1981.

Planning for Group Time

NOTE: All music, fingerplays, stories, poems, and games listed here may be used at other times during the session as appropriate. See Core Library, "Basic Resources," p. 95, for publishers and addresses. See p. 99 for record company addresses. In parodies, hyphenated words match music notes of the tune used.

Music

Songs

SPRINGTIME (a parody)

(tune: "Did You Ever See a Lassie?")
Adaptation by JoAnne Deal Hicks

My—eyes can see it's spring-time, it's spring-time, it's spring-time.
My—eyes can see it's spring-time, the grass is so green!
The green grass, the flow-ers, the sun-shine and show-ers.
My—eyes can see it's spring-time, and I am so glad!

My—ears can hear it's spring-time, it's spring-time, it's spring-time.
My—ears can hear it's spring-time, the birds sweetly sing.
The birds sing, the lambs bleat, the frogs croak, the bees buzz.
My—ears can hear it's spring-time, and I am so glad!

My-bod-y can feel it's spring-time, it's spring-time, it's spring-time.
My—bod-y can feel it's spring-time, the air is so warm.
The warm air, the breez-es, no frost and no freez-es.
My—bod-y can feel it's spring-time, and I am so glad!

NOTE: This parody may also be sung to the tune of "Ach du Lieber, Augustine." If you do, omit the pause (shown by the dash) and sing "my-eyes," "my-ears," "my-bod- ..." on the first note, and, in the fourth line, "time and" on one note.

POPCORN (a parody)

(tune: "Frère Jacques")
Adaptation by JoAnne Deal Hicks

Pop, pop, pop-ping. Pop, pop, pop-ping. Our pop-corn. Our pop-corn.
Pop-ping, pop-ping, pop-corn, pop-ping, pop-ping, pop-corn.
Our pop-corn, our pop-corn ... (or Pop, pop, pop, ... Pop, pop, pop)

From *More Piggyback Songs for Infants and Toddlers*, Warren
"Popcorn," p. 92
"Mr. Oil," p. 92
"Oh Rainbow, Oh Rainbow," p. 28
"When I Look into the Sky," p. 22

From *The Goat With the Bright Red Socks*, Birkenshaw and Walden
"These Are My Eyes, Eyes, Eyes," p. 3

From *Elephant Jam*, Sharon, Lois, and Bram
"Jenny Jenkins," p. 122

From *Sally Go Round the Sun*, Fowke
"Monkey See and Monkey Do," p. 17

From *Stepping Along in Music Land*, Murray
"My Five Senses," p. 1
"Coloured Sticks," p. 33
"Little Green Man," p. 42
"Colour Song," p. 44
"Make a Rainbow," p. 46

From *What Shall We Do and Allee Galloo*, Winn
"Two Little Blackbirds," p. 39

From *Do Your Ears Hang Low*, Glazer
"Lavender's Blue," p. 60
"Long-legged Sailor," p. 72

From *Eye Winker, Tom Tinker, Chin Chopper*, Glazer
"Jennie Jenkins," p. 42
"The Little White Duck," p. 46

Records and cassettes

Bob Homme. *The Giant Concert of Concerts Presents the Friendly Giant*. (A & M Records)
"Ribbon Concert"

Bob Schneider. *When You Dream a Dream*. (Capitol Records)
"In the Morning"
"Over the Rainbow"

Fingerplays and Poems

From *Don't Eat Spiders*, Heidbreder and Patkau
"Sun, Sun," p. 9

From *Finger Rhymes*, Dutton
"Grandma's Spectacles," p. 6
"Where Is Thumbkin?" p. 10
"Whoops! Johnny," p. 21

From *Round and Round the Garden*, Williams
"Clap Your Hands," p. 45
"Ten Little Fingers," p. 18

From *Read Aloud Rhymes for the Very Young*, Prelutsky and Brown
"Hide and Seek Shadow," p. 25
"Look," p. 25
"Poor Shadow," p. 25
"Yellow Butter," p. 67

From *Finger Plays and Action Rhymes*, Jacobs
"Grandma," p. 17

From *The New Wind Has Wings*, Downie
"Windshield Wipers," p. 78
"Indian Summer," p. 100

From *Where the Sidewalk Ends*, Silverstein
"Colours," p. 24

From *A New Treasury of Children's Poetry*, Cole
"Little Black Bug," p. 23

I HAVE SO MANY PARTS TO ME

I have two hands to clap with (CLAP)
One nose with which to smell (SNIFF)
I have one head to think with (TAP HEAD)
Two lungs that work quite well. (TAKE A DEEP BREATH)
I have two eyes that let me see (POINT TO EYES)
I have two legs that walk (WALK IN PLACE)
I have two ears that help me hear (CUP HANDS TO EARS)
A mouth with which to talk. (POINT TO MOUTH)

BEAR HUNT

(LEADER GIVES A LINE—OTHERS REPEAT. PAT ON THIGHS IN RHYTHM)

Would you like to go on a bear hunt?
Okay—all right—come on—let's go!
Open the gate—close the gate. (CLAP HANDS)

Coming to a bridge—can't go over it—can't go under it
Let's cross it. (THUMP CHEST WITH CLOSED FISTS)

Coming to a river—can't go over it—can't go under it
Let's swim it. (PRETEND TO DO CRAWL STROKE)

Coming to a tree—can't go over it—can't go under it
Let's climb it! (PRETEND TO CLIMB TREE AND LOOK AROUND)
No bears! (PRETEND TO CLIMB DOWN)

Coming to a wheat field—can't go over it—can't go under it
Let's go through it! (RUB PALMS TOGETHER TO MAKE SWISHING NOISE)

Oh! Oh! I see a cave—it's dark in here— (COVER EYES)
I see two eyes—I feel something furry— (REACH OUT HAND)
It's a bear! Let's go home! (RUNNING MOTION WITH FEET)
(REPEAT ABOVE ACTIONS IN REVERSE USING FAST MOTIONS)
Slam the gate. (CLAP HANDS)
We made it!

GRANDMOTHER'S GLASSES

These are grandmother's glasses (MAKE GLASSES OVER EYES)
This is grandmother's cap (PEAK HANDS ON HEAD)
This is the way she folds her hands (FOLD HANDS)
And puts them in her lap. (PLACE IN LAP)

These are grandfather's glasses (MAKE GLASSES OVER EYES)
This is grandfather's hat (FLAT HAND ON HEAD)
This is the way he folds his arms (CROSS ARMS ON CHEST)
And sits there just like that. (LOOK STRAIGHT AHEAD)

LOOK LOOK

Look up, look down
Look all around
Look here, look there
Look everywhere.

LITTLE BOY BLUE

Little Boy Blue, come blow your horn,
The sheep's in the meadow, the cow's in the corn,
Where's the little boy that looks after the sheep?
He's under the haystack, fast asleep.

Stories

(To read, read–tell, or tell. See Book Centre on p. 134 for complete list.)
When choosing stories for reading or telling in this section, choose ones with very vivid visual images and with visually stimulating pictures. Stinson's *Red Is Best* and Brown's *Walk With your Eyes* are good examples of books that meet these criteria.

Games

(See "Learning Games," pp. 50–59, and teacher-made games in this part of the guide for directions.)

1. Can you remember?
2. Look and see
3. I see something, what do you see?
4. Who's missing?
5. Grouping and sorting by association
6. Did you ever see a lassie?
7. Sequence
8. Guess who?
9. Match-them
10. Alike, different, and the same
11. Easter egg hunt: Hide plastic or paper eggs, or familiar objects for the children to find.
12. Pin the tail on the donkey: Older children might enjoy this game.

★ **CAUTION:** Use "hold-it" or magnets with magnetic flannelboard or double-sided masking tape on paper instead of pins.

Routine Times

1. At snack or meal times emphasize the use of eyes in talking about food. Teacher: "What are we having for a snack?" Child: "Carrots." Teacher: "How do you know they are carrots?" Child: "They look like carrots." Teacher: "What colour (or shape or size) are they?" Child: "Orange and long. . . ." Teacher: "That's right, our eyes help tell us what they are."
2. When busing or walking (where crossing streets is involved), talk about how our eyes help us to drive or to walk safely. Traffic lights, road signs, median lines. Teacher: "Could you drive if you were blind?" What would you need to help you walk, if you were blind?
3. When walking or busing children on a sunny day, talk about the use of sunglasses and the sun visor while in the car or bus. On a rainy or foggy day or late afternoon in winter, discuss how the use of headlights, streetlights, and windshield wipers helps us to see.
4. At rest time talk about the eyelids and how we close them to keep the light out and give our eyes a rest.

Large Muscle Activities

1. Take a "magic circle walk." (See p. 342 for description.)
2. Throw a large ball into a wastepaper basket.
3. Toss beanbags into a box.
4. Try to kick a ball to a fence or to another designated spot.
5. Bowling: Make an alley with large hollow blocks. Use detergent bottles for pins. Plastic bowling sets are available commercially.
6. Woodworking: Emphasize how we use our eyes when measuring, sawing, and hammering. Buy eye protectors to use at woodworking tables.
7. Try to hit a ball with a bat or small plank (for older children); plastic bats and whiffle or cloth balls would be safest.

   NOTE: This activity requires adult supervision at all times.

8. Johnny can you . . . jump the brook? Put two lengths of rope in a parallel line about 15 cm apart and let each child "jump the brook." Increase the distance between the ropes after each child has had a turn.
9. Have the children imitate animal walks (with pictures as cues) to encourage them to translate visual ideas into action.
10. Bring a bright light into a large room with a white wall and turn off all the other lights. Have the children stand facing the wall and with their backs to the light. Then ask them to stand or dance in different ways to see their shadows.
11. Use a 75-watt spotlight (available in most hardware stores) and a screen to create shadow people and animals.

Extended Experiences

1. Take a sightseeing trip or walk to see what you can see.
2. Visit an optometrist or an eye doctor or have him or her visit the group.
3. Take slides or movies of your group and show them, or buy or borrow commercially made films, slides, or filmstrips.

   ★ CAUTION: Leave a light on in the room or the door ajar—especially for the younger children.

4. Visit the children's section of your nearest library.
5. Have a blind person with a seeing-eye dog visit your centre.

   ★ CAUTION: This activity is perhaps best for older children as the children must be told they cannot touch the dog while he is visiting because he is specially trained to see for and guard his owner.

6. Invite a lapidist or rockhound to bring a "black" light and some fluorescent rocks and minerals to be viewed in a dark room.
7. If you have access to a video camera, take a video of the children. Turn off the microphone and ask the children to mime actions for the film. (It would be useful to set a theme for the mimes.) When you show the video, have the children guess what their friends are imitating.

Teacher Resources

Pictures and Displays

▷ Display pictures of eyes or people looking at things.
▷ Display pictures of a blind person with a seeing-eye dog.
▷ Display an eye chart on a wall.
▷ Display things we use with our eyes: mirror, magnifying glass, telescope, microscope, kaleidoscope, or View Master.

Books and Periodicals

Many picture books and pamphlets are published at the Canadian Optometric Association. Often these are available from your local optometrist.

Martin, Paul D. *Messengers to the Brain: Our Fantastic Five Senses.* Washington, DC: National Geographic Society, 1984.

Rivlin, Robert. *Deciphering the Senses: The Expanding World of Human Perception.* New York: Simon & Schuster, 1984.

Sully, Nina. *Looking at the Senses.* Batsford, GB: David and Charles, 1982.

Suzuki, David. *Looking at Senses.* Don Mills, Ont: Stoddart, 1986.

Films and Videos

Consult the *National Film Board Catalogue* and your community library

Community Resources and Organizations

▷ Eye doctor
▷ Optometrist

▷ Nurse—school nurse may lend you an eye chart
▷ Local association for the blind
▷ Children's librarian at nearest library
▷ Check with local rock and mineral club for a lapidist or rockhound
▷ Parent with a movie camera or Polaroid camera
▷ Photographer
▷ Canadian National Institute for the Blind

3 Sound

★★★★★★★★★★★★★★★★★★★★★★

Basic Understandings

(concepts children can grasp from this subject)

▷ We hear with our ears.
▷ We listen to many sounds.
▷ We learn many things by listening.
▷ Sounds are made by things that vibrate.
▷ Sounds are air vibrations that go into the ear.
▷ The outside of the ear acts as a funnel to catch the vibrations that go into the ear.
▷ Some animals hear better than we do, for example, dogs.
▷ Some animals hear sounds different from those that we can hear.
▷ Some people cannot hear at all; they are deaf. Some are hard of hearing (cannot hear well).
▷ Most people who are deaf "hear" by *feeling* sound vibrations (waves).
▷ We can recognize some things by the sounds they make—dogs, birds, motors.
▷ Some sounds help to warn us of danger—sirens, horns, whistles, bees, rattlesnakes, growling animals, cracks of lightning, thunder.
▷ Some sounds help us—alarm clock bells, chimes, voices, telephone bells, doorbells.
▷ We can make sounds as well as hear them.
▷ Some sounds we like; some sounds we do not like.
▷ Some sounds are loud, soft, high, low, pleasant, or harsh.
▷ We need to take good care of our ears.

> ★ CAUTION: When presenting this concept, avoid giving children ideas by telling them, "Don't stick things in your ears." Instead, say, "We must keep our ears clean by washing them. We must not hurt our ears or the ears of other people."

▷ Some people who cannot hear "talk" without making a sound. They use sign language; they move their hands in a special way. Sometimes they can read other peoples' lips and can know what they are saying.

Additional Facts the Teacher Should Know

1. For the sense of sound, people need nerves in the inner ear to relay vibration messages to the brain. The outer ear acts as a funnel in channeling sound vibrations to the eardrum, which separates the outer ear from the middle ear. Behind the eardrum are three small bones that carry sound to the inner ear where the organ of balance and the organ of hearing are found. Each of these organs has a nerve that connects it with the brain.

2. The eustachian tube connects the middle ear with the throat and ordinarily allows a balance of air pressure on both sides of the eardrum.

3. Some people are born deaf. Some become deaf because of injury or nerve damage; others become deaf because of repeated infections that result in scar tissue on the eardrum. This scar tissue can interrupt the flow of sound vibrations. When a cold settles in the inner ear (often due to blowing the nose too hard), medicine may be needed to stop the infection. Sometimes it becomes necessary for a doctor to lance the eardrum (puncture a small hole) to relieve the pressure of the infection and allow for drainage so that the eardrum will not burst. While the eardrum heals rapidly, a star-shaped scar may form after breaking, if the eardrum is not lanced. As scar tissue forms with repeated infections, a person may become more "hard of hearing." Surgery can repair the eardrum, allowing for improved hearing, but usually it is not indicated if the cause of deafness is nerve damage. Be alert to the need to notify a parent or a doctor if a child develops an earache at school.

4. Some children may be hearing impaired. If a child repeatedly loses interest during story time or does not respond readily to questions, the child may have a hearing loss. Consult with the parent(s) and recommend that the child go to a doctor for examination and testing. Many public health departments will come to a children's centre to screen for hearing problems.

Methods Most Adaptable for Introducing this Subject to Children

1. Play a tape recorder, with previously recorded sounds, to see if the children can identify them.
2. Have a variety of sound-producing objects for the children to identify without seeing or touching them; for example, drop objects or make sounds behind a screen.
3. Use a piano or other musical instrument to illustrate the concepts "high," "low," "soft," and "loud." If you use a stringed instrument, demonstrate the vibrations. This can also be done with an open, empty box encircled with several rubberbands.
4. A visitor might play a musical instrument or a child might bring in a music box to share.
5. A siren might blow or a sudden storm with lightning and thunder might occur.
6. You might obtain a telephone teaching unit from the telephone company for the children to use or bring in a homemade telephone for the home-living centre.

Vocabulary

ear(s)	talk	tone	pleasant
hear	hum	high	harsh
deaf	sing	low	tape recorder
sound	whistle	loud	telephone
buzz	whisper	soft	stereo
listen	shout	noise	speaker
vibration	ring	silence	microphone

NOTE: There are real phones that ring and have a dial tone or a busy signal. Children can actually hear one another through the receiver. There is often no charge for borrowing this equipment from the telephone company.

Learning Centres

Discovery Centre

1. Pop popcorn: Listen for the sounds of crackling hot oil and popping kernels.
2. Record children talking or singing on a tape recorder and play it back.
3. Play previously taped segments of
   a. Sounds around the house—for example, a mixer, vacuum cleaner, doorbell, door shutting, toilet flushing, water running, dryer, washing machine
   b. Sounds of nature—for example, a bird chirping, cricket, dog barking, rain, wind blowing through evergreens, crunch of leaves
   c. Street sounds—for example, a police whistle, cars, bus, siren, brakes, clatter of garbage can lids
4. Have rhythm band instruments available for exploring different sounds.
5. Tune bottles or glasses of water to various pitches. Play a tune and let the children experiment with them (supervise for safety).
6. Make a double set of sound tubes from unbreakable plastic or metal film cans. Fill with various ingredients (in varying amounts), such as flour, rice, beans, pebbles, salt, a peachstone, and others. After shaking the container and listening to them, the children can match those that sound alike or can arrange the containers from loudest to softest. Plastic prescription bottles (labels removed) may be used. Glue all container lids shut when filled.
7. Go on a listening walk.
8. Set out step bells, tone blocks, and a xylophone for children to try out.
9. Use a tuning fork to help teach about vibrations.
10. Examine, operate, and make musical instruments (see illustration, p. 144).
11. Examine a typewriter, a see-through music box, or an alarm clock.
12. Examine a stethoscope. Let the children listen to each other's heartbeat or to the heartbeat of a guinea pig.
13. Invite the children to explore a sound tray filled with objects that can be used to make sounds. Include:

bell	coconut shell	tone block and mallet
feather	gong	eggbeater
whisk broom	triangle and striker	crisp paper
comb	alarm clock	tissue
seashell	castanet	cotton ball

14. Encourage children to compare the sounds of items being dropped, struck, or handled—for example, wood against wood, metal against metal, metal against wood, paper being torn and crumpled.

Dramatic Play Centres

Home-living centre

1. In this centre, put an alarm clock that ticks loudly.
2. Encourage the use of the telephone. Make paper cup telephones, put one paper cup telephone in this centre and another in the block centre or in other dramatic play centres, such as a store or an office. Make certain there is more than one telephone in this centre to encourage co-operative interaction.
3. Invite children to listen for kitchen sounds, such as a wooden or metal spoon stirring different kinds of foods in pans or bowls made of metal, glass, plastic, and so on.
4. Add sound-making tools, such as a toy-sized, hand-operated eggbeater, a small hand sweeper, and a broom. Note sounds when used.

Exploring sounds. Left: Reacting to sound made by drawer-pull cymballs. **Right:** Listening to a watch ticking. **Foreground:** Trying to match the sounds of different instruments.

Block-building centre

1. Set out small wooden, metal, or unbreakable plastic fire engines. Encourage some of the children to build a fire station, either a small one (made with wooden blocks) or one large enough for them to play in (made with hollow blocks). Allow the children to imitate sirens.
2. Set out airplanes and encourage the making of runways for takeoffs and landings. Children can imitate the airplane motor as they use the toys.

   NOTE: Other vehicles that are often associated with a sound and that could be used include an ambulance or rescue car and a police car.

3. Set out other motor and machine block accessories.

Other dramatic play centres

1. Make a train from cardboard, wooden boxes, or a row of small chairs. An occasional conductor's call, "All aboard," and/or piano background sounds for a train whistle or engines will add to the dramatic play. Authentic train whistles are available at a reasonable price from VIA Rail.
2. Doctor's office: Set out stethoscopes to give opportunities to listen to heartbeats.
3. Carpenter's shop: Encourage the use of woodworking tools and invite the children to listen or describe sounds their saws, hammers, or sandpaper blocks make.

Learning, Language, and Readiness Materials Centre

Commercially made games and materials

(See "Basic Resources," pp. 79, 100, for manufacturers' addresses.)

1. *Construction and manipulative toys:* Include a variety of musical instruments. Be sure that the instruments are durable and that they play notes that are in tune. Best choices are xylophones, drums, maracas, bells, and triangles. Toy pianos are not appropriate; play telephones are.
2. *Outdoor toys:* Wind chimes (made of metal) can add a touch of sound to an outdoor play environment.
3. *Miscellaneous:* Sturdy cassette tape recorders.

Teacher-made games and materials

NOTE: For a detailed description of "Learning Games," see pp. 50–59.

1. Listen and hear
2. Listening (or telephone): You may wish to try whispering
3. Guess who? or Who am I? Imitate an animal
4. Guess what? or What am I? Imitate a tool or machine sound
5. Match-them: Match sound tubes (see the discovery centre, p. 143, no. 6)
6. What can you hear? Recall sounds
   a. Of a zoo
   b. Of a kitchen
   c. Of a street
7. What did you hear? (Echo): Invite children, one at a time, to duplicate a sound, describe it, or identify it
8. Rhyming words: older children, especially, like to string rhyming words together. Choose words that have many possible matches—cat, rat, mat . . .
9. Matching pitch: Sing a child's name (high or low) and see if he or she can match the pitch

Art Centre

- 1. Offer basic media: Listen for sounds when using tools and materials.
- 2. Make shakers or rattles from gourds or boxes filled with seeds, rice, or sand. These can be painted. Empty hand-size lotion bottles can be decorated with contact paper or pictures.
- 3. Make drums from yogurt or ice cream containers or coffee cans:
   a. Colour or paint them
   b. Wind yarn around the outside or cover with wallpaper
   c. Make a beater by piercing a rubber ball with a sharpened piece of doweling
- •• 4. Make tambourines: Use bells and paper plates or throw-away pie plates. Let children paint or crayon the paper plates or glue paper or fabric scraps on the metal ones.
- 5. Make sand blocks from wooden blocks with sandpaper tacked on. Paint blocks (see p. 34).
- 6. Make jingle paddles and let children paint them with water base paint (see p. 37).
- 7. Make sound trumpets from the top portion of liquid rinse or bleach bottles (be sure they are well washed).

Book Centre

- ••• Arthur, Catherine. *My Sister's Silent World.* Chicago: Children's Press, 1979.
- •• Bloom, Freddy. *The Boy Who Couldn't Hear.* London: Bodley Head, 1977.
- ••• Branley, Franklin. *High Sounds, Low Sounds.* New York: Thomas Y. Crowell, 1967.

•• Brown, Margaret Wise. *The Country Noisy Book.* New York: Harper & Row, 1942.
•• _____ . *The Indoor Noisy Book.* New York: Harper & Row, 1943.
••• _____ . *The Little Brass Band.* New York: Harper & Row, 1955.
•• _____ . *The Quiet Noisy Book.* New York: Harper & Row, 1950.
•• _____ . *The Seashore Noisy Book.* New York: Harper & Row, 1941.
• _____ . *Shhhhhh-Bang!* New York: Harper & Row, 1943.
•• _____ . *The Summer Noisy Book.* New York: Harper & Row, 1940.
•• _____ . *The Winter Noisy Book.* New York: Harper & Row, 1947.
• Bruna, Dick. *I Can Make Music.* New York: Methuen, 1984.
•• Curry, Peter. *I Can Hear.* Los Angeles: Price Stern, 1984.
•• Flack, Marjorie. *Ask Mr. Bear.* New York: Macmillan, 1971.
• Forrester, Patricia. *The Magnificent Moo.* New York: Macmillan, 1983.
• Hearn, Emily. *Woosh! I Hear a Sound.* Willowdale, Ont.: Annick Press, 1983.
• Hutchins, Pat. *The Good Night Owl.* New York: Macmillan, 1972.
••• Isadoro, Rochel. *Ben's Trumpet.* New York: Macmillan, 1979.
•• Keats, Ezra Jack. *Whistle for Willie.* New York: Viking Press, 1964.
••• Kuskin, Karla. *The Philharmonic Gets Dressed.* Markham, Ont: Fitzhenry & Whiteside, 1986.
••• McGovern, Ann. *Too Much Noise.* Boston: Houghton Mifflin, 1967.
•• Nicol, B.P. *Once: A Lullaby.* Windsor, Ont: Black Moss Press, 1983.
•• Parramon, J.M. and J.J. Puig. *Sound.* New York: Barron, 1986.
•• Perkins, Al. *The Ear Book.* New York: Random House, 1968.
••• Peterson, Jean. *I Have a Sister, My Sister Is Deaf.* New York: Harper & Row, 1977.
•• Polland, Barbara Kay. *The Sensible Book: A Celebration of Your Five Senses.* Millbrae, CA: Celestial Arts Publishing, 1974.
• Scarry, Richard. *Splish Splash Sounds.* New York: Western Publishing, 1986.
•• Showers, Paul. *How You Talk.* New York: Thomas Y. Crowell, 1967.
•• _____ . *The Listening Walk.* New York: Thomas Y. Crowell, 1961.
••• Spier, Peter. *Gobble, Growl, Grunt.* Garden City, NY: Doubleday, 1971.
•• Stecher, Miriam, and Alice Randall. *Max the Music Maker.* New York: Lothrop, 1980.
••• Stevenson, James. *Clams Can't Sing.* New York: Greenwillow Press, 1980.
•••• Wolf, Bernard. *Anna's Silent World.* New York: Lippincott, 1977.
•• Zion, Gene. *Harry and the Lady Next Door.* New York: Harper & Row, 1960.

Planning for Group Time

NOTE: All music, fingerplays, poems, stories, and games listed here may be used at other times during the session as appropriate. See Core Library, "Basic Resources," p. 95, for publishers and addresses. See p. 99 for record company addresses. In parodies, hyphenated words match music notes of the tune used.

Music

Songs

From *Sally Go Round the Sun,* Fowke
"Oranges and Lemons," p. 31
"Do Your Ears Hang Low?" p. 139

From *More Piggyback Songs for Infants and Toddlers*, Warren
"I Hear the Animals," p. 73
"Farm Sounds," p. 80
"Can You Clap," p. 84
"Old Volcano," p. 90

From *Stepping Along in Music Land*, Murray
"Five Senses," p. 1
"Strike Up the Band," p. 8
"Ten Little Notes," p. 58
"Mr. Clock," p. 1 (Book II)

Rhythms and singing games

1. All records and songs are appropriate for listening to sound. Use your favourites and point out high sounds, low sounds, loud and soft sounds, fast and slow tempos, rhythms, and moods (happy, sad, dreamy, excited). Use a piano, xylophone, autoharp, and tone bells to show sounds, tempo, and moods.
2. Rhythm band: All instruments available using any good march tune.
3. Rhythm band instruments separately:
   a. Bells: "Sleigh Ride" or "Jingle Bells"
   b. Drums: Any good marching music or authentic Native Canadian music
   c. Sand blocks: "I've Been Working on the Railroad"
   d. Marching: "Little Brass Band"
4. Listening and moving for an interpretation of music: Find the following pieces of classical music and have the children move to the music listening for the suggested mood.
   ▷ "Brahm's Lullaby," Strauss
   ▷ any waltz by Strauss
   ▷ any march by Sousa
   ▷ "Pomp and Circumstance March," Elgar
   ▷ "Papegano's Aria," Mozart
   ▷ "Ein Fogelfanger Bin Ich, Ja," Mozart

Records and cassettes

Bob Homme. *The Giant Concert of Concerts Presents the Friendly Giant.* (A & M Records)
"Band Concert"
"Buzzy Concert"

Bob Schneider. *When You Dream a Dream.* (Capitol Records)
"Band of Songs"
"Grandpa's Song"

Raffi. *The Corner Grocery Store.* (Troubadour Records)

Sharon, Lois, and Bram. *Smorgasbord.* (Elephant Records)

Fingerplays and Poems

From *Read Aloud Rhymes for the Very Young*, Prelutsky and Brown
"Whistling," p. 6
"Chook, Chook," p. 42
"Quack, Quack," p. 43
"A Little Talk," p. 43
"Ears Hear," p. 84

From *Round and Round the Garden*, Williams
"Clap Clap Hands," p. 10
"Knock at the Door," p. 30
"I Hear Thunder," p. 37

From *Hand Rhymes*, Brown
"Here is the Beehive," p. 14
"Quack, Quack, Quack," p. 22

From *Mischief City*, Wynne-Jones
"Talking," p. 6
"They Are Having a Party Downstairs," p. 19
"The Vacuum Monster," p. 27

From *Let's Do Fingerplays*, Grayson
"Clap Your Hands," p. 10
"Things That Go" (series), pp. 21-28
"Hickory Dickory Dock," p. 31
"Kitty, Kitty," p. 42
"Raindrops," p. 47
"The Finger Band," p. 86
"Noise Makers" (series), pp. 86-90
"I Am a Fine Musician," p. 87
"Hammering," p. 88
"Shake, Shake, Knock, Knock," p. 88
"Balloons," p. 89
"Pound Goes the Hammer," p. 89

HERE IS A BEEHIVE

Here is a beehive (MAKE A BEEHIVE WITH FISTS)
Where are the bees? (PRETEND TO LOOK AROUND FOR THEM)
Hiding inside (TRY TO SEE INSIDE THE BEEHIVE)
Where nobody sees!

Soon they come creeping, (UNLOCK FISTS SLOWLY)
Out of the hive
One, two, three, four, five (EXTEND FINGERS ONE AT A TIME)
BZZZZZZZZZZZZZZZZZ (FLUTTER HANDS ALL AROUND VIGOROUSLY)

Stories

Choose stories for reading aloud that have lots of interesting sounds and rhythms in the words such as Scarry's *Splish Splash Sounds* or Hearn's *Woosh, I Hear a Sound*.

Games

(See "Learning Games," pp. 50–59, and teacher-made games in this part of the guide for directions.)
1. Guess who? Guess what? Imitate animals sounds and tool sounds
2. Listening or telephone: Use play telephones; guess who's on other phone
3. Listen and hear: Have some objects that make noise behind a screen, such as an alarm clock, bell, rattle, eggbeater, or crumpled paper
4. Simon says or Sally says: crow like a rooster, bark like a dog
5. What do you hear? A language development game for discovering sounds; ask children what sounds they could hear if they were in the country, at the seashore, in the city, in a park

Routine Times

1. At meal or snack times serve crunchy foods like carrot sticks and celery sticks, crisp crackers, some dry cereal.
2. At meal or snack times talk about chewing quietly with the mouth closed and not slurping beverages and soups.
3. At pickup time suggest moving as quietly as possible without talking, and occasionally walking on tiptoe.
4. At rest time listen for sounds; when sitting or lying on blankets outside or with windows open when weather permits.
5. At rest time use one of the suggested records or play a quiet lullaby.
6. When walking or busing listen for sounds—birds, sirens, hammers.
7. When playing outside make note of sounds—a squeaky trike, a chirping cricket, an approaching helicopter, the thud of a falling block, and so on.

Large Muscle Activities

1. Take a listening walk outdoors and listen for sounds made by animals, insects, people, machines, bells, and sirens.
2. Organize a marching band.

Extended Experiences

1. Invite a parent or a musician to bring an instrument and play it for the children.
2. Visit a school during band, orchestra, or choir rehearsal. Arrange with the person in charge in advance to select two or three short pieces that the children would enjoy. Perhaps they would practice and play one or two pieces that the children know best (if music is provided in advance). An eight to ten-minute program would be sufficient. Also ask that some of the instruments be played separately and identified.
3. Visit a church to hear an organ and the church bells.
4. Borrow the telephone company teaching unit and talk about how to answer the telephone, how to dial the telephone, and how to lay the receiver down carefully. Younger children should be taught not to play with the telephone, and older children should be encouraged to learn their own telephone number.

Teacher Resources

Pictures and Displays

▷ Display pictures of ears and of things that make sounds, such as animals, clocks, machines, bells. Ask children to imitate the different sounds.
▷ Display a few musical instruments.
▷ Make available drinking glasses tuned to various pitches by filling with varying amounts of water.

Books and Periodicals

(See the list of music resource books on pp. 76–77.)
Martin, Paul D. *Messengers to the Brain: Our Fantastic Five Senses.* Washington, DC: National Geographic Society, 1984.

Rivlin, Robert. *Deciphering the Senses: The Expanding World of Human Perception.* New York: Simon & Schuster, 1984.

Sully, Nina. *Looking at the Senses.* Batsford, GB: David and Charles, 1982.

Suzuki, David. *Looking at Senses.* Don Mills, Ont: Stoddart, 1986.

Films and Videos

Consult the *National Film Board Catalogue* and your community library

Community Resources and Organizations

▷ Local telephone company, teaching unit
▷ Local school band, orchestra, or chorus director
▷ Church organist
▷ Hearing-aid companies (often give free ear charts and pamphlets)
▷ Canadian Hearing Society
▷ Canadian Amateur Musicians Association

4 Taste

★★★★★★★★★★★★★★★★★★★

Basic Understandings

(concepts children can grasp from this subject)

▷ We taste through parts of our tongue called taste buds.
▷ Each food has a particular taste.
▷ Some foods taste sweet, sour, salty, or bitter. Some foods combine these tastes.
▷ We may add flavouring to a food when preparing it, to make it taste better.
▷ The flavour of a food or a drink is a combination of the way it tastes and the way it smells.
▷ Some foods taste good; sometimes we do not like the flavour.
▷ Sometimes we have to get used to a new taste by trying it several times. We may learn to like the taste of it.

Additional Facts the Teacher Should Know

1. For a sense of smell and taste, human beings need the olfactory nerves in the nose and the taste buds on the tongue. If these are not properly developed, humans will have difficulty with taste discrimination. The senses of smell and taste are based on a sensitivity to chemicals. Different nerve endings are sensitive to particular chemical stimuli—for example, salts, sugars, acids. Some children may be born without a sense of taste or smell, either of which will affect their ability to discriminate flavours.

2. Most young children do not have a keen sense of taste and therefore do not require as much seasoning in their food. The way the food is displayed and the size of the servings can affect children's attitudes toward eating and trying new foods. Try to serve foods from the four food groups in an attractive manner. Keep the portions small. With new foods, only one bite may be expected. If foods are served family-style, children gain independence in serving themselves and can more easily express their food taste needs. Sometimes the texture of a food can affect the child's attitude toward it.

3. Children can be encouraged to learn to like different foods by inviting a parent who represents a different ethnic group to come and help make a simple recipe that is a favourite food of their family. Consult your Public Health Department regarding laws regulating the preparation of foods in your centre. Encourage the children to keep food preparation surfaces sanitary, to keep hands clean while cooking, and to handle equipment safely. For recipes, see book list in Teacher Resources, p. 159. (For related information and activities, see the chapters on colour, sense of smell, and sense of touch.)

★ CAUTION: Many children have special diets, either for health or religious reasons. Be sure you are aware of any special diets before planning any of the activities in this section.

Methods Most Adaptable for Introducing this Subject to Children

1. Prepare a favourite food that has a distinctive flavour and odour.
2. Introduce a story about food like *Bread and Jam for Frances.*
3. Have a tasting party.
4. Have a parent visit the school and bring or prepare a typical food from his or her traditional recipe.

Vocabulary

taste	salty	bad	seasoning
taste bud	bitter	tart	salt
tongue	spicy	cold	pepper
sweet	hot	pleasant	cinnamon
bland	flavour	disagreeable	sugar
sour	good	delicious	

Learning Centres

Discovery Centre

1. Make a milkshake. Add chocolate, strawberry, vanilla, or banana flavouring.
2. Make a pitcher of lemonade. Taste it before and after adding the sugar.
3. Make popcorn. Taste with and without salt.
4. Mix cinnamon and sugar. Shake the mixture onto enriched white-bread toast or raisin toast.
5. Have a shaker full of sugar and a shaker full of salt. Let the children shake a little on their clean hands and taste it. Talk about how the tastes are alike and how they are different.
6. Melt bitter chocolate. Taste it. Add sugar. Taste it.
7. Start with strong tea or unsweetened fruit drink. Taste it. Add sugar. Taste it.
8. Bake pumpkin cupcakes, using your favourite recipe. Let children taste some of the ingredients and the final product.
9. Mix up a muffin batter. Add blueberries to some of the batter, chopped dates or nuts to some, peanut butter to some, and mashed banana to some. Identify and compare before baking.
10. Compare cooked and uncooked foods and fresh and canned foods as to flavour.
11. Have a tasting party: Set out bite-size portions of a variety of foods that have distinctive flavours—salty, sweet, sour, bitter, spicy, bland. Let children match processed cheese shapes with corresponding cracker shapes. To increase the discussion about foods, consider colour, texture, and odour when providing foods for the children to taste—for example, orange carrot coins, green pickle slices, yellow cubes of cheese, red radish roses, candy orange slices, shavings of bitter chocolate. Serve strong tea, grapefruit juice, pink lemonade, chocolate milk to drink.

★ **CAUTION:**   Before serving foods to children be aware of their allergies (chocolate, egg, milk) and special dietary needs (sugar-free [diabetics], salt-free [high blood pressure], or food additives [hyperactivity]).

Dramatic Play Centres

Home-living centre

1. Encourage the preparation of foods in the housekeeping area.
2. Collect empty cartons and cans to put on the shelves to encourage preparation, serving, and tasting of food.
3. Put up pictures in this area of people preparing and eating foods (include pictures of community helpers who serve, sell, grow, deliver, cook, prepare, or handle food or food products).
4. Allow the use of tea or a fruit drink for a tasting tea.
5. Provide utensils and ingredients to make a no-cook food—for example, rolling dates in sugar, instant puddings, no-bake cookies, or candy.

Other dramatic play centres

1. At snack time set up a bakery store and let the children "buy" their snacks. Provide a variety of cookies, rolls, or cupcakes. Provide hats and aprons for the bakers and servers, and "money" for the customers. A cash register will also be needed.
2. Set up an ice cream stand for snack time. Give a choice of ice creams or sherbets to be scooped into cones, or offer a choice of ice creams to be put in dishes. Offer a choice of syrups or fruits to put on top.
3. For snack or meal times have a cafeteria with a variety of raw vegetables, crackers, dry cereals, fruits, sandwiches, and drinks available. TV trays, cash register, and "money" will be needed.

Learning, Language, and Readiness Materials Centre

Commercially made games and materials

(See "Basic Resources," pp. 79, 100 for manufacturers' addresses.)
1. *Puzzles:* Puzzles showing a variety of foods.
2. *Small toys for imaginative play:* Plastic food and cooking utensils. Try to find food that looks realistic and is non-toxic—for example Fisher Price food and cooking utensils. Sturdy toy stoves and refrigerators. Do not buy any of the electric toys as they require very close supervision and discourage independent play.
3. *Outdoor toys:* Child-size gardening equipment for setting up a small garden in the playground. Choose equipment that is strong enough to be useful and small enough to be used by small hands.
4. *Flannelboards and flannelboard aids:* There are a number of flannelboard kits about food and nutrition. Check with your local educational supplier (see list on p. 79).

Teacher-made games and materials

NOTE: For a detailed description of "Learning Games," see pp. 50–59.

1. Name it: Have a tray of fresh fruits and vegetables available. Identify them by name and allow the children to taste and smell them. Blindfold each child and have each identify a fruit or vegetable by taste alone. This game is best for snack time.

2. Look and see: Make flannelboard figures of foods that have different tastes. Ask children which is missing—salty food, spicy, sweet, or sour?

3. Lick, chew, and taste: Select appropriate foods to illustrate tastes.

4. Grouping and sorting: Categories could be salty, sweet, spicy, sour. Use labeled boxes, flannelboard or cardboard game board, with areas divided with a picture of a child/food identifying taste—for example, carton of salt, piece of candy, peanut, pickle—glued to each section.

5. Guess what? Describe a food; be sure to include its taste. For instance, say, "It is yellow, smaller than an orange, and tastes sour. What is it?"

Art Centre

NOTE: Many teachers are using food (such as dried pasta and instant pudding) for art activities. In a time when we have food banks in most major cities, this is quite inappropriate as it gives children a subtle, but powerful message, that food is cheap and easily disposable. Therefore, the following activities do not use foods in any recognizable form, except for cooking and eating activities.

- 1. Save coloured water obtained from boiling brown onion skins (yellow) and red onion skins (purple) to let the children watercolour with brushes on different sizes and types of paper.

- 2. Prepare ahead of time some coloured salt (pickling, table, or ice-cream salt) by mixing with dry tempera or a mixture of liquid and tempera. When salt is dry, let children paint their picture with thinned glue and sprinkle on the desired colour(s) for a textured painting.

- 3. Make a book of pictures cut from magazines of foods that taste good. Caption with what children say about their choices of pictures as they cut and paste them.

    NOTE: For younger children you may have a precut or preselected pile of pictures for them to choose for their book.

- 4. Save seeds and eggshells from food preparation to be dried out. Use as collage materials later in the week for an extended experience.

- 5. Offer a variety of the basic media (fingerpaint, clay, paint) in colours of special foods tasted or cooked that day so children will have colours they need to tell about their experiences through art.

- 6. Provide gummed coloured geometric shapes for children to make a "lick and stick" picture.

Book Centre

••• Aliki, Diogenes. *A Medieval Feast.* Toronto: Fitzhenry & Whiteside, 1983.
•• _____. *My Five Senses.* New York: Thomas Y. Crowell, 1962.
•• Andrews, Jan. *Fresh Fish and Chips.* Toronto: Women's Press, 1973.
••• Armitage, Rhonda. *The Lighthouse Keeper's Lunch.* New York: Deutsch, 1979.
•••• Brown, Marcia. *Stone Soup.* New York: Macmillan, 1947.
••• Croll, Carolyn. *Too Many Babas.* New York: Harper & Row, 1979.
•• Curry, Peter. *I Can Smell, I Can Taste.* Kingswood, Surrey, GB: World's Work, 1982.
• DePaola, Tomie. *Pancakes for Breakfast.* New York: Harcourt Brace Jovanovich, 1978.
••• _____. *The Popcorn Book.* New York: Holiday, 1978.
•••• Ferrier, Shannon. *The Kids Bakebook,* Toronto: Lorimer, 1986.
•••• _____. *Kids in the Kitchen.* Toronto: Lorimer, 1986.
•••• _____. *More Kids in the Kitchen.* Toronto: Lorimer, 1986.
•••• Ferrier, Shannon, and Tamara Shuttleworth. *The Kids Food Cookbook.* Toronto: Lorimer, 1986.

- Greenway, Kate. *A—Apple Pie.* New York: Warne, 1987. (Revised Edition)
●●● Hoban, Russell. *Bread and Jam for Frances.* New York: Harper & Row, 1964.
●●● Kohl, Virginia. *The Duchess Bakes a Cake.* New York: Scribner, 1955.
- Krauss, Ruth. *The Carrot Seed.* New York: Harper & Row, 1945.
- Levinson, Riki. *Touch! Touch!* Toronto: Fitzhenry & Whiteside, 1987.
●●● Lottridge, Celia. *One Watermelon Seed.* Toronto: Oxford University Press, 1986.
●●●● MacEwan, Gwendolyn. *The Chocolate Moose.* Toronto: New Canada Publications, 1981. (Read-Tell)
●●● McCloskey, R. *Blueberries for Sal.* New York: Viking Press, 1948.
●●● Orbach, Ruth. *Apple Pigs.* New York: Philomel, 1981.
- Oxenbury, Helen. *Eating Out.* New York: Dial Press, 1983.
●● Parramon, J.M., and J.J. Puig. *Taste.* New York: Barron, 1985.
●●●● Pasternak, Carol, and Alan Sutterfield. *Stone Soup.* Toronto: Women's Press, 1975. (Read-Tell)
●●● Polland, Barbara Kay. *The Sensible Book: Celebration of Your Five Senses.* Millbrae, CA.: Celestial Arts Publishing, 1973.
- Poulet, Virginia. *Blue Bug's Vegetable Garden.* Chicago: Children's Press, 1973.
●● Rayner, Mary. *Mrs. Pig's Bulk Buy.* New York: Macmillan, 1981.
●●● Rice, Eve. *Benny Bakes a Cake.* New York: Greenwillow Press, 1981.
●●● _____ . *Sam Who Never Forgets.* New York: Greenwillow Press, 1977.
●●● Robart, Rose. *The Cake that Mack Ate.* Toronto: Kids Can Press, 1986.
- Tetherington, Jeanne. *Pumpkin, Pumpkin.* New York: Greenwillow Press, 1986.
- Vincent, Gabriel. *Breakfast Time, Ernest and Celestine.* New York: Greenwillow Press, 1985.
●●● Wallace, Ian, and Angela Wood. *The Sandwich.* Toronto: Kids Can Press, 1985.
●● Watson, Clyde. *Tom Fox and the Apple Pie.* New York: Thomas Y. Crowell, 1972.
●●●● Wheeler, Bernelda. *I Can't Have the Bannock, But the Beaver Has A Dam.* Winnipeg, Man: Pemmican, 1985. (Read-Tell)

NOTE: Select one of the foods mentioned in the book for the children to taste before, during, or after the story as appropriate.

Planning for Group Time

NOTE: All music, fingerplays, poems, stories, and games listed here may also be used at other times during the session as appropriate. See Core Library, "Basic Resources" p. 95, for publishers and addresses. See p. 99 for record company addresses. In parodies, hyphenated words match music notes of the tune used.

Music

Songs

From *The Goat with the Bright Red Socks*, Birkenshaw and Walden
"Those Rumbling, Tumbling Down in the Stomach Junk Food Blues," p. 34
"The Good Food Song," p. 35

From *Stepping Along in Music Land*, Murray
"Gingerbread Boy," p. 19
"Table Manners," p. 26
"Making Butter," p. 8 (Book II)
"Making Bread," p. 9 (Book II)
"Be a Honey Bee," p. 17 (Book II)

From *Sally Go Round the Sun,* Fowke
"Oats and Beans and Barley Grow," p. 14
"My Aunt Jane," p. 122
"Found a Peanut," p. 138

From *What Shall We Do and Alee Galloo,* Winn
"Pease Porridge Hot," p. 58

From *Do Your Ears Hang Low?* Glazer
"The Donut Song," p. 24

NOTE: Combine the singing of the songs above with a sample taste of the food to which you are referring or, if at a time other than music time, sing the song as the activity is being carried out, such as popping corn or making applesauce.

WHAT FOODS DO YOU LIKE? (a parody)
(tune: "Oats, Peas, Beans")
Adaptation by JoAnne Deal Hicks

VERSE 1: Eggs and milk and ba-con strips. Eggs and milk and ba-con strips.
Do you, do you, do you, do you . . . like eggs and milk and ba-con strips?
(AS YOU SING THE QUESTION, POINT TO INDIVIDUAL CHILDREN IN THE GROUP.)
VARIATIONS FOR OTHER VERSES ARE GIVEN BELOW. REPEAT AND ADAPT AS IN THE FIRST VERSE.

VERSE 2: Dan-ish rolls and or-ange juice
VERSE 3: Pea-nut but-ter, jel-ly too
VERSE 4: Ap-ples, grapes, and can-ta-loupe
VERSE 5: Cheese and pie with cold ice-cream
VERSE 6: Corn and peas and broc-co-li

NOTE: This song may be adapted, as above, to include many combinations of foods. Encourage the children to help you select the different foods.

Records and cassettes

Raffi. *The Corner Grocery Store.* (Troubadour Records)

Sandy Tobias Oppenheim. *If Snowflakes Fell in Flavours* (Berandol Records)

Sharon, Lois, and Bram. *Smorgasbord.* (Elephant Records)

Fingerplays and Poems

APPLES

Away up high in the apple tree, (POINT UP)
Two red apples smiled at me. (FORM CIRCLES WITH FINGERS)
I shook that tree as hard as I could; (PRETEND TO SHAKE TREE)
Down came those apples, and mmmmmm, were they good! (RUB TUMMY)

From *Don't Eat Spiders,* Heidbreder and Patkau
"Nutty Chat," p. 19
"Don't Eat Spiders," p. 23
Sticky Maple Syrup," p. 29
"The Apple and the Worm," p. 38

From *Mischief City,* Wynne-Jones
"Don't Drink the Bathwater," p. 18
"Invasion from the Planet Pizza," p. 32

From *Round and Round the Garden,* Williams and Beck
"Five Fat Sausages," p. 8
"Five Fat Peas," p. 29
"Pat-a-Cake," p. 38
"Here are the Lady's Knives and Forks," p. 43
"I'm a Little Teapot," p. 44

From *Read Aloud Rhymes for the Very Young,* Prelutsky and Brown
"The Picnic," p. 31
"The Toaster," p. 35
"Crunch and Lick," p. 67
"Yellow Butter," p. 67
"The Meal," p. 68
"Two Sad," p. 68
"Table Manners," p. 69
"Toothsome," p. 69
"Tickles, Tickles," p. 79

From *Fingerplays and Action Rhymes,* Jacobs
"Cake," p. 47

From *A New Treasury of Children's Poetry,* Cole
"Mix a Pancake," p. 39
"The Cupboard," p. 38
"Soft Boiled Egg," p. 89
"I Eat my Peas with Honey," p. 104

From *Where the Sidewalk Ends,* Silverstein
"I Must Remember," p. 14
"Pancake?" p. 34
"Boa Constrictor," p. 45
"Peanut Butter Sandwich," p. 84
"Spaghetti," p. 100
"Me Stew," p. 122

From *The New Wind Has Wings,* Downie
"Eating Fish," p. 18

NOTE: Most of the above are about food; finding it, serving it, or eating it.

LUNCH

by Darlene Hamilton

Crunch, munch
There's food for our lunch!
Today we have berries, or you may have cherries,
There's salad with peas, a sandwich with cheese.
Or—a slice of browned roast on your own buttered toast.
Crunch, munch, eat your lunch!

TASTES

by Darlene Hamilton

Syrup and honey are sweet.
Pickles and lemons are sour.
Peanuts and crackers a treat
For a snack most any hour!

Stories

(To read, read–tell, or tell. See the Book Centre on p. 154 for complete list.)
Stories for the theme of taste can be greatly varied. Wood and Wood's *The Sandwich* deals with problems around food and culture. Parramon and Puig's *Taste* introduces some of the scientific ideas underlying the sense of taste.

Games

(See "Learning Games," pp. 50–59, and teacher-made games in this part of the guide for directions.)
1. Name it
2. Look and see
3. Listen: Have one child be the baker with a plate of cookies or other baked goods. Blindfold the baker. Point to a child who says, "Please may I have a cookie?" The baker says, "Yes, you may, _____" and guesses the child, who then takes a cookie. If the baker guesses wrong, he or she guesses again until he or she gets the name correct. The child whose name was guessed then becomes the baker. Continue until all have had a cookie. VARIATION: Farmer with apples; squirrel with nuts
4. Grouping and sorting
5. Guess what?

Routine Times

1. At snack or meal times, feature foods that can be grouped or classified.
   a. Fruits—apples, oranges, fresh pineapple, bananas, cherries, berries
   b. Vegetables—carrots, green pepper, cauliflower, celery, peas, corn
   c. Bread—enriched white, whole wheat, rye, raisin, pumpernickel
   d. Milk—fresh, canned, powdered, buttermilk, chocolate
   e. Meats—fish, eggs, wieners, hamburger, pork chops, roast lamb
2. At snack or meal times, combine the serving of food with a dramatic play activity (see other dramatic play centres, stories, songs, and poems in this part of the guide).
3. Offer snacks with different flavours, such as salty pretzels, sour lemon wedges, sweet candy orange slices, semi-sweet chocolate. Talk about putting food on the tongue to see how it tastes. Discuss how food tastes different when seasoned or when sugar is added.

Extended Experiences

1. Visit a bakery, buy some freshly baked enriched bread rolls. Take back to the centre and eat. Bake your own bread at the centre. Let frozen dough rise and then let children twist their own design for their roll. Identify each child's roll by making a chart of the pan or by labelling with toothpicks.
2. Invite parents who represent different ethnic groups to come and help prepare nutritious snacks or food with the group. Make detailed preparations in advance for food/utensils needed and simplify procedures for the youngest in the group.
3. Invite a dentist to come and show the children how to brush their teeth and to discuss ways to keep teeth clean and breath fresh.
4. Visit a local farm, where the children can see food growing and being prepared before it is sent to wholesalers.
5. Visit a local fisherman to see fish as it is caught, before being sent to fish stores and processors.
6. Visit a local restaurant for a tour. (Many fast-food chains offer excellent tours, as long as you do not come at meal times.)

Teacher Resources

Books and Periodicals

Ferrier, Shannon. *Kids in the Kitchen.* Toronto: Lorimer, 1986.

_____ . *More Kids in the Kitchen.* Toronto: Lorimer, 1986.

_____ . *The Kids Bakebook.* Toronto: Lorimer, 1986.

Ferrier, Shannon, and Tamara Shuttleworth. *The Kids Food Cookbook.* Toronto: Lorimer, 1986.

Martin, Paul D. *Messengers to the Brain: Our Fantastic Five Senses.* Washington, DC: National Geographic Society, 1984.

Rivlin, Robert. *Deciphering the Senses: The Expanding World of Human Perception.* New York: Simon & Schuster, 1984.

Sully, Nina. *Looking at the Senses.* Batsford, GB: David and Charles, 1982.

Suzuki, David. *Looking at Senses.* Don Mills, Ont: Stoddart, 1986.

Films and Videos

Consult the *National Film Board Catalogue* and your community library

Community Resources and Organizations

▷   Home economist
▷   Eye, ear, nose, and throat doctors
▷   Dentists/dental hygienists
▷   Milk Marketing Board
▷   Other food marketing boards

Government Agencies

Provincial, territorial, and federal ministries/departments of agriculture

5 Smell

★★★★★★★★★★★★★★★★★★★★★★

Basic Understandings

(concepts children can grasp from this subject)

▷ We smell odours through our noses.
▷ We learn about some things by the way they smell.
▷ Some things smell good (have a nice odour) and some things smell bad (have a bad odour).
▷ We take baths so that we will be clean and smell nice.
▷ The smell of smoke tells us something is burning.
▷ We can tell some foods by the way they smell; we can sometimes tell what we will be eating at the next meal by the way it smells while it is cooking.
▷ Most animals can find things by smelling for them. It helps them find food, their friends, and their enemies.
▷ Flowers have a nice odour (perfume) that attracts bees and helps them find the nectar (food) they like to eat.
▷ Skunks give off a bad (disagreeable) odour to protect themselves and drive others away.

Additional Facts the Teacher Should Know

1. The senses of smell and taste are based on a sensitivity to chemicals. Different nerve endings are sensitive to particular chemical stimuli—for example, salt, sugar, acids. Because of the position of the olfactory nerve endings high in the inner back part of the nasal passages of the nose, it is sometimes necessary to sniff or smell closely to detect a delicate fragrance.
2. The tongue, like the fingers, has a higher number of nerve endings per square centimetre of surface than many other areas of the skin. Being also sensitive to chemicals makes it more highly sensitive to a variety of stimuli. Often the smell of food enhances its taste (if you hold your nose sometimes you cannot taste what you are eating). If food smells bad it may also warn you that it is spoiled. Sometimes when children have a cold or are ill their sense of smell may be hampered. The nostrils have fine hairs inside that help filter dust and particles and keep them from going into the lungs when we breathe.
3. Some children may be born without a sense of smell. That is, the olfactory nerve endings located in the nose are not properly developed. Children who do not have a sense of smell also have a poor sense of taste and are unable to distinguish the differences in bland foods in particular. (See the parts of the guide on food and animals for related activities.)

Methods Most Adaptable for Introducing this Subject to Children

1. Plan to cook pumpkin cupcakes (use your own favourite recipe) and ask each child to smell the ingredients before they are added.
2. Children may smell an unpleasant odour, such as from a skunk, factory waste, or garbage, or a pleasant odour, such as from flowers or cooking.
3. Set out smell tubes (see teacher-made games on p. 163).
4. Use a sleep mask (wrapped with fresh tissue for each child) to blindfold children and then ask them to identify a variety of different objects by smell. Be sure to choose objects that can be easily distinguished by their odour.

Vocabulary

odour	scent	perfume	unpleasant
smell	sniff	delicious	spicy
nose	smoky	pleasant	sweet
musty	fragrance	disagreeable	tongue
aroma			

Learning Centres

Discovery Centre

1. Take a smelling walk. Talk about the odours you smell and whether they are pleasant or unpleasant.
2. Cooking food is especially good for discovering smells. Bake bread, rolls, pumpkin cupcakes, cinnamon or peanut butter cookies, or make pancakes, waffles, or popcorn.
3. Set out a tray of fresh, cleaned fruits and vegetables. Identify the foods and let the children touch, smell, and taste them.
4. If possible, observe flowers or flowering trees or bushes nearby. Talk about how bees are attracted by the sweet smelling odour and how they carry pollen from flower to flower. Watch out for bees.
5. Close windows to keep out bad odours; open windows to let in fresh air.
6. Match smelling tubes (see teacher-made games on p. 163).
7. Burn scented candles or incense with different fragrances. Let children guess what they think the fragrance smells like.
8. Bring in a vase of flowers or a potted flowering plant.
9. Encourage the children to explore the room to discover how different things smell, even those with no apparent odour, such as leather, rubber boots, wood, flowers, polished furniture, aquarium, pet cages, cedar chips, painted objects.
10. Collect other fragrant items for a smell tray. Include leather, fur, cedarwood, incense, perfume sachet, rubber foam, carpet, linoleum, magazine and newspaper, cotton, tissues, cork, soap, pine cones, evergreen.
11. After a smelling walk, talk about smells that are specific to your community; that is, how does a city smell in comparison to a farm area? Or how does a small farming village smell in comparison to a fishing village?

★ CAUTION: Remember that some children may be allergic and/or sensitive to some smells. Before choosing items for centres, check on the allergies of children.

Dramatic Play Centres

Home-living centre

1. Pretend to bake and cook. Have play dough available for baking in the housekeeping corner. Teacher could comment on how good it smells.
2. Provide a dressing table with empty bottles of perfume, lotion, and creams for playing dress up.

   ★ CAUTION:　Be sure containers are unbreakable/empty.

3. Put a bouquet of real flowers on the table.
4. Set out a small carton of scented tissues.

Block-building centre

1. Encourage fire engine play by saying, "I smell smoke. I think there is a fire over here. Please come and put it out!"
2. Encourage older children to build a gasoline station. Talk about how gasoline smells.
3. Suggest that children build a fishing boat. Talk about how it would smell.

Other dramatic play centres

1. Set up a florist shop with artificial flowers, plastic corsages, and plants (add a touch of perfume to articles to make them more authentic). Provide a cash register, pencil, pad, telephone table, and chairs.
2. Set up a perfume store, adding appropriate fragrant items or a spice store.

   ★ CAUTION:　Make sure all items are unbreakable and bottles are empty.

3. Set up a bakery. (See the chapter on taste, p. 151.)

Learning, Language, and Readiness Materials Centre

Commercially made games and materials

(See "Basic Resources," pp. 79, 100, for manufacturers' addresses.)
Miscellaneous: Scratch and sniff stickers, scented washable marking pens—for example Sanford's Mr. Sketch Scented Instant Watercolour Markers.

NOTE:　Many of the items listed under taste are also usable in this section as the two senses are so closely linked (see p. 153).

Teacher-made games and materials

NOTE:　For a detailed description of "Learning Games," see pp. 50–59.

1. Sniff and smell.
2. Match-them: Have two sets of smelling bottles filled with distinctive odours for the children to match. Include cloves, peppermint, coffee, cinnamon, garlic, chili, vanilla, cocoa, perfume. Small, opaque plastic bottles obtained from a pharmacy or unbreakable film tubes are best. Puncture two or three holes in each lid. Glue a circle of nylon fabric inside the lid to keep ingredients from spilling out, but allowing the odour to rise.
3. Name it: Have a tray of fresh fruits and vegetables. Identify them by name and allow children to hold and sniff them. Blindfold children and have them identify the fruits or vegetables by odour alone. (See **CAUTION**, p. 52, regarding blindfolds.)

Art Centre

•• 1. Cook brown and red onion skins in separate pans of water. Save yellow (brown) and red (purple) liquid obtained after boiling to be used with paintbrushes in art centre later.
• 2. Make your own library paste; add fragrant edible essences, such as oil of cloves or wintergreen. Use in art centre when paste is required.
• 3. Make a collage of pictures of things you like to smell.
• 4. Printing with vegetables can make interesting designs *if* you use unedible ends, rinds, or sections of vegetables with a distinct odour used by the cook this week—for example, green peppers, cabbage, onions. Use vegetable as you would any other printing tool, bouncing it in paint and then stamping it on a paper surface.

Book Centre

••• Aliki, Diogenes. *My Five Senses.* New York: Thomas Y. Crowell, 1962.
•• Allington, Richard. *Smelling.* Milwaukee: Raintree, 1985.
•• Berry, Joy. *Teach Me About Smelling.* New York: Grolier, 1986.
• Curry, Peter. *I Can Smell, I Can Taste.* Kingswood, Surrey, GB: World's Work, 1982.
•• Moncure, Jane, B. *What Your Nose Knows!* Chicago: Children's Press, 1982.
•• Parramon, J.M., and J.J. Puig. *Smell.* New York: Barron, 1985.
•• Pluckrose, Henry. *Smelling.* New York: Watts, 1986.
••• Polland, Barbara Kay. *The Sensible Book: Celebration of Your Five Senses.* Millbrae, CA: Celestial Arts Publishing, 1974.

Planning for Group Time

NOTE: All music, fingerplays, poems, stories, and games listed here may be used at other times during the session as appropriate. See Core Library, "Basic Resources," p. 95, for publishers and addresses. See p. 99 for record company addresses. In parodies, hyphenated words match music notes of the tune used.

Music

Songs

THE SMELLING SONG (a parody)

(tune: "Did You Ever See a Lassie?")
Adaptation by JoAnne Deal Hicks

TEACHER SINGS: Have you ev-er smelled a rose-bud, a rose-bud, a rose-bud?
Have you ev-er smelled a rose-bud? Oh . . . how does it smell?

CHILDREN ANSWER: (Teacher may substitute another word for rosebud. Allow the children to respond verbally. Adjectives and adverbs that they might use are: spicy, sweet, good, sour, badly burned.)

From *Sally Go Round the Sun,* Fowke
"Oranges and Lemons," p. 31
"The Little Skunk," p. 138

From *Piggyback Songs for Infants and Toddlers,* Warren
"Scrub a Dub Dub Song," p. 18
"This Is the Way We Take a Bath," p. 19
"Hair Washing Song," p. 19

Records and cassettes

Bob Homme. *The Giant Concert of Concerts Presents the Friendly Giant.* (A & M Records)
"Seafood Concert"

Raffi. *The Corner Grocery Store.* (Troubadour Records)
"The Corner Grocery Store and Popcorn"

Sandy Tobias Oppenheim. *If Snowflakes Fell in Flavours.* (Berandol Records)
"Don't Disturb My Olfactory Nerve"

Fingerplays and Poems

From *Sally Go Round the Sun,* Fowke
"To Market to Market," p. 101
"Bubble Gum, Bubble Gum," p. 109
"Ink, Ink," p. 110

Stories

Stories about the sense of smell are difficult to find. When choosing stories in this area, try to find stories that relate to other experiences the children have had in relation this theme. Curry's *I Can Smell, I Can Taste* is a good choice because it interrelates the two senses of smell and taste and can be tied in with fragrant cooking experiences—for example, cooking cinnamon cookies.

Games

(See "Learning Games," pp. 50–59, and teacher-made games in this part of the guide for directions.)
1. Name it
2. Sniff and smell

Routine Times

1. Snack or meal times is a natural time to talk about the odour of foods. You might want to plan some foods with distinctive odours, such as popcorn, peanut butter, bacon, cinnamon toast, chocolate milk.
2. When toileting talk about the clean soapy smell of washed hands.
3. When busing or walking talk about the smell of the earth after a rain, the smell of gasoline when stopping for a fill-up, the delicious odours from a bakery, the smell of newmown hay or grass, the perfume of flowers or flowering bushes.

Extended Experiences

1. Take a walk and call attention to or look for things that have an odour; talk about whether it is a pleasant or an unpleasant odour.
2. Visit a bakery to see and smell the baked goods. Buy something for a snack.
3. Visit a flower shop or greenhouse. Enjoy the many fragrances and talk about the colours that you see. If possible, buy some flowers to take back to the centre.
4. If the centre is in a smaller town or suburb, make arrangements to visit a neighbour's flower or vegetable garden where the children would be welcome to explore.

Teacher Resources

Pictures and Displays

▷ Put up pictures of noses (people's and animals') with a picture display of good things to smell. Include pictures of flowers, perfume and baked goods.

▷ Display smelling bottles.

> ★ CAUTION: Be certain all are unbreakable.

▷ Fresh flower arrangements: Choose flowers with a characteristic fragrance—mums, roses, carnations.

Books and Periodicals

Ferrier, Shannon. *Kids in the Kitchen.* Toronto: Lorimer, 1986.

_____ . *More Kids in the Kitchen.* Toronto: Lorimer, 1986.

_____ . *The Kids Bakebook.* Toronto: Lorimer, 1986.

Ferrier, Shannon, and Tamara Shuttlework. *The Kids Food Cookbook.* Toronto: Lorimer, 1986.

Martin, Paul D. *Messengers to the Brain: Our Fantastic Five Senses..* Washington, DC: National Geographic Society, 1984.

Rivlin, Robert. *Deciphering the Senses: The Expanding World of Human Perception.* New York: Simon & Schuster, 1984.

Sully, Nina. *Looking at the Senses.* Batsford, GB: David and Charles, 1982.

Suzuki, David. *Looking at Senses.* Don Mills, Ont: Stoddart, 1986.

Films and Videos

Consult the *National Film Board Catalogue* and your community library

Community Resources and Organizations

▷ Milk Marketing Board
▷ Other food marketing boards

Government Agencies

▷ Provincial, territorial, and federal ministries/departments of agriculture
▷ Local parks and recreation departments

6 Touch

★★★★★★★★★★★★★★★★★★★★★★

Basic Understandings

(concepts children can grasp from this subject)

▷ We feel with our skin.
▷ We may touch things with almost any part of our body, but we usually use our fingers. (We can feel with our tongue, lips, feet, and arms.)
▷ Some things feel soft, hard, smooth, rough, cold, hot, wet, or dry.
▷ Our skin helps keep us safe. It tells us when we are near something too hot; it tells us if we are too cold, or if we are hurt.
▷ We can "feel" happy or sad, sick or well, sleepy or wide awake, energetic or tired.
▷ We can feel the sun's rays, cool shade, wind, raindrops, snow, and hail.
▷ We can tell if we are moving or standing still. This is called the kinesthetic sense.
▷ We can feel pain (or discomfort) inside our bodies. This is called the organic sense.
▷ When people say hello or goodbye they often touch, shake hands, kiss, or hug.

Additional Facts the Teacher Should Know

1. Touch is a broad term for several senses, those of pressure, pain, and temperature. The sense of touch is made possible by nerve endings scattered through the skin. Some nerve endings make our bodies sensitive to temperatures (cold or heat), others to pain, and still others to sensations from touch or pressure.

2. When stimulated, different nerve endings (receptors) send electrical impulses to the sensory area of the brain. When received there, the brain interprets what has happened by the kind of signal stimulus and its source. In almost a reflex chain reaction, a message is sent back to the muscles to withdraw or react to the stimuli whether pressure, pain, extreme temperature, or other. These nerve endings are also found in our mouth and inside our bodies on muscles or organs making possible sensitivity to pressure or distress internally, such as stomach pain, sore throat, earache, and others. Fingers, because of a higher concentration of nerve endings per square centimetre surface area, are more sensitive to stimuli (change) and therefore have a better sense of touch than most other areas of the body. Some people do not have a sense of touch and may therefore cut or burn themselves without knowing they are doing so. Some people have a very low threshold of pain, which means a little pain is very uncomfortable; others have a high threshold of pain, which means they can tolerate a good deal of pain.

3. This theme area can provide an appropriate arena for introducing some material on streetproofing. While discussing touch, one can talk about proper touching and improper touching and help children become sensitive to the differences. It is important to prepare this material carefully and to send home complete information on what you have covered, so that parents will understand what has been talked over with their children. The teacher resources section at the end of the chapter lists sources for information for these discussions.

Methods Most Adaptable for Introducing this Subject to Children

1. Fill a box or sack with items for the child to feel and identify. Use a commercially made "feel box" or make your own (see illustration, p. 169).
2. While playing outdoors encourage children to explore sand, rocks, bark, mud, water, ice and snow, twigs, fresh and dry leaves, sprouts, buds, seeds, roots, shells through touch.
3. Make a "feel" book with different kinds of fabrics or materials—sandpaper, corduroy, satin, velvet, leather, fur.

Vocabulary

rough, smooth	many, few	furry	soapy
hard, soft	big, little	bumpy	satin
cold, hot	sleepy, awake	finger	velvet
limp, crisp	tired, peppy	feel	fur
wet, dry	sick, well	touch	corduroy
happy, sad	sticky, slick	prickly	sandpaper
thick, thin	heavy, light	skin	cardboard

Learning Centres

Discovery Centre

1. Provide objects for the children to feel which have been warmed by a heating pad or cooled in a refrigerator.
2. Make or buy a feeling book with the animals or other figures made of various textures, such as silk, corduroy, sandpaper, smooth contact paper, cotton. Individually or in small groups identify the materials and help the children feel the differences and describe them as well. Use adjectives, such as soft, furry, slippery, shiny, smooth, rough.
3. Buy or make a feel box with two each of 10 cm squares of various types of fabrics and materials. Ask children to match the samples without looking.
4. Have a tub of very warm water and one of very cold water side by side. Have children put one hand in each tub of water. Reverse hands for change in feel. Have towels available to dry hands. Add soap (liquid detergent) to warm water for another feel. VARIATION: In season add ice or snow.
5. Let children explore a variety of items in a touch-and-feel tray, comparing texture, size, weight, number, and consistency by touch. Encourage them to discover how each item feels, first with bare hands, and then wearing rubber or cotton gloves. Include:

fur (soft, furry)
coil (springy, cold)
bark (rough, bumpy)
shells (smooth, hard)
carpet (soft, stiff)
cactus (prickly, sharp)
yarn ball (soft)
cotton (soft, light)
feather (soft, light)
rope/twine (scratchy)
cellophane (crisp, thin)

brushes (bristly, soft)
pine cone (prickly, rough)
fabrics (offer variety)
wood (smooth, hard)
plastic (smooth, flexible)
styrofoam (smooth, scratchy)
sandpaper (scratchy, rough)
rubber foam (spongy, soft)
paper (crisp, soft, smooth)
metal (cold, smooth)

6. Encourage children to observe the different ways people greet each other, such as shaking hands, kissing, hugging, nodding. Films, pictures, and observation at home, on the street, or on TV will afford the opportunity.

7. Allow children to experiment with touch when exploring a stringed instrument or a horn with valves. Demonstrate and talk about how pianists or instrumentalists use their fingers or mouth to make their instruments play. Note that they often "feel" for these places (keys, strings, valves) without looking.

8. Put textured items into a container which conceals its contents, such as a can covered with a stocking, a bag closed with a drawstring or elastic, a closed paper sack, or a box with only a fist-size opening. VARIATIONS: The task might be (i) to retrieve two like objects by feeling a concealed group of items; (ii) to match one concealed item with one visible; (iii) to match one item concealed with one selected from a visible group.

9. Conceal familiar objects in rolled-up socks and have children feel and name them—for example, a pocket comb, a clothespin, a fork, etc.

Touching. Children are exploring objects by touching and feeling them. See pp. 11–13 for list of items to include in a touch-and-feel science tray.

Dramatic Play Centres

Home-living centre

1. Wash doll clothes in warm soapy water and rinse in cool clear water. Talk about the temperature of the tubs of water. Feel liquid soap. How does it feel? Hang the clothes up to dry. How do they feel? Damp. Let the clothes dry. How do they feel? Dry. How do you know? They *feel* damp or dry. Talk about the various fabrics.
2. Wash dolls and dry them with big bath towels.
3. Wash dishes and rinse them.
4. Pretend the dolls are sick and have a fever. Do their foreheads feel hot? Take their temperature. Call the doctor. Give sponge baths to lower their temperature.
5. Put on blankets and sweaters when the dolls are cold.

Block-building centre

1. Set out vinyl, wooden, and plastic cars.
2. Provide wood shavings for hay and a piece of green indoor–outdoor carpet for grassy area.
3. Talk about how blocks feel—warm, smooth, curved, square.

Other dramatic play centres

1. At woodworking bench have woods of various textures. Talk about rough and smooth. Provide sandpaper for smoothing the edges and sides of the wood of various objects made by children.
2. Set up a clothing store. Hang up the dress-up clothes on rolling clothes racks or clothes trees. Have a hat bar, shoe corner, and glove and scarf counter. Talk about the various fabrics and textures of the clothes. A full-length mirror, small mirrors, and hand mirrors would add to the discussion of the clothes: How do they look and how do they feel? Cash register, sacks, and "money" are needed, too. Boxes and shopping bags would also be useful. Include many textures—feathered hats, denim, satin, fur, net, velours, leather.

Language, Learning, and Readiness Materials Centre

Commercially made games and materials

(See "Basic Resources," pp. 79, 100, for manufacturers' addresses.)
1. *Construction and manipulative toys:* Montessori graded cylinders, tactile letters and letter cards, flannelboard letters, rocks, shells, fossils.
2. *Outdoor toys:* Sandbox toys.
3. *Miscellaneous:* Sand and water play tables.

Teacher-made games and materials

NOTE: For a detailed description of "Learning Games," see pp. 50–59.

1. Make a box for touching: Cut a sturdy cardboard box so child cannot see in but can put a hand through a hole on each side (see illustration, p. 52). Put pairs of matched materials of different textures, cut in 4 cm squares, in the box—for example, two pieces of sandpaper, two of velvet, satin, corduroy, plastic upholstering material, cardboard, carpet (two each of several different textures and piles), formica, corktiles. Children reach in and find the two that match by feel only.

2. Name it or scramble: Use many different types of textured objects.
3. Look and see: Using a screen or box for touching, put several articles that can be identified by touch alone out of sight, letting children see them first. Remove one article and decide, by touch alone, which one is missing.
4. Reach and feel: Use items that can be guessed by touch alone, such as pencil, crayon, ball, clothespin, string, bottle cap, blunt-nosed scissors, box, stone, spoon. Place one article in each of several sacks or sock-covered cans. Let each child select one to see if he or she can identify it. Avoid using anything sharp.
5. Grouping and sorting by association: Have several objects made of fur, leather, plastic, or cloth, and let children group them.
6. Alike, different, and the same: Use various squares from "match-them." Put two alike and one different together and ask a child to show you the one that is different. Talk about the differences. Ask children to do this with their eyes closed or use a small screen or the "feel" box. Can be alike in colour, shape, but should be different in texture.

Art Centre

- 1. Paint with tempera on corrugated paper or sandpaper.
- 2. Paint eggshell halves with tempera. When dry, use a rolling pin to break them into chips. Use these later to make a collage.
- ••• 3. Make a sandpainting: With fingers, paintbrush, or cotton swabs, put paste or white glue on paper in the design desired. Colour sand with tempera; place in containers with large holes in the top. Shake sand onto the paper with glue on it. Shake excess sand off painting onto newspaper. Fold newspaper to make a slide for returning excess sand to container if not mixed colours.
- 4. Fingerpaint with various media—starch, whipped soapsuds. Add powdered tempera for colour. Add sawdust, salt, for different textures.
- •• 5. Dip chalk in water or liquid starch, and colour on sandpaper.
- 6. Make play dough with flour and salt. Use rock or kosher salt for a grainier texture. Let children measure and feel ingredients during preparation.
- ••• 7. With fingertips draw designs in a tray of salt.
- •• 8. Use potter's clay; should be quite moist and soft.
- ••• 9. Gather leaves and other objects while taking a "feeling walk." Make a crayon rubbing by placing a sheet of thin white paper over one or more objects, rubbing the paper with the side of the crayon (remove paper from used crayons or use block crayons for this). Any interesting material, such as screen wire, grained wood, nylon net (open mesh), coins, or paper clips, may also be used.
- •• 10. Make a collage of textured materials—eggshells, yarn, corrugated paper, buttons.
- •• 11. Woodworking: Use hammer, saw, and sandpaper to make a wood design or just experience the feeling one gets when using these tools.

Book Centre

- •• Aliki, Diogenes. *My Five Senses.* New York: Thomas Y. Crowell, 1962.
- •• _____. *My Hands.* New York: Thomas Y. Crowell, 1962.
- ••• Baylor, Byrd. *Everybody Needs a Rock.* New York: Charles Scribner's Sons, 1974.
- ••• Brighton, Catherine. *My Hand's World.* New York: Macmillan, 1984.
- ••• Burningham, John. *Would You Rather!* London: Jonathan Cape, 1978.
- • Ets, Marie Hall. *Talking Without Words.* New York: Viking Press, 1970.
- •• Hoban, Tana. *Is It Rough! Is It Smooth! Is It Shiny!* New York: Greenwillow Press, 1984. (Read–Tell)
- ••• Holzinthaler, Jean. *My Hands Can.* New York: E.P. Dutton, 1978.
- ••• Kline, Suzy. *Don't Touch.* Niles, IL: Whitman, 1985.

- Kunhardt, Dorothy. *Pat the Bunny.* New York; Western Publishing, 1962.
- Levinson, Riki. *Touch! Touch!* Markham, Ont: Fitzhenry & Whiteside, 1987.
- • • Munsch, Robert. *50 Below Zero.* Willowdale, Ont: Annick Press, 1986.
- • • Parramon, J.M., and J.J. Puig. *Touch.* New York: Barron, 1985.
- • • Polland, Barbara Kay. *The Sensible Book: A Celebration of Your Five Senses.* Millbrae, CA: Celestial Arts Publishing, 1974.
- • • • Ryder, Joanne. *A Wet and Sandy Day.* New York: Harper & Row, 1977.
- • • • Sivulich, Sandra. *I'm Going on a Bear Hunt.* New York: E.P. Dutton, 1973.
- • • Steiner, Charlotte. *My Bunny Feels Soft.* New York: Alfred A. Knopf, 1958.
- • • • Stren, Patti. *Hug Me.* New York: Harper & Row, 1977. (Read–Tell)
- • • • Witte, Eve. *Touch Me Book.* Los Angeles: Children's Music Centre, 1961.

Planning for Group Time

NOTE: All music, fingerplays, poems, stories, and games listed here may also be used at other times during the session as appropriate. See Core Library, "Basic Resources," p. 95, for publishers and addresses. See p. 99 for record company addresses. In parodies, hyphenated words match music notes of the tune used.

Music

Songs

From *Baby Beluga Book*, Raffi
"To Everyone in All the World," p. 21
"This Old Man," p. 32

From *Elephant Jam*, Sharon, Lois, and Bram
"Michael Finnegan," p. 13
"Arabella Miller," p. 45
"Head 'n Shoulders, Baby," p. 52

From *Piggyback Songs for Infants and Toddlers*, Warren
"Never Play with Matches," p. 46
"One Blue Square," p. 48
"Toes Are Tapping," p. 51
"Good Morning Song," p. 52

From *What Shall We Do and Allee Galloo*, Winn
"My Hat It Has Three Corners," p. 54

Rhythms and singing games

Clapping: Use any suitable music or record with distinct rhythm patterns. Vary the patterns by striking the hands on the thighs or on the floor as well as clapping hands together.
Drums: Use fast and slow tempos and vary the rhythms in patterned beats—for example, clap, clap, clap-clap or clap, clap-clap, clap or clap-clap-clap, clap, clap.

Records and cassettes

Raffi. *The Corner Grocery Store.* (Troubadour Records)
"My Way Home"

Sandy Tobias Oppenheim. *If Snowflakes Fell in Flavours* (Berandol Records)
"Let's Play a Statue Game"
"If Snowflakes Fell in Flavours"
"Peanut Butter"

Fingerplays and Poems

From *Don't Eat Spiders*, Heidbreder and Patkau
"Sticky Maple Syrup," p. 29
"Today and Yesterday," p. 48

From *Mischief City*, Wynne-Jones
"Holes," p. 24

From *Round and Round the Garden*, Williams and Beck
"Clap Clap Hands," p. 10
"Clap Your Hands," p. 45

From *Read Aloud Rhymes for the Very Young*, Prelutsky and Brown
"Showers," p. 12
"Little Wind," p. 12
"Mud," p. 13
"Cat Kisses," p. 18
"Slippery Sam," p. 45
"Pussy Willows," p. 57

From *Where the Sidewalk Ends*, Silverstein
"Hug o' War," p. 19
"Rain," p. 40
"Standing," p. 152

Stories

The choice of stories to illustrate touch can be great fun, as it is possible to incorporate movement and cognitive experiences in to the story time. Sivulich's *I'm Going on a Bear Hunt* can be adapted for children to act out a bear hunt and can include different experiences using touch. In contrast, Baylor's *Everybody Needs a Rock* can stimulate thinking about how important things we touch are to us.

Games

(See "Learning Games," pp. 50–59, and teacher-made games in this part of the guide for directions.)
1. Together together: Find your nose, clap your hands
2. Sally says or Simon says: Touch your head, touch your toes
3. Did you ever see a lassie? Pat your knees, rub your elbow
4. Follow the leader: Touch parts of the body
5. Reach and feel: If your group is small enough to avoid a long wait for a turn

Routine Times

1. At snack or meal times talk about the coolness of the foods or beverages—juice, milk, ice creams, sherbets, and the warmth of the cooked foods. It feels cool to your hand when you lift the glass and cool or warm when it touches your lips, tongue, and mouth.
2. At snack or meal times provide many different textures of food and talk about how it feels—smooth like ice cream, or rough like carrots and celery, or sticky like peanut butter, rough like nuts.

3. When washing hands talk about the temperature of the water and the slippery soap. Provide a few drops of hand lotion for children if they want it.
4. When brushing teeth talk about how brushing makes the teeth feel clean and smooth.
5. When dressing to go outside, talk about what is appropriate to wear and why. When coming inside on a cold day, talk about the warm room. When coming in on a hot day talk about the cool air-conditioning or the cool breeze from the fan.
6. When busing the children, talk about the use of the heater or air-conditioner to make everyone feel as comfortable as possible. Also speak of the use of windows to keep out snow or rain or to let in cool breezes.

Large Muscle Activities

1. Take a "feeling walk." Have the children select different objects because of their texture. If walk must be taken on or near private property, the children may have to only look at the objects. But describe how they might feel—smooth, rough, shiny, furry, wet, dry.
2. Waterplay outdoors in appropriate season (see the chapter, "Water Around Me," p. 509).
3. Dig in the sand. Fill and dump sand in various containers. Allow children to dampen sand and make sand molds in various-shaped containers.
4. Dig in the mud. Make mud pies. Walk barefoot in the mud.
5. Play in the snow, (see chapter, "Winter," p. 319).
6. Run in the wind. (For other activities on windy days, see the chapter, "Spring," p. 331.)
7. Walk in the rain, with or without an umbrella (see the chapter, "Spring").
8. Roll down a hill or on the grass.
9. Play ball with rubber, plastic, styrofoam, yarn, or nylon stocking balls.
10. Play with horseshoes, ring toss/quoits (plastic, rubber, rope).
11. Play beanbag toss games.

Extended Experiences

1. Some zoos have a petting farm or a petting zoo for children. Take the children to one.
2. Bring a live pet like a bunny, kitten, hen, or turtle for children to touch (see chapter, "Pet Animals," p. 389).
3. Ask a blind person to visit and bring a book written in Braille. Ask the person to explain how to read the books and how important the sense of touch is.
4. Take a feeling walk in the room or outdoors to discover how things feel by touch.

Teacher Resources

Pictures and Displays

▷ Show pictures of hands doing things, people shaking hands, hugging, or kissing, and of interesting things to feel.
▷ Have objects of different sizes, colours, and textures on a table for children to explore. Include a book written in Braille. Explain its use.
▷ The Five Senses Bulletin Board Kit (Constructive Playthings)
▷ Your Skin and Mine: Film, record, and book (Thomas Y. Crowell)

Games

Safely Home, Playtoy Industries. A streetproofing game that is not too alarmist in its presentation of the issue.

Books and Periodicals

NOTE: Check your local library for the latest books on streetproofing. New books are being published all the time, but attempt to choose books that are not too alarmist.

Ferrier, Shannon. *Kids in the Kitchen.* Toronto: Lorimer, 1986.
——————. *More Kids in the Kitchen.* Toronto: Lorimer, 1986.
——————. *The Kids Bakebook.* Toronto: Lorimer, 1986.
Ferrier, Shannon, and Tamara Shuttleworth. *The Kids Food Cookbook.* Toronto: Lorimer, 1986.

NOTE: Cooking can be a tactile experience.

Martin, Paul D. *Messengers to the Brain: Our Fantastic Five Senses.* Washington, DC: National Geographic Society, 1984.
Rivlin, Robert. *Deciphering the Senses: The Expanding World of Human Perception.* New York: Simon & Schuster, 1984.
Sully, Nina. *Look at the Senses.* Batsford, GB: David and Charles, 1982.
Suzuki, David. *Looking at Senses.* Don Mills, Ont: Stoddart, 1986.

Films and Videos

Consult the *National Film Board Catalogue* and your community library

Community Resources and Organizations

▷   School for the blind
▷   Borrow some books in Braille
▷   Canadian National Institute for the Blind
▷   Carleton University, Ottawa is conducting a survey of resources for streetproofing children. Contact the university for further information

Government Agencies

▷   Provincial, territorial, and federal ministries/departments of social services (streetproofing)
▷   Local police officers (streetproofing)

PART

2

Families

**Part
Two:
Families**

Contents

Introduction

Basic Understandings

(concepts children can grasp from this subject)

What is a family?

▷ A family is a group of people who may live together; they usually take care of one another.

▷ Some children are born into a family and some are adopted.

▷ Some families have several children, some only a few, some just one, and some none.

▷ Some families have two children born at one time, usually on the same day. These are called twins; three are called triplets, four are quadruplets, and five are quintuplets.

▷ Some children live with only one parent, guardian, or other person. This could be a father, mother, grandparent, aunt, uncle, or friend of the child.

▷ A person may live alone or with only a pet.

▷ Families may have other relatives besides those living *in* their family group, such as grandmothers, grandfathers, aunts, uncles, and cousins. Sometimes these relatives also live *with* the family.

▷ The family group may be changed for many reasons—for example, by divorce, death, adoption, (re)marriage, when young people leave to marry, old age, separation caused by hospitalization, military service, term in prison, or job requirements.

▷ Each member of a family is special. In some ways they are alike, and in some ways they are different from one another.

▷ Each family has a special beginning and way of life (culture)—for example, Italian, Asian, Scandinavian, European, Jamaican.

▷ My family is like some families but different from some others.

▷ A mother is a woman (parent) who has a child (or children).

▷ A father is a man (parent) who has a child (or children).

▷ Boys are called sons by their parents. Girls are called daughters.

▷ Boys and girls in the same family are called brothers and sisters.

▷ Children are called different group names at different ages—for example, infant, baby, toddler, preschooler, kindergartner, school-age, preteen, teenager, adolescent, or young adult.

What is a home?

▷   A home is a place where a family lives, usually where they eat, sleep, play, and work.

▷   Families live in many different kinds of homes—for example, a single house, apartment, row house, townhouse, condominium, duplex, cottage, igloo, mobile home, tent, house-boat, chalet, (log) cabin, trailer, or penthouse.

▷   Homes may be located in the city, town, suburbs, on a farm, in the country, on a river, on an island, in a valley, in a desert, on a mountain, on a reserve, or in the woods.

▷   The space or ground around a home differs in size and form. There may be much space, little, or none.

▷   The space around a house may be surfaced, bordered by water, or may have ground that allows for grass, flowers, shrubs, or bushes to grow depending on the climate, place, and cost.

▷   Homes may be made from many materials; for example, wood planks, or logs, bricks, stones, mud, grass, leaves, branches, sheet metal, stucco, hides, canvas, ice blocks, or concrete blocks.

▷   A group of houses where families live near each other is called a neighbourhood, settlement, community, commune, or subdivision.

▷   Most houses have one or more rooms, each named for how it is used—for example, bedroom, living room, bathroom, dining room, kitchen, recreation room, utility room.

▷   Often each room in a house has special furnishings to make the family more comfortable and the room more useful.

▷   A family needs a place to live, food to eat, clothes to wear, and people to care for them if they cannot take care of themselves.

Additional Facts the Teacher Should Know

1.   The family is the core of the child's life. As teachers we must remember that the family is the child's primary influence and that we must respect the family and its values. Our role as adults working with young children is to be a resource for the family. The traditional view of the family is changing, but we can still be with children and their families to help them celebrate the joy of family life in a wide variety of forms and cultural traditions.

2.   In addition to presenting children with materials that will help them explore their own and other family traditions, teachers may also be called upon to help support children through family crises. The school and preschool centre is often the second place a child will turn when they face a crisis. As adults working with young children, teachers need to be prepared to support children when they are facing some stress in their lives. The section on "books to read with children" contains books that may be used to help children understand a stressful situation. They should be used with care and sensitivity. When possible, a short note should be sent home to the parents describing the content of the books used. This will help them answer questions that may arise at home after the children have been exposed to these books. The "teacher reference" section covers book that may aid you as a teacher when you are working with children facing some crisis.

3.   Chapters 7 and 8 focus on the enjoyment of varied family lifestyles. Obviously, crisis in the family is not an appropriate educational theme, but to deal effectively with family issues you will need resources for dealing with children's concerns that cover the entire spectrum of family life.

Books to Read with Children

New baby

- • Alexander, Martha. *When the New Baby Comes, I'm Moving Out.* New York: Dial Press, 1979.
- • Andry, Andrew, and Suzanne Kratha. *Hi, New Baby.* New York: Simon & Schuster, 1970.
- • Brown, Myra. *Amy and the New Baby.* New York: Watts, 1965.
- • Burningham, John. *The Baby.* New York: Thomas Y. Crowell, 1974.
- •• Hazen, Barbara. *Gorilla Wants to Be the Baby.* New York: Atheneum, 1978.
- • Hoban, Russell. *A Baby Sister for Francis.* New York: Harper & Row, 1964.
- •• Knotts, Howard. *Great Grandfather, the Baby and Me.* New York: Atheneum, 1978.
- • von Konigslow, Andrea Wayne. *That's My Baby.* Willowdale, Ont. Annick Press, 1986.
- ••• Wasson, Valentina. *The Chosen Baby.* Philadelphia: J.B. Lippincott, 1977.
- •• Wolde, Gunilla. *Betsy's Baby Brother.* New York: Random House, 1975.

Divorce and separation

- ••• Lexau, Joan. *Emily and the Klunky Baby and the Next Door Dog.* New York: Dial Press, 1972.
- •• Schick, Eleanor. *City in Winter.* New York: Collier, 1970.
- ••• Sharmat, Marjorie. *Sometimes Mama and Papa Fight.* New York: Harper & Row, 1980.
- ••• Stinson, Kathy. *Mom and Dad Don't Live Together Any More.* Willowdale, Ont: Annick Press, 1984.
- •• Winthrop, Elizabeth. *Are You Sad, Mama?* New York: Harper & Row, 1979.
- • Zindel, Paul. *I Love My Mother.* New York: Harper & Row, 1975.

Moving

- •• Cohen, Miriam. *Will I Have a Friend?* New York: Macmillan, 1967.
- •• McCloskey, Robert. *Make Way for Ducklings.* New York: Viking Press, 1969.
- • Scarry, Richard. *My House.* New York: Golden Press, 1976.
- ••• Zolotow, Charlotte. *A Tiger Called Thomas.* New York: Lothrop, Lee and Shepard, 1963.
- ••• —————— . *Janey.* New York: Harper & Row, 1973.

Hospitalization and illness

- • Bemelmans, Ludwig. *Madeline.* Markham, Ont: Penguin, 1977.
- ••• Cairo, Shelley. *Our Brother Has Down's Syndrome.* Willowdale, Ont: Annick Press, 1985.
- •• Rey, M., and H.A. Rey. *Curious George Goes to the Hospital.* Boston: Houghton Mifflin, 1966.
- • Scarry, Richard. *Nicky Goes to the Doctor.* Racine, WI: Western Publishing, 1971.
- ••• Segal, Lore. *Tell Me a Mitzi.* Don Mills, Ont: Collins, 1970.
- ••• Williams, Barbara. *Albert's Toothache.* New York: E.P. Dutton, 1974.
- •• Wolde, Gunilla. *Betsy and the Chicken Pox.* New York: Random House, 1976.

Death

- ••• Aliki, Diogenes. *The Two of Them.* New York: Greenwillow Press, 1979.
- ••• Brown, Margaret. *The Dead Bird.* Reading, MA: Addison-Wesley, 1965.
- ••• Buscgalia, Leo. *The Fall of Freddy the Leaf.* New York: Henry Holt, 1982.
- ••• Doll, Elizabeth. *My Daddy Is a Policeman.* Englewood Cliffs, NJ: Prentice-Hall, 1973.
- ••• Viorst, Judith. *The Tenth Good Thing About Barney.* New York: Atheneum, 1971.

Teacher Resources

Elkind, David. *The Hurried Child.* Reading, MA: Addison-Wesley, 1981.

Interviewing

Evans, D.R., M. Hearn, M.R. Uhlemann, and A.E. Ivey. *Essential Interviewing.* Monterey, CA: Brooks/Cole, 1979.

Garrett, Annette. *Interviewing.* New York: Family Service Association, 1972.

Stierlin, H., I. Rucker-Embden, N. Wetzel, and M. Wirsching. *The First Interview With the Family.* New York: Bruner Mazel, 1980.

Divorce and separation

Despert, Louise. *Children of Divorce.* Garden City, NY: Doubleday, 1962.

Stuart, I., and E. Lawrence, eds. *Children of Separation and Divorce.* New York: Grossman, 1972.

Hospitalization and illness

Petrillo, M., and S. Sanger. *The Emotional Care of Hospitalized Children.* Philadelphia: J.P. Lippincott, 1972.

Ramos, Suzanne. *Teaching Your Child to Cope With Crisis.* New York: David McKay, 1975.

Death

Furman, Erna. *A Child's Parent Dies.* New Haven, CT: Yale University Press, 1974.

Kubler-Ross, Elizabeth. *On Death and Dying.* New York: Macmillan, 1969.

Zeligs, R. *Children's Experience of Death.* Springfield, IL: Charles C. Thomas, 1974.

7 Living in Families

★★★★★★★★★★★★★★★★★★★★★

Basic Understandings

(concepts children can grasp from this subject)

▷ Some families buy their homes, their food, and their clothes; others may build their homes, grow their own food, and make their own clothes.

▷ Homes and clothes may also be rented or borrowed.

▷ Some family members need to work to earn money to buy things the family needs, such as food, clothes, housing (see "Families at Work," p. 199).

▷ Family members can divide the work at home in many ways:

a. Sometimes mother *takes care of the children*
b. Sometimes father *takes care of the children*
c. Sometimes both parents do this at different times or at the same time
d. Sometimes a guardian, or family friend, or a member of the family, like grandma, *takes care of the children*
e. Sometimes a person is employed by the family to *take care of the children*

> **NOTE:** Insert *takes care of the house, prepares the food, does the laundry*, and other tasks in place of italicized words in a, b, d, and e above.

▷ Most families have tools and machines to help them work at home (see "Tools and Machines," p. 537).

▷ Some families own a car that they use to go to work, to school, to shop, to visit friends and relatives, or to transport them to other places they wish to go.

▷ Some families own a truck, motorcycle, bicycle, boat, airplane, snowmobile, van, motorscooter, helicopter, minibus, that they may use to carry themselves or other people or objects for work or fun.

▷ Families each do some things in their own way—for example, customs, dress, childrearing, and lifestyle. They have certain things they believe and ways of showing them in their worship and celebrations.

▷ Families celebrate certain days together, with special preparations and plans for things to do. These celebrations often include parties, gifts, dinners, birthdays, weddings, Mother's Day, Father's Day, St. Valentine's Day, anniversaries, special religious days, and other occasions, both happy and sad.

▷ We should try to learn about other people's ways and what they believe so that we can understand and respect them as they are.

▷ Some families have pets that they care for.
▷ Families may do many things together at home—for example, eat, sleep, cook, clean, play, work.
▷ Families can have good times together at home by playing games, singing, or having barbecues.
▷ Families may do many things together away from home, such as shopping, riding, picnicking, walking, and visiting friends, relatives, parks, zoos, and other interesting places.
▷ Some children will have two homes, one with their father and one with their mother.

Additional Facts the Teacher Should Know

1. Good early-childhood centres encourage the family to share in the opportunities for learning they offer each child. At its best, the home is the primary educator of the child and programs at the centres are supplemental. Therefore teachers should use interviews, home visits, and background information sheets to help them learn as much as possible about a child and his or her family that is relevant to their teaching job.
2. Today's society in Canada is made up of many cultures and many lifestyles within these cultures. Divorce, remarriages, adoptions, placement in foster homes resulting from death or illness of a parent, or child abuse are just a few of many events that may have far-reaching effects on your children. Children may not have the same last name as their parents. They may not have the same skin colour, culture, or religious background as the family with whom they are currently living.
3. The staff needs always to be supportive of children in helping them understand themselves, their relationship with their family or the group in which they are residing, their peers, and their need to identify with their own culture grouping. (See Additional Facts the Teacher Should Know in the chapter "I'm Me, I'm Special," and the introduction to "Family Celebrations.")
4. The staff should know:

   a. Where each child lives and with whom.
   b. How many adults are in the home.
   c. How many children are there in the family and what are their approximate ages.
   d. What are the blood relationships of others in the family to the child.
   e. How do the children in the family relate to one another.
   f. What are the child's skills and handicaps.
   g. Is the child toilet trained, able to feed himself, or herself, dress, communicate his or her needs.
   h. What language(s) does the child speak.
   i. To what ethnic and religious grouping do the child and family belong.

   The purpose for asking or noting this information is to aid you in assessing a child's needs and to assist you in choices relating to dealing with behaviour. This information may also allow the staff to give support and understanding when it is needed.
5. In your centre's newsletter for parents, include an activities column describing activities the children enjoy at school that can also be done at home. For example, list favourite cassettes, records, and books; give the recipe for play dough; print the words of a song; describe a game that does not need equipment or a lot of children, etc.
6. Children should be encouraged to take pride in their culture and pride in their country. The staff should provide opportunities for children to share knowledge and experiences. The centre needs to accept each child and provide opportunities for each to express her or his feelings, whether happy, sad, angry, hurt, dejected, or anxious.
7. Other chapters in the guide related to this one are "I'm Me, I'm Special" and "Families at Work."

Methods Most Adaptable for Introducing this Subject to Children

1. Individual or group time conversation. "Who brought you to school today?" "Does your grandmother live nearby?"
2. Post pictures on the walls or on a bulletin board of families doing things together—for example, sharing, helping one another. Change the pictures or at least part of them in the presence of children. Invite them to help you. If this is not possible, take two or three children at a time on a picture walk around the room. Make sure that the pictures are of different family constellations and have examples of people from the different cultures represented in your centre.
3. When a grandparent brings the child or visits one day.
4. Someone mentions that Mother's Day or Father's Day is coming soon.
5. A brother or sister brings or picks up one of the children.
6. You may read a story about a family or about mothers, fathers, babies, grandparents.
7. A child announces that a new baby has been born in their family, or relates a family happening.
8. Encourage children to talk about activities that they have done with their families—for example, going to a movie, watching television at home, having a family barbecue, playing a game, going to a restaurant for dinner.

Vocabulary

mother	grandmother	great-aunt	cousin
father	grandfather	great-uncle	care for
family	children	baby	live with
sister	mommy	home	share
brother	daddy	husband	like
step-mother	guardian	wife	belong to
step-father	foster-mother	friend	love
step-sister	foster-father	babysitter	adoption
step-brother	housekeeper	"nanny"	divorce
God-mother	great-grandmother	aunt	separation
God-father	great-grandfather	uncle	foster home
twins			

Learning Centres

Discovery Centre

1. Invite a mother and an infant to visit. Observe the size of the baby's hands, feet, mouth, how it eats, sleeps, and dresses. Encourage the children to ask questions and offer information. Allow touching of baby's feet rather than head or hands for health and safety reasons. Talcum powder can be dusted on the baby's feet and hands and prints made on a dark piece of paper. Compare baby's prints with prints made of children's hands and feet.

2. Demonstrate the use of a baby bottle and plate food warmer. This would be especially appropriate to do when a mother comes to visit with a baby and feeds the infant during snack time. Children can be allowed to taste baby foods at this time. Many nursing mothers and babies are relaxed and natural even in a group setting. Invite a nursing mother to visit your centre to show an alternative to bottle feeding.

3. Compare the texture of pureed foods (fruit, meat, or vegetables) with the same foods that are raw or cooked whole. You may wish to puree food with a blender or a simple non-electric food mill that children can turn.

4. Put up a simple map of your area. If most of the children live within a close radius, insert a bulletin board pin and a name tag at the place each child's home is located (see "I'm Me, I'm Special," p. 107.)

5. For housecleaning see "Tools and Machines," p. 538.

6. Borrow a pair of hamsters, guinea pigs, rats, mice, or gerbils and observe. Let animals mate and then raise a family.

> ★ **CAUTION:** Do this only if you can find a home for the pets when observation is completed.

7. Talk about animals that mate for life, such as foxes, and those that do not, such as cats or elephants.

> **NOTE:** Most large birds of prey keep the same mate each year unless one dies. Canada geese and swans do *not* remate if their mate dies.

8. Learn unusual names of some bird babies, such as:

chicken—chick	swan—cygnet	owl—owlet
duck—duckling	pigeon—squab	eagle—eaglet
turkey—poult	goose—gosling	

Learn names of other animal babies (see the animal chapters, pp. 376, 390, 402, 412).

9. Bake cookies: If a kitchen is available, let the children (two or three at a time) help make simple drop cookies or hand-rolled cookies. If a kitchen is not available, supply plain cookies, several colours of frosting, varied decorations, and let the children decorate the cookies. Eat for party, snack, or lunch.

Dramatic Play Centres

Home-living centre

1. Encourage adult/parent role playing by providing dress-up clothes and dramatic play props. Consider the interchangeability of props and clothes for males and females

   a. Parents/guardians: Include aprons, hats, purses, shoulder bags, wallets, wigs, vests, jewellery, shoes, jackets, ties, keys, brief cases, first-aid kit, sleepwear, evening wear, day clothes, lunch buckets, jumbo-plastic-tool kits, gloves, coats, and boots.

   b. Grandparents: Include eyeglass frames, wigs, sweaters, bedroom slippers, newspapers, magazines, magnifying glasses and cancs. Be careful not to stereotype grandparents as in need of chronic care—many grandparents are active, vibrant people in their middle years.

   > **NOTE:** All children should be allowed to dress up as they choose.

   c. Babies: Use life-size dolls representing all the cultural groups that are available. Dress them in real baby clothes (size six-months-to-one-year). Have lots of blankets. Include a few small hand towels for bathing babies. Allow children to bring a few baby items from the display table to use in the centre with supervision. A cradle, crib, bed, buggy, and rocking chair will also add to the dramatic play possibilities in this centre.

2. Allow children to wash and dry doll dishes, outdoors if weather is nice. Provide tea towels, dishcloths, rack, plastic dishpans, and liquid soap.
3. Encourage children to clean the cupboards, tidy the toy shelves, vacuum the carpet, dust the furniture, and sweep the floor in the home-living centre using dustpan, broom, mop, dusters, and toy vacuum.
4. Encourage the children to wash and dry doll clothes. Pretend to iron when dry.

    ★ **CAUTION:**   Clothes and bedding may need a real washing and ironing by an adult after this.

5. Allow children to give washable dolls a bath. Provide washcloths, bath towels, and talcum powder with puff.
6. Allow a simple food to be prepared in the centre.
7. Play tea party. Take turns being hosts and visitors. For a special treat, pour water or fruit juice into cups. Cut bread, bananas, or other soft finger foods into small pieces to serve on dishes.

    ★ **CAUTION:**   Be sure all dishes and utensils actually used for eating and drinking are sterilized. Paper cups and plates are recommended.

8. Provide food preparation tools commonly used at home by parents—for example, egg-beater, rubber spatula, rolling pin, measuring cups and spoons. Add play dough to use with tools.
9. Allow opportunities for children to use rulers, measuring tape, plastic hammer, wrench, or saw to do parents' jobs around house.

Block-building centre

1. Set out wooden or rubber family figures.
2. Add a moving van or label a truck as one.
3. Encourage use of blocks for building of rooms and new houses.
4. Add a camper, mobile home, tent, and a variety of boats to encourage recreational play.
5. Set out multiethnic family figures for block accessories.

Other dramatic play centres

1. Set up a dollhouse adjacent to the block area with movable furniture and multiethnic family figures.
2. Hand puppets of family figures (multiethnic) can be used with a three-way play screen or in connection with hollow blocks and planks.
3. Arrange for a hat bar with various types of helper hats to try on. An unbreakable hand mirror, cash register, money, and bags will encourage participation.
4. Set up a shoe store with men's, women's, and children's shoes for customers to try on. Add cash register, money, chair and shoe boxes.
5. Arrange for a clothing store with mittens, gloves, shirts, skirts, scarves, purses, jewellery, and other appropriate items grouped into areas or on separate shelves. A small coat or hat tree is a helpful addition. Set up a checkout counter similar to stores noted above.
6. Set up a grocery store. Include shopping bags, grocer's hat and apron, money, plastic foods, and empty food cans and cartons among the props.
7. Encourage children to move (relocate) the home-living centre or set up a second home. Provide cartons to pack, suitcases to carry clothes, and wagons to move the furniture.

    NOTE: Choose any of the above or another family-related facility, depending upon your children's opportunity, experience, and your community—for example, hamburger stand, cafe, library. (See the section on Dramatic Play Centres in the chapter, "Families at Work.") What you highlight may reflect the visitors, trips, or interests of the children.

8. Make a tabletop or floor terrain for building a community. Duplicate a terrain similar to one familiar to children. For instance, if you are located in an inner-city area, incorporate more concrete into your model. The illustration that follows allows for play areas, a park, a farm, and a lake area. Children will enjoy building homes, stores, driving with small cars or trucks on roads, adding trees, boats, animals around the lake, with endless variations. If roads are not too defined, children are allowed more alternatives in use of space. The terrain is easily stored when folded in half. Best for older children who can work together.

Cut out two sides of a stereo carton or desk carton. Tape at centre to allow folding to store. Tape edges for durability. Paint with green enamel, leaving roads neutral colour of cardboard or paint white. Paint lake blue.

NOTE: Make a tape hinge with masking tape or paper mailing tape *before* painting the surface.

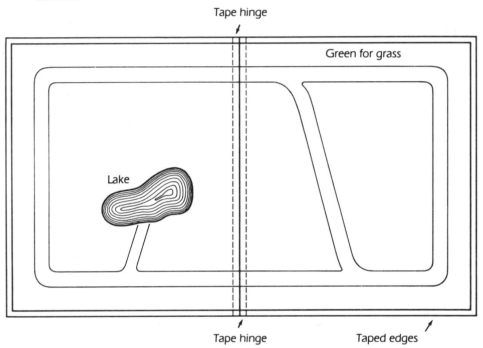

Learning, Language, and Readiness Materials Centre

Commercially made games and materials

(See "Basic Resources," pp. 79, 100, for manufacturers' addresses.)
1. *Puzzles:* Puzzles should include families of a variety of races, cultural origins, and colours. Be sure to include some puzzles with small knobs on the pieces. It is acceptable to use puzzles with animal families, being sure to draw a clear differentiation between the animals and humans. Try Animal Parents and Baby Puzzles (Judy/Instructo); Just Like Us Jigsaw Puzzles (Louise Kool).
2. *Dolls and puppets:* Dolls and puppets of people of various ages and cultural origins, that can be used to make up different family constellations. Be sure when using dolls in traditional costumes to make it clear to the children that the costumes are usually used for special celebrations and are not everyday wear. Try Family Puppets (Galt), Realistic Flexible Doll Families (Wintergreen).
3. *Small toys for imaginative play:* Toys that are accurate models of household objects and materials can enhance imaginative play. Try Complete Food Centre (Lakeshore).

4. *Costumes:* Offer a wide variety of costumes and old clothes in the dress-up centre. Try to have clothes that are suitable for people of different ages. Be sure the clothes are cleaned frequently and kept in good shape—no loose threads. Try Grandma's Dress-up Trunk (Wintergreen).
5. *Flannelboards and flannelboard aids:* Most commercial suppliers have excellent flannelboard sets showing different types of families and family activities.
6. *Posters:* Posters of family activities are available from most commercial suppliers. Make sure you are choosing posters that show a variety of families, diversity in family roles, and families having fun together.

Teacher-made games and materials

NOTE: For a detailed description of "Learning Games," see pp. 50–59.

1. Name it or scramble: Use diaper, bottle warmer, bottle, pacifier
2. Look and see: Use rattle, pacifier, bath toy, wash cloth
3. Reach and feel: Use plastic baby bottle, rattle, pacifier, soft rubber toy, cotton ball
4. Who am I? Describe a mother, baby, daddy, grandmother
5. If: If the baby cries what could it mean? If the milk in baby's bottle gets too hot what can you do?
6. Grouping and sorting by association:

    a. Set out dress-up clothes. Ask children to separate into various groupings: sleepwear, parents' clothes, baby clothes
    b. Set out rubber or wooden farm animals and have children find the young that belong to the adult animals—for example, a cow and calf

7. Match-them: Make sets of picture cards with two each of:

    a. Family members, baby items, furniture
    b. Use several pairs of mittens, shoes, socks; divide into two piles; let children find the match to the one they choose

8. Guess what? Ask child, "What can a baby do?" "What can you do that a baby cannot?" "What can a grownup do that you cannot?"

Art Centre

1. Doll blankets: With pinking shears cut 30.5 cm squares from old sheets. Thumbtack to a square of white interior insulation board and let the children decorate them with coloured markers. When dry remove them from the board and use with box cradles as blankets for dolls (or take them home).
2. Play dough: Use rolling pins and cookie cutters with self-hardening play dough. Bake cookies in play oven and use for tea parties in the doll corner (when they become hard). See the recipe in "Basic Resources," p. 27.
3. Cutting and pasting: Select many pages of figures from old catalogues to represent mothers, fathers, and different-aged children. If possible let the children cut around the figures they choose to represent their own family and paste them onto a cardboard or other stiff backing. The figures usually need to be precut for three-year-olds.

    NOTE: An easy way for older children to cut them out is to outline the figures with felt pens and then to cut along the coloured lines.

4. Encourage the children to make a collage gift or a get-well card for a child or staff member when appropriate, as an expression of caring.
5. Make a gift and greeting card for Mother's Day or Father's Day.

Book Centre

- • Adoff, Arnold. *Black Is Brown Is Tan.* New York: Harper & Row, 1973.
- • Alexander, Martha. *Nobody Asked Me If I Wanted a Baby Sister.* New York: Dial Press, 1971.
- • _____ . *Out! Out! Out!* New York: Dial Press, 1968.
- • • Alderson, Sue Ann. *Bonnie McSmithers You're Driving Me Dithers.* Edmonton: Tree Frog Press, 1974.
- • • Bell, Bill. *Saxophone Boy.* Montreal: Tundra Books, 1980.
- • Bemelmans, Ludwig. *Madeline.* Markham, Ont: Penguin, 1977.
- • • Cairo, Shelley. *Our Brother Has Down's Syndrome.* Willowdale, Ont: Annick Press, 1985.
- • Brown, Margaret Wise. *The Runaway Bunny.* New York: Harper & Row, 1942.
- • Clifton, Lucille. *Don't You Remember?* Markham, Ont: Fitzhenry & Whiteside, 1987.
- • • dePaolo, Tomie. *Nana Upstairs, Nana Downstairs.* New York: G.P. Putnam's Sons, 1973.
- • Dumas, Jacqueline. *And I'm Never Coming Back.* Willowdale, Ont: Annick Press, 1986.
- • Eastman, P.D. *Are You My Mother?* New York: Random House, 1960.
- • • Fernandes, Eugene. *A Difficult Day.* Toronto: Kids Can Press, 1983.
- • • Flack, Marjorie. *Wait for William.* Boston: Houghton Mifflin, 1935.
- • _____ . *Ask Mr. Bear.* New York: Macmillan, 1971.
- • • Gaeddert, Lou Ann. *Noisy Nancy Norris.* Garden City, NY: Doubleday, 1971.
- • Galloway, Priscilla. *When You Were Little and I Was Big.* Willowdale, Ont: Annick Press, 1985.
- • • Geisel, Theodore. *The Cat in the Hat.* New York: Random House, 1957.
- • • • Hutchins, Hazel. *Ben's Snow Song: A Winter Picnic.* Willowdale, Ont: Annick Press, 1987.
- • • Hutchins, Pat. *Tutch.* New York: Macmillan, 1971.
- • Keats, Ezra Jack. *Pete's Chair.* New York: Harper & Row, 1976.
- • • Krumins, Anita. *Who's Going to Clean Up the Mess?* Toronto: Three Trees Press, 1985.
- • • Lasker, Joe. *He's My Brother.* Chicago: Albert Whitman, 1974.
- • • Laurence, Margaret. *Six Darn Cows.* Toronto: James Lorimer, 1986. (Read–Tell)
- • • Levinson, Rikki. *I Go With My Family to Grandma's.* New York: E.P. Dutton, 1986.
- • Lim, John. *At Grandmother's House.* Montreal: Tundra Books, 1977.
- • MacKay, Jed. *The Big Secret.* Willowdale, Ont: Annick Press, 1985.
- • • Morgan, Allan. *Daddy Care.* Willowdale, Ont: Annick Press, 1986.
- • • Munsch, Robert. *I Love You Forever.* Scarborough, Ont: Firefly Books, 1986.
- • • Munsil, Janet. *Dinner at Auntie Rose's.* Willowdale, Ont: Annick Press, 1984.
- • Ormerod, Jan. *Moonlight.* Markham, Ont: Penguin, 1987.
- • • Quinlan, Patricia. *My Dad Takes Care of Me.* Willowdale, Ont: Annick Press, 1987.
- • • Schlein, Miriam. *The Way Mothers Are.* Chicago: Albert Whitman, 1963.
- • • Segal, Lore. *Tell Me a Mitzi.* Don Mills, Ont: Collins, 1970.
- • • Sharmat, Marjorie. *Sometimes Mama and Papa Fight.* New York: Harper & Row, 1980.
- • Simon, Norma. *What Do I Do?* Chicago: Albert Whitman, 1969.
- • _____ . *What Do I Say?* Chicago: Albert Whitman, 1967.
- • • Slobodkin, Louis. *Excuse Me—Certainly.* New York: Vanguard Press, 1959.
- • • Stamm, Claus. *Three Strong Women.* Markham, Ont: Penguin, 1987.
- • Staunton, Ted. *Simon's Surprise.* Toronto: Kids Can Press, 1986.
- • • Steptoe, John. *Stevie.* New York: Harper & Row, 1969.
- • • _____ . *Daddy Is a Monster . . . Sometimes.* New York: Harper & Row, 1980.
- • • Stinson, Kathy. *Mom and Dad Don't Live Together Any More.* Willowdale, Ont: Annick Press, 1984.
- • Viorst, Judith. *Alexander and the Terrible, Horrible, No Good, Very Bad Day.* Don Mills, Ont: Collier Macmillan, 1972.
- • von Kongigslow, Andrea Wayne. *That's My Baby.* Willowdale, Ont: Annick Press, 1986.
- • • Wasson, Valentina. *The Chosen Baby.* Philadelphia: J.B. Lippincott, 1977.
- • • Watts, Bernadette. *David's Waiting Day.* Scarborough, Ont: Prentice-Hall, 1978.

- • Yashima, Taro. *Umbrella.* New York: Viking Press, 1958.
- • Zindel. *I Love My Mother.* New York: Harper & Row, 1975.
- • Zolotow, Charlotte. *William's Doll.* New York: Harper & Row, 1972.
- • _____ . *Mister Rabbit and the Lovely Present.* Markham, Ont: Fitzhenry & Whiteside, 1977.

NOTE: In your library, look for books about families by Russell Hoban, Lois Lenski and Joan Lexau, as each has several good books on this subject.

Planning for Group Time

NOTE: All music, fingerplays, poems, stories, and games listed here may be used at other times during the session as appropriate. See Core Library, "Basic Resources," p. 95, for publishers and addresses. See p. 99 for record company addresses.

Music

Songs

From *Singing Bee*, Hart
"Hugh Little Baby," p. 12
"Bye Bye Baby Bunting," p. 14
"Lazy Mary," p. 62
"The Farmer in the Dell," p. 79
"Billy Boy," p. 111

From *Stepping Along in Music Land*, Murray
"My Grandpa," p. 3
"Shopping," p. 6 (Volume II)
"He's My Dad," p. 21 (Volume II)

From *More Piggyback Songs*, Warren
"Happy Father's Day," p. 36
"Where Is Daddy?" p. 36

From *The Goat With the Bright Red Socks*, Birkenshaw and Walden
"This Is My City," p. 1
"What Has this City Got?" p. 22
(substitute names and sites from your own city)
"What Makes a House a Home?" p. 20
"Who Is My Neighbour?" p. 21

Records and cassettes

Anne Murray. *There's a Hippo in My Tub.* (Capitol Records)

Bob Schneider. *When You Dream a Dream.* (Capitol Records)
"Grandpa's Song"
"Help Each Other"

Fred Penner. *Special Delivery.* (Troubadour Records)
"My Grandfather's Clock"
"Mail Myself to You"

Raffi. *The Corner Grocery Store.* (Troubadour Records)
"My Way Home"

Sandy Tobias Oppenheim. *If Snowflakes Fell in Flavours.* (Berandol Records)
"Clearing the Table Is My Job"

Sharon, Lois, and Bram. *Elephant Show Record.* (Elephant Records)
"Go to Sleep Now My Pumpkin"
_____ . *Smorgasbord.* (Elephant Records)
"Father Papered the Parlour"

Fingerplays and Poems

From *Read Aloud Rhymes for the Very Young*, Prelutsky and Brown
"Mother Cat's Purr," p. 19
"The Old Woman," p. 24
"The Way They Scrub," p. 27
"My Sister Laura," p. 28
"Hamsters," p. 54 (if you have hamsters in the centre)
"Table Manners," p. 69
"Night Fun," p. 70
"Bedtime," p. 70

From *Mischief City*, Wynne-Jones
"Talking," p. 6
"I Must Be Talking Martian," p. 8
"Baby," p. 13
"I Wasn't Angry When I Thought About Maxine," p. 16
"They're Having a Party Downstairs," p. 19
"Monster Parents," p. 28

From *Finger Rhymes*, Brown
"Grandma's Spectacles," p. 7
"The Baby Mice," p. 14
"Five Little Mice," p. 16

From *Round and Round the Garden*, Williams and Beck
"My House," p. 14
"Here's a Ball for Baby," p. 39
"Here's the Lady's Knives and Forks," p. 43

From *Pieces*, Dixon
"What Colour Is Love?" p. 26

From *Fingerplays for Nursery and Kindergarten*, Poulson
"Mrs. Pussy's Dinner," p. 58

From *Fingerplays and Action Rhymes*, Jacobs
"Baby Toes," p. 5
"Grandma," p. 17

From *A New Treasury of Children's Poetry*, Cole
"Rock, Rock, Sleep, My Baby," p. 44
"Two in a Bed," p. 53
"On Mother's Day," p. 163

From *Where the Sidewalk Ends*, Silverstein
"For Sale," p. 52
"What a Day," p. 118
"Me and God," p. 163
"Dreadful," p. 141

From *The New Wind Has Wings*, Downie
"Song for Naomi," p. 80

Stories

The choice of stories to read children in the family area should reflect the current interests and concerns of the children and their families. The themes of the stories should cover a wide range of feelings. Remember to include stories in which families have fun and also solve problems. For instance, Alderson's *Bonnie McSmithers You're Driving Me Dithers* gives children an opportunity to talk about solving problems related to rambunctious behaviour; Krumin's *Who's Going to Clean Up this Mess!* gives a humourous view of family roles and the sharing of jobs around the house.

Routine Times

1. Let children prepare the daily snack, such as pouring their own milk or juice, peeling and slicing bananas, scraping and cutting carrots, cutting up slices of bread, washing and counting out grapes. All this must be done under close supervision. Use table knives.
2. One day for a snack or at meal time serve only baby food. Provide one jar for each child of such items as apricots, plums, peaches, fruit dessert. (The jars may be saved as paint containers for the easel.) You may wish to puree your own baby food.
3. For a snack serve teething biscuits, milk, and baby food. A mother with a baby could be asked to bring some formula so the children could taste it.
4. You may wish to demonstrate using the bottle warmer at this time.
5. Have the children wash off the tables with a damp sponge before and after snack or meal times. Also straighten the chairs and sweep the floor.
6. When driving or walking with children, point out various homes you see.

Large Muscle Activities

1. Family play: Take or wear dress-up clothes outdoors. Set up a house of hollow blocks or large cardboard cartons, a sheet over a jungle gym, or arrangement of packing boxes. Tricycles and wagons can be family cars for going to work, shopping, or taking trips.
2. Encourage taking dolls for a walk in baby carriages or strollers.
3. Woodworking: Let children use the workbench in pairs. Use play hammers, balsa wood, large-headed plastic nails. *Junior Handyman* equipment in a tool box (by Creative Playthings).
4. Sandplay: In hot weather use wet sand to bake cookies and cakes. Use orange crates or cardboard cartons for stoves. Have a mud picnic. Bake mudpies in the sun, mix seeds and grass with mud for puddings. Sprinkle with sand. Decorate with pebbles. Use leaves for sandwiches. Serve to each other or to dolls and pretend to eat.
5. Hang clothes washed in the dramatic play centre earlier today to dry outside.
6. Set up a car and truck wash. Use a bucket of water, rags, and hose lengths.
7. Paint the outside of the centre. Provide large paintbrushes and small buckets of water. Empty commercial paint cans with handles work fine!
8. Set up a simulated bowling alley with plastic pins and balls.
9. See dramatic play centre suggested activities for those that would be suitable to play outdoors when the weather and temperature permit.

Extended Experiences

1. Take a trip to visit someone's parent at work who is a police officer, firefighter, letter carrier, grocer, teacher, hairstylist, or postal worker.
2. If your centre is in a residential area, take a walk around your block to look at and identify different kinds of housing. Consider safety and feasibility. Talk about what each home is made of, the number of floors, design, colour, style. Contrast how each is

different, how some are similar or the same, how the homes may differ inside—number of family members, age, number of rooms, furnishings, and so on.

3. Visit a store that sells clothes, shoes, hats, furniture, kitchenware, appliances, tools, to see where things are purchased that we need in a family. Choose a store where children can see and will be welcomed in small groups; choose a time of day when there may be few shoppers (see Trips and Excursions in "Basic Resources," p. 70).

4. Occasionally it is possible to plan a trip to the home of a teacher or child. Select those that are different in style or type and plan a special activity related to the trip... exploring a backyard, seeing a pet.

5. Invite a parent with a baby less than one year old to visit. Have children bathe the baby if possible; also feed it, change its diaper, rock it. Discuss what the baby can or cannot do —sit, walk, stand, talk, crawl. Does it have teeth? Hair? Fingernails? Why does it cry? What does it eat?

6. Invite grandparents to come and show pictures of themselves as children and tell interesting experiences or stories. Invite them to help with some of the centre activities —read a story; help with food preparation, creative arts, or woodworking; or repair or make a piece of equipment used by the children.

7. Invite a parent, especially a father if you do not have a male on your staff, to share a special talent, such as playing a musical instrument, or to show an interesting hobby collection.

8. Have a big or little brother or sister visit.

Teacher Resources

Pictures and Displays

▷   Select pictures of various family lifestyles from magazines showing as many ethnic groups as possible. Mount on coloured cardboard or construction paper and hang them around room.

▷   Use commercially available family pictures.

▷   Use pictures of baby animals and their parents and the homes in which they live.

▷   Show some hospital-made footprints of a baby; also the bracelet that babies and mothers wear for identification.

▷   Display some real baby items near the home-living centre. Include nursing bottles, rattles, pacifiers, baby food, diapers, ointments, powder, teething rings, spoons, bottle warmer, bottles, brush, plastic pants, soft rubber toys, bath toys.

> ★ **CAUTION:**   Supervize closely so that the children do not actually put the nipples and spoons in their mouths. You will want to reserve the use of the bottle warmer for a demonstration by the teacher or parent (see Extended Experiences, no. 5, above).

Books and Periodicals

Parent magazine.

Workshop Models for Family Life Education. New York: Family Service Association, 1977.

Active Learning in the Early School Years. Toronto: Federation of Women Teachers' Associations of Ontario, 1986. (Sections on Parents and Community)

The You and Me Series. Scarborough, Ont: Nelson Canada, 1986.

Films and Videos

The Canadian Filmstrip Company, 1987:
▷ *All About Me*
▷ *Get Ready, Baby's Coming!*
▷ *Learning About Myself*
▷ *Learning About Families*

Community Resources and Organizations

▷ YMCA
▷ YWCA
▷ YMHA
▷ Children's Aid Society or child welfare associations
▷ Family service associations
▷ Community health centres

Government Agencies

▷ Federal Ministry of Health and Welfare
▷ Provincial or territorial ministries responsible for social services; such as welfare, health, etc.

8 Families at Work

★★★★★★★★★★★★★★★★★★★★★★★

Basic Understandings

(concepts children can grasp from this subject)

▷ Some family members need to work to earn money to buy things the family needs, such as food, clothes, housing.

▷ Other family members work at home as full-time parents and homemakers.

▷ Family members can divide the work at home in many ways (see "Living in Families").

▷ Some people have a special place to work at home (workshops, studios, offices), while other people walk, drive, or commute to work by car pool, train, subway, bus, plane, monorail, van, helicopter, or truck.

▷ Some people work at different times of the day and night. Sometimes their time to work changes from day to day, week to week, or month to month (shifts) or they may be on call depending on weather or need. (See "Day and Night")

▷ Some people wear special clothes or uniforms when they work to protect their clothes, to keep them safe, or to tell who they are and what they do. Other uniforms are worn to carry tools or to keep workers or what they work with clean.

▷ Many people use tools or machines in their work. (See "Tools and Machines" and the "Transportation" section)

▷ Some people use animals or work with animals on their jobs.

▷ Some people grow their own food, build their own houses, and make their own clothes; others pay someone else to do these jobs for them.

▷ Most people are paid for their work outside the home. Some are given money and some are given cheques, which they can cash for money.

▷ People can put cheques or money in the bank to keep it safe until they need it.

▷ Some people may trade work to get what they want done. One person may paint a house for someone in exchange for fixing her car.

▷ Every job and each worker is important. We need everyone to help in his or her own way and do what he or she can do best.

▷ It is important that each person does his or her own job as well as he or she can and that he or she tries to do their share of the work.

▷ We all depend on each other for the things or services we need.

▷ A person who does one kind of work very well is called a "specialist."

▷ Most jobs can be done by either a man or a woman, if they choose to do that kind of work and have the ability and training to do it.

▷ Often people have to go to school or take special training to learn how to do their job or to be licensed to do their work.

▷ Some people are taught how to do their job while they work at their job.
▷ Helpers in our community include:
   a. People who help to keep us well: doctors, dentists, nurses, pharmacists, public health officers, exercise instructors, paramedics, nutritionists
   b. People who build things for us: carpenters, architects, bricklayers, construction workers, developers, engineers, and road, ship, and bridge builders
   c. People who keep us safe: police officers, firefighters, crossing guards, weather watchers, emergency broadcasters, service-and-rescue patrollers, water, road, health, food and equipment inspectors, air traffic controllers, forest rangers, flight attendants, lifeguards, camp counsellors

   NOTE: An inspector is a person who makes sure things are done or made the right way for our safety and protection.

   d. People who help us to know what is happening to others: teachers, writers, journalists, radio and television announcers, politicians, civil servants, librarians, legislators, ministers, rabbis, priests
   e. People who fix things: appliance repair persons, utility maintenance workers, plumbers, carpenters, shoe repair persons, car mechanics, electricians, office equipment repair persons, piano tuners
   f. People who sell or provide things we need: farmers, salespersons, clerks, realtors, grocers, clothiers, hardware merchants, shoe salespersons, retailers, manufacturers
   g. People who provide entertainment or a place for us to play: park and recreation personnel, neighbours, movie theatre owners, artists, musicians, hobby and craft shop personnel, actors, dancers, singers, clowns, circus performers
   h. People who help us when we travel: service station attendants, tour guides, stewards, conductors, bus drivers, travel counsellors, flight attendants, taxi drivers, language interpreters, tourist information officers, police officers.
   i. People who plan for food (grow, sell, cook, serve, deliver, prepare or handle food or food products): farmers, grocery clerks, truckers, produce retailers, frozen food plant personnel, fishermen, harvesters, migrant workers, caterers, restaurant managers, waiters/waitresses, cooks, bakers, meat packers, food packagers, butchers
   j. People who provide services for us: couriers, bookkeepers, bankers, caterers, drycleaners, laundry workers, tailors, carpet cleaners, carwashers, babysitters, movers, taxi drivers, housekeepers, valets, luggage handlers, shippers, hairstylists
   k. People who make new things: manufacturers of paper, rubber, cars, cards, toys, garments, auto parts, steel furniture, plastic, glass, etc.; dressmakers, engineers, inventors, designers, artists, writers, sculptors, builders, carpenters, jewellers, chefs, architects

Additional Facts the Teacher Should Know

1. People work for many reasons:
   a. To earn money to buy necessities and luxuries for themselves, their family, and friends
   b. As an outlet for creativity
   c. To be of service
   d. For diversity of activity
   e. To produce goods
   f. For adventure and discovery
2. Today, women constitute a principal part of both the labour force and professions. This can largely be attributed to their being given the opportunity and encouragement to train and be educated in most fields.
3. Many women have chosen to remain single and pursue a career; combine marriage with a career; combine marriage and motherhood; or combine marriage and motherhood with a career. Some women who have chosen marriage and motherhood and have been widowed or divorce, have pursued careers out of financial necessity.

4. More and more husbands and wives work together as associates in business—as lawyers, doctors, dentists, architects, and others. Some will share jobs. Many share family responsibilities.

5. Some men—writers, musicians, artists, educators, and those with businesses in their homes—elect to share the work of the home and childcare with their wives by mutual agreement for the satisfactions that come with closer relationships within the family. If the father is a single parent, this combined role may be a necessity.

6. Men have also taken jobs once previously held only by women, such as nurses, flight attendants, hairstylists, teachers in early childhood education, secretaries, and telephone operators. Since both sexes may now hold almost any job, the names of some jobs need to be modified or changed to eliminate the sex differentiation where it once existed. For example, to avoid stereotypes in occupational roles remember to use:

firefighter for fireman	*salesperson* / *sales clerk* for salesman, saleslady
police officer for policeman	*insurance agent* for insurance man
business executive / *business manager* for businessman	*person* for man, woman
leader / *civil servant* for statesman	*humanpower* for manpower
supervisor for foreman	*adulthood* for manhood, womanhood
flight attendant for steward, purser, stewardess	*chairperson* for chairman
homemaker for housewife	*camera operator* for cameraman
maintenance crew member for maintenance man	*housekeeper* / *houseworker* / *servant* for maid, houseboy
logger for lumberman	
newspaper carrier for newspaper boy/girl	*courier* for deliveryman

7. Preschool children can learn the names of various occupations and can understand a simple explanation of what each person does. It is wise to begin with jobs held by parents of the children in your centre or those which your children come in contact with in their daily living. You may choose to focus on one occupational grouping at a time. See the groupings listed in "Basic Understandings," p. 200.

NOTE: Many of the recent changes in today's lifestyles are reflected in current children's storybooks, poems, fingerplays, and toys; but you will still need to edit and modify references that reflect sexism as you use otherwise suitable materials. Occasionally in telling a story you may simply change the leading character to the opposite sex to reflect this change and avoid stereotyping what boys are like or girls are like, reflecting instead what young children are like! You might also include a woman's name or man's name in a list of helpers or workers in a story to suggest that *both* might exist in that situation. Father might be baking or fixing pancakes, bathing the baby, or doing the laundry. Mother may be repairing a chair or painting the house. We have tried to make those modifications in this book, but when referring to other books available we have been limited in such editing and therefore leave this responsibility to you. Remember too that some parents may be unemployed. Be sensitive to these families when planning the section.

8. Children can learn something of our basic economic system—that we get paid for our work and can exchange our pay for services for something we want or need and that there is a basic interdependence in our society. If given paper money and play coins to use when "shopping" and when various dramatic centres are set up to pay for services, such

as service station (use of credit cards), post office (pay for stamps), or grocery store (paying for food at check-out counter) *or* in a direct, real-life experience when buying a needed item at a pet store or grocery store when group takes a trip, children get experience in purchasing goods or services.

★ **CAUTION:**   Coins are not suitable for children under three.

9. Many services are provided by volunteers, such as food bank workers, hospital volunteers, phone line operators, etc. Visits from volunteers with whom children may come into contact would add another perspective to your unit on work. Older children may be able to take on a volunteer project (For example, children may be asked to bring in a toy that they no longer use to be sent to a local children's hospital.) Explain that often children cannot take their own toys into a hospital and that the hospital may need toys that can be kept especially for sick children.

10. Some occupations have been highlighted in other sections of this book where more appropriate. You may wish to refer to them in the following chapters: "Tools and Machines," "I'm Me, I'm Special," "Living in Families," and in the "Transportation" section.

Methods Most Adaptable for Introducing this Subject to Children

1. On a table, display tools highlighting one kind of occupation, such as doctor's/dentist's surgical mask, stethoscope, play thermometer, empty unbreakable pill bottle, hot water bottle, or ice bag.
2. Read a book about a community helper (see Book Centre list).
3. Invite a person, dressed in the uniform or garb of her/his profession to come and show the children the "tools" of that occupation and how they are used.
4. Post pictures of one grouping of community helpers on a bulletin board near entrance or cloakroom.
5. Plan a trip to a place of business as part of developing an interest in another subject—for example, grocery store—food; pet store—pets.
6. The children may observe an interesting job (workers near the playground or seen when the children are on a walk).

Vocabulary

work	spend	cheque	cash
job	buy	bank	names of occupations
pay	sell	money	names of businesses
earn	trade	coins	task each person does
save	barter	change	

Learning Centres

Discovery Centre

1. Talk with visitors to find out how they earn money and what they do when at work.
2. Help children discover nonsexist occupational roles by introducing children to women and men who hold similar jobs.
3. Find pictures of various jobs held by parents of your children. Put a photo of each child by a picture of his/her parent's job. Take polaroid pictures or cut from illustrative business brochures or magazines. Encourage parents and children to help collect pictures

if feasible. Include in this group those who are jobless or who have nonpaying jobs, showing other kinds of jobs they do, such as caring for family.

4. Set up an "our special visitor" or "work" discovery centre area where tools of a special kind of worker are displayed and can be explored and explained each day by a parent, special community resource person, or teacher. This might be a bake centre, special kind of art centre, a workbench, or a sewing centre. Plan for opportunities for children to pursue the activity at their level of ability.
5. Display bank books, chequebooks, and unbreakable piggy banks from your community.
6. Examine a stethoscope, simple microscope, thermometer.
7. Borrow a real telephone from the telephone company for children to explore.
8. Borrow a used typewriter for children to use. Encourage the children to type their names by finding and pressing the letters on the keys.

Dramatic Play Centres

Home-living centre

1. Place money in purses and wallets so children are able to buy goods being sold in other dramatic play areas (don't give coins to children under three).
2. Provide lunch boxes or paper bags and laminated food pictures or plastic fruits and vegetables for the lunch that a person might take to work.

Role playing. An indoor climbing gym can be used as a ladder when children pretend to be firefighters. The girl firefighter is using a vacuum-cleaner hose and wearing a felt hat (see pattern, p. 468). The boy is using a cardboard tube with rope attached and wearing a real firefighter's helmet. A cut up length of garden hose is also a useful prop for would-be-firefighters.

3. Have tricycles, wagons, or ride-on cars for family members to drive to work or to go shopping.

4. For work-at-home suggestions see home-living centre in the chapter, "Living in Families."

Block-building centre

1. Set out model accessories of community workers and family members and pictures of the job areas being emphasized to encourage the building of appropriate groups and structures, such as families and play people/community workers/women workers—available in catalogues and at retail toy stores.

2. Set out various model toy trucks and machines. Encourage road building and building of structures to complement the occupation(s) being emphasized.

3. Use hollow blocks or large brick blocks and ride-on cars, trucks, and machinery to encourage dramatic play on a different scale. Provide child with appropriate props (see "Basic Resources," pp. 20–23).

4. When spotlighting animal doctors, set out animals (pets, zoo, woods, and farm) that a veterinarian or zoo keeper might care for.

5. Set up a tabletop terrain; see illustration, p. 190.

Other dramatic play centres

NOTE: Suggestions for dramatic play materials to highlight various community helpers have been included in other sections of the book. Should a special visitor, trip, or opportunity make it desirable to use one of those listed below, you will find more detailed suggestions on the pages noted. The "Basic Resources" section on dramatic play props and prop patterns may also be helpful.

1. With a three-way play screen, cash register, sacks, and money you can have a store. Vary the products sold each day, groceries, gifts, hats, shoes (see "Living in Families," p. 185).

2. Doctor, baker, grocer, nurse (see patterns, pp. 22–23).

3. Pilot, railroad engineer, post officer worker, firefighter, ship captain (see Part Six, "Transportation," p. 431).

4. Grocer, truck driver, farmer.

5. Astronaut (see "Air Transportation," p. 450).

6. Carpenter, painter, plumber, gas station attendant (see "Tools and Machines," p. 542).

7. Veterinarian: Set up similarly to a physician's office but have cages and pens to house animals that must remain to be cared for in the clinic.

8. Art museum or art gallery: Make choice depending upon the children's past experience. Let the children plan, arrange, and rearrange their art work in a special corner in various ways. Hang pictures on a line, mount and tape to construction paper mats, or thumbtack to a bulletin board. See kiosk illustrated in "Basic Resources," p. 73, for ideas on how to display wood, paper, clay, and styrofoam sculpture on surfaces or in boxes.

9. Set up a business office: Telephones, small tables and chairs (to serve as desks), typewriter, stapler, paper, paper clips, pads and pencils, ink pads and rubber stamps, envelopes and postage stamps. Be sure to monitor use of staplers and small items like paper clips and elastic bands.

10. Play library: In the Book Centre provide a long table for checking books in and out, file cards, ink pad, and date stamp. Small, stiff stock card rectangles with child's name printed on them can be used for library cards/book cards.

11. Mail delivery route: Set out large brown envelopes with names or drawn objects identifying them to which the children can deliver matching postcards. Provide a mail hat and bag for the carrier to wear. For older children the envelopes and cards could also have addresses for various locations around the room.

Learning, Language, and Readiness Materials Centre

Commercially made materials

(See "Basic Resources," pp. 79, 100, for manufacturers' addresses.)
1. *Puzzles:* A variety of puzzles showing people working. Try to find puzzles that show men and women in atypical jobs. Be sure to include some puzzles that have small knobs on the pieces—for example, Multi-Ethnic Career Puzzle or See Inside Puzzle set, both available from Wintergreen.
2. *Small toys for imaginative play:* A variety of small cars, trucks, and figures that are identified with various types of work—for example Fisher Price Farm, Wedgie Play People, and Community Workers Action Figures (available from Wintergreen). Canada Post has excellent models of postal trucks and mailboxes available in main post offices and postal boutiques.
3. *Toys for riding:* Riding toys that are painted to look like various working vehicles—for example, a tractor, an ambulance, a fire engine, etc.
4. *Dolls and puppets:* Puppets that represent a variety of careers—for example Washable Career Puppets available from Louise Kool and Wintergreen.
5. *Costumes:* A variety of props and costumes that represent different occupations—for example, straw hats for farmers, slickers for fishers, firefighters hats, white coats for doctors and nurses, etc.
6. *Flannelboards and flannelboard aids:* Flannelboard sets that represent different occupations. Be sure to choose sets that show people from both sexes and a variety of races in many positions.

Teacher-made games and materials

NOTE: For detailed description of "Learning Games," see pp 50–59.

1. Name it:
   a. Use community helper models or pictures of people at various jobs
   b. Use hats: police officer, firefighter, baker, nurse
   c. Use tools from various jobs—whistle, stethoscope, rolling pin, empty milk carton, wrench
2. Look and see: Use materials listed in 1(a), (b), and (c)
3. Which: Use materials listed in 1(a), (b), and (c)
4. Alike, different, and the same:
   a. Two people wearing uniforms and one not
   b. One male police officer, two female police officers
   c. Doctor, nurse, and letter carrier
5. Grouping and sorting by association:
   a. Group all those who wear uniforms on the job
   b. Match the tool with the helper
6. Who am I? Describe various jobs mentioning what the person wears and does
7. Listen and hear: Typewriter, hammer, whistle, eggbeater; sounds may be taped and replayed leaving space on the tape for the child to think and guess before final answer is given or not given
8. Let's tell a story: Use a picture of someone at work; choose picture with action to invite imaginative response

Art Centre

1. Play dough: Use rolling pins and baking pans from the home-living centre. Provide baker's hats (see patterns, p. 22). Encourage the decoration of baked goods. Have pictures of cakes, pastries, and colourful food on plates. Children may score clay with tongue depressors, potato mashers, or other utensils.

2. Make a book of families at work: Cut out pictures of workers at various jobs and paste on construction paper. Fasten together or place in a three-ring notebook.
3. Artist: provide a variety of art media for several days. Expand special activities to correspond if class has a visiting artist.
4. Carpenter: Set out carpenter aprons, balsa wood in various shapes and sizes, plastic hammers, saws, and nails with workbench at the woodworking centre.
5. Use various objects and implements to create different painting effects—for example spools of thread, old spatulas, pill bottle lids, old movie reels, and old tools all would create interesting effects if used in place of fingers and paint brushes.

Book Centre

- Capdevila, Roser. *Books About Us Series: Shopping, The City, What We Do.* Willowdale, Ont: Annick Press, 1986.
- Florian, Douglas. *People Working.* New York: Thomas Y. Crowell, 1983.
- •• Gaitskell, Susan. *Emily.* Toronto: Three Trees Press, 1986.
- •• Kraus, Robert. *Herman the Helper.* New York: Windmill Books, 1974.
- ••• Leines, Katherine. *Ask Me What My Mother Does.* Danbury, CT: Watts, 1978.
- ••• Lobel, Arnold. *On market Street.* Richmond Hill, Ont: Scholastic–TAB, 1985.
- •• Marino, Dorothy. *Where Are the Mothers?* Philadelphia: J.B. Lippincott, 1959.
- ••• Morgan, Allen. *Matthew and the Midnight Tow Truck.* Willowdale, Ont: Annick Press, 1984.
- •• Rockwell, Anne. *I Like the Library.* New York: E.P. Dutton, 1977.
- •• _____ . *The Supermarket.* New York: Macmillan, 1979.
- •• Rockwell, Harlow. *My Doctor.* New York: Macmillan, 1973.
- •• Scarry, Richard. *Nicky Goes to the Doctor.* New York: Western Publishing, 1972.
- ••• Schop, Janice. *Boys Don't Knit!* Toronto: Women's Press, 1986.
- ••• Stamm, Claus. *Three Strong Women.* Markham, Ont: Penguin, 1987.
- ••• Tresselt, Alvin. *Hide and Seek Fog.* New York: Lothrop, Lee & Shepard, 1965.
- ••• Udry, Janice. *What Mary Jo Shared.* Chicago: Albert Whitman, 1966.
- ••• Yeoman, John. *The Wild Washerwomen.* Markham, Ont: Penguin, 1986.
- ••• Zaffo, George. *The Big Book of Real Trucks.* New York: Grosset & Dunlap, 1950.

Planning for Group Time

NOTE: All music, fingerplays, poems, stories, and games listed here may also be used at other times during the session as appropriate. See Core Library, "Basic Resources", p. 95, for publishers and addresses. Record company addresses can be found on p. 99.

Music

Songs

From original songs in this book, JoAnne Deal Hicks
"Who's Who," p. 192

From *Sally Go Round the Sun*, Fowke
"Oats and Beans and Barley Grow," p. 14
"Miss Polly Had a Dolly," p. 40

From *Do Your Ears Hang Low?* Glazer
"Michael Row the Boat Ashore," p. 74

From *Piggyback Songs*, **Warren**
"Housework song," p. 36
"To the Hospital," p. 46
"Community Helpers," p. 46
"The Policeman," p. 47

From *More Piggyback Songs*, **Warren**
"The Helpful O," p. 61
"Firefighters," p. 62
"I Am a Fireman," p. 62
"I Am a Policeman," p. 62

From *Elephant Jam*, **Sharon, Lois, and Bram**
"Dr. Knickerbocker," p. 72
"The Muffin Man," p. 79
"Lots of Fish in Bonvist's Harbour," p. 108

From *Singing Bee*, **Hart**
"Pat a Cake," p. 72
"Doctor Foster," p. 41
"Simple Simon," p. 48
"Hippity Hop to the Barber Shop," p. 55
"To Market, To Market," p. 99

From *What Shall We Do and Allee Galloo*, **Winn**
"Tommy Was a Soldier," p. 11

From *Eye Winker, Tom Tinker, Chin Chopper*, **Glazer**
"Shoemaker, Shoemaker," p. 69
"When I Was a Shoemaker," p. 87

Records and cassettes

Bob Homme. *The Giant Concert of Concerts by the Friendly Giant.* (**A & M Records**)
"Seafood Concert"
"Pretty Things Concert"

Bob Schneider. *When You Dream a Dream.* (**Capitol Records**)
"A Computer Man"

Raffi. *The Corner Grocery Store.* (**Troubadour Records**)
"The Corner Grocery Store"

Sharon, Lois, and Bram. *The Elephant Show Record.* (**Elephant Records**)
"Take Me Out to the Ballgame"

NOTE: See also pp. 34–38 in "Basic Resources" for suggestions for music, music accessories, and rhythm band instruments to be used with dancing or a band. When using rhythm instruments let children take turns being the conductor or leader. See also the chapter on "Sound" for a suggested list of records. If you do not own or have access to the records listed, ask a friend to tape segments of music while playing a piano or another instrument. You can use these tapes later with the children.

Fingerplays and Poems

From *Round and Round the Garden*, **Williams and Beck**
"Pat a Cake," p. 38
"Here's the Church," p. 41

From *Don't Eat Spiders*, **Heidbreder**
"The Newfoundland Cod," p. 35

From *Read Aloud Rhymes for the Very Young*, Prelutsky and Brown
"My Father Owns a Butcher Shop," p. 79
"Ears Hear," p. 84

From *Where the Sidewalk Ends*, Silverstein
"Helping," p. 101
"Bang-Klang," p. 120

Stories

The choice of stories on the family or related areas to read to the children should reflect the current interests and experiences of the children. The themes of the stories should cover a wide range of occupations and should include stories in which both men and women are successful and involved in a variety of jobs. Gaitskell's *Emily* describes the life of a famous artist (Emily Carr) and helps children think about slightly unconventional ways and places of working. Scarry's *Nicky Goes to the Doctor* is useful for discussion of doctors and hospitals, especially if one of the children has visited one recently.

Games

(See "Learning Games," pp. 50–59, and teacher-made games in this part of the guide for directions.)
  1. Together, together: Act out jobs; paint a house, write a book, conduct an orchestra
  2. Sally says: Be a painter, a carpenter, a dancer

Routine Times

  1. At snack or meal times play restaurant. Allow children to take turns waiting on tables.
  2. At snack or meal times play flight attendant and serve snacks or meals to passengers on a pretend airliner.
  3. At pickup time play moving van. Have children return toys to shelves using wagons, rolling platforms, or ride-on trucks as vans.
  4. Have the children look for people at work—sanitation workers, painters, crossing guards, road crews, telephone maintenance crews, letter carriers.

Large Muscle Activities

  1. Athletes: Play catch; toss a ball into a basket or toss rolled-up socks into a laundry basket.
  2. Painters: Provide children with pails of water and large paintbrushes. Let children paint the outside of the centre or a fence with the water.
  3. Carpenters: Move woodworking bench and materials outside.
  4. Baker: Wet some of the sand. Encourage children to bake cakes, cookies, and so on, by providing some pans, spoons, and bowls. Decorate bakery products with dry sand, pebbles, and leaves.
  5. Car wash: Provide sponges and pails of water near the tricycles and other wheel toy storage area.
  6. Crossing guard: This is a good opportunity to use safety signs with wheel toys.
  7. Firefighters: Take the firefighter hats and the hoses to be used with the hollow blocks for dramatic play outside.
  8. Garage or service station: See "Ground and Road Transportation." Provide chamois or wipe rags, oil cans, hoses for gas, pumps for air in tires, and old credit cards.
  9. Parking lot attendant: Set aside an area for parking cars (motor toys).

Extended Experiences

1. Take a trip to visit a child's parent at work—telephone operator, firefighter, hairstylist, artist, postal worker, grocer, librarian, manufacturer.
2. Take a walk and look for people doing different kinds of work.
3. Ask parents to visit and to talk about their jobs. Ask them to dress as they would for their jobs and to bring one or more tools they use to share them with the children.
4. Invite someone who comes to the centre on business to talk about his/her job—plumber, meter reader, florist—or tape an interview and let the children guess who it might be. Perhaps a few interested children could be allowed to look through the door of a delivery truck. (It may not be possible for children to enter a Canada Post truck and some other kinds of trucks.)
5. Plan to have letters delivered to children at the centre by the regular letter carrier. Address one manila envelope containing all the notes or picture postcards to the teacher so all will arrive the same day. Let the carrier hand the teacher the envelope in front of the children. Invite him/her to stay a moment to meet the children. Used picture postcards could be recycled by pasting a new message over the previously written note. Choose special cards to fit the interests of individual children. Parents and friends could be encouraged to save their old postcards for your centre prior to this activity.
6. Show a film or filmstrip of a job which would be of interest to the children.

Teacher Resources

Pictures and Displays

▷ Put up pictures of various jobs. Be sure to include both men and women of the various ethnic groups.
▷ Athletes: Display various kinds of balls—basketball, football, golf ball, baseball, tennis ball, bowling ball; Put up pictures of the various professional ball players near the display.
▷ Musicians: Display pictures of an orchestra, a band, and musical instruments
▷ Writers: Display books, magazines, newspapers, paper, pencil or pen, typewriter
▷ See other related parts of the guide—"Transportation"; "I'm Me, I'm Special"; "Tools and Machines."
▷ Display a city scene.
▷ Display coins, dollar bill, bank cheques, passbook, pay envelope, identification card.
▷ See Discovery Centre and Other Dramatic Play Centres for other suggestions.

Books and Periodicals

Amato, Sheila, and Pat Staton. *Making Choices! Women in Non-Traditional Jobs.* Toronto: Green Dragon Press, 1987.

Films and Videos

Check the *National Film Board Catalogue* for films and videos on work and related subjects

Community Resources and Organizations

▷ YMCA
▷ YWCA
▷ YMHA
▷ An employment agency
▷ A service club
▷ Parents
▷ Workers in the community

Government Agencies

▷ Federal Ministry of Labour
▷ Ontario Women's Directorate
▷ Provincial or territorial ministry in charge of labour and employment
▷ Canada Manpower office

Who's Who?
A Question and Answer Song

JoAnne Deal Hicks

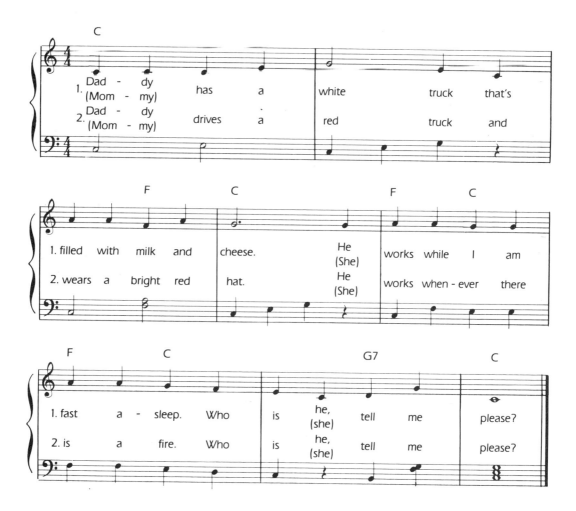

VERSE 3:

Mom-my drives a blue car and wears a sil-ver star.
(Dad-dy)
Her clothes are blue, her hat is blue. Who is she, tell me who?
(His)   (his)   (he)

VERSE 4:

Mom-my wears some white shoes, her u-ni-form is white.
(Dad-dy)   (his)
She helps the doc-tor day and night, who is she? Yes you're right!
(He)   (he)

NOTE: Use with flannelboard figures.

PART 3

Family Celebrations Throughout the Year

★★★

213

Contents

Part Three: Family Celebrations Throughout the Year

Introduction

In Canada, we have many celebrations and holidays throughout the year. In addition, many families have celebrations that are unique to their culture and/or family practices. As educators we can enhance the experience of the children with whom we work by inviting them to bring aspects of their families' celebrations to the school.

Although many celebrations are standard across the country, there may be local variations in the way some are observed, such as in Vancouver, where Halloween is celebrated with backyard fireworks displays, or in Newfoundland, where mummers (people in disguises) visit homes at Christmas. And further, there may be celebrations that are unique to a specific community—such as the Calgary Stampede, Kitchener's Oktoberfest, and Quebec City's Winter Carnival. The Teacher Resources section will provide you with information about a particular holiday or special event in your area.

Each of the three chapters in Part III begins with a "Calendar of Events." The calendar identifies a selection of special events over a given period of months and lists their corresponding dates according to the solar calendar (Western tradition) rather than the lunar calendar (Eastern tradition). Most of these special events are featured in the chapter, some in greater depth than others. Those that are dealt with in depth should be used as models for planning celebrations with children.

When planning your program, it is important to remember that although celebrations may have interesting and important historical roots, some of these may be beyond the understanding of young children. We must, therefore, plan in a way that not only respects the origins of the celebration, but also acknowledges the children's level of understanding. (Remember, there are some religions and cultures that have very definite restrictions on how children participate in any celebration. It is wise to check with parents, perhaps during an initial interview, to ascertain if their family has any specific practices. If they do, then a plan can be devised as to how the celebrations should be handled.)

Furthermore, it is important to ensure that your calendar of events reflects the backgrounds of the children in your program as well as the uniqueness of our country and its regions. Check with the children's parents to see if there are any special holidays or celebrations that they would like to see included.

Finally, there are three basic concepts that children can take away from any celebration:

▷ Celebration is important and fun
▷ There are many different kinds of celebrations and ways of celebrating, all of which are good
▷ There are many different reasons for celebrating

Books and Periodicals

Adler, D.A. *A Picture Book of Passover.* New York: Holiday House, 1982.

_____. *The Picture Book of Jewish Holidays.* New York: Holiday House, 1981.

Allen, G.P. *Days to Remember.* Toronto: Ontario Ministry of Culture and Recreation, 1979.

Barber, Mary, and Flora McPherson. *Christmas in Canada.* Don Mills, Ont: J.M. Dent, 1972. (Read-Tell)

Barer-Stein, T. *You Eat What You Are.* Toronto: McClelland and Stewart, 1979.

Casal, U.A. *The Five Sacred Festivals of Ancient Japan.* Rutland, VT: Charles Tuttle, 1967.

Coffin, T.P. *The Book of Christmas Folklore.* New York: Seabury Press, 1973.

Crean, Patrick. *The Fitzhenry and Whiteside Fireside Book of Canadian Christmas.* Markham, Ont: Fitzhenry & Whiteside, 1986.

Greenfeld, H. *Chanukah.* New York: Holt, Rinehart and Winston, 1976.

_____. *Passover.* New York: Holt, Rinehart and Winston, 1978.

Hirsch, M. *I Love Hanukkah.* New York: Holiday House, 1984.

Ickis, Marguerite. *The Book of Religious Holidays and Celebrations.* New York: Dodd Mead, 1977.

_____. *The Book of Festivals and Holidays the World Over.* New York: Dodd Mead, 1978.

Joy, M. *Highdays and Holidays.* Boston: Faber & Faber, 1981.

Kalman, Bobbie, et al. *We Celebrate Family Days.* Toronto: Crabtree Publishing, 1986.

_____. *We Celebrate Hanukkah.* Toronto: Crabtree Publishing, 1986.

_____. *We Celebrate the Harvest.* Toronto: Crabtree Publishing, 1986.

_____. *We Celebrate Valentine's Day.* Toronto: Crabtree Publishing, 1986.

_____. *We Celebrate Winter.* Toronto: Crabtree Publishing, 1986.

Kehoe, J. *A Handbook for Enhancing the Multicultural Climate of the School.* Vancouver: Western Educational Development Group, 1984.

Kessel, J.K. *St. Patrick's Day.* Minneapolis, MI: Carolrhoda Books, 1982.

Laurence, Margaret. *The Christmas Birthday Story.* Toronto: McClelland and Stewart, 1980. (Read–Tell)

Manning-Saunders, R. *Festivals.* London: Heinemann, 1973.

Montpetit, Raymond. *Les temps de fêtes au Québec.* Montreal: Les Éditions de l'Homme, 1978.

Nicker, B. *Celebrate the Sun.* Toronto: McClelland and Stewart.

Parry, Caroline. *Let's Celebrate: Canada's Special Days.* Toronto: Kids Can Press, 1987.

Ryan, Mary. *Multicultural Festivals.* St. Johns, NB: New Brunswick Human Rights Commission, 1979.

Stephan, B. *Decorations for Holiday Celebrations.* New York: Crown, 1978.

Wernecke, H.H. *Christmas Customs Around the World.* Philadelphia: Westminster Press, 1979.

Community Resources and Organizations

▷ Chamber of commerce
▷ Municipal offices
▷ Tourist board or tourist information offices
▷ Historical boards or associations
▷ Service clubs
▷ Public library
▷ Cultural organizations or associations
▷ Provincial ministries of culture, recreation, and multiculturalism

Native Canadian Celebrations

Canadians are fortunate to have a rich and varied Native heritage. Yet we often overlook this wonderful aspect of our culture or treat it as an eccentric part of Canadian life. It is, therefore, important to include Native people's celebrations in any program that introduces children to Canadian celebrations.

When planning your program, it is important to remember that:

▷ There is not a single Native culture in Canada; rather there is a mosaic of cultures as varied and exciting as the many tribes and groups in the country.
▷ Celebrations in Native cultures tend to be tied to significant events such as births, initiations, marriages, harvests, hunts, eclipses, etc. Most of these celebrations are religious ceremonies.
▷ Native people's celebrations are not as closely related to the calendar year as other Canadian celebrations.

Books and Periodicals

Cambell, Maria. *People of the Buffalo.* Vancouver: Douglas & McIntyre (How They Lived in Canada Series), 1976.

Cass, James. *Ekahotan, the Corn Grower: Indians of the Eastern Woodlands.* Toronto: D.C. Heath and the Royal Ontario Museum (Native Peoples of Canada Series), 1983.

————. *Mistatin, the Buffalo Hunter: Indians of the Plains.* Toronto: D.C. Heath and the Royal Ontario Museum (Native Peoples of Canada Series), 1983.

————. *Ochechak, the Caribou Hunter: Indians of the Subarctic.* Toronto: D.C. Heath and the Royal Ontario Museum (Native Peoples of Canada Series), 1983.

————. *Oyai, the Salmon Fisherman and Woodworker: Indians of North Pacific Coast.* Toronto: D.C. Heath and the Royal Ontario Museum (Native peoples of Canada Series), 1983.

Embree, J. *Let Us Live.* Don Mills, Ont: J.M. Dent, 1977.

Harper, Kenn, ed. *Christmas in the Big Igloo.* Yellowknife: Outcrop, 1983.

Jennes, Diamond. *The Indians of Canada* (7th ed.) Toronto: University of Toronto Press, 1977.

Kirkland Lake Native People's Research Committee. *My People Anishinabe.* London, Ont: Scholar's Choice, 1977.

Leechman, J.D. *Native Tribes of Canada.* Agincourt, Ont: Gage, 1956.

Ridington, Jillian, and Robin Ridington. *People of the Longhouse.* Vancouver: Douglas & McIntyre (How They Lived in Canada Series), 1982.

_____. *People of the Trail.* Vancouver: Douglas & McIntyre (How They Lived in Canada Series), 1978.

Siska, Heather Smith. *People of the Ice.* Vancouver: Douglas & McIntyre (How They Lived in Canada Series), 1980.

Steltzer, Ulli. *A Haida Potlatch.* Vancouver: Douglas & McIntyre, 1984.

Updike, R. Lee, and R.D. Symons. *The First People: An Artist's Reconstruction of Five Native Canadian Cultures.* Saskatoon: Western Producer Prairie Books, 1978.

Community Resources and Organizations

The following organizations should be able to help you find out when and where Native Canadian celebrations are held in your area:

Alberta Native Friendship Centres
10176–117th Street
Edmonton, Alta
T5K 1Z3
(403)482-6051

British Columbia Association of Indian
  Friendship Centres
1617 West 4th Ave
Suite 101
Vancouver, BC
V6J 1L8
(604)738-8412

Calgary Native Friendship Society
140–2nd Avenue SW
Calgary, Alta
T2P 0B9
(403)264-1155

Canadian Native Friendship Centre
10827–144A St
Edmonton, Alta
T5K 1X3
(403)482-7632

Central Okanagan Indian Friendship Society
442 Leon Ave
Kelowna, BC
V1Y 6J3
(604)763-4905

Hamilton Regional Indian Centre
133 King St E
Hamilton, Ont
L8N 1B1
(416)527-5677

Ininew Friendship Centre
P.O. Box 1499
Cochrane, Ont
P0L 1C0
(705)272-4497

Manitoba Association of Friendship Centres
213 Notre Dame
Suite 605
Winnipeg, Man
R3B 1N3
(204)943-8082

Micmac Native Friendship Society
2281 Brunswick St
Halifax, NS
B3K 2Y0

N'Amerind Friendship Centre
260 Colborne St
London, Ont
N6B 2S6
(519)672-0131

National Association of Friendship Centres
200 Cooper St
Suite 4
Ottawa, Ont
K2P 0G1
(613)563-4844

Native Canadian Centre
16 Spadina Rd
Toronto, Ont
M5R 2S7
(416)964-9087

Ne'Chee Friendship Centre
152 Main St
Kenora, Ont
P9N 1S9
(807)468-5440

Niagara Regional Native Centre
219 Church St
St. Catharines, Ont
L2R 3E8
(416)685-9433

N'Swakamok Friendship Centre
66 Elm St
Sudbury, Ont
P3C 1T5
(705)674-2128

North Bay Indian Friendship Centre
980 Cassells St
North Bay, Ont
P1B 4A6
(705)472-2811

Northwest Territories/Yukon Friendship
Centres
P.O. Box 923
Fort Smith, NWT
X0E 0P0

Odawa Native Friendship Centre
600 Bank St
Ottawa, Ont
K1S 3T6
(613)238-8591

Ojibwe and Cree Cultural Centre
84 Elm St S
Timmins, Ont
P4N 1W6
(705)267-7911

Ontario Federation of Indian Friendship
Centres
234 Eglinton Ave E
Suite 207
Toronto, Ont
M4P 1K5
(416)484-1411

Saskatchewan Association of Friendship
Centres
1950 Briad St
Regina, Sask
S4P 1X9
(306)525-0561

Sault Ste. Marie Friendship Centre
29 Wellington St E
Sault Ste. Marie, Ont
P6A 2K9
(705) 256-5634

Society of the Victoria Native Friendship
Centres
533 Yates St
Penthouse
Victoria, BC
V8W 1K7
(604) 384-3211

Thunder Bay Friendship Centre
401 North Cumberland St
Thunder Bay, Ont
P7A 4P7
(807)344-0706

Union of New Brunswick Indians
35 Dedam St
Fredericton, NB
E3A 2V2
(506)472-6281

Union of Nova Scotia Indians
111 Memberton St
P.O. Box 961
Sydney, NS
B1P 6J4
(902)423-8331

Yukon Indian Cultural Education Society
22 Nisutlin Dr
Whitehorse, YT
Y1A 3S5
(403)667-7631

222 PART THREE □ FAMILY CELEBRATIONS THROUGHOUT THE YEAR

Potlatch

Potlatch, a Chinook word which means "to give," is the principal spiritual and social ceremony of the Pacific coastal nations. It is a festival of gift-giving that is held to celebrate the succession of a new chief upon the death of an old chief, an important marriage in the tribe, or a girl's initiation into womanhood or a young man's into manhood. During the celebration there is much dancing and singing that conveys the meaning of the gifts or, if a name is being passed on, the history of the family name and its origins. Ceremonial gear includes hand-carved masks, rattles, and dance screens, headdresses, and totem poles. Some of the tribes that comprise the Pacific coastal nations include the Kwakiutl, Haida, Westcoast (Nootka), Tlingit, Tsimshian, Chinook, Bella Coola, and Coast Salish.

Extended Experiences

1. Masks, rattles, and headdresses can be made in the art centre. To make a headdress, paper feathers can be cut out, painted, and stapled to a paper head band. Plastic mustard squeeze bottles filled with pebbles make excellent rattles.
2. The children can also make special gifts in the art centre to be given during the celebration (see Steltzer under Teacher Resources).
3. Pictures of carved masks, totem poles, and other coastal Indian art can be displayed throughout the centre.
4. Make salmon sandwiches for the celebration. (Salmon and berries are natural resources in the Pacific coastal region.)

Teacher Resources

Cass, James. *Oyai, the Salmon Fisherman and Woodworker: Indians of the North Pacific Coast.* Toronto: D.C. Heath and the Royal Ontario Museum (Native Peoples of Canada Series), 1983.

Johnson, Eve. "Masked Resurrection" in *Equinox.* Camden East, Ont: Telemedia Publishing, July/August, 1982.

Ridington, Jillian, and Robin Ridington. *People of the Trail.* Vancouver: Douglas & McIntyre (How They Lived in Canada Series), 1978.

Steltzer, Ulli. *A Haida Potlatch.* Vancouver: Douglas & McIntyre, 1984. (Steltzer was invited to a potlatch and used her camera to record the preparations for the doings, both the making of gifts and the gathering of foods, and later the potlatch itself—the speakers, the singers, the dangers, and the spectators.)

Powwows

The largest powwow held in Canada each year is the *Kainai Indian Days Celebration* that takes place on the Blood Indian Reserve in southern Alberta. It is held in July to honour the end of the traditional sun-dance ceremony, which gives thanks to the spirits. During this massive powwow, which is open to all Canadians, there are dancing and dance competitions, potlatch, performance art, a weekend rodeo, a parade, a baseball tournament, and a small midway replete with food and merchandise concessions. (One of the food specialities is Indian fry bread.) The dancers specialize in one of three dance styles—traditional dancing, which is a tap-step along the floor in slow stately rhythm; fancy dancing, which is twisting and spinning in rapid beats, blending Native movement with contemporary Canadian styles; and grass dancing, a sacred warrior-society dance in which the dancer wears a special costume that symbolizes grass. Some of the Plains tribes that participate in the powwow include the Assiniboine from Saskatchewan, the Shuswap and Kootenay from British Columbia, and Cree, Blackfoot, Peigan, Sarcee, and Blood from Alberta. It is a celebration of Native Canadian culture and heritage.

Another annual powwow is held at the Wikwemikong Band Reserve on Manitoulin Island in Ontario. The celebration involves four days of tribal ceremonies by several Indian nations and presents Native artisans at work. The summer powwow usually takes place around the first weekend of August. All Canadians are welcome.

The Six Nations Indian Reserve in Brantford, Ontario holds an Indian pageant each year. This is a reenactment of Native history and culture. The annual event takes place throughout the month of August and is open to all Canadians. The six tribes that make up the Iroquois Nations are the Seneca, Cayuga, Oneida, Onondaga, Mohawk, and Tuscarora tribes.

Extended Experiences

1. Water-based paints can be used to decorate the children's faces for the celebration.
2. Masks, rattles, and headdresses can be made in the art centre (see Potlatch).
3. Using a pompom drum, encourage the children to try the different styles of dancing described above.
4. Display pictures of elaborate costumes, headdresses, Native people dancing, and teepees.

Teacher Resources

Campbell, Maria. *People of the Buffalo.* Vancouver: Douglas & McIntyre (How They Lived in Canada Series), 1976.

Cass, James. *Mistatin, the Buffalo Hunter: Indians of the Plains.* Toronto: D.C. Heath and the Royal Ontario Museum (Native Peoples of Canada Series), 1983.

Pringle, Heather. "Ceremonial Circuit" in *Equinox.* Camden East, Ont: Telemedia Publishing, July/August, 1987.

9 Celebrations: January to March

★★★★★★★★★★★★★★★★★★★★★

Calendar of Events

(based on the solar calendar)

▷ New Year's Day—January 1
▷ Orthodox Christmas—January 7
▷ Sir John A. MacDonald's Birthday—January 11
▷ Chinese/Vietnamese New Year's Day—varies from January 21 to February 19
▷ Ashura—sometime during February
▷ Groundhog Day—February 2
▷ St. Valentine's Day—February 14
▷ Basanth—late February or March
▷ Hina Matsuri—March 3
▷ St. Patrick's Day—March 17
▷ Purim—usually in March
▷ Basanta—usually in March
▷ Holi or Basaat—late March or early April

Included in this chapter are an example of a solar calendar New Year's Day celebration, a mainly Western tradition, and an example of a lunar calendar New Year's Day celebration, a mainly Eastern tradition.

New Year's Day

Basic Understandings

(concepts children can grasp from this subject)

▷ New Year's Day is celebrated by most Canadians on January 1st. January 1 is the first day of the solar calendar year.
▷ People usually begin the new year with a resolution that the coming year will be happier and more prosperous than the one just ended.
▷ Many people celebrate the new year by giving a party with food, drink, dancing, and merriment. At midnight on new Year's Eve, whistles are blown, car horns are honked, bells are rung, and people shout "Happy New Year," kiss, and sing "Auld Lang Syne." The

parties may be in homes, hotels, or public places such as Parliament Hill in Ottawa or the local city hall.

▷   Many families celebrate by attending a Watch Night service at church.

▷   Most businesses are closed on this holiday so that people can visit friends and relatives.

Additional Facts the Teacher Should Know

1. The custom of celebrating New Year's on January 1st began in the 1500s when the Georgian calendar was established. It is a solar calendar and is based on the time it takes for the earth to travel around the sun—365¼ days. Every four years an extra day is added to February and then that year is referred to as leap year. The twelve months in our calendar have names, and most were taken from Roman gods. January, for example, was named for the god of doors and gates; Janus had two faces, one looking forward and the other backward.

2. Noisemaking is often a part of New Year's celebrations. This practice goes back to the ancient custom of driving out evil spirits. In Scotland, men and boys parade in the streets and circle friends' homes and drown out the demons by shouting. In Denmark, they "smash in the New Year" by banging on the doors of their friends' homes and "let in the New Year" by setting off fireworks. In Japan, dancers rattle bamboo sticks. In Nigeria, drums beat and ceremonial dances are performed.

3. The Germans believe that the way you live the first day of the year will affect the way you live the others, so the house is made spotless. In Spain, there is a similar belief applied to food. If you eat good food the first day, you will have plenty all year long.

4. Some New Year's customs involve children. In Belgium, children take wafers with raised crosses on them, called "nules," to friends. In Italy, children receive gifts of coins and hang mistletoe on the door for luck. In Switzerland, children play hide-and-seek with their parents and when found shout "Happy New Year." In Portugal, children sing songs in their neighbourhood, for which they receive coins and treats.

5. For young children, the New Year's celebration is often a disappointment, as it is essentially an adult celebration. All the talk and excitement lead children to expect something special, beyond a family or neighbourhood party. For very young children the concept of a new year is beyond their understanding. For most young children the idea of a resolution is also incomprehensible. In your holiday newsletter to parents, it is helpful to include a few New Year's activities for children that can be done at home.

6. Many children's centres are closed for an extended holiday from before Christmas until after New Year's Day. Often little emphasis is made by teachers of young children on this holiday in their curriculum planning because Canadian New Year's celebrations seldom involve children except when they gather with or visit relatives. However, when the children return to school, invite them to recall and discuss how *they* celebrated the New Year's holiday. Through sharing they can learn more about the holiday and begin to recognize that children, and in fact everyone, celebrate New Year's with traditions that are sometimes similar, sometimes completely different, but always very interesting.

Extended Experiences

1. Display pictures of New Year's celebrations, including parties and parades.

2. Display a new calendar. Talk about the fact that it is the beginning of a new year. Children who can recognize numbers can be shown the numbers for last year and for this year, such as 1988 and 1989. Include a lunar calendar, available from an Asian shop or import store.

3. Ask children to tell what they did on New Year's Day. Did they do something special with their family?

4. Read "They're Having a Party Downstairs" and "Mrs. Night" from *Mischief City* by Wynne-Jones in group time. They will help you talk about New Year's, parties and changes in the calendar.

Orthodox Christmas

Many families celebrate Christmas on January 7, if they belong to one of the Orthodox Christian religions. In most cases this is primarily a religious celebration, but it usually includes a special family meal. Check if there are any children in your program who celebrate Christmas on this date. Invite them to tell the other children about the special family and religious celebration.

The celebration of Orthodox Christmas begins on January 6—Christmas Eve—when the first star is sighted in the sky. Usually children will watch the sky for a star and will be in charge of letting the rest of the family know when to start the celebration. The meal on Christmas Eve consists of twelve courses, each representing one of the twelve Christian apostles. After the supper the children will receive gifts, traditionally nuts and apples. The family goes to church at midnight. A procession in the neighbourhood of the church is a part of the celebration of the mass.

Basic Understandings

(concepts children can grasp from this subject)

▷ Some people celebrate Christmas in January. It is essentially the same holiday as other people celebrate in December.

▷ Some children call Santa Claus "St. Nicholas." He is a similar figure but has different names.

▷ Stars gradually appear in the evening as the clear blue sky darkens. We can watch the sky to see how many stars can be seen on different nights.

Extended Experiences

1. Serve a traditional Ukranian, Serbian, Greek, Russian, or Croation snack.
2. If your program runs until after the winter sunset, take the children outside to watch for the first star on January 6 or on a clear evening.
3. Arrange to visit an Orthodox church. The priest can tell the children about Orthodox Christmas and show them some of the special artifacts that are used in the celebration.
4. Arrange to have a visitor come from a local cultural organization whose culture celebrates Orthodox Christmas. The visitor can tell the children about the ways in which children participate in the celebration.

Teacher Resources

Barer-Stein, T. *You Eat What You Are.* Toronto: McClelland and Stewart, 1979.

Burke, M. *The Ukranian Canadians.* Scarborough, Ont: Nelson, 1982.

Chernin, H. *Letters to St. Nicholas.* Association of Ukranian Writers, 1981.

Chimbos, P.D. *The Greek Experience in Canada.* Toronto: McClelland and Stewart, 1980.

Czuboka, M. *Ukranian Canadian, Eh!* Winnipeg: Communigraphics, 1983.

Loeb, L., ed. *Down Singing Centuries: Folk Literature of the Ukraine.* Winnipeg: Hyperion Press, 1980.

Nicker, B. *Celebrate the Sun.* Toronto: McClelland and Stewart.

Stechishin, S. *Traditional Ukranian Cookery.* Winnipeg: Trident, 1984.

Symchych, V., and O. Vesey. *The Flying Ship and Other Ukranian Folk Tales.* Toronto: Holt, Rinehart and Winston, 1976.

Wernecke, H.H. *Christmas Customs Around the World.* Philadelphia: Westminster Press, 1979.

Chinese/Vietnamese New Year's Day

Basic Understandings

(concepts children can grasp from this subject)

▷ New Year's Day is celebrated by many Chinese or Vietnamese Canadians on the first day of the lunar calendar year. In terms of the solar calendar year, this takes place sometime between January 21 and February 19.

▷ The celebration of the Chinese/Vietnamese New Year once lasted as many as fifteen days; now it lasts for only a few days.

▷ The holiday, which has been celebrated for many, many years, begins with a special family dinner on New Year's eve. The dinner includes fish (the symbol for prosperity and surplus), pork, eggs (the symbol for well-being and rebirth), and many vegetables (at least ten in one dish; this dish is called *schu-chieng-tzi* (szhoo-jing-tsi) in Mandarin. Special foods (sweets and desserts) are baked and cooked for the occasion, such as watermelon seeds baked with cinnamon and salt, rice cakes, and dried fruit.

▷ Red is the symbol of happiness to all Chinese. This colour is always used for New Year's decorations, candles, and gift wrappings.

▷ On this holiday, children receive gifts of money from older people, such as their grandparents, parents, aunts, uncles. The gift money is given in red envelopes, often with gold lettering or pictures on them. If grandparents or relatives live too far away, children may find their envelopes under their pillow when they awaken.

▷ Even numbers are considered lucky, especially the numbers two and ten. Therefore, two oranges, tangerines, or apples are often given and eaten on this day. Ten different dishes are often served for the New Year's feast.

▷ Homes are decorated with brightly coloured good luck scrolls or banners that are usually hung in pairs on doorways or windows. These good luck greetings are often written in couplets and hung in pairs on each side of the front doorway (see pp. 230, 237).

▷ It is important to Chinese children and their parents to wear new clothes, especially new shoes, on New Year's Day to bring them good luck.

▷ *Kung-Hi, Fot-Choy* (Cantonese) or *Kung-Hsi, Fah-Tsai* (Mandarin) is the most common New Year's greeting, meaning "Have a happy, rich, and prosperous New Year!" Sometimes children say *Kung-Hi* or *Kung-Hsi*, "I wish you joy" and adults then say *"Sui Hi"* or *"Sui-Hsi,"* "May joy be yours!"

▷ The New Year's holiday usually includes a big parade the night of the first full moon of the New Year. Many firecrackers are fired. A lion dance or dragon dance performed by adults is an important part of this New Year's parade. Children often carry fish or flower lanterns. During the parade, the sound of drums, gongs, cymbals, and fireworks can be heard. It is very noisy and colourful. People cheer, set off fireworks, and tease the dragon, who pretends to bite the teasers. Dragons are make-believe animals and to the Chinese they are friendly beasts and mean good luck.

▷ The Vietnamese celebration of New Year's is called "Tet." This is a time for family reunions and the payment of outstanding debts.

▷ The heads of Vietnamese families light candles at the family altars in remembrance of family ancestors. In addition, food and special papers decorated with herons are also placed at the family altar.

▷ Later in the day fireworks are exploded before a special family meal. At this meal, special foods are eaten—in particular, rice cake.

Additional Facts the Teacher Should Know

1. In Canadian cities with a large Chinese/Vietnamese population (such as Vancouver, Toronto, Montreal, and Halifax) special holidays, festivals, and parades are held every year to which anyone is welcome. All children enjoy visits to these public celebrations. Children may also be welcome at Chinese or Vietnamese restaurants where special festivities are often planned for customers.

2. Many Chinese and Vietnamese refer to an astrological calendar that is a combination of mathematical cycles and symbolic tradition. To record time, the Chinese developed a six hundred-year cycle based on smaller cycles of sixty years each. Within the smaller cycles, each "year" is given an animal's name as well as an element. (According to one legend, the twelve animals were selected on the basis of a cross-country race. The twelve, in order of finish, were: rat, ox, tiger, hare (rabbit), dragon, serpent (snake), horse, ram, monkey, rooster, dog, and boar.) The five elements symbolically connected to the calendar are: water, wood, fire, earth, metal. Many Chinese and Vietnamese call each "year" in this cycle by its animal name, such as the Year of the Horse; some believe that all people born in that year, and other years bearing that name, have traits in common. This is similar to the widespread belief in North America in the signs of the zodiac. The Chinese calendar, like the Hebrew, is lunar, and each month has twenty-nine to thirty days. Every thirty months a double month is added; the calendar does not have the Christian B.C. and A.D.

3. Recorded Chinese culture dates back over 4500 years. It is said that a primitive society on the Asian continent existed as far back as 600 000 years ago.

4. The Chinese New Year begins on *Yuan Tan*, the first day of the first moon, which can occur anywhere from January 21 to February 19. The festival once lasted until the full moon, about fourteen or fifteen days. Each day had its special activities, but today a family or community may shorten the celebration because of work and school schedules.

Chinese Fortune Calendar

Year of **Rat**	1984	1996	**Rat**	1	3	5	2	4	Series of
Year of **Ox**	1985	1997	**Ox**	2	4	1	3	5	elements:
Year of **Tiger**	1986	1998	**Tiger**	3	5	2	4	1	1. metal
Year of **Hare**	1987	1999	**Hare**	4	1	3	5	2	2. wood
Year of **Dragon**	1976	1988	**Dragon**	5	2	4	1	3	3. water
Year of **Snake**	1977	1989	**Snake**	1	3	5	2	4	4. fire
Year of **Horse**	1978	1990	**Horse**	2	4	1	3	5	5. earth
Year of **Sheep**	1979	1991	**Sheep**	3	5	2	4	1	
Year of **Monkey**	1980	1992	**Monkey**	4	1	3	5	2	
Year of **Cock**	1981	1993	**Cock**	5	2	4	1	3	
Year of **Dog**	1982	1994	**Dog**	1	3	5	2	4	
Year of **Boar**	1983	1995	**Boar**	2	4	1	3	5	

24 years of a 60-year cycle;
5 of the series of 12 = 60 years.

Each combination of animal with element occurs only once in a 60-year cycle.

On the Feast of Lanterns, or Feast of the Full Moon, a huge parade is staged with fireworks, gongs, drums, and people dressed in costumes carrying lighted lanterns; the parade features a golden dragon and a lion dance.

5. At one time some Chinese believed their activities were ruled by the *Yang* and *Yin* principle: the positive and the negative, the male and the female, life and death, the rebirth of spring and the dormancy of winter. The noise and the light created on the Feast of the Lanterns are thought by some to demonstrate the *Yang* forces driving out the evil spirits that have accumulated during the past year.

6. The dragon is one of the four divine creatures that the Chinese believe dispel spirits. It is worshipped as the ruler of rivers, lakes, and seas. Its legendary appearance combines the head of a camel, horns of a deer, neck of a snake, claws of a hawk, belly of a frog, and scales of a fish. The dragon is the symbol of goodness and strength and it virtually leads the way into a good year.

7. In preparation for the New Year holiday, the house is thoroughly cleaned, new clothes are purchased, and special sweets are baked. Doors or gates are often lacquered red to keep out evil spirits and to bring the family joy and happiness. Red is the featured colour of this holiday. Five signs of happiness are printed or written on red paper and hung by windowsills and door frames for luck. Two is considered the perfect number, so they are often hung in pairs; poems are written in couplets, double portions of food are served, and two presents are given at one time.

8. Characters representing Chinese words are written from top to bottom and right to left, although now this is beginning to change. If you decide to make a scroll or card with the New Year's greeting *Kung-Hi, Fot-Choy*, be sure to write it in a single column with the character for *Kung* on the top.

	Good luck for the new Spring!	May you have prosperity!	Have a happy New Year!
MANDARIN:	Hsin-chwun-dah-jee	Kaw-ng hsee fah tsai	Hsin nee-an quai loh
CANTONESE:	Sahn chee-un dai-gaht	Gaw-ng hay faht choy	Sahn nee-in fai lohk

9. The industry and science of silk weaving is attributed to the Chinese. They are also credited with inventing the compass, paper, printing, gunpowder, firecrackers, finger-plays, and the use of herbs as medicines. The Great Wall of China is an astonishing architectural and engineering feat. The Chinese have developed the arts of lacquering, calligraphy, painting, printing, weaving, knot tying (macramé), embroidering, paper folding, and paper cutting. They have also made outstanding use of bronze and of porcelain chinaware. We have woven into this guide suggestions for using some of these contributions, which will help the children have a broader knowledge of the Chinese culture.

Methods Most Adaptable for Introducing this Subject to Children

1. A display of Chinese/Vietnamese art or artifacts, such as chinaware, sculpture, jade, rings, greeting cards, paper cuts, silk, fans, masks, Chinese or Vietnamese characters written on a banner, five signs of luck, and firecrackers.
2. A Chinese or Vietnamese calendar that has the New Year date circled.
3. News clippings, postcards, or a coloured portfolio about the Chinese or Vietnamese New Year.
4. Display and show how to use an abacus or chopsticks.
5. Use the chart on p. 229 to determine which animals represent the years in which the children and the teachers were born. (If you can not find the year you need add or subtract twelve to the year in which the person was born until you find a date on the chart. For example, one of the authors was born in 1947. Adding twelve, you have 47 + 12 = 59 + 12 = 71 + 12 = 83. Therefore, he was born in the Year of the Boar.)
6. Following the return of children after our New Year's holiday, talk about their New Year's celebration. Invite a Chinese/Vietnamese parent or student from a nearby university or college to come and make a New Year's treat that the children can eat. Encourage the visitor to demonstrate the use of chopsticks or to share some artifact or treasure.
7. Introduce a game like Chinese checkers, pick-up sticks or the seven-piece puzzle to the children. (See "Learning Games" and talk about where the "seven-piece puzzle" originated.)

Vocabulary

Animals used to name years

Chinese	wind chimes	cake	above
holiday	lunar, moon	banner	fan
lantern	solar, sun	debt	tea
dance	calendar	red	rice
celebrate	parade	tease	jade
festival	almanac	lacquer	incense
feast	first	abacus	chow mein
fireworks	fifteen	embroidery	dragon
firecracker	compass	lucky	chinaware
chopsticks	gong	sign	silk

Chinese words used in English:
　kowtow, to bow down to another person
　catsup (*keh-chop*), tomato juice (sauce for meat)
　typhoon (*dai-fong*), big wind
　chop suey, bits and pieces (miscellaneous)

Kung-Hi, Fot-Choy (Cantonese) pronounced Gaw-ng HAY, FAHT—choy = "Have a happy and prosperous New Year!"

Kung-Hsi, Fah-Tsai (Mandarin) pronounced Kaw-ng HSEE, FAH-tsai (as in sigh) = "Have a happy, rich, and prosperous New Year!"

Kung-Hi (Cantonese) pronounced Gaw-ng HAY = "I wish you joy"

Kung-Hsi (Mandarin) pronounced Kaw-ng HSEE = "I wish you joy" and usually followed by:

Sui-Hi (Cantonese) pronounced soo-ee-HIGH = "May joy be yours!"

Sui-Hsi (Mandarin) pronounced soo-AY-see = "May joy be yours!"

Yuan Tan (Cantonese) pronounced Ywahn Dahn = New Year

Yuan Tan (Mandarin) pronounced Yuhn DAHN = New Year

Hsin Nien (Mandarin) pronounced SYIN nee-an = New Year

Hsien Nien (Cantonese) pronounced SAHN nihn = New Year

NOTE: Chop suey is not a traditional Chinese food. According to one legend, it was first prepared from leftovers for a group of miners in California. It means "bits and pieces." Now it is available in most Chinese restaurants. Fortune cookies are probably a commercialized product, too. Rice Krispies squares or crunchies made from marshmallows, butter, and Rice Krispies or Rice Krispies, syrup, brown sugar, and peanut butter are actually North American versions of an Asian confection called rice puff squares. In Korea and China they are made from rice syrup and puffed (popped) rice. Sometimes roasted peanuts are added to the rice puffs or popped corn to add a nutty flavour. Soybeans are also popped and combined with rice syrup. Sesame seeds are browned and mixed with rice syrup to make a delicious chewy bar.

Learning Centres

Discovery Centre

1. Silkworms in their various stages of development are a fascinating adventure for children. (Some museums and science centres display silkworms.)
2. Examine mulberry leaves. Use a magnifying glass.
3. Display Chinese chinaware, glassware, a *wok*, and chopsticks. Compare likenesses and differences with our own utensils. Notice that the chinaware is transparent when held up to the light.
4. Taste sweet-and-sour sauce and soy sauce. Smell ginger root and star anise. (The latter smells and tastes like licorice. It grows in southwest China on an evergreen tree and the fruits blossom into a star shape.)
5. Examine a block print and show children how to use it.
6. Burn incense so children can smell and experience what it is like.
7. Examine a compass: Let children hold it and move around the room with it in order to watch the needle move. Tell them the Chinese invented it a very long time ago.
8. Experiment with sound: Tap gongs or finger cymbals, bells of various sizes, listen to wind chimes, or hit blocks of wood (see "Sound," p. 141). Teacher might thumb-strike a piece of crystal.
9. Explore authentic Chinese paper lanterns, kites, and paper cuts so children can discover how they are made.
10. Let children examine Chinese scrolls, children's books, silk paintings, paper kites, greeting cards, pieces of jade, paper cuts, banners, fans, masks, costumes, and authentically

dressed dolls. These may be borrowed from friends or purchased from an Asian or import store. This will need to be supervised closely as items are quite fragile.

11. Bamboo pen: Show hole for gluing goat's hair or camel's hair.

   NOTE: There are camels in northern China.

12. Display a tea set from China and one from North America. Look for likenesses and differences.

13. Make egg drop soup and taste it.

EGG DROP SOUP

(Egg Flower Soup)

15 mL/1 tbsp. cornstarch
30 mL/2 tbsp. cold water
1 egg
680 mL/3 cups clear chicken broth
   (can use bouillon cubes or strained chicken noodle soup)

Optional: 5 mL/1 tsp. chopped parsley or scallion to suggest leaves.

Directions:

Pour chicken broth into or prepare broth in a metal saucepan, bring to a boil
Add the water to the cornstarch in a baby food jar, cover with the lid, and shake vigorously
Open the jar and pour the cornstarch mixture into the broth; stir with fork until smooth
Break an egg into a small bowl and beat with a fork
Slowly pour the beaten egg into the broth

Allow children to watch and take turns helping to pour the egg into the broth. Then they can see the flowers form when the egg cooks in shreds as it is dropped into the broth: it sinks and then rises to float on the surface in bud-like pieces. Stir until all egg has been added and cooked; remove from heat, and serve. Make sure each child gets some flowers spooned into his or her cup.

Dramatic Play Centres

Home-living centre

1. Have two separate metre lengths of cotton or nylon with ties attached at each corner to wrap dolls to be carried (on a child's back).

2. Quilted jackets, mandarin collars, frog closings, silk scarves.

3. Provide a low table or cut off the top of a large carton.

4. Tablecloths and tea sets for tea party might be available. (A red tablecloth would be especially appropriate.)

5. Set out place mats of straw or woven paper.

6. Set out chopsticks and bowls on the cupboard shelves.

   NOTE: Allow spoons. Chinese children also use spoons until they are skilled in using chopsticks.

7. Set out plastic flowers in a simple wooden or metal vase.
8. Remove chairs and set out cushions.
9. Include a feather duster, feather hats, and feather fans.
10. Sturdy (or replaceable) lanterns or scrolls may be hung around the room by the children.

Block-building centre

1. Add a Pagoda Tower Builder. Available from educational suppliers.
2. Add boats and freeform shapes of blue construction paper for lakes, rivers, and ponds.
3. Discuss how sailors know what direction to sail when they cannot see the land. Let children use the compass in this centre.

> **NOTE:** An inexpensive directional compass (available at variety stores) makes an ideal accessory in the block centre when children have assembled boats of large wooden and/or cardboard hollow blocks.

4. Post pictures of Vietnamese or Chinese architecture such as the Great Wall of China.
5. Set out animals representing the Chinese calendar years, such as a rat, ox, tiger, rabbit, dragon, snake, horse, sheep, monkey, cow, dog, and boar.
6. Set out proportional block arches.
7. A large rectangular empty box makes a good boat. (For other suggested ideas see the dramatic play sections in the chapters on water and water transportation.)

Learning, Language, and Readiness Materials Centre

Commercially made games and materials

(See "Basic Resources," p. 79, for manufacturers' addresses.)
1. *Puzzles:* Many oriental gift shops have fascinating and inexpensive puzzles that can be used for this theme. Be sure that the puzzles are easy to assemble and contain pieces large enough so that they do not present a choking hazard.
2. *Outdoor toys:* Kites are available in most toy stores and also in oriental gift shops. Be sure to choose a simple kite that will fly easily. There are some very attractive kites with dragon themes that are easy to fly and are relevant to the New Year's celebration.
3. *Miscellaneous:* An abacus.

Teacher-made games and materials

(For detailed description of "Learning Games," see pp. 50–59.)
1. Tic-tac-toe (called "Circles and Squares" in China): Draw nine equal-sized squares on a piece of white or light-coloured cardboard. Give each child five round counters or cubes to place on the cardboard, one at a time, alternately. The object of the game is to get three in a row first. Each child should have a different colour or shape.

> **NOTE:** Children might be encouraged to make their own game if the larger and smaller squares of cardboard can be precut and made available. Teacher may provide commercial sets or make them.

2. Match-them: Make up sets of two each of the twelve animals for which the Chinese years are named. Let children find the two that match.
3. Alike, different, and the same: Use the above sets made in no. 2. Compare other characteristics.
4. I see something red: Each child finds something red.

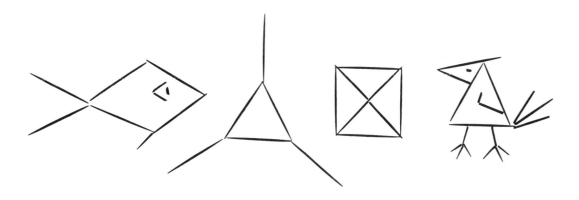

5. Toothpick puzzlers: Arranging coloured toothpicks can be an interesting and challenging discovery. Children may even wish to glue down their creations on a piece of paper after exploring the material on a piece of dark felt or dark paper. See illustration above.

6. Pick-up sticks: A rather difficult game for the very youngest; requires blunt or sanded ends on the pick-up sticks (sometimes available in a thicker stick). Requires great patience. It can be played with chopsticks and is much easier.

7. Seven-piece puzzle: Children fit the pieces together to make a square. other designs and shapes can be made with the pieces. You can make your own out of poster board. For youngest children draw pattern on another cardboard and let them match the shapes to it.

8. Chinese checkers: Older children may be able to grasp the concept of how this game is played. Supervize carefully as marbles may be swallowed.

9. Toteetum: Small cube has a dowel inserted into one end and either numbers or picture characters are painted on each side. The child spins the toteetum and predicts what side will come up. Similar to a dice game of chance. Flipping coins is also a somewhat universal game. Spinning a wooden plate on its edge and predicting which side will come up is still another pastime. These games of chance may not be acceptable by some measures of judgment.

Art Centre

•• 1. Blow art: Older children will enjoy blowing into a straw to shoot or push the paint into a spidery branchlike painting. Give children only brown or black paint. Then by sponge-daubing bright colours on these creations they can be made to look like flower blossoms or leaves on a bush or tree. Blow art sometimes resembles skyrockets bursting in the air.

> ★ **CAUTION:**   Children should be advised to hold the straw above the paper and should practice blowing through the straw.

• 2. Create a picture with shapes: Begin with Chinese puzzle shapes or parquetry.

• 3. Clay work: Relate the beginning of all pottery and chinaware to the use of clay and/or the materials used to make porcelain. Encourage the children to expand their use of clay by making available some simple tools such as palate sticks, cuticle sticks, or coffee stirrers in designing their creations.

• 4. Paper folding: Some simple plans for paper folding appear on p. 236. (Origami is the Japanese term.) Show children how to fold and pleat the paper and let them make what they choose. Simple books of *origami* are available (see Teacher Resources) that may suggest other possibilities.

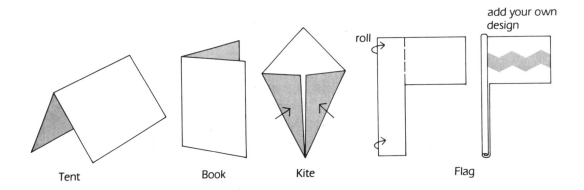

Tent   Book   Kite   Flag

•• 5. Paper cutting: Use after seeing some examples of paper cuts. Encourage the children to cut a picture or explore the use of paper and scissors. Give them paste or glue if they need it to complete their creations. Some may also wish to continue with the use of the materials by asking to paint their cut-outs.

••• 6. Make lanterns for decorations: Use lightweight construction paper (cutting paper). If a piece of paper is 22 cm x 30 cm or 21.6 cm x 28 cm it can be folded lengthwise and cut by slashing along the folded edge. When opened and rolled lengthwise into a diamond-like cylinder, it appears to be a colourful lantern. Wallpaper makes an interesting patterned lantern, although children may wish to colour or paint a plain piece of paper and then cut as described, as the Chinese do. Fingerpainting (monoprint), using crayons, or painting a design on a rectangular piece of paper can also be done. This may be rolled into a cylinder (without cutting) to make still a different type of lantern. Add a strip of paper to form a handle as shown in the diagram below. Two paper cups attached mouth to mouth with paper clips is another kind of lantern.

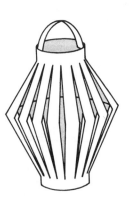 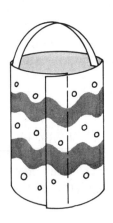 

•• 7. Charcoal and chalk: It is interesting to observe and to discover that if the Chinese ink stick is rubbed in a porcelain dish with a drop or two of water, it forms ink for the brush that is used to write Chinese characters. This stick is made from charcoal and oil mixed into a kind of crayon.

•• 8. Printing: Show children some wood-block designs and prints. Let children print some with blocks that you have made or use those that are commercially available.

••• 9. Weaving: The Chinese are masters in the use of bamboo, rattan, flax, and, of course, silk. Simple weaving may be done on a weaving frame (with rug yarn), or with a slashed piece of paper by lacing other coloured paper strips through the paper frame. Mesh bags or loosely woven pieces of drapery offer still other possibilities for weaving yarn. For a needle use an inexpensive bodkin.

Paper folding
During a celebration of the Year of the Dragon, toys, books, and cards from China are displayed. The woman is showing the children how to make objects by paper folding.

••• 10. Make a good luck sign: Let the children design their own good-luck picture to hang like a scroll.

	Good Fortune	Prosperity	Long Life	Happiness
MANDARIN:	Foo	Loo	Hsiao	Hsi
CANTONESE:	Fulk	Luk	Sow	Hay

Other experiences in this centre using art media

1. Make an Asian kite: Below are several kites ranging from the very simple to the more complex. The carp kite is typically Japanese but the box- and egg-shaped hollow kites are also representative of Chinese kites. They are often made with silk or paper and may be made into many shapes other than fish, such as butterflies, box shapes, and dragons. Note some of the pictures in the books listed in this guide.

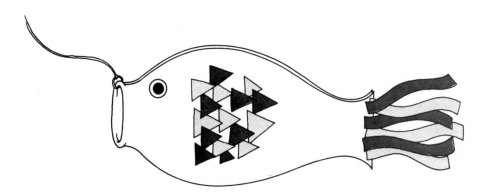

••   a. Carp kite: Cut two matching fish shapes of lightweight paper and glue together along the outside edges to form a hollow fish. Glue a ring of pipecleaner around the mouth edge. Overlay tissue triangles and glue to the body of the fish. Glue streamers to the tail. Attach a string to the mouth so that when the kite is pulled the wind will pass through the fish.

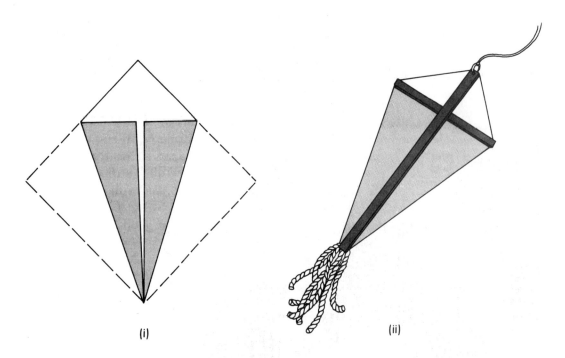

(i)   (ii)

••   b. Paper-fold kite: Use a square of lightweight paper and lay it flat with one corner pointing up. Fold in left and right corners to centre (see (i) above). Add tassels or tails to lower corner. Attach a crosspiece of cardboard or wood for support (see (ii) above).

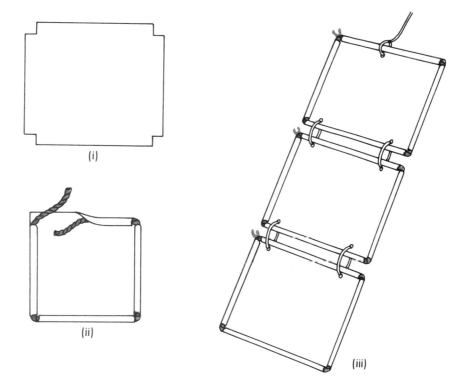

c. Flat kite: Begin with a rectangular piece of paper. Notch each corner as shown in (i) above. Role each edge of the paper to form a tube. Thread one length of yarn through all four tubes and secure the ends with a knot. The resulting shape is square. Punch four holes in the square, two on one side and two on the parallel side. Make several of these squares and connect them by slipping yarn through the holes. Each section of the kite can be decorated. Attach a string to one end.

Carp kites
Directions for making a simple version of these kites will be found on the opposite page.

Book Centre

••• Flack, Marjorie. *The Story About Ping.* New York: Viking Press, 1970.
•••• Handforth, Thomas *Mei Li.* Garden City, NY: Doubleday, 1938.
••• Lattimore, Eleanor. *Little Pear.* New York: Harcourt Brace Jovanovich, 1968.
•••• Lim, John. *At Grandmother's House.* Montreal: Tundra Books, 1977. (Read–Tell)
••• Sendak, Maurice. *Chicken Soup with Rice.* New York: Scholastic School Book Service, 1960.
••• Wallace, Ian. *Chin Chiang and the Dragon's Dance.* Vancouver: Douglas & McIntyre.

Planning for Group Time

NOTE: All music, fingerplays, poems, stories, and games listed here may also be used at other times during the session as appropriate. See Core Library, "Basic Resources," p. 95, for publishers and addresses. Record company addresses are found on p. 99.

Music

Songs

NOTE: Most of the songs that are appropriate for this section are difficult for Canadian children to sing. The Oriental songs in children's song books are often insulting to people of Oriental heritages and their music. Songs of celebration are very appropriate for this section. Songs such as "Puff the Magic Dragon" are very inappropriate for this section, in spite of the fact that it is a good song which may be used for other celebrations such as Halloween.

Rhythms and singing games

1. Use drums and have a dragon dance: Make a dragon head out of papier-mâché or a paper sack; use a tablecloth or a bedspread to cover dragon's body; attach a tail.
2. Play Asian music: Use finger cymbals, tone blocks, gong, bells, or guitar.

Fingerplays and Poems

NOTE: Tell children that the Chinese are credited with using fingerplays hundreds of years ago. Show children how to make shadow pictures using their fingers. For example, make a bird, a dog, or a rabbit.

From *Let's Do Fingerplays*, Grayson
"Old Shoes, New Shoes," p. 18
"Shiny Shoes," p. 19

Stories

(To read, read–tell, or tell. See Book Centre for complete list.)

When choosing stories for this theme, choose stories that introduce new ideas and customs to children who are not from a Chinese or Vietnamese background, but that respect the experience of children who are. Lim's *At Grandmother's House* is an excellent book for achieving this dual goal.

Games

(See "Learning Games," pp. 50–59, and teacher-made games in this chapter for directions.)

1. Look and see: Use animals of the Chinese Fortune Calendar year.
2. Scramble: Use animals of year; also chopsticks, *daruma* doll, kite, fan, Vietnamese picturebook, and so on.
3. I see something red game.

Routine Times

1. Serve rice and chicken, pork or shrimp with broccoli for meal time.
2. Foreign foods are offered in specialty stores or international food sections of grocery stores. Inquire about what is available in your city or community and plan to serve some at snack or meal times.

   NOTE: Expanded travel by business people, students, and tourists has broadened the opportunities for tasting and learning about food that is prepared and eaten in different parts of the world. It has also nurtured an appreciation and a desire in many people to eat these foods as a regular part of their diets.

3. At snack or meal times eat some of the food that has been prepared earlier by a Chinese/Vietnamese visitor or a parent. Observe as the food is made or help to make it.
4. Give each child a double portion or two of everything at snack or meal time since even numbers are considered lucky in the Chinese tradition. Two of anything means double happiness. Two sections of a mandarin orange or tangerine would be especially appropriate.
5. If possible, buy some dried fruits for the children for snack or meal times such as dried apples. One student interviewed remembered a particular octagon-shaped tin that was always brought out for the New Year and the divided sections were filled in with different dried fruits and foods.
6. Play some Chinese music for rest time, or play it as background music when the children are using art materials and participating in free-choice activities.

Large Muscle Activities

1. Flip-a-stick: Children count the number of lengths of their stick that make the distance they have flipped. First to get to an attainable score wins. Actually better just to let each take a turn and continue to practise.
2. Marble game (needs careful supervision): In China, children used to toss marbles, stones, or seed pods into the air and catch them before they fell in a game similar to "jacks." Quite difficult, but interesting to note origin of our game.
3. Coordination games (very difficult): Pat stomach as you circularly stroke your head or vice versa. Have children cross hands and wrists and see if they can lift the finger pointed to.
4. Chinese jump rope (another game with many variations): One variation involves raising the elastic rope higher and higher to see how high children can jump. (Use waist-band elastic.)
5. Paper, scissors, and stone (two can play): On the count of three, both players show one of the following:

Paper will cover a stone	(HAND EXTENDED FLAT FOR PAPER)
Scissors will cut paper	(INDEX AND MIDDLE FINGER EXTENDED TO FORM V, WIGGLE AS IF CUTTING WITH SCISSORS)
Stone will dull scissors	(HAND MAKES A FIST FOR A ROCK)

   The child showing the most powerful subject wins or scores a point.

   NOTE: Sometimes called "cloth, scissors, and stone."

6. Blowing game: By paper folding, children in Asia make little frogs. They place them on a tabletop, and blow them across the table to see whose frog gets there first. If the tabletop can have a ledge made along the sides, ping-pong balls can be blown across the surface instead.

7. Flip ball: Perhaps you have a parent with craft skills. If so, ask this person to make you a flip ball using the instructions in *Folk Toys Around the World and How to Make Them* by Joan Joseph (New York: Parents' Magazine Press, 1972).

Extended Experiences

1. Visit a Chinese or Vietnamese restaurant.

2. Invite a parent or a Chinese student to visit and bring a Chinese treat to share with the children. If the recipe is simple enough and there is no danger involved with hot grease, knives, or cleavers, the children might help to make it. Sometimes part of the preparation can be done beforehand and described to the children when completing the final steps.

3. Children will enjoy learning the skill of manipulating chopsticks. Soup crackers or miniature marshmallows make good items to be picked up and eaten by children.

> **NOTE:** Many Chinese children are nearly six before they can manipulate chopsticks adroitly. Younger children in China are given spoons.

Teacher Resources

Pictures and Displays

1. Note display items suggested in the Discovery Centre. Consult the yellow pages of your phone book for your nearest import–export store.

2. Check with discount stores for toys from UNESCO or toys marked UNIWORLD. Be selective, as some are better than others.

3. Seek out and collect artifacts from your children's parents, friends, or persons who may have travelled extensively. Teachers in the public school systems with a particular interest in cultural awareness may prove helpful. When possible invite them to bring these artifacts so that they can supervize the exploration of them and be available to answer questions about them. See "Basic Resources," p. 71, about visitors in the classroom.

4. Obtain an Asian lunar calendar from an import–export store.

Books and Periodicals

Joy, M. *Highdays and Holidays.* Boston: Faber & Faber, 1981.
Manning-Saunders, R. *Festivals.* London: Heinemann, 1973.
Shepard, S.M. *Asian Food Treats.* Vancouver: Douglas & McIntyre, 1984.
U.S. Committee for UNICEF. *Joy Through the World.* New York: A.O. Bragdon, 1985.
Wyndham, Robert. *Chinese Mother Goose Rhymes.* Cleveland: Collins-World, 1968.

Community Resources and Organizations

▷ Art museums for Chinese or Vietnamese artifacts
▷ Parents, teachers, students, armed forces personnel, or other persons who have lived or visited in an Asian country or who may themselves be Asian
▷ An import–export store
▷ A Chinese or Vietnamese restaurant and its staff

▷ A university group of Asian students who may serve a traditional New Year's dinner or participate in an International Night displaying artifacts and sharing dances, dress, or drama

▷ Other special celebrations, such as parades or festivities planned in restaurants for the Vietnamese/Chinese New Year

Ashura

(A-shoora)

This holiday of thanksgiving is celebrated sometime during February by Moslems to commemorate their joy in Noah and his family's survival of the Flood and the sparing of humankind. According to legend, Noah asked his wife to prepare a special pudding on the day he was able to set foot on land after the flood. She gathered dates, figs, grapes, nuts, and currants in great quantities and prepared the largest pudding ever made. The pudding was called *Ashura*. On this holiday a similar pudding is prepared and eaten by Moslems as an expression of thanksgiving.

Extended Experiences

1. Allow children to play with a toy ark (houseboat) and pairs of animals in the block centre. Place on shelves miniature painted animal sets including models of pairs of farm and wild animals.

   NOTE: Noah's Ark: pull toy, 32 pieces; two take-apart Noah's Ark models (one has 39 pieces). (ABC School Supply).

2. Offer the children an opportunity to make a simple pudding adding any or all of the following fruits—dates, figs, grapes, nuts, currants, and so on.
3. Judy puzzle: Noah's Ark, 19 pieces.
4. A large cardboard box could also be set out for an ark the children may build. Hollow-block ramps can be used to march up into it.

Groundhog Day

Groundhog Day can provide variety and diversion in the middle of winter's dreariness. Legends say that if groundhogs come out of their holes from winter hibernation on February 2 and see their shadows they will return to their holes and we will have another two months of winter weather. If the day is cloudy and the groundhog does not see his shadow then spring weather will come early. Canada's special groundhog lives in Wiarton, Ontario, and is named Wiarton Willy. The town of Wiarton has special celebrations on February 2 every year. Celebration of Groundhog Day could also be a part of exploration of the winter theme.

Basic Understandings

(concepts children can grasp from this subject)

▷ Some people believe that animals can help people find out about the weather.
▷ Groundhogs sleep or hibernate for most of the winter.
▷ Shadows are created when there is a strong light behind a person, object or animal.

Extended Experiences

1. Tell children the story of the groundhog. Encourage the children to check on the playground to see if the groundhog would see his shadow in your area, by looking for the shadows of other children and their own shadows.
2. Provide scraps of brown nylon fur in the art area so that children could make their own pictures of groundhogs with glue and stiff cardboard backing.
3. Serve raw vegetables at snack time as a special groundhog snack.

St. Valentine's Day

St. Valentine's Day is a very commercial celebration, but its theme of kindness and love can be presented to children in a gentle manner that will help them appreciate the people whom they like and love. With the thematic colour for Valentines being red, activities in the colour chapter can also be used or modified for use with the Valentine's Day celebrations. Generally it is advised to spend a very short time on this celebration. A maximum of two days is appropriate. If cards are being given out in the school stress that every child should be given a card. It is helpful to parents to send home a description of the centre's plans for St. Valentine's Day and a list of all the children's names, but emphasize that it is not necessary to send cards.

Book Centre

•• Greydanus, Rose. *Valentine's Day Grump.* Mahwah, NJ: Trail Assocs., 1981.
•• Kalman, Bobbie, et al. *We Celebrate Valentine's Day.* Toronto: Crabtree Publishing Co., 1986.
••• Prelutsky, J. *It's Valentine's Day.* New York: Scholastic, 1985.

Songs

From *Piggyback Songs*, Warren
"The Postman Brings a Valentine," p. 15
"Will You be My Valentine," p. 16
"Valentine Game," p. 16
"Counting Valentines," p. 17
"Three Red Valentines," p. 18
"Heart Hopping," p. 18
"A Red Heart," p. 18
"I Love You," p. 18

From *More Piggyback Songs*, Warren
"Valentines Red," p. 23
"My Valentine," p. 23

From *Elephant Jam*, Sharon, Lois, and Bram
"Skinnamarink," p. 58

From *Tunes for Tots*, Warner and Berry
"Be My Valentine," p. 34

Fingerplays and Poems

From *Don't Eat Spiders*, Heidbreder
"A Million Valentines," p. 32
"Valentine Helicopter," p. 33

Teacher Resources

Joy, M. *Highdays and Holidays.* Boston: Faber & Faber, 1981.
Manning-Saunders, R. *Festivals.* London: Heinemann, 1973.

Basanth
(Buh-sahnth)

Usually this Muslim holiday for the first day of spring (lunar calendar) falls in late February or March (solar calendar) and is heralded by the new moon. It is celebrated in some parts of Eastern Europe and Africa as well as Asia. In Pakistan, Punjabi kites—special, elaborate, colourful kites without tails—are flown on this national holiday. Stout string stiffened or coated with starch and powdered glass allows boys to cut down each other's kites during competitions. Usually kites are flown from rooftops or high hills to avoid trees. Businesses and shops are often closed for the festivities.

Extended Experiences

1. A simple kite might be made by the children (see p. 238.)
2. Prepare and serve a Pakistani treat. See Teacher Resources, below, for suggestions.

Teacher Resources

Humayun, S.N. *Muslim Cookery.* Ottawa: Ottawa Muslim Women's Auxiliary, 1985.
Hardwick, F.C. ed. *From Beyond the Western Horizon.* Vancouver: Tantalus, 1974.
Shepard, S.M. *Asian Food Treats.* Vancouver: Douglas & McIntyre, 1984.

Hina Matsuri
(HEE-nah MAT-soo-ree)

Traditionally, peach blossoms are a symbol of wedded happiness and also of the qualities of mildness, softness, and peacefulness.

Hina Matsuri, the Japanese Doll Festival or Peach Festival, begins on March 3rd. It is a time when peach blossoms are usually in full bloom. Treasured heirloom dolls are exquisitely dressed in colourful embroidered silk costumes and are arranged very carefully on a tier-like platform in a special room or place in the home. Emperor and empress dolls are placed on the top shelf and ladies-in-waiting and their attendants are arranged on lower shelves. On the bottom shelf are placed lacquered miniature furniture and little musical instruments. Peach blossoms are arranged all around them.

The dolls (*hina ningyo* pronounced HEE-nah NIN-GEE-yaw) are highly treasured, and because of the time it takes to produce them, they become almost priceless. They are handed down from generation to generation. During the festival family friends are invited over to see the collections and to have special treats. Often soup, fish, rice boiled with beans, special diamond-shaped cakes, and fruit-shaped candies are served with tea.

This is a special day in Japan for girls. There is a complementary holiday for boys on May 8 called *Tan-Go-No-Sekku.*

Extended Experiences

1. Invite all children to bring in a doll or stuffed animal for this celebration. Tell them the story of *Hina Matsuri* and have a doll festival in your setting, displaying all the children's dolls or animals.
2. Serve fish and rice for lunch. Serve Japanese rice cakes for snack.

Teacher Resources

Allen, G.P. *Days to Remember*. Toronto: Ontario Ministry of Culture and Recreation, 1979.

Casal, U.A. *The Five Sacred Festivals of Ancient Japan*. Rutland, VT: Charles Tuttle, 1967.

Ickis, M. *The Book of Religious Holidays and Celebrations*. New York: Dodd Mead, 1966.

_____. *The Book of Festivals and Holidays the World Over*. New York: Dodd Mead, 1970.

Kehoe, J. *A Handbook for Enhancing the Multicultural Climate of the School*. Vancouver: Western Educational Development Group, 1984.

Takashima, R., and M. Haji. *The Art of Japanese Cooking for All Seasons*. Vancouver: Haji, 1985.

Takata, T. *Nikkei Legacy: The Story of Japanese Canadians from Settlement to Today*. Toronto: NC Press, 1983.

St. Patrick's Day

On March 17th each year, the Irish, Irish-Canadians, and Newfoundlanders celebrate St. Patrick's Day by "wearin' of the Green." This holiday commemorates St. Patrick who, legend tells us, went about Ireland as a missionary, preaching Christianity. St. Patrick also was credited with ridding Ireland of snakes. On St. Patrick's Day, Canadians of Irish origin wear shamrock pins and/or some article of green clothing.

Songs

From *Piggyback Songs*, Warren
"On St. Patrick's Day," p. 21
"Top of the Morning to You," p. 21

From *More Piggyback Songs*, Warren
"March 17th," p. 29
"Leprechauns," p. 29
"Do You Know What a Shamrock Is?" p. 30
"I'm a Little Leprechaun," p. 30
"Leprechaun's March," p. 30

From *Tunes for Tots*, Warner and Berry
"The Leprechaun," p. 35

Extended Experiences

1. Learn about the colour green. (See the chapter on "Colour").
2. Discover that the shamrock is the national symbol of Ireland. (The shamrock is a low-growing plant with three leaves, similar to the field clover that grows in the United States and Canada.)

3. Several weeks before St. Patrick's Day, cut a large flat green sponge in the shape of a shamrock. Dampen the sponge and sprinkle generously with grass seed. Keep moistened and by St. Patrick's Day, it will be covered with green grass.
4. Post pictures of Ireland and help other children find it on the globe. Ireland is called the "Emerald Isle" because its land is covered with beautiful green grass.
5. Post pictures you may have of a St. Patrick's Day parade.
6. Have a parade at music time.
7. Play "The Irish Washer Woman" and let the children dance or move to this fast music tempo.
8. Display the Irish flag or a picture of one. Older children may be able to cut and paste, paint, or crayon one. The flag is rectangular with three equal vertical blocks of colour, which are, from left to right, green, white, and reddish orange.
9. Invite a parent to bring Irish linen, a Kerry cloak, a clay pipe, or a tall hat to show the children. English and Gaelic are spoken in Ireland. Perhaps this parent could teach the children a few words of Gaelic. (Gaelic is a very unusual and difficult language, so the words should be kept simple.)

Teacher Resources

Allen, G.P. *Days to Remember.* Toronto: Ontario Ministry of Culture and Recreation, 1979.
Ickis, M. *The Book of Religious Holidays and Celebrations.* New York: Dodd Mead, 1966.
───────. *The Book of Festivals and Holidays the World Over.* New York: Dodd Mead, 1970.
Kane, A. *Songs and Sayings of an Ulster Childhood.* Toronto: McClelland and Stewart, 1983.

Purim

(POOR-ihm)

For Jewish families *Purim* is *the* festival of merriment. It is an obligation to eat, drink, and be merry. It is a springtime religious festival and comes on the 14th day of the Hebrew month Adar, which usually falls in March. It is celebrated to mark the victory of the Jews in Persia, as written in the *Megillah* (Book of Esther).

The story of *Purim* tells of Esther, a Jewish woman who was married to the King of Persia. Haman, the Prime Minister of Persia, hated the Jews and tricked the king into agreeing that all the Jews in Persia should be killed. Esther heard of the plan and told the king how Haman had tricked him. When the king heard this, he had Haman put to death, and then gave the Jews their freedom. *Purim* is also called the Feast of Lots, because Haman drew lots to see which day would be best suited to enact his sinful plan.

The day before *Purim* is one of fasting. On the day of the holiday, the *Megillah* is read. Every time the name Haman is mentioned, the children yell, stamp their feet, and twirl a noisemaker called a *grager*.

Jewish children today have *Purim* parties and enjoy dressing up in biblical costumes and acting out the story of Esther. In Israel, children go from door to door singing loudly and reciting humourous poems.

Usually money and food are given to the poor. In the afternoon there is a feast with gifts of food for friends and relatives. *Hamantaschen* (Hah-mehn-tah-shen), which are three-cornered cakes with poppy seeds and honey or dried fruit fillings, are traditionally served. Some say the triangular shapes resemble Haman's hat (jailers wore tricornered hats in those days) and others say they are "Haman's pockets" because he had to pay out of his pocket for his wicked plan.

Extended Experiences

1. Listen to a story that the teacher could read or tell using the following book:
   Adler, D.A. *The Picture Book of Jewish Holidays*. New York: Holiday House, 1981.
2. Sing a Jewish song or listen to Israeli music on a record.
3. Invite a Jewish parent to bring a *grager* to show the children or buy one at a Hebrew bookstore.
4. Display different kinds of noisemakers used at birthday parties, New Year's Eve, and Halloween. Also display a *grager* and a *shofar*.
5. Make *hamantaschen* using recipes below, or ask a Jewish parent to bake some and bring for a snack or to come and help the children make their own.

Directions:

Roll canned biscuits to 6 mm thickness
Brush tops with melted butter
Place a teaspoon of the chosen filling in the centre
Pull up the edge to form a tricorner, pinching the corners to let some of the filling show
Brush the tops with honey or beaten egg
Bake on a greased cookie sheet for 20 min at 350°

Fillings:

a. Poppyseed filling:
   Melt 15 mL/1 tbsp. of butter with 15 mL/1 tbsp of honey;
   add 5 mL/1 tsp lemon juice, 115 mL/½ cup ground almonds, and 225 mL/1 cup poppyseeds;
   stir until blended.
b. Dried fruit filling:
   In the top of a double boiler, mix 115 mL/½ cup each of raisins, pitted chopped prunes, chopped dried apricots, and fresh bread or cake crumbs;
   add 115 mL/½ cup honey;
   stir over boiling water until honey melts;
   if too thin, add more crumbs; cool.
c. Plum jam filling:
   Beat together 340 mL/1½ cup plum jam, grated rind, and juice of 1 lemon, 115 mL/½ cup chopped almonds, and 115 mL/½ cup bread or cake crumbs.

Teacher Resources

Adler, D.A. *The Picture Book of Jewish Holidays.* New York: Holiday House, 1981.
Edmonton Hadassah WIZO Association *The Great Hadassah WIZO Cookbook.* Edmonton: Hurtig, 1982.
Temes, S.R. *Welcome to My Kitchen.* Toronto: Temes, 1985.
Weinfeld, W., ed. *The Canadian Jewish Mosaic.* Rexdale, Ont: John Wiley & Sons, 1981.

Basanta

(Buh-SAHN-tah)

This is a spring Hindu holiday celebrated three weeks earlier than Holi. In Sanskrit, *basanta* means yellow, which is the sacred colour of the Hindus. In India, this festival is held in recognition of *Saraswati*, the Hindu goddess of sixty-four arts and sciences and also the wife of the god *Brahma*.

Extended Experiences

1. If you have East Indian friends, you might ask them to share some artifacts with the children, such as a beautiful silk sari, interesting pieces of ivory, silver, or clay, possibly with mirrors embedded in them, or perhaps an exquisitely embroidered painting. Often ivory and wood are carved into elephants. Most young children are familiar with and fascinated by this animal and have seen it in picture books if not in zoos or circuses.
2. At Christmas time, charming clay elephants, bells, and camels made of mirror-faceted clay are available as tree ornaments at import shops. Other such items are available during the rest of the year.
3. Prepare and serve an Indian dish. Consult Teacher Resources for recipes.

Teacher Resources

Hardwick, F.C., ed. *From Beyond the Western Horizon.* Vancouver: Tantalus, 1974.
Nimji, N. *India Today: Traditional Cuisine with Western Convenience.* Calgary: Nimji, 1986.
Shepard, S.M. *Asian Food Treats.* Vancouver: Douglas & McIntyre, 1984.

Holi or Basaat

(Hoh-lee or Buh-saht)

This is a spring festival and the gayest of the Hindu holidays. It usually occurs late in March or early April before the monsoon (big rain) begins. It is on the fifteenth day of the light half of the moon in the Hindu month of *Phalguna*. Children squirt coloured water at each other. Water games sometimes involve teams of participants. Favourite Hindu colours, red, crimson, and saffron are most often used in water pistols or large pumps. In India, wreaths are often made to place around cows' necks or to be hung near windows and doors.

In Bengal, India, gifts are given and preparations made before eating special foods on this holiday, which is connected with Indian worship of *Krishna*, a Hindu god. Coloured powders are used in the festivities. East Indian children who live in North America enjoy throwing confetti when celebrating this holiday.

Extended Experiences

1. A special fun time for young children during this holiday might be to throw confetti, to make simple wreaths or necklaces with coloured paper to hang near doors or windows, or to squirt water at each other when dressed appropriately (raincoats or swimsuits).
2. Children can squirt water and then sprinkle dry tempera on a mural laid on the floor, and watch colours run together.

Teacher Resources

Hardwick, F.C., ed. *From Beyond the Western Horizon.* Vancouver: Tantalus, 1974.

Nimji, N. *India Today: Traditional Cuisine with Western Convenience.* Calgary: Nimji, 1986.

Shepard, S.M. *Asian Food Treats.* Vancouver: Douglas & McIntyre, 1984.

10 Celebrations: April to September

★★★★★★★★★★★★★★★★★★★★★★

Calendar of Events

(based on the solar calendar)

▷ Pesach (Passover)—late March or early April
▷ Easter—between March 22 and April 25
▷ April Fool's Day—April 1
▷ St. George's Day (Newfoundland)—April 23
▷ Baisakhi—April or May
▷ Tango-No-Sekku—May 8
▷ Mother's Day—second Sunday in May
▷ Victoria Day—third Monday in May
▷ St. Anthony's Day—second Sunday in June
▷ Father's Day—third Sunday in June
▷ Fête Nationale (formerly Fête de St. Jean Baptiste) (Quebec)—June 24
▷ Discovery Day (Newfoundland)—June 24
▷ Canada Day—July 1
▷ Memorial Day (Newfoundland)—July 12
▷ Civic Holiday (Manitoba, New Brunswick, Northwest Territories—first Monday in August
▷ Simcoe Day (Ontario)—first Monday in August
▷ Saskatchewan Day—first Monday in August
▷ British Columbia Day—first Monday in August
▷ Heritage Day (Alberta)—first Monday in August
▷ Harvest Moon Festival—August 15
▷ Discovery Day (Newfoundland)—third Monday in August
▷ Labour Day—first Monday in September
▷ Rosh Hashanah—two days in September or early October
▷ Yom Kippur—late September or early October (ten days after Rosh Hashanah)

Historical and Political Holidays

From June 24th to the first Monday in September, there are many holidays that are of historical and political significance for Canadians. Most of these have little meaning for young children and take place on statutory holidays. Try to find out if there are any special activities in your community that would be of interest to young children and make use of them in your program.

Pesach (Passover)

(PES-ah)

A yearly festival, celebrated by Jewish people for eight days every March or early April, Passover is the symbol of liberty, recalling the ancient Israelites' march to freedom from Egyptian slavery, as told in the biblical book Exodus. During Passover, Jews eat *matzo*, or unleavened bread, rather than bread made with yeast. It is eaten in memory of the fact that they had no time to leaven the bread when they fled from Egypt. *Matzo* is made from potato starch and *matzo* meal instead of flour.

On the first or second night a *Seder* (service) is held. At this service special foods are eaten that are not eaten at any other time of the year. Orthodox Jews use a special set of dishes, cooking utensils, and silver at this time, too. During the *Seder*, a special supper is served. A traditional platter is always placed on the Passover table beside the *Haggadah*, the book containing the story of Passover. The platter contains parsley, saltwater, a hard-cooked egg, a horseradish root, a lamb shank, *moror* (bitter herbs or horseradish sauce), and *haroset*, all symbolic in the Passover story, which is recited during the *Seder*. Close to this platter is a white napkin interleaved with three sheets of *matzo*. Two of the *matzo* are used in the ceremony and the third one, called the *afikomen*, is hidden. Whoever finds it gets a reward, and then it is divided so everyone can eat a piece for good luck.

Wine is an important part of Jewish feasts. At the *Seder*, a glass of wine that no one touches is poured for the prophet Elijah, who, the Jews expect, will come one day to announce the coming of the Messiah. After dinner the door of the home is opened and Elijah is invited to enter.

Vocabulary

freedom	*Seder*	*matzo*	cake
Passover	supper	macaroons	fruit

Book Centre

•• Adler, D.A. *A Picture Book of Passover*. New York: Holiday House, 1982.
•• _____ . *The Picture Book of Jewish Holidays*. New York: Holiday House, 1981.
••• Greenfeld, H. *Passover*. New York: Holt, Rinehart and Winston, 1978.
•••• Simon, Norma. *My Family Seder*. New York: United Synagogue Book Service, 1961.
•••• _____ . *Passover*. New York: Thomas Y. Crowell, 1965.

Extended Experiences

1. Invite a Jewish parent to visit the group and tell about the holiday, showing pictures or items of interest.
2. Prepare a Jewish food appropriate to the celebration.
3. Compare *matzo* and saltines: How they are alike and different in taste, colour, texture, and shape.

4. Compare *matzo* and square sandwich bread made with yeast, as to shape, colour, texture, and taste.

5. Compare two glasses of water, one of which has one teaspoon of salt added. Give each child a hard-cooked egg. Let each child dip the egg in the plain water and take a bite, then dip in the saltwater and take a bite.

6. Compare dried fruits with whole fruits if available. Soak dried fruits in water and compare with whole fruits as to texture, size, and taste.

7. Make a compote of dried fruits: Simmer three cups of soaked fried fruit in 340 mL/1½ cups water to which has been added 170 mL/¾ cup sugar, thin slices of lemon, a stick of cinnamon, and 3 or 4 whole cloves tied in cheesecloth. Cook for 20 minutes or until tender. Discard spices and add 225 mL/1 cup whole blanched almonds. Chill before serving.

8. Make Passover macaroons: Beat 3 egg whites until they hold a stiff peak. Beat in 30 mL/2 tablespoons superfine sugar until mixture is glossy. Fold in 150 mL/⅔ cup sugar mixed with 90 mL/6 tablespoons *matzo* meal and 225 mL/1 cup ground almonds or coconut. Drop tablespoonfuls of the mixture on a cookie sheet lined with silicone paper. Bake in 300° over for 20 minutes. Cool and peel off the paper.

9. Adapt the following games as noted:

    a. I see something square: Show *matzo*; look for square things.
    b. Chew, lick, and taste: Use a variety of crackers including *matzo*.
    c. How many? Count prune, peach, and apricot pits.
    d. Match-them: Use prune, peach, and apricot pits or pictures of these fruits.
    e. Grouping and sorting by association: Use items in (d) above.
    f. Alike, different, and the same: Use items in (d) above.

Teacher Resources

Adler, D.A. *The Picture Book of Jewish Holidays.* New York: Holiday House, 1981.

Edmonton Hadassah WIZO Association. *The Great Hadassah WIZO Cookbook.* Edmonton: Hurtig, 1982.

Temes, S.R. *Welcome to My Kitchen.* Toronto: Temes, 1985.

Weinfeld, W., ed. *The Canadian Jewish Mosaic.* Rexdale, Ont: John Wiley & Sons, 1981.

Easter

Easter is the most joyous Christian festival. It commemorates for the Christian the resurrection of Christ. Since this event is recorded in the Bible as occurring at the time of the Jewish Passover, it was originally celebrated at that time. But in 325 A.D., the Council of Nicaea determined that Easter would be the first Sunday after the first full moon which appears after the spring equinox (March 21st). Easter always occurs between March 22nd and April 25th.

Basic Understandings

(concepts children can grasp from this subject)

▷ Easter Sunday is a special, joyful day celebrated in the Christian churches and their church schools.

▷ Many children go to church or attend sunrise services outdoors on Easter Sunday with their parents.

▷ Churches are often decorated with white lilies, a symbol of *purity and light.*

Additional Facts the Teacher Should Know

1. Many Easter traditions and customs come from ancient pagan celebrations. The word "Easter" comes from the name of an Anglo-Saxon goddess, *Eostre*, who represented light or spring. The Anglo-Saxon tribes held a festival in her honour every April. Just as the earth is dressed in a new cloak of greenery, people often wear new clothes for Easter. In Europe, people take a walk through the fields. In America, there are Easter parades. Probably this custom originated with Emperor Constantine, who had his leaders don their most elegant robes on Easter to honour Christ's resurrection. There was an old belief that if a person wore a new article of clothing for the first time on Easter, he or she would surely have luck for the rest of the year.

2. The legend of the Easter bunny is definitely not religious. The legendary Easter rabbit or bunny, after a long winter nap, is supposed to hide brightly coloured eggs in the new green grass. He may bring dyed eggs, wooden eggs, even fancy sugar eggs. The idea of Easter eggs came to us from ancient Egypt and Persia. The eggs are a sign of new life. Newly hatched chicks and ducklings and baby rabbits are also associated with spring.

3. Except for the association of Easter and what it means to Christians, with the potential for a new beginning, most child-related activities, including the Easter bunny, are not religiously oriented to this holiday.

Book Centre

••• Adams, A. *The Easter Egg Artisto.* New York: Scribner, 1976.
••• Friedisch, P. *The Easter Bunny That Overslept.* New York: Lothrop, Lee and Shepard, 1957.
•• Shaugnessy, Maureen. *We Celebrate Easter.* Toronto: Crabtree Publishing, 1985.
••• Williams, Margery. *The Velveteen Rabbit.* New York: Messner, 1983.

Songs

From *Singing Bee*, Hart
"Hot Cross Buns," p. 140
"The Easter Bunny," p. 141

From *A Treasury of Songs for Children*, Glazer
"Hot Cross Buns," p. 122

From *Piggyback Songs*, Warren
"The Bunny Patch," p. 24
"Did You Ever See a Bunny?" p. 24
"Easter Bunny Hippity Hop," p. 25
"Down the Bunny Trail," p. 25

From *More Piggyback Songs*, Warren
"Did You Ever See a Bunny?" p. 31
"Easter Bunny," p. 31

From *Tunes for Tots*, Warner and Berry
"I Wish I Was a Bunny," p. 37
"Easter Morning," p. 38

Fingerplays and Poems

From *Hand Rhymes*, Brown
"Little Bunny," p. 21

Teacher Resources

Joy, M. *Highdays and Holidays.* Boston: Faber & Faber, 1981.
Manning-Saunders, R. *Festivals.* London: Heinemann, 1973.
Patterson, L. *A Holiday Book for Easter.* Champaign, IL: Garrard Pub. Co., 1966.
Stephan, B. *Decorations for Holiday Celebrations.* New York: Crown, 1978.

April Fool's Day

April 1st is known as April Fool's Day, or All Fools' Day. No one knows how it began, but it is the day people like to play tricks on one another. For example, someone ties a string to a wallet and hides out of sight. When someone else comes along and tries to pick it up, the person holding the string jerks the wallet out of reach and yells, "April Fool." Also, one may be tricked into believing something is true when it is not, such as saying to someone, "You have a red spot on your chin!" When the person goes to the mirror to see for himself/herself, you say, "April Fool!"

In France, a person who has a joke played on him or her is called an "April fish" (*poisson d'Avril*), and in Scotland, this person is referred to as an April *gowk*. A *gowk* is a word of Scandinavian origin meaning a fool or simpleton.

The kind of humour involved in April fool jokes is best understood by the older child. Some four- and five-year-olds can begin to understand this kind of humour.

Teacher Resources

Joy, M. *Highdays and Holidays.* Boston: Faber & Faber, 1981.
Manning-Saunders, R. *Festivals.* London: Heinemann, 1973.

Baisakhi

(Bi-e-SAH-kee)

In India, the Hindu New Year, *Baisakhi*, comes in April or May. Hindus believe that bathing in the Ganges will protect them from evil. Then they go to the temple and listen to the reading of the calendar of the New Year. Women and girls wear colourful saris on this day. Elaborate feasts are held; gifts are exchanged, prayers are offered to family gods.

Extended Experiences

1. Display pictures or artifacts from India.
2. Invite a mother or student to show the children how to wrap a sari.
3. Ask the parent or student if they would play the sitar, bells, cymbals, or tabla for the children.

Teacher Resources

Hardwick, F.C., ed. *From Beyond the Western Horizon.* Vancouver: Tantalus, 1974.
Nimji, N. *India Today: Traditional Cuisine with Western Convenience.* Calgary: Nimji, 1986.
Shepard, S.M. *Asian Food Treats.* Vancouver: Douglas & MacIntyre, 1984.

Tan-Go-No-Sekku

(Tahn-goh-noh-seh-koo)

This holiday is celebrated on May 8th. Historically this was a day to celebrate military strength and to expel the evil spirits that caused poverty and misfortune. Today it is a day to celebrate the beginning of summer weather and the warmth and good crops that it brings. Japanese boys fly kites, fight mock battles with swords made of iris leaves and display puppets. This is a special day in Japan for boys. There is a complementary holiday for girls on March 3 called *Hina Matsuri.*

Extended Experiences

1. Set up a white sheet on a curtain rod and shine a bright light on the sheet from behind. Show the children how shapes can be seen as shadows on the screen. Provide them with bristol board, scissors, and sticks to assemble shapes to be used as shadow puppets behind the sheet. They can stand behind the screen and move their puppets in time to music, while other children and teachers watch.
2. Serve fish and rice for lunch. Serve Japanese rice cakes for a snack.
3. Make and fly carp kites. Instructions are on p. 238 in the section on Chinese/Vietnamese New Year's celebrations.

Teacher Resources

Allen, G.P. *Days to Remember.* Toronto: Ontario Ministry of Culture and Recreation, 1979.

Casal, U.A. *The Five Sacred Festivals of Ancient Japan.* Rutland, VT: Charles Tuttle, 1967.

Ickis, M. *The Book of Religious Holidays and Celebrations.* New York: Dodd Mead, 1966.

_____. *The Book of Festivals and Holidays the World Over.* New York: Dodd Mead, 1970.

Kehoe, J. *A Handbook for Enhancing the Multicultural Climate of the School.* Vancouver: Western Educational Development Group, 1984.

Takashima, R., and M. Haji. *The Art of Japanese Cooking for All Seasons.* Vancouver: Haji, 1985.

Takata, T. *Nikkei Legacy: The Story of Japanese Canadians from Settlement to Today.* Toronto: NC Press, 1983.

Mother's Day

Mother's Day is an important family celebration, to which teachers can contribute. In the week preceding Mother's Day, which is celebrated on the second Sunday in May, it is appropriate to sing songs about mothers, prepare small gifts, and read stories about mothers.

It is essential to be sensitive to the needs of children who do not live with their mothers or whose mothers are dead. Try to find out if their is any mother figure for whom the child would like to prepare a special card or gift or suggest that they can do something special for their father on this day.

Songs

From *Piggyback Songs,* Warren
"I Love You," p. 18

From *Elephant Jam*, Sharon, Lois, and Bram
"Skinnamarink," p. 58

From *Tunes for Tots*, Warner and Berry
"Mother," p. 39

NOTE: These songs are easy to learn. Children enjoy learning the songs to sing to their mothers on Mother's Day.

Victoria Day

Victoria Day, which takes place every third Monday in May, is a holiday of historical importance for many Canadians, but it does not have great meaning for young children. For children it is usually important because of neighbourhood and community fireworks displays and because it is the beginning of many summer activities. (For example, many Canadians will begin to plant their gardens after the Victoria Day holiday.) It is useful to talk about fireworks and how they can be fun if they are used safely.

Extended Experiences

This is a good time to begin planting a garden inside or outside your centre (see the Teacher Resources).

Teacher Resources

Chickadee magazine.
Hardy, Ralph, et al. *The Weather Book.* Toronto: Little, Brown, 1982.
Owl magazine.

Father's Day

Father's Day, which takes place on the third Sunday in June, is an important family celebration, to which teachers can contribute. In the week preceding Father's Day, it is appropriate to sing songs about fathers, prepare small gifts, and read stories about fathers.

It is essential to be sensitive to the needs of children who do not live with their fathers or whose fathers are dead. Try to find out if there is any father figure for whom the child would like to prepare a special card or gift or suggest that they can do something special for their mother on this day.

Songs

From *More Piggyback Songs*, Warren
"Happy Father's Day," p. 36
"Where's Daddy?" p. 36

From *Elephant Jam*, Sharon, Lois, and Bram
"Skinnamarink," p. 58

NOTE: These songs are easy to learn. Children enjoy learning the songs to sing to their fathers on Father's Day.

Harvest Moon Festival

This festival is held on August 15th, or in the middle of the eighth month of the lunar calendar. Traditionally this is a Chinese festival, but it is also celebrated by other Asians as a time of thanksgiving for the harvest of summer crops. According to legend this is also the moon's birthday. The moon on this night is considered to be the largest and fullest of the year. Specially decorated moon cakes are baked of pale yellow flour. Round fruits, such as oranges, are arranged on four plates that surround a fifth plate on which moon cakes are placed. Red candles and incense are burned and music is played everywhere. The holiday lasts for three days.

Extended Experiences

1. Invite an Asian parent to make moon cakes as a special treat, or to assist and supervize the children in preparing them, or purchase moon cakes at a Chinese bakery.
2. Serve oranges and moon cakes for a snack, arranging them as described. Pre-peel oranges.
3. Burn incense and play recordings of Asian music.
4. Make night and day pictures using chalk, gummed moon and star shapes, white paint on dark paper (see "Day and Night," p. 503).

Rosh Hashanah
(ROHSH-hah-shah-nah)

The Jewish New Year, *Rosh Hashanah*, is celebrated on two days in September or early October. The day is marked by the blowing of the *shofar* (ram's horn) calling the people to prayer. The *shofar* was blown when the people were called together to be told of the Ten Commandments by Moses. It is the opening of the most important time of the Jewish religious year, the ten-day period leading to the Day of Atonement, called *Yom Kippur* (YOHM-kip-POOR).

At sundown on New Year's Eve the family eats a special meal. The *challah* (bread) for this meal is shaped like a ladder symbolizing prayers ascending to God on its rungs or indicating that people can go up or down in the world, the choice depends on them. However, the twisted-shaped (braided) *challahs* (plural) are eaten on the Sabbath as well as on other Jewish holidays.

On this day, by tradition, the life of every person is judged by the Lord and is written in the Book of Life or the Book of Death. Therefore, it is the custom for friends to greet each other with the words, "May your life be inscribed for a happy New Year" or "May a good year be recorded for you." The ten days starting with *Rosh Hashanah* are known as the "days of repentance." It is a time to examine one's deeds for the last twelve months and resolve to do better. Those who are truly sorry can ask God's forgiveness and thereby be inscribed in the Book of Life on *Yom Kippur.* During the "days of repentance" Jews call on those they have wronged and ask for forgiveness.

Extended Experiences

1. Eat apple wedges dipped in honey. Talk about sweet things. Taste some. Talk about sour things. Taste some. (See the chapter on "Taste").

2. Buy a loaf of *challah* bread. It is usually a special braid-shaped loaf eaten by families on the Sabbath and other special holidays, but may now be available in the shape of a ladder or round loaves that are more customary during this holiday. If neither is available, ask a Jewish friend or parent to bake several small loaves of the different shapes for you to share with the children.

3. Taste *tayglach* (honey balls) or honey cake made by a Jewish parent or a bakery. Make cans of cinnamon, ginger, allspice, and nutmeg available for the children to smell. Have the children guess which one is in the honey balls by smelling and tasting.

4. Record the sound of the *shofar* (difficult to play) on a tape recorder as well as the sounds of other kinds of horns—(car, trumpet, tuba, French horn. Have pictures of instruments, or real ones, to show as you play the tape. When children are familiar with the sounds play the tape without the pictures and let the children guess which is which.

5. Read or tell either of the following stories:
   •• Adler, D.A. *The Picture Book of Jewish Holidays.* New York: Holiday House, 1981.
   ••• Cone, Molly. *The Jewish New Year.* New York: Thomas Y. Crowell, 1966.

6. Invite a Jewish parent to visit and tell about *Rosh Hashanah.* Bring a *shofar* to blow.

7. Visit a synagogue and see the *shofar* there.

Teacher Resources

Adler, D.A. *The Picture Book of Jewish Holidays.* New York: Holiday House, 1981.

Edmonton Hadassah WIZO Association. *The Great Hadassah WIZO Cookbook.* Edmonton: Hurtig, 1982.

Temes, S.R. *Welcome to My Kitchen.* Toronto: Temes, 1985.

Weinfeld, W., ed. *The Canadian Jewish Mosaic.* Rexdale, Ont: John Wiley & Sons, 1981.

Yom Kippur

(YOHM-kip-poor)

Yom Kippur is the holiest day of the Jewish year. It is reverently called "The Sabbath of Sabbaths" and occurs 10 days after *Rosh Hashanah.*

Nine days after *Rosh Hashanah* is the "Day of Atonement," which is marked by twenty-four hours of prayer, fasting, and asking God to forgive sins. At sundown the night before *Yom Kippur* the family gathers for a festival meal. Candles are lit (one is in memory of departed ones) and the family members ask each other to forgive any wrongdoings. After the meal the family goes to the synagogue to pray. White, symbol of purity, is worn by the officials and white cloths cover the altar and the Ark, the holy chest which holds the scrolls of the *Torah,* a part of Jewish sacred scriptures. The men and boys wear white skull caps. Often white flowers are placed on the altar. From early morning the next day until sundown a service is held at the synagogue. People fast, pray, and ask God's forgiveness. At sundown a *shofar* (ram's horn) is blown, marking the closing of the gates of judgment for another year.

Extended Experiences

1. Read or tell the following story:
   •• Adler, D.A. *The Picture Book of Jewish Holidays.* New York: Holiday House, 1981.

2. Invite a Jewish parent to visit and tell about *Yom Kippur.* Bring a *shofar* to blow.

3. Visit a synagogue and see the *shofar* there.

Teacher Resources

Adler, D.A. *The Picture Book of Jewish Holidays.* New York: Holiday House, 1981.

Edmonton Hadassah WIZO Association *The Great Hadassah WIZO Cookbook.* Edmonton: Hurtig, 1982.

Temes, S.R. *Welcome to My Kitchen.* Toronto: Temes, 1985.

Weinfeld, W., ed. *The Canadian Jewish Mosaic.* Rexdale, Ont: John Wiley & Sons, 1981.

11 Celebrations: October to December

★★★★★★★★★★★★★★★★★★★★★

Calendar of Events

(based on the solar calendar)

▷ Sukkot—in September or October
▷ Thanksgiving—second Monday in October
▷ Harvest Home Festival—October 15
▷ Halloween—October 31
▷ Remembrance Day—November 11
▷ Shichigosan—November 15
▷ Hanukkah—early December
▷ Christmas—December 25
▷ Boxing Day—December 26
▷ Kwanzaa—from December 26 to January 1

Sukkot

(SOO-cot)

Sukkot, a Jewish holiday observed in September or October, celebrates the harvest and commemorates the forty-year period after the Exodus from Egypt, during which the Jews wandered in the wilderness and lived in huts made of branches. A hut or a booth called *sukkah* (succah) is built of boards or canvas in the garden near the house or at the synagogue. The top of the *sukkah* is made of pine branches through which the stars can shine at night. Flowers, vegetables, and fruits are woven into the branches or hung by children in the hut for decoration. During the festival, as many meals as possible are eaten in the *sukkah* and always include harvest fruits and vegetables. "Apple slice" and rolled strudel are frequently served. It is customary to invite guests, especially those who do not have a *sukkah* of their own. Some people like to sleep in the *sukkah* at night. *Sukkot* is celebrated for eight days by Orthodox and Conservative Jews both in and outside of Israel. On the last day of *Sukkot*, Jews thank God for the *Torah* in a ceremony called *Simhat Torah* ("rejoicing in the law"). Although associated with *Sukkot*, this is actually a separate holiday that comes after *Sukkot*. The sacred scrolls of the *Torah* are taken from the ark and carried around the synagogue. Everyone joins in. Boys and girls carry flags. On top of the flagstaffs are candles in hollowed-out apples. After the parade, the children are given nuts and candies.

NOTE: "Apple slice" is a baked dough with apples like a strudel.

Extended Experiences

1. See the Discovery Centre and Learning Language Centre sections for the Thanksgiving and harvest celebrations for suggestions on activities involving apples, nuts, and other harvest foods.
2. Taste Jewish "apple slice" or rolled strudel.
3. Children might enjoy building a *sukkah* out of a large refrigerator cardboard box. Cut a door in one side and wide slits in the roof to appear like slats so that children can look up through the roof. Plastic flowers, fruits, vegetables, branches, and leaves can be placed on the roof. Snacks of raisins, nuts, and citrus fruits can be eaten inside.
4. Add the following books to your book centre to read–tell at storytime:

• • • •   Edelman, Lily. *The Sukkah and The Big Wind.* New York: United Synagogue Book Service, 1956.

• • • •   Morrow, Betty, and Lewis Hartman. "Sukkot, A Double Thanksgiving," in *Jewish Holidays.* Champaign, IL: Garrard, 1967, pp. 33–45.

• • • •   Simon, Norma. *Our First Sukkah.* New York: United Synagogue Book Service, 1959.

• • • •   _____. *Simhat Torah.* New York: United Synagogue Book Service, 1960.

Thanksgiving

Basic Understandings

(concepts children can grasp from this subject)

▷   It is a celebration of the end of a harvest.
▷   In the fall some of the fruits and vegetables harvested include pumpkins, apples, and nuts.
▷   A family celebrates the end of the harvest with a special Thanksgiving dinner. The dinner usually includes a roasted turkey and pumpkin pie.
▷   In the pioneer days, native families and pioneer families sometimes celebrated together and shared the food they harvested.

Additional Facts the Teacher Should Know

1. The Thanksgiving celebration has its roots in Britain where it was common to hold holidays of thanksgiving for any number of things, not only a bountiful harvest.
2. According to the *Canadian Encyclopedia,* the very first Thanksgiving in the New World was celebrated in Newfoundland by explorer Martin Frobisher in 1578. He and his ship's crew gave thanks for having survived their dangerous venture into the Hudson Strait while in search of a northwest passage to China.
3. The first annual Thanksgiving Day was proclaimed by the Canadian Parliament on November 6, 1879 as "a bountiful harvest with which Canada has been blessed."
4. In 1957, Parliament permanently fixed the second Monday in October as Canada's day for Thanksgiving.

5. The first Thanksgiving celebration in the United States took place in 1621 at Plymouth. There, fifty-one Pilgrims and ninety-one Natives of the Wampanoag tribe shared deer meat and popcorn with maple syrup. The celebration lasted for three days, during which the people ran races, had wrestling matches, paraded their warrior/soldiers, and played games like stool ball—a type of croquet.

Methods Most Adaptable for Introducing this Subject to Children

1. Thanksgiving provides an opportunity to look at pioneer life. Rural teachers can celebrate the joys of life in a rural community with the children. Urban teachers can use this as an opportunity to introduce children to the satisfactions of life in a farming community. It is an ideal time to celebrate the importance of Canadian farmers for all Canadians.
2. Present a puppet show or flannelboard story of the first Thanksgiving.
3. Learn a Thanksgiving song.
4. Ask the children what they are thankful for.
5. Display pictures of pioneers, harvests, and Thanksgiving feasts.
6. Display a cornucopia with real or artificial gourds, vegetables, and fruits.

Vocabulary

Thanksgiving	harvest	feast	cranberry
give thanks	fruit	dinner	harvest
cornucopia	vegetable	food	pumpkin
pioneers	farm	tractor	crops
log cabin	apple	turkey	

Learning Centres

Discovery Centre

1. Examine turkey feathers and eggs. Note how they differ from those of a chicken. Scramble two turkey eggs.
2. Vegetable dyeing: Dip pieces of white cloth or white turkey feathers into solutions made by boiling the following plants in water and allowing to cool. Turkey feathers are available from some craft stores, butchers, and poultry farms.

goldenrod stalks and flowers—yellow	spinach leaves—green
sumac leaves—yellow-brown	blackberries—blue
onion skins—yellow or red	sunflower seeds—blue
beets—red violet	hickory bark—brown
dandelion roots—magenta	walnut hulls—brown
rhubarb leaves—light green	cranberries—pink or red

NOTE: If supervision is minimal, boil solutions in advance. If turkey feathers are used, wash them first in soap and water to remove oil. Rinse.

3. Cooking: Prepare a food with the children that is related to Thanksgiving, using the recipes from your favourite cookbook. Make cranberry salad, Waldorf salad, popcorn balls, pumpkin pie, or pumpkin muffins. Bake potatoes. Use watercress or leeks in snacks or salads.
4. Examine dried fruits: Show samples of fresh grapes and raisins (include other fruits, such as apples, peaches, plums, and apricots, if available). What happens if raisins are put in water? What happens if grapes are put in the sun to dry?
5. Set out an ear of corn. Shell. Let children pop, butter, and salt the corn.

Dramatic Play Centres

Home-living centre

1. Set out artificial fruit and vegetables. Encourage preparation of a big feast. Teacher may mount pictures of turkeys, potatoes, or pie on heavy cardboard or cut food sections from TV dinner boxes for children to use in preparing a Thanksgiving dinner.
2. Baking: Provide play dough, rolling pins, cookie cutters, and child-size pans or aluminum pot-pie pans for baking pies, cookies, or bread.
3. Dress-up clothes: Add types used by early settlers—ankle-length skirts, plain white aprons, pellon collars, dark dresses, long-sleeved shirts, and black jackets.

Block-building centre

1. Encourage children to build houses to play in and to play families coming for a Thanksgiving Day visit.
2. Transportation toys: Trains, planes, buses that bring visiting grandparents.
3. Build farms: set out animals, tractors, trucks. Provide spools, small rocks, and other small articles for crops to harvest and take to the market.
4. Toy logs: Older children may build log cabins. Flexible plastic and rubber family figures can be dressed in pioneer or Native Canadian clothing made from felt and imitation leather if teachers have skill and time.

Learning, Language, and Readiness Materials Centre

NOTE: See also the chapter on "Fall" for other appropriate materials related to harvest.

Teacher-made games and materials

NOTE: For detailed description of "Learning Games," see pp. 50–59.

1. Name it: Identify fruits and vegetables and other Thanksgiving symbols
2. Look and see: Use fall fruits and vegetables or other reminders of Thanksgiving
3. Reach and tell: Use fruits, vegetables, or Thanksgiving symbols
4. Sniff and smell: Use fruits and vegetables (see chapter on "Smell")
5. Chew, lick, and taste: Use fruits, vegetables (see chapter on "Taste")
6. Match-them: Use real objects or make cards using decorative seals
7. Grouping and sorting by association: Use matching cards made for "match-them" or real fruits and vegetables to mix and sort
8. Alike, different, and the same: Use the picture cards or real objects. Set out two that are alike and one that is different; for instance, two green apples and one red. Vary the size, such as two big pumpkins and one small one
9. How many? Count real objects or use pictures or flannel cut-outs
10. Count turkeys, pumpkins, pioneers
11. Make designs on small cards to be reproduced by matching with parquetry blocks

Art Centre

- 1. Sand drawing and painting: Show the children how to smooth sand in a sandbox or tray using a long flat stick and then how to draw with a round stick or a finger in the smooth sand. Sand can also be washed and dried in an oven, mixed with dry tempera, and placed in shaker dispensers to be used in sand painting on a surface. After the children have drawn a picture with glue on lightweight cardboard or stiff paper, they can sprinkle on sand from the shakers. Let dry, then turn upside down and tap to remove excess sand.

•• 2. Texture designs can be made by children, crayoning on newsprint over precut shapes of sandpaper or corrugated cardboard. Other textures can be introduced by the teacher for interesting effects and designs.

- 3. Paste precut pieces of various coloured tissue paper onto construction paper. (Children may discover that by overlapping pieces, tissue has the appearance of fall leaves.)

•• 4. Collage: Glue dried seeds, sticks, or grasses onto paper.

- 5. Printing: Use fruits or vegetables (teacher should prepare them in advance). Cut one-half inch from the large end of a sturdy fat carrot or celery stalk for circles and crescent shapes, or half of a grapefruit shell. Dip fruit or vegetable into desired paint colour and press onto paper.

   NOTE: Use parts of fruit or vegetables that are ordinarily discarded or not edible.

•• 6. Border designs: Describe a border as "shapes lying in a row." Give the children an assortment of strips of coloured and white paper printing scraps. Let each child select from a tray of assorted precut geometric shapes of construction paper the shapes he or she needs to design a border. Find examples in pictures of art objects or children's clothes. Allow the children to print a border, using small spools, bits of wood-molding scraps, dowels, plastic lids, rolls of corrugated paper, or bits of sponge cut in shapes, which have been dipped into shallow pans of thickened paint. Have several colours of paint from which to choose.

•• 7. Burlap pictures: Cut squares from burlap bags or colourful burlap material.
   a. String embroidery large-eyed, blunt needles with fine, bright coloured yarn. Let children sew a design or picture.
   b. Duplicate "porcupine quill art" by letting the children do the above project using coloured toothpicks instead of yarn.

•• 8. Rugs (dollhouse or block accessory size) may be simulated by fringing loosely woven upholstery fabrics. Cut in rectangles and squares and show the children how to unravel the threads to make a fringe. See (i) below. Some children may be able to do some simple weaving with loops on a frame or with yarn lengths on a home-made frame (ii). The teacher will need to secure the edges of the upholstery fabric and the weaving by stitching them on a sewing machine, so they will not fray.

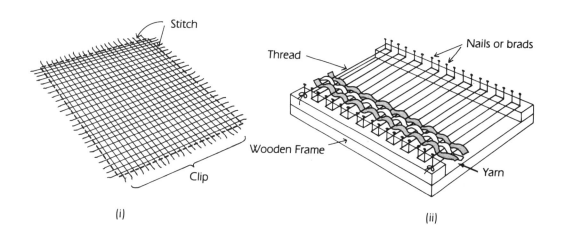

(i)   (ii)

Book Centre

• • • • Climo, Linda. *Chester's Barn*. Montreal: Tundra Books, 1982.

• • Graboff, *Old MacDonald Had a Farm*. Richmond Hill, Ont: Scholastic—TAB.

• • Kroll, *The Biggest Pumpkin Ever*. Richmond Hill, Ont: Scholastic—TAB.

• • • • Kurelek, William, and Margaret Engelhardt. *They Sought a New World*. Montreal: Tundra Books, 1985. (Read–Tell)

• Roth, H. *Babies Love Autumn Days*. Markham, Ont: Fitzhenry & Whiteside, 1986.

Planning for Group Time

NOTE: All music, fingerplays, poems, stories, and games listed here may be used at other times during the session as appropriate. See Core Library, "Basic Resources," p. 95, for publishers and addresses. Record company addresses can be found on p. 99. In parodies, hyphenated words match the music notes of the tune used.

Music

Songs

THANKSGIVING DINNER (a parody)
(tune: "Frère Jacques")
Adaptation by JoAnne Deal Hicks

VERSE 1: We eat tur-key, we eat tur-key. Oh, so good. Oh, so good.
Al-ways on Thanks-giv-ing, al-ways on Thanks-giv-ing.
Yum-yum-yum. Yum-yum-yum.

VERSE 2: Mashed po-ta-toes. Mashed po-ta-toes. Oh, so good. Oh, so good.
Al-ways on Thanks-giv-ing, al-ways on Thanks-giv-ing.
Yum-yum-yum. Yum-yum-yum.

VERSE 3: Pie and ice-cream. (REPEAT AS IN VERSE 2)

VERSE 4: Home-made bis-cuits. (REPEAT AS IN VERSE 2)

VERSE 5: Tur-key dress-ing. (REPEAT AS IN VERSE 2)

From original songs in this book by JoAnne Deal Hicks
"My Special Friend," p. 105
"Fruitbasket Song," p. 561
"Sing a Song of Applesauce," p. 562

From *A Treasury of Songs for Children*, Glazer
"Come Ye Thankful People Come," p. 53

From *Piggyback Songs*, Warren
"A Thanksgiving Song," p. 43
"Ha Ha Turkey in the Straw," p. 44

From *More Piggyback Songs*, Warren
"Harvest Time," p. 41
"Thanksgiving Day," p. 47
"Let Us Give Thanks," p. 47

"To Grandma's House," p. 48
"Mr Turkey," p. 48
"Smells Like Thanksgiving," p. 48

From *Baby Beluga Book*, Raffi
"Biscuits in the Oven," p. 9
"Oats and Beans and Barley Grow," p. 12
"Thanks a Lot," p. 18

From *Elephant Jam*, Sharon, Lois, and Bram
"Sweet Potatoes," p. 103

From *Tunes for Tots*, Warner and Berry
"Turkey Gobbler," p. 26
"We Are Thankful," p. 27
"Pick a Big Pumpkin," p. 28

Rhythms and singing games

Dramatize different methods of going to grandmother's (aunt's, cousin's, or friend's) house, such as walk, run, ride trike, fly, go by train, bus, car.
Strutting: Children may strut like a turkey, using appropriate music.
Hop, skip, jump: Use the record *Rhythmic Activities*, Volume 1 (RCA).
Drums: Reproduce chants or poems to music or drumbeats; walk, jump, hop, skip to drumbeats.
Dance: Toe-heel, toe-heel to Native music.

Fingerplays and Poems

MR. TURKEY

Mr. Turkey's tail is big and wide. (SPREAD HANDS WIDE)
He swings it when he walks. (SWING HANDS BACK AND FORTH)
His neck is long, his chin is red. (STROKE CHIN AND NECK)
He gobbles when he talks. (OPEN AND CLOSE HAND)

Mr. Turkey is so tall and proud. (STRAIGHTEN SELF UP TALL)
He dances on his feet. (MAKE FINGERS DANCE)
And on each Thanksgiving Day, (HANDS IN PRAYER)
He's something good to eat. (PAT STOMACH)

Games

(See "Learning Games," pp. 50–59, and teacher-made games in this chapter for directions.)
Play traditional circle games similar to those that pioneer children might have played.

1. Hokey pokey
2. Mulberry bush
3. Skip to my lou
4. Oats, peas, beans
5. Looby lou
6. Did you ever see a lassie?
7. Go round and round the village

8. A-hunting we will go
9. Bluebird through my window
10. London Bridge

Routine Times

1. At snack or meal time have a cornucopia with real or artificial food as a centrepiece.
2. Plan a Thanksgiving dinner the last day your group meets before Thanksgiving. Serve small portions if the meal is lunch or snack.
3. In settings where it is appropriate, pray or offer grace before the Thanksgiving dinner or snack.
4. Talk about table manners, especially saying "thank you."
5. Talk about food—its colour, texture, size, shape, taste, and odour as you are eating during snack or meal time. (See chapters on "Colour," "Smell," and "Taste".)
6. At snack or meal time use foods prepared by the children such as pumpkin muffins, popcorn, pumpkin pie, cranberry sauce, or Waldorf salad.
7. Serve foods for snacks or meal time that Native people first introduced to the settlers. *Snack-time foods:* popcorn, peanuts (use peanut butter on crackers), strawberries, pineapple chunks, cocoa, fresh or dried fruit (apples, figs, grapes, peaches). *Lunchtime foods:* cornbread cakes with maple syrup, corn, sweet potatoes, nuts, squash, turkey, tomatoes, beans, pumpkin pudding, barbecued meat, fish, potato cakes, succotash. For salad: apples, raisins, nuts, and celery combined, carrot sticks. For dessert: fried bread, pudding, or fruit.
8. At lunchtime, talk about what it would be like not to have forks—only hands or wooden spoons—with which to eat.
9. At pickup time, use a wagon to carry toys and equipment back to storage area or shelves. Point out that this is how the early settlers moved their things. Have a picture of a covered wagon.

Large Muscle Activities

1. See "rhythms and singing games."
2. Catch the turkey: All the children are turkeys except one who is a pioneer. The settler chases the turkeys until he catches one. The child who is caught becomes the settler. This game will probably interest only a few of the older children.
3. Skill games: Include games young pioneers or Native children may have played.
   a. Run to a destination and back.
   b. Walk a log, balance beam, or chalkline drawn on cement or on the floor.
   c. Play follow the leader.
   d. Play with balls of various sizes.

Extended Experiences

1. Take a trip to the grocery store to look at or buy Thanksgiving foods—turkeys, pumpkins, apples, nuts, celery, onions, potatoes, cranberries.
2. Visit a turkey farm. Ask permission from owners to make a loud noise such as blowing a whistle or horn to get turkeys to "gobble." Ask permission to collect turkey feathers or ask owner to save some for you to use in discovery, creative arts, and language arts centres.
3. Have a grandmother or grandfather visit and tell about Thanksgiving Day when she or he was a child.

Teacher Resources

Joy, M. *Highdays and Holidays.* Boston: Faber & Faber, 1981.
Manning-Saunders, R. *Festivals.* London: Heinemann, 1973.
Stephan, B. *Decorations for Holiday Celebrations.* New York: Crown, 1978.

Harvest Home Festival

The Harvest Home Festival is held on October 15th in England. This is the approximate time (late September to mid-October) that the first Thanksgiving feast was held at Plymouth. It would not be surprising that these colonists from Scromby, England, should model their celebration after a traditional holiday of their homeland. The Harvest Home Festival is the basis of Canadian Thanksgiving.

In England, this holiday is likely a remnant of influence from the Roman Empire. The Romans celebrated their Thanksgiving in early October. It was dedicated to Ceres, goddess of the harvest, and the holiday was called *Cerelia*. The English often held a parade, with a queen who had been selected to ride in a carriage drawn by white horses; unlike the Romans, however, they did not wish to honour the Roman goddess but instead showed their gratitude for a fine harvest by attending church services.

In ancient times, other harvest festivals were held in Chaldea, Egypt, and in Greece.

Halloween

Basic Understandings

(concepts children can grasp from this subject)

▷ In Canada and the United States, Halloween is celebrated on October 31.
▷ Pumpkins are commonly used to make jack-o'-lanterns.
▷ Halloween colours are orange, black, and white.
▷ On Halloween children dress up to disguise themselves (hide who they are) from their friends and visit them to get a treat, or else they play a trick on their friends.
▷ Halloween is celebrated during the time of harvesting apples, pumpkins, and nuts, and when leaves change colour. These foods and materials are often used as decorations and for games at parties.

Additional Facts the Teacher Should Know

History of Halloween

1. The night of October 31 is Halloween. "Hallow" means "saint." November 1 is a church festival, All Saints' Day. Thus the word "Hallowe'en" is short for "All Hallows Evening." On this date the Roman Catholic Church celebrates the feast of all those who were known to have lived a good life but who were not included on the church's calendar of

saints. October 31 was believed to be the one night during the year when ghosts and witches were most likely to wander about. In the early years of Britain, October 31 was the last day of the year and celebrations were similar to those for New Year's Eve.

2. Legend says that some thought this was the date when the souls of the dead were liberated from purgatory, which according to Roman Catholic theology is a place or state after death for making amends (or to atone) for sins. It was believed the released souls were allowed to visit their homes, and thus has evolved the present-day custom of "trick or treaters" coming to neighbourhood homes dressed as skeletons. The carved pumpkin was another symbol of death.

3. Another legend says there was once a miserly man named Jack, who was consigned to roam the earth until Judgment Day, because he was too stingy to get into heaven and too prone to playing practical jokes on the devil to go to hell. So, Jack carried his lantern (jack-o'-lantern) as he roamed.

4. Still another legend concerns a circle of dough, better known as the doughnut. According to this story, an English cook invented this "soul cake" to remind English beggars about eternity. The cook cut a hole out of a piece of dough and then dropped the dough into a pan of deep fat. Its circular shape was to be a reminder of the constancy of eternity. The people who received this doughnut were supposed to pray for the dead of the family who gave it to them.

5. Some say that the Halloween customs of bonfires, pranks, tricks, and jack-o'-lanterns were first introduced to Canada in the early 1900s by Irish immigrants. In recent years, schools, parents, and communities have encouraged parties and parades to discourage the pranks of the past and now many children and teenagers collect funds for UNICEF on Halloween. Their younger brothers and sisters dress up in costumes and masks and only ring doorbells where porch lights are lit to invite children to stop. Treats are prepared at such homes and given in return for the children's performing a trick or feat. Some communities, through the schools, encourage children to learn a trick to perform for a treat, for example, a poem, riddle, song, or physical feat, deemphasizing malicious mischief and calling it a "trick *for* a treat."

About preschool celebrations of this holiday

1. Small children should be helped to realize that Halloween is a time for fun and surprises rather than a time for superstition and fright. For young children perhaps the main emphasis should be on pumpkins and their uses, jack-o'-lanterns, tricks, and disguises (guess who?) with suggestions to paint faces, wearing hats or animal costumes rather than wearing masks, or portraying skeletons, witches, or goblins. A two-year-old feels disguised wearing a lampshade (as one author put it). Save the witches and ghosts for the older children who, it is hoped, will be better able to tell what is real or unreal, fantasy and fiction or fact.

2. Many children will enjoy making masks but refuse to wear them. For this reason, masks that can be held in front of them are often better. Stress the fun of surprise in guessing who is who.

3. In recent years this holiday has been marred by vandalism as well as by the poisoning of children. Children should be encouraged to visit only the friends and neighbours that their parents suggest.

Methods Most Adaptable for Introducing this Subject to Children

1. A trip to a farm where pumpkins are raised
2. A trip to the store to buy apples, nuts, and several pumpkins
3. Read or tell a story about Halloween or a pumpkin
4. Pictures on the bulletin board of pumpkins growing, a jack-o'-lantern, or a pumpkin pie
5. Bring several pumpkins to be cut and scooped out by the children

Vocabulary

pumpkins	orange	costume	ghost
jack-o'-lantern	black	riddle	joke
candle	pie	eyes	scare
trick	cat	nose	surprise
grin	owl	mouth	guess
seeds	mask	witch	harvest
treat			

Learning Centres

Discovery Centre

1. Bake sugar cookies, cutting pumpkins or other related shapes. (Tupperware has a jack-o'-lantern cutter.) Children may frost these or prebaked cookies with orange frosting. Chocolate chips and raisins or small marshmallows also can be made available for decorating.
2. Make pumpkin custard from the meat of a pumpkin. Use recipe for pumpkin pie filling, but pour in custard cups and bake. Place custard cups in baking pan. Fill pan with 2.5 cm of hot water. Bake at 350° for 30 minutes (or until knife inserted comes out clean).
3. Make orange Jell-O or chocolate Shake-a-Pudding or orange Kool-Aid.
4. Observe pumpkins growing on the vine. Note variations in colour, size, shape, quality, weight, and how pumpkins differ from squash.
5. Make jack-o'-lanterns from pumpkins. Let the children draw on the eyes, nose, and mouth shapes they want with a wax marking pencil. Teacher does the cutting. Children can take turns scooping out the seeds. For a special treat darken the room and light a candle inside a pumpkin. An adult should always be present, careful to watch children nearest the jack-o'-lantern. Short candles smoke less than tall ones. Drip candle wax into the pumpkin to secure the candle or nail from the underside of the pumpkin to hold the candle.
6. Wash and dry pumpkin seeds for planting, baking, frying, or dyeing for use in making collages. When making the jack-o'-lantern, notice how the seeds grew inside the pumpkin.
7. Discover differences between raw and cooked pumpkin. Taste some of each.
8. Discover uses of pumpkins—puddings, pies, decorations, halloween jack-o'-lanterns.
9. Observe difference between cut apples and carrots that are dipped in lemon juice (prevents browning) and those that are not.
10. Display masks used by community helpers in their work. Include picture books and mounted pictures that illustrate how and why they are worn. Include some of the following: oxygen mask, ski mask, football helmet with face guard, motorcycle helmet, face shields or goggles for welders or sanders, airpacks worn by firefighters, a sleep mask, a hospital-type mask, dark sunglasses, a gas mask. Let children try on some of the masks and see if they can guess or think why each is worn.

Dramatic Play Centres

Home-living centre

1. In this centre or behind a three-way play screen, have a costume shop with a mirror, or buy Halloween costumes and accessories like those listed:

a. Disguises for younger children:

Hats, these are often enough for the youngest children
Mail carrier, mail carrier's hat and bag
Safety officer, police officer's hat and tickets
Cowboy/cowgirl, felt hat and stick horse
Mother or lady, coloured or veiled hats, women's high heels, purse, car keys
Father or man, vest, tie, wallet, hat, car keys, shoes

b. Disguises for older preschoolers:

Scarecrow, patchy blue jeans, pants and shirt, fringe sleeves, collar, and pant legs, battered hat, old pair sneakers (cut so toes show)
Bride, white dress (gathered or gored skirt with elastic waist), veil, lace curtain train, artificial flowers for hair and bouquet, rings
Animals, dyed "sleepers," stuffed tails with loop to fasten to belt, ears attached to skull cap
Ballerina, a tank top, sleeveless T-shirt top, or a body suit, with a ruffled tutu to tie around waist, pipe cleaner tiara, ribbons to tie around shoe and ankle
Man, black mustache (can be painted on with mascara), old hat, black tie
Pirate or Buccaneer, tie a bandana around head, attach curtain rings to ears with tape, notch pair of old blue jeans, wrap waist with a sash, wear a bolero and add a cardboard or rubber knife
Clown, pointed hat, crepe paper, or cloth ruffles to tie around neck, wrists, and ankles or button on to a clown suit
Queen or king, gilt cardboard crown covered with sequins and beads. Use same materials to make a tiara for a queen. Old lace tablecloth or velvet curtain can be draped or pinned for a cloak or robe. King needs cardboard sword or scepter

Block-building centre

1. Set out farm helper figures with wooden or rubber family, tractors, trucks, and wagons.
2. Encourage farm play. Supply spools and coloured cubes or small plastic vegetables to be harvested, loaded into trucks, and driven on the road to market.
3. Talk about how you get to the biggest city near you (if you live in a small town), such as up and down hills, over bridges, and through tunnels (see the chapter "Ground and Road Transportation").

Learning, Language, and Readiness Materials Centre

Teacher-made games and materials

NOTE: For detailed description of "Learning Games," see pp. 50–59.

1. Name it: Use Halloween objects—mask, owl, black cat, pumpkin.
2. What's missing: Use hats, masks, or Halloween objects.
3. I see something: I see something about Halloween in the room and describe what it is. Let the children guess and do the same for you.
4. Grouping and sorting: Have a group of orange and black objects and sort by colour.
5. Guess who? Describe a child in the group by saying, "I see someone who is wearing a blue dress and has brown eyes." A variation is to describe a community helper or a story character.
6. Listening: Tell the children that it is hard to guess who is visiting us if they're dressed up, but sometimes you can tell who they are by listening to their voices. The child pointed to may say, "Hello," or "trick for a treat."

button-on pumpkin

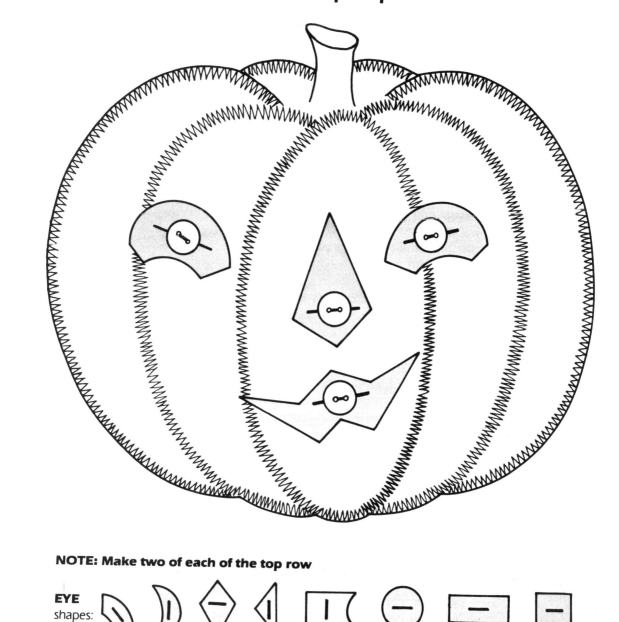

NOTE: Make two of each of the top row

EYE shapes:

NOSE shapes:

MOUTH shapes:

7. Alike, different, and the same: Cut several orange pumpkins and black cats out of felt, cardboard, or upholstery plastic. Vary the size, shape, and form of those made. Ask children to match two that are identical, to select one that is different, or to find several that are similar.

8. Make a felt pumpkin plus black felt triangles, circles, crescents, ellipses, and squares to arrange a variety of jack-o'-lantern faces. See p. 273 for shape suggestions.

9. Cut a pumpkin out of orange upholstery plastic or other heavy fabric. Use a satin zigzag stitch to secure the edges and make pumpkin crevice lines. Sew on buttons (at least 1.3 cm in diameter) where the eyes, nose, and mouth could be. Children can then button on felt or plastic shapes to create their own jack-o'-lanterns. Sew buttons as if for a coat, leaving a long shank for easier buttoning. Sew buttons on both sides of fabric to make it sturdier and reversible! For illustration of pumpkin and face pieces see p. 273.

> **NOTE:**   The felt pumpkin invites the most creative use. The button-on pumpkin combines the possibility of another learning skill to the child's creative use, and is best for older children. The very young will want to keep theirs, so you may explain that it belongs to the centre, but after they have experimented with this one they can make one like it out of paper shapes to take home.

10. How many? Children may need to talk about how many eyes, noses, mouths are needed for a face in above activities or during creative experiences in the art centre.

Art Centre

- 1. Use orange and black paint at the easels to encourage Halloween art.
- 2. Fingerpaint in orange or make a monoprint. When dry, cut into pumpkin shapes.
- 3. Tint play dough with orange tempera. (For basic recipe of play dough, see p. 27.) VARIATION: Allow children to knead red and yellow powdered paint or food colouring into the play dough.

Art Centre. Right: Felt shapes encourage a child to create different faces for a felt pumpkin. **Centre:** Black cat silhouettes, in various poses, challenge the child to describe each pose and to match poses that are identical. **Left:** Child is sorting items that are orange by placing them within a circle of orange yarn.

Other experiences in this centre using art media

- 1. Create a paper jack-o'-lantern: Allow child to select a paper pumpkin from a variety of sizes, shapes, shades of orange. (These may be precut or predrawn for the youngest.) Child attaches snippings or precut geometric shapes for eyes, nose, and mouth. Identify shapes —crescents (moonshaped), triangles, squares, circles, and half-circles—as you give them to the children. Features for the jack-o'-lantern may be precut from black gummed paper for the youngest to stick on. Talk about how many eyes, noses, and mouths we have and show on a felt pumpkin a variety of faces possible by inverting and reversing the same shapes.

  NOTE: Do not post or make a sample as it may limit their creativity. The older children may be able to draw their own pumpkins, to cut them out themselves, and to cut the desired feature shapes.

- ••• 2. Make a "handle mask": Let the children cover a bent wire clothes hanger with an old top to a nylon stocking or panty hose. Precover for the youngest child. Have children create a face by gluing on scraps of felt, cloth, and yarn. (See below.) Child can hold in front of face. For fun, the teacher may make wild guesses as to who the child is—for example, Robbie the Rabbit, Freddie the Frog. The child is always identifiable behind the mask although he may think he's hiding.

  ★ CAUTION: Be sure to bend the open end hook back on itself to form the handle and eliminate a sharp point. (See illustration below.)

- ••• 3. Make a paper plate mask: attach a tongue depressor or popsicle stick to the bottom of a paper plate with tape or staples and let child decorate a face (similar to idea no. 2). Guess person by clothes or exposed hair. (See above.)
- •• 4. Make a seed collage picture: Arrange pumpkin seeds on dark-coloured paper. To add variety you may also dye seeds different colours, using food colouring of desired intensity and one teaspoon vinegar to a cup of water. Spread on paper towel to dry before using.
- •• 5. Make a trick or treat bag: Prefold a cuff around a large-size sack, inserting a thin strip of cardboard. On opposite sides staple an orange or black strip of bias tape, rope, string, ribbon, or cord for a handle. Encourage children to cut or tear Halloween shapes, such as pumpkins, owls, cats, cornstalks, or nuts, out of construction paper and glue onto sack. Crepe-paper streamers, strips of black and orange paper, fringed borders, or yarn also make attractive decorations.
- ••• 6. Make Halloween banners for a parade: Use crepe-paper streamers or tissue taped to the end of a small upholstery cardboard core or tube (available free at any upholstery shop). Glue or tape on the face of a pumpkin, clown, cat, or any other nonfrightening face.
- ••• 7. Make rattles or noisemakers out of small empty boxes. Put in a few stones or spools, tape shut, paint or decorate, fasten to stick or carry in hand.

- 8. Make sack pumpkins: Fill a small white or brown paper sack with torn newspapers. Have some pretorn as children tire of tearing and want to proceed. Twist top and secure with a rubber band. Then let children paint all sides of the pumpkin orange and the twisted stem green. When dry you may let older children add eyes, nose, and mouth by gluing on shapes to create a fat sack jack-o'-lantern. Some may wish to twist a strip of green crepe paper around the top for a gay stem. Youngest may leave plain to make a pumpkin patch prop to play "Halloween pumpkin patch," p. 278.

•• 9. Make a pumpkin patch picture: This activity is fun following a trip to a pumpkin patch. Let the children paint a piece of brown or beige construction paper with glue. Give each child several cotton balls to roll in a shallow pan of *dry* orange tempera for use as pumpkins and supply several lengths of green yarn to be twisted around among the pumpkins like a creeping vine.

  ★ CAUTION: Be sure the children wear aprons for this activity.

••• 10. Make Halloween sack puppets (for most mature young children): A two-step process—paint sacks orange for a pumpkin, black for a cat, or leave brown or beige for an owl. Precut appropriate shapes children might choose or need. You may let children snip their own snippings (see illustration below).

Book Centre

••• Adams, A. *A Woggle of Witches*. New York: Charles Scribner's Sons, 1971.
••• Asch, F. *Popcorn*. New York: Parents, 1979.
••• Balian, Lorna. *Humbug Witch*. Nashville, Tenn: Abingdon Press, 1965.
••• Bourgeois, Paulette. *Franklin in the Dark*. Toronto: Kid's Can Press, 1986.
•• Keats, Ezra Jack. *Hi Cat!* New York: Macmillan, 1970 (paper, 1972).
••• Miller, Edna. *Mousekin's Golden House*. Englewood Cliffs, NJ: Prentice-Hall, 1964.
• Mueller, Virginia. *A Hallowe'en Mask for Monster*. Chicago: Albert Whitman, 1986.
•••• Slobodkin, Louis. *Trick or Treat*. New York: Macmillan, 1967 (paper, 1972).
••• Zolotow, Charlotte. *A Tiger Called Thomas*. New York: Lothrop, Lee & Shepard, 1963.

Planning for Group Time

NOTE: All music, fingerplays, poems, stories, and games listed here may be used at other times during the session as appropriate. See Core Library, "Basic Resources," p. 95, for publishers and addresses. Record company addresses can be found on p. 99. In parodies, hyphenated words match the music notes of the tune used.

Music

Songs

From *Stepping Along in Music Land,* Murray
"Hallowe'en Is Coming," p. 49

From *Piggyback Songs,* Warren
"Friendly Ghost," p. 40
"Do You Have the Spooky Ghost?" p. 40
"One Little Two Little Three Little Pumpkins," p. 41
"Jack-O'-Lantern," p. 41
"The Goblin in the Dark," p. 42
"Halloween Is Here," p. 42

From *More Piggyback Songs,* Warren
"I'm Jack-O'-Lantern," p. 44
"Mr. Pumpkin," p. 45
"Sometimes I Like to Walk in the Dark," p. 46
"Ghosts and Witches," p. 46
"Ghosts and Goblins," p. 46

From *Tunes for Tots,* Warner and Berry
"Boo," p. 21
"Hee, Hee, Hee," p. 23
"It's Halloween," p. 24
"Who Do You See on Halloween?" p. 25

THE HALLOWE'EN PARTY (a parody)
(tune: "Mary Had a Little Lamb")
Adaptation by JoAnne Deal Hicks

Pump-kins have such hap-py grins, hap-py grins, hap-py grins.
Pump-kins have such hap-py grins. It's Hal-low-e'en at last.

Cats have come with long, black tails, long, black tails, long, black tails.
Cats have come with long, black tails. It's Hal-low-e'en at last.

Ghosts have come to school to-day, school to-day, school to-day.
Ghosts have come to school to-day. It's Hal-low-e'en at last.

Witch-es have their witch-es' brooms, witch-es' brooms, witch-es' brooms.
Witch-es have their witch-es' brooms. It's Hal-low-e'en at last.

HALLOWE'EN (a parody)
    (tune: "This is the Way")
    Adaptation by JoAnne Deal Hicks

I saw a pump-kin face so **glad**, face so **glad**, face so **glad.**
I saw a pump-kin face so **glad,**
It's Hal-low-e'en in Oc-to-ber!

VARIATIONS: 1. Repeat verse 1 inserting "face so **mad**," or . . . "face so **sad**."
            2. Repeat the same sequences (three verses), including the above variation of emotions,
               but substitute "ghost with" or "cat with" for the word pumpkin.

NOTE: Flannel cut-outs depicting these emotions or things could be displayed on a flannel-
         board as the song is being taught.

HALLOWE'EN PUMPKIN PATCH (a parody)

    (tune: "Farmer in the Dell")
    Adaptation by JoAnne Deal Hicks

Several children are selected to sit in the centre of the room to represent pumpkins in a
pumpkin patch. Each child holds a cut-out of a particular pumpkin shape. Some are tall and
thin, short and fat, round, oblong, flattop, and so on. Also, colours should vary from bright
orange to light orange to green-tinged orange.

NOTE: Real pumpkins may be used if you caution the children to "Handle with Care!"

The other children are told, "When the song begins, one of you will be selected to go to
the pumpkin patch and choose the pumpkin shape you like best! When you have made your
choice, you and the person holding the pumpkin shape will rejoin the circle and sing along
with the rest of the group as we walk around the pumpkin patch.

VERSE 1: We see a pump-kin patch. We see a pump-kin patch.
         Hi-ho, it's Hal-low-e'en, we see a pump-kin patch.

Teacher selects child who is to choose a pumpkin. When he/she makes the selection, rest of
group sings:

VERSE 2: He'll (She'll) take that pump-kin home. He'll (she'll) take that pump-kin home.
         Hi-ho, it"s Hal-low-e'en, he'll (she'll) take that pump-kin home.

The two children now rejoin the group and all walk around the pumpkin patch singing verse
1. Repeat until every child has had an opportunity to select a particular pumpkin . . . or until
interest lags.

NOTE: Farmers usually give children pumpkins to take with them after a group visits on a
         tour. If not, explain that we would need to pay the owner for pumpkins chosen as
         we do in a store.

Rhythms and singing games

Costume parade: Use any good marching record and parade around the room, or if more than
one room in your centre, parade through building.

Fingerplays and Poems

From *Hand Rhymes*, Brown
"Jack-O'-Lantern," p. 10
"Five Little Goblins," p. 12

From *Don't Eat Spiders*, Heidbreder
"Here Comes the Witch," p. 36
"Hallowe'en Night," p. 37

MY PUMPKIN

by Darlene Hamilton

Here's my orange pumpkin (HAVE HANDS OUTSPREAD)
Big and fat and round (MAKE CIRCLE WITH HANDS)
It's the very best one (HOLD UP ONE FINGER)
I could find downtown (POINT IN THAT DIRECTION)

Now I need to make a nose ("CUT" NOSE ON YOUR FACE)
A mouth . . . some eyes (CIRCLE EYES LIKE GLASSES)
Or mother will use it (MOTION TO REMOVE)
To cook and bake some pies (ACT LIKE STIRRING)

JACK-O'-LANTERN

by Darlene Hamilton

See my jack-o'-lantern (POINT)
Smiling right at you (SMILE)
You don't need to be afraid (LOOK FRIGHTENED)
It can't holler **Boo!**

PUMPKINS

By Darlene Hamilton

A pumpkin is big (CIRCLE HANDS OVER HEAD)
A pumpkin is round (CIRCLE ARMS IN FRONT)
A pumpkin has a great big smile (OUTLINE SMILE ON MOUTH)
But doesn't make a sound. (PUT FINGER OVER LIPS)

MY JACK-O'-LANTERN FRIEND

Anonymous

(USE APPROPRIATE ACTIONS)
All children have a happy friend, who comes just once a year.
He has two eyes, a nose, a mouth, and grins from ear to ear.
He has a light that's tucked inside. He's big and round and yellow.
And, when we light the candle bright, he's such a jolly fellow.
Now, who is he? Of course, you're right! He's jack-o'-lantern, big and bright!

PETER, PETER, PUMPKIN EATER

Use the traditional poem by Mother Goose with the picture from nonsense Rhymes Picture Set (The Child's World)

Games

(See "Learning Games," pp. 50–59, and teacher-made games in this chapter for directions.)
1. Name it
2. What's missing?
3. I see something
4. Guess who?
5. Listening

Routine Times

1. At snack time, drink orange juice through black licorice straws (cut ends to open).
2. Cheese pumpkins can be served at snack or meal times.

    a. Cheese slices cut in shapes of pumpkins. Serve plain or on bread or crackers.
    b. Let children grate processed cheese and mold into pumpkins. Eat immediately.

    NOTE: Wash hands first!

3. Jack-o'-lanterns made of a variety of foods may be served at snack or meal times during Halloween week:

    a. apples with raisins for eyes, nose, mouth. Use the end of the peeler to make holes in which to poke raisins.
    b. Cut out a face in an apple using sharp point of knife. Dip in lemon juice or comparable substitute.
    c. Use whole peeled oranges for pumpkins. Slice out a wedge and insert a small apple wedge for mouth, raisin eyes, and a miniature marshmallow for a nose. One can be divided in halves, if flat side of each is placed down.

4. Carrot strips and raisins may be served at snack or meal times.
5. For snacks, eat Halloween cookies which the children have baked or decorated.
6. Play "Guess who?" while waiting for snacks or meals. (See Teacher-made games, no. 5, p. 272).

Large Muscle Activities

(See also rhythms and singing games, p. 278.)
1. Costume Parade: March around the room (if the centre has more than one group, parade through other rooms)
2. Beanbag game

Extended Experiences

1. Take a trip to the store to buy several pumpkins—one pumpkin per five children. Encourage children to select their favourite one, noting colour, weight, shape, flaws, size, and price. Each group of five might choose their own and give necessary coins to cashier (with supervision of teacher, volunteer, or parent). This will give all the children an opportunity to participate in the total experience. If you can walk to the store, take a wagon to carry the pumpkins back to the centre.
2. Trip to a pumpkin farm: Select pumpkins for the centre and, if possible, one for each child.

Teacher Resources

Joy, M. *Highdays and Holidays.* Boston: Faber & Faber, 1981.
Manning-Saunders, R. *Festivals.* London: Heinemann, 1973.
Stephan, B. *Decorations for Holiday Celebrations.* New York: Crown, 1978.

Shichigosan
(Shee-CHI-goh-sahn)

Shichigosan is the Japanese Feast of the Living Children. Celebrated on November 15, it is a day of thanksgiving honouring seven-year-old girls, five-year-old boys, and all three-year-old children, because they have survived three critical periods of childhood. The children are presented by their parents at a shrine. After their presentation, they have their picture taken and receive a gift of "candy for a thousand years." This is long sticks of red and white candy in a bag printed with pictures of a crane and a tortoise (symbols of good fortune and long life). The children are also given balloons.

Traditionally, this is the first time that a three-year-old girl wears her hair fully dressed in the fashion of her mother, the first time a five-year-old boy wears a long *kimono*, and the first time a seven-year-old girl puts on a stiff *obi*, or wide *kimono* belt. Japanese–Canadian children are more likely to wear bright-coloured clothes to reflect their joy and thankfulness.

Extended Experiences

1. Allow the children to play with balloons.
2. Display some Japanese dolls in traditional dress.
3. See the Chinese/Vietnamese New Year section for other information regarding Asian customs, toys, and games.
4. Include a tortoise or a crane in stories read or games played, mentioning their significance to Japanese people.

Hanukkah
(HAHN-na-kuh)

Basic Understandings

(concepts children can grasp from this subject)

▷ *Hanukkah* is a festival of light observed by Jewish people.
▷ *Hanukkah* celebrates religious freedom for the Jews.
▷ Candles are lit each night in a special candleholder called a *menorah* (meh-NOR-ah). The candle known as the *shamash* (SHAH-mush) is lit every night. In addition, one candle is lit the first night, two the second, and so on, until there are nine in the *menorah* on the last night.
▷ Families enjoy eating potato pancakes called *latkes* (LOT-kuhs).
▷ Children like to play games with a *dreidel* (DRAY-dull).
▷ Gifts are generally given to children—one each night. Frequently *gelt* (coins) is given. Bags of chocolate coins covered with gold foil are in favour in Jewish Canadian families.

Additional Facts the Teacher Should Know

1. *Hanukkah*, a festival of light, comes in late November or December and begins on the 25th day of the Hebrew month *Kislev*. The Hebrew calendar is a lunar one, so the exact date of *Hanukkah* varies each year. The Hallmark Date Book, distributed free where Hallmark cards are sold, or the current UNICEF wall calendar identifies the Jewish holidays. *Hanukkah* celebrates a great victory for the Jews approximately 2100 years ago.

A variety of menorahs.

2. Antiochus, a Syrian king, drove the Jews from their temple in Jerusalem and ordered them to worship Greek gods or be put to death. The Jews fought back and under the leadership of the Maccabees finally regained Jerusalem and set about purifying their temple, which the Syrians had defiled. When it was ready they proclaimed a holiday and called it _Hanukkah_, which means "dedication." The celebration lasted eight days.

3. There is a legend about the first _Hanukkah_ which relates how only one little jar of oil was found to light the holy lamp in the temple for the festival. It should have lasted only one day, but it miraculously lasted eight days until new oil was ready. This is probably why _Hanukkah_ is celebrated for eight days.

4. Today, each family has a _menorah_, a candelabrum with eight branches made of wood, brass, silver, or gold. The first _menorahs_ used little pots of oil, but today candles are used. There is also a place for a smaller candle called the _shamash_. It is usually in the centre and a little higher than the others but can be forward, behind, or to the right of the others if on the same level. It is lit first and then is used to light the others. The candles are placed in the _menorah_ beginning on the right and moving to the left each day with the required number of candles. Then the candles are lit from left to right beginning with the new candle. Forty-four small candles are needed for the eight-day festival, because each night you must use new candles.

5. Potato pancakes called _latkes_ are frequently served during _Hanukkah_. They are dipped in sour cream or served with applesauce. Christians have a similar custom of eating pancakes on Shrove Tuesday. Gifts are given to Jewish children at the beginning of the holiday or one each night. The intent is to spread light and joy. Although _Hanukkah_ is celebrated during the same season as Christmas and gifts are given to children as part of both celebrations, _Hanukkah_ is _not_ the Jewish Christmas. Christmas is a Christian holiday; and _Hanukkah_ is a Jewish holiday. Each celebration is important to a child in his or her own faith for a very different reason. Also at _Hanukkah_ time, Jewish children enjoy playing the _dreidel_ game while adults play cards. The _dreidel_ is a four-sided top with Hebrew letters on each side representing the words in the phrase "A Great Miracle Happened There," referring to the oil lasting for eight days during the first _Hanukkah_.

6. Very young children, whether Jewish or non-Jewish, do not always comprehend the history of their faith or the deeper meanings involved in their celebrations. But they can learn the name of the celebration and begin to understand some of the outward symbols

for the inner meanings. Jewish children should be given the opportunity to develop a good concept of self and pride in one's family and heritage by sharing their beliefs and customs. Non-Jews can learn that not everyone believes the same thing, and we must respect each person's right to his/her own beliefs. All can learn they have some beliefs in common and some that differ.

Methods Most Adaptable for Introducing this Subject to Children

1. Display of *Hanukkah* candelabra, *dreidel*, or pictures.
2. Sing a song or read a story about *Hanukkah.*
3. Discussion of festivals of various religions or national groups.
4. Discussion of the fact that different peoples have festivals centring around the use of candles and other lights during the gray winter with its long, dark nights.
5. Invite a Jewish parent to display *Hanukkah* decorations and *menorah.*

Vocabulary

candle	*shamash* (SHAH-mush), helper candle
light	*ner tamid* (nehr-TAH-MEED), everlasting light
first, eighth	*dreidel*
gelt	Maccabee (Jewish soldier-hero)
menorah	*latke*

Learning Centres

Discovery Centre

1. Make potato *latkes*:

LATKES

450 mL/2 cups raw grated potato
1 small grated onion
5 mL/1 tsp. salt
1 pinch of pepper
15 mL/1 tbsp. flour (matzo meal)
7.5 mL/1/2 tbsp. baking powder

Peel the potatoes and soak in cold water.
Grate them and pour off the liquid. Add the grated onion, salt, and pepper.
Mix flour and baking powder and add to potato mixture.
One or two well-beaten eggs *may* be added.
Drop by spoonfuls onto a hot, well-greased griddle (fry pan). Spread thin with back of spoon.
Turn when very brown. Drain fat.

NOTE: A potato pancake mix may also be used. *Latkes* are especially good served with applesauce or dipped in sour cream.

2. Make *Hanukkah* cookies: Use your favourite sugar cookie recipe. Cookie cutters in the shapes of a candle, a *dreidel*, a lion, or a Star of David (six-pointed star) are available in Hebrew bookstores or a specialty store, or you may borrow some from a Jewish parent.

3. *Hanukkah* salad may be made by constructing a fruit candle as follows—a slice of canned pineapple for a base; stand one-half of a banana in the pineapple for a candle; place a maraschino cherry on top of the banana for flame (slit banana to insert).

4. Light: Candles and the light they give may lead to the discovery and discussion of many different kinds of light, such as electricity (lamp), gas (yard light), fire (firelight), sun (sunlight), kerosene (lantern), and battery (flashlight). Help children find these in their environment and/or collect pictures illustrating these to put on the wall or in a scrapbook.

5. Post pictures or display often-used lights. Include small electric lamp, traffic lights, neon lights, flashlight, candle (teacher-supervized!), porch light. If you have adequate supervision light a candleholder with chimney, demonstrate how the chimney keeps the candle from being blown out. Demonstrate how a candle snuffer is used to put out a flame.

Learning, Language, and Readiness Materials Centre

Teacher-made games and materials

NOTE: For detailed description of "Learning Games," see pp. 50–59.

1. How many? Count candles on flannelboard *menorah*.
2. I see something: Find round things like a *latke*.
3. Chew, lick, and taste: A *latke* and a pancake.
4. *Dreidel* Game I: Materials needed— *dreidel* (see pattern, p. 285) and tokens, nuts in the shell, or wrapped candies. Procedure: Everyone playing puts in a token. Children, in turn, spin the top and play for the tokens, nuts, or candies. If the letter *nun* (‫נ‬) faces up, the child gets nothing. If the letter *heh* (‫ה‬) appears, she or he gets half of the tokens. If the *shin* (‫ש‬) appears, she or he must put a token in the group pile from her or his stock. If the *gimel* (‫ג‬) appears, the child wins. Singing the parody "Dreidel Game," p. 287, may help the children remember. (See also *Dreidel* Game II, p. 287.)

How to make a **dreidel:** use bristol board or a file folder to make a cube 5 cm square (or any size between 5 cm and 10 cm). Use the pattern and example shown on the next page. A dowel with one end pointed can be inserted through the holes in the top and bottom of the cube. Adjust cube up or down on dowel until it is balanced enough to spin easily. Wood or cardboard can be used if you have the necessary tools.

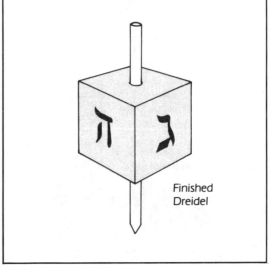

Finished
Dreidel

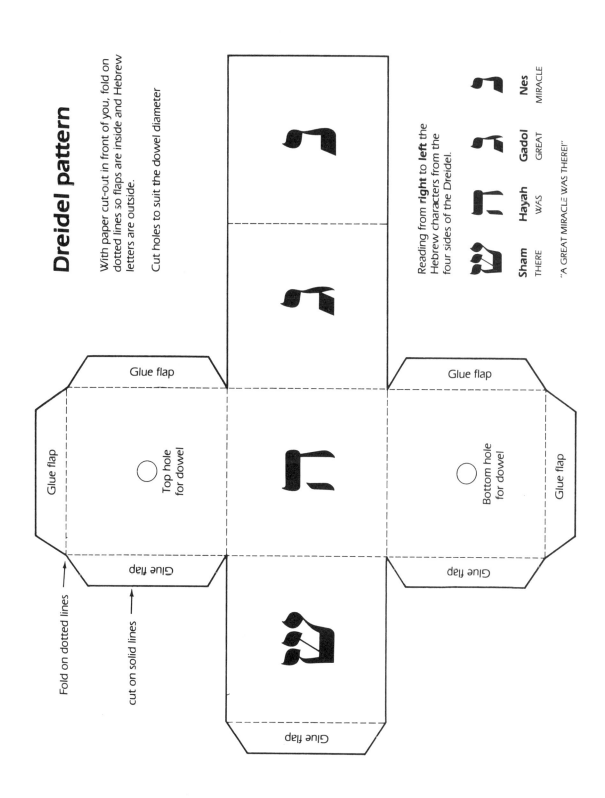

Dreidel pattern

With paper cut-out in front of you, fold on dotted lines so flaps are inside and Hebrew letters are outside.

Cut holes to suit the dowel diameter

Reading from **right** to **left** the Hebrew characters from the four sides of the Dreidel.

Sham   **Hayah**   **Gadol**   **Nes**
THERE   WAS   GREAT   MIRACLE

"A GREAT MIRACLE WAS THERE!"

Fold on dotted lines

cut on solid lines

Glue flap

Glue flap

Glue flap

Glue flap

Glue flap

Glue flap

Top hole
for dowel

Bottom hole
for dowel

Art Centre

- 1. Easel paint: Feature orange, white, and dark blue paint.
- •• 2. Paint and crayon: Make enough *dreidels* for each child in the group and let each paint or crayon every side of the cube. Teacher puts letters on or children use gumbacked letters.
- ••• 3. Pasting *menorahs*: Eight long strips of paper, straws, pipecleaners, yarn, or felt can be pasted on background paper to represent candles. One short one should be cut for the *shamash*. Pieces of cotton dipped in yellow paint, short lengths of yellow yarn, clippings of yellow paper, or cotton swabs dipped in yellow, red, or orange paint will offer a variety of possibilities for making flames. Gold or silver glitter can be used to cover a line of glue placed under the candles to represent a metal candleholder. Gold or yellow paper rectangles can be pasted on for bases.
- 4. Paper chains: Use royal blue and white construction paper for making chains in the traditional manner. Teacher can precut strips or children with cutting experience can cut their own strips.
- 5. Sponge prints: Cut sponges in the shape of the Star of David, *dreidel*, lion, or candle. (See patterns on p. 289.)

Other experiences in this centre using art media

1. Greeting cards:

- a. Spatter-paint *Hanukkah* symbols, using white paint on royal blue construction paper. Fold paper in half to form card before painting.
- •• b. Use sponge stamps to print a combination of symbols on a card. (See no. 5, in Art Centre above.)
- ••• c. Cut and paste two triangles one inverted over the other to form Star of David (six-pointed star) or paste precut *dreidels* to a prefolded card. Encourage children to make a border and, if they are able, to letter their names inside.

- ••• 2. Gifts can be made for parents, for Jewish children in local hospitals, or to exchange. Candleholders can be made of styrofoam or wooden spools mounted on a board and painted. Make eight places for candles, plus an extra one for the *shamash* which is used to light the others.

Book Centre

••• Adler, D.A. *The Picture Book of Jewish Holidays.* New York: Holiday House, 1981.

••• Chanover, Hyman, and Alice Chanover. *Happy Hanukkah Everybody.* New York: United Synagogue Book Service, 1954.

••• Garvey, Robert. *Holidays Are Nice.* New York: Ktav Publishing House, 1960.

••• Greenfeld, H. *Chanukah.* New York: Holt, Rinehart and Winston, 1976.

•••• Kalman, Bobbie, et al. *We Celebrate Family Days.* Toronto: Crabtree Publishing, 1986.
_____. *We Celebrate Hanukkah.* Toronto: Crabtree Publishing, 1986.

••• Morrow, Betty, and Lewis Hartman. "Hanukkah, Feast of Lights," in *Jewish Holidays.* Champaign, IL: Garrard Publishing, 1967, pp. 41–47 (Holiday Book Series).

••• Simon, Norma. *Hanukkah in My House.* New York: United Synagogue Book Service, 1960.

•• _____. *Hanukkah.* New York: Thomas Y. Crowell, 1966.

Planning for Group Time

NOTE: All music, fingerplays, stories, poems, and games listed here may also be used at other times during the session as appropriate. See Core Library, "Basic Resources," p. 95, for publishers and addresses. Record company addresses can be found on p. 99. In parodies, hyphenated words match the music notes of the tune used.

Music

Songs

DREIDEL GAME (a parody)

(tune. "This Is the Way")
Adaptation by JoAnne Deal Hicks

The drei-del game is fun to play, fun to play, fun to play,
The drei-del game is fun to play, on Ha-nuk-kah in the morn-ing.

The "shin" turns up, you put one in, put one in, put one in . . .

The "heh" turns up, then you get half, you get half, you get half . . .

The "nun" turns up, then you get none, you get none, you get none . . .

"Gim-mel" turns up, then you get all, you get all, you get all . . .

From original songs in this book by JoAnne Deal Hicks
"Happy Hanukkah," p. 276
From *A Treasury of Songs for Children*, Glazer
"Hanukkah Song," p. 108
From *Singing Bee*, Hart
"Hanukkah Song," p. 144

Records and cassettes

There are many lovely folk songs that are appropriate to the celebration of *Hanukkah*. Visit a local Jewish bookstore to pick up current records and/or tapes that will be useful for this celebration. Some community libraries also have suitable tapes, but go early as they are used a great deal in the *Hanukkah* season.

Games

Dreidel Game II: Children form a circle holding hands. One child is chosen to be a *dreidel* in the centre. Children walk around in a circle while child in centre turns in place for first half of melody (use any Israeli music). Then both the circle and the *dreidel* stop. The child in the centre chooses another child to spin by holding hands and turning together in the centre while circle moves again for the last half of the melody. The chosen child stays in the centre for the start of a new game and the first child rejoins the circle. Repeat until every child who wishes can be a *dreidel*. Form a second circle if time will not allow everyone a turn.

Routine Times

1. During snack or meal times serve *latkes,* candle salad, or sugar cookies in the shape of the Star of David, a lion, a candle, or a *dreidel.*
2. When walking or busing look for a synagogue or a temple.

Large Muscle Activities

(See "Games" above.)

Extended Experiences

1. Visit a temple or synagogue to see the eternal light (*ner tamid*).
2. Invite a Jewish parent, student, or friend to come to the classroom. Ask them to share with the children any of the following:

    a. A *menorah*: show how it is lighted and explain how it is used.
    b. A *dreidel*: show how to play the *Dreidel* Game, and explain the letters.
    c. Some *Hanukkah* sugar cookies for snack time, or bring *Hanukkah* cookie cutters and help the children make and bake cookies. Discuss the reason for shapes chosen.
    d. Some *latkes,* serve with sour cream or applesauce. The visitor might be asked to help supervize and to assist the children in making *latkes.*

Teacher Resources

Pictures and Displays

▷ Children around the world: "Ziva of Israel," set of three, SVE (Singer)
▷ Holidays picture packet: "Hanukkah" (David C. Cook)
  Holidays of the year: "Hanukkah" (Vanguard Visuals Company)
▷ UNICEF wall calendar (Canadian UNICEF Committee, 443 Mt. Pleasant Road, Toronto, Ontario M4S 2L8)

Books and Periodicals

Adler, D.A. *The Picture Book of Jewish Holidays.* New York: Holiday House, 1981.

Cavanah, Frances, and Lucy Pannell. *Holiday Round Up.* Philadelphia: Macrae Smith, 1968.

Dobler, Lavinia. *Customs and Holidays Around the World.* New York: Fleet Press, 1963.

Edmonton Hadassah WIZO Association *The Great Hadassah WIZO Cookbook.* Edmonton: Hurtig, 1982.

Margalit, Avi. *The Hebrew Alphabet Book.* New York: Coward, McCann, 1965.

Mervis, Rabbi Leonard J. *We Celebrate the Jewish Holidays.* New York: Union of American Hebrew Congregations, 1953.

Purdy, Susan. *Festivals for You to Celebrate.* Philadelphia: J.B. Lippincott, 1969.

Siegel, Richard, Michael Strassfield, and Sharon Strassfield. *The Jewish Catalog.* Philadelphia: Jewish Publication Society of America, 1973.

Temes, S.R. *Welcome to My Kitchen.* Toronto: Temes, 1985.

United Synagogue Book Service, 155 Fifth Avenue, New York 10010. For storybooks, song books, and records listed in Book Centre and Music.

Weinfeld, W., ed. *The Canadian Jewish Mosaic.* Rexdale, Ont: John Wiley & Sons, 1981.

Community Resources and Organizations

▷ Jewish parents in your centre, students in a nearby college or university
▷ Rabbi or director of Hebrew education
▷ Hebrew bookstore
▷ Temple gift shop

Lion   Star of David

Menorah

Happy Hanukkah

JoAnne Deal Hicks

Christmas

Basic Understandings

(concepts children can grasp from this subject)

▷ December 25th is Christmas Day and is a national holiday in Canada.

▷ Christmas is the Christian celebration of the birth of Jesus (the Christ Child).

▷ Christians believe God sent His Son to earth as a special gift of love, and like the Wise Men who brought gifts to him as a token of their love, esteem, and respect, they give to others in Jesus's name.

▷ Christmas symbols are evergreen trees, stars, candles, crèches, bells, wreaths, holly, angels, sleighs, Christmas stockings, tree ornaments, reindeer, elves, Santa Claus.

▷ Colours used at Christmas come from some of the symbols we use, for example, red for holly berries, cranberries, and Santa's suit; green for evergreen trees, wreaths, and holly; and silver or gold for the bright star the Wise Men followed.

▷ In Canada, traditional activities of the Christmas season include carol singing, special church services, gift making and giving, family gatherings at festive dinners and special parties, and sending greetings and cards to friends.

▷ Many children believe in Santa Claus.

   a. Stories, songs, and poems suggest that Santa and Mrs. Claus live at the North Pole and that Santa spends the whole year making and painting toys, which he delivers in a sleigh pulled by eight reindeer, to good boys and girls while they are asleep on Christmas Eve.

   b. We may see many persons dressed like Santa Claus during the Christmas season.

   c. Anyone can be a Santa's helper or play Santa to another person if he or she gives a gift secretly (anonymously).

Additional Facts the Teacher Should Know

1. Christmas is a time set aside by Christians throughout the world to celebrate the birth of their Saviour, Jesus Christ. The word "Christmas" is derived from the early English term, *Christes masse*, which means Christ's Mass. No one knows when it was first celebrated except that it began in the early Roman Church.

2. It is important for teachers to be sensitive to the customs and practices around Christmas that vary from family to family and region to region. For some families Christmas is solely a religious celebration, for others it is solely a secular celebration, for others it is a combination of the two, and for others it is not an occasion for celebration. Unless your program is based in a setting which teaches a particular religious philosophy, it is wise to focus on the secular aspects of Christmas and to leave the religious celebrations to each family. It is acceptable to present the religious aspects of Christmas as long as they are presented in the context of being the beliefs and stories of one group of people. This parallels the presentation of religious beliefs that has been recommended in other parts of the celebration chapters. It is critical to be aware of the children who do not celebrate Christmas in any form. It is equally important to be aware of the children for whom Christmas may be very stressful, because of financial and/or family stresses. Close consultation with parents before any holiday celebrations are commenced will be helpful in designing a holiday program that is acceptable to all the families in your program. Another important influence in the planning your Christmas program is the media. Children are bombarded with the commercial celebration of Christmas for many weeks before the holiday. We can counterbalance this by stressing the gentler aspect of Christmas and emphasizing the themes of kindness that underlie all Christmas history and legends.

3. Christmas is a statutory holiday in Canada. The secular and religious celebrations of Christmas have been strongly influenced by the practices of our ancestors from all over the world. Most Canadians celebrate Christmas in the same way, but there are regional differences and traditions that are very important to the people of each region. Although you are likely aware of the main practices in your community, you may find that you can make the celebration of Christmas in your setting more personal by researching the particular practices of the children in the centre. There are some regional Canadian Christmas customs, about which children enjoy learning. For example, in Vancouver boats of all sizes are decorated with lights and sail around the harbours and inlets with the people on board singing Christmas carols. In the Arctic, Inuit people will often have a community Christmas dinner of caribou, seal, or Arctic char and bannock. Usually, the dinner is followed by a tournament of traditional games. The last person to remain undefeated in the games is the champion of the Christmas games for the year. Games include archery, target shooting, and dog-team races. In Newfoundland, some communities have the ancient European tradition of mummery, which has been becoming more popular in the past few years. Mummers dress in elaborate costumes and will go from house to house performing short Christmas skits and plays. In larger communities, mummers are now performing in halls and theatres. If they visit homes they are usually fed Christmas delicacies. In many communities across the land there are Santa Claus parades.

4. Many Christmas customs, celebrations, and legends have a pagan beginning. When the pagans of Northern Europe became Christians they made their sacred evergreen trees a part of the Christian festival and decorated them with gilded nuts and candles to represent stars, moon, and sun.

5. The most popular legend about the first Christmas tree concerns Martin Luther, a German clergyman who found a small fir tree, glistening with snow, in the woods on a starry night. He took it home for his children and placed many lighted candles on it to represent the stars. Holly and mistletoe became symbols of Christmas, also. To children the Christmas tree represents much of the excitement and colour of the holiday season. Children may share in its decoration. The family usually gathers around it on Christmas to open their gifts. A Scandinavian legend loved by children is "The Friendly Beasts." According to this story all dumb animals are able to speak at midnight on Christmas Eve.

6. Although Santa Claus is not a part of the religious celebration of Christmas, he is a very real part of the very young child's Christmas and is one of the most beloved figures in the legends of childhood. The modern mythical Santa, it is said, developed from a real person, St. Nicholas, the patron saint of school boys, who, dressed in his bishop's robes, brought gifts to them. Clement C. Moore's *A Visit from St. Nicholas* probably gives the best modern-day description of the saint. Reindeer appear in this poem (which is probably from a Scandinavian legend). Children seem to want to believe in Santa Claus even if they are not consciously taught this myth. This belief must be respected even if it is not encouraged. As children mature in their understanding, they begin to realize that Santa Claus is the embodiment of the wonderful spirit of Christmas and of giving gifts anonymously.

7. Children should be encouraged to realize that Christmas is a time to share and to give gifts, not just an occasion when they receive presents themselves. They can be helped to play Santa Claus by preparing gifts to be given anonymously to others. Surprises and secrets are especially fun (making gifts for parents, friends, or other special persons). The Christmas season is the most exciting time of all for young Christian children. In many homes, children hang up stockings on Christmas Eve that they hope to find filled with treats in the morning.

8. It is often fun for children to explore the traditions of other countries. If children in your class were born outside Canada, it is especially enjoyable to examine the customs of their country and to incorporate some of their customs into your program. Some customs and practices from around the world follow.

Cookie trees. These are usually wooden trees made of graduated lengths of dowels for branches, threaded through a thick dowel trunk-post. Some are made to be flat, others are branched on all sides. A sheaf of wheat is tied to the top of the tree with a ribbon. Cookies are hung on the branches with yarn or fine twine, and small lady apples are pierced on the end of each branch, like fruit growing on the tree.

Sweden□St. Lucia is a special Christmas time holiday. Because of the long period of darkness in midwinter all kinds of lights are welcomed. Candle-making and giving is therefore an important part of the Swedish Christmas holiday. *Pepparkakor* (ginger cookie) trees, brass angel candle chimes, candles, and live green Christmas trees are other Swedish traditions related to Christmas. Evergreen trees are decorated with intricate straw figures (stars, animals, sunbursts, snowflakes, and people) and always include at least one bird in a nest. Other paper decorations include miniature flags of blue and yellow, the national colours of Sweden. Brightly painted horses, pigs, goats, and wooden figures as well as straw mobiles and straw centrepieces in the form of crowns are other decorations for this holiday.

Jultomte, an old gnome, is said to give gifts on Christmas Eve. Dipping Day, *doppa i grytan* (dip-in-the-pot), comes on the day before Christmas. The custom recalls a famine winter when the only food available was black bread and broth. Today it is an aid to a mother who is busy baking and cooking for the family gathering. Dipping dark rye bread into the broth of the simmering sausages assuages appetites so that the family can more patiently wait and look forward to the evening meal. The Christmas Eve family dinner includes *lutfisk* (a white fish), saffron or caraway bread, and pork of some kind (sausages and ham). All are commonly eaten before the family goes to church services. (Most Swedes, however, prefer attending *Julotta* services on Christmas morning.) The holiday ends the day after Holy Kings' Day, January 6th, with the burning of the tree or the replanting of the tree in the yard.

Denmark□Rye or wheat is placed on every gable and gateway and in the barn for the birds to eat. Rooms and windows in Danish homes are decorated with evergreen. Trees are decorated with heart-shaped woven paper baskets or baskets shaped like miniature hats, which are filled with candy. Flat linked paper chains, inverted cones, triple bells, and garlands of tiny flags are other tree decorations made from paper, using red and white, the Danish national colours, with a touch of gold. *Nisse*, a tiny bearded sprite, is said to deliver presents to children. On Christmas Eve children walk around the Christmas tree singing carols. Then they all sit down to hear the Christmas Story told to them by their parents. The legend of the Friendly Beasts (animals able to speak on Christmas Eve) is also often told in Denmark. Goose and *grød* (rice pudding) are traditional foods served at Christmas.

Norway☐Norwegians say there should be different kinds of cookies for every day of the Christmas season, fourteen in all! They probably consider Christmas Eve through the Twelfth Night festival the Christmas season (Little Christmas to Big Christmas).

The Christmas tree is usually topped with a replica of the aurora borealis. Paper fishnets, cranberries, and popcorn are other decorations. Sheaves of rye and wheat are tied on posts or high buildings to feed the birds. As in other Scandinavian countries, traditional church services are held on Christmas Day with family dinners often on Christmas Eve.

England☐Noted for the first Christmas cards, yule logs, fruitcake, plum pudding, mincemeat pie, mistletoe, holly, and bells. Dickens's *A Christmas Carol* is commonly read during the holidays. Christmas trees are planted in tubs indoors to be returned to the garden after the holidays so they can be used again and again. Trees are topped with the British crown or an angel and may be covered with angel hair and artificial snow. Other decorations often include candy and sugarplums tucked into ribbon- and flower-decorated cornucopias or silver-filagreed doily baskets. Swags of red and gold ribbon are also used, and tiny packages wrapped in velvet, ribbons, or even brocade. Father Christmas gives gifts to children on Christmas. These are placed by the fireplace, but gifts to others are given on Boxing Day, December 26th. Bells are traditionally rung from every tower and church belfry at midnight on Christmas Eve, announcing Christ's birth. Carolers gather in town squares under the village trees. Earlier bells toll warning to the Prince of Evil that the Prince of Peace's birth will soon be announced.

Wales☐Carol singing is accompanied by the harp. Each town offers prizes for the best carols composed each year. Goose is often eaten. Taffy making is an important custom for the holidays, as well as the preparation and eating of plum pudding.

Ireland☐Candles burn brightly in windows to light the way of the Holy Family. All wanderers are given a meal and coins.

Greece☐People sing carols while beating drums and striking triangles. Carolers are given figs, cookies, walnuts, almonds, oranges, tangerines, pomegranates, and money. *Christpsomo* (bread of Christ) is a simple cake decorated with nuts and covered with powdered sugar. When the cakes are soaked in diluted honey they are called *melomacaromas*. Christmas is primarily a religious festival with no Christmas trees or presents. Greeks give presents on St. Basil's Day, January 1, commemorating one of the four fathers of the Orthodox Church.

Italy☐The crèche (or *presepio*) is the centre of the Italian Christmas celebration. *Presepios* include artistically crafted figures of the Holy Family, shepherds, and domestic animals. Gifts at Christmas are for the family and thought to be brought by *Gesù-Bambino*, the Christ child, not by Santa Claus. Christmas letters or notes, written and decorated by little children as a surprise for their parents, include promises to be good, helpful, and obedient or are notes of praise. These are hidden under the father's plate or tucked in his napkin or under the tablecloth, and read ceremoniously by him when the whole family is gathered and the meal is finished. Another form of *presepio*, which is equivalent in popularity to the Christmas trees in America, is the *ceppo*, a pyramid-shaped tripod fitted with three shelves. Candleholders for fat votive candles are fastened to the tripod sections at the corner of each shelf, making nine candleholders. The top shelf of the *ceppo* contains a star or angel, and the middle shelf holds small gifts for the children, secretly placed there by the parents. On the bottom shelf are beautiful ceramic or hand-carved figures of the Holy Family and sometimes a few lambs, a donkey, and a cow. Sometimes fringes or tassels decorate the edges of the shelves. In some families each child has his or her own small *ceppo*. On Christmas Eve the candles are lit beside the *presepio* or on the *ceppo*, and the children dance around it with tambourines while singing. During the holidays children go door to door reciting Christmas selections and receive coins to buy special treats.

Spain☐A *nacimiento* or manger scene is found in almost every home (literally, the word means birth). It is often lighted with candles and children dance around it with tambourines while singing. Figures included in the nativity scene are a gray donkey, a Spanish bull, shepherds, and an angel. Some include a home for Herod and others have the Wise Men approaching from the East. Festivities end on the twelfth day of Epiphany, January 6th. On this date the *Magi* (the Three Kings) are supposed to leave gifts for children on their way to visit the Christ child. Children leaves shoes on balconies with *cebada* (barley) for the tired camels. A favourite sweet served is *dulces de almend* (a sweet almond pastry). Elaborate parades are held in big cities on that day, honouring the Three Kings.

Germany☐Credited with the first Christmas tree. Crafting wooden toys and giving home-made gifts are still important customs. Such items are often used to decorate Christmas trees. Advent wreaths, candles, calendars, and other traditions are related to the religious celebration of Christmas in Germany. Tree decorations also include *lebkuchens* (layb-KOO-h'kens), gingerbread cookies shaped like men and women, animals, stars, hearts, and other hand-carved ornaments. *Christkind* (Christ child) (sometimes called "Kriss Kringle") is the bearer of gifts—nuts, apples, and sweets—to children. Some homes give each other secret homemade gifts from the Christmas Angel once every week during Advent. *Stollen* (SHTUHL-len), a fruit-studded coffee cake, is often served at Christmas.

Netherlands☐St. Nicholas Day is December 6th, when St. Nicholas is said to arrive in this country by ship. He comes wearing a white bishop's robe, a scarlet cassock, a tall red hat called a mitre, and white gloves. He then mounts a white horse and delivers gifts to children. On Christmas Eve, inexpensive gifts are given, each one wrapped mysteriously and elaborately. Sometimes they are in a series of boxes, one within the other. Every gift is accompanied by a verse or rhyme.

Czechoslovakia☐Christmas celebrations begin on December 6th. The holiday ends with the visit of the *Tri Kralu* (Three Kings). The manger, the *jeslicky*, is always in the church or home. Young pig or goose is often served for dinner. "Good King Wenceslaus" is a traditional carol. Delicately dyed cornhusks are used to create nativity scenes. Sometimes tree ornaments are fashioned from bread dough and painted elaborately. Other ornaments are made from paper, straw, eggshells, and woven baskets. They can appear as little houses, heart-shaped windows, peasant dolls, clowns, birds, violins, or angels. Traditionally, children feed animals a portion of their Christmas dinner so the animals will give more milk, lay more eggs, and so on. It is said *Svatej Nikulas* comes down from heaven on a golden rope and leaves gifts on December 5th. On Christmas Eve, families gather around the trees and fortunes are told. In Czechoslovakia (and Austria) hand-carved, heirloom crèches called Bethlehems or cribs have been placed under Christmas trees for generations. Originally, these were carved during long winter months by miners in their slack season and sometimes had as many as 100 pieces or more. These scenes were characterized by their inclusion of entire miniature villages, reflecting both the misery and joy of the people.

France☐*Crèche* is the French word for cradle and has come to be the term used for any manager scene including the figures of Mary, Joseph, and the baby Jesus. It can also include a donkey, cow, sheep, shepherds, and approaching Magi. It was popularized in the thirteenth century by monks who were concerned that people did not realize the true meaning of Christmas because they could not read and church services were held in Latin. Inspired after seeing shepherds sleeping in a nearby field with their sheep they gathered live animals and asked people to take the parts of Mary, Joseph, and the shepherds in a living portrayal of the biblical story. They invited children to come to the manager and sing lullabies to the baby Jesus. The custom became very popular and gypsies are said to have carried it throughout southern Europe. Churches in France often have a living *crèche* with real people and animals. Sometimes smaller *crèches* are decorated with holly, moss, laurel, and stones. *Santons*, or little saints, are made to be added to miniature *crèches* in the home. They are painted terracotta figures placed around the manger, representing families and tradespeople of a particular village. Trees are decorated with many different-coloured stars. On Christmas Eve, toys, candies, and fruits are added to the tree. Most gifts are not given until St. Nicholas Day, December 6th, and then primarily to children. *Père Noël*, Father Christmas, is tall and slim and leaves gifts on Christmas Eve in shoes that have been placed before the fireplace. Drama and puppet shows are often part of the children's holiday. A special French treat is *bûche de Noël*, traditionally a yule log confection made of crushed chestnuts or cake molded into a log and decorated with plenty of mistletoe and holly. Variations today may resemble a log-type frosted cake like a jelly roll confection, but made with creamy filling and pistachio nuts. Baked ham and roast fowl are often served.

Rumania□On Christmas Eve boys carry long bags in which to pack gifts as they offer greetings to families, singing *colinde* (carols). A *steaua* (a star placed on a pole with little bells under it) announces the approach of the singers. Strings of cranberries, paper chains, cookies, pretzels, and apples are put on the Christmas tree with straw heaped beneath it.

Yugoslavia□Wheat is planted on a plate on December 10th. By Christmas Day, the resulting miniature field of wheat serves as a decoration and sits on the windowsill. Tables are strewn with straw as a reminder of the manger. Roasted suckling pig is eaten. *Kolaches*, ring-shaped coffee cakes filled with prunes or apricots, are made and three candles are placed within the ring. The first candle is lit on Christmas Eve, the second on noon of Christmas Day, and the third on New Year's Day. A *kolache* is not cut until January 6th, but then with an elaborate ceremony. Quite often the children write to Jesus and the angels, who bring gifts on Christmas morning.

Poland□Christmas is often called Little Star (*Gwiazdka*). No food is served on Christmas Eve until the appearance of the first star, in commemoration of the star of Bethlehem, a signal for the beginning of the festivities. Gilded nuts, sweets wrapped in coloured paper, frosted cookies, bits of ribbon, straw, beads, eggshells, and even feathers are made into clowns, chickens, fish, pitchers, and stars to give Polish Christmas trees a special look. Straw is placed under the tablecloth because the Christ child was born in a manger. Sometimes villagers dressed as animals go about singing carols and are rewarded with food and drink. Boys, singing carols, often wander from house to house with small boxes of the manger scene or lighted stars mounted on poles.

South Africa□Christmas is a summer holiday; there is no school. Christmas greeting cards often show robins. There are open-air lunches of turkey or roast beef, mincemeat pie, suckling pig, and yellow rice seasoned with turmeric. The Christmas holiday is usually a weeklong carnival. People dressed in gay, fancy clothing sing, dance, and parade in the streets, often accompanied by pipe and string bands.

Ghana□Yam and rice festivals and tribal dances are part of the cultural celebrations before Christmas. Christmas is a symbol of hope. Flowers and palm branches are used as decorations during Advent. Groups go together to buy cows, sheep, or goats to slaughter for the Christmas Day Feast. Father Christmas does not come from the North Pole but from the jungles. *Egbona hee! Egbona hee! Egogo vo!* means "Christ is coming! Christ is coming! He is near!" It is a common greeting. There are also fireworks. The church has a decorated tree and candles but usually individual homes do not. Foods eaten include rice and *fufu*, which is a dish of yams pounded into a kind of paste, and stew-porridge, with bean or okra soup. Sheep, goats, cows, hogs, and chickens are served as meat for the day. Some people prefer fish. Gifts are given, Christmas cards are sent, and enemies are reconciled. Love and forgiveness are emphasized.

Japan□The Japanese tree is decorated with faintly tinted Christmas cards, finely lined woodcuts, dolls, tangerines, paper fans, wind chimes, and tiny toys and dolls. Green and red paper balls, holly, and red Japanese lanterns are other decorations used. Christmas pageants are performed in Japanese dress. Party boxes or bags of Japanese cakes are shared. It is a church-centred holiday because seldom are all family members Christian. It is often a day of caring for others in hospitals. Japanese usually decorate a "back," which is a backdrop or cloth on which is fastened a scene of the shepherds or Wise Men with the Holy Family. Cardboard banners in assorted colours quote Bible verses about the birth of Jesus. Glass wind chimes are hung on the Christmas tree (usually a pine tree). A flat cake made from pounded, cooked rice called *mochi* is a favourite Christmas treat. It was once offered at sacred shrines but as a symbol of happiness it is now eaten on other festive occasions.

Taiwan□Poinsettias bloom from November to March. Streamers and paper chains are made. Big red and gold ideographs, messages written with Chinese characters, are beautiful and magnificent. Candy like solid marshmallow is made of rice flour and sugar and decorated with Christmas symbols. Greeting cards are hand-painted, often on fabric which is then glued to cards. Christmas is not a legal holiday; therefore it is usually celebrated on the weekend nearest December 25th.

China□The Christmas tree is called the "Tree of Life." It is decorated with paper lanterns and foil-covered paper that is made into fans, tassels, and chains. Glass ornaments lacquered with brilliant colours are also used for decorations, as well as Chinese lanterns, holly leaves and berries, tinsel, and mellow lights. Sending postcards or greeting-card giving is more common than giving gifts. Gifts are given to Christian relatives, who may get silks, jewels, or more valuable gifts; to Christian friends or distant relatives, who might get food or cut flowers; and to the poor. *Lan Khoong* (nice old father) or *Dun Che Lao Ren* (Christmas old man) are Chinese Santa Claus equivalents. The Christmas meal is often shared with the church family, as usually few members of a family are Christians. On Christmas Eve there is a lantern parade. The biggest feast is saved for New Year's Day, which is traditionally a bigger holiday in China. Many Chinese greeting cards are exquisitely painted fabric pictures. Usually the Holy Family is painted with the features and dress of the Chinese.

Panama□*Nacimientos* (manger scenes) in churches and private homes are very elaborate and artistic. They often include houses, trees, waterfalls, and grass duplicating a small Bethlehem scene. At school Christmas gifts and greeting cards are made by hand. Plays and pageants are given. Children send letters to the baby Jesus. Straw is woven into sunbursts, birds, fish, butterflies, people, and animals and are used as tree decorations. The poinsettia plant, native to that country, is called *Flor de la Noche Buena* (flower of the Holy Night).

Mexico□Houses are decorated with coloured paper lanterns, garlands, or wreaths of Spanish moss and evergreen. Pine branches and moss cover the area of the room where the table holding the nativity scene is located. The crèche or *pesebre* has a shepherds, sheep, small huts, and trees. The figures of Mary, Joseph, and an empty cradle are placed in the stable. The manger is not filled with the baby Jesus figure until Christmas Eve. Santa Claus and Christmas trees are rare. Children receive toys and gifts on Epiphany. On the night of January 5th they put their shoes on a window ledge before going to sleep. On Christmas Eve they receive candies and trinkets.

In many other Spanish-speaking countries of South and Central America or the West Indies, Bethlehem scenes, including the manger and the Holy Family figures, are given similar focus and emphasis for worship during the Christmas holidays. For example, in Cuba such scenes are surrounded with eggs and cookies and decorated with fruit and flowers. In Costa Rica, a special small room known as a *portal* is filled with such a scene and visitors come to view each family's manger. In Honduras, *nacimientos* are set up in almost every home and are made from materials varying from very elaborate to very rustic, depending upon the means or skill of the individual family. Families come to view portals much as they do in Costa Rica. In Ecuador, the brightly painted *pesebre* figures are often made of bread dough and placed in simple cardboard box mangers. In most such countries each child places her or his most valuable possession near the *nacimiento* her or during this season and it becomes a part of the scene.

Syria☐The Christmas holiday begins with St. Barbara's Day on December 4th and ends with the Epiphany celebration on January 6th. St. Barbara is a saint honoured for her goodness, faith, and love. She is a fine example to all Christian children. On the eve of this holiday special sweets are served made from wheat, nuts, honey, and sugar. Wheat is cooked with sugar and flavoured with rosewater. These treats are taken to the poor or to the homes of those in whose families someone has died recently. A party is given on St. Barbara's Day that includes dancing, singing, and games. In a special ceremony, girls, one by one, go to an elderly woman who annoints their eyes with a salve. The legend of St. Barbara suggests that her miserly father did not approve of her giving to the poor. When he caught her, he threatened her with a sword and it is said that God turned the sword into a crochet hook. When her father demanded to see the food she had hidden in her lap, it had become roses. Parents hope this holiday and legend will teach children to be unselfish and to care and share with those less fortunate. Children are encouraged to do this by sharing with others. Chicken, oranges, nuts, and pastries are special foods eaten during the Christmas holidays in Syria. Children save money to give to the poor. On January 1st presents are exchanged. It is a day for circumcision of male children. Children go door to door to receive Turkish sweetmeats. January 2nd is a woman's visiting day. It is said that in southern Syria every tree bends its trunk and inclines its branches on Christmas in homage to the Christ child. The gentle camel of Jesus is said to travel over the desert bringing presents to children. According to legend this camel was the youngest camel of those that travelled with the Wise Men. Children customarily leave water and wheat for the camel on this night. Candles are also placed in windows to guide the camel over the hills.

India☐Bundled branches of rice straw are put in water and soaked, then plastered with mud. Green pieces of oleander are stuck in and candles put on the ends of the branches to form a Christmas tree. Paper chains and mica (a thin, sheetlike, fragile mineral) are scattered over the tree for decoration. Candles are put in candleholders in the windows of churches. Little candles are sometimes lighted and placed all along the roof.

Methods Most Adaptable for Introducing this Subject to Children

1. Children may pin pictures of Christmas activities on bulletin boards, helped by a supervizing adult who can discuss the pictures as they are chosen. (Use push-pins, which are much easier for children to manipulate than thumbtacks.)
2. Take a picture walk during free playtime. One teacher may accompany several children to look and discuss what they see.
3. A child or teacher may share or talk about a Christmas picture, book, or object.
4. Children may make decorations for the room or the Christmas tree.
5. Take a shopping trip to buy a tree for the room or to see a decorated store window.

Vocabulary

Christmas	caribou	lights	Christmas Eve
gift	bells	twinkle	Santa Claus
turkey	merry	tinsel	St. Nicholas
bannock	wreath	candle	Père Noël
star	holly	Arctic char	reindeer
bell	night	candy cane	decorations
carol	glitter	elf (elves)	stocking
sing	pine cone	wrap	chimney
sleigh	evergreen	Christmas tree	present
mantel	snow	poinsettia	mummers
jingle	ornament	mistletoe	parade
carol boat			

Learning Centres

Discovery Centre

1. Collect different species of evergreen branches and pine cones. Feel and smell. Identify and compare shape, size, colour. Count. Use a magnifying glass. Note likenesses and differences—find two that are alike.
2. Remind parents that the winter sky has particularly brilliant stars that will stimulate a child's sense of wonder.
3. Christmas ornaments and wrappings have delightful sensory appeal. Discuss colour, shape, size, texture.
4. Cookies may be mixed, cut with cutters, baked, frosted, and decorated. Choices may depend upon the maturity of the group or the time available.
5. Collect old Christmas cards. Encourage the children to sort them by colour, type of picture, shapes, etc.

Dramatic Play Centres

Home-living centre

1. See Art Centre regarding a small Christmas tree for children to use in the dramatic play centre.
2. Set out replicas of traditional Christmas foods from various cultures. Encourage the children to prepare a family or community dinner.
3. Provide decorations (preferably made in the art centre) for the children to decorate the home-living centre.

Block-building centre

Children may need or request large cardboard brick blocks to make chimneys and fireplaces.

Other dramatic play centres

1. Santa: A rocking boat is an excellent prop for a sleigh. Hollow blocks can be made into stalls for the reindeer. Children can pretend to be reindeer or use stick horses as props. Provide children with a burlap sack, to be filled with small toys for their sleigh. Add sleigh bells and a red stocking cap for anyone wishing to play Santa.
2. Jack-in-the-box: Children hide in a large cardboard box one at a time and pop out while teacher and remaining group recite this poem.

> Down in the box there is a little man
> Who waits and waits as quiet as he can
> Until he opens the lid of his box
> A-n-n-n-n-nd (PAUSE) . . . UP HE POPS!

NOTE: A box with a top that has been cut on three sides and hinged on the fourth is the best. Box may be painted or decorated.

Learning, Language, and Readiness Materials Centre

Teacher-made games and materials

NOTE: For detailed description of "Learning Games," see pp. 50–59.

1. Name it or scramble: Use Christmas ornaments or models of symbols such as tree, Santa, Christmas stocking
2. Look and see: Use Christmas ornaments or symbols
3. Ponder posters: Use trees, Christmas balls, or stars with one or more different from the others in colour and position (see illustration below).
4. Alike, different, and the same: Children can choose from felt shapes that are: alike—all trees; different—trees of different sizes and shapes; or same—two trees exactly alike

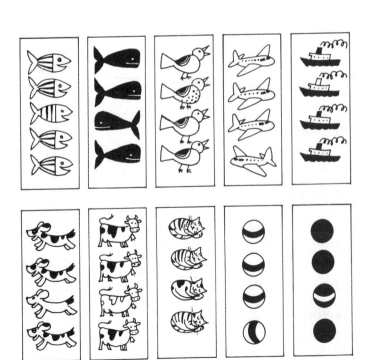

5. Christmas tree: Make a large two-dimensional felt Christmas tree about one foot high. Use felt stars, balls, and bells to decorate. Yarn or trimming braid may be used for garlands. Children may decorate tree as many times and in as many ways as they wish. The felt tree can be placed on a flannelboard or laid in a flat box and the trimmings placed in the lid (see p. 306 for a song that may be used with this tree).

6. Match-them and counting: Count or match one, two, three, four trees, bells, pine cones, sprays of evergreens, pictures or models of cars, dolls, or toys

7. Grouping and sorting by association: Mount Christmas stickers on small squares or circles of cardboard; sort into a partitioned box or into separate labelled boxes

8. See also group games for Christmas, pp. 307–308, for other teacher-made games two or three children can play with an adult at a table or on a mat.

Art Centre

- 1. Put out red and green easel paint only, to emphasize the basic Christmas colours.
- 2. Any creative art project may be made especially Christmas-like by using red and green in such media as blotto-painting, and string-painting, or by sprinkling glitter from small shakers on the finished product.
- 3. Invite children to experiment with long sprigs of evergreen as paintbrushes. Let them use a dark-coloured paint on white paper or white paint on dark-coloured paper. Makes a delicate painting.
- 4. Fingerpaint with red or green on large sheets of paper. When these are dry, children can, if they wish, cut Christmas designs such as big bells and trees from their fingerpaint paper as a second experience. Fingerpaintings may also be matted with a tree, bell, or Christmas tree ball shaped opening in the mat.
- •• 5. Spatterpaint Christmas shapes: Use white paint on red or green paper or vice versa. Child may select another colour.
- •• 6. Decorate windows: Use Christmas stencils, a sponge, and Glass Wax. Invite some children to help you.
- •• 7. Styrofoam sculpture: Invite children to use small pieces of styrofoam, precut by teacher from scraps, with coloured pipecleaners or lengths of scrap telephone wire to make interesting decorations to hang on the tree or set in the room or on the tables at snack time.
- •• 8. Set out wooden toothpicks with styrofoam balls. Children may wish to make 3-D stars. Colour the toothpicks with food colouring, a box at a time. This is much cheaper than purchasing coloured toothpicks.
- ••• 9. If the children are cutting out Christmas trees at a cut-and-paste table, set out paper punches, pencils, cuticle sticks, or meat skewers for anyone who may wish to punch holes in their trees. Have available variegated tissue and shiny metal-coloured paper at the table. Let children discover what happens when the punched-out trees are placed over other paper. It appears as though the tree has Christmas lights in it, or is lighted with coloured lights. Children may wish to paste the coloured paper to the backs of their trees.
- •• 10. If folded blank cards are available with a collage tray of various scrap materials for additives, children will enjoy designing their own cards or tree decorations.
- •• 11. Let children decorate green triangles or irregular Christmas tree shapes with collage trimmings such as lace, yarn, ribbon, felt scraps, buttons. Bits of coloured foil snipped by children can also be added.

  VARIATIONS:

  a. Yesterday's fingerpaintings can be cut into tree forms and decorated as described above.

  b. An egg carton lid can be used as a collage base. If children brush thinned white glue over its entire inside surface, they can then press down collage items selected to form their shadow-box picture. Dry and hang.

- 12. Children may paint their own wrapping paper by using printing tools such as sponge or wood or cork shapes precut by the teacher into Christmas designs. Older children may print on tissue paper if stamping pads are used. Usually newsprint or a plain paper shopping bag works best. Use paint sparingly in shallow trays or make pad of paint-soaked paper towels. VARIATION: A child-sized rolling pin can be covered with flocked vinyl wallpaper or a piece of textured upholstery. Secure with rubber bands. When rolled over a paint-soaked pad it can be used like a brayer to create designed wrapping paper. Other such brayer-type rollers which can be used similarly are hair rollers or spool brayers (see illustration, p. 30). The spool brayer can be used to create striped or plaid wrapping paper, greeting cards, or gift tags. Offer the children a variety of quality paper scraps from a print shop.

- 13. Provide a small artificial tree and appropriate-sized durable decorations to be used by one or two children at a time. Allow them to decorate, remove, and redecorate when and as they wish.

   NOTE: Move tree when children need it to expand their dramatic play, such as into home-living centre, or into the block-building centre when builders have completed a fireplace, a room, or a home and feel they need a tree to complete their furnishings.

Other experiences in this centre using art media

TREE DECORATIONS

- 1. Gallon milk bottle lids and other small plastic lids can be used as a base on which to glue or stick small Christmas stickers. Pictures cut from old greeting cards can also be used. Punch a hole for a ribbon or yarn hanger. Invite children to lick and stick.

- 2. Tree garlands can be made from lengths of yarn with Christmas seals stuck back to back at intervals enclosing the yarn.

- 3. Make available compartment sections of egg cartons for the children. These individual, bell-like sections may be covered with a circle of aluminum foil, painted, or decorated with magic markers. Real jingle bells, available from variety stores, can be threaded on a pipecleaner through the bell-like sections. Several may be attached to a ribbon or a piece of yarn to hang on the tree.

- 4. Pipecleaners and coloured plastic telephone wire can be twisted into wire sculptures to make candy cane ornaments and other tree ornaments.

- 5. Let children cut out decorations from playdough with cookie cutters, or older children might mold some. When dry, these can be painted with tempera and hung on the tree.

- 6. Invite children to roll, tear, cut, and crumple aluminum foil into various free-form sculptures. Set out some dowel sticks or pencils. (If a strip of foil is coil-wrapped around a pencil and slightly crumpled, it looks like an icicle.)

- 7. Colour glue by adding powder paint to white glue. Let children pour the glue into any mold they choose which has been lined with a piece of plastic wrap. Allow to dry for four days. Peel off paper. These ornaments can be hung by yarn if the teacher drills a hole in each.

- 8. Children will enjoy selecting pieces of styrofoam packing to string on yarn or string for frosty garlands. Threaded bobby pins make good needles. VARIATION: They may wish to punch holes in bits of coloured construction paper or use precut lengths of straw to alternate with the styrofoam and add colour to their garlands.

- 9. Cranberries and Cheerios can be strung to hang on trees for feeding the birds. Popcorn is frustrating for young children to string because the kernels break. Few children like raw cranberries.

   ★ CAUTION: Use blunt yarn needles. Allow adequate space and permit only one or two children to sew at a time.

••• 10. Brightly coloured flocked vinyl wallpaper can be cut into shapes to be hung on a Christmas tree for decorations. To make them sturdy mount on heavy cardboard.

GIFT IDEAS

• 1. Children can make hand prints on art paper. (A better-quality paper is more suitable for framing.) If a kiln is available, make hand prints from ceramic clay. Before firing, punch one or two holes at the top through which yarn or bright ribbon can be threaded later and tied in a bow for hanging.

•• 2. Show children how they can place a photo of themselves face-down in a glass caster and cover it with a round piece of cardboard. Children can then fill the caster cup with salt dough or plaster of Paris. When the dough is dry, paste or glue felt over the dough, invert with the felt side down, and use as a paperweight.

••• 3. Another paperweight can be made by filling the bottom of a milk carton 1.9 cm deep with plaster of paris or salt dough. Children may choose different kinds of seed pods, to be pushed into the plaster as close together as possible. Gum tree seeds, pine cones, arborvitae cones, and acorns work well. When plaster is dry, tear carton to remove, spray with clear plastic or antique gold, and glue felt to the bottom.

NOTE: Felt helps protect wood surfaces against scratches.

••• 4. A simple candleholder can be molded by children using a 7.6 cm ball of sawdust dough or salt dough (see recipes, pp. 27–28). Children need to flatten the bottom and to use a real candle to make the candle hole the size they wish. Allow to dry, paint white or another colour, sprinkle with glitter.

★ **CAUTION:** Be sure candle hole will hold candle straight.

•• 5. Pinecones are easily decorated by young children. Brush tip of each scale with glue and then sprinkle with glitter and sequins. The teacher may spray each cone with green, silver, or gold paint before the children decorate it, which will make a more ornate product or will give children greater choice in selecting the colour, size, and shape of their cone tree.

•• 6. Centrepieces: Children will enjoy creating their own holiday centrepieces to share with their families if given a variety of materials, such as pine cones, to be painted, glittered, or decorated. Children can use sequins, evergreen twigs or small branches, holly, discarded Christmas wrapping bows and bits of ribbon, doilies, and a container. Cardboard fruit cartons or berry boxes can be wrapped or laced with strips of yarn or ribbon. Crumpled aluminum foil or sturdy wrapping paper can also be used to cover the container.

••• 7. An abstract or "accidental" design can be made by children either by dripping or squirting streams of thinned acrylic paint (polyresin base) on a solid-coloured piece of upholstery fabric, or by placing shavings from a batik crayon on the same kind of fabric and pressing with a warm iron under waxed paper. If colour combinations are planned by the teacher, and not too many colours are used, the result cannot fail and may be beautiful enough to be permanently stretched over a wood frame.

Book Centre

NOTE: When choosing books for the book centre, try to respect the traditions of the children in your program. Pick books that are consistent with the philosophy of your centre, keeping in mind the discussion on pp. 2–3.

••• Barry, Robert. *Mr. Willoughby's Christmas Tree.* New York: McGraw-Hill, 1963.
••• Bianco, Pamela. *The Doll in the Window.* New York: Henry Z. Walck, 1953.
••• De Brunhoff, Jean. *Babar and Father Christmas.* New York: Random House, 1946.

• • • Duvoisin, Roger. *One Thousand Christmas Beards.* New York: Alfred A. Knopf, 1955.

• • _____ . *Petunia's Christmas.* New York: Alfred A. Knopf, 1952.

• • _____ . *The Christmas Whale.* New York: Alfred A. Knopf, 1945.

• • • Ets, Marie Hall. *Nine Days to Christmas.* New York: Viking Press, 1959. (Read for *Las Posadas.*)

• • Freeman, Don. *Corduroy.* New York: Viking Press, 1958, (paper, 1970; film, record, cassette).

• • Hoff, Syd. *Santa's Moose.* Markham, Ont: Fitzhenry & Whiteside, 1986.

• • • Joslin, Sysyle. *Baby Elephant and the Secret Wishes.* New York: Harcourt Brace Jovanovich, 1962.

• • • • Kalman, Bobbie, et. al. *We Celebrate Family Days.* Toronto: Crabtree Publishing, 1986.

• • • • _____ . *We Celebrate Christmas.* Toronto: Crabtree Publishing, 1986.

• • • Karasz, Ilonka. *The Twelve Days of Christmas.* New York: Harper & Row, 1949.

• • • Keats, Ezra Jack. *The Little Drummer Boy.* New York: Macmillan, 1968 (paper, 1972).

• Khalsa, Dayal, Kaur. *Merry Christmas Baabee.* Montreal: Tundra Books, 1985.

• • • Kroeber, Theodora. *A Green Christmas.* Berkeley, Calif.: Parnassus Press, 1967.

• • • • Kurelek, William. *A Northern Nativity.* Montreal: Tundra Books, 1976. (Read–Tell)

• Lenski, Lois. *I Like Winter.* New York: Oxford University Press, 1950.

• • Lipkind, William and Nicholas Mordvinoff. *Christmas Bunny.* New York: Harcourt Brace Jovanovich, 1953.

• • • Miller, Edna. *Mousekin's Christmas Eve.* Englewood Cliffs, N.J.: Prentice-Hall, 1965 (paper).

• • Moore, Clement C. *The Night Before Christmas.* New York: Random House, 1961 (paper, 1970).

• • Piper, Watty. *The Little Engine That Could.* New York: Platt & Munk, 1930.

• • Politi, Leo. *Pedro, the Angel of Olvera Street.* New York: Scribner's 1972.

• • _____ . *The Nicest Gift.* New York: Scribner's, 1964.

• • _____ . *Rosa.* New York: Scribner's, 1964 (also in Spanish).

• • • • Rockwell, Anne. *Befana.* New York: Atheneum, 1974. (Read–Tell)

• • • Speare, Jean, and Ann Blades. *A Candle for Christmas.* Vancouver: Douglas & McIntyre, 1986.

• • • • Swede, George. *Dudley and the Christmas Thief.* Toronto: Three Trees Press, 1986.

• • Templeton, Bill. *How Mrs. Claus Saves Christmas!* Toronto: Collins, 1978.

• • Woolaver, Lance, *Christmas With the Rural Mail.* Halifax: Nimbus Publishing Ltd., 1979.

Planning for Group Time

NOTE: All music, fingerplays, poems, stories, and games listed here may be used at other times during the session as appropriate. See Core Library, "Basic Resources," p. 95, for publishers and addresses. Record company addresses can be found on p. 99. In parodies, hyphenated words match music notes of the song used.

Music

Songs

There is a wealth of lovely and suitable songs for this subject. When choosing songs from among your favourites, remember the criteria for choice of songs on p. 35 (in "Basic Resources").

From *Singing Bee,* Hart
"Santa's Chimney," p. 146
"Jingle Bells," p. 150
"Pat-a-Pan," p. 152
"We Wish You a Merry Christmas," p. 153

From *Piggyback Songs,* Warren
"Ten Little Reindeer," p. 11
"On Christmas Day," p. 12
"Guess Who?" p. 12

From *More Piggyback Songs,* Warren
"Christmas Time Is Here," p. 12
"Christmas Time Is Near," p. 13
"Christmas Time," p. 13
"The Merry Christmas Band," p. 15
"S-A-N-T-A," p. 16
"Santa's Coming," p. 16
"He'll Be Driving Eight Brown Reindeer," p. 17
"Rudolph's Light," p. 17
"Christmas Cookies," p. 18
"Merry Christmas Everywhere," p. 18
"Gingerbread Boy," p. 19
"Gingerbread," p. 19

From *Tunes for Tots,* Warner and Berry
"Sleigh Bells," p. 30
"Christmas Bells," p. 31
"Santa," p. 32

From *Stepping Along in Music Land,* Murray
"Christmas Presents on Parade," p. 51

From *A Treasury of Songs for Children,* Glazer
"Christmas Is Coming," p. 50

From a book of traditional songs or sheet music in your own collection
"Twinkle, Twinkle, Little Star"
"Jingle Bells"
"Up on the House Top"
"Here Comes Santa Claus"
"Santa Claus Is Coming to Town"
"Rudolph, the Red-Nosed Reindeer"
"Merry Christmas to You" (tune: "Happy Birthday to You")
"'Twas the Night Before Christmas"
"Away in a Manger"

DOWN THE CHIMNEY SANTA CAME (a parody)
(tune: "London Bridge")

VERSE 1: Guess whose beard is long and white? long and white? long and white?
          Guess whose beard is long and white? Dear old San-ta!
VERSE 2: Guess whose suit is red and white? . . . Dear old San-ta!
VERSE 3: Guess who comes on Christ-mas Eve? . . . Dear old San-ta!
VERSE 4: Down the chim-ney, San-ta came, . . . Dear old San-ta!
VERSE 5: With a doll that says "Ma-ma," . . . Dear old San-ta!
VERSE 6: With a train that goes "Choo-choo," . . . Dear old San-ta!
VERSE 7: With a truck that goes "Beep-beep," . . . Dear old San-ta!

NOTE: Repeat in each verse, as in verse 1. Encourage the children to help you think of
          other verses to fit the tune.

Rhythms and singing games

Make a felt cutout of a Christmas tree about 23 cm wide by 30.5 cm high and tack it to a bulletin board or a heavy piece of cardboard. Also using felt, make the decorations that are mentioned in capital letters in the parody below. While the teacher and children sing the song, one or more children may add the decorations to the tree.

HERE'S OUT LITTLE PINE TREE (a parody)
(tune: "I'm a Little Teapot")
Adaptation by Darlene Hamilton

Here's out lit-tle pine TREE
　　tall and straight.
Let's find the things
　　so we can dec-o-rate
First we want to put
　　a STAR on top!
Then we must be care-ful
　　the BALLS don't pop
Hang on all the TIN-SEL
　　shin-y and bright
Put on the CANES
　　and hook them just right
Fin-ally put some PRES-ENTS
　　for you and for me
And we'll be read-y
　　with our CHRIST-MAS TREE!

brush star with
glue and sprinkle
with glitter

glue rope tinsel
to length of felt

cut shape
of tree
from piece
of felt

candy cane:
stripe white felt
with marker
or paint

place gifts
and toys in front
of felt tree

Records and cassettes

New tapes and records are issued every year and as many recordings are taken out of circulation every year. As a result, a tape and record list would be out of date before this book goes to print. There is always a good choice of records and tapes. Keep in mind that children enjoy listening to complex melodies and rhythms, but that recordings chosen for singing along must have songs that are within the range and ability of the children.

NOTE: See also Large Muscle Activities, which soon follows, for other musical participation games.

Fingerplays and Poems

From *Let's Do Fingerplays*, Grayson
"Christmas Is A-Coming," p. 92
"Santa Claus," p. 92
"Christmas Bells," p. 92
"Christmas Tree," p. 93
"Here Is the Chimney," p. 94

CHRISTMAS IS HERE

Here is the wreath that hangs on the door, (MAKE A CIRCLE WITH ARMS OVER HEAD)
Here is the fir tree that stands on the floor, (MAKE A TRIANGLE WITH THUMBS AND FOREFINGERS)
Here is the book from which carols are sung, (PALMS TOUCHING AND FACING UPWARD LIKE BOOK PAGES)
Here is the mantel from which stockings are hung. (PLACE ONE BENT ARM OVER THE OTHER BENT ARM IN FRONT OF BODY, DROP ONE ARM LIKE A HANGING STOCKING)

Here is the chimney that Santa comes down. (MAKE AN UPRIGHT RECTANGLE WITH THUMBS AS THE BASE AND FINGERS FOR THE SIDES)
Here is the snow that covers the town, (FINGERS FLUTTER DOWN)
Here is a box in which is hid (CLOSE RIGHT FIRST WITH THUMB INSIDE AND PLACE LEFT HAND ON TOP)
A Jack that pops up, when you open the lid. (LIFT LEFT HAND UP AND POP OUT THUMB)

CHILDREN'S CHRISTMAS TREE

Here the children's Christmas tree (MAKE TRIANGLE WITH THUMBS FOR THE BASE AND THE FINGERS FORMING THE PEAK)
Standing straight and tall.
Here's the pot to put it in (CUP HANDS TOGETHER)
So it will not fall.

Here are two balls bright and gay (MAKE CIRCLES WITH THUMB AND INDEX FINGER OF EACH HAND)
One ball—two balls—see? (HOLD UP TO SEE)
And two tall candles red! (HOLD INDEX FINGERS UP STRAIGHT FOR CANDLES)
To trim our Christmas tree. (REPEAT TRIANGLE FOR TREE)

Stories

(To read, read-tell, or tell. See Book Centre for complete list.)

A Candle for Christmas is a sensitive story about a family that is reunited for Christmas. The illustrations reflect the contrast between a northern winter landscape and safe and secure indoor family scenes. The story can be edited for younger children.

Games

(See "Learning Games," pp. 50–59, and teacher-made games in this chapter for directions.)
  1. Guess what? (Christmas riddles): Teacher describes a Christmas symbol or a toy and the children guess; for instance, "I'm brown and white, have four legs and antlers, and pull Santa's sleigh. Who am I?"

2. Merry Christmas (variation of listening): Children are seated in semi-circle. Teacher chooses one child to hide eyes by putting his or her head in teacher's lap (otherwise they can't resist peeking). Teacher points to one of the children in the semi-circle, who says, "Merry Christmas to you!" or "Hi Santa!" Child who just said "Merry Christmas" then hides his or her eyes. Child must guess voice. This game requires that the children know each other well.

3. Santa and his reindeer (or elves): Children are seated in semi-circle. Teacher chooses one child to be Santa. She or he puts his head in teacher's lap. Teacher points to one of the children (reindeer or elf). This child hides. Santa is then told to look at the remaining reindeer or elves to see if she or he can tell who is missing. The hidden reindeer or elf then becomes the new Santa.

Routine Times

1. Use the fingerplays while the children are coming to the table for snack time. Milk may be coloured red or green with food colouring. (Let the children drop in the colour themselves.) They may eat the cookies that they have baked or frosted.

2. When washing hands, let children make thick soap suds and make lovely Santa beards! Mirrors add to the fun if you do not normally have them on the wall by the wash basins.

3. Christmas carols may be played softly on the piano or record player during rest time.

4. When walking or busing, look for Santa and Christmas decorations.

Large Muscle Activities

(Traditional tunes are used in games 1 to 4 below. All pages noted are from the *Music Resource Book*, Lutheran Church Press.)

1. Did you ever see a toy?—adaptation of "Did you ever see a lassie?" p. 86. Children watch child in the circle who acts out the motions of any toy (truck, doll, or racing car), and then they try to guess the name of the toy.

2. Here we go round the Christmas tree—adaptation of "Here we go round the mulberry bush," p. 92. "This is the way to chop the tree, carry it home, stand it up, put on the lights."

3. See the puppets, p. 45—pretend to be puppets; move with words describing an action.

4. Santa's pack: Let children all choose a toy to "be" and carry. Child who plays Santa calls out name of toy to be added to his pack in his invisible sleigh. Child joins Santa in a follow-the-leader trip around the room, leaving toys where they belong on shelves. Adapt to suit your group and space. VARIATION: Can also be played like Fruit Basket Upset with record or piano music to signal change (delivery) of toys. Santa may choose children to join him by touching them or motioning when music stops. All go to place and new Santa can be chosen.

Extended Experiences

1. Organ recital: If you are fortunate enough to know an organist, perhaps he or she will allow the children to watch and listen for a few minutes while he or she practices Christmas music at a nearby church.

2. Visit a Santa: Visit a department store to see a Santa, or interesting store windows planned especially for children. Plan smaller groups for such an excursion. Extra adults will be necessary to help supervise the group. VARIATION: Have a Santa visit your group. Plan for him or her to share or bring a treat. (You may provide it!)

3. Choose a real tree for your centre and after the holiday plant it in your school yard or in the yard of a teacher or parent as soon as weather permits. (England)

4. Plan a display of Christmas cards from other countries. Check with parents, armed forces personnel, ministers, and students from other countries, all of whom might have such cards. Examine and note how they are alike or different and notice particularly the stamps on the envelopes.

5. Plan to decorate an evergreen tree or potted branch with treats for the birds. Your favourite garden centre or tree nursery will be helpful with seed suggestions.

   NOTE: Let children string, hang, or fill containers with popped corn, cracked corn, cubes of cheese, doughnuts (stale or fresh), rolled oats, melon rinds, raisins, cranberries, pork fat, crumbs, cabbage or lettuce leaves, pumpkin or water-melon seeds, grain, peanut butter (if mixed with cornmeal so it will not choke the birds), and uncooked peas. (Scandinavia)

6. Make some Danish rice pudding. (Denmark)

7. Hang colourful Swedish Christmas wall hangings over your walls. (Sweden)

8. Make and decorate some Christmas cookies. Select cookie cutters shaped like shepherds, sheep, Wise Men, donkeys, and baby Jesus and other nativity figures. (Germany, Poland)

9. Invite children to share food, mittens, and other items with those less fortunate than themselves. St. Barbara's Day (December 4th) would be a good date. (Syria and Japan)

10. Display a hand-carved crèche borrowed from a friend. (Austria, Czechoslovakia)

11. Buy or borrow a few wooden, straw, or other unbreakable Christmas tree ornaments imported from another country. (Germany, Panama, or Scandinavian countries)

12. Invite a Japanese friend to paper-fold some fish, stars, or butterflies (symbols of Christ) for your tree. (Japan)

13. Display pictures of trees showing decorations of different ethnic groups.

14. View a *nacimiento* (crèche which usually includes a whole village scene), a *pesebre* (manger), or *ceppo* (tree-like group of shelves for gifts and crèche) in the home of a Spanish-American, Mexican, or Italian family, during the *novena* of *Las Posadas*. You might try to prepare a *nacimiento* in a corner of your room with the children's help. (Mexico, Spain, Italy, South American countries)

15. Invite a harpist (student) to play Welsh carols or other Christmas music. (Wales)

16. Share simple gifts on the Twelfth Night, January 6th (see p. 303 for suggestions regarding gifts). (Many countries)

17. Borrow a *pepparkakor* tree from a Swedish friend. *Pepparkakor* is the name for ginger cookies. Hang Christmas treats on the tree and serve snacks one day (see p. 293 for a description of the tree). (Sweden)

18. Encourage the children to draw a picture letter for their parents. Older children might choose a piece of paper labeled "I love you because you ..." or "I promise to help by ..." to be folded up and sealed inside a decorated envelope to be placed by their father's plate at dinner. (Italy)

19. Make small cone-shaped containers for treats from flocked vinyl wallpaper scraps to decorate a tree. Staple on small sprays of flowers as you attach ribbon or yarn handles. Staple silver or small white plastic doilies into decorative baskets and attach twisted silver cord or braid for handles. (England)

Teacher Resources

Allen, G.P. *Days to Remember.* Toronto: Ontario Ministry of Culture and Recreation, 1979.

Barber, Mary, and Flora McPherson. *Christmas in Canada.* Toronto: J.M. Dent, 1972. (A Story to Tell)

Barer-Stein, T. *You Eat What You Are.* Toronto: McClelland and Stewart, 1979.

Coffin, T.P. *The Book of Christmas Folklore.* New York: Seabury Press, 1973.

Crean, P. *The Fitzhenry and Whiteside Fireside Book of Canadian Christmas.* Markham, Ont: Fitzhenry & Whiteside, 1986.

Harper, Kenn, ed. *Christmas in the Big Igloo.* Yellowknife: Outcrop, 1983.

Hunter, D., and J. Shipley. *Making Your Own Traditions: Christmas Fast and Easy Crafts and Recipes for Parents and Kids.* Traditions, 1984.

Ickis, Marguerite. *The Book of Festivals and Holidays the World Over.* New York: Dodd Mead and Co., 1970.

Joy, M. *Highdays and Holidays.* Boston: Faber & Faber, 1981.

Laurence, Margaret. *The Christmas Birthday Story,* Toronto: McClelland and Stewart, 1980. (A Story to Tell)

MacDougall, S. *Christmas Cooking for Santa.* MacDougall, 1984.

Manning-Saunders, R. *Festivals.* London: Heinemann, 1973.

Nicker, B. *Celebrate the Sun.* Toronto: McClelland and Stewart.

Stephan, B. *Decorations for Holiday Celebrations.* New York: Crown, 1978.

Wernecke, H.H. *Christmas Customs Around the World.* Philadelphia: Westminster Press, 1979.

Kwanzaa
(Keh-WAHN-zah)

This special holiday, celebrated by some Black families from December 26th to January 1st, is in recognition of traditional African harvest festivals. In the African language Kiswahili, *Kwanzaa* means "first fruits." The holiday originally began as an alternative to the highly commercialized version of Christmas. It starts on Christmas Day and lasts for an entire week, with special parties on successive days, and often ends with a community-wide harvest feast and party on the seventh day. Small gifts are traditionally given on each day. The *Kwanzaa* holiday stresses the unity of the Black family. Often, homemade or homegrown gifts, such as pecan pralines, molasses peanut brittle, molasses bread, and fruit are given.

Seven lessons associated with observing this holiday and a key word for each are listed below:
1. *umoja* (unity)
   We must stand together.
2. *kujichagulia* (self-determination)
   We must decide in our own way.
3. *ujima* (cooperation)
   We must work together.
4. *ujamaca* (sharing by all)
   We must share what we have.
5. *kuumba* (creativity)
   We need to use creativity in reflecting pride in and in caring for our community.
6. *nia* (purpose)
   We must have a purpose in life to make a better world.
7. *imani* (faith)
   We need to have faith which will result in works and action.

Customs of the traditional African Holiday

1. Lighting candles called *mishumaas* to remind people to live and build together.
2. Placing candles in the *kinara* (candleholder) on a straw mat called the *mkeka* in the centre of the table.
3. Holding a feast on the last day of *Kwanzaa* during which everyone drinks from a unity cup called the *kikombe.*
4. Giving each child an ear of corn. This corn is called *mihindi.*
5. Giving gifts on the last day. These love gifts are called *zawadi.*

The following recipe is a traditional African treat. It is associated with *John Canoe,* the celebration that African slaves held at Christmas time. It also can be enjoyed by children during *Kwanzaa.*

SWEET POTATO CANDY

.45 kg/1 lb. sweet potatoes (450 mL/2 cups)
450 mL/2 cups sugar (225 mL/1 brown, 225 mL/1 white)
5 mL/1 tsp. lemon juice
225 mL/1 cup marshmallows (optional)

For flavouring, you may add:
    pineapple juice
    orange juice
    vanilla or cinnamon

Wash and boil sweet potatoes.
Cool, peel, and mash potatoes in a colander to remove strings.
Place in a pan and add lemon juice, sugar, and marshmallows.
Cook over low flame, stirring constantly until very thick.
Set aside to cool.
Add vanilla and/or other flavouring.
Spoon out candy into paper cups.
Dust with powdered sugar, or sprinkle with sugar candies such as candy beads.

Extended Experiences

1. Allow your children to make love gifts for a friend or family member.
2. Serve fruit or make sweet potato candy.
3. Mount pictures of Black families doing things together for the holidays.
4. Eat ears of corn if meals are served at your centre, light candles, and have a *Kwanzaa* party.
5. For further information about this holiday, write: Institute of Positive Education, 7528 Cottage Grove Avenue, Chicago, IL 60619.
6. Chase, William D. *Chase's Calendar of Calendar Events.* revised edition. Flint, MI: Appletree Press, 1986.

PART 4

Seasons

★★★

Contents

Introduction

Basic Understandings

(concepts children can grasp from this subject)

▷   In North America we have four seasons—winter, spring, summer and fall.

▷   Each season has a different type of weather.

▷   In Canada we can have different weather across the country in the same season. For example: in January (winter) flowers can be growing in the sun in Victoria, rain can be falling in Vancouver, warm winds (called chinooks) can be blowing down on the Prairies, wet snow can be falling in Toronto and Montreal, and heavy snow can be falling in the Maritimes.

▷   We do some things in specific seasons.

▷   We wear clothes that are comfortable and safe in each season.

▷   Our homes are built to keep us comfortable in different seasons.

Additional Facts the Teacher Should Know

It is difficult for children to comprehend the full significance of any of the seasons. The concepts of seasons are best introduced when there is some noticeable change in the weather or when there is some seasonally related local activity; for example, when the lawn outside the centre is re-seeded, or the roads are repaired, or the last crops of the season are harvested.

Book Centre

•   Anno, M. *Anno's Counting Book.* New York: Thomas Y. Crowell, 1977.

•••   Aska, Warabe. *Who Goes to the Park.* Montreal: Tundra, 1984.

•••   _____. *Who Hides in the Park.* Montreal: Tundra, 1986. (Trilingual: English, French, Japanese)

•   Coleridge, S. *January Brings the Snow.* New York: Dial Press, 1986.

•••   Gibbons, G. *The Seasons of Arnold's Apple Tree.* New York: Harcourt Brace Jovanovich, 1984.

•••   Harris, D.J., and V. van Kamper. *Four Seasons for Toby.* Richmond Hill, Ont: North Winds Press, 1987.

•••   Littlewood, Valerie. *The Season Clock.* Markham, Ont: Penguin Books, 1986.

••••   Newman, Fran, and Claudette Boulanger. *Snowflakes and Sunshine.* Richmond Hill, Ont: North Winds Press, 1979.

•••   Patience, John. *The Seasons in Fern Hollow.* New York: Outlet Book Co.

- Pienkowski, Jan. *Weather.* New York: Messner, 1983.
- Rockwell, Anne. *First Comes Spring.* New York: Thomas Y. Crowell, 1985.
- Spier, P. *Dreams.* New York: Doubleday, 1986. (an interesting book about clouds)
- Tafuri, Nancy. *All Year Long.* New York: Greenwillow Press, 1983.
- Wolff, A. *A Year of Beasts.* New York: Dutton, 1986.
    _____. *A Year of Birds.* New York: Dodd Mead, 1984.

NOTE: See p. 337 in the chapter on Spring for additional references.

12 Winter

★★★★★★★★★★★★★★★★★★★★★★

Basic Understandings

(concepts children can grasp from this subject)

Winter is a season that comes after fall and before spring. There are many changes in nature in winter.

Earth changes

▷ When it gets very cold, water freezes (gets hard), making ice, such as snow, sleet, icicles; also, materials that contain water will freeze.
   a. Sleet is frozen raindrops.
   b. Snow is frozen crystals of water.
   c. Ice is a frozen mass of water.
▷ In many areas the weather is warmer and it rains instead of snowing.
▷ We have blizzards when a strong wind blows for a long time during a heavy snowstorm. It causes deep snowdrifts and makes it hard for people to see or move around outside.
▷ Daylight hours get shorter in Canada in winter; in parts of the North there are some days with no daylight at all.
▷ Children have more chance to see the moon and stars before going to bed or when they wake up early (see "Day and Night" p. 499).
▷ Usually, the winter weather is colder, chillier, and damper, and the wind is more likely to feel cold than in other seasons of the year.
▷ The length of the winter season will be longer or shorter depending on the kind of weather there is where we live.

Plants

▷ Where it is very cold most plants stop growing for a while. (They seem to die but their seeds, roots, or bulbs often live underground, protected from the frost by dirt and a blanket of snow.)
▷ Where it rains instead of snowing, flowers and trees continue to bloom and grow all year round.
▷ Some shrubs and trees grow and bloom all year round and are called "evergreens."
▷ Some trees lose their leaves and become bare.
▷ Some indoor plants seldom bloom except during the winter—for example, the Christmas cactus.
▷ When frozen, plants wilt and turn brown.

Animals

▷ Some animals hibernate (rest or sleep for a long time) during the winter.

▷ Animals hibernate in trees, underground, in caves.

▷ Birds migrate (fly away) to a warmer climate where they can find food during the winter months.

▷ Sometimes, wild animals grow thicker fur, down, or hair in winter to keep them warm.

▷ Some animals' fur changes colour in the winter to help camouflage and hide them when it snows.

▷ A few animals, such as ants and squirrels, store food for winter.

▷ Some animals enjoy playing in the snow and on the ice.

▷ Special care must be taken of some animals in winter, such as sweaters for short-haired pet dogs, protection for livestock against blizzards, food for birds who remain, or for those who return too early when there is a late snow in spring.

People

▷ Depending upon how cold it is children and adults need to wear heavier, warmer, or special clothes in winter, for play and work, such as boots, sweaters, scarves, mittens, caps, hats, coats, thermal underwear, snow suits, parkas.

▷ Children and adults enjoy playing in snow or on ice, such as sledding, skating, skiing, tobogganing, snow mobiling, or ice fishing.

▷ Where it is very cold, people often spend more time indoors in winter—baking, using fireplaces, giving parties, reading, playing games, sipping hot chocolate.

▷ People need to clear snow from sidewalks and streets in order to walk or drive safely.

▷ Cold weather, rain, snow, and freezing sometimes make it difficult to build or paint houses or to pour cement.

▷ Drivers have to put antifreeze in their cars to prevent the water in their radiators from freezing when it is very cold. Sometimes they need snow tires and chains such as when driving on snow or on ice.

▷ People are more likely to catch colds and flu in winter when we have less sunshine.

▷ When it gets too cold outside we need to heat the buildings where we live, work, or play, and turn on the heaters in buses, cars, and trucks.

▷ People whose job is to catch fish often cannot work in the winter because of the cold weather. However, some people do go ice fishing.

▷ Farmers are not as busy with crops during the winter, but they have many important tasks with their animals. They must keep them warm, well fed, and clean.

Additional Facts the Teacher Should Know

1. It is difficult for young children to comprehend the full significance of any of the seasons. However, they can understand that winter is a time when certain changes take place in our environment and certain events, activities, and holidays occur.

2. Winter is one of the four seasons of the year. In most of Canada winter extends from approximately December 21st to March 20th. Winter in the southern hemisphere is from June 21st to September 22nd. These are the official dates determined by solar and lunar phases. It is easier for young children to understand changes in weather; such changes usually present better times to introduce the themes of the seasons.

3. The four seasons vary in time and length all over the world as the sun's rays strike the earth differently at any one time. Because it gets dark early in this season, winter is a good time to learn about day and night (see "Day and Night", p. 499). The stars are visible in the winter while the young child is still awake. Parents should be encouraged to help the child find and enjoy them.

4. Each snowflake is unique—no two are alike! All snowflakes are hexagonal (have six sides). You can help children appreciate their uniqueness and beauty by providing them with magnifying glasses and enlarged photographic reproductions. The exact way in which they grow depends on what is happening in the atmosphere when they are formed. Snow that comes from very high and very cold clouds, where rapid freezing takes place, have simple crystals. Snow falling from and through warmer air builds up more elaborate patterns.

5. Snow festivals are celebrated in many northern countries including Canada. The most famous Canadian winter carnival is in Quebec City, but there are many local carnivals and festivals. Check with your Chamber of Commerce and/or tourist board to find out if any special winter celebrations are planned for your area.

6. The Ice Follies and Ice Capades are just two of the troupes that tour and perform in ice skating shows in arenas. These shows are enjoyed by whole families. Some children travel with their families to ski resorts and winter recreation parks for special fun with ice and snow. All children enjoy snow if it is a part of the winter weather where they live.

7. Mistletoe, holly, poinsettia plants, and evergreens are the most common plants and flowers used for decoration during the Christmas season. Both mistletoe and poinsettia plants are poisonous to humans if eaten, so if you use these plants for decoration take proper precautions. Tell the children that "some plants are good to eat and some are not good to eat and will even make us sick." If you live where it is too cold for plants to grow outside you may wish to plant bulbs or seeds indoors. This will give the children an opportunity to understand that plants need warmth and light to grow.

8. Most birds migrate in fall or early winter because food becomes scarce, not because it is cold. Birds grow an undercoating of down that keeps them warm. However, when ponds freeze and snow covers the ground and many bugs and insects die or hibernate, birds have limited sources of food. Children might enjoy helping feed birds during the winter (see illustration). However, if you start a bird-feeding station you should maintain it all through the winter or else the birds who remain because of your efforts may be stranded and die.

Make a bird feeder from a three-litre size plastic bleach jug. Cut out two sides so the birds can fly through. Weight jug with coarse pebbles and fill it with birdseed. Wire it securely to a tree limb.

9. Suet or bacon fat can be melted and mixed with wild birdseed in equal proportions. This mixture can be poured into half walnut shells, aluminum pie plates, margarine containers, paper cups, or on pine cones; wires can be attached to the containers through punched holes and then tied to the tree.

10. Pour melted fat over birdseed mixture in small paper cups. Insert wire or pipecleaners into the mixture with 5 cm or so protruding. When hardened, peel away the paper and hang on a tree. Stale bread or doughnuts can be hung on the branches or crumbled and thrown on the ground. Chicken scratch, livestock grain, and apple peelings are also appreciated by birds. If you do not have a suitable tree or bush, food can be spread out on the top of a box. A simple V-shape roof nailed to the box would provide protection from the wind while eating. Dishes holding food should be nailed or tied down because some birds push and shove while crowding around food.

11. Children may wish to help our small animal friends by building a shelter for them. Dead branches heaped over an old stump, a pile of rocks, logs, or rail piles make good escape cover or winter dens. Old drain tiles buried under rocks and earth make artificial burrows. Children can put nuts and seeds out for squirrels, and leafy vegetables, beans, and carrots for rabbits. Interest in animals that live well in ice and snow may be developed through pictures of polar bears, penguins, and seals. (See also "Animals of the Woods.")

12. Citrus fruits grown in Florida, Texas, southern California and Mexico are the most prevalent ones available in the winter. Grapefruit, oranges, and tangerines are plentiful and make good snacks peeled and sectioned or squeezed and drunk. Many young children do not like grapefruit or its juice by itself, but if it is combined with other fruit or juices it is acceptable in small amounts. Cranapple juice is also available now. (Other parts of the guide related to Winter include "My World" and "Animals.")

Methods Most Adaptable for Introducing this Subject to Children

1. Note changes in weather, trees, birds, animals, etc.
2. Notice when it snows for the first time.
3. Take a pan of water outside on a freezing day. Observe the results.
4. Observe that some trees have bare branches and some don't.
5. Prepare a bird feeder or animal shelter.
6. Read a story about winter or the four seasons.
7. Bring in a large dishpan or baby's bathtub filled with snow.

Vocabulary

winter	trees	temperature	snowflake
snow	bare	road salt	hockey
cold	evergreens	snow shovel	mistletoe
ice	birds	snowplow	holly
icicle	snowmobile	snowblower	poinsettia
rain	tobaggan	ski	snow tires
fog	snow shoes	sled	parka
blizzard	animals	skate	long johns
snowstorm	feeder	sleet	mittens
snow squall	hibernate	Jack Frost	ski jacket
freeze	migrate	igloo	snow suit
			toque

Learning Centres

NOTE: Many suggestions are made for climates where there is snow. If you live in a milder climate, adapt each suggestion to rain (see "Water Around Me"); or use ice or frost from freezer or refrigerator where feasible. If, however, mountains are nearby, you can take along a cooler and pack some snowballs/snow/icicles for children to see when you return.

Discovery Centre

1. Take a pan of water outside when the temperature is below freezing. Observe what happens. After it has frozen bring the pan inside again; what happens?
2. Fill a juice can and a half-pint milk carton with water. Staple milk carton shut. Take both outside in freezing weather or place in a freezer. Observe what happens. VARIATION: Set out a small carton of milk to freeze. When frozen give children a spoonful to taste.
3. Bring a pan of snow inside for measuring and exploring.
4. Bring icicles inside and place in a suitable container to observe as they melt.
5. Outside, observe snowflakes that fall on children's coat sleeves or catch some on a dark velvet cloth. Use magnifying glass if available.
6. Make snow cones by packing clean crushed ice in paper cups with an ice-cream scoop or large spoon and pouring fruit-flavoured gelatin powder or syrup over the ice. Let children choose the flavour they want. Other flavourings and diluted food colouring may also be added if you like.
7. Store some snowballs or cartons of snow in the deep freeze so that the children can discover the snow is still frozen in late winter or early spring when the snow has melted and disappeared completely outside. Discuss why.
8. Make ice cream, using your favourite recipe. Talk about why the cream freezes.
9. Let children mix food colouring with snow.
10. Look for animal or bird tracks in the snow.
11. Buy as large and as accurate a thermometer as you can and let the children observe, under supervision indoor-outdoor thermometers: allow children to compare the two and see the similarities and differences. They can see that as it gets colder the mercury goes down.

Playing with snow. If weather does not permit the children to play outdoors in the snow, bring the snow indoors for a discovery experience.

12. Make a large cardboard thermometer. (See Discovery Centre p. 556, no. 5.) Use extra wide cardboard and paste pictures of children in appropriate clothes beside the related temperatures: snowsuit, cap, and mittens for under 5° celsius; a warm jacket, hat, and mittens for temperatures of 5° to 10°; a light jacket or sweater for 15°.
13. Make Jack wax. Pour two cups of maple syrup in a saucepan and boil until the softball stage is reached. Pour the hot syrup over crushed ice in a salad bowl. Twirl the wax onto forks.
14. Go outside on a cold day to see water vapour when children breathe and talk.
15. To show that plants need sunlight force a hyacinth bulb. In the fall plant hyacinth bulbs outside in a buried pot. Dig it up in January and bring it inside. Put it in a warm, dark place. Soon yellow leaves will appear. Move the plant to a sunny ledge and watch the leaves turn green and the plant grow and blossom.

NOTE: See the Discovery Centre sections in the chapters on water and animals.

Dramatic Play Centres

Home-living centre

1. Set out heavy blankets, sweaters, warm jackets, hats, snowsuits, and parkas for the dolls, suggesting the need for warmer clothes in the winter.
2. Put up pictures of snow, rain, and activities related to each. Include pictures of children dressed for freezing temperatures or rainy weather, using some that are appropriate to your area's climate.

Block-building centre

1. Set out animal figures and suggest that unit blocks be used to build a barn, a stable, or another animal shelter.
2. A bulldozer can be a make-believe snowplow and dump trucks can be used to haul away the snow.
3. Toy logs can be set out for older children to build houses as the first settlers did their first winter.
4. Blocks can be used to build igloos.

Learning, Language, and Readiness Materials Centre

Commercially made games and materials

(See "Basic Resources," pp. 79, 100, for manufacturers' addresses.)

1. *Puzzles:* Snowflake puzzles and other puzzles with winter themes.
2. *Small toys for imaginative play:* Snowplows, snowmobiles, and sleds made of vinyl, plastic or metal.
3. *Outdoor toys:* Dog sleds and model snowmobiles. Plastic child-sized snow shovels and pails for digging and playing in the snow.

    NOTE: Choose a sturdy vinyl that is less likely to crack in the cold.) Child-sized hockey sticks and vinyl hockey pucks.

4. *Dolls and puppets:* Glove puppets. Winter clothes for dolls.
5. *Flannelboards and flannelboard aids:* Weather cutouts—for example, storm clouds, sun, etc.

6. *Posters:* Weather boards

   NOTE: Choose boards that can be changed each day, preferably by one of the children.)

7. *Miscellaneous:* Large indoor–outdoor thermometer in an unbreakable case.

Teacher-made games and materials

NOTE: For a detailed description of "Learning Games," see pp. 50–59.

1. What's missing? Use a styrofoam snowball, plastic or paper snowflake, pair of mittens, pair of earmuffs, ski mask.
2. Match them: Show children a styrofoam snowball. Say, "This snowball is round. Find me something else that is round." or "This plastic snowball is white. Find me something else that is white." "These mittens are red. Find me something else that is red."
3. Match-them: Scramble several pairs of mittens. Have children find a matching pair.
4. Reach and feel: Use objects similar to those in no. 1.
5. Show me: Use objects similar to those in no. 1. "Show me the one we wear on our hands." "Show me the one that keeps our ears warm."
6. Make a winter calendar for one or all of the months, making each day a 5 cm square. Use decorative seals to mark the special holidays, birthdays, and other events that will have meaning for the children at your centre. Surround the calendar with paper snowflakes 5 cm in diameter (see Pictures and Displays). As each day goes by, cover it with one of the snowflakes. In areas where there is no snow, mark off the days with poinsettias or evergreen trees or raindrops/clouds.

Art Centre

- 1. Feature white paint at the easel for painting snow pictures.
- 2. Provide white chalk and coloured construction paper for making snow pictures.
- • 3. Paint pine cones white or green and glue to styrofoam bases. Use as decorations on the snack or library table or use to add a winter effect to unit block building of houses or roads. Bare twigs stuck in styrofoam could be used as deciduous trees in the same manner.
- 4. Mix up soap flakes and water into a thick paste using a hand beater or electric mixer. Add a small amount of liquid starch and white powdered tempera for a more permanent, attractive product. Let children create designs by painting the thick mixture on with a brush or rub it on with a tongue depressor.
- ••• 5. Children who have had a great deal of experience with clay and dough may discover they can make snow sculptures.
- ••• 6. When outdoors encourage children to mold or sculpt with snow to make free-form figures.
- •• 7. Paste cotton balls on construction paper to make a snowy day picture.
- •• 8. Make a star shape out of sponge or cut a green pepper in half around the middle. Notice the unusual star shape. Let children dip the green pepper in white paint and print snowflakes on coloured construction paper.
- •• 9. Make styrofoam sculptures using precut free-forms cut from scrap styrofoam with styrofoam balls, toothpicks, bits of yarn, leather, feathers. Use toothpicks and pipecleaners with glue to assemble or to add attachments.

Book Centre

- ••• Branley, Franklin. *Big Tracks, Little Tracks.* New York: Thomas Y. Crowell, 1960.
- ••• Branley, F.M. *Snow is Falling,* rev. ed. Markham, Ont: Fitzhenry & Whiteside, 1986.
- •• Breinburg, P. *Sally Ann in the Snow.* London: Bodley Head, 1977.

•• Burningham, John. *Seasons.* New York: Bobbs-Merrill, 1970 (paper).

••• Burton, Virginia Lee. *Katy and the Big Snow.* Boston: Houghton Mifflin, 1959 (paper).

•••• Carrier, Roch. *The Hockey Sweater.* Montreal: Tundra Books, 1984. (Also available in French as *Le Chandail de Hockey.*) (Read–tell)

••• Duvoisin, Roger. *The House of Four Seasons.* New York: Lothrop, Lee & Shepard, 1956.

••• Freeman, Don. *Ski Pup.* New York: Viking Press, 1963.

••• Hartley, Deborah. *Up North in Winter.* Markham, Ont: Fitzhenry & Whiteside, 1986.

•• Hoff, Syd. *When Will It Snow!* New York: Harper & Row, 1971.

••• Hutchins, Hazel. *Ben's Snow Song: A Winter Picnic.* Willowdale, Ont: Annick Press, 1987.

•• Ipcar, Dahlov. *Black and White.* New York: Alfred A. Knopf, 1963.

••• Kalman, Bobbie. *We Celebrate Winter.* Toronto: Crabtree Publishing, 1986.

• Keats, Ezra Jack. *The Snowy Day.* New York: Viking Press, 1962.

•••• Kidd, Bruce. *Hockey Showdown.* Toronto: James Lorimer, 1986. (Read–Tell)

•••• Kurelek, William. *A Prairie Boy's Winter.* Montreal: Tundra Books, 1973. (Read–Tell)

• Lenski, Lois. *I Like Winter.* New York: Henry Z. Walck, 1950.

• McKie, Roy, and P.D. Eastman. *Snow.* New York: Random House, 1962.

••• Miller, Edna. *Mousekin's Woodland Sleepers.* Englewood Cliffs, NJ: Prentice-Hall, 1970.

••• Morgan, Allan. *Sadie and the Snowman.* Toronto: Kids Can Press, 1986. (Also available in French.)

••• Munsch, Robert. *50 Below Zero.* Willowdale, Ont: Annick Press, 1986.

••• _____. *Thomas's Snowsuit.* Willowdale, Ont: Annick Press, 1985.

• Podendorf, Illa. *The True Book of Seasons.* Chicago: Childrens Press, 1972.

••• Priest, Robert. *The Short Hockey Career of Amazing Jany.* Toronto: Aya Press, 1986.

• Shaw, Charles. *It Looked Like Spilt Milk.* New York: Harper & Row, 1947.

•• Tresselt, Alvin. *It's Time Now!* New York: Lothrop, Lee & Shepard, 1969.

••• _____. *The Mitten.* New York: Lothrop, Lee & Shepard, 1964.

••• _____. *White Snow, Bright Snow.* New York: Lothrop, Lee & Shepard, 1947.

••• Waldren, K.C. *A Winter's Yarn.* Red Deer, Alta: Red Deer College Press, 1986.

••• Zolotow, Charlotte. *Hold My Hand.* New York: Harper & Row, 1972.

• _____. *Summer Is.* (all seasons) New York: Abelard-Schuman, 1967.

Planning for Group Time

NOTE: All music, fingerplays, poems, stories, and games listed here may also be used at other times during the session as appropriate. See Core Library, Basic Resources, p. 95, for publishers and addresses. Record company addresses can be found on p. 99. In parodies, hyphenated words match music notes of the songs used.

Music

Songs

WINTER (a parody)

(tune: "Pussy Cat, Pussy Cat")
Adaptation by JoAnne Deal Hicks

Win-ter is here; it's so co-ld to-day. Win-ter is here, it's too co-ld to play.
We must stay in-side, for there's much too much snow.
We sit by the win-dow and hear the wind blow!

From *Piggyback Songs*, Warren
"Songs About Winter," pp. 11–18

From *More Piggyback Songs*, Warren
"Songs About Winter," pp. 11–24

From *Singing Bee*, Hart
"The North Wind Doth Blow," p. 33
"Over the River and Through the Wood," p. 142

From *Elephant Jam*, Sharon, Lois, and Bram
"The Wind," p. 28

From *Stepping Along in Music Land*, Murray
"Seasons," p. 52
"Winter Won't You Go," p. 53

From *Sally Go Round the Sun*, Fowke
"The Wind the Wind," p. 65

Rhythms and Singing Games

Snowflakes: give children white scarves or white crepe paper streamers or precut white paper snowflakes.
a.   Play fast tempo music and let children pretend to be snowflakes on a windy day.
b.   Play slow tempo music and let children pretend to be softly falling snowflakes.

Ice skating: Play the *Skater's Waltz* and let the children pretend to be ice skaters.

Sleigh ride: Using a rope as a harness and stick horses, let the children pretend to be horses pulling a sleigh through the snow. Six horses could pull at a time and the rest of the children could be sitting in the sleigh. (Line up several rows of three chairs each, as needed.) Those in the sleigh can have bells to shake in time with the music.

Records and cassettes

Sandy Oppenheim, *If Snowflakes Fell in Flavours*. (Berandol Records)
"If Snowflakes Fell in Flavours"

Fingerplays and Poems

From *Let's Do Fingerplays*, Grayson
"Mittens," p. 18
"My Zipper Suit," p. 18
"The Mitten Song," p. 20
"Big Hill," p. 23
"Snowflakes," p. 48
"Snow Men," p. 48
"Shiver and Quiver," p. 58

From *Don't Eat Spiders*, Heidbreder
"Vancouver," p. 18
"Sticky Maple Syrup," p. 29
"Polar Bear Snow," p. 31

From *Hand Rhymes*, Brown
"Snowflakes," p. 17
"The Snowman," p. 18

From *Read Aloud Rhymes for the Very Young*, Prelutsky and Brown
"Little Wind," p. 12
"The Moon's the North Wind's Cooky," p. 51
"The Wind and the Moon," p. 51
"The More It Snows," p. 74
"The Mitten Song," p. 74
"Winter Sweetness," p. 74
"Jack Frost," p. 75
"It Fell in the City," p. 75
"First Snow," p. 76
"January," p. 76
"Icy," p. 76
"Snowman," p. 77
"Snow," p. 77

Stories

(To read, read–tell, or tell. See Book Centre for complete list.)
When you are choosing stories in the winter time, choose a combination of stories that reflect your weather and also teach children about weather in other parts of the country. For example, in Victoria you may want to read Scheffler's *A Walk in the Rain* (see Book Centre in "Spring") and contrast it with telling stories based on Kurelek's *A Prairie Boy's Winter.*

Games

(See "Learning Games," pp. 50–59, and teacher-made games in this chapter for directions.)
  1. What's missing?
  2. Match-them
  3. Reach and feel
  4. Show me

Routine Times

  1. At snack or meal times serve fruits that are available in winter such as oranges, grapefruit, tangerines; talk about the fact that these are grown where it is warmer and are brought on ship, boat, train and/or truck to stores in the city.
  2. At snack or meal times serve foods that are white in colour, such as milk, marshmallows, enriched white bread, popcorn, potatoes, or rice. And talk about the relationship between the colour of snow and the colour of the food.
  3. At rest time pretend to be hibernating animals sleeping through the cold winter.
  4. When walking or busing the children to and from the centre call attention to any signs of winter: frost, snow, bare trees, evergreens, people dressed warmly, frozen ponds, water vapour from nose and mouth.
  5. When dressing to go outside you might talk about the weather. Look at the outdoor thermometer and decide how cold it is and what you need to wear. If you made a cardboard thermometer with pictures of the children in appropriate clothing at the various levels of degrees this might help them decide. Set the cardboard thermometer at the same position as the outdoor thermometer and see which picture is closest to it. You might recite "The Mitten Song," "Mittens," or "My Zipper Suit," from *Let's Do Fingerplays*, as the children are putting on these articles of clothing.

Large Muscle Activities

  1. Provide children with child-size snow shovels and let them shovel the play yard walks, trike paths, and other paved surfaces. Show children where to put the snow. It could be

loaded into wagons and carried to another part of the yard for snow sculptures or the activities suggested in no. 2.

2. Provide children with some of the sand toys or kitchen pans and utensils that would be appropriate for using with snow as they would with sand—pails, shovels, spoons, molds, pie plates, measuring cups.

3. If the snow is the wet kind that sticks together, make a snow sculpture, molding it into interesting shapes as you would with clay or dough.

4. Show children how to make angels by lying down on you back in the snow and moving your arms up and down.

5. If you have a hill in your play yard and the snow is good for sledding, provide the children with cardboard squares from packing boxes, flying saucers, old trays, or sleds. Establish traffic patterns for going up and coming down. It is ideal to have an adult at the top and one at the bottom of the hill to help regulate traffic. However, if only one adult is available for this area it is best that she or he be stationed at the bottom of the hill so, he/she can direct those who have completed their slide where to climb back up if they want another turn. The adult could instruct the children at the top of the hill to wait until called, such as "Go, _____," allowing one child at a time to proceed, thereby avoiding rear-end collisions.

6. Throwing snowballs at others should be discouraged. Provide a suitable target for those who wish to throw snowballs. The target should be away from the general play area.

7. Children's ski-skates (available commercially) or snowshoes are fun to wear outside after a new snow.

8. Follow-the-leader can be played in fresh snow by children following the footsteps in the snow made by the leader. Zigzag or circle patterns of footsteps can be made. If an adult is the leader remember to take small steps, especially if the snow is deep. Try hopping and jumping as well as walking.

9. Snowball toss: Make snowballs and see how many you can toss into a basket, a box, or a waste basket. If no snow is available, use styrofoam balls as snowballs. Count the balls. White nylon balls can be made from nurses' white discarded pantyhose.

Extended Experiences

1. Take a walk and look for things that tell us it is winter—snow, ice, bare trees, icicles, frozen pond, evergreen trees, people dressed warmly.

2. Visit a site where your children could safely go sledding if your facility does not have a suitable slope.

3. Visit a frozen pond. If the ice is thick enough let the children walk on ice. Sleds and flying saucers pull easily over frozen ice, so bring them along.

4. If you know someone with a horse and sleigh you might wish to arrange a ride for the children.

5. Show a filmstrip: "Winter Is Here," from the captioned filmstrip series *The Seasons* and "Winter Adventures," from the series *Seasons' Adventures* (Singer SVE).

6. Have a snow picnic.

Teacher Resources

Pictures and Displays

▷ Set out winter issues of, or mount pictures from, *Owl*, and *Chickadee, National Geographic*, and *Equinox* magazines.

▷ Post pictures of snow, frozen ponds, bird or animal feeders and shelters, hibernating animals, winter sports like skiing, skating, hockey.

▷ Make a mobile of plastic snowflakes (available commercially where tree decorations are sold) or cut your own, using folded paper squares, circles, or hexagons, cutting only the folded edges. When opened they may be painted with glue and covered with glitter or artificial snow and then allowed to dry. Snowflakes may also be cut from heavy duty aluminum foil wrap. When opened, flatten these aluminum foil snowflakes between the pages of a book. Remember no two snowflakes are alike, so make yours different.

> **NOTE:**   Snowflake stencils could be cut out of cardboard and designs stencilled on the windows using sponges and Glass Wax or Bon Ami. Commercial stencils are available at the grocery and department stores at Christmas time.

▷ Decorate windows and walls with snowflakes cut as suggested above.
▷ Doilies to put under the juice or milk cup at each place at snack or meal times can be made from 10 cm thick sections of a pine cone. Glue this to a larger thin circle of wood or cork. Glue a small candle to the centre of the cone. Float the candle base in water. Light candles. Several can be floated if a large enough container is available. Exercise care with candles around young children.
▷ Make a snow scene: A mirror makes a good frozen pond. Surround the pond with cotton batting. Pine cones of various sizes and shapes can be used as trees. Paint green or white if you wish. Bare twigs can be the bare deciduous trees. Little figures of skiers, skaters, toboggans, birds, and rabbits or other small animals can be added to the winter wonderland.

Books and Periodicals

Chickadee magazine
Cleary, Val. *Seasons of Canada.* Willowdale, Ont: Hounslow Press, 1979. (Good for pictures of all the seasons in all parts of the country.)
Hardy, Ralph, et al. *The Weather Book.* Toronto: Little, Brown, 1982.
Holford, Ingrid. *The Guiness Book Weather Facts and Feats,* 2nd ed. Enfield, Middlesex, G.B.: Guiness Superlatives, 1982.
Owl magazine
Stokes, Donald W. *A Guide to Nature in Winter.* Camden East, Ont: Equinox Books, 1986.

Films and Videos

Consult your local library for resources

Community Resources and Organizations

▷ Natural history museums: Often exhibits are changed to reflect the change in seasons or there are different sections to the exhibits that show winter habitats
▷ A frozen pond in a park nearby or an ice arena
▷ Snow sculptures created by university or civic groups
▷ A local television or radio weather reporter

Government Agencies

Provincial, territorial and federal departments or ministries concerned with meteorology and the environment

13 Spring

★★★★★★★★★★★★★★★★★★★★★★★

Basic understandings

(concepts children can grasp from this subject)

Spring is a season of the year that comes after winter and before summer. There are many changes in nature in the spring.

Earth changes

▷ In areas where there is ice and snow, these both melt.
▷ Days are longer (sunrise is earlier and sunset later than in winter).
▷ The temperature is usually warmer, the wind blows hard, and there are often thunderstorms.
▷ East, west, and central parts of Canada have very different types of weather within the period called spring. In some areas it may still be quite cold; in others it may be rainy, windy, and warmer.
▷ The ground thaws as the rain warms and softens it. Spring showers and warm sunshine help seeds to sprout and begin to grow.
▷ There may be many storms like late snow storms in the spring when warmer weather suddenly becomes colder.
▷ The length of the season may seem longer or shorter depending on the weather where you live.

Plants

▷ Seeds sprout and plants begin to grow.
▷ Leaf buds turn into leaves on trees and on bushes.
▷ Blossoms appear on some plants (fruit trees, spring bulbs, dandelions, and pussywillows).
▷ Grass turns green and starts to grow.
▷ Some indoor plants can be planted outdoors for the summer months, such as geraniums, ivies, cacti, rubber plants, begonias.

Animals

▷ Animals that hibernate (sleep during the winter) wake up and come out of their sleeping places.

▷   Most animals have babies in the spring.
▷   Birds migrate to their summer homes and build nests.
▷   Birds and animals often grow new coats of feathers or fur, to adjust to weather and new
     colourings of surroundings.

People

▷   We do not need to wear such warm clothing in spring.
▷   Farmers prepare their fields for seed planting.
▷   City workers clean the streets and prepare park and gardens for new plants and flowers.
▷   Highway workers begin to repair roads in the cities and highways.
▷   Children and animals frolic outdoors.
▷   Spring is a time of beginning again—housecleaning, planting.

Festivals

Spring festivals are celebrated all over the world. Some are related to religious holidays and others to the arrival of spring and the planting of crops. One such special nonreligious festival is the Tulip Festival held in Ottawa.

Additional Facts the Teacher Should Know

1. In the northern hemisphere, spring is March 21st to June 20th. (In the southern hemisphere it is September 23rd to December 21st.) These are the official dates determined by solar and lunar phases. It is easier for young children to understand changes in weather. These changes are usually better times to introduce the themes of the seasons.

2. The equinox is the time of year when the centre of the sun is directly over the equator. The word "equinox" means equal night. During an equinox the days are the same length as the nights all over the world. The sun appears to cross the equator twice a year, so there are two equinoxes. The spring, or vernal equinox occurs around March 20th as the earth tilts its northern hemisphere toward the sun. The autumnal equinox comes about six months later, around September 23rd, as the earth tilts back and the sun "moves" south. This change in the earth's position produces variations in the patterns of warm and cold air masses to such a degree that storms are frequent at the time of the equinoxes. As the sun "travels" north, its rays strike the northern countries more directly each day, and the weather grows steadily warmer. The time from the end of the vernal equinox to the beginning of the autumnal equinox is longer than the interval between the autumnal equinox and the following vernal equinox. This difference amounts to seven days each year, or six days in leap years. It is caused by the elliptical shape of the earth's path around the sun. The earth must move faster when it is nearer the sun.

   NOTE: See Additional Facts the Teacher Should Know in "Day and Night" for illustrations of the equinoxes, and other related chapters on animals, water, and colour.

Methods Most Adaptable for Introducing this Subject to Children

1. Talk about what happens in the spring—new leaves, flowers blooming, seeds sprouting, baby animals, birds returning, and nest building.
2. Read a story about the change of seasons or spring (see Book Centre).
3. Let the children select pictures of spring and spring activities and put them on the bulletin boards. (They can do this easily with push-pins rather than thumbtacks.)

4. Discovery table—a bird's nest or eggs, a blooming crocus which has been dug up and put in a pot, sprouting seeds.

> **NOTE:** Return these to a pond when observation period is over.

5. Force a flowering shrub or tree branch by bringing it inside late in February so that it will bloom early. Use the same procedure with a bulb.

6. Children should be encouraged to watch for signs of spring—the first robin, a bulb sprouting, leaf or flower buds unfurling, the first dandelion, frogs croaking, grass turning green, a crocus blooming, snow melting.

Vocabulary

kite	plant	born	blossom
crocus	robin	dandelion	wind
bulb	tulip	bouquet	seed
sprout	tadpole	garden	flower
daffodil	polliwog	rain	leaf
earth	spring	showers	bloom
migrate	hatch	bud	

Learning Centres

Discovery Centre

Plants

1. Provide child-size gardening equipment (real garden tools of small size are much more sturdy and satisfactory than toys) and, if yard space allows, plant a vegetable or flower garden. This can be a most educational and rewarding plant growing experiment. If the teacher plans extended experiences, children will be able: to observe plants' gradual growth, to learn the care needed, and to harvest, cook, and eat their crop, if vegetables, or pick and arrange, if flowers. Ideally, a plot in the play yard that can be easily cared for routinely by the children when they are outdoors is far better than a garden that must be maintained by a teacher until a crop can be harvested. Allow children to care for this garden by watering and weeding. Radishes and lettuce are rewarding because they mature quickly and are edible. Marigold seeds are fairly dependable for quick flowers.

   ★ **CAUTION:** Careful supervision is necessary as tools have sharp edges.

2. Discover how seeds grow. Line the inside of a large straight-sided jar with brown blotting paper. Dampen this paper and place a variety of seeds of different sizes about halfway down the side of the jar between the jar and the blotting paper. The seeds will sprout at different times, which will help to maintain the children's interest. Radish seeds seem to sprout almost immediately. Bean sprouts are more likely than other seeds to mold before they have a chance to sprout. Carrot, lettuce, and corn seeds are also satisfactory. Just enough water should be kept in the jar to touch the bottom of the blotting paper. If the blotting paper dries out, the sprouts will die quickly.

3. Seeds may be placed in shallow pans and the corresponding vegetables or fruits displayed so that the children may see what grows from the seed—for instance, grapefruit seeds, a tiny grapefruit tree newly sprouted, and a grapefruit. The real object is better than a photograph or picture. VARIATION: Plant seeds or seedlings in peat pots. This allows plants to be taken home and placed directly into the ground there. If they are planted, however, in a paper or plastic cup without making a hole in the bottom, roots are more likely to rot from being overwatered even though maintenance may be supervised by a willing parent.
4. Grow grass by sprouting bent grass on a damp sponge or wet blotter.
5. Provide a magnifying glass for the close examination of buds, new leaves, tree seeds, and insects.
6. Force a hyacinth bulb: Set several bulbs into the soil in a large pot and bury so that the tops of the bulbs are about 20.3 cm below the surface of the ground. This may be done in late October or November. After ten or twelve weeks, bring inside and place in a cool, dark place until the sprouts are about 10.2 cm high—keep watered. Bring into the light occasionally and observe that the yellow sprouts turn green very soon, and the buds and blooms appear. Fertilize in sprout stage with Jobe Sticks. You should have hyacinths blooming in February.

   ★ CAUTION: Be sure to store fertilizer away from the children.

7. If children plant bulbs in the fall, they can watch the plants develop and bloom naturally in April. For instance a lily bulb forced to bloom is more satisfactory than just buying one that has already bloomed.
8. Watch a sweet potato sprout. It is interesting to observe that the part of the potato in the water makes roots while the top produces sprouts with leaves.
9. Plant seeds in eggshells. Marigold or pumpkin seeds produce very gratifying results and may be taken home and planted by the children, by gently crushing the eggshell before putting it in the ground. The seeds are easily tended by placing the eggshells in an egg carton and keeping the lid on until the seeds sprout. Water with a teaspoon.
10. A spring walk will enable the children to find and observe many new and growing things. Take a magnifying glass and paper bags in which to collect *treasures.*

Animals

1. Care for a baby animal such as a gerbil, guinea pig, or rabbit. Be sure there is a home that will welcome this creature when you no longer wish to keep it in the classroom. (See the "Animal" section for care and feeding.)
2. Incubate and hatch an egg. Children need to learn to respect and care for living things. Make a calendar to check off days—twenty-one days for chicks and twenty-eight days for ducklings. Quail eggs are another possibility.
3. Prepare and observe an ant house (commercially available through catalogues listing science supplies).
4. Earthworms may be housed in a jar of loose earth and fed on a small amount of minced lettuce.

   ★ CAUTION: Do not drown them with too much water. Use as little as possible.

5. Provide insect cages for insects the children may catch. Observe for a day or so and then turn the insects loose. Many children seem to feel that "a bug is to squash"; careful handling and concern for these small creatures must be emphasized constantly (see the chapter on insects, p. 423).
6. Visit a farm to see new baby animals (see "Farm Animals," p. 375).
7. Go to a pond or brook to find frog eggs or tadpoles. You might be just in time to watch the eggs hatch into tadpoles. Spring peeper tadpoles turn into frogs in one season and

into bullfrogs in two seasons. The huge bullfrog tadpoles are great to observe. Be sure to keep these creatures in pond water. It is advisable to return them to their natural environment, since they are becoming an endangered species.

Weather

1. On a windy day, fly a kite (see the section on "Chinese/Vietnamese New Year," p. 238) or blow bubbles outdoors. The children could let milkweed seeds out of the pods. Make paper pinwheels or fly paper airplanes or helicopters (see "Air Transportation," p. 455). Release fluffy feathers into the air.
2. Go for a walk during a spring shower. Look for a rainbow.
3. Make a rainbow (see "Colour", p. 528).
4. Use a cardboard thermometer (see "Mathematics" p. 556).
5. Make a weather calendar: Each day in March, have a child check on the weather and paste the appropriate symbol on the day—sun, clouds, rain, or snow. There is usually quite a variety.

Senses

1. Listen for sounds of spring—bird and animal calls, thunder, wind, raindrops, insects buzzing.
2. Uniquely delightful spring smells are fresh air, different flower fragrances, spring rain, the smell of soil, fresh-cut grass.
3. Create the opportunity to feel pussywillows, new grass, animal fur, blossoms, wind and air currents, seeds.
4. Look for all signs of spring. (See Methods Most Adaptable for Introducing this Subject.)
5. If you have access to a spotlight or a filmstrip projector, let children experiment with making shadow pictures. View-Master projectors are quite inexpensive.

Dramatic Play Centres

Home-living centre

1. Replace some winter articles such as hats, scarves, and mittens with different spring hats, gloves, stoles, and rainwear.
2. Suggest that the house could be spring-cleaned or rearranged.
3. The doll clothes could be washed and hung out to dry.
4. Provide flowers, real or artificial, to make bouquets.

Block-building centre

1. Block corner: Set out unbreakable chicks, ducks, rabbits—suggest building pens, hutches, and fences. Include sets of mother animals and their young.
2. Inexpensive small plastic flowers could be used to lay out a park or garden by letting children insert into flat pieces of styrofoam to hold upright as if growing.

Other dramatic play centres

1. Locate rabbit, duck, chicken, or baby animal Halloween costumes for children to wear to pretend to be animals. Attaching a tail, wings, or ears will suffice. Appropriate face masks can be made from wire coat hangers, sacks, or paper plates (see "Halloween").

2. Commercial or homemade sock puppets can be used for a puppet show behind a box, three-way screen, or puppet stage.
3. Hand puppets can be made from small paper sacks, and the children can either paste on ears and faces or mark them with felt-tip pens. Children's white socks make nice puppets, too.
4. Arrange a hat store from hats children make in the art centre or commercial hats available from toy stores.

Learning, Language, and Readiness Materials Centre

Commercially made games and materials

(See "Basic Resources," pp. 79, 100, for manufacturers' addresses.)
1. *Puzzles:* Rainy day, flower, farm and fishing puzzles.
2. *Construction and manipulative toys:* Fishing game with magnets or loops, sewing pictures of fish and flowers.
3. *Outdoor toys:* Soft foam balls, plastic bats, skipping ropes, perforated plastic balls, plastic hoops, Skilts (wooden blocks with long rope handles that can be used as stilts), pogo sticks, plastic coated nylon beanbags, rubber quoits, wagons, model road signs.
4. *Flannelboards and flannelboard aids:* Cutouts of flowers, sun, clouds, farm equipment, fishing equipment.
5. *Posters:* Weather chart.
6. *Miscellaneous:* Thermometer (see above), small plastic watering tin; bug cages (Reliable produces "Bug Keepers"); butterfly and fish nets; ant farms (available from educational supply companies); magnifying glasses and viewers

Teacher-made games and materials

NOTE: For a detailed description of "Learning Games," see pp. 50–59.

1. Children may cut out and paste spring pictures on pages, to be assembled into a book about spring or to put up on the bulletin board. Use pictures from seed and flower catalogues.
2. Make "match-them" or classification cards by mounting large gummed seals of birds, animals, flowers, butterflies, or rabbits. Make "match-thems" of animals and their young or animals and what they eat.
3. How many? Make circle counters for counting or sorting colours and other subjects by mounting the gummed seals listed in no. 2 on cardboard discs or octagons (see p. 55 for illustration of discs).

Art Centre

•• 1. Add interest to easel painting centre by using pastel colours (add colour to white paint).
•• 2. Spatter-paint over animal or flower shapes. Children can make their own stencils by choosing or arranging geometric shapes cut from innertubes or plastic upholstery scraps.
•• 3. Pastel soap painting: Colour soap flakes with tempera to make pastel shades for painting. A little liquid starch added to this stiff mixture makes it less fragile when dry.
•• 4. Blow painting (to illustrate wind): Place spoonful of paint on paper and, using halves of drinking straws, blow on the paint for a splatter-type picture.
••• 5. Sponge-paint blossoms on crayoned tree trunks drawn on construction paper.
• 6. Mud-paint outdoors with bare feet.
•• 7. Large kindergarten chalk used on pastel construction paper creates a lovely effect. Do this activity at the easel to avoid smearing. Spray with hair spray or fixative when finished.

•• 8. Dipping pastel chalk in water before applying to construction paper makes a more permanent product.

••• 9. Make rainbows using flat sides of crayon stubs or Chunk-O-Crayons (Milton Bradley).

•• 10. Use animal- or flower-shaped cookie cutters with play dough.

••• 11. Cut and paste pictures from flower and seed catalogues, wallpaper books, and old greeting cards.

••• 12. Tear free-form shapes from white construction paper (pieces as large as possible). Paste on blue paper. Just for fun, suggest that the children tell you what the picture looks like after it is finished. Make up their own *It Looked Like Spilt Milk* book with these pages (see Book Centre, below).

•• 13. Colour sawdust or rice with tempera or food colouring. Sprinkle on construction paper that has been brushed or squirted with white glue.

•• 14. Make collages from seeds, twigs, and soft maple and elm pods.

•• 15. Pastel styrofoam from egg cartons makes a lovely spring collage material.

•• 16. Vegetable prints: Save sliced ends of green peppers, celery, cabbage, lemons, limes, or apples. Dip in tempera (make stamp pad) and print on paper. Use sponge shapes or corrugated cardboard rolled across the paper (both ways) if more feasible than food scraps.

••• 17. Pressed flowers: Use on spring mural or greeting cards.

••• 18. Draw two posts on paper, and paste a piece of string or yarn across between them. Children like to paste pieces of cloth on this line to look like clothes hanging on a clothesline in the wind.

•• 19. Precut tissue paper circles. Children may wad these up, dip in paste, and fasten to paper to represent crocuses in green grass or blossoms on a tree.

••• 20. Individual pussywillows make tiny animals. Let children design their own "pussy-willow creatures" using other collage materials, crayons, or paint.

••• 21. Make egg carton caterpillars, paint green or another colour. Add toothpicks with balls of play dough or small pipe cleaners for antennae. Children may paint or decorate with gummed paper according to their own imagination.

••• 22. Make a butterfly from a cylindrical clothespin: Use precut rectangles of tissue paper for wings. Children may decorate with bits of gummed paper on other collage items. Birds can be made from small plastic bags stuffed with tissue; attach cut paper wings and tails with tape. Encourage children to explore insect, bird, and butterfly books.

••• 23. Make pinwheels or paper gliders (see p. 455 for directions and illustrations).

•• 24. Make kites (see p. 238 for illustrations).

• 25. Paste precut coloured-paper ovals in the centre of a sheet of construction paper. Let children finish the picture by adding eyes, wings, bills, tails, and feet to make chicks and other animals.

•• 26. Make rabbits, clouds, and lambs by pasting cotton balls on paper.

Book Centre

• Adelson, Leone. *All Ready for Summer.* New York: David McKay, 1955.

•• Atkinson-Keene and Patterson. *Fun Times.* Toronto: Greey de Pencier, 1986.

•• Baum, Arlene and Joseph. *One Bright Monday Morning.* New York: Random House, 1962.

••• Birnbaum, A. *Green Eyes.* New York: Western Publishing, 1973.

••• Bulla, Clyde. *A Tree Is a Plant.* New York: Thomas Y. Crowell, 1960.

•• Burningham, John. *Seasons.* New York: Bobbs-Merrill, 1970.

••• Burton, Virginia Lee. *The Little House.* Boston: Houghton Mifflin, 1969.

••• Clifton, Lucille. *The Boy Who Didn't Believe In Spring.* New York: E.P. Dutton, 1973.

•• Clifton, L. *The Boy Who Didn't Believe in Spring.* New York: E.P. Dutton, 1978.

••• Duvoisin, Roger. *The House of Four Seasons.* New York: Lothrop, Lee & Shepard, 1956.

••• _____ . *Two Lonely Ducks.* New York: Alfred A. Knopf, 1955 (counting book).

•• Ets, Marie Hall. *Gilberto and the Wind.* New York: Viking Press, 1963.

•• Flack, Marjorie. *Tim Tadpole and the Great Bullfrog.* Garden City, NY: Doubleday, 1959 (paper).

• Foster, Joanna. *Pete's Puddle.* New York: Harcourt Brace Jovanovich, 1950.

•• Francoise. *Springtime for Jeanne-Marie.* New York: Scribner's, 1965 (paper).

••• Gans, Roma, and Franklyn M. Branley. *Flash, Crash, Rumble, Roll.* New York: Thomas Y. Crowell, 1964.

••• _____ . *It's Nesting Time.* New York: Thomas Y. Crowell, 1964 (filmstrip, record, cassette).

•• Garelick, May. *Where Does the Butterfly Go When It Rains?* Reading, MA: Addison-Wesley, 1961 (Scholastic Book Service, paper, 1970).

•• Gay, Zhenya. *The Nicest Time of the Year.* New York: Viking Press, 1960.

• Ginsburg, M. *The Chick and the Duckling.* New York: Macmillan, 1972.

• Hill. *Rain.* Toronto: Methuen, 1986.

• Hines, Anna. *Taste the Raindrops.* New York: Greenwillow Press, 1983.

• Hutchins, Pat. *The Wind Blew.* New York: Macmillan, 1974.

• Hutchins, P. *The Wind Blew.* New York: Macmillan, 1974.

•• Ipcar, Dahlov. *The Song of the Day Birds and the Night Birds.* Garden City, NY: Doubleday, 1967.

••• Jordan, Helene. *How a Seed Grows.* New York: Thomas Y. Crowell, 1960 (paper).

••• _____ . *Seeds by Wind and Water.* New York: Thomas Y. Crowell, 1962.

••• Kalman, Bobbie. *We Celebrate Spring.* Toronto; Crabtree Publishing, 1986.

•• Keats, Ezra Jack. *A Letter to Amy.* New York: Harper & Row, 1968.

••• Krauss, R. *The Carrot Seed.* New York: Harper & Row, 1945.

• Lenski, Lois. *Spring Is Here.* New York: Henry Z. Walck, 1945.

• Leonard, Marcia. *Little Puppy's Rainy Day.* New York: Bantam, 1987.

••• Lifgren, Ulf. *The Wonderful Tree.* New York: Delacorte Press, 1970.

•• Lionni, Leo. *Inch by Inch.* New York: Astor-Honor, 1962.

••• McCloskey, Robert. *Make Way for Ducklings.* New York: Viking Press, 1969 (paper).

••• Miller, Edna. *Mousekin Finds a Friend.* Englewood Cliffs, NJ: Prentice-Hall, 1967 (paper).

•• Politi, Leo. *Juanita.* New York: Scribner's, 1948.

•• Rey, Margaret. *Curious George Flies a Kite.* Boston: Houghton Mifflin, 1958.

••• Selsam, M. *Egg to Chick.* New York: Harper & Row, 1970.

•• Scheer, Julian. *Rain Makes Applesauce.* New York: Holiday House, 1964.

•• Scheffler, Ursel. *A Walk in the Rain.* New York: G.P. Putnam's Son's 1986.

• Shaw, Charles G. *It Looked Like Spilt Milk.* New York: Harper & Row, 1947.

••• Shulevitz, Uri. *Rain Rain Rivers.* New York: Farrar, Strauss & Giroux, 1969.

• Spier, P. *Peter Spier's Rain.* Garden City, NY: Doubleday, 1982.

• Stock, C. *Sophie's Bucket.* New York; Lothrop, Lee & Shepard, 1985.

••• Tresselt, Alvin. *Follow the Wind.* New York: Lothrop, Lee & Shepard, 1950.

•• _____ . *Hide and Seek Fog.* New York: Lothrop, Lee & Shepard, 1965.

••• _____ . *Hi, Mr. Robin.* New York: Lothrop, Lee & Shepard, 1950.

••• _____ . *It's Time Now.* New York: Lothrop, Lee & Shepard, 1969.

•• _____ . *Rain, Drop, Splash.* New York: Lothrop, Lee & Shepard, 1965.

••• _____ . *The Frog in the Well.* New York: Lothrop, Lee & Shepard, 1958.

•• _____ . *Under the Trees and Through the Grass.* New York: Lothrop, Lee, & Shepard, 1962.

•• Udry, Janice. *A Tree Is Nice.* New York: Harper & Row, 1956.

• Zolotow, Charlotte. *One Step, Two.* New York: Lothrop, Lee & Shepard, 1955.

• _____ . *Summer Is Here.* New York: Abelard-Schuman, 1967.

••• _____ . *The Storm Book.* New York: Harper & Row, 1952.

•• _____ . *When the Wind Stops.* New York: Abelard-Schuman, 1962.

Planning for Group Time

NOTE: All music, fingerplays, poems, stories, and games listed here may also be used at other times during the session as appropriate. See Core Library, "Basic Resources," p. 95, for publishers and addresses. Record company addresses can be found on p. 99.

Music

Songs

From *Piggyback Songs*, Warren
"Songs about Spring," pp. 19–30

From *More Piggyback Songs*, Warren
"Songs about Spring," pp. 25–32

From *Singing Bee*, Hart
"Rain, Rain," p. 49
"Nuts in May," p. 80
"Over the River and Through the Wood," p. 142

From *Elephant Jam*, Sharon, Lois, and Bram
"The Wind," p. 28

From *Stepping Along in Music Land*, Murray
"Butterfly, Butterfly," p. 47
"Seasons," p. 52
"New Day in Spring," p. 54

From *Sally Go Round the Sun*, Fowke
"The Wind the Wind," p. 65

From *A Treasury of Songs for Young Children*, Glazer
"It's Raining It's Pouring," p. 132

Rhythms and singing games

From appropriate music listed under Songs
Allow children to be waddling ducks, hopping rabbits, pecking chickens, and so forth.
"Bunny Hop": Make headbands with paper rabbit ears and tails attached (see p. 37, no. 3 for tails).
"Easter Parade": Use hats the children have made in the art centre.

Records and cassettes

Anne Murray. *There's a Hippo in My Bathtub.* (Capitol Records)
"You Are My Sunshine"

Bob McGrath. *If You're Happy and You Know It*, Volume I. (Kids Records)
"Mr. Sun"
"Take Me Out to the Ballgame"

Raffi. *Baby Beluga.* (Troubadour Records)
"Over in the Meadow"

Sandy Oppenheim. *If Snowflakes Fell in Flavours.* (Berandol Records)
"Hey Little Bird"
"Muck"

Fingerplays and Poems

From *Don't Eat Spiders*, Heidbreder
"Sun, Sun," p. 9
"Vancouver," p. 18
"Bird's Nest," p. 25
"Sticky Maple Syrup," p. 29

From *Hand Rhymes*, Brown
"The Caterpillar," p. 28

From *Round and Round the Garden*, Williams and Beck
"Round and Round the Garden," p. 6
"The Apple Tree," p. 12
"I Hear Thunder," p. 37
"The Cherry Tree," p. 46

From *Read Aloud Rhymes for the Very Young*, Prelutsky and Brown
"Showers," p. 12
"Little Wind," p. 12
"The Rain," p. 12
"Rainy Day," p. 13
"Mud," p. 13
"Sun After Rain," p. 13
"Little Seeds," p. 14
"A Spike of Green," p. 14
"Singing in the Spring," p. 23
"A Kite," p. 33
"The Butterfly," p. 33
"Ode to Spring," p. 56
"The Spring Wind," p. 56
"Pussy Willows," p. 57
"April," p. 61
"Umbrellas," p. 61

From *Let's Do Fingerplays*, Grayson
"Animal Antics," section, pp. 30–38
"Kitty, Kitty," p. 42
"Chickens," p. 42
"My Garden," p. 46
"Pitter-Pat," p. 46
"Raindrops," p. 47
"Five Little Froggies," p. 62
"Five Little Kittens," p. 64
"Two Little Ducks," p. 71
"Two Little Blackbirds," p. 73

Stories

(To read, read–tell, or tell. See Book Centre for complete list.)
As spring is a season of contrasts, it is fun to choose stories in pairs that will show the contrasts—for example, Zolotow's *The Storm Book* and Baum's *One Bright Monday Morning*.

Games

(See "Learning Games," pp. 50–59, and teacher-made games in this chapter for directions.)

1. Name it or scramble: New leaf, bud, blade of grass, bird's nest, pussywillow, daffodil
2. I see something that tells it's spring: outdoors or in the room
3. Reach and feel: Bag of spring items
4. Listen and hear: Sounds of spring outdoors or with window open
5. Who am I? Riddles, simple descriptions of baby animals
6. Alike, different, and the same: Use plastic models of young animals, eggs, flowers, or similar flannelboard figures
7. Listening: "Hen and Chicks"—mother hen (chosen child) leaves the room; one or more children are chosen to be a chick; when mother hen returns, they peep softly until she finds them by the sound
8. Come, chick, chick, chick: "Come, chick, chick, chick. Here's food for you to eat." Repeat these two lines as children pretend they are chicks and come to the teacher for food from teacher's hands. Substitute other animal names
9. Pin the tail on the bunny (Pin the tail on the donkey): Use circles of masking tape to stick tail on, or sew a magnet on a yarn pom-pom and put bunny on a metallic board or cookie sheet (see p. 48 for description of magnetized flannelboard).

Routine Times

1. Decorate the snack table with garden flowers or potted spring bulbs that have been forced.
2. Eat snacks or meals outside. Have a picnic.
3. Eat vegetables you have grown for snacks or at meal times.
4. Use spring fingerplays at snack or meal times.
5. Eat eggs in different ways—deviled eggs, egg salad.
6. Use spring placemats that children have made and decorated.
7. When dressing, talk about the weather and what clothing is needed.
8. Look for signs of spring while walking or busing.
9. Rest outside in suitable weather. Look at clouds; listen for birds, wind, thunder, insects.

Large Muscle Activities

1. Shadow tag
2. Leap frog
3. Follow the leader
4. Fly a kite
5. Play with balloons
6. Encourage water play (see "Water," p. 512)
7. Dirt and sand play (see "Water," p. 515)
8. Have a treasure hunt, outdoors if possible.
9. Water-paint the cement walk or walls and equipment outside using large paintbrushes and buckets to hold water

Extended Experiences

1. Visit a local greenhouse to see Easter lilies and other spring blooming plants.
2. Visit a local farm to see newborn animals, spring planting, or beehives.
3. Visit a hatchery and obtain chicken or duck eggs to hatch.
4. Visit a zoo that may have newborn animals and/or a pet farm section.

5. Go to a park on a nature walk or to an open field to fly a kite.
6. Visit a feed and seed store or a farm implement company.
7. Explore a "magic circle." Give each child or group a yard length of string to outline a circle on the ground. Let them use a magnifying glass to see what can be found in their area. Encourage them to look carefully under stones and in grass for items.
8. A small shallow stream of water is a safe place to observe water creatures like tadpoles, frogs, crayfish, and minnows.

Teacher Resources

Pictures and Displays

▷   Make a tree for all seasons: Obtain an attractive bare tree branch and secure with sand or pebbles in a large coffee can. Children may glue tissue paper blossoms on it in the spring and follow through the seasons with tree leaves in summer, fruit, nuts, coloured leaves, or seed pods in autumn, and the bare branch for winter.

▷   An "insect motel" to use on a collecting trip or for a temporary display can be made simply by cutting a 5 cm by 10 cm rectangular window from the side of a small cylindrical ice cream carton. Roll a piece of screen wire to fit inside and cover the window. A string may be attached to the lid for carrying. This will save many an insect guest from too much handling. Nylon hose pulled over a milk carton from which two large windows have been cut is also useful. Another insect keeper can be made from a piece of screen rolled into a cylinder, with empty tuna cans placed on each end.

▷   Make frames for children's finger paintings by cutting ovals or rectangles from large white mat board or cardboard, and superimpose on the paintings. Reuse for other art works.

Books and Periodicals

Chickadee magazine
Cleary, Val. *Seasons of Canada*. Willowdale, Ont: Hounslow Press, 1979. (Good for pictures of all the seasons in all parts of the country)
Cooper, Terry Touff, and Marilyn Ratner. *Many Hands Cooking: An International Cookbook for Boys and Girls*. New York: Thomas Y. Crowell, 1974. Holiday Date Bits (Israel), p. 37; Kaju (India), p. 39; Tofu Toss (Japan), p. 4; Ancient Day Salad (Egypt), p. 38.
Equinox magazine
Hardy, Ralph, et. al. *The Weather Book*. Toronto: Little, Brown, 1982
Holford, Ingrid. *The Guiness Book of Weather Facts and Feats*, 2nd ed. Enfield, Middlesex, GB: Guiness Superlatives, 1982
National Geographic magazine
Owl magazine
Seed catalogues
Spring issues of farm and garden journals or magazines

Films and Videos

Consult your local library for resources from their collection, the National Film Board and the CBC

Community Resources and Organizations

▷ County extension offices
▷ Dairy councils
▷ Greenhouses or garden centres
▷ Florist shops
▷ Hardware stores—small-size, sturdy garden tools (not toys)
▷ Local television or radio weather reporters

Government Agencies

Provincial, territorial and federal ministries/departments concerned with meteorology and the environment

14 Summer

★★★★★★★★★★★★★★★★★★★★★★★

Basic Understandings

(concepts children can grasp from this subject)

Summer is a season of the year that comes after spring and before fall. There are many changes in nature in the summer.

Earth changes

▷ In some areas there is not much rain. It can be hot or warm every day.
▷ When it gets very dry there is a risk of forest fires.
▷ In the summer there are often thunder and lightning storms.
▷ Sometimes, in the summer, ponds, streams, and lakes dry up or become smaller.
▷ Breezes blowing across nearby ponds, oceans, lakes, or rivers help to keep people and animals cool.
▷ On very windy days dust storms may form.
▷ Cement, sand, and brick hold the heat from the sun and are hot to touch, walk on, or live by.
▷ In Canada, the daylight hours in summer are longer and there are fewer hours of darkness.
▷ In some parts of Canada, summer weather lasts a long time, while in other areas the hot weather period is very short.

Plants

▷ Many trees, flowers, and shrubs bloom and grow in the summertime.
▷ Fruit, nuts, and vegetables grow best in summer and ripen enough to eat.
▷ Often grass, trees, flowers, and other plants need to be watered if there is not enough rain.
▷ Some plants wither and dry up in the hot sun.
▷ Leafy bushes, trees, and vines offer shade for homes, people, and animals.

Animals

▷ Some animals shed their heavy coats of fur in summer. Sometimes people help their pets by cutting their hair to make them cooler; for example, sheep and poodles.

▷   Some animals change from lighter to darker colours in summer to match where they live; examples are birds, rabbits.

▷   In summer animals need water to drink and in which to bathe. They also need shade and places in which to cool off (ponds, streams, and lakes).

▷   Some animals and birds raise their young, feed them, protect them, and teach them to find food and defend themselves (see chapter on "Animals").

People

▷   Because it is often hot we need to wear less clothing in summer.

▷   Some children go barefoot.

▷   People often lie in the sun to get suntanned. We must be careful, however, to wear a sun protection lotion so as not to get sunburned and damage our skin.

▷   Children and adults like to swim, go boating, water-ski, and play in the sand in summer.

▷   We often go to parks, have picnics, go on hikes, and play games outdoors in the summer, such as baseball, tennis, miniature golf, ball.

▷   Often food becomes ripe and can be canned, preserved, frozen, stored, or eaten by people in summer.

▷   Many families go camping, go on vacations (take trips), or have more time to do things together in summer.

▷   We should not waste water in summer.

▷   We often need to turn on fans, water coolers, and air conditioners in the buildings where we live, work, and play in order to keep cool.

▷   We may turn on the air conditioners in cars, trucks, buses, and tractors in order to be more comfortable when traveling in the summer.

▷   Some communities in which we live have special programs or activities at schools, parks, pools, churches, or community centres. Children often go with families to county fairs that are usually held in late summer.

▷   Many schools close for the summer. Others stay open and offer special classes.

▷   Farmers are very busy planting and carrying for their crops.

▷   Fishermen spend a great deal of time at sea catching a lot of fish.

▷   Families with gardens must care for their plants and flowers in the summer.

Additional Facts the Teacher Should Know

1. Summer is one of the four seasons which in most of Canada is approximately from June 21 to September 20. These are the official dates determined by solar and lunar phases. It is easier for young children to understand changes in weather. These changes are usually better times to introduce the themes of the seasons.

2. Summer weather is not the same for all the provinces. The north does not have as high temperature readings for such a prolonged time as does the south where temperatures of 70° and above occur almost daily from the middle of May to the middle of September. Therefore, it is expected each teacher will keep in mind the uniqueness of his/her area when teaching about this season. It is difficult for young children to grasp the full meaning involved in the concept of summer but they can begin to understand some of the changes which take place at this time of year. They can also learn about some of the most common activities families enjoy together at this time.

3. Children may be very easily burned in the hot summer sun. Be sure the children do not spend too much time in the direct sun. Have them wear sun hats or visors and play in shaded areas.

Other parts of the guide related to the subject of summer are "Animals," "Colour," "Water," and "Transportation."

Methods Most Adaptable for Introducing this Subject to Children

1. Take a walk and look for some of the signs that tell us it is summer, such as lawn sprinklers turned on, dogs panting, people dressed in lightweight clothes, trees leafed out, flowers blooming, and noisy crickets.
2. Read a story about summer.
3. Children may be talking about vacations or special activities their families are planning.
4. Everyone is talking about how hot it is.
5. Make lemonade to drink outside in the shade of a tree.
6. Display pictures of summer activities, for instance, at the beach, in the swimming pool, boating, and picnicking.

Vocabulary

summer	fan	parade	hose
sprinkler	fireworks	lemonade	cool
water cooler	lawns	plant	water
air conditioner	leaves	flower	shells
hot	march	fruit	beach
ice	flag	ripe	sand
dry	holiday	shade	swim
ice cream cone			

Learning Centres

Discovery Centre

1. A discovery table: Children can bring in things they have found, such as flowers, shells, fruits and vegetables, a bird's nest, insects.
2. If you planted a garden in the spring continue to care for it. Check to see if the soil is hard or damp. If it is hard it should be hoed and watered. If you don't have a garden, check seed packages and see if there is still time to start a garden in your area.
3. A melon-tasting feast: Bring in a watermelon, honeydew melon, and a cantaloupe. Cut each melon. Compare colour, odour, taste, and texture. Compare seeds.
4. A berry tasting party: Set out bowls of whole, washed blackberries, blueberries, raspberries, and strawberries. Compare size, colour, shape, odour, and taste.
5. Set out fresh vegetable tray: Include a potato, carrot, onion, tomato, celery, radish, cucumber (whatever is available and in season). Let children explore. Talk about colour, shape, taste, odour and texture. Let children help wash, slice, peel.
6. Listen for crickets, they make a noisy, shrill sound when it gets hot. Try to find one.
7. Look for a rainbow after a sudden summer shower.
8. After several hours of rain look for worms on the sidewalks.
9. Insects and spiders are plentiful in summer and the children will discover many, especially butterflies and fireflies. Look under rocks (see "Insects and Spiders" for related discovery activities).
10. Plant and care for some flowers: Marigolds, geraniums, and zinnias are very hardy and grow in almost all parts of the country.

11. Borrow or purchase several types of plants (see list below). Help children discover that different plants need different amounts of water and begin to understand the phrase "No plant likes wet feet!" by allowing them to water and observe several plants.

    a. Cactus or rubber plant: Water once a week or every ten days.
    b. Boston fern: Water every other day (needs to be root-bound).
    c. Philodendron: Water every other day.
    d. Azalea (planted in peat moss): Water daily.

    > **NOTE:** Plants should never stand in water. It is better to water more often, and very little at one time. Feel soil; if dry it needs water. For a 10 cm pot with plant, add 28 mL/⅛ to 56 mL/¼ cup water. For a 15 cm pot with plant, add 225 mL/ 1 cup every other day. Leaves do NOT need to be misted (leaves washed) because indoors there is no breeze or sun to dry and leaves can rot. To help the children remember, make a chart for watering plants that has symbols to identify which plants need attention on which days.

12. Make or buy a bird bath and put it in a quiet part of the play yard. Make certain the children can observe it from their classroom window.
13. Set out a View-Master with appropriate reels.
14. Make strawberry or peach ice cream: Use your favourite recipe.
15. Make lemonade–squeeze lemons. Taste with and without sugar.
16. Display a shell collection: Provide a magnifying glass for closer viewing or hide some shells in a small box of sand and let the children find and arrange them.
17. If feasible, allow children to remove their shoes to walk in the grass, step on cement walk on blacktop, or step on dirt or on a smooth board. Which is warmer? Cooler? Smoother? Rougher? Softer? Harder? VARIATION: Ask children to touch and compare the temperature of a metal bar, piece of wooden equipment, the ground, all in the sun. Which is cooler? Touch the same objects in the shade. What is different? Why?

    > ★ **CAUTION:** Make certain there is no glass or any sharp object where children will be walking or stepping.

18. If you have flowers or flowering bushes, such as lilacs, in the school yard, allow children to pick some buds with stems and place them in a container of water. Set them in a window where they can get sun. Observe what happens.
19. If some equipment such as a tire, wooden box, or a board has been left sitting over a grassy area for several days, move it and let the children discover what happened to the grass underneath that was without sun and air. Leave uncovered. Observe.
20. When busing children for an excursion in summer, turn on the air conditioner (if you have one) in the car and talk about what happens to the air in the car if we leave the windows closed.

Dramatic Play Centres

Home-living centre

1. Set out beach hats, hats with visors, straw hats, beach towels, terry robes, thongs, and sandals.
2. Place travel folders, brochures on local parks, and road maps out on shelves to encourage planning of family trips.
3. Set out boxes of artificial flowers with a variety of containers and allow children to make floral arrangements.

Swinging at the playground. Children enjoying outdoor play activities.

Block-building centre

1. Set out cars, campers, trains, ships, and planes to encourage travel play.
2. Set out farm equipment to encourage planting, cultivating, and harvesting of crops. Provide small plastic foods to carry to market.

Other dramatic play centres

1. Set up a tent on the playground for the children to use for camping out.
2. Set up a water table, large tub with water, or tractor tire cut in half, forming two circular troughs for sailing boats or water play.
3. Add new equipment to the sandbox to increase interest in this area; for example, sieves, funnels, pails, and shovels.

Learning, Language, and Readiness Materials Centre

Commercially made games and materials

(See "Basic Resources," pp. 79, 100, for manufacturers' addresses.)

1. *Puzzles:* Rainy day, flower, farm and fishing puzzles.
2. *Construction and manipulative toys:* Fishing game with magnets or loops, sewing pictures of fish and flowers.
3. *Outdoor toys:* Soft foam balls, plastic bats, skipping ropes, perforated plastic balls, plastic hoops, Skilts (wooden blocks with long rope handles that can be used as stilts) pogo sticks, plastic coated nylon bean bags, rubber quoits, wagons, model road signs. Pails, sifters, shovels for sand play. Light plastic garden hose and simple spinning lawn sprinkler. Rugged outdoor play tunnel. Child-sized wheelbarrows. Small garden tools that can be used by children.
4. *Flannelboard and flannelboard aids:* Cutouts of flowers, sun, clouds, farm equipment, fishing equipment.
5. *Posters:* Weather chart.
6. *Miscellaneous:* Thermometer (see above), small plastic watering tin.

Teacher-made games and materials

NOTE: For a detailed description of "Learning Games," see pp. 50–59.

1. Look and see: Use different-shaped and coloured sea shells, a variety of plastic foods, transportation toys.
2. Reach and feel: Use a swim mask, bathing cap, and sand shovel.
3. Summer fun: The children can make a picture book of summer by cutting out appropriate pictures and mounting on paper, punching, and fastening together.

Art Centre

- 1. Summer is all colours! Move art media outdoors whenever possible. Feature a wide choice of colours at the easel especially if the group has been with you all year.
- • 2. Sponge-paint blossoms on crayoned tree trunks; trunks and branches can be made by using the broad side of short crayons which have the paper wrappings removed.
- • 3. Blow-painting: Drops of bright coloured paint blown with a straw over paper.
- • 4. Sand-painting: Sand can be washed, mixed with dry tempera, and dried in the oven. Child draws a design on paper with glue squeezed from tip of white glue bottle. Sprinkle coloured sand over the glue. When dry, shake off excess. Sand should remain on glue. A brush can also be used to apply the glue.
- • 5. Make wet-sand sculptures by using various containers as molds or mold with the hands.
- • • 6. Glue cupcake papers or crumpled tissue paper to green construction paper to simulate flowers in the grass; also let children tear, cut, or slash paper for grass.
- • • • 7. Burlap pictures: Cut squares from burlap bags or colourful burlap material. Thread wide-eyed embroidery needles with brightly coloured yarn. Let children sew a design on the burlap.
- • 8. Simulated porcupine quill art: Weave coloured toothpicks into burlap squares.
- 9. Make drawing in sand or damp earth with a stick.

Book Centre

- • Alexander, Martha. *No Ducks in our Bathtub.* New York: Dial Press, 1973.
- • • Atkinson-Keene and Patterson. *Unexpected Wonders.* Toronto: Greey de Pencier, 1986.
- • Burningham, John. *Seasons.* New York: Bobbs-Merrill, 1970.

• • • •   Cole, S. *When the Tide Is Low.* New York: Lothrop, Lee & Shepard, 1985. (Read–Tell)
  •   Crisitini, E., and L. Puricelli. *In My Garden.* New York: Picture Book Studio, 1985.
• • •   Goudey, Alice. *The Day We Saw the Sun Come Up.* New York: Scribner's, 1961.
• • •   Hughes, S. *Lucy and Tom at the Seaside.* London: Victor Gallancz, 1976.
• • • •   Kessler, Leonard. *Last One in Is a Rotten Egg.* New York: Harper & Row, 1969. (Read–Tell)
• • •   Kinney, Jean. *What Does the Sun Do?* Reading, MA: Addison-Wesley, 1967.
  •   Krauss, Ruth. *The Growing Story.* New York: Harper & Row, 1947.
• • • •   Kurelek, William. *A Prairie Boy's Summer.* Montreal: Tundra Books, 1975. (A book for reading to children.)
  •   Lenski, Lois. *On a Summer Day.* New York: Henry Z. Walck, 1953.
• • •   Lobel. *The Rose in My Garden.* Toronto: Methuen, 1986.
  •   Loree, Kate. *Pails and Snails.* New York: E.M. Hale, 1967.
• •   Lund, Doris. *The Paint Box Sea.* New York: McGraw-Hill, 1972.
• • •   MacDonald, Golden. *The Little Island.* Garden City, NY: Doubleday, 1946 (paper, 1974).
• • •   Orange, A. *The Flower Book.* New York: Lerner, 1975.
• • •   Plantos, Ted. *Heather Hits Her First Home Run.* Windsor, Ont: Black Moss Press, 1986.
• • •   Podendorf, Illa. *True Book of Seasons.* Chicago: Childrens Press, 1972.
• •   Ryder, J. *A Wet and Sandy Day.* New York: Harper & Row, 1977.
  •   Schick, Eleanor. *City in the Summer.* New York: Macmillan, 1969 (paper, 1974).
• •   Tresselt, Alvin. *I Saw the Sea Come In.* New York: Lothrop, Lee & Shepard, 1965.
• •   _____. *Sun Up!* New York: Lothrop, Lee & Shepard, 1949.
• •   Udry, Janice. *A Tree Is Nice.* New York: Harper & Row, 1956.
• •   Wondriska, William. *The Stop.* New York: Holt, Rinehart & Winston, 1972.
• •   Zion, Gene. *Harry by the Sea.* New York: Harper & Row, 1965.
  _____. *The Plant Sitter.* New York: Harper & Row, 1976.
• • •   Zolotow, Charlotte. *Summer Is. . . .* New York: Thomas Y. Crowell, 1983.

Planning for Group Time

NOTE: All music, fingerplays, poems, stories, and games listed here may be used at other times during the session as appropriate. See Core Library, "Basic Resources," p. 95, for publishers and addresses. Record company addresses will be found on p. 99. In parodies, hyphenated words match music notes of the song used.

Music

Songs

SUMMERTIME FUN (a parody)
(tune: "Pussy Cat, Pussy Cat")
Adaptation by JoAnne Deal Hicks

I like to boat, and to ski is such fun.
I like to fish, then to lie in the sun.
I like to swim . . . and when I am done
I'm hap-py, so hap-py that sum-mer's be-gun.

From *Piggyback Songs,* Warren
"Songs about Summer," pp. 31–36

From *More Piggyback Songs,* Warren
"Songs about Summer," pp. 33–38

From *Singing Bee*, Hart
"Nuts in May," p. 80
"Over the River and Through the Wood," p. 142

From *Stepping Along in Music Land*, Murray
"Butterfly, Butterfly," p. 47
"Seasons," p. 52

From *Sally Go Round the Sun*, Fowke
"The Wind the Wind," p. 65

From *A Treasury of Songs for Young Children*, Glazer
"It's Raining It's Pouring," p. 132

Rhythms and singing games

A parade can provide a change of pace in the summer program. Choose any excuse for a parade. Have the children choose their costumes and what they wish to carry in the parade. Also have them choose which songs they will sing in the parade (from choices offered by the teachers). Parade around the room, the halls, the offices, and the playgrounds. Warn other people working in your centre that you are planning a parade.

Records and cassettes

Anne Murray. *There's a Hippo in My Bathtub.* (Capitol Records)
"Teddy Bears Picnic"
"You Are My Sunshine"

Bob McGrath. *If You're Happy and You Know It*, Volume I. (Kids Records)
"Mr. Sun"
"Take Me Out to the Ballgame"

Raffi. *Baby Beluga.* (Troubadour Records)
"Dayo"
"Over in the Meadow"

———. *The Corner Grocery Store.* (Troubadour Records)
"Going on a Picnic"

Sandy Oppenheim. *If Snowflakes Fell in Flavours.* (Berandol Records)
"Hey Little Bird"
"Muck"

Fingerplays and Poems

From *Let's Do Fingerplays*, Grayson
"An Airplane," p. 22
"The Train," p. 22
"The Bus," p. 25
"Row, Row, Row Your Boat," p. 26
"My Turtle," p. 32
"There Was a Little Turtle," p. 33
"My Garden," p. 46
"Who Feels Happy?" p. 76
"The See Saw," p. 78
"The Window," p. 78

From *Don't Eat Spiders*, Heidbreder
"Sun, Sun," p. 9
"Bird's Nest," p. 25

From *Hand Rhymes,* Brown
"The Caterpillar," p. 28

From *Round and Round the Garden,* Williams and Beck
"Round and Round the Garden," p. 6
"The Apple Tree," p. 12
"I Hear Thunder," p. 37
"The Cherry Tree," p. 46

From *Read Aloud Rhymes for the Very Young,* Prelutsky and Brown
"Little Wind," p. 12
"Mud," p. 13
"Sun After Rain," p. 13
"Little Seeds," p. 14
"A Spike of Green," p. 14
"Shore," p. 30
"We Build a Castle Near the Rocks," p. 31
"The Picnic," p. 31
"Picnic Day," p. 32
"Joyful," p. 32
"August Heat," p. 32
"Wouldn't You?" p. 33
"A Kite," p. 33
"The Butterfly," p. 33
"In the Summer We Eat," p. 58

Stories

(To read, read–tell, or tell. See Book Centre for complete list.)
There are many children's activities that are specific to the summer. Children enjoy hearing stories about these activities and then planning how they may do similar things. Plantos's *Heather Hits Her First Home Run* is a good example of a story that serves this purpose.

Games

(See "Learning Games," pp. 50–59, and teacher-made games in this chapter for directions.)
1. Guess what? Describe what you like to do outside in summer—swimming, going on picnics, going to zoos. Together think of summer-related activities.
2. I'm taking a vacation: Describe something you will put into your suitcase. "I need it after I eat and before I go to bed ... I use it in my mouth, with toothpaste" (toothbrush). Continue to give other hints until children guess. VARIATION: "I am going in something that ..." (describe airplane, car, bus).

Routine Times

1. At snack or meal times use foods harvested from the children's garden. Also offer special summer treats like watermelon, strawberries, tomatoes, corn on the cob, and cherries.
2. At meal time have a picnic in the park.

Large Muscle Activities

1. Walk a balance beam, log, or chalk mark drawn on the floor.
2. Run to a destination and back.
3. Take a hike.

4. Toss and catch a beach ball.
5. Have a parade (see Rhythms and singing games).
6. Run in the spray from a lawn sprinkler.
7. Add some new homemade sand toys and tools to the sandbox accessories or purchase some new items, such as sand combs (Childcraft), or sand tools, pails, sifters, measuring cups and spoons, sprinkling cans, boats. See sand and water equipment section of most early childhood equipment catalogues.

Extended Experiences

1. Go to a park on a picnic.
2. Watch a parade.
3. Visit the zoo or a circus (see chapter on zoo animals).

Teacher resources

Pictures and Displays

Pictures of parades, the beach, summer flowers, and summer activities.

Books and Periodicals

Chickadee magazine
Cleary, Val. *Seasons of Canada.* Willowdale, Ont: Hounslow Press, 1979. (Good pictures of all the seasons in all parts of the country)
Coleman, Mary Jane. *Foliage, Plants for Modern Living.* Kalamazoo, MI: Merchants Company Publisher, 1974
Equinox magazine
Hardy, Ralph, et al. *The Weather Book.* Toronto: Little Brown, 1982
Holford, Ingrid. *The Guiness Book of Weather Facts and Feats,* 2nd ed. Enfield, Middlesex, GB: Guiness Superlatives, 1982
Hunt, W. Ben. *Golden Book of Indian Crafts and Lore.* New York: Golden Press, 1961
National Geographic magazine
Owl magazine

Films and Videos

Consult your local library for resources from the National Film Board and the CBC

Community Resources and Organizations

▷ Cherry or peach orchard; farm
▷ Television or radio weather reporter

Government Agencies

Provincial, territorial, and federal ministries or departments concerned with meteorology and the environment

Fall

★★★★★★★★★★★★★★★★★★★★★★★

Basic Understandings

(concepts children can grasp from this subject)

Fall is a season of the year that comes after summer and before winter. Autumn is another word for fall. There are many changes in nature in the fall.

Earth changes

▷ The daylight hours become shorter and the night (hours of darkness) longer because the sun rises later and sets earlier.
▷ The temperature slowly drops and the weather becomes cooler, especially at night.
▷ Frost may appear at night or in the early mornings. We can see our breath.
▷ The soil gets harder and sometimes freezes.
▷ There are usually more rainy or cloudy days than in summer.

Plants

▷ Most leaves begin to change colour; some trees remain green and are called "evergreens."
▷ Parts of some plants fall to the ground, such as leaves, apples, nuts, pine cones, and other seeds.
    a. Some leaves change colour but do not drop until replaced by new leaves in the spring —for example, pin oak.
    b. Evergreen trees remain green all year round, but they stop growing in the fall and won't grow again until spring.
▷ In some areas grass and plants turn brown and wither.
▷ Some bulbs are dug up and stored and others are planted for spring blooming.
▷ Some plants are brought inside to prevent freezing, such as geraniums, ivy, cactus, rubber plants, and those in hanging baskets.
▷ In fall many foods ripen and are picked. This is called "harvesting." Examples are pumpkins, apples, cranberries, acorn squash, potatoes, and nuts.

Animals

▷ Some birds and butterflies fly (migrate) south where they can find food more easily.
▷ Some animals get ready to sleep or rest a long time (hibernate) by eating much food or storing it in their homes.
▷ Some animals grow thicker fur or a special undercoating to help keep them warm.

People

▷ We begin wearing warmer clothes, such as sweaters and heavy jackets, caps, and mittens.
▷ People need to build fires or turn on heaters or furnaces.
▷ Many people set out bird feeders and food for the birds after the snow begins.
▷ In many areas farmers harvest many foods and sow winter crops.
▷ Activities include raking leaves, homecomings, football, and Halloween.

Additional Facts the Teacher Should Know

1. It is difficult for a preschool child to grasp the full meaning involved in the concept of fall because it is not something she/he can see, touch, or hold, except by various parts. However, children can learn that it is a time of year when various changes take place in the plants and animals in our environment.

2. Fall is one of the four seasons of the year; in Canada it occurs from approximately September 21st to December 20th (see p. 500.) These are the official dates determined by solar and lunar phases. It is easier for young children to understand changes in weather. These changes are usually better times to introduce the themes of the seasons. The four seasons do not occur at the same time all over the world because the sun's rays are striking the earth differently at any one time, resulting in very different climates. Also countries with large geographic areas, such as Canada, have a wide range of climates during a given season.

3. Squirrels are rodents or gnawing animals that are related to rats and beavers. They can be found in many parts of the world and in most parts of Canada, in woods and city parks. Their obvious activity of collecting seeds and nuts for the winter has long been a sign of fall. (For additional information, see "Animals" chapters.)

4. Chipmunks are like small squirrels, but they live in cleverly hidden burrows 15 to 20 cm under the ground. They make several passageways, storage areas, and a large sleeping area. There are several kinds living in North America and Asia. In Canada, they are usually seen in the woods. The most common are reddish or grayish brown with black and white stripes down their backs. They are about 25 cm long with flat, bushy tails. They eat seeds, nuts, berries, insects or grubs. Chipmunks hibernate from November until spring; however, they may come out of hibernation at intervals. The male and female chipmunk live together in the burrow. Three to five chippers are born by April.

5. In the fall the monarch butterfly, which is orange and black, hatches from a caterpillar which has black, yellow, and white stripes around its body. The monarch's larva can be found in the fields near milkweed, which it likes to eat and which, incidentally, gives the caterpillar a bad taste to birds. If you find one and wish to observe it, put it in a container or box with a screen over the top opening for ventilation. Place a stick in the container at a 45-degree angle for it to use to suspend its chrysalis. Provide it with fresh milkweed leaves daily. It will eat a good deal just before it spins a chrysalis of a lovely apple-green colour, edged at the large end with gold. A monarch butterfly will emerge in less than two weeks and should be allowed to fly away. These butterflies migrate after they emerge and return in the spring to lay their eggs. The change from caterpillar to butterfly is called "metamorphosis." (See "Insects and Spiders".)

6. Woolly bears are the caterpillars of the Isabella tiger moth and are found in many parts of Canada. They are black and reddish brown. They hibernate through the winter, then spin their cocoons in April or May. Near the end of May the moths are hatched. Some people say they are weather predictors. The thicker the fur or the wider the black bands, the colder the winter will be; but no one has ever proved it. Do not bring a wolly bear inside if you want to see it change into a moth; it is too warm inside. Build a small wire cage out of window screening about the size of a large coffee can, leaving it open at one end. Place the open end down over a patch of clover or dandelions and put the woolly bear inside the cage. The children will then be able to watch without losing or disturbing the caterpillar. (See "Insects and Spiders".)

7. Migration is the movement of animals from one place to another. Animals which migrate are birds, fish, and butterflies. In the fall, birds migrate from the north to the south, where they can find food. Some birds which migrate are Canada geese, robins, swallows, and mallards. Not all birds migrate when it turns cold; cardinals, English sparrows, chickadees, juncos, and nuthatches are examples of birds that remain during the winter months. Some birds (such as Canada geese) have stopped following their natural migration patterns because they are being fed and cared for by people. This is an unfortunate example of people interfering with nature. These birds have a special snowsuit of soft down, which they grow when it turns cold to help keep them warm through the winter.

8. Hibernation is a sleep or half-sleep state many animals remain in during the winter months. At this time the animal's body functions slow down and it is able to live through the cold winter when it would not be able to find food. Some may lie in a deep sleep and others may move around on warm days. Animals do not grow during hibernation and may lose as much as one-third of their weight. Only those animals that can store up enough food to last through the winter are able to hibernate. Bears are said to hibernate but their body temperature does not drop as much as it does in a true hibernating animal. Certain frogs, turtles, toads, and lizards bury themselves in the earth below the reach of frost. The horseshoe crab sinks in the mud beneath deep water until May or June. Spiders and snails hibernate under rocks. The woodchuck (groundhog), racoon, and praying mantis also hibernate. (See "Animals of the Woods" and "Zoo Animals" for more information about some of these animals.)

9. Trees in Canada are divided into two main groups. Those that lose their leaves in the fall are called "deciduous" trees. The leaves of the pin oak turn brown in the fall but do not drop until spring. Conifers or cone-bearing trees remain green all year round and are called "evergreens."

10. Fruits that ripen in the fall are purple grapes, apples, persimmon, beechnut, and milkweed.

11. Flowers that bloom in the fall are chrysanthemums, goldenrod, purple asters, barberry, heather, thistle, and wild sunflower.

Methods Most Adaptable for Introducing this Subject to Children

1. Take a walk and look for things or changes that tell us it is fall, such as leaves, nuts, milkweed pods, woolly bears, birds flying south.
2. A child brings in a pretty leaf, an apple, pine cone, or chrysanthemum and you can say, "This is one of the things (or signs) that tell us it is fall." Let the children take turns holding the item and help them to observe, describe, and compare it with other items.
3. Read a book about fall or the four seasons.
4. Set out a new fall puzzle or flannelboard-figure kit.

Vocabulary

fall	chrysalis	high, low	evergreen
autumn	change	warm, cool	red
hibernate	bird(s)	frost	orange
migrate	squirrel	thermometer	yellow
harvest	chipmunk	tree	green
caterpillar	woolly bear	leaves	brown
butterfly	chrysanthemum	nuts	
cocoon	temperature	pine cone	

Learning Centres

Discovery Centre

1. Have a table where children can put things they bring in that tell us it is fall. There should be small boxes, an insect house, magnifying glass, pictures of fall, and resource books. October and November issues of *Owl* and *Chickadee* magazines are especially suitable. Help the child identify the object she or he has brought in and discover its outstanding characteristics, such as colour, shape, size, weight, texture, name, and use. If it is an animal or insect, add habits, what it eats, what it does, how it moves, sounds it makes, and safety precautions. Find these things in the pictures or resource books you have provided. (Use with learning, language, and readiness materials and activities.)

2. Display: Take-a-walk-in-the-fall picture charts with companion book *Fall Is Here* (The Child's World).

3. Display: Life-cycle-of-a-monarch sequence chart (The Child's World).

4. Display: How-seeds-travel-from-plants-and-seeds picture fold-outs (The Child's World).

5. Find a milkweed pod and open it. Talk about how seeds travel—wind, on clothing, animals' fur, mouth.

6. Apples can be cut in half crosswise to reveal a star-shaped seed case with seeds. Talk about the various parts, colour, texture, and shape. Buy yellow, red, and green apples. Ask how they are alike and how they are different.

   ★ CAUTION: Make a cardboard sheath for the paring knife and keep it in the sheath and out of the children's reach when not in use.

7. Make applesauce: The teacher should pare, core, and cut the apples in advance. Put apples, water, and sugar in saucepan and cook on a stove, electric skillet, or hot plate. The children can help with the measuring, stirring, and mashing. A dash or two of nutmeg, cinnamon, or ginger may be added. Serve warm or cool with a cookie or cracker or save until meal time. Have whole apples available and talk about differences in size, texture, and appearance.

   ★ CAUTION: High heat is required for cooking the apples. Extra supervision is necessary. Try to have extra help and then limit this centre to three or four children at a time, or use a microwave oven to cook the apples.

8. Buy and compare several kinds of corn—popcorn, corn on the cob, canned, frozen, and cream style. Compare the size, taste, and texture as appropriate. Pop some corn to serve as a snack. Use an electric popper with a glass lid or a wire basket popper so children can see corn popping. (See chapter on "Sight" for songs and other related experiences with popcorn.)

★ **CAUTION:**   High heat is required. Close supervision will be necessary.

9. Buy as large and as accurate a thermometer as you can. Indoor–outdoor models are excellent as children can see differences or similarities between the two. They can see that as it gets colder the mercury goes down and vice versa. (See also no. 11, p. 360).

10. Obtain a kitchen food scale or balance pans so children can weigh nuts, apples, or pumpkins. Which weighs more, an apple or a nut? A pumpkin or five apples? Children may want to weigh themselves or other objects in the classroom. Of course other scales will be needed for this.

11. When outdoors watch for birds flying south, if you live in a migration pattern and have a good view of the sky. As a beginning experience you might simply announce, "Look, the birds are flying south, where it will be easier for them to find food." With children who have had more experience, you might use a compass to find north and then draw a directional cross on the sidewalk in chalk or paint it on a block of wood. Use N, E, S, W for the four points. Help children decide which direction is south from where they are. On a windy day, you could tie a scarf to a stick and hold it over the compass cross and see which way the wind is blowing.

12. Discover that wet leaves leave a print on the sidewalk.

13. Falling leaves, nuts, and apples may lead to an interest in gravity.

Dramatic Play Centres

Home-living centre

Set out sweaters, coats, and blankets for dolls to indicate the change in the weather.

Block-building centre

1. Set out farm animals. Suggest through conversation or pictures the need to build barns or buildings for the animals.

2. Make a barn of large hollow blocks or large cardboard boxes. Sing "Ha Ha," "Turkey in the Straw" from *Piggyback Songs* by Warren (p. 44).

Learning, Language, and Readiness Materials Centre

Commercially made games and materials

(See "Basic Resources," pp. 79, 100, for manufacturers' addresses.)

1. *Puzzles:* Puzzles of leaves, wind, rain, and harvest time.
2. *Outdoor toys:* Child-sized rakes, kites.

   ★ **CAUTION:**   Only use kites if you can take the children to an area where they can run with the kites away from power and telephone lines.)

3. *Flannelboards and flannelboard aids:* Cutouts of leaves, clouds, umbrellas, kites, and warm clothing.
4. *Posters:* Weather chart.
5. *Miscellaneous:* Thermometer (see no. 9 above), small plastic watering tin.

Teacher-made games and materials

NOTE: For a detailed description of "Learning Games," see pp. 50–59.

1. What's missing? Use several objects from the discovery table, such as a pine cone, nut, or leaf.
2. Show me: Use a nut, yellow leaf, and apple. "Show me the one you eat." "Show me the one that is round."

3. Match-them: "This leaf is yellow; each of you (or name one child) find me something in this room that is yellow." "This nut is round; find me something in this room that is round." Use sets of two cards with identical pictures of fall objects to match.

4. What am I? "I am thinking of something that is tall and green and has needles; what is it?" "I am thinking of something that has gray fur and likes to eat nuts; what is it?" "I am thinking of something that is big and round and orange; what is it?"

5. Reach and feel: Use fall objects.

6. Grouping and sorting by association:

   a. Buy several kinds of nuts in quantity or use those you find. Identify the nuts for the children and compare the size, colour, and texture. Mix the nuts together in a large bowl or container and provide as many smaller bowls or containers as there are kinds of nuts. Let the children sort the nuts.

   b. Sort leaves by colour or by shape. Use the ones you find or precut some from coloured construction paper.

   c. Sort pine cones by size or type.

7. Alike, different and the same: Make card sets with pictures of leaves, trees, birds, squirrels, chipmunks, fall fruits, and vegetables. Put out two cards that are alike and one that is different.

8. Count nuts, seeds, pine cones, or leaves. Beginning concepts are one to three and experienced children may count to ten with understanding.

9. Division: Apples can be cut in halves or quarters for a snack.

10. Make a calendar for September, October, and/or November with large 5 cm square blocks for the days. Paste appropriate pictures on the square for each holiday you are planning to celebrate. Remember to highlights trips and birthdays. You might add to the decoration of the room and the children's understanding if you cut a large tree from brown construction paper and put it beside the calendar. Cut enough leaves of various colours to put on the tree to correspond with the number of days on the calendar. Each day take one of the leaves off the tree and cover up the day that is on the calendar. When the month is over the tree will be bare, coinciding with the way trees will look in your community. Choose to do this during the fall month when leaves usually drop in your area.

11. Make a large cardboard thermometer with movable elastic or ribbon mercury. (See "Mathematics," p. 556). Talk about the kinds of clothes we wear when the temperature is at various positions (or degrees) on the thermometer. Pictures of children wearing appropriate clothes can be cut from catalogues and pasted on the cardboard. Wider cardboard should be used for the thermometer to accommodate the pictures of clothing. Also you could set the temperature on the cardboard thermometer at the same degree as on the real thermometer. The next day you can look at the outdoor thermometer again, compare it with the cardboard thermometer, and help children decide if it is warmer or colder than yesterday.

Art Centre

- 1. All art media: Feature the fall colours seen in your area in the easel paints, fingerpaints, chalk, crayons, and play dough.

- • 2. Spatter-painting: Place a leaf that a child has found on a piece of paper. Let the child spatter-paint over the leaf, using a vegetable brush rubbed over wire screening fastened to a cigar box or wooden frame. When dry, remove the leaf.

- • 3. Allow children to arrange various leaves, twigs, nutshells, and dried grasses on a piece of construction paper. Spatter-paint the arrangement. When dry, remove the articles and an interesting design will remain.

- • 4. Teacher may make a leaf stencil by tracing around a well-shaped leaf on cardboard and then carefully cutting out the leaf. The stencil can be used to make leaf designs by spatter-painting or daubing on paint with sponges. Upholstery plastic or rubber innertubing makes a washable, reusable stencil.

•• 5. Roll-on painting: The teacher should cut out sleeves of various upholstery fabrics with deep cut designs. Wrap the fabric swatches around small rolling pins and fasten in place with two rubber bands. Drop small amounts of selected fingerpaint or thick poster paint on a piece of paper. Let the children choose the roller designs and colours they wish. There will be interesting blends of colour. If they are ready, help the children to see the relationship between the colours put on and the ones resulting from the blending.

•• 6. Crayon rubbings: Fasten a nicely shaped leaf with a good vein pattern onto an easel using double-sided Scotch tape in at least two places. Thumbtack a sheet of newsprint over the leaf. Have child rub firmly over leaf with the flat side of a crayon (from which the paper has been removed). Leaf outline and vein pattern should appear.

• 7. Pasting leaves: Use those that are found outside or teacher may precut leaves from coloured construction paper. Paste leaves on paper as the children wish.

• 8. Tearing leaves: Children may make their own leaves by tearing them out of tissue paper. These paper leaves could be used in pasting leaves.

•• 9. Hand printing leaves: Children dip each hand, palm down, in separate fall colours and then press palms down on paper in different positions. Hands may be washed and two other colours chosen. When finished, the effect is like varicoloured leaves.

• 10. Leaf printing: Use any of the following methods to make leaf prints.

• a. Cut flat sponges into leaf shapes. Children dip them in selected paint and press on paper in desired pattern.

• b. Cut sponges into any small shape and let children daub paint with sponges on the paper desired. Use separate sponge for each fall colour. Result looks like vari-coloured leaves.

••• c. Place leaves the children bring (or precut some from construction paper) on blue print paper. Expose to the sun for five to ten minutes. The outline of the leaf will remain when the leaf is removed.

••• 11. Caterpillar: Remove the lid from an egg carton and cut the bottom portion in half lengthwise to make two caterpillars. Children may paint their caterpillars colours of their own choosing. Pipecleaners or hair curler picks make good antennae (feelers). For variation, cotton balls may be dipped in dry powdered paint and glued to the humps to give the caterpillar a fuzzy appearance.

••• 12. Fall mural: Children first draw tree trunks by holding an unwrapped crayon sideways and using downward strokes. Branches can be added by a few upward strokes fanning out from the top of the trunk. Leaves may then be added to the trees by using the methods suggested above. A ground cover may be made by pasting on dried grasses, nutshells, and twigs.

Book Centre

• Adelson, Leon. *All Ready for Winter.* New York: E.M. Hale, 1952.
• Bacon. *Wind.* Toronto: Methuen, 1986.
• Bancroft, Henrietta. *Down Come the Leaves.* New York: Thomas Y. Crowell, 1961.
• Burningham, John. *Seasons.* New York: Bobbs-Merrill, 1970.
••• Duvoisin, Roger. *The House of Four Seasons.* New York: Lothrop, Lee & Shepard, 1960.
• Fisher, Aileen. *I Like Weather.* New York: Thomas Y. Crowell, 1963.
• Friskey, Margaret. *Johnny and the Monarch.* Chicago: Childrens Press, 1946.
• Hill. *Rain.* Toronto: Methuen, 1986.
• Hines, A. *Taste the Raindrops.* New York: Greenwillow Press, 1983.
• Hutchins, P. *The Wind Blew.* New York: Macmillan, 1974.
•• Krauss, Ruth. *The Growing Story.* New York: Harper & Row, 1947.
•• Kumin, Maxine. *Follow the Fall.* New York: G. P. Putnam's Sons, 1961.
• Lenski, Lois. *Now It's Fall.* New York: Henry Z. Walck, 1948.

- Leonard, Marcia. *Little Puppy's Rainy Day.* New York: Bantam, 1987.
- ••• Locker, T. *Sailing with the Wind.* New York: Dial Press, 1986. (Read–Tell) (Notable for its beautiful pictures.)
- ••• Marino, Dorothy Bronson. *Buzzy Bear's Busy Day.* New York: Franklin Watts, 1965.
- •• Miles, Betty. *A Day of Autumn.* New York: Alfred A. Knopf, 1965 (paper).
- ••• Podendorf, Illa. *True Book of the Seasons.* Chicago: Childrens Press, 1972.
- ••• Tresselt, Alvin. *It's Time Now.* New York: Lothrop, Lee & Shepard, 1969.
- •• Udry, Janice. *A Tree Is Nice.* New York: Harper & Row, 1956.
- • Wing, Helen. *The Squirrel Twins.* Chicago: Rand McNally, 1961.
- • Zion, Gene. *All Falling Down.* New York: Harper & Row, 1951.

Planning for Group Time

NOTE: All music, fingerplays, poems, stories, and games listed here may also be used at other times during the session as appropriate. See Core Library, "Basic Resources," p. 95, for publishers and addresses. Record company addresses can be found on p. 99.

Music

Songs

From *Piggyback Songs*, Warren
"Songs About Fall," pp. 37–44

From *More Piggyback Songs*, Warren
"Songs About Fall," pp. 39–48

From *Singing Bee*, Hart
"The North Wind Doth Blow," p. 33
"Rain, Rain," p. 49

From *Elephant Jam*, Sharon Lois, and Bram
"The Wind," p. 28

From *Sally Go Round the Sun*, Fowke
"The Wind the Wind," p. 65

From *A Treasury of Songs for Young Children*, Glazer
"It's Raining, It's Pouring," p. 132

Rhythms and singing games

Dramatize falling leaves, migrating birds, shaking down apples with the songs above. Other activities might include crawling or tunneling to music, to simulate animals burrowing underground to hibernate for the winter.

Records and cassettes

Bob McGrath. *If You're Happy and You Know It*, Volume I. (Kids Records)
"Take Me Out to the Ballgame"

Raffi. *Baby Beluga.* (Troubadour Records)
"Over in the Meadow"

Fingerplays and Poems

From *Let's Do Fingerplays*, Grayson
"This Little Squirrel," p. 35
"Little Bird," p. 37
"Falling Leaves," p. 47
"October," p. 47
"Whirling Leaves," p. 47

From *Don't Eat Spiders*, Heidbreder
"Falling Leaves," p. 10
"Vancouver," p. 18

From *Round and Round the Garden*, Williams and Beck
"Round and Round the Garden," p. 6
"The Apple Tree," p. 12
"I Hear Thunder," p. 37
"The Cherry Tree," p. 46

From *Read Aloud Rhymes for the Very Young*, Prelutsky and Brown
"Showers," p. 12
"Little Wind," p. 12
"The Rain," p. 12
"Rainy Day," p. 13
"Mud," p. 13
"Sun After Rain," p. 13
"A Kite," p. 33
"The Moon's the North Wind's Cooky," p. 51
"The Wind and the Moon," p. 51
"Umbrellas," p. 61

BABY SEEDS

In a milkweed cradle, snug and warm, (CLOSE FINGERS INTO FIST)
Baby seeds are hiding safe from harm,
Open wide the cradle, hold it high, (OPEN HAND AND HOLD IT UP IN THE AIR)
Coming along wind, help them fly. (WIGGLE FINGERS)

WHISKY FRISKY

Whisky Frisky
Hippity hop,
Up he goes
To the tree-top.

Whirly, twirly,
Round and round
Down he scampers
To the ground.

Furly, curly
What a tail!
Tall as a feather,
Broad as a sail!

Where's his supper?
In the shell;
Snappy, cracky,
Out it fell.

WALKING AROUND THE BLOCK

We went walking around the block together
Leaves were scarlet, leaves were brown
It was fun in sunny weather
Squirrels darting—squirrels scampering
Acorns dropping—brown birds chattering
Leaves were crunching with our feet
Smell of pine was sharp and sweet
We held pine cones in our hand
It was fun when we walked together
Walked around the block in autumn weather
Walked around the block in sunny weather
All of us liked it
All of us thought it was fun!

CRUNCHY LEAVES

We make such a crunchy sound
In the leaves upon the ground.
Crunchy, crunchy, hear the noise
Made in leaves by girls and boys.

LITTLE SQUIRREL

I saw a little squirrel
Sitting in a tree;
He was eating a nut
And wouldn't look at me.

ROLY-POLY CATERPILLAR

Roly-poly caterpillar (WALK FINGER ACROSS LEFT PALM)
Into a corner crept, (FOLD UP FINGERS OF LEFT HAND OVER CATERPILLAR)
Spun around himself a blanket, (MAKE WINDING MOTION AROUND HAND)
Then for a long time slept. (PRETEND TO SLEEP; CLOSE EYES)

Roly-poly caterpillar (PRETEND TO WAKE; OPEN EYES)
Wakening by and by,
Found himself with beautiful wings, (PUT THUMBS TOGETHER; FLUTTER FINGERS LIKE WINGS)
Changed to a butterfly. (FLY THE BUTTERFLY AWAY)

GRAY SQUIRREL

Gray squirrel, gray squirrel,
Whisk your bushy tail,
Gray squirrel, gray squirrel,
Whisk your bushy tail.

Wrinkle up your funny nose,
Hold a nut between your toes,
Gray squirrel, gray squirrel,
Whisk your bushy tail.

Stories

(To read, read–tell, or tell. See Book Centre for complete list.)
There are many fall stories about the wind. Try reading Bacon's *Wind* or Zion's *All Falling Down* to your group and follow this by having them imitate the wind in sound and in movement.

Games

(See "Learning Games," pp. 50–59, and teacher-made games, pp. 359–60, nos. 1, 2, 3, 4, 5, 7 in this chapter for directions.)
1. What's missing?
2. Show me
3. Match-them
4. Reach and feel
5. What am I?
6. Alike, different, and the same

Routine Times

1. During snack or meal times feature foods that are harvested in fall—popcorn, apple wedges (spread peanut butter on them for variation), nuts, applesauce, corn, squash, sweet potatoes, pumpkin pie, pumpkin custard, or pumpkin cupcakes. Use your favourite recipes.

   NOTE: Children who are deprived of food at home may find it difficult to use food as a cognitive medium as suggested in discovery activities and teacher-made games and materials. For these children, these activities might best be carried out in combination with snack or meal times with the idea the food will be consumed immediately afterward. Sorting nuts or other similar use of foods may also be successfully offered as cognitive media after a meal time. Otherwise, use pictures of food or plastic models.

2. While busing or walking children to and from school, look for signs that it is fall.
3. Before dressing to go outside you might talk about the weather. Look at the indoor-outdoor thermometer and talk about what we need to wear today.
4. Encourage resting by suggesting the children pretend to be hibernating animals getting ready to sleep through the cold winter.

Large Muscle Activities

1. Raking leaves: If your centre is in an area where trees grow, you may wish to rake leaves into a pile and run and jump in them. If your play yard does not have trees that drop their leaves, you may plan a trip to a nearby park or to a child's home where there are some. Children enjoy scuffling through the leaves to hear the crunchy, crackling noise. Songs about leaves may be sung at this time. Leaves can be raked into a pile and jumped into. Child-size leaf rakes are desirable, or shorten handles of adult-size leaf rakes by cutting and sanding the edges.
2. Kicking football: Children with above-average large muscle control may enjoy kicking a football off a tee. Using a whiffle football (plastic with holes cut in it), show the children how to set the ball on the tee and, if necessary, demonstrate how to kick.

   ★ CAUTION: Be sure to place the tee so that the ball will be kicked away from where other children are playing. If a regulation-size football is used, do not inflate to its full extent.

Extended Experiences

1. Take a walk to look for things that show us it is fall. Collect leaves, nuts, milkweed, pine cones, caterpillars, and other finds. Bring back to the centre for the science and nature table, creative arts activities, and learning games. Take sacks to collect pebbles, twigs, dry grasses or flowering weeds, or seeds. Also look for chipmunks or squirrels collecting nuts and try to spot migrating birds.
2. A trip to an apple orchard to pick apples.
3. A trip to a grocery to buy apples, gourds, nuts, popcorn, or pumpkins for the various planned activities.
4. Visit a farm or agricultural museum to see harvesting and planting equipment.
5. Visit a natural history museum showing animals in fall.

Teacher Resources

Pictures and Displays

▷ Mount pictures of trees in fall, squirrels, chipmunks, monarch butterflies, harvest fruits and vegetables, children in sweaters and coats, animals hibernating, birds migrating, Halloween, Thanksgiving, and other fall holidays and celebrations in appropriate places.

▷ Place a bowl or vase of plastic or real fall flowers on a windowsill, snack table, or library table for the children to enjoy.

▷ A basket or cornucopia of plastic or real fruits that ripen in the fall could be placed on a low table for the children to enjoy and talk about.

Books and Periodicals

Chickadee magazine

Cleary, Val. *Seasons of Canada.* Willowdale, Ont: Houslow Press, 1979. (Good for pictures of all the seasons in all parts of the country)

Equinox magazine

Hardy, Ralph, et al. *The Weather Book.* Toronto: Little Brown, 1982

Holford, Ingrid. *The Guiness Book of Weather Facts and Feats,* 2nd ed. Enfield, Middlesex, GB: Guiness Superlatives, 1982

National Geographic magazine

Owl magazine

Sterling, Dorothy. *Fall Is Here.* Garden City, NY: Doubleday, 1966

Zim, Herbert S., and Alexander C. Martin. *Trees.* New York: Western Publishing, 1952 (paper)

Films and Videos

Consult your local library for resources

Community Resources and Organizations

▷ Provincial agricultural representative
▷ Department of agriculture at a local college or university

Government Agencies

Provincial, territorial and federal ministries or departments concerned with meteorology and the environment

PART 5

Animals

★★

Contents

411 19. Zoo Animals

421 20. Insects and Spiders

Introduction

Basic Understandings

(concepts children can grasp from this subject)

▷ Anything that is alive and is not a plant is an animal.

▷ There are many different kinds of animals in the world (at present, approximately three million).

▷ Some of the different kinds of animals are birds, fish, insects, worms, shell creatures, reptiles, amphibians, and mammals.

▷ All animals need food and water to live. Some animals eat plants; some eat other animals (meat); some, like people, eat both meat and plants.

▷ Animals get their food in many different ways and places:

1. Out of the air—frogs catch flying insects
2. In the water—ducks catch fish
3. On the ground—cows eat grass
4. Out of the ground—birds eat worms
5. Above the ground off bushes, plants, or trees—rabbits eat lettuce, raccoons eat berries
6. From their keeper or owner—lions in a zoo, pets in a home, chickens on a farm are given food
7. From their mother or father (parents)—baby kittens nurse from their mother

▷ Some animals are born alive, while others are hatched from eggs.

▷ Most animals do not look like their parents at birth, but they change and grow up to look like them later.

▷ Animals differ from each other in colour, in size, in body covering, in body parts, but they are similar to each other within family groups.

▷ Each animal moves about in its own special way. Some of the ways animals move are:

swim, float	jump, leap, or hop
fly	climb
walk, run, trot, gallop	swing
slither, slide, creep, or crawl	burrow or tunnel

▷ Each animal makes a different sound. Some of the sounds they may make are:

bark	growl	chatter	chirp
whinny	snort	squeal	whistle
grunt	bleat	honk	hiss
crow	quack	moo	purr
roar	mew	trumpet	cluck

NOTE: Try to imitate actual sounds. See Additional Facts the Teacher Should Know.

▷ Animals have different kinds of coverings such as:

fur	hair	skins (hides)	feathers
shell	scales	plates	down

▷ Animals can provide people with many things:

1. Pleasure, comfort, and companionship—as pets to love and play with
2. Assistance—to help the disabled and/or physically challenged
3. Protection—as watchdogs and guard dogs
4. Labour—to help people carry, push, pull, or lift something
5. Wool and feathers—for clothing, hats, and decorations
6. Food—eggs, honey, and milk.

▷ Some animals we hear about are make-believe, such as dragons and unicorns
▷ Some animals, such as dinosaurs and dodo birds, are extinct
▷ Each kind of animal is given a different name for the male, the female, the offspring, and the group (see animal charts)
▷ Some animals need people to help them:

1. By caring for them in captivity in zoos, homes, animal hospitals, or on farms
2. By helping them to live in their natural homes:

   a. By assisting wild animals to find food and water especially in times of hardship
   b. By protecting them from other animals, from machines, from people, from enemies, and from weather
   c. By building or fencing off special places for them to live
   d. By having rules for fishermen and hunters

▷ Sometimes animals are referred to by the place where they live—farm animals, animals of the woods, zoo animals, and pets (animals we have at home)
▷ Many animals, especially birds, insects, and wild animals, are coloured to look like the place where they usually live; because they match tree bark, leaves, ground, rocks, or grass, other animals or hunters cannot find them easily and they are safe
▷ Animals live in different kinds of homes—water, burrow, nest, or tree
▷ A veterinarian is a doctor for animals
▷ An animal hospital or clinic is a place where sick and injured animals can be taken to get help
▷ The Humane Society (animal shelter) is a place where lost animals or animals without owners are cared for until they are claimed or a home is found for them; some will not be claimed and may be killed

Additional Facts the Teacher Should Know

1. Most animals we have seen or heard about have backbones and are called *vertebrates*.
2. Insects and spiders, examples of animals without backbones, are called *invertebrates*.
3. Mammals are warm-blooded vertebrates that are born alive, covered with fur or hair. They feed (nurse) their babies with milk from their own bodies. The duckbill platypus and the spiny anteater produce their young as eggs, but they, too, nurse the young once they are hatched.

4. Reptiles and amphibians are cold-blooded vertebrates. Reptiles such as snakes crawl on their bellies while others such as lizards, turtles, alligators, and crocodiles crawl on very short legs. Reptiles are covered with dry scales, are *not* slimy, and most lay eggs on dry land. Four groups of reptiles now living are—lizards, snakes, turtles, alligators and crocodiles. Amphibians live both in water and on land. Their skins are bare and moist, with no scales, fur, or feathers. Frogs, toads, and salamanders are amphibians. Cold-blooded animals must bury themselves underground or hibernate in a cave in cold weather (see "Fall" and "Winter").

5. Most baby animals are cared for by their parents when young; some must take care of themselves from birth. Some baby animals eat the same kind of food that their parents eat; others get milk from their mother's body (nurse or suckle).

6. To avoid misinformation or misconceptions while teaching about the sounds animals make, try to imitate the sounds the animal really makes. If possible, listen to good records and tapes with accurate reproductions of these sounds. (See Voice under "Description and Characteristics" in the animal charts.)

7. At times you may want to assure that children have heard the correct animal sound, but do not forget that it is great fun for children to try to imitate animals. A rousing chorus of animal sounds can add a great deal to animal stories.

8. When reading or telling stories in which animals have human qualities it is important to assure that the children understand the stories are imaginative and are allegories for real situations. Asking questions, such as, "What would you do if you were this animal?" or "What it would it be like if your dog actually could talk and wear your clothes?" will remind children that the stories are fanciful, without spoiling the fun of the story.

Teacher Resources

Durrell, Gerald. *The Stationary Ark.* London: Collins, 1976.

Forsyth, Adrian. *Mammals of the Canadian Wild.* Camden East, Ont: Equinox Books, 1986.

Grey Owl. *The Adventures of Sajo and the Beaver People.* Toronto: Macmillan, 1973.

Headstrom, Richard. *Suburban Wildlife.* Camden East, Ont: Equinox Books, 1986.

Hendrikson, Robert. *Animal Crackers.* Markham, Ont: Penguin, 1983.

The Larousse Encyclopedia of Animal life. London; Hamlyn, 1967.

Seton, E.T. *Wild Animals I Have Known.* Ottawa: University of Ottawa Press, 1977.

Tremain, Ruthven. *The Animal's Who's Who.* New York: Charles Scribner's Sons, 1982.

Whitaker, Murel, ed. *Great Canadian Animal Stories.* Edmonton: Hurtig, 1978.

16 Farm Animals

★★★★★★★★★★★★★★★★★★★★★★★

Basic Understandings

(concepts children can grasp from this subject)

▷ A farm is a piece of land, usually larger than a city lot, used to raise crops or animals. It is ordinarily located outside a city or town.

▷ There are many kinds of farms—poultry, grain, dairy, livestock, fruit, and vegetable. At one time a farmer used to raise crops *and* animals. Some farmers still do. But more often only one main crop or one kind of animal is raised—wheat, corn, potatoes, beans, peaches, berries, sheep, turkeys, ducks, hogs, etc.

▷ Horses and cattle are sometimes raised on ranches. The people who work on ranches are called ranch-hands or ranchers.

▷ Animals usually raised on a farm are cows, horses, sheep, goats, pigs, chickens, ducks, turkeys, and geese.

▷ Most farm animals need to be fenced into fields so they do not stray into a roadway or into another farmer's field. Fences prevent animals escaping to other fields where they might eat the wrong foods.

▷ To protect them from bad weather, farm animals usually have special houses, such as barns, sheds, stables, coops, or pens, to sleep in at night.

▷ Sometimes the farmer raises food for the farm animals—hay, alfalfa, corn, oats, and barley.

▷ The farmer, family, and employees work long hours to care for their animals and their crops. At certain seasons of the year (during planting, cultivating, irrigating, harvesting, butchering, breeding, and marketing) they are much busier than at other seasons.

▷ A herd is a group of one kind of animal living together.

▷ Farm animals help the farmer:

1. Horses provide transportation; pull wagons
2. Chickens lay eggs
3. Cows and goats give milk
4. Cats catch mice; dogs guard other animals
5. Sheep grow wool
6. Bees make honey

▷ The farmer uses many tools and machines to take care of farm animals (see "Tools and Machines").

▷ Many farm families like to show their best animals at fall fairs or exhibitions. Sometimes they win ribbons or prizes.

▷ At rodeos, ranch hands show how well they can rope (lasso) calves and ride horses.

Additional Facts the Teacher Should Know

Chickens

▷ Brood (family group)
▷ Hen (female)
▷ Rooster (male)
▷ Chick (young)
▷ They are covered with feathers which vary in colour depending on the breed; two pieces of red flesh called wattles hang behind and below their bills
▷ They communicate through clucks; roosters crow
▷ Chickens eat corn, grains, and gravel
▷ Although they have wings, they can only fly short distances
▷ The average hens lays 218 eggs a year
▷ The average chicken has a life span of 8 to 14 years

Cattle

▷ Herd (family group)
▷ Cow (female)
▷ Bull (male)
▷ Heifer (young female)
▷ Calf (young male)
▷ They are covered with a fairly course hair that varies in colour depending on the breed; both cows and bulls have horns; cows have large udders with teats that hold their milk
▷ They communicate through moos and bellows
▷ Cattle eat grass, hay, corn, grains, and lick salt
▷ The average life span is 20 years

Hogs

▷ Herd (family group)
▷ Sow (female)
▷ Boar (male)
▷ Piglet or shoat (young)
▷ Their long heavy bodies are covered with short bristly hair that varies in colour depending on the breed; they have large snouts and short curly tails
▷ Hogs communicate through squeals and grunts, snorts and oinks
▷ They eat almost anything
▷ The average life span is 9 to 15 years

Horses

▷ Herd or band (family group)
▷ Mare (female)
▷ Stallion or gelding (male)
▷ Filly (young female)
▷ Colt (young male)
▷ Foal (newborn)
▷ They are covered with a coat of hair, which varies in colour; they have long manes and tails

▷ Horses communicate through whinnys or neighs
▷ They eat oats, hay, grass, clover, barley, carrots, and lick salt
▷ The average life span is 20 to 30 years

Sheep

▷ Flock (family group)
▷ Ewe (female)
▷ Ram (male)
▷ Lamb (young)
▷ They are covered with a thick coat of wool, which varies in colour depending on the breed; some rams have horns
▷ Sheep communicate through bleats and baahs
▷ They eat grain, grasses, and corn
▷ The average life span is 13 years.

Goats

▷ Herd or band (family group)
▷ Nanny (female)
▷ Billy (male)
▷ Kid (young)
▷ They are covered with thick coarse hair, which varies in colour depending on the breed
▷ They communicate through bleats
▷ Goats eat a variety of grains and grasses
▷ The average life span is 8 to 10 years

Methods Most Adaptable for Introducing this Subject to Children

1. At meal time, discuss animal-food products from farms.
2. Children take a trip to a farm.
3. Tell or read–tell a farm storybook like *Big Red Barn.*
4. See a truck or cattle car full of farm animals.
5. Make a picture display of farm scenes.
6. Have a parent who is a veterinarian or a farmer visit.
7. Make egg salad sandwiches or an omlette. This can lead to a talk about the original source of eggs, milk, butter, and cream.

Vocabulary

saddle	trough	pasture	ranch
cowboy/cowgirl	stable	corncrib	hay
cattle	pig pen	field	silo
sheep	poultry	dairy	stall
brand	livestock	fence	barn
hayloft	harness	farm	herd
feeder			

Add to the above list words that pertain to farm animals observed by your group. Include the names, body parts, sounds, and foods eaten by animals you are observing.

Learning Centres

Discovery Centre

1. Make butter.
2. Churn butter using a butter churn.
3. Examine raw eggs; then poach, scramble, soft boil, hard boil, and bake them. Compare.
4. Make cottage cheese:

   1 litre of milk
   1 rennett tablet

   DIRECTIONS:

   Heat milk to lukewarm.
   Dissolve rennet tablet in a small amount of the milk.
   Stir rennet mixture into remaining milk.
   Let stand in a warm place until set.
   Drain through a strainer lined with cheesecloth.
   Bring corners of cloth together and squeeze or drain mixture.
   Rinse mixture with cold water and drain again.
   Add a little butter and salt.

5. Make pudding: Pour hot milk into a plastic container. Add instant pudding mix. Seal container, then shake. Let pudding cool before eating.
6. Take a pony ride at a farm or in a park.

   NOTE: Must have adequate adult supervision and animals must be used to children. Do not insist any child ride who does not *wish* to.

7. Explore wool: Examine wool clippings, lanolin, dyed yarn, yarn spun into thread, wool cloth, sheepskin, wool articles (mittens or scarves). Order a folder with attached samples from a wool company.
8. Explore a loom or other spinning and weaving equipment.
9. Examine feathers: Note difference between tail or wing feathers and downy fluffs. See if feathers will float. Talk about why they float. What are feathers for? (To keep birds warm or cool, to help ducks float on water.) Use a magnifying glass to examine feathers.
10. Examine blown out or hard boiled eggs: Compare size, shape, and colours of chicken, duck, goose eggs. Put feathers with each kind of egg in a cigar box with a picture or model of bird so that children can make a proper association.
11. Various grains that farm animals eat can be examined under a magnifying glass or viewed in a sealed pill bottle.
12. Examine leather: Identify an article's source, such as pigskin gloves, snakeskin belt, calfskin shoes, horsehide baseball, sheepskin coat or collar. Point out that some endangered animals are now protected by law.
13. Hatch an egg in an incubator.
14. Taste goat milk, cream, skimmed milk, whole milk, cottage cheese, sour cream, honey-butter, margarine, buttermilk. Smell sour milk.

Dramatic Play Centres

Home-living centre

1. Post pictures of baking, showing eggs and milk next to a mixing bowl.
2. Show picture of a chicken with eggs or a cow being milked.

3. Mount on cardboard, pictures of fried eggs, bacon, meat for children to pretend to cook and to serve. Cover pictures with clear adhesive plastic for greater durability.
4. Display marble or plastic eggs (unbreakable plastic eggs are available through toy companies. Occasionally, coloured plastic eggs are available at discount stores at Easter). Eggs may be put in refrigerator or cupboard. Cut or break egg carton in half.
5. Add empty milk cartons and empty evaporated milk or pudding cans with "cut" edge taped for safety. If possible choose labels showing whole food in natural state.
6. Add pie plates, frying pans with spatulas, muffin tins, eggs, and dairy products for cooking.
7. Collect coloured pictures from grocery store advertising inserts to make food cards or books for grocery lists.

Block-building centre

1. Set out block accessories such as model farm animals (including cats and dogs), tractors, dump trucks, farm fences, trees, troughs, and people.
2. Hang pictures of farm activities including a farmer milking cows or harvesting crops to feed livestock. Also include pictures of chickens, goats, pigs, and other farm animals.
3. Set out a shoebox filled with excelsior for hay to "feed" farm animals.
4. Add some blue paper cut in free-form shapes to use as lakes and ponds.
5. Set out coloured cubes and coloured spools to be used for loading and unloading trucks and wagons.
6. Encourage use of large hollow blocks for building barns. Children may pretend to be animals.
7. Make silo from coloured paper or foil wrapped around a cardboard cylinder.
8. Add buckets, work gloves, old saddle or child harness, dishpans for feeding chickens, work hats, step ladders (to go to hayloft).

Other dramatic play centres

1. Set out clothes and props for farmer or ranch-hand (see p. 18).
2. Make paper sack costumes or hand puppets designed to look like farm animals (see p. 276); provide Halloween costumes of farm animals such as ducks, chicks, and rabbits. Appropriate coat hanger masks can be used (see "Halloween" p. 275).

Learning, Language, and Readiness Materials Centre

Commercially made games and materials

(See "Basic Resources," pp. 79, 100, for manufacturers' addresses.)
1. *Puzzles:* Puzzles with a variety of farm animals. Be sure some of the puzzles have knobs.
2. *Small toys for imaginative play:* Model animals and farms: Durable plastic or wooden animals and farm buildings made of non-toxic materials. Choose models with pieces that are of a good size to fit into children's hands. Try to find models of animals that are similar to animals the children are likely to see. Playmate: A 137 by 97 cm mat for play with small trucks, tractors and cars that shows a farm scene. Miniature animals (for example, Britain's Toy Animals) could be used to make a farm diorama.
3. *Toys for riding:* Tractors.
4. *Dolls and puppets:* Dolls in farm work clothes. Puppets that are models of a variety of farm animals. Remember that farmers are both men and women and that male and female farm costumes and puppet characters should be available.
5. *Miscellaneous:* Animal dominoes.

Teacher-made games and materials

NOTE: For a detailed description of "Learning Games," see pp. 50–59.

1. Match-them: Match farm animals with what they give us; parents with their babies.
2. Look and see: Homemade felt animal shapes or farm animal pictures mounted on felt are very satisfactory to use on a flannelboard. Use food with animals, mother with young, and so on.
3. Make cardboard classification cards at least 25 cm by 30 cm on which to place pictures of animals as children classify them. Decorate cards, each with a different picture or drawing in the centre (house, lake, grass, and barn) or models of these. This activity may also be done by using appropriate pictures of houses, cages, or barns pasted on the end of shoe boxes.
4. Offer a box of geometric felt shapes with a square of dark felt flannelboard. Child may make into animal shapes.
5. Match-them: Use homemade animal-word identification cards. Cut several cardboard rectangles about 12 cm by 12 cm. Glue picture of animal on upper half of the card. Letter name of animal beneath picture. Cut several more cardboard rectangles 3 cm by 10 cm. Letter animal name. Children can match lettered name on small card to that lettered on large card. Game may be varied for younger children by making "match" cards (these might be 6 cm by 10 cm) using the animal picture instead of the animal name. Check dimestores and shopping centres for sticker-picture books such as farm fun or animal homes for use in making game cards. School supply stores stock packages of gummed animal seals.
6. Count animal parts in pictures of animals or live animals in discovery centre and stationary supply stores.
7. Grouping and sorting by association: Use plastic animals. Classify by their outer coverings, by their products, by their homes. Sort into boxes labelled with a picture of that animal.
8. Have the children tell a story about a farm or what they saw on a visit to a farm. Then, write it down and post it with farm picture.

Art Centre

- 1. Offer clay for modeling.
  2. Collage pictures:
- ••• a. Geometric-shaped construction paper collage: Let children experiment several days prior with felt shapes or magnetic geometric shapes until they get the idea that everything is a shape or combination of shapes
- •• b. Yarn collage: Include clipped yarn, yarn fluffs, and various lengths and colours of yarn
- •• c. Texture collage: Be sure to include spotted fabric shapes
- •• d. Grain and seed collage: Use grain seeds or other products gathered from a farm for a collage. Consider if appropriate to your group
- •• e. Scrap collage: Dye eggshells and use in collage pictures
- 3. Complete the picture: Let children mount a cut-out of farm animals, including cats and dogs, on plain paper or cardboard. Let them colour in the rest of the picture for a background scene. Children may choose to cut out of wallpaper book. Introduce questions: "What is your animal?" "What is it doing?"

Book Centre

- Anastsaiu, S. *The Farmyard.* Toronto: James Lorimer, 1985.
- •• Anderson, C.W. *Blaze and the Gray Spotted Pony.* New York: Macmillan, 1968.

Teacher-made games. Plastic animals are grouped and sorted into a box with sections.

•• _____ . *Lonesome Little Colt*. New York: Macmillan, 1961.
 • Anglund, Joan. *Brave Cowboy*. New York: Harcourt Brace Jovanovich, 1959.
••• Beskow, Elsa. *Pelle's New Suit*. New York: Harper & Row, 1929.
••• Borenstein, Ruth. *Of Course a Goat*. New York; Harper & Row, 1980.
 • Chase, E.N., and B. Reid. *The New Baby Calf*. Richmond Hill, Ont: Scholastic-TAB, 1984.
••• Climo, Lindee. *Chester's Barn*. Montreal: Tundra, 1983.
••• Cole, J. *A Calf Is Born*. New York: William Morrow, 1975.
••• Cumming, P. *A Horse Called Farmer*. Charlottetown, PEI: Ragweed Press, 1984.
 •• De Paola, Tomie. *Charlie Needs a Cloak*. Englewood Cliffs, NJ: Prentice-Hall, 1973.
 •• Flack, Marjorie. *Angus and the Ducks*. Garden City, NY: Doubleday, 1939.
 • Forrester, V. *The Magnificent Moo*. New York: Macmillan, 1983.
••• Galdone, P. *Cat Goes Fiddle-i-fee*. New York: Ticknor and Fields, 1985. (Fun to use in conjunction with the song.)

- ● ● ● _____. *The Little Red Hen.* New York: Seabury Press, 1973.
- ● ● Gay, M.L. *The Garden.* Toronto: James Lorimer, 1985.
- ● ● ● Gemming, E. *Born in a Barn.* New York: Coward, 1974.
- ● Gerstein, M. *Follow Me!* New York: William Morrow, 1983.
- ● ● Ginsburg, Mirra. *Good Morning Chick.* New York: Greenwillow Press, 1980.
- ● ● Hale, S. *Mary Had a Little Lamb.* New York: Holiday, 1984. (Fun to use in conjunction with learning the song)
- ● ● ● Holl, A. *The Rain Puddle.* New York: Lothrop, Lee & Shepard, 1965.
- ● Hutchins, P. *Rosie's Walk.* New York: Macmillan, 1968.
- ● Isenbart, H. *Baby Animals on the Farm.* New York: G.P. Putnam's Sons, 1984.
- ● Jeffers, S. *All the Pretty Horses.* Richmond Hill, Ont: Scholastic-TAB, 1985.
- ● ● ● ● Jesseau, P. *Willow: The Story of an Arabian Foal.* Kapuskasing, Ont: Penumbra Press, 1985.
- ● ● Kent, Jack. *Little Peep.* Englewood Cliffs, NJ: Prentice-Hall, 1981.
- ● ● Kivitz, M. *Little Chick's Story.* New York: Harper & Row, 1978.
- ● ● ● ● Krasiloosky, Phyllis. *The Cow Who Fell in the Canal.* Garden City, NY: Doubleday, 1972. (Read–Tell)
- ● ● ● ● Laurence, Margaret. *Six Darn Cows.* Toronto: James Lorimer, 1986. (Good for reading to children.)
- ● ● ● Lobel, A. *How the Rooster Saved the Day.* New York: Greenwillow Press, 1977.
- ● ● ● _____. *A Treeful of Pigs.* New York: Greenwillow Press, 1979.
- ● ● ● ● Locker, T. *The Mare on the Hill.* New York: Dial Press, 1985. (Beautiful pictures for use along with telling the story.)
- ● ● Lyon, G. *A Regular Rolling Noah.* New York: Bradbury, 1986.
- ● ● ● ● Martin Jr., Bill, and John Archambault. *Barn Dance.* New York: Henry Holt, 1986. (Read–Tell)
- ● ● McCloskey, Robert. *Make Way for Ducklings.* New York: Viking Press, 1969.
- ● ● McMillan, B. *Here A Chick, There a Chick.* New York: Lothrop, Lee & Shepard 1983.
- ● McPhail, D. *Farm Morning.* New York: Harcourt Brace Jovanovich, 1985.
- ● Miller, J. *A Farm Alphabet Book.* Englewood Cliff, NJ: Prentice-Hall, 1984.
- ● ● ● Petersham, Maud, and Miska Petersham. *The Box with Red Wheels.* New York: Macmillan, 1973 (paper).
- ● ● Pienkowski, J. *Farm.* New York: Heinemann, 1985.
- ● ● ● Potter, B. *The Tale of Little Pig Robinson.* New York: David McKay, 1930.
- ● ● ● ● Provenson, A., and M. Provenson. *Our Animal Friends at Maple Hill Farm.* New York: Random House, 1984. (Read–Tell)
- ● ● ● Robart, Rose. *The Cake That Mack Ate.* Toronto: Kids Can Press, 1986.
- ● ● Roffey, M. *Home Sweet Home.* New York: Coward, 1983.
- ● ● Rojankovsky, Feodor. *Animals on the Farm.* New York: Alfred A. Knopf, 1967.
- ● ● ● Sawyer, R. *Journey Cake, Ho!* New York: Viking Press, 1953. (Read–Tell)
- ● ● ● Selsam, Millicent. *All About Eggs.* Reading, MA: Addison-Wesley, 1952.
- ● Tafuri, N. *Early Morning in the Barn.* New York: Greenwillow Press, 1983.
- ● Tresselt, Alvin R. *Wake Up Farm.* New York: Lothrop, Lee & Shepard, 1955.
- ● ● ● Wildsmith, B. *Daisy.* New York: Pantheon, 1984.
- _____. *Goat's Tail.* New York: Alfred A. Knopf, 1986.

Planning for Group Time

NOTE: All music, fingerplays, poems, stories, and games listed here may be used at other times during the session as appropriate. See Core Library, "Basic Resources," p. 95, for publishers and addresses. Record company addresses can be found on p. 99.

Music

Songs

From *The Goat With the Bright Red Socks*, Birkenshaw and Walden
"The Goat With the Bright Red Socks," p. 25

From *Tunes for Tots*, Warner and Berry
"Farm Sounds," p. 80
"Oink, Oink," p. 81

From *More Piggyback Songs*, Warren
"I Hear the Animals," p. 73
"All Around the Barnyard," p. 80
"Farm Sounds," p. 80
"I Like Baby Animals," p. 81
"Farm Animals," p. 81
"Are You Listening to the Animals?" p. 82
"Can You Guess What I Am?" p. 82

From *A Treasury of Songs for Children*, Glazer
"The Farmer in the Dell," p. 82
"Go Tell Aunt Rhody," p. 99
"The Gray Goose," p. 102
"Mary had a Little Lamb," p. 161
"Turkey in the Straw," p. 226

From *Singing Bee*, Hart
"All the Pretty Horses," p. 11
"This Little Pig," p. 26
"Baa, Baa Black Sheep," p. 47
"Goosey, Goosey Gander," p. 57
"Bingo," p. 82
"See the Pony Galloping, Galloping," p. 98

From *Do Your Ears Hang Low?* Glazer
"The Horse Stood Around," p. 37
"I Had a Little Rooster," p. 43

From *What Shall We Do and Allee Galloo*, Winn
"The Little Pony," p. 53
"Wake Up You Lazy Bones (Hunt the Cows)," p. 74

Records and cassettes

Bob McGrath. *If You're Happy and You Know It*, Volume I. (Kids Records)
"Baa, Baa Black Sheep"
"Home on the Range"
"The Farmer in the Dell"

Raffi. *The Corner Grocery Store.* (Troubadour Records)
"Cluck, Cluck Red Hen"

Sharon, Lois, and Bram. *Smorgasbord.* (Elephant Records)
"Did You Feed my Cow?"
"Riding Along"

Fingerplays and Poems

From *Oranges and Lemons*, King
"The Farmer's in His Den," p. 32
"The Scarecrow," p. 36

From *Round and Round the Garden*, Williams and Beck
"Piggy on the Railway," p. 12
"This Little Pig," p. 36

From *Finger Rhymes*, Brown
"Five Little Pigs," p. 8

From *Hand Rhymes*, Brown
"Quack, Quack, Quack!" p. 22

From *Read Aloud Rhymes for the Very Young*, Prelutsky and Brown
"Higglety, Pigglety, Pop!" p. 5
"The Pigs," p. 36
"Mary Middling," p. 36
"There Was a Small Pig Who Wept Tears," p. 36
"Chook, Chook," p. 42
"Five Little Chickens," p. 42
"Quack, Quack!" p. 43
"A Little Talk," p. 43
"Ducks in the Rain," p. 43
"The Donkey," p. 46

From *Where the Sidewalk Ends*, Silverstein
"The Farmer and the Queen," p. 32

From *Let's Do Fingerplays*, Grayson
"When a Little Chickens Drinks," p. 36
"This Little Calf," p. 38
"Two Little Ducks," p. 71
"Two Mother Pigs," p. 72

Stories

(To read, read–tell, or tell. See Book Centre for complete list.)

Margaret Laurence's *Six Darn Cows* is an excellent example of a story to read or tell to children, as it captures the flavour of farm life for urban children and will be familiar and fun for rural children.

Routine Times

1. Serve animal cookies and milk at snack time.
2. At snack or meal times have the children eat scrambled, deviled, or hard-boiled eggs that they prepared earlier (in the discovery centre).
3. Serve cheese wedges, cottage cheese, and a variety of milk and juice drinks at snack time.
4. Talk about source of foods and make up a guessing game as you eat.

Children at a farm. Trips to a farm will help urban children understand what happens on farms and will also help them become comfortable with large farm animals.

5. If you have a rest period, encourage the children to curl up like a cat or a dog.
6. In dismissing children to leave the room or go outside, say, "You can gallop like a horse, hop like a bunny, waddle like a duck...."

Large Muscle Activities

1. Allow wagons, trikes to be used as tractors for hauling (could clean up twigs on the farm).
2. Large hollow blocks, cardboard packing boxes, cylinders, or laundry barrels can be used for farm animal houses, barns, silos.
3. Using large balls, let children pretend to be goats and butt the balls with their heads.
4. Imitate how animals walk.
5. Allow digging and plowing in one area of yard.
6. Add water to sand and dirt and encourage the exploration of these elements that are so important to growing things.
7. Let the children pretend to ride horses by providing stick horses.

Extended Experiences

1. Trips children can take:

   a. Dairy

      ★ **CAUTION:**   May be too much machinery for very young children

   b. Ice-cream shop
   c. Dairy section of the grocery store
   d. Fair or exhibition (visit farm section to see most common farm animals)
   e. Farms (turkey, sheep, dairy, horse, or chicken)

2. Bring a farm animal pet to school (turkey, lamb, or young goat).
3. Show a filmstrip.

Teacher Resources

Pictures and Displays

▷ Hang a mobile of shapes with a picture of an animal on one side and its products on the back. Mount pictures on circles, squares, or triangles for mobile.
▷ Put out *Instructo Series*, Scott, Foresman, Society for Visual Education, or other pictures of food and animals (include farm animals only, at first).
▷ Bulletin board ideas (each in a separate section):

   a. Ranch, ranch-hand, cattle
   b. Poultry farming
   c. Grain fields
   d. Dairy farm, swine farm, beef farm
   e. Fruit orchards

   NOTE: Vary the choice of number of sections with pictures available and the size of the bulletin board and your focus of interest.

Books and Periodicals

Farm journals
Durrell, Gerald. *The Stationary Ark.* London: Collins, 1976.
Hendrikson, Robert. *Animal Crackers.* Markham, Ont: Penguin, 1983.
The Larousse Encyclopedia of Animal Life. London: Hamlyn, 1967.
Tremain, Ruthven. *The Animal's Who's Who.* New York: Charles Scribner's Sons, 1982.

Films and Videos

Consult your local library for audio-visual resources

Community Resources and Organizations

▷ Veterinarian
▷ Farmer
▷ Fairs and exhibitions
▷ Marketing boards for various farm products

Government Agencies

Provincial, territorial and federal ministries or departments concerned with agriculture

Who Can Feed the Animals?
A Question and Answer Song

JoAnne Deal Hicks

NOTE: Teacher sings the question to the children, showing flannelboard pictures of the necessary food and feeding utensils to "help" the children with their answers. For the youngest children teach one verse at a time.

17 Pet Animals

★★★★★★★★★★★★★★★★★★★★★★★★

Basic Understandings

(concepts children can grasp from this subject)

▷ Any tame animal that is kept just for fun as a special friend is called a pet.
▷ Children should choose pets carefully because:

1. Pets have special needs due to their size, diet, need for exercise, and need for protection
2. Some pets are more playful than others and therefore make better companions
3. Some pets need more care than a child can give and parents may not wish to assume the responsibility

▷ Sometimes you cannot keep a pet where you live.

1. Big pets, such as ponies, lambs, and goats, need large, fenced areas in which to exercise
2. Some pets, like exotic pets, may be noisy and/or dangerous and should live where they will not need to be confined
3. Some pets need special equipment, such as cages or tanks, in order to be kept in a house
4. Sometimes motels, apartments, and condominiums do not allow people to keep pets
5. Some pets are more dangerous than others (they may bite or scratch)
6. An animal should not be kept in a cage if it cannot be happy there
7. Some pets cost more money than others to feed and care for because their food may be hard to get or may be too expensive
8. We need permission from our families for most pets

▷ All pets need to be loved and cared for.
▷ Sometimes pets get sick or injured. Doctors for pets are called veterinarians.
▷ Some common house pets are dogs, cats, gerbils, goldfish, parakeets, hamsters, guinea pigs, and canaries.
▷ Other pets include rabbits, crickets, chameleons, horned toads, white mice or rats, and guppies.
▷ Pets need to be handled gently and carefully.
▷ Pets often need baths, their hair brushed, their toenails clipped, and their eyes washed out. This should always be done with adults. They also need opportunities to eat, sleep, and play much like children do.

▷ Some pets, like dogs and cats, have to wear a licence tag, so if they are lost they can be returned to their owners.

▷ Some pets need to be immunized (have shots like children do) so they cannot give or get diseases from other animals or people.

▷ Sometimes children and parents exhibit their pets at pet shows. Prizes and ribbons are given for pets that are well-mannered and well-groomed (prepared for showing).

Additional Facts the Teacher Should Know

Cats

▷ Tom (male)
▷ Queen (female)
▷ Kitten (young)
▷ They are covered with a thick fur coat; some of the coats have long hair and some have short hair; the coats vary in colour depending on the breed
▷ Cats communicate by meowing and purring, hissing and growling
▷ They eat small animals, mice, birds, milk, and fish
▷ The average life span is 16 years.

Dogs

▷ Dog (male)
▷ Bitch (female)
▷ Pup (young)
   breed
▷ They can be covered with long-hair coats or short-hair coats which vary in colour
▷ Dogs communicate by barking and howling, whimpering and growling
▷ They eat meat, bones, fish, and dog chow
▷ The average life span is 14 years

Gerbils

▷ Gerbil (male, female, and baby)
▷ They are covered with a coarse, light brown, black-tipped fur coat; they have slightly protruding eyes and large ears
▷ Gerbils are usually silent; as babies, however, they may issue a sound like a whispering squeak or sniff
▷ They eat lettuce and rabbit food pellets
▷ The average life span is 1 to 2 years

Hamsters

▷ Hamster (male, female, baby)
▷ They are covered with short and smooth golden brown and white fur; they have black eyes, a big bulge behind the cheek for storing food, large ears, poor eyesight, and almost no tail
▷ Hamsters communicate through squeaks and growls
▷ They eat bread, raw vegetables, grain, seeds, lettuce, and a few drops of cod-liver oil
▷ The average life span is 2 to 3 years

Guinea Pigs

▷   Boar (male)
▷   Sow (female)
▷   Piglet (young)
▷   Some have long-haired coats and others have short-haired coats; the colour of the coat varies depending on the breed; they have no tail
▷   Guinea pigs communicate through squeals, grunts, whistles or squeaks
▷   They eat fresh greens with grain, apples, cauliflower, celery tops, corn, tomatoes, and other vegetables
▷   The average life span is 8 years

Parakeets

▷   Cock (male)
▷   Hen (female)
▷   Chick (young)
▷   Clutch (family group)
▷   Parakeets are birds with green and yellow feathers, although some have blue, gray, and white feathers depending on the breed
▷   They communicate with chirps and whistles
▷   They eat fresh spinach, carrots, celery tops, or dandelion greens
▷   The average hen lays 3 to 5 eggs per year
▷   The average life span is 10 years

Pet animals. Learning how to care for and handle a pet is an important part of a child's relationship with animals.

Methods Most Adaptable for Introducing this Subject to Children

1. A child brings a new or favourite pet to share with the group.
2. As a result of a dog or cat "following" a child to school, or being seen by a child on the way to school.
3. A child tells about the birth of pet babies at home.
4. Following a trip to a pet shop to purchase a pet and its food for the classroom.
5. Display pictures of children with pets showing the pets playing, sleeping, eating or the children caring for the pets (see Pictures and Displays, p. 399).
6. Read a new pet story or poem, or teach a song about a pet
7. Present a new puzzle or game about pets (see commercially made games).
8. On the introduction of a new classroom pet by teacher.

Vocabulary

pet	biscuit	whiskers	born
cage	water bottles	feathers	home
bone	exercise wheel	fur	house
bed	love, care	coat	indoor
tail	pellets	claws	outdoor
supplies	drink	paws	feed
feeding dish			

Include the names, sounds, body parts, and foods eaten by the pets you are observing. Also include breed or species of pet, such as collie, parakeet, or goldfish, as appropriate.

Learning Centres

Discovery Centre

1. Questions to ask while observing a pet in the classroom:
   What kind of animal is it?
   What does it look like?
   What does it eat?
   How does it eat?
   How does it sleep?
   When does it sleep?
   What is it doing?
   What sounds does it make?
   How does it move?
   How could it best be handled? Why?
2. Compare with another kind of pet. How are they different? How are they the same? Why?

Pet animal centre. If it is feasible, set up a pet animal centre like the one above. All the children can share the responsibility of caring for the pets. This is particularly good for children who may not be able to have pets in their homes.

★ CAUTION: Be sure that when animals are brought to school they are used to children and are known to be friendly to them. If the animal will stay for half or all day, have a place for it to be safe from the children for periods of time. Also provide food, water, and a place to eliminate. Someone who knows the animal should be present to help handle it. If baby animals are considered, try to provide at least two of them. This prevents the overtiring of just one well-discovered and enjoyed baby animal. It also means less waiting for a turn.

3. Set out a variety of food—plants, meat, human food—to discover which the animal will select. Talk about why? What body parts does it need to eat the food it chose? What body parts would it need to eat other food?
4. Compare animals by using toy animals or pictures and by grouping them into categories (big/brown/furry/hoofed or pets/farm/zoo/forest).
5. Make cookies shaped like cats, bunnies, chickens. Let children experiment with making their own shapes. Decorate with coloured frosting, or paint cookies with egg yolk and one tablespoon water with food colouring added to desired intensity. Use new, clean watercolour brushes to apply. Give each child one or two tablespoons of frosting in a plastic cup with a spreader. A coffee stirrer is great.

★ CAUTION: Do not use same bowl of frosting or spreader for everyone. Children will want to taste.

6. Make a display of common pet supplies: an unbreakable pet feeding dish, pet toys (bone, ball, or rubber mouse), leash, licence tags, brush, empty cage, cedar chips, and empty containers of cat, dog, fish, or bird food. Ask children which pet uses the various supplies (pictures on boxes will provide a hint). The pictures you post above the display of appropriate pets eating and sleeping or of children caring for pets may also suggest answers.

Dramatic Play Centres

Home-living centre

1. Provide stuffed animals for "pets" or invite children to bring in their favourite ones.
2. Include a pet bed, box, or basket with blanket or cushion in it. You may make it large enough for a child to be a pet.
3. Add a few pet toys—ball, rubber bone or mouse, ball on a string. Use unbreakable pet feeding bowls and plastic baby bottles for feeding toy pets.
4. Make a pet store using stuffed toys and empty pet food boxes.

Block-building centre

1. Set out rubber, wooden, cardboard, or unbreakable plastic models of pets on the block shelf.
2. Hang pictures showing children with their pets' homes in order to encourage an interest in building homes, or fences for pets.

Learning, Language, and Readiness Materials Centre

Commercially made games and materials

(See "Basic Resources," pp. 79, 100, for manufacturers' addresses.)
1. *Puzzles:* Puzzles with a variety of pet animals. Be sure some of the puzzles have knobs.
2. *Small toys for imaginative play:* Model animals—durable plastic or wooden animals made of nontoxic materials. Choose models with pieces that are of a good size to fit into children's hands. Try to find models of animals that are likcly to see.
3. *Dolls and puppets:* Puppets that are models of a variety of domestic animals. Stuffed animals such as dogs, cats, mice, etc.
4. *Miscellaneous:* Animal dominoes.

Teacher-made games and materials

NOTE: For a detailed description of "Learning Games," see pp. 50–59.

1. Name it: Use models or pictures of pets.
2. Who am I? Describe various pets.
3. Which is (larger): Change adjective, use pictures or toy animals.
4. Look and see: Use pet pictures or models.
5. Match-them: Use on individual or large flannelboards; match pets with foods they eat, parent with its young, or pet with its home.
6. Guess what? Use recordings of animal sounds.
7. Count pets in a picturebook—how many cats? Count body parts of pets in classroom. Make counting discs or squares with gummed seals of pets on cardboard.
8. Use commercial game cards, such as "snap," "animal rummy," or "kiddie cards," for matching cards. Modify games to suit your group or a child's ability.

Art Centre

- 1. Clay dough: Do not set out rollers or cookie cutters, just set out clay and coffee stirrers or palate sticks for cutting or marking. This will allow for making forms rather than limit products to baked goods.
- 2. Use potter's clay: Note preparation instructions on box or bag.
- ••• 3. Finish the picture: Give children paper with circle or oval shape drawn or pasted to it and encourage them to use crayons to "finish" the picture. Ask them what it makes them think of—animal object, animal face? (This is better when it follows an experience with felt shapes.)
- ••• 4. Some five and five-and-a-half year olds can make representative picture books of animal drawings using crayons. It is wise for teachers to label the pictures with the names children supply in talking about their pictures so that their parents can identify them.
- ••• 5. Cut and paste: Make a pet book. Teacher can add story line for a group book or children can mount pictures they like until they have enough for their own books. Staple pages together.
- 6. Make an animal picture collage.

  - ••• a. Geometric paper collage: Encourage children to make a picture of their favourite pet or a pet they would like to own. (Make available precut geometric shapes for the inexperienced cutter.)
  - ••• b. Texture collage: Be sure to include trays of clipped yarns, scraps of felt, fur, textured cloth, bits of rope or yarn for tails, and buttons for eyes.
  - ••• c. Yarn collage pictures: Use a paintbrush to spread thinned glue over a page. "Draw" with yarn lengths, securing them as you go. Child can fill in with clipped yarn. Include the colours of most pets (black, brown, white, gray, or beige) so that the children will have available the colours of pets they know. Heavy cotton rug or ribbon yarn fluffs are the best.

- •• 7. Styrofoam sculpture: Provide children with an assortment of precut styrofoam pieces (curved and square), styrofoam balls of various sizes, and decorations, such as pieces of yarn, bits of leather, felt, buttons, and coloured toothpicks, to make their favourite pet animal (real or imagined).

Other experiences in this centre using art media

- •• 1. Encourage children to make "match-them" game, which they can keep, using matching gummed animal seals with pictures of food they eat or match two seals of the same animal. Mount on circles or octagonal shapes as there is no up or down on either of them.
- •• 2. Bookmarks: Children can cut out small pictures of pets boldly encircled with a magic marker, or they can lick and stick favourite gummed labels of pets on strips of cardboard (cover stock scraps from a printer) for a bookmark to share with group, or give as gift to a parent or older brother or sister.
- •• 3. Pull toy for a pet:

  a. Tie colourful ends of bread wrappers or tissue into a pompon with about 61 cm of string attached (for kitten).
  b. Dye spools using vegetable dye in pans; thread with string for pull-toy for a pet.

- •• 4. Stick puppets: Let children cut out pictures of pets boldly encircled with a magic marker to avoid cutting difficult appendages. Then let them glue to oval or round shapes of cardboard. For a handle, slip tongue depressors between the picture and the cardboard. This can be made by younger children if the teacher precuts cardboard and picture.
- ••• VARIATION: Make a collage-like face on a paper plate using styrofoam shreds, yarn, clipped yarn, and buttons. Use very thin packing paper strips or straws for whiskers and tail. Melt crayons into bottle lids to use as eyes, noses, or mouths; ruffled crepe paper for

manes, clipped construction paper, tissue, or overlapping circles of velveteen or satin for scales or feathers. Glue plastic stick handle or staple stiff cardboard handle to back of plate. These puppets may be used as masks: Children can grasp the handle and hold plate in front of their face.

Book Centre

•• Alexander, Martha. *No Ducks in Our Bathtub*. New York: Dial Press, 1973.
• Aliki, Diogenes. *At Mary Bloom's*. New York: Greenwillow Press, 1983.
•• Ambrus, V. *Grandma, Felix and Mustapha Biscuit*. New York: William Morrow, 1982.
••• Anderson, C.W. *Billy and Blaze*. New York: Macmillan, 1964 (paper, 1971).
•• Asch, F. *The Last Puppy*. Englewood Cliffs, NJ: Prentice-Hall, 1983.
•••• Atwood, M., and J. Barkhouse. *Anna's Pet*. Toronto: James Lorimer, 1986. (Read–Tell)
••• Bemelmans, L. *Madeline's Rescue*. New York: Viking Press, 1953.
•• Bliss, C., and A. Bliss. *That Dog Melley*. New York: Hastings, 1981.
• Bonsall, C. *Mine's the Best*. New York: Harper & Row, 1984.
•• Brandenberg, F. *Aunt Nina and Her Nieces and Nephews*. New York: Greenwillow Press, 1983.
••• Burningham, J. *Cannonball Simp*. New York: Cape, 1966.
••• Cohen, M. *Jim's Dog Muffin*. New York: Greenwillow Press, 1984.
••• Chalmers, M. *Six Dogs, Twenty-Three Cats, Forty-Five Mice and One Hundred and Sixteen Spiders*. New York: Harper & Row, 1986.
• De Regniers, B.S. *It Does Not Say Meow*. Boston: Houghton Mifflin, 1972.
•• Eastman, P.D. *Go Dog, Go*. New York: Random House.
••• Fisher, Aileen. *Listen Rabbit*. New York: Thomas Y. Crowell, 1964.
• Flack, Marjorie. *Angus and the Cat*. Garden City, NY: Doubleday, 1971.
• _____. *Angus Lost*. Garden City, NY: Doubleday, 1941.
••• Gackenbach, D. *A Bag Full of Pups*. Boston: Houghton Mifflin, 1981.
• Ginsburg, Mirra. *Three Kittens*. New York: Crown, 1973.
•• Graham, M.B. *Benjy's Boat Trip*. New York: Harper & Row, 1977.
_____. *Benjy's Dog House*. New York: Harper & Row, 1973.
• Hazen, Barbara. *Where Do Bears Sleep?* Reading, MA: Addison-Wesley, 1970.
••• Hearn, E. *Race You Fanny!* Toronto: Women's Press, 1986.
• Hoban, T. *One Little Kitten*. New York: Greenwillow Press, 1979.
• _____. *Where Is It?* New York: Macmillan, 1974.
••• Holl, A. *One Kitten for Kim*. Reading, MA: Addison-Wesley, 1969.
•••• Holmes, E.T. *The Christmas Cat*. New York: Thomas Y. Crowell, 1976. (Read-Tell)
••• Keats, E.J. *Hi Cat!* New York: Macmillan, 1970.
••• _____. *Pet Show*. New York: Macmillan, 1972.
••• _____. *Whistle for Willie*. New York: Viking Press, 1964.
•••• _____, and Pat Cherr. *My Dog Is Lost*. New York: Thomas Y. Crowell, 1960.
••• Kerr, J. *Mog and the Baby*. London: Collins, 1980.
••• _____. *Mog, The Forgetful Cat*. London: Collins, 1970.
••• Kovalski, Maryann. *Brenda and Edward*. Toronto: Kids Can Press, 1984.
••• Levchuk, H. *The Dingles*. Vancouver: Douglas and McIntyre, 1985.
••• Muir, Mary Jane. *Gynn*. Richmond Hill, Ont: North Winds Press, 1985.
•••• Noble, C. *The Day Jimmy's Boa Ate the Wash*. New York: Dial Press, 1980.
••• Parish, Peggy. *Too Many Rabbits*. New York: Macmillan, 1974.
••• Potter, B. *The Tale of Tom Kitten*. New York: Warne, 1935.
•• Rice, E. *Benny Bakes a Cake*. New York: Greenwillow Press, 1981.
• Risom, Ole. *I Am a Puppy*. New York: Western Publishing, 1970.
• _____. *I Am a Kitten*. New York: Western Publishing, 1970.
•• Robinson, T. *Button*. Markham, Ont: Penguin Books, 1976.
••• Schaffer, Marion. *I Love My Cat*. Toronto: Kid's Can Press, 1980.
•• Selsam, M. *How Kittens Grow*. New York: Four Winds Press, 1975.

•• _____ . *How Puppies Grow.* New York: Four Winds Press, 1972.

•• Selsam, Millicent. *How the Animals Eat.* New York: E.M. Hale, 1955.

•• Simon, Norma. *Where Does My Cat Sleep?* Chicago: Albert Whitman, 1982.

••• Thayer, J. *The Outside Cat.* Toronto: Hodder and Stoughton, 1957.

• Tresselt, Alvin. *Wake Up Farm.* New York: Lothrop, Lee and Shepard, 1955.

••• Ungerer, T. *Cristor.* New York: Harper & Row, 1958.

•••• Waber, Bernard. *The House on East 88th Street.* New York: Houghton Mifflin, 1975. (Fun to read for contrast to other stories about conventional house pets.)

• Welch, M. *Will That Wake Mother?* New York: Dodd Mead, 1982.

•• Wheeler, Bernelda. *A Friend Called Chum.* Winnipeg: Pemmican Publications, 1984.

• Wheeler, C. *Marmalade's Nap.* New York: Alfred A. Knopf, 1983.

• _____ . *Marmalade's Picnic.* New York: Alfred A. Knopf, 1983.

• _____ . *Marmalade's Snowy Day.* New York: Alfred A. Knopf, 1982.

• _____ . *Marmalade's Yellow Leaf.* New York: Alfred A. Knopf, 1985.

••• Wildhelm, H. *I'll Always Love You.* New York: Crown, 1985.

• Wildsmith, Brian. *Birds.* New York: Franklin Watts, 1968.

•• _____ . *Cat on the Mat.* Toronto: Oxford University Press, 1986.

• _____ . *Fishes.* New York: Franklin Watts, 1970.

•• _____ . *Give a Dog a Bone.* New York: Pantheon, 1985.

•• _____ . *Pelican.* New York: Pantheon, 1983.

• Williams, Gweneira. *Timid Timothy.* Reading, MA: Addison-Wesley, 1944.

••• Yashima, Mitsu, and Taro Yashima. *Momo's Kitten.* New York: Viking Press, 1961.

•• Zion, Gene. *Harry by the Sea.* New York: E.M. Hale, 1965.

•• _____ . *Harry the Dirty Dog.* New York: Harper & Row, 1956.

•• _____ . *No Roses for Harry.* New York: Harper & Row, 1958.

Planning for Group Time

NOTE: All music, fingerplays, poems, stories, and games listed here may be used at other times during the session as appropriate. See Core Library, "Basic Resources," p. 95, for publishers and addresses. Record company addresses found on p. 99.

Music

Songs

From original songs in this book by JoAnne Deal Hicks
"Animal Nonsense Song," p. 400, verses 2, 4, 5, 7, 8

From *Singing Bee*, Hart
"I Love Little Pussy," p. 46
"Pussy Cat, Pussy Cat," p. 50
"Three Little Kittens," p. 72
"Bingo," p. 82
"Where Oh Where Has My Little Dog Gone?" p. 115

From *Elephant Jam*, Sharon, Lois, and Bram
"Little Peter Rabbit," p. 55
"Alison's Camel," p. 66 (the words can be changed to include other pets and of course other children)
"Tingalayo," p. 89 (pets in other countries)
"Candy Man, Salty Dog," p. 118

Rhythms and singing games

From *Songs for the Nursery School*, MacCarteney
Use appropriate actions with songs, pp. 25, 27, 30, 35, 36

From *Music Resource Book*, Lutheran Church Press
"Six Little Ducks," p. 62

Rhythmic activity; Pretend to move like various pet animals.

Records and cassettes

Bob McGrath. *If You're Happy and You Know It*, Volume I. (Kids Records)
"My Dog Rags"

Fingerplays and Poems

From *Read Aloud Rhymes for the Very Young*, Prelutsky and Brown
"The House Cat," p. 18
"Cat Kisses," p. 18
"At Night," p. 18
"Mother Cat's Purr," p. 19
"The Puppy Chased the Sunbeam," p. 40
"How a Puppy Grows," p. 40
"Chums," p. 40

From *Hand Rhymes*, Brown
"Kittens," p. 24
"There Was a Little Turtle," p. 4

From *Mischief City*, Wynne-Jones
"I'm Collecting Monsters," p. 4

From *Let's Do Fingerplays*, Grayson
"Kitten Is Hiding," p. 32
"There Was a Little Turtle," p. 33
"My Rabbit," p. 34
"Golden Fishes," p. 35

Stories

(To read, read-tell, or tell. See Book Centre for complete list.)

It is appropriate to read stories about pets who are well cared for by their owners. Wheeler's *A Friend Called Chum* and Muir's *Gynn* are good examples of this type of story.

Routine Times

Serve commercial animal cookies or those baked and frosted by children at snack or meal times.

Large Muscle Activities

1. Set out boxes and barrels for children to crawl into and through to imitate animal behaviour.
2. Play ball (roll or toss two or more).
3. Play follow the leader: The group moves as directed, imitating ways pets move—hop, crawl, leap, run, walk, climb, slither. The children may take turns being leader and choosing actions. Teacher may suggest actions as necessary. This activity is best done with a small group.

Extended Experiences

1. Take a trip to teacher's home or a child's home to see a pet.
2. Visit pet store to view supplies as well as pets.
3. Visit a pet farm, pet library, or petting zoo.
4. Visit pet section in variety store (in group of eight or less at a time). They often have baby gerbils or hamsters, fish, birds, and sometimes chameleons or lizards.
5. Invite a representative of the Humane Society or a veterinarian to bring an animal and talk to the children about the care of pets. Alert them to what the children may be able to understand or need to hear. Keep it simple.
6. View short filmstrip about a pet (no more than ten minutes). Edit it if it is too long to suit your group.

Teacher Resources

Pictures and Displays

▷ If children have access to magazines, encourage them to bring pictures of their favourite kind of pet or to share a book with a picture of pets that they like. Mount or group on a bulletin board. Set books out in book centre. If they are not suitable for book centre, share them at group time and highlight briefly without reading them entirely. Charity organizations or church groups may be enlisted to assist you in obtaining magazines with pictures of animals.

▷ Group pictures of a specific kind or family of pets—all kinds of cats, black pets, furry pets, or caged pets. Sometimes a large, abstract-shaped, coloured piece of paper or a small yarn circle can help group pictures on a bulletin board or wall display.

▷ Snapshot display: Our pets at home. Encourage the children to bring snapshots of pets they have or have had. Label with child's name, name of pet, and kind of pet. You may need to begin the display with pictures of pets you have had. Post near group time area so children can point and share at that time. VARIATION: Let child select picture of a pet he or she would *like* to have. Let child cut or mount, label each with child's name.

★ CAUTION: When returning the picture to the child, put in envelope and pin to outer garment to avoid loss.

Books and Periodicals

Chickadee magazine
Equinox magazine
Hendrikson, Robert. *Animal Crackers.* Markham, Ont: Penguin Books, 1983
National Geographic magazine
Owl magazine
Tremain, Ruthven. *The Animal's Who's Who.* New York: Charles Scribner's Sons, 1982

Films and Videos

Consult your local library for audio-visual resources

Community Resources and Organizations

▷ Veterinarian
▷ Animal clinic
▷ Humane Society
▷ Pet owners and breeders associations

Animal Nonsense Song
A Dramatic Play Song

JoAnne Deal Hicks

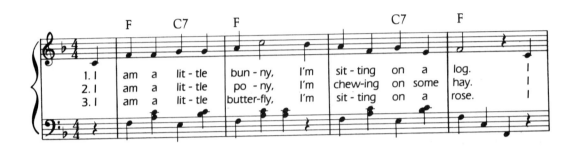

VERSE 4: I am a lit-tle kit-ten, I'm sit-ting on a rug,
I purr and purr and purr and purr, then curl up like a bug.

VERSE 5: I am a lit-tle yel-low duck, I wad-dle down the road,
I quack and quack and quack and quack, and chase a hop-ping toad.

VERSE 6: I am a lit-tle chick-en, I'm strut-ting through the weeds,
I peck and peck and peck and peck, I'm look-ing for some seeds.

VERSE 7: I am a lit-tle tur-tle, I hide with-in my shell,
I creep a-long and creep a-long, and fall in-to a well.

VERSE 8: I am a lit-tle dog-gie, I'm chew-ing on a bone,
I bark and bark and bark and bark, in-to the tel-e-phone.

NOTE: Children enjoy pantomiming the various actions.

18 Animals of the Woods

★★★★★★★★★★★★★★★★★★★★★★★★★★★

Basic Understandings

(concepts children can grasp from this subject)

▷ A woodland or forest is an area of ground with many trees and bushes. It often has streams of water or a pond.

▷ Wild animals who live in this area are called animals of the woods or forest animals.

▷ The most common forest animals are beavers, skunks, deer, foxes, bears, raccoons, porcupines, chipmunks, moose, and birds.

▷ Most animals of the woods are coloured or marked to match the leaves, bark, rocks, or grass where they usually live.

▷ Small forest animals are often frightened by loud noises and people.

▷ Some animals, like snakes, may eat only once a week. Other animals, like birds, hunt and eat almost all day long.

▷ A wild animal often feeds and rests in its home.

▷ We should not throw glass, cans, paper, or garbage in ponds and streams because this pollution is killing woodland animals.

▷ We can sometimes see some animals of the woods in a zoo or a park.

▷ Animals often found in city parks are squirrels and birds.

> **NOTE:** Include basic understandings listed for "Animals," page 371, as appropriate. See chapters on the seasons regarding hibernation, migration, and other seasonal habits of forest animals.

Additional Facts the Teacher Should Know

1. When teaching this subject, encourage children to observe and protect animals in their own surroundings. Frogs and toads have not been included as animals to be observed (captured) because pollution is decreasing the numbers of these animals. Also, by bringing the eggs or polywogs into the classroom, you are further decreasing their chances to survive. Animals that have been in captivity for even a short time stand little chance of survival when returned to their natural habitat.

2. Snakes are not included in this chapter because they are hard to feed, and because it is difficult for the average person to tell the harmless ones from the poisonous ones.

3. Trying to catch wild animals is dangerous, as most animals will bite when they feel trapped or threatened, and may carry rabies.

Beaver

▷   Beaver (male and female)
▷   Kit (young)
▷   They have a coat of soft, dense, waterproof fur that is dark brown in colour; a long paddle-shaped tail that is used as a balance on land and a rudder in the water; and powerful webfooted hind legs
▷   Beavers communicate by making crying sounds; they slap their tails on the water to warn of danger
▷   They eat leaves and bark and store large amounts of food for the winter
▷   The average life span is 9 to 12 years

Deer

▷   Buck (male)
▷   Doe (female)
▷   Fawn (young)
▷   Herd (family group)
▷   They have a thick reddish-brown coat of fur with a white underbelly, and antlers
▷   They are usually silent; however, if frightened utter loud hoarse, high-pitched shrieks and snorts
▷   Deer eat leaves, twigs, fruits, grasses, and farm crops in the summer, and nuts, acorns, mosses, lichens, and seeds in the winter
▷   The average life span is 15 years in nature; 25 years in captivity

Foxes

▷   Fox (male)
▷   Vixen (female)
▷   Kit (young)
▷   Skulk (family group)
▷   They have a pointed muzzle, large ears, and a long thick fur coat which varies in colour depending on the breed; they also have a long bushy tail
▷   They are generally silent; however, during the mating season a male will respond to a female's shrill calls with a few short barks
▷   Foxes eat rabbits, small rodents, wild birds, poultry, insects, turtles, snakes, fruits, frogs, and fish
▷   The average life span is 12 years

Raccoons

▷   Buck (male)
▷   Raccoon (female)
▷   Cub (young)
▷   They have pointed muzzles, a black mask, a long stripped bushy tail, thick dense brownish-gray fur tipped with black, and dexterous fingers
▷   When annoyed they snarl or growl; otherwise they have a shrill whistling night cry
▷   Raccoons eat fruits, nuts, grains, mice, frogs, lizards, fish, birds, eggs, insects, larvae, clams, crayfish, and grasshoppers, and always wash their food before they eat
▷   The average life span is 8 to 13 years

Skunks

▷ Skunk (male and female)
▷ Kitten (young)
▷ They have a thick black fur coat with a white stripe down the middle of the back to the tip of the tail, sharp teeth, small eyes, and a blunt nose
▷ Skunks communicate with growls, screeches, purrs, sniffs, cooing, and whistling. When they are annoyed they stamp their front paws—this is a warning that they are about to spray their strong, repulsive scent
▷ They eat insects, worms, grubs, mice, turtle eggs, rodents, small plants, fruit, and berries
▷ The average life span is 8 to 10 years

Bears

▷ Boar (male)
▷ Sow (female)
▷ Cub (young)
▷ Stock (family group)
  408 to 520 kg for the grizzly
▷ They have massive heads, large muzzles, huge paws with long claws, and thick long shaggy fur of varying colours depending on the type of bear and the season
▷ Black bear cubs hum and moan, older bears whine and grunt; grizzly bears cough and roar
▷ They eat plants, animals, grass, mice, lizards, insects, worms, honey, fish, and larvae
▷ The average life span is 20 years in nature, 40 years in captivity

Methods Most Adaptable for Introducing this Subject to Children

1. Observe a bird, squirrel, toad, or turtle while on a walk or when these animals come to a feeding station.
2. If the school is a country day school, you may possibly see a red fox, raccoon, or small deer near a stream in the woods.
3. Occasionally in a small town or city, you may see a skunk or smell its characteristic odour after a rain.
4. In winter, point out footprints of an animal in the snow.

Vocabulary

forest	fur	claws	cave
woods	hide	footprint	log
stream	hoofs	hibernate	lodge
burrow	odour	pollution	trees
nest	wild	den	rock
hole			

Include the names, sounds, body parts, and foods eaten by the most common animals of the woods that you observe.

Learning Centres

Discovery Centre

1. Leaf through selected issues of *National Geographic, Owl, Chickadee,* and *Equinox* magazines.
2. Display food that forest animals eat—acorns and other nuts, eggs, seeds, berries, and fruit. (Use artificial berries and fruit.)
3. Borrow a caged squirrel, a descented skunk, a raccoon, a snake, or any other animal for a short visit accompanied by its owner.
4. Take a walk to a park, a pond, a field, or a wood to see what animals live there. Observe them from a respectful distance. Older children may use binoculars or a telescope. Take a paper bag for collecting litter.
5. Bring a pet rabbit to school.

Dramatic Play Centres

Block-building centre

1. Add painted, model forest animals available in variety stores.
2. Provide small twigs and branch sections for use in building animal homes or environs.
3. Set out unbreakable plastic trees or bushes.
4. Children may tear or cut free forms of blue construction paper for lakes, ponds, or streams.
5. Provide strips or squares of green carpet or upholstery for grass.
6. Papier-mâché rocks or crumpled tan or gray construction paper may simulate rocky areas without the danger presented when using real rocks or stones.

   NOTE: Additional activities and materials may be found in the following chapters: squirrels—"Fall"; birds—"Fall," "Winter," and "Spring"; rabbits—"Spring."

Other dramatic play centres

Animal bag masks or animal hand or face puppets may be used by older children with verbal skills. Animal faces may be made on large or small grocery bags, depending on use (see illustration, p. 276).

Learning, Language, and Readiness Materials Centre

Commercially made games and materials

(See "Basic Resources," pp. 79, 100, for manufacturers' addresses.)
1. *Puzzles:* Puzzles with a variety of forest animals. Be sure some of the puzzles have knobs.
2. *Small toys for imaginative play:* Model animals—durable plastic or wooden animals made of nontoxic materials. Choose models with pieces that are of a good size to fit into children's hands. Try to find models of animals that are similar to animals the children are likely to see.
3. *Dolls and puppets:* Puppets that are models of a variety of forest animals.
4. *Miscellaneous:* Animal dominoes, animal lotto games and animal card games. Bird feeders. Binoculars (available from Fisher-Price).

Teacher-made games and materials

NOTE: For a detailed description of "Learning Games," see pp. 50–59.

1. Match-them: Use mounted forest animal seals or Canadian Wildlife stamps
2. How many? Use felt animal shapes, flannel-backed pictures of animals, or plastic models of forest animals
3. Grouping and sorting by association: Group animals by their coverings, their actions, or their body parts (fur/fin/feather; flies/runs/swims; no legs/two legs/four legs)
4. Adapt games in "Farm," "Pets," or "Zoo" to forest animals

Art Centre

- 1. Paint or crayons: Offer green, yellow, black, tan, and brown
- 2. Model with play dough or natural clay
•• 3. Collage: Yarn, paper, geometric cloth or paper shapes, fur, feathers, and assorted materials for creating animals
•• 4. Collage turtle: Precut turtle shapes from green, brown, or black construction paper. Set out empty halves of walnut shells, individual egg carton sections, paints, and glue. Children choose colours and materials they wish to use to make their own turtle. Dotted lines indicate positioning of nut shell on top side. Walnut shells can be cut in half with a sharp knife by following the seam line. Save meats for cooking.

Bottom side

•• 5. Design arrangements: Set out hammer and nail sets, magnetic or felt geometric shapes for creating "animals"

Book Centre

•• Alexander, Martha. *I'll Protect You from the Jungle Beasts.* New York: Dial Press, 1973.
• Bartoli, J. *In a Meadow, Two Hares Hide.* Chicago: Albert Whitman, 1978.
••• Bauman, H. *Chip Has Many Brothers.* New York: Philomel, 1985.
••• Brinklol, J. *Fireflies.* New York: Macmillan, 1985.
••• Burke, M. *Tales from the Beechy Woods.* Burlington, Ont: Hayes, 1983.
•• Burningham, John. *Harquin, the Fox Who Went Down to the Valley.* Don Mills, Ont: Academic Press, 1979.
• Caldone. P. *Over in the Meadow.* Englewood Cliffs, NJ: Prentice-Hall, 1986.
••• Cleaver, E. *The Enchanted Caribou.* Toronto: Oxford University Press, 1985.
• Cook, Bernadine. *The Little Fish That Got Away.* Reading, MA: Addison-Wesley, 1956.
• Crisitini, E. *In the Pond.* New York: Picture Book Studio, 1985.
• _____. *In the Woods.* New York: Picture Book Studio, 1985.
• D'Aulaire, I., and E. D'Aulaire. *Animals Everywhere.* Garden City, NY: Doubleday, 1954.
•• Ets, Marie Hall. *Play with Me.* New York: Viking Press, 1955.
•• Flack, Marjorie. *Tim Tadpole and the Bullfrog.* Garden City, NY: Doubleday, 1934.
•• _____. *Ask Mr. Bear.* New York: Macmillan, 1932.
••• Freeman, Don. *Fly High, Fly Low.* New York: Viking Press, 1957.
• Gay, Zhenya. *Look!* New York: Viking Press, 1957.
• _____. *Who Is It?* New York: Viking Press, 1957.
•• Hazen, Barbara. *Where Do Bears Sleep?* Reading, MA: Addison-Wesley, 1970.
••• Holl, Adelaide. *Remarkable Egg.* New York: Lothrop, Lee & Shepard, 1968.
••• Kassian, O. *Slip the Otter Finds a Home.* Toronto: Greey de Pencier, 1984.
• Keats, Ezra Jack. *Over in the Meadow.* New York: Four Winds Press, 1971.
••• Langstaff, J. *Over in the Meadow.* New York: Harcourt Brace Jovanovich, 1967.
••• Lane, M. *The Beaver.* New York: Dial Press, 1982.
••• McCloskey, Robert. *Blueberries for Sal.* New York: Viking Press, 1948.
••• _____. *Make Way for Ducklings.* New York: Viking Press, 1941.

● ● ● Nicoll, Helen. *Meg and Mog.* Markham, Ont: Penguin Books, 1976.

● Obed, E.B., and W. Ritchie. *Little Snowshoe.* St. John's, Nfld: Breakwater, 1984.

● ● ● Oppenheim, J. *Have You Seen Birds.* Richmond Hill, Ont: Scholastic-TAB, 1986.

● ● Paul, A.W. *Owl at Night.* New York: G.P. Putnam's Sons, 1985.

● ● ● Potter, Beatrix. *The Tale of Peter Rabbit.* London: Warne, 1972. (All of Potter's books are excellent.)

● ● Rockwell, Anne, and Harlow Rockwell. *Toad.* Garden City, NY: Doubleday, 1972.

● ● Roy, R. *Three Ducks Went Walking.* Boston: Houghton Mifflin, 1979.

● ● Ryder, J. *Fireflies.* New York: Harper & Row, 1977.

● ● ● St. George, J. *The Hallowe'en Pumpkin Smasher.* New York: G.P. Putnam's Sons, 1978.

● ● ● Spier, P. *The Fox Went Out on A Chilly Night.* Garden City, NY: Doubleday, 1961.

● Tafuri, N. *Have You Seen My Duckling?* New York: Greenwillow Press, 1984.

● _____ . *Rabbit's Morning.* New York: Greenwillow Press, 1985.

● ● ● Tresselt, Alvin. *Beaver Pond.* New York: Lothrop, Lee & Shepard, 1970.

● ● ● _____ . *Frog in the Well.* New York: Lothrop, Lee & Shepard, 1958.

● ● ● ● Wallace, I. *The Sparrow's Song.* Markham, Ont: Penguin Books, 1986. (Read–Tell)

● ● ● Waterton, B. *A Salmon for Simon.* Vancouver: Douglas & McIntyre, 1978.

● ● Wheeler, Bernelda. *I Can't Have the Bannock, But the Beaver Has A Dam.* Winnipeg: Pemmican Publications, 1984.

● ● Zolotow, Charlotte. *Mister Rabbit and the Lovely Present.* Markham, Ont: Fitzhenry & Whiteside.

Planning for Group Time

NOTE: All music, fingerplays, poems, stories, and games listed here may be used at other times during the session as appropriate. See Core Library, "Basic Resources," p. 95, for publishers and addresses. Record company addresses can be found on p. 99.

Music

Songs

From original songs in this book by JoAnne Deal Hicks
"Animal Nonsense Song," p. 400, verses 1 and 7

From *Tunes for Tots*, Warner and Berry
"The Owl," p. 78
"Down in the Meadow," p. 83
"Guess the Animal (Turtle)," p. 86
"The Birds," p. 88

From *Baby Beluga Book*, Raffi
"Over in the Meadow," p. 28

From *More Piggyback Songs*, Warren
"Crawl, Crawl Little Snake," p. 74
"Little Tadpole," p. 75
"Birds Fly High," p. 75

From *A Treasury of Songs for Young Children*, Glazer
"The Frog Went a Courtin'," p. 92

From *Singing Bee*, Hart
"Over in the Meadow," p. 44
"El Coquito," p. 136

Rhythms and singing games

Choose appropriate piano or phonograph music for movements of animals, such as bunnies, squirrels, bears, foxes, mice, and birds. Use scarves for wings and tails. Sew a loop of elastic to a small chiffon coloured square for a wristlet. It can be worn at wrist or fastened to strap or belt.

Records and cassettes

Fred Penner. *Special Delivery.* (Troubadour Records)
"The Fox"

Raffi. *Baby Beluga.* (Troubadour Records)
"Over in the Meadow"

⸻. *The Corner Grocery Store.* (Troubadour Records)
"Les Loups-Garous"
"Y un Rat"

Sandy Oppenheim. *If Snowflakes Fell in Flavours.* (Berandol Records)
"Hey Little Bird" (Good for singing to children.)

Fingerplays and Poems

From *Let's Do Fingerplays,* Grayson
"Animal Antics," pp. 30–37
"Chickadees," p. 60
"Five Little Froggies," p. 63
"This Little Rabbit," p. 35
"My Rabbit," p. 34
"Little Mousie," p. 80
"Five Little Squirrels," p. 63
"Telegraph Poles," p. 66
"Two Little Blackbirds," p. 73

NOTE: See "Spring" for rabbits and "Fall" for squirrels.

From *Don't Eat Spiders,* Heidbreder
"A Big Bare Bear," p. 5
"How to Catch a Bird," p. 11
"Bird's Nest," p. 25

From *Oranges and Lemons,* King
"Five Little Speckled Frogs," p. 32
"Goldilocks and the Three Bears," p. 40

From *Round and Round the Garden,* Williams and Beck
"Foxy's Hole," p. 9
"Two Little Dicky Birds," p. 31
"The Little Bird," p. 47

From *Finger Rhymes,* Brown
"There Was a Little Turtle," p. 4
"The Baby Mice," p. 14
"Five Little Mice," p. 16
"Two Blackbirds," p. 19
"The Squirrel," p. 25

From *Hand Rhymes,* Brown
"Little Bunny," p. 21

From *Read Aloud Rhymes for the Very Young,* Prelutsky and Brown

THE TURTLE

Unknown

The turtle crawls on the ground and makes a rustling sound.
He carries his house wherever he goes,
And when he is scared, he pulls in his nose and covers his toes!

FIVE LITTLE TURTLES

by Bonnie Flemming

One little turtle all alone and new,
Soon it finds another and then there are two.
Two little turtles crawl down to the sea,
Soon they find another and then there are three.
Three little turtles crawl along the shore,
Soon they find another and then there are four.
Four little turtles go for a dive,
Along swims another and then there are five!

NOTE: Use felt or flannelboard turtles.

ANIMAL HOMES

by JoAnne Deal Hicks

The cow has a barn, a chick has her pen,
The pony her stable, a fox her den.
The bear likes her cave, a guppy her bowl.
The rabbit her hutch, the wee mouse her hole.
The bee has a hive, a bird has its nest,
The spiders their web, but **my** home is best!

IF A SQUIRREL COULD

by JoAnne Deal Hicks

If a squirrel could bark like a dog,
If a squirrel could hop like a frog,
If a squirrel could squirm, or if he could crawl,
Then he just wouldn't be a squirrel at all!

HERE IS A BUNNY

Here is a bunny with **ears** so funny, (BEND 2 FINGERS OVER THUMB)
And here is a **hole** in the ground. (MAKE HOLE WITH LEFT HAND ON HIP)
When a noise he hears, he pricks up his **ears** (HOLD "EARS" STRAIGHT)
And **hops** into his hole so round. (HOP BUNNY OVER AND POP IN HOLE)

Stories

(To read, read–tell, or tell. See Book Centre for complete list.)
Most of the stories written for this subject are quite fanciful. Try to chose stories with interesting illustrations and with plausible characters. Wheeler's *I Can't Have Bannock, But the Beaver Has a Dam* is an interesting and untraditional choice.

Games

(See "Learning Games," pp. 50–59, and teacher made games in this chapter for directions.)
  1. Look and see: Use flannel-backed pictures of woods animals
  2. Alike, different, and the same: Use materials prepared for match-them
  3. Reach and feel: Use fur, feather, acorn, twig, and grass

Routine Times

  1. At snack times or meals offer nuts, peanuts in shell (for children over 4 only), sunflower seeds, toast squares, carrot or celery sticks, lettuce or cabbage leaves, raisins, apples, bananas, berries, animal crackers.
  2. At nap time encourage children to curl up like sleeping animals.

Large Muscle Activities

  1. Caves: Packing boxes or barrels placed horizontally on the playground allow children to pretend to be animals in caves
  2. Tree homes: Laundry or fat fibre barrels with a hole sawed in one side, painted, and mounted vertically on wooden frames outdoors
  3. Burrows or tunnels, using fabric tunnels (available from IKEA and educational suppliers)
  4. Beaver dams: Children can gather sticks (or use tongue depressors) to use in the sandpile; provide water
  5. Gopher or rabbit holes: Low cardboard boxes turned upside down with a hole cut in the top. Make up games using these on rainy days
  6. Nuts: Collect acorns or other nuts that have fallen from trees, or wad brown tissue paper for use by children pretending to be squirrels
  7. Nests: Allow children to use twigs and small branches in the sandpile to build animal homes; remove each day and store in a sack
  8. Forest animal models: Place in or near the sandpile. Aid in developing creative play involving animals of the woods
  9. Follow the leader: Imitate the way the various animals move or walk

Extended Experiences

  1. Trip to a museum that has displays of forest animals.
  2. Trip to a zoo or a park that has animals of woods and stream.
  3. Trip to an aquarium or marina if group is interested in fish.
  4. Trip to see a beaver dam. Avoid trip after a heavy rain as dams may be damaged. A naturalist or taxidermist may advise you where you may see one, or where to find squirrels, raccoons, and foxes.
  5. Explore a stream or wooded area if one is nearby.
  6. Woodlands party or picnic. Make name tags using forest animal stickers or wildlife stamps. Have children bring stuffed animals or puppets if they wish. Serve foods listed under Routine Times, no. 1.
  7. Invite a parks and wildlife director or a forester to tell your group how they can help forest animals. Two or three suggestions are best. Perhaps she or he could bring a "Prevent Forest Fires" poster to share.

Teacher Resources

Pictures and Displays

▷ Forest products companies often picture forest animals in their magazine advertisements
▷ Display plastic forest animal models in a forest scene. Use as a table centrepiece for a forest party
▷ Display stuffed forest animals children may share, such as teddy bears, rabbits, skunks, squirrels, chipmunks, and deer
▷ Wildlife stamps (Canadian Wildlife Federation)

Books and Periodicals

Chickadee magazine
Durrell, Gerald. *The Stationary Ark,* London: Collins, 1976
Equinox magazine
Forey, Pamela. *An Instant Field Guide to Mammals.* New York: Crown, 1986
Grey Owl. *The Adventures of Sajo and the Beaver People.* Toronto: Macmillan, 1973
Godfrey, E.W. *The Birds of Canada.* Ottawa: Queen's Printer, 1966
Hendrikson, Robert. *Animal Crackers.* Markham, Ont: Penguin, 1983
The Larousse Encyclopedia of Animal Life. London: Hamlyn, 1967
National Geographic magazine
Owl magazine
Seton, E.T. *Wild Animals I Have Known.* Ottawa: University of Ottawa Press, 1977
Tremain, Ruthven. *The Animal's Who's Who.* New York: Charles Scribner's Sons, 1982
Whitaker, Muriel, ed. *Great Canadian Animal Stories.* Edmonton: Hurtig, 1978

Films and Videos

Consult your local library for audio-visual resources

Community Resources and Organizations

▷ Forester or parks and wildlife supervisor
▷ Department of biology or zoology at a university
▷ Taxidermist
▷ Museum curator
▷ City or provincial park director

Government Agencies

▷ Canadian Wildlife Service, Environment Canada
▷ Provincial, territorial, and federal ministries or departments concerned with the environment, forestry, and natural resources

19 Zoo Animals

★★★★★★★★★★★★★★★★★★★★★★★

Basic Understandings

(concepts children can grasp from this subject)

▷ A zoo is a place where people can safely see wild animals in captivity.

▷ At a zoo, animals from all over the world are kept in cages, in fenced off areas, or in special houses that are like their former homes (caves, hillsides, woods, or waterways).

▷ At zoos, certain families of animals are grouped near each other:

1. Cats (tigers, panthers, lions, cheetahs, leopards)
2. Monkeys and apes (gorillas, orangutans, chimpanzees, spider monkeys)
3. Bears (black, brown, grizzly, polar, panda)
4. Birds
5. Reptiles and snakes
6. Fish

▷ Animals found in most zoos are giraffes, elephants, lions, tigers, monkeys, apes, zebras, bears, and hippopotami.

▷ Other animals sometimes included in a zoo are alligators, crocodiles, rhinoceroses, camels, goats, deer, seals, foxes, wolves, peacocks, ostriches, panthers, leopards, and tortoises.

▷ It is necessary to cage wild animals because most of them are not safe to play with. Also a cage offers protection for the animals and keeps them from straying.

▷ Tame animals are usually safe to play with (except when eating or sleeping). Wild animals are *not* safe to play with except by owners who have tamed and trained them.

▷ It is not safe to feed zoo animals as they may bite and seriously injure children and adults.

▷ We pay money to go into some zoos. This money helps to pay for the feeding, care, and purchase of the animals.

▷ Many people work in a zoo to keep the animals healthy, safe, fed, and exercised. Other people sell tickets, food, and rides or care for the walks, roads, plants, and flowers.

▷ Some zoos have a pet farm or a children's zoo where children may pet, touch, feed, or ride the animals.

   NOTE: Include basic understandings listed for "Animals," p. 371, as appropriate.

Grouping and sorting by association. The children above are playing the game "grouping and sorting by association," using different animals (see "Basic Resources," p. 55). The child at left is selecting zoo animals to place in one of the homemade cages, while the child in the centre is placing her choices of pets around the house and yard. The child at right is reaching for a calf to place with other farm animals on the farmyard space.

Additional Facts the Teacher Should Know

Elephants

▷ Cow (female)
▷ Bull (male)
▷ Calf (young)
▷ Herd (family group)
▷ They have wrinkled gray skin, long powerful trunks, two ivory tusks, a thin tail with course hairs at the tip, and huge flapping ears
▷ Elephants roar when they're enraged, trumpet when they're warning intruders, purr or squeal when content, and thump the ground with their trunks when suspicious
▷ They eat leaves, roots, fruit, bark, tubers, twigs, grasses, and bamboo shoots. In captivity, an elephant eats 18 to 90 kg of hay per day as well as 300 kg of fresh greens, and drinks 136 to 227 l of water
▷ The average life span is 50 to 60 years (maximum 70)

Giraffes

▷ Cow (female)
▷ Bull (male)
▷ Calf (young)

▷ Corps or herd (family group)
▷ They have buff-coloured coats with complex patterns of various shades of brown, long necks, horns, and long legs
▷ They communicate by making gurling whimpers, cries, moos, or snoring; the bull's mating call is a snorting cough
▷ Giraffes eat shoots of acacia and mimosa, and favour legumes
▷ The average life span is 20 years in nature, 28 years in captivity

Lions

▷ Lioness (female)
▷ Lion (male)
▷ Cub (young)
▷ Pride (family group)
▷ They have tawny yellow brown fur, powerful front legs, sharp retractible claws, excellent hearing and sight, and the males have a large mane
▷ They roar frequently
▷ Lions eat meat; they hunt their prey singly or in groups
▷ The average life span is 20 to 25 years in nature, up to 30 years in captivity

Monkeys

▷ Monkey (female, male, young)
▷ Troop or colony (family group)
▷ They have dark brown fur coats with black faces, the under parts are gray or buff; well-developed colour vision, slender bodies, small heads, and long limbs
▷ They communicate with chatters, shrieks and howls
▷ Monkeys eat plants, fruits, shoots, leaves, eggs, insects, small animals, and sometimes nuts depending on the breed
▷ The average life span is 25 to 30 years in captivity

Zebras

▷ Mare (female)
▷ Stallion (male)
▷ Foal (young)
▷ Herd (family group)
▷ They have black-and-white striped hides, black noses, and short bushy manes
▷ Their honking and barking is loud and shrill
▷ Zebras eat grasses and herbs in the wild, carrots, potatoes, oats, and apples in captivity
▷ The average life span is 20 to 30 years in captivity

Tigers

▷ Tigress (female)
▷ Tiger (male)
▷ Cub (young)
▷ Ambush (family group)
▷ They have coarse short-haired coats that are tawny yellow with black vertical stripes, large paws, and large heads
▷ Tigers roar; they also make a strange bell-like noise called "titting" when hunting
▷ They eat meat—up to $4\frac{1}{2}$ kg per day in captivity.
▷ The average life span is 12 to 19 years in captivity.

Methods Most Adaptable for Introducing this Subject to Children

1. Set new model zoo animals out on the shelves or on a table.
2. Read or tell a story about a zoo or zoo animals.
3. Show a picture in a newspaper about a zoo or a zoo animal pet in the community.
4. Bulletin board display (see Pictures and Displays).

Vocabulary

wild	watch	claws	fence
tame	circus	hoofs	arena
keeper	zoo	fur	perform
tricks	tour	mane	striped
safari park	gate	cave	spotted
cage	pool	tank	protect
sharp	veterinarian		

Include animal names, sounds, body parts, and foods eaten by the zoo animals observed by your group.

Learning Centres

Discovery Centre

1. Display some nonperishable models of foods that wild animals eat: hay, grass, leaves, bark, bananas (see pp. 412–13).
2. Borrow from school, church, or public library a short zoo animal educational film or filmstrip.
3. Use View-Master reels of zoo animals.

Dramatic Play Centres

Home-living centre

1. Post pictures to suggest family going to the zoo (children and their doll families).
2. Set out souvenir pennants, made in the art centre, to carry to the zoo.
3. Provide stuffed zoo animal toys, such as teddy bears, tigers, and pandas.

Block-building centre

1. Set out rubber, plastic, or wooden models of zoo animals.
2. Place hay or excelsior in a box for children to feed or bed down animals.
3. Set out wooden snap clothespins for fences.
4. Hang pictures of animals in a zoo. These may suggest that children build enclosures for wild animals with the hollow or unit blocks.

Other dramatic play centres

1. Use cartons as cages or caves for children to crawl inside. Cut cardboard to make barred windows.
2. Set out cable spools or nail kegs for platforms for performing animals and ruffled collars for clowns, performing seals or dogs. Let children pretend to be trained animals using balls and hula hoops. Offer balloons.
3. Set out homemade "top" hat, black felt hat, or plastic derby for master of ceremonies.

   NOTE: Teacher may need to become zookeeper or master of ceremonies if children become too hilarious.

4. Tour train: Set up as described in "Ground and Road Transportation" p. 467. Post large pictures of zoo animals or outdoor scenes for passengers to see. Sell tickets.
5. Laminate pictures of raw meats for "pretend" feeding of zoo animals.
6. Have small buckets available for feeding and watering the animals.
7. Set out work gloves and a large ring with keys for opening cages (variety-store sheriff's lock and keys are great).
8. Allow children to use short lengths of rubber hose (dishwasher or sink hose, or hygienic syringe tubing) for washing elephants and cages.

Learning, Language, and Readiness Materials Centre

Commercially made games and materials

(See "Basic Resources," pp. 79, 100, for manufacturers' addresses.)
1. *Puzzles:* Puzzles with a variety of zoo animals. Be sure some of the puzzles have knobs. Lauri produce particularly good animal puzzles.
2. *Small toys for imaginative play:* Model animals—durable plastic or wooden animals made of nontoxic materials. Choose models with pieces that are of a good size to fit into children's hands. Try to find models of animals that are similar to animals the children are likely to see. Zoo or circus animal playsets (available from Fisher-Price or Li'l Playmates).
3. *Dolls and puppets:* Puppets that are models of a variety of zoo animals.
4. *Miscellaneous:* Animal dominoes, simple board and matching games with animals.

Teacher-made games and materials

NOTE: For a detailed description of "Learning Games," see pp. 50–59.

1. Match-them: Zoo animal model with picture of the animal. Large size animal gummed seals may be glued to the backs of old playing cards for this purpose.
2. Alike, different, and the same: Name animals that have similar characteristics, such as claws, teeth, tails, and fur. Have children separate small model animals into groupings of zoo, pet, farm animals. Compare animals by size, colour, family to designate which are alike, which are different.
3. Grouping and sorting by association: By fur, feathers, or fin or those that swim, fly, crawl, or walk, using models or pictures.

Art Centre

• 1. Make pennants for zoo visitors. Put large paper triangles (pennant shaped) on easel with large edge at child's left. Children may staple to cardboard sticks when dry.
• 2. Make place cards with zoo animal stickers. Children may use magic markers to edge, stripe, polka dot, and letter name, if they can. Use for zoo party.
•• 3. Crayon picture of favourite zoo animal.

••• 4. Make caged animal pictures: cut out and paste animal pictures on a plain piece of paper; cut stripes and glue on picture as bars. Precut pictures are offered to youngest children. Wallpaper books and discarded picture books are good sources of pictures. Glue on bars by gluing only along top and bottom of page.

• 5. Collage picture: Provide spotted and striped fabric for zoo animals, Easter basket grass, fur bits, yarn, rope, leather scraps, and cotton balls.

• 6. Yarn collage: Provide yarns of various sizes and colours.

••• 7. Box sculpture: Let children stack or fasten together small boxes for use in making animals. Attach with masking tape. Supply rope or yarn for tails, buttons for eyes, scrap leather or felt scraps for tongues.

Other experiences in this centre using art media

1. Puppets:
•   a. Stick: see "Pet Animals" p. 395.
•••   b. Sock: Glue on bits of felt for eyes, ears, manes, and tails, use white glue.
••   c. Paper bag: Use the largest brown paper bags, cut hole in bottom for head, cut armholes, decorate like a zoo animal (see illustration, p. 276).

••• 2. Zoo cages: Paint shoe boxes. Paste, glue, or draw a zoo animal picture on the inside bottom of each box. Then glue construction paper strips over opening or punch with nail holes along two opposite edges and thread pipe cleaners through. Put excelsior or straw in the bottom of the cage and small bottle caps for feeding dishes (glue to bottom of cage). Wheeled cages can be made by using milk bottle caps or other discarded items like plastic discs or wheels. (Teacher may make for display.)

••• 3. Decorate reinforced nail kegs that are sturdy enough to climb and stand on. Use water base paints and paste ons. This is to be used by children in dramatic play areas when they are imitating wild animals performing.

Book Centre

•••• Blanchet, M. Wylie. *A Whale Named Henry.* Madeira Park, BC: Harbour Publishing, 1983. (Read–Tell)

••• Bowen, E. *The Good Tiger.* New York: Alfred A. Knopf, 1965.

•• Browne, A. *Gorilla.* New York: Alfred A. Knopf, 1985.

• Campbell, R. *Dear Zoo.* New York: Macmillan, 1984.

•• Cantieni, B. *Little Elephant and Big Mouse.* New York: Picture Book Studio, 1981.

• Carle, Eric. *Do You Want to Be My Friend?* New York: Thomas Y. Crowell, 1970.

•• Carle, E. *1, 2, 3 to the Zoo.* New York: World, 1968.

• D'Auliare, I., and E. D'Auliare. *Animals Everywhere.* Garden City, NY: Doubleday, 1954.

•• de Regniers, Beatrice Schenk. *Circus.* New York: Viking Press, 1966.

••• Dr. Seuss. *If I Ran the Zoo.* New York: Random House, 1950.

••• Doughty, J. *Andy and the Lion.* New York: Viking Press, 1938.

• Flack, Marjorie. *Ask Mr. Bear.* New York: Macmillan, 1971.

• Freeman, Don. *Dandelion.* New York: Viking Press, 1964 (filmstrip and record).

•• _____. *The Seal and the Slick.* New York: Viking Press, 1974.

•• Gantschev, I. *Journey of the Storks.* New York: Picture Book Studio, 1983.

••• Graham, Margaret Bloy. *Be Nice to Spiders.* New York: Harper & Row, 1967.

• Hoban, T. *Big Ones, Little Ones.* New York: Greenwillow Press, 1976.

• _____. *A Children's Zoo.* New York: Greenwillow Press, 1985.

•• Ipcar, Dahlov. *Black and White.* New York: Alfred A. Knopf, 1963.

••• Isenberg, B., and S. Wolf. *The Adventures of Running Bear.* Boston: Houghton Mifflin, 1982.

•••• Johnson, Crockett. *Ellen's Lion: Twelve Stories.* Markham, Ont: Fitzhenry & Whiteside, 1984. (Good for reading to children.)

• Krauss, Ruth. *Bears.* New York: Harper & Row, 1948.

••• Lewis, R.B. *Aunt Armadillo.* Willowdale, Ont: Annick Press, 1985.

••• Mahy, M. *The Boy Who Was Followed Home.* New York: Dial Press, 1986.

••• Morgan, A. *Barnaby and Mr. Ling.* Willowdale, Ont: Annick Press, 1984.

 •• Munsil, Janet. *Zach at the Zoo.* Willowdale, Ont: Annick Press, 1986.

••• Peet, B. *Pamela Camel.* Boston: Houghton Mifflin, 1984.

  • Pienkowski, J. *Zoo.* New York: Heinemann, 1985.

 •• Rice, E. *Sam Who Never Forgets.* New York: Greenwillow Press, 1977.

  • Rojankovsky, Feodor. *Animals in the Zoo.* New York: Alfred A. Knopf, 1962.

  • _____. *The Great Big Animal Book.* New York: Western Publishing, 1950.

 •• Slobodkina, Esphry. *Caps for Sale.* Reading, MA: Addison-Wesley, 1957.

  • Wildsmith, Brian. *Circus.* New York: Franklin Watts, 1970.

Planning for Group Time

NOTE: All music, fingerplays, poems, stories, and games listed here may be used at other times during the session as appropriate. See Core Library, "Basic Resources," p. 95, for publishers and addresses. Record company addresses can be found on p. 99.

Music

Songs

From *Singing Bee,* Hart
"Eletelephony," p. 124

From *More Piggyback Songs,* Warren
"I Know a Bear," p. 79

From *Baby Beluga Book,* Raffi
"Baby Beluga," p. 5
"Joshua Giraffe," p. 41

From *Elephant Jam,* Sharon, Lois, and Bram
"Elephant and Giraffe: A Game," p. 12
"One Elephant, Deux Elephants," p. 34
"Elephant Rhyme," p. 42
"Five Little Monkeys," p. 48
"Three Little Monkeys," p. 49
"Alison's Camel," p. 66
"Monte sur un Elephant," p. 95

From *Tunes for Tots,* Warner and Berry
"The Monkey," p. 82
"Giraffe," p. 84
"Camel," p. 85
"Penguin," p. 87

A TRIP TO THE ZOO

(tune: "Frère Jacques")
Adaptation by JoAnne Deal Hicks

See the li-on, see the li-on, in his cage, in his cage.
Lis-ten to his roar-ing. Lis-ten to his roar-ing. . . . I can too, I can too!
(ALLOW CHILDREN TO ROAR)

See the mon-keys, see the mon-keys, in their cage, in their cage.
Hear them as they chat-ter, chit-ter, chit-ter, chat-ter. I can too, I can too!
    (ALLOW MONKEY CHATTERING)

See the big bear, see the big bear, in his cage, in his cage.
He can stand on one leg. He can stand on one leg. I can too, I can too!
    (CHILDREN STAND ON ONE LEG)

See the black snake, see the black snake, curled up small, curled up small.
He can be so qui-et. He can be so qui-et. So can I . . . so can I!
    (CHILDREN CURL UP ON FLOOR)

Rhythms and singing games

▷ From your own rhythm record sets: Select appropriate music for elephants, bears, monkeys, etc.

▷ From your own favourite music book: Choose appropriate music for giraffe stretching, kangaroo hopping, and so on.

▷ Adapt "This is the Way We Wash Our Clothes" to: This is the way the elephant walks, the lion stalks, the monkey climbs, and so on.

Records and cassettes

Anne Murray. *There's a Hippo in My Tub.* (Capitol Records)
"There's a Hippo in My Tub"
"Animal Crackers"

Raffi. *Baby Beluga.* (Troubadour Records)
"Baby Beluga"
"Joshua Giraffe"

Sharon, Lois, and Bram. *Elephant Show Record.* (Elephant Records)
"One Elephant Went Out to Play"

_____. *Smorgasbord.* (Elephant Records)
"Three Little Monkeys"

Fingerplays and Poems

From *Read Aloud Rhymes for the Very Young*, Prelutsky and Brown
"The Elephant Carries a Great Big Trunk," p. 10
"Holding Hands," p. 11
"Wild Beasts," p. 16
"I Can Be a Tiger," p. 17
"When You Talk to a Monkey," p. 22
"Before the Monkey's Cage," p. 22
"Way Down South," p. 46
"Giraffes Don't Huff," p. 58

From *Hand Rhymes*, Brown
"Two Little Monkeys," p. 9

From *Round and Round the Garden*, Williams and Beck
"The Ostrich," p. 13

From *Don't Eat Spiders*, Heidbreder
"Hippopotamus," p. 6
"Ellie the Elephant," p. 21

TWO LITTLE MONKEYS

Two little monkeys, jumping on the bed, **jump, jump, jump.**
　　　　(USE TWO INDEX FINGERS DOING JUMPING MOTION)
One fell off and bumped his head.
　　　　(ONE INDEX FINGER FALLS—OTHER HAND IS PLACED ON HEAD)
We took him to the doctor, and the doctor said:
　　　　(WALK INDEX FINGERS TO DOCTOR)
That's what you get, for jumping on the bed.
　　　　(SHAKE ONE INDEX FINGER—POINTING AT GROUP)

Stories

(To read, read-tell, or tell. See Book Centre for complete list.)
Stories about zoo animals in their natural habitat are effectively used for this subject such as
Gantschev's *Journey of the Storks.*

Games

(See "Learning Games," pp. 50–59, for directions.)
　1. Guess who? Children cover faces, one child is chosen to be "it"—makes zoo animal sound
　　　—children guess
　2. Reach and feel: Use model zoo animals in a bag
　3. Who am I? Describe zoo animal
　4. Which is larger? Compare sizes of rubber or plastic animals or pictures of animals; for
　　　more accurate comparison, select pictures and models that are scaled to natural size
　5. Look and see: Use model zoo animals, cut up old picture books or order zoo animal
　　　cutouts

Routine Times

At snack or meal time:
　1. Have a zoo party with centrepieces of stuffed wild animal toys.
　2. Eat animal crackers.
　3. Let older children "sell" real popcorn at the zoo as snack for the day.

　　　★ **CAUTION:**　　Encourage children to chew it carefully and wash it down with a drink of
　　　　　　　　　　　　water.

　4. Popsicles: Freeze juice in cubes with coffee stirrers inserted for handles. Children may
　　　"buy" these as treats.

Large Muscle Activities

　1. Add cartons to make zoo train cars.
　2. Encourage "monkeys" to do tricks on climbing gyms using monkey grip for safety
　　　(thumbs under, fingers over).
　3. Play "may I?" with several moving at once. Children may take three elephant steps, two
　　　lion leaps, three alligator glides, one kangaroo hop, and so on.
　4. Play "teddy bear": "Teddy bear, teddy bear turn around."
　5. Pantomime a walk through a zoo: Children choose an animal to pantomime; cages can be
　　　backs of school chairs; children crouch behind the chair and if teacher is musical, the
　　　piano makes magnificent sound effects to accompany the children's pantomime of the
　　　animals.

Extended Experiences

1. Plan a trip to a:

    a. Zoo or circus
    b. Museum that displays zoo animals
    c. Pet farm

2. Souvenir stand: Sell pennants made in the art centre (p. 415), or balloons.
3. Popcorn stand: Sell bags filled with popcorn for snack. Provide cash register, play money, vendor's hat and apron (see "Basic Resources," p. 22).
4. Invite a zookeeper to visit the class with a zoo pet.

Teacher Resources

Pictures and Displays

▷   Display a group of stuffed toy wild animals
▷   Display pictures of a circus

Books and Periodicals

Chickadee magazine
Durrell, Gerald. *The Stationary Ark.* London: Collins, 1976
Equinox magazine
Hendrikson, Robert. *Animal Crackers.* Markham, Ont: Penguin Books, 1983
The Larousse Encyclopedia of Animal Life. London: Hamlyn, 1967
Metropolitan Toronto Zoo. *ZooBook* series. (16-page booklets of information and photographs concerning species found at the Metro Zoo) Toronto: D.C. Heath Canada, various dates.
National Geographic magazine
Owl magazine
Seton, E.T. *Wild Animals I Have Known.* Ottawa: University of Ottawa Press, 1977
Tremain, Ruthven. *The Animal's Who's Who.* New York: Charles Scribner's Sons, 1982

Films and Videos

Consult your local library for audio-visual resources

Community Resources and Organizations

▷   Museum curator
▷   Zookeeper or zoo park personnel
▷   Instructors of zoology from a nearby university

20 Insects and Spiders

★★★★★★★★★★★★★★★★★★★★★★★★

Basic Understandings

(concepts children can grasp from this subject)

▷ There are many kinds of insects (over half a million).

▷ Insects are found in nearly all parts of the world. Some even live in ice and snow.

▷ Insects differ in many ways—size, shape, colour, kinds of eyes, mouths, and number of wings, as well as the food they eat.

▷ Insects have six legs (three pair) and, if winged, four wings (two pair).

▷ Bees, wasps, butterflies, moths, flies, grasshoppers, ants, dragonflies, ladybugs, mosquitoes, beetles, crickets, bugs, and fireflies are insects we often see.

▷ A spider is not an insect. It is called an arachnid.

▷ Spiders have eight legs (four pair) and no wings.

▷ Most spiders spin webs for their homes, for their young, or to help catch insects for food.

▷ Insects and spiders live all around us in the grass, in the trees, on the flowers, and in the dirt.

▷ Some insects (bees, ants, termites, and certain wasps) live in colonies.

▷ All insects and spiders come from eggs.

▷ When some insect babies hatch out of their eggs they are called larvae (caterpillars in the case of butterflies). Others, like grasshoppers, hatch looking like a grownup insect only smaller.

▷ Young spiders are called spiderlings.

▷ Some insects and spiders are beautifully coloured (morpha butterfly, golden garden spider, harlequin cabbage bug).

▷ Some insects (mosquitoes) spread disease.

▷ Insects sometimes eat our food while it is growing in the fields. Farmers and gardeners do not like this.

▷ Insects help us by making honey (bees) and pollinating fruits and flowers.

▷ Spiders help us by eating insect pests.

▷ Birds, snakes, frogs, and toads eat great numbers of insects.

NOTE: Include basic understandings listed under "Animals," p. 371, as appropriate.

Additional Facts the Teacher Should Know

Insects

1. Insects are invertebrates and have no backbone. There are more kinds of insects than any other kind of animal. They have a segmented body, jointed legs, and an external skeleton. They never have more than three pairs of legs, their body is divided into three parts (head, thorax, and abdomen), and the adults usually have two pairs of wings. Some insects are harmful. They may eat crops or cause the spread of disease. Many insects are helpful. They help pollinate fruits and flowers. Insects are food for birds, frogs, toads, and snakes. They provide us with many products including honey and medicinal substances.

2. Insects have two sets of jaws, but they do not move as ours do. They grind or move sideways. Some insects use their mouths for chewing and others for piercing and sucking. Some insects use their legs for more than walking. They use them for swimming, jumping, or digging. Some have forelegs that are adapted for grasping and holding prey. Others have legs with hairs or suction discs to help them walk on water. Other special leg structures are combs for cleaning antannae or eyes; hearing organs and other special sensory structures, such as taste, smell, and chemical receptors; noise-making organs; silk glands.

3. Insects breathe although they require very little oxygen. They get oxygen through their body walls or through special openings for breathing. They can also get oxygen from their food.

4. An insect's blood can be colourless, pale yellow, green, or red depending on what it has eaten. One part of a tube that carries its blood pulsates and is called the heart. Insects have a central nervous system and a primitive kind of brain. They are more sensitive to touch than people are. They have touch receptors all over their bodies, and each has two "feelers." Insects can also hear. Some can hear sounds that humans cannot. They can taste. Insects have a keen sense of smell and use it to recognize other insects of their own kind, to find their way, to find a mate, and to locate food. Most insects have two kinds of eyes and in some ways can see better than humans. They mate to reproduce, and their reproductive organs are named similarly to humans: testes, ovaries, vagina.

5. Insects do not have a voice like humans, but they do make sounds with other parts of their bodies. Some tap their heads against the sides of their burrows. Others may hum or buzz by vibrating their wings or their thorax, or they may squeak by forcing air out through their breathing holes. Insects may also make a sound by rubbing one part of their body against another part. For example, some crickets and grasshoppers rub a "scraper" on one wing cover across a "file" on another wing cover.

6. Insects outgrow their skeletons. They shed the one that is too little and form a new, larger one. Insects come from eggs, and many can be seen by the human eye. Baby insects are usually called larvae. Most insects have a pupal stage. The pupae of butterflies are called chrysalises because they are studded with bright metallic spots. The pupae of many species are usually enclosed in a cocoon that the larvae make before they enter this stage. Most cocoons are made of silk, often with bits of leaves, wood, earth, or excrement worked into them. Some are waterproof and airtight, but others have valves, or openings, with lids at one end to help the emergence of the adult. Cocoons may be found in dirt, under tree bark, beneath stones, rolled up in leaves, hanging from twigs, or tucked into crevices. When an insect struggles free of the cocoon it may have to wait until its wings dry before it can fly away.

7. In order to observe the opening of a cocoon or a chrysalis, create a cage from a rectangular piece of wire mesh screen and two cylinder-shaped shallow cans or pans. For sides to the cage, select a piece of screen large enough to overlap 6 cm when coiled inside one of the two pans (or cans). Use the second pan or can as a lid. Cake pans or large tuna cans work well. Twigs with the cocoon or chrysalis should be placed in a vertical position inside the cage. A cocoon found during the cold months of the year and brought into a warm room will develop a month ahead of the regular season. It should be kept in a cool

place, and then in the spring placed in the cage for observation. Sprinkle the cocoon occasionally with a little water to keep it pliable. If several cocoons of the same mother are placed in the cage at the same time and allowed to develop into adult moths, the eggs laid may hatch and grow into small caterpillars.

8. If the cocoon of a praying mantis is found, place it in a large, transparent container with tiny holes punched through the lid. Because large numbers of praying mantises are hatched at the same time, this is necessary if you do not want them all over the room. Children enjoy watching the actions of these young insects who are just like the adult except that they do not have any wings. They are absolutely harmless.

9. Any insect developed from a cocoon or chrysalis should be set free after a few days. Otherwise, when they try to fly they will break their wings on the cage and die.

Caring for caterpillars

1. Children often find caterpillars at various times during the spring, summer, and early fall months. If found on a tree or bush, put some of the leaves of the plant in the cage with them. Different caterpillars eat the leaves of different kinds of plants. They also may not be ready to spin a cocoon. When they are ready to do this, they will leave the food alone and hunt for a suitable place.

   NOTE: Children can be taught to handle caterpillars carefully. Too many children tend to destroy every tiny creature they see.

2. If the caterpillar of the tomato sphinx (tomato worm) is brought in, put it in a fruit jar with some dirt, as it burrows into the ground to pupate. The caterpillar of the polyphemus moth may be put in a glass jar containing twigs and leaves. Clean out the jar daily. When the caterpillar is ready to spin its cocoon, it will use the twigs and side of the jar as its foundation and spin the leaves into its cocoon. After it is spun, the cocoon may be removed from the jar and put in a cool place. It should be dampened from time to time. If placed in a warm place and kept moist you can force its development and it will come out as a full-grown moth.

3. Twigs should be placed in the jar with the cecropia and monarch caterpillars. With the monarch butterfly, the leaves from a milkweed plant should be placed in the jar. The caterpillar spins a pad of silk on a leaf or twig, hangs from it, and sheds its larval skin, leaving the green chrysalis. This is an extremely interesting stage of development to observe. Some woolly bear caterpillars hibernate in the larval stage under dead leaves and bark. They will spin a cocoon in the spring and a tiger moth will emerge in late May. Other varieties spin a cocoon in the fall (see "Fall" for further information).

   NOTE: Silkworms are great to observe. The entire metamorphosis takes less than two months from hatching eggs to laid eggs. Earthworms are *not* a stage of insect development. They are annelids.

Spiders

1. Spiders are not insects. They have no backbones and do not have antennae. They usually spin silken webs. They have four pairs of legs instead of three. The one pair of legs nearest the head is used primarily for holding and moving things. The other three pairs are used for walking. Spiders have only two body parts. Spiders are found in almost all parts of the world.

2. Most spiders have poison glands and fangs. They use them for defense or for killing prey. Generally, however, spiders are not dangerous to people because they usually do not attack human beings unless they are provoked or cornered. If they do bite, the wound is usually not serious.

3. Silk is made in abdominal glands inside the spider's body and comes out of tubes called spinnerets. It hardens and forms strands that are fine but very strong and elastic. This silk is used to make webs to preserve food and protect the eggs it lays.

4. A spider's blood is clear. Its heart is like that of the insect. It can breathe through body openings like that of the insect or through book lungs. They are called book lungs because they look like an open book.

5. There are male and female spiders. All spiders come from eggs. Like insects, spiders have to shed the skeleton that is too small in order to grow larger. Many spiders lay eggs in a cocoon fastened to a twig, or a stone, or a web. Spiders hatch inside the cocoon. The baby spiders or larvae grow very rapidly and become spiderlings. If the temperature is warm, the spiderlings may tear their way out of the cocoons and almost immediately begin feeding.

6. Adult spiders spend much of their time seeking food. Some chase the insects they will eat, some spit sticky material on them to immobilize their victims, some wait in holes for the insects to fall in and be trapped, and some spin webs to catch the insects.

7. All spiders spin a dragline behind them and attach it at various intervals. Using the dragline, a spider drops from a surface, hangs suspended in mid-air, and then climbs back up or floats gently down. Draglines are also used to lay down the framework of webs. Webs come in many shapes.

8. Spiders can be put in a jar with holes in the lid (not big enough for them to get out of). Cover the bottom of the jar with soil. Place leaves and twigs on the soil, or lean a small branch with smaller branches coming off it against the jar or stick in the soil. These will provide food and will be a centre of interest for the children to observe how this animal handles its food. Water is supplied by putting a piece of moist blotting paper or a piece of moist sponge in the jar.

Methods Most Adaptable for Introducing this Subject to Children

1. Pictures of insects and spiders and their homes should be prominently displayed to encourage conversations between teacher and child about them.

2. An ant farm could be prepared and put out for display. While outside, the children could look for ant hills and make closer observations with a magnifying glass.

3. In the appropriate season, the children, with the help of the teacher, could collect insects or spiders and keep them as described earlier or in a plastic bug keeper for a day.

4. Go on a walk to look for insects or spiders and their homes.

5. Follow a child's discovery of a water bug or other bug outdoors with other discovery activities.

6. Locate a cricket by its sound (in season).

7. A child may bring in a specimen—look up in a book how to care for it.

Vocabulary

insect	grasshopper	moth	antennae (feelers)
larva	spider	wasp	butterfly
pupa	pollinate	beetle	ladybug
cocoon	spiderling	cricket	ant
caterpillar	mosquito	firefly or	bee
hatching	dragonfly	lightning bug	fly

Include the names, sounds, body parts, and foods eaten by the insects you are observing.

Learning Centres

Discovery Centre

1. An insect or spider collection could be brought to school as well as books that help to identify the names of these animals.
2. Parents should be notified that the class is especially curious about spiders and insects in a particular week, and that they can do much to stimulate their children's interest and answer their questions.
3. Present a honeycomb and let the children taste the honey it contains.
4. Observe an ant farm (available from Battat).
5. Find a caterpillar, care for it, and observe what happens.
6. Compare a moth and a butterfly (see no. 7).
7. Observe a dead fly or other insect under a microscope or magnifying glass (a tripod giant magnifier is available in educational catalogues).
8. Listen to a cricket (if you have one) during quiet or rest time.
9. Observe an insect caged in a commercially available bug cage.
10. Look at View-Master reels of insects and butterflies.

Learning, Language, and Readiness Materials Centre

Commercially made games and materials

(See "Basic Resources," pp. 79, 100, for manufacturers' addresses.)
Miscellaneous: Insect Cages—reliable makes a cage called a bug keeper.
Butterfly and insect kites are available in kite stores and Oriental gift and variety stores.
Butterfly nets are available in some variety and toy stores.

Teacher-made games and materials

NOTE: For a detailed description of "Learning Games," see pp. 50–59.

1. Match-them: Sets of animals and foods they eat; include bugs for turtles and birds and flowers for bees.
2. Make match-them cards with butterfly or insect stickers. These can be used for counting and sorting.

Art Centre

- 1. Teacher can cut easel paper in the shape of butterfly wings. Paint as usual.
- 2. While children are fingerpainting play a record of "Flight of the Bumblebee." Suggest that they might pretend their fingers are bumblebees buzzing around bushes or chasing something (could be animal or person).
- 3. Fingerpaint creepy-crawly pictures.
- •• 4. Make insect bodies of clay or play dough. Use sticks, pine needles, pipe cleaners, or paper for legs and wings.
- ••• 5. Let children creatively arrange crayon shavings on a butterfly- or bug-shaped piece of wax paper, cover with a plain piece of wax paper, and press with an iron set at low heat. (Use iron with caution.) Alternative: Mount melted crayon pictures under a butterfly- or bug-shaped mat opening.
- •••• 6. String beads, paper circles, and/or disc-shaped styrofoam packing pieces.
- • 7. Allow children to use straws, toothpicks, and pipe cleaner segments for appendages if they make insects with their clay and need them.

●● 8. Other bugs/spiders can be made from circles/ovals of corrugated cardboard and decorated. Pipe cleaners may be inserted through holes for legs. Single egg carton cups can also be similarly used for insect bodies. Allow children to lick and stick coloured geometric gummed shapes on "bugs" or paint their "bugs" appropriately.

●● 9. Make available half lengths of the bottom of egg cartons (elongated variety) for the children to paint. Set out appropriate colours of paint. Short lengths of pipe cleaners or hair-curler pins may be used as "feelers."

●● 10. Make thumb print insects. Let children crayon legs to make the thumb prints look like insects.

Book Centre

●●●● Aardema, Verna. *Why Mosquitoes Buzz in People's Ears: A West African Tale.* Markham, Ont: Fitzhenry & Whiteside, 1978.

●● Brinckloe, Julie. *The Spider's Web.* Garden City, NY: Doubleday, 1974.

●● Carle, Eric. *The Very Hungry Caterpillar.* Cleveland: Collins and World, 1970.

●●● Caudill, Rebecca. *A Pocketful of Crickets.* New York: Holt, Rinehart & Winston, 1964.

●●● Freschet, Bernice. *The Web in the Grass.* New York: Charles Scribner's Sons, 1972.

● Garelick, May. *Where Does the Butterfly Go When It Rains?* Reading, MA: Addison-Wesley, 1961.

●●● Ginsburg, Mirra. *Mushroom in the Rain.* New York: Macmillan, 1974.

●● Graham, Margaret Bloy. *Be Nice to Spiders.* New York: Harper & Row, 1972.

●●● Heller, Ruth. *How to Hide a Butterfly.* New York: Grosset & Dunlap, 1986.

● Lionni, Leo. *Inch by Inch.* New York: Astor-Honor, 1962.

●●● Mizumura, Kazue. *If I Were a Cricket.* New York: Thomas Y. Crowell, 1973.

●● _____. *Way of an Ant.* New York: Thomas Y. Crowell, 1970.

●●● Selsam, Millicent. *Terry and the Caterpillars.* New York: Harper & Row, 1962. (Tell)

●●● Waber, B. *A Firefly Named Torchy.* Boston: Houghton Mifflin, 1970.

●●● Wagner, J. *Aranea: A Story About a Spider.* New York: Bradbury, 1978.

Planning for Group Time

NOTE: All music, fingerplays, poems, stories, and games listed here may also be used at other times during the session as appropriate. See Core Library, "Basic Resources," p. 95 for publishers and addresses. Record company addresses can be found on p. 99.

Music

Songs

From *Tunes for Tots*, Warner and Berry
"Bees," p. 74
"Butterfly, Fly," p. 76

From *Piggyback Songs*, Warren
"The Little Caterpillar," p. 26
"Butterfly, Butterfly," p. 27
"Fly Fly Butterfly," p. 27

From *More Piggyback Songs*, Warren
"Pretty Butterfly," p. 75
"Bugs," p. 75

From *Stepping Along in Music Land*, Murray
"Wiggly Worm," p. 27
"Butterfly, Butterfly," p. 47
"How Many Bees," p. 57

From *A Treasury of Songs for Children*, Glazer
"The Blue Tail Fly," p. 41
"Eency Weency Spider," p. 76
"Shoo Fly," p. 201

From *Singing Bee*, Hart
"Caterpillar," p. 22

BUGS

(tune: "Frère Jacques")
Adaptation by JoAnne Deal Hicks

Big bugs, small bugs, big bugs, small bugs.
See them crawl. See them crawl.
Creep-y, creep-y, crawl-ing. Nev-er, nev-er fall-ing.
Bugs, bugs, bugs. Bugs, bugs, bugs.

Thin bugs, fat bugs. Thin bugs, fat bugs.
See them crawl, on the wall.
Creep-y, creep-y, crawl-ing. Nev-er, nev-er fall-ing.
Bugs, bugs, bugs. Bugs, bugs, bugs.

Rhythms and singing games

From original songs in this book by JoAnne Deal Hicks
"The Tiny Weaver," p. 430: creepy, crawly music. Pretend to be caterpillars. Play "fluttering" music for butterflies. Play a chromatic scale on the piano for bees (white note followed by black notes on upper register of piano keyboard).

Records and cassettes

Anne Murray. *There's a Hippo in My Tub.* (Capitol Records)
"Inchworm"

Bob Homme. *The Giant Concert of Concerts by the Friendly Giant.* (A & M Records)
"The Buzzy Concert"

Bob McGrath. *If You're Happy and You Know It Sing Along*, Volume I. (Kids Records)
"The Incey Wincey Spider"

Fred Penner. *Special Delivery.* (Troubadour Records)
"There Was an Old Lady"

Sandy Oppenheim. *If Snowflakes Fell in Flavours.* (Berandol Records)
"Did You Ever Hear an Ant Say Can't?"

Fingerplays and Poems

From *Let's Do Fingerplays*, Grayson
"Five Little Ants," p. 63
"Grasshoppers," p. 65
"Bumblebee," p. 73

From *Don't Eat Spiders*, Heidbreder
"Don't Eat Spiders," p. 23
"The Giant Snail," p. 41

From *Round and Round the Garden*, Williams and Beck
"The Incy Wincy Spider," p. 17

From *Hand Rhymes*, Brown
"Here Is the Beehive," p. 14
"The Caterpillar," p. 28

From *Read Aloud Rhymes for the Very Young*, Prelutsky and Brown
"Snail's Pace," p. 20
"The Butterfly," p. 33
"Wings," p. 39
"Fuzzy Wuzzy Creepy Crawly," p. 62
"Only in My Opinion," p. 62
"Ants," p. 62
"Ants Live Here," p. 62
"Grasshopper Green," p. 63
"Dragonfly," p. 63
"But I Wonder....," p. 63
"Firefly," p. 65
"An Explanation of the Grasshopper," p. 72
"Under the Ground," p. 73
"The Underworld," p. 73
"Tell Me Little Wood Worm" p. 79

From *Where the Sidewalk Ends*, Silverstein
"One Inch Tall," p. 55

EENSIE WEENSIE SPIDER

Adaptation of Southern Folksong

The tiny, tiny spider went up the water spout. ("WALK" FIRST AND SECOND FINGERS UP ARM)
Down came the rain and washed the spider out. (BRUSH HAND DOWN ARM)
Out came the sun and dried up all the rain. (MAKE CIRCLE WITH ARMS OVERHEAD)
And the tiny, tiny spider went up the spout again. ("WALK" TWO FINGERS UP ARM)

THE ANT HILL

(THE RIGHT HAND WITH THE THUMB CLOSED INSIDE IS THE ANT HILL. THE FINGERS WILL BE THE ANTS. LIFT EACH FINGER AS IT IS COUNTED, BEGINNING WITH THE THUMB)

Once I saw an ant hill, with no ants about.
So I said, "Little ants, won't you please come out?"
Then as if they had heard my call, one, two, three, four, five came out.
And that was all.

Stories

(To read, read-tell, or tell. See Book Centre for complete list.)
Stories chosen for this subject should help children get rid of any fears they may have of insects, such as Aardema's *Why Mosquitoes Buzz in Peoples' Ears*. They can also give children information about insects, such as Gaerlick's *Where Does the Butterfly Go When It Rains?*

Routine Times

1. Use fingerplays, poems, and songs about insects or spiders while children are coming to the table for lunch or snacks.
2. Serve honey and biscuits at snack or meal times.

Extended Experiences

1. Go for a walk in a nearby park, around the block, or around the playground area to find bugs (under rocks, in cracks in sidewalks, in bushes—shake bushes into an open umbrella).
2. Have someone bring a butterfly collection to show.

Teacher Resources

Pictures and Displays

▷ Display magazines with special articles on insects:

 a. *National Geographic* magazine
 b. *Owl* magazine
 c. *Chickadee* magazine
 d. *Equinox* magazine

▷ Use the 3-D bugs and caterpillars made in creative art for table decor.
▷ Put up pictures of spiders, caterpillars, moths, and butterflies from your own personal files.
▷ Display and use commercial picture packets:

 a. Monarch Butterfly, Insects/Bees, Science Themes No. 1 (David C. Cook)
 b. Bees/Ants, Science Themes No. 2 (David C. Cook)
 c. Insects, Instructo Flannelboard Set, 12 prints
 d. Colour Study Prints, Insects and Spiders (The Child's World)
 e. Sequence Charts, Life Cycle of Monarch Butterfly (The Child's World)
 f. Basic Science Series No. 1, Common Insects (SVE)
 g. Basic Science Series No. 2, Moths and Butterflies (SVE)

Books and Periodicals

Equinox magazine
National Geographic magazine
Owl magazine
Chickadee magazine
Klots, A., and E. Klots. *Insects of North America.* Garden City, NY: Doubleday, 1972

Films and Videos

Consult your local library for audio-visual resources

The Tiny Weaver

A Listening Song or Dramatic Play Accompaniment

JoAnne Deal Hicks

NOTE: Teacher may wish to sing this song to the group after exploring the subject of spiders. Use pictures from **National Geographic, Owl, Chickadee,** or **Equinox** magazines. Allow children to join in singing the words as they become familiar with them.

PART

6

Transportation

★★★

Contents

21 Many Ways to Travel

★★★★★★★★★★★★★★★★★★★★★★

Basic Understandings

(concepts children can grasp from this subject)

▷ Transportation means moving people or things from one place to another.

▷ People can move from one place to another:

  a. By their own movements—walking, running, swimming, or crawling.
  b. By riding an animal or being pulled by one in a wagon or carriage.
  c. By riding in or on a machine—car, train, plane, ship, or bus.

▷ Some machines that move or carry us need motors, wind, water, steam, gas, oil, or people to make them go.

▷ When we travel or transport things:

  a. We first decide what we need to move—people or things.
  b. We think about where we need to move them or ourselves.
  c. We decide the best way to move them or ourselves.
  d. We buy a ticket, pay a fare, or give instructions to the person or animal that is going to take us.
  e. We may turn a key or a switch or pull a throttle if we are to start the machine in which we are traveling.

▷ Machines most often used for moving people or things are cars, trucks, buses, taxis, trains, airplanes, ships, and boats.

▷ The person who steers most transportation machines is called the driver.

▷ A driver must have a licence and follow certain rules. Drivers who break the rules may get a ticket from a law enforcement officer, pay a fine (money), or have their licences taken away.

▷ We usually must pay money to transport people or things:

  a. People may buy tickets to ride on trains, airplanes, ships, or buses.
  b. People may pay fares (money) to ride in a taxi, bus, subway, ferry, or street car.
  c. People who own their own car (or other machine) must take care of it and buy gasoline and oil for it.
  d. Sometimes drivers must pay a toll (money) to drive on roads or drive in tunnels or drive over bridges. The money collected is used to help build and care for the roads, tunnels, and bridges.

▷ We can travel or carry things on the ground, in the air, or through the water.
▷ When people walk on the sidewalks we call them pedestrians; when pedestrians cross streets they must be careful and obey the crossing guard, police officer, or traffic lights.
▷ People can do many things while traveling as passengers: eat, sleep, rest, talk, read, and sometimes stand, walk, or use rest rooms.
▷ Drivers must pay attention to their driving and passengers must be careful not to disturb or distract the driver.
▷ All drivers must follow signs and signals for safety:

    a. Railroad engineer: semaphores, flags, and whistles.
    b. Pilot: windsocks, radar, and radio signals.
    c. Ship captain: whistles, buoys, flags, and radio signals.
    d. Crossing guard and/or police officer: road signs and traffic lights.

▷ There are many specially trained people who help us with transportation, such as conductors and flight attendants.

Additional Facts the Teacher Should Know

1. This chapter will deal with concepts and activities that involve all methods of moving people or things from one place to another. It will deal with movements of self, use of animals to ride or pull, and transportation by air, water, road, rail, or in space. Subsequent chapters dealing specifically with transportation by air, rail, road, water, and space have been developed for use where special interest in one form of transportation is indicated. First experiences with transportation should begin with ways the child can move and carry things. Use of wheel toys that can be pushed, pulled, or pedalled enlarge the concepts of moving things and people. Cars or buses used for transporting the children to and from the centre would provide additional experiences with transportation. If your centre is near a railroad track, beneath a flight pattern, near a river or near an ocean you will have natural exposure to these means of transportation.
2. The basic concepts listed are understandably broad and are not intended to be taught outside of the children's opportunities to experience them. For example, you would not suggest activities involving toll booths, ferries, or trolleys if they do not exist in your community, unless a child in your group has had experience with them. Select those that will have the most meaning for your group.

Methods Most Adaptable for Introducing this Subject to Children

1. A child or teacher at the centre takes a trip.
2. Read a story about transportation.
3. Put up pictures or display scale models of trains, airplanes, ships, boats, cars, trucks, buses, or spaceships.
4. Visitor: If one of the children's father or mother works for a transportation agency have him or her visit the classroom, dressed in working attire, and talk about the job. If possible, the visitor could bring something that he or she uses on the job to show the children. Many transportation companies have representatives from their public relations departments who will visit centres.

Vocabulary

transportation	fare	suitcase	go
passenger	toll	baggage	start
schedule	taxi	boat	car
airplane	tourist	pack	run
move	travel	ride	crawl
carry	driver	walk	drive
trip	train	ship	truck
bus	carry	stop	streetcar
ticket			

Learning Centres

Discovery Centre

1. Help children discover that there are many ways to move things or people—carry by hand, animal, car, train, truck, airplane, or ship. Discuss the methods by which a product, like milk, is carried by people, animals, cars, trains, planes, and ships. If possible, have pictures of each mode of transportation used.
2. Encourage children to observe signs, crossing guards/police officers, stop lights, and parking meter signs when taking a trip and crossing streets. Provide picture books, films, or licence rule manuals to help children discover some of these signs and signals.
3. Display hats and pictures of people at work to help children discover that some people wear uniforms or special clothes when they work on their transportation job and some do not.
4. Display one each of a model train, car, truck, bus, ship, boat, and airplane on a table. Encourage discussion about transportation. Discuss likenesses and differences and why each is necessary.
5. Display pictures and/or models of animals used to carry people or things, such as horses, elephants, burros, dogs, camels.

Dramatic Play Centres

Home-living centre

1. Have several overnight bags available so they can be packed for a trip with dressup clothes or doll clothes.
2. Have several travel brochures with colourful pictures and timetables on a shelf for the children to look at.
3. Put play money in purses so tickets can be purchased or fares or tolls paid.
4. Hang travel posters here and in the block-building centre.

Block-building centre

1. A steering wheel or dial panel, planks, and hollow blocks will all provide opportunities for many kinds of transportation play. A dial panel (see illustration, p. 467) can be made out of wood or a heavy cardboard box. See other transportation chapters for specific suggestions for its use.
2. Set out items to be transported in both large and small trucks, such as animals, blocks, cars, and containers full of buttons, beads, spools, twigs, and pebbles.
3. Commercial materials that will add to dramatic play with transportation are listed below:

   a. Unit blocks to build roads, bridges, stations, garages, docks, and airports
   b. Unit block transportation vehicles—cars, trucks, planes, taxis, boats, ships
   c. Unit block people to transport and transportation helpers
   d. Unit block animals to transport
   e. Hollow blocks and building boards for larger-scale building
   f. Four-way traffic light (Childcraft)
   g. Traffic signs—unit block size and wheel toy size
   h. Wheel toys—doll carriage, wagons, trikes, wheelbarrows
   i. Oversize vehicles—trucks, planes, trains, and boats
   j. Ride—on vehicles
   k. Cash register and play money (metal and paper)

4. Post pictures of highways, bridges, docks, airports, railroad stations, or launching pads in block-building area to encourage use of unit blocks as related to transportation.

Other dramatic play centres

1. Two rows of chairs with an aisle between might suggest travel by bus, train, subway, trolley, or airplane. If space is limited one row may be sufficient. Provide money, tickets, and conductor's hat or make a hat using pattern on p. 468.
2. Ask parents and staff to bring in used airline or rail tickets to use in the mock vehicles.
3. Empty cardboard cartons from large appliances, such as refrigerators and stoves, make excellent centres for buses, fire engines, trains, etc. The children can decorate them using paints and large pieces of construction paper.

Learning, Language, and Readiness Materials Centre

Commercially made games and materials

(See "Basic Resources," pp. 79, 100, for manufacturers' addresses.)
1. *Puzzles:* A variety of puzzles with transportation themes. Excellent puzzles are made by Galt, Simplex and Ravensburger.
2. *Construction and manipulative toys:* Wooden steering wheels and wheels that match large wooden blocks encourage the construction of a variety of transportation vehicles.
3. *Small toys for imaginative play:* Vinyl models of various vehicles for younger children. Metal models of various vehicles for older children. A printed vinyl playmat that represents the layout of a small town, that can be used in conjunction with model vehicles and blocks, for example Chieftan Products' Roadway Playmat (900).
4. *Toys for riding:* A variety of toys for riding both indoors and outdoors. Be sure to choose toys that are replicas of vehicles the children are likely to see not models of television vehicles. Choose vehicles that are sturdy and that do not have sharp edges. Make sure they are easy to steer and that you have a variety of sizes to fit different children.
5. *Costumes:* Hats and coats that represent various employees of the transportation industry.

Teacher-made games and materials

NOTE: For a detailed description of "Learning Games," see pp. 50–59.

1. Look and see: Use sturdy models of the various transportation vehicles.
2. Reach and feel: Use sturdy models of different types of transportation vehicles.
3. Can you remember? Use transportation toys.
4. How many? How many ways can you get from one side of the room to the other? Get to school? From one city to another? Get a car across the river? Get across the ocean?
5. Who am I? Describe someone who works for an airline, railroad, bus company, or trucking firm, for example, "I fly an airplane; who am I?"
6. Grouping and sorting by association: Place several models of each type of transportation vehicle in a box or on a tray. Let children sort into appropriate groups. Label boxes or make an appropriate garage, hangar, or harbour into which vehicles can be sorted.
7. Alike, different, and the same: Use scale models or sets of picture cards of the various transportation vehicles. Toy catalogues or model catalogues available at some hobby centres may provide you with the pictures for this game. Have children find two just alike. As children gain experience, add one that is different to pairs that are alike and ask child to "find the one that is different," such as two cars and a bus.
8. Colour, shape, size, and number: At every opportunity, when observing real transportation vehicles or using scale models, talk about the colour, shape, size, and number characteristics as appropriate; examples: "What *colour* is the caboose?" "Put away the *big* truck." "How *many* propellers does your airplane have?" "*Count* the wheels on the car."

Art Centre

••• Pasting: Children could help make a picture book of transportation for the Book Centre by cutting pictures out of magazines, catalogues, or brochures and pasting them on coloured construction paper. These pages could then be punched and placed in a three-ring notebook.

NOTE: Cut one side and the bottom rectangle out of six large grocery bags. When all six are cut, stack and fold them to form a book. Staple at the folded edge to make a large flat scrapbook of twelve pages.

Book Centre

••• Bauer, C. *My Mom Travels a Lot.* Markham, Ont: Penguin, 1985.
•• Curry, Peter. *Trucks, Planes, Boats, Trains.* New York: Price Stern, 1984.
••• Douglas, Barbara. *The Great Town and Country Bicycle Chase.* New York: Lothrop, Lee & Shepard, 1984.
•• Hall, Donald. *Ox-Cart Man.* New York: Viking Press, 1979.
••• Hutchins, Pat. *Rosie's Walk.* New York: Macmillan, 1971.
• Keats, Ezra Jack. *Skates.* New York: Franklin Watts, 1973.
• Lenski, Lois. *Davy Goes Places.* New York: Henry Z. Walck, 1961.
••• Mitsumara, Anna. *Anno's Journey.* Toronto: Academic, 1987.
••• Pearson, Susan. *Karin's Christmas Walk.* New York: Dial Press, 1980.
• Prater, John. *You Can't Catch Me.* London: Bodley Head, 1986.
• Rockwell, Anne. *Things That Go.* New York: E.P. Dutton, 1986.
• _____. *My Travel Book.* Burlington, Ont: Hayes Publishing, 1986.
•• Sawyer, Ruth. *Journey Cake, Ho.* New York: Viking Press, 1953.
••• Shannon, George. *The Piney Woods Peddlar.* New York: Greenwillow Press, 1981.
••• Svend, Otto, S. *Inuk and His Sledge Dogs.* London: Pelham, 1979.
•• Wildsmith, Brian. *Daisy.* New York: Pantheon, 1984.
••• Wright, Ethel. *Saturday Walk.* Sidney, OH: Scott, 1954.

Planning for Group Time

NOTE: All music, fingerplays, poems, stories, and games listed here may also be used at other times during the session as appropriate. See Core Library, "Basic Resources," p. 95, for publishers and addresses. Record company addresses can be found on p. 99. In parodies, hyphenated words match the music notes of the tune used.

Music

Songs

TAKE A TRIP (a parody)

(tune: "Twinkle, Twinkle, Little Star")
Adaptation by Wendy Flemming

Take a bus or take a train,
Take a boat or take a plane.
Take a tax-i, take a car,
May-be near or may-be far.
Take a space ship to the moon,
But be sure to come back soon.

NOTE: To add interest use pictures, figures, flannelboard, or models.

GET ON BOARD

Get on board lit-tle chil-dren
Get on board lit-tle chil-dren
Get on board lit-tle chil-dren
There's room for many and more.
There's room for Bet-ty. There's room for Tom-my. (and so on)

There's room for man-y and more.
There's room for man-y and more.

NOTE: Can be sung when playing train, plane, bus, or ship. It is a good way to involve those who may be watching.

From *Piggyback Songs*, Warren
"We Sail a Ship," p. 31
"Off We Go—A Traveling Song," p. 33
"Twinkle Twinkle Traffic Light," p. 47

From *More Piggyback Songs*, Warren
"Buckle Up," p. 67
"When I Cross the Street," p. 67
"Safety," p. 67
"Choo Choo Train," p. 89

From *Baby Beluga Book*, Raffi
"Morningtown Ride," p. 46

From *What Shall We Do and Allee Galloo*, Winn
"Run Children, Run," p. 70

NOTE: There are many songs that may be used in this section. Please see the following chapters for further and more complete suggestions.

Rhythms and singing games

1. Hoofbeats can be imitated by using walnut or coconut shells or wooden tone blocks when records or songs about horses or donkeys are played.
2. Play a variety of tempos on the piano or from segments of action records that will encourage the children to walk, run, tiptoe, and jump.
3. The sounds made by airplanes, trains, cars, trucks, buses, or boats can be suggested by the music of certain records or piano music or appropriate rhythms. Allow children to respond creatively. (See "Basic Resources," p. 42.)
4. Stick horses. Allow children to use stick horses when galloping or trotting music is used.

ROUND AND ROUND THE VILLAGE

Sing this song using different ways of moving around a village.

Let's fly a-round the vil-lage. (PRETEND TO BE AN AIRPLANE)
Let's walk a-round the vil-lage. (ALSO USE JUMP, HOP, SKIP, OR GALLOP)
Let's drive a-round the vil-lage. (PRETEND TO BE CARS, TRUCKS, OR BUSES)
Let's swim a-round the pool. (PRETEND TO DO THE CRAWL)
Let's row a-round the lake. (PRETEND TO ROW A BOAT)
Let's pad-dle down the riv-er. (PRETEND TO PADDLE A CANOE)

AS I WAS WALKING DOWN THE STREET

(Adaptation of "Rig-a-Jig-Jig")

As I was walk-ing down the street, down the street, down the street
A lit-tle friend I went to meet, hi-ho, hi-ho, hi-ho.

Skip-pet-y-skip and a-way we go, a-way we go, a-way we go
Skip-pet-y-skip and a-way we go, hi-ho, hi-ho, hi-ho!

NOTE: Change verse to include running, jumping, hopping, flying in the sky, rowing down a stream, and other action verbs.

Records and cassettes

Bob Homme. *The Giant Concert of Concerts by The Friendly Giant.* (A & M Records)
"Railroad Concert"

Bob McGrath. *If You're Happy and You Know It Sing Along,* Volume I. (Kids Records)
"The Wheels on the Bus"
"Little Wheel a Turnin'"
"She'll Be Comin' Round the Mountain"

Fred Penner. *Special Delivery.* (Troubadour Records)
"Car Car Song"
"En Roulant"

Raffi. *The Corner Grocery Store.* (Troubadour Records)
"Swing Low, Sweet Chariot"
"Jig Along Home"
"Sur le Pont d'Avignon"

Sharon, Lois, and Bram. *Smorgasbord.* (Elephant Records)
"Mango Walk"
"Riding Along (Singing a Cowboy Song)"

Fingerplays and Poems

From *Let's Do Fingerplays*, Grayson
"Things That Go," pp. 22–26
"Big Hill," p. 23

From *The New Wind Has Wings*, Downie
"Donkey Riding," p. 15

From *A New Treasury of Children's Poetry*, Cole
"The Sidewalk Racer," p. 135

From *Where the Sidewalk Ends*, Silverstein
"Where the Sidewalk Ends," p. 64
"Traffic Light," p. 121

From *Rhymes for Fingers and Flannelboards*, Scott and Thompson
"The Airplane," p. 21
"Five Little Sailors," p. 23

Stories

(To read, read–tell, or tell. See Book Centre for complete list.)
The choice of stories for introducing the transportation section should reflect the children's experiences. Although they may have been exposed to most modes of transport through television, they will become more interested in the subject if you start with stories that relate to their own experiences.

Games

(See "Learning Games," pp. 50–59, and teacher-made games in this chapter for directions.)
1. Look and see
2. Reach and feel
3. Can you remember?
4. How many?
5. Who am I?
6. Grouping and sorting by association

Routine Times

1. During snack or meal times, talk about how the various foods you are eating were brought to the centre.

   a. How does the food get from the kitchen to the tables?
   b. How does the food get from the store to the kitchen?
   c. How does the food get from garden, dairy, or canning factory to the store?

2. At snack or meal times ask children to help by *transporting* food, dishes, silver, water, and other food or utensils as needed.
3. At pick-up time, point out to the children that carrying things in our hands and walking are forms of transportation. Suggest also the use of wagons and rolling platforms as means of transporting blocks and toys to shelves to be put away.

4. While riding or walking look for different kinds of *vehicles,* for example, cars, trucks, buses, trains, airplanes, boats.
5. When riding in a bus or car, talk about safety in a car or bus: Use safety belts if available, lock the doors, be considerate of the driver; as appropriate, talk about traffic signals and rules.

Large Muscle Activities

1. An old discarded steering wheel from a junked car, boat or tractor, remounted on a large wooden box big enough for three or four children to stand in, makes an excellent dramatic play vehicle. If built to look like no one vehicle it will be more versatile. A couple of broomhandle clips mounted on the side will allow for hanging a hose when it is a fire engine or a coil of soft rope for a lifeline or old bicycle tire for a life preserver when it is a boat.

NOTE: Set it up on cement blocks outside and drill a few drain holes in the bottom of the box so it will weather without rotting.

2. Encourage use of wheel toys for transport of each other or things around the play yard. Add traffic signs and signals.
3. Remind children of traffic rules, such as one-way traffic or boundaries.

Extended Experiences

1. Visit a railroad station, bus terminal, or airport. Time your visit to see arrivals and departures.
2. Ride on a bus, trolley, train, or boat (whatever is possible in your area that would interest your group), considering safety factors involved.
3. Visit a park or other public site that may have a ship, locomotive, or airplane as a permanent display, with pieces of play equipment or mounted so that children are free to explore.
4. Visit a hobby shop that has a model car racetrack or model train on display.

Teacher Resources

Pictures and Displays

▷ Pictures of trains, cars, trucks, buses, boats, ships, wheel toys, or children walking or running could be mounted and displayed on walls.
▷ Land Transport Around the World (Grolier).

Books and Periodicals

Allen, Kenneth. *The Children's Book of Cars, Trains, Boats, and Planes,* 1978.

Films and Videos

Check with your local library for the list of current materials available from the National Film Board and the CBC

Community Resources and Organizations

▷ Travel agencies for posters, brochures, and timetables
▷ A travel agent
▷ Public relations personnel of various airlines, steamship lines, or railway companies for pictures, calendars, brochures, and timetables
▷ A VIA Rail agent
▷ An airline's representative
▷ Hobby centres for models and catalogues
▷ A transportation company
▷ Societies interested in transportation; for example, a model train club, a flying club, a steam train "buffs" club, a car racing club, a hang-gliding club, a shipping and ship travel club

Government Agencies

Provincial, territorial, and federal ministries of transportation and/or communication

22 Air Transportation

★★★★★★★★★★★★★★★★★★★★★★★★

Basic Understandings

(concepts children can grasp from this subject)

▷ Airplanes carry people and things from one place to another by flying in the sky.
▷ Some airplanes are small and carry one or two people and some are very big and carry many, many people.
▷ Some people own their own private airplanes.
▷ People can buy tickets (pay money) to ride in an airplane.
▷ Most airplanes take off and land on runways at an airport.

    a. Sea planes can take off and land on water.
    b. Ski planes can take off and land on snow.
    c. Some planes land in fields.
    d. Helicopters land on fields, parking lots, and buildings.

▷ The person who flies the airplane is called the pilot; his/her assistant is called the co-pilot.
▷ Flight attendants ride in the cabin on a passenger plane to help make the passengers comfortable and serve them snacks or meals.
▷ The air terminal is the building at the airport where people may buy tickets and wait for airplanes. It often has a lounge, rest rooms, restaurant, snack bar, telephones, car rental and ticket agents, gift shops, and news stands.
▷ The control tower is a tall building where an air traffic controller can view all the runways. It has radar which helps the controller guide pilots in safe takeoffs and landings.
▷ Hangars are buildings at the airport that house airplanes when they are not in use.
▷ Hangars are like garages, but they are large enough to hold aircraft.
▷ Some small towns have small, but important airports with little sheds for buildings and limited equipment.
▷ There are many different kinds of aircraft—passenger planes (airliners), cargo planes (for freight only), sea planes, helicopters, gliders, ski planes, and jets.
▷ Rockets and missiles carry people and things into outer space, to the moon, and to other planets.
▷ Windsocks tell pilots which way the wind is blowing.
▷ Each airplane has a number, symbol (logo), or flag so we know who owns it. International aircraft have the flags of their countries painted on the sides.
▷ Airplanes have seat belts for safety, just as automobiles do.

▷ People depend on airplanes to travel long distances quickly, to bring them food, to carry mail and to bring them other goods.

▷ Most aircraft travel from one place to another on the earth. There are craft called space ships, satellites, and space shuttles that travel to other planets.

▷ Satellites and space shuttles help us receive telephone calls and special television programs.

Additional Facts the Teacher Should Know

1. How can something that is heavier than air fly? An airplane flies because of the work done by the propellers, the wings, and the engine. A glider does not have an engine but is towed (lifted) into the air by another airplane to which it is attached by a cable. When the glider is at the proper height the cable is released and the glider flies (glides) back to earth. Airplanes are powered by gasoline engines, turbine engines, jet engines, or rockets. These engines provide power to turn the propellers or provide forward thrust for the airplanes. Forward thrust causes air to flow over the wings, which are curved on top and flat on the bottom. As airplanes are thrust forward, air flowing over the curved part of the wing has farther to go than air flowing across the flat underside. The air that has to go farther therefore goes faster to meet the slower air beneath. Because the air goes faster it does not push down as much as the slower air pushes up. The faster airplanes go forward, the greater the lift; therefore, airplanes fly.

2. Not all modern planes have propellers. Many jet planes do not, nor do rockets or missiles. Gases from burning fuel in the engine rush out from a hole in the rear of each engine (these can be seen in the pods under the wings) with terrific force and the plane is pushed forward. Forward thrust can be demonstrated by blowing air into a balloon and then letting the balloon go. As the air rushes out the open end the balloon goes in the opposite direction. Jet engines use the oxygen from air, but rockets must carry their own oxygen supply. The first plane to fly faster than the speed of sound was a jet. When a plane or rocket flies faster than the speed of sound a loud boom is heard and the plane or rocket is said to be "breaking the sound barrier." Vibrations from the sonic boom may cause houses to shake, windows and dishes to break or rattle, and objects to fall.

3. Three controls are used in flying an airplane. They are the control stick, the rudder pedals, and the throttle. In smaller, older planes the control stick has a knob on the end for the pilot to grasp, but newer and larger craft have a small steering wheel. There are two ways to turn an airplane to the right and to the left—by moving the stick or turning the wheel to the left or right and by pushing the rudder pedals down. Usually a pilot works both the stick and rudder pedals together. There are two different ways to make an airplane go up or down. When the control stick is pushed forward the airplane moves toward the earth; if the stick is pulled back, the airplane climbs. The second way involves the throttle, which controls the speed of the engine. Pushing the throttle in makes the engine go faster, increasing the lift, and the airplane goes higher. If the throttle is pulled back, the engine slows down, increasing the downward force, and the plane descends.

4. Most takeoffs and landings are made by pilots with permission obtained by two-way radio communication with the air traffic controller in the tower at the airport. In good weather with good visibility pilots land planes under their own control. However, the control officer in the tower can bring in an airplane with the use of radar and other instruments when visibility is poor. Bringing a plane in by radar is called a ground control approach (GCA) and instrument landing systems (ILS) means a radio highway approach.

5. Airports range in size from small landing fields with one runway, a windsock, and no landing lights (no night service) to the huge international airports serving several

airlines, including those flying to and from other countries. The largest airports have terminals built on a circular layout and are virtually mini-cities.

6. At the larger airports each airline has its own ticket counter, baggage claim centre, boarding gates, and customer service staff. Tickets are now written and confirmed by computer. Tickets arc presented by customers at customer service stations near boarding gates, where they receive boarding passes. When it is time for boarding a plane customers must go through a security checkpoint. Because of many recent hijackings and hidden bombs, all persons must walk through a magnetometer or scan-screen which detects the presence of metal. All coats, purses, and hand-carried luggage are checked by security guards or placed in a scan-ray machine to detect metal. Once through the security checks travelers walk through tunnels called gangways or telescopic gangways to waiting planes.

7. Customers' baggage is placed on a conveyor belt which takes it out to a service area where it is placed on baggage tugs or luggage carts and taken to waiting planes. A ramp with a conveyor belt carries it up into the baggage compartment.

8. All foods and drinks served on the airplane are catered by food services. The food is prepared in advance and brought to the airplane before takeoff. The small kitchens, or galleys, are used for preparing drinks and setting up trays which are taken to passengers in their seats by flight attendants. Special diet menus can be ordered by passengers if the airline has been alerted to their specific needs.

9. Helicopters cannot fly as fast as airplanes but they can take off and land straight up and down, making them excellent for rescue work in mountains and valleys where runways do not exist. They have two sets of propellers called "rotors." Most have one big rotor overhead and a smaller one on the tail. One set of rotors turns clockwise and the other set counterclockwise, keeping the helicopter in balance.

10. Ski planes are equipped with giant skis that allow them to glide over snow. Sea planes are equipped with pontoons, allowing them to land and float on water. They both also have sets of wheels which can be lowered to allow them to land on runways. Some sea planes can land on their bellies.

11. Airplanes have many parts—wings, propellers, engine, control stick or steering wheel, tail, rudder, and wheels. The cockpit is where the pilot sits to fly the plane. The cabin is where the passengers sit. Transcontinental planes have galleys, rest rooms, and lounges. Some planes have seats that can be converted to upper and lower berths for sleeping.

12. As the concepts of space and space exploration are often beyond their comprehension, many children find the discussion of space transport either boring or frightening. Be sure that the children are interested before introducing much of the material in this section. Often children will be most interested in imaginative and nonscientific play in relation to space. Many of the activities and resources relating to space travel will be most successful if the teacher does not take them too seriously and focuses on having fun with the concepts rather than worrying about how much the children are learning about space exploration. Often children are interested in the sun, the moon and the stars.

Methods Most Adaptable for Introducing this Subject to Children

1. A child or one of the teachers or a child's relative at the centre takes a trip by airplane.
2. Put up pictures or display scale models of various kinds of planes.
3. Read a story about airplanes.
4. Visitor: If one of the children's parents works for an airline have him/her visit and tell about the job or arrange for a visitor from a representative of an airline, or travel agency.
5. Observe planes or helicopters from the playground.

Vocabulary

aircraft	spaceship	helicopter	seat belt
airplane	space shuttle	satellite	astronaut
airport	terminal	cockpit	fasten
runway	hangar	fly	takeoff
flight attendant	tower	jet	landing
airline	baggage	wing	windsock
glider	ski plane	pod	air controller
pilot	sea plane	propeller	

Learning Centres

Discovery Centre

1. Display model airplanes of various kinds. Help children identify the airplanes and discover the uses made of each kind. Recognize likenesses and differences. Look for symbols (logos), numbers, and flags for identification. These should be models that would withstand manipulation. Demonstrate with models how airplanes take off and land.
2. Help children understand how a propeller works by providing pinwheels, either commercial or homemade (see pattern on p. 455).
3. Help children understand how a jet engine works by blowing up a balloon and letting it go. The escaping air pushes the balloon forward.
4. Make a windsock to take outside to find out which way the wind is blowing. Sew a tube of material or the sleeve of a shirt to a circle of wire or embroidery hoop. Fasten the hoop to a stick which can be used as a handle or stuck in the ground. Airplanes must take off and land into the wind. The windsock tells the pilot which way the wind is blowing.

Dramatic Play Centres

Home-living centre

1. Have airline schedules and travel brochures in this centre to encourage the planing of a trip by airplane. Suitcases should be available to pack and money placed inside the purses to be used for purchasing tickets.
2. Used airline tickets and travel posters from travel agents and government tourist offices can be brought in for this centre.

Block-building centre

1. Build a runway with long planks or unit blocks. Have wooden or unbreakable model airplanes available for takeoffs and landings.
2. Add cars, people, and baggage to various models and types of airplanes on shelves. These will suggest to children who may have had some experience with airplanes the idea of building an airport terminal, runway, tower, or hangar where they could be used.

3. Pictures of terminals, airplanes being loaded and boarded, or airplanes flying may also encourage an interest in air transportation in the block centre.
4. Provide cylindrical and cone-shaped blocks for children who wish to build space stations and rocket ships. Display authentic space pictures on walls in this area.
5. Styrofoam cones, balls, wreaths, and sheets would provide some short-term exploration.
6. When block buildings fall, talk about gravity.

Other dramatic play centres

1. A walking board or plank laid across a wooden box or sturdy cardboard carton could make an airplane. Add a steering wheel or dial panel (see illustration, p. 467). Propellers can be cut out of cardboard and taped to the edge of the plank. A step unit can be pushed up to the plane for passengers to get on or off the plane. A wagon or rolling platform can be used to take passengers' luggage to and from the plane.
2. Set up two rows of chairs with an aisle between. Section off a galley with a three-way play screen or other room divider. Provide TV dinner trays with laminated food cut-outs and paper cups for the flight attendants to serve to the passengers.
3. Set up two short rows of chairs with an aisle between for airport limousine or minibus. Driver can wear a chauffeur's cap. Sky-cap can manage luggage.
4. Boxes and bags of various sizes can be used as airplane cargo. They can be packed and delivered to a mock terminal or stores.
5. Binoculars or telescopes may be made by the teacher for use by the group.
   Materials needed:

   a. Rolls from paper towels, waxed paper, plastic wrap, or aluminum foil are used to make telescopes
   b. Rolls from toilet paper are needed to make binoculars

   Procedure: The various tubes are of different diameters and some of them actually telescope. The teacher should find pairs that fit one inside the other (for example, a wax-paper roll and a paper-towel roll). Let the children paint or decorate them. The teacher would also need to fasten the toilet paper rolls together in pairs for binoculars after they had been painted by the children.
6. Teacher may construct a rocket ship for the children to use indoors.
   Materials needed:

   a. Cardboard cone
   b. Cardboard fins
   c. Spools
   d. Wires, earphones
   e. Large cardboard boxes of different sizes (large enough for a child to get into)
   f. Wooden or metal knobs (handles from cupboard doors), old dials

   Procedure: Using the illustration on the following page as a guide, the teacher cuts a door in the biggest box and a whole in the top of it. The next biggest box is fastened over this, open side down. A cone is made from a large sheet of posterboard and fastened to the top of the second box. Fins are made from a piece of posterboard, cut in two diagonally, and attached to the side of the lower box. Dials, knobs, spools, and wires are attached inside the boxes wherever the teacher wants. The children can paint each section with wide brushes and tempera, or the whole spaceship can be covered with silver paper or painted with gray or aluminum paint. Instead of standing upright, the rocket ship could be horizontal on the floor. A rocket ship can also be made by arranging large packing boxes on the playground and adding a nose cone, fins, and instruments as on the one for indoors.

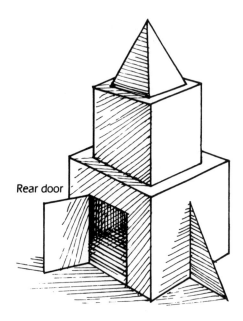

Rear door

7. Teacher may provide a homemade space helmet for children to use.
   Materials needed:

   a. Round ice-cream cartons, plastic bleach or water jugs, and cartons or paper bags large enough to go on a child's head
   b. Discarded garden or vacuum cleaner hose which has been washed
   c. Paper cups, wire, electrical cord, pipecleaners, boxes, leather straps or canvas webbing, and plastic holders from pop cans

   Procedure: Using the illustration as a guide, the teacher cuts the end and a face hole or eye holes from a plastic water jug and smoothes edges, then cuts a hole for the hose. Children fix helmets any way they choose. They may be painted with tempera or coloured with felt pens. A hose may be attached from a hole in the back or front of a shoebox, which is worn on the child's back and secured over his or her shoulders by means of straps.

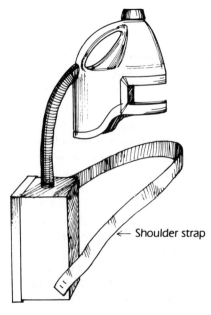

← Shoulder strap

Learning, Language, and Readiness Materials Centre

Commercially made games and materials

(See "Basic Resources," pp. 79, 100, for manufacturers' addresses.)
1. *Puzzles:* A variety of puzzles with transportation themes. Excellent puzzles are made by Galt, Simplex and Ravensburger.
2. *Construction and manipulative toys:* Wooden steering wheels and wheels that match large wooden blocks encourage the construction of a variety of transportation vehicles.
3. *Small toys for imaginative play:* Vinyl models of vehicles for younger children. Metal models of vehicles for older children. Replicas of airports, for example, Fisher Price Jet Port.
4. *Toys for riding:* A variety of toys for riding both indoors and outdoors. Be sure to choose toys that are replicas of vehicles the children are likely to see, not models of television vehicles. Choose vehicles that are sturdy and that do not have sharp edges. Make sure they are easy to steer and that you have a variety of sizes to fit different children.
5. *Costumes:* Hats and coats that represent various employees of the airline industry.

Teacher-made games and materials

NOTE: For a detailed description of "Learning Games," see pp. 50–59.

1. Look and see: Use scale metal or unbreakable plastic replicas of different kinds of airplanes which show detail.
2. Can you remember? Use different kinds of airplane models.
3. Alike, different, and the same: Make two sets of each type of airplane available. Mix the sets together and have children find the ones that match. Put two matching planes and a different one together. Ask children to point to the one that is different.
4. Colour, shape, size, and number: At every opportunity when observing real planes or working with models or pictures, talk about size, colour, shape, and number. Count wheels, pontoons, propellers, jet pods, wings, and tails.

Art Centre

•• 1. Make several different kinds of airplane stencils. Let children spatter-paint airplanes on blue construction paper, choosing colours and models they wish to use to make their airplanes.
  • 2. Children could help make a picture book of airplanes by pasting precut pictures of different kinds of airplanes onto construction paper. The pictures could then be put in a colourful contact photo album with lift up plastic covers (these are available at a reasonable price in variety and drug stores).
••• 3. At the woodworking table set out wheels (discs of wood cut from dowels, bottle caps, and plastic caps) and precut shapes of soft wood that children can nail together to make airplanes. Propellers can be precut from plastic lids or plastic bottles.
  4. Decorate a large paper grocery bag with paints, scraps of tissue paper and crayons. Attach a 1.8 m to 3 m string to one corner of the open end of the bag. When children run with the bag it goes aloft as a kite.
••• 5. Gliders can be made by paper folding (see illustration on the next page). The teacher may make some, showing the children how to make the folds. Once the children have the idea they will design some of their own.

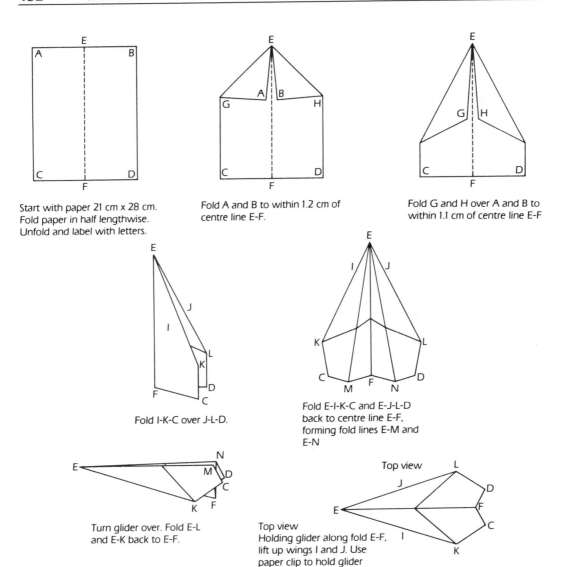

Start with paper 21 cm x 28 cm.
Fold paper in half lengthwise.
Unfold and label with letters.

Fold A and B to within 1.2 cm of
centre line E-F.

Fold G and H over A and B to
within 1.1 cm of centre line E-F

Fold I-K-C over J-L-D.

Fold E-I-K-C and E-J-L-D
back to centre line E-F,
forming fold lines E-M and
E-N

Turn glider over. Fold E-L
and E-K back to E-F.

Top view
Holding glider along fold E-F,
lift up wings I and J. Use
paper clip to hold glider
together (optional).

Top view

Book Centre

•• Assanthiany, Sylvie, and Louise Pelletier. *Grandma's Visit*. Toronto: James Lorimer, 1987.
   (Also available in French as *Grand-Maman*)

• Barton, Byron. *Airport*. New York: Thomas Y. Crowell, 1982.

•• *Bill's Balloon Ride*. Toronto: Methuen, 1986.

• Bruna, Dick. *Miffy Goes Flying*. New York: Price Stern, 1984.

•• Crews, Donald. *Flying*. New York: Greenwillow Press, 1986.

• Florian, D. *Airplane Ride*. New York: Thomas Y. Crowell, 1984.

• Gay, Michael. *The Little Helicopter*. New York: Macmillan, 1986.

••• Gelman, Rita Golden, and Jack Kent. *Why Can't I Fly?* Richmond Hill, Ont: Scholastic-TAB,
   1985.

•• Gramatky, Hardie. *Loopy*. New York: G.P. Putnam's Sons, 1941.

• Khalsa, Dayal Kaur. *Bon Voyage, Baabee*. Montreal: Tundra Books, 1983.

• Lenski, Lois. *The Little Airplane*. New York: Walck, 1938.

•••• Ransome, Arthur. *The Fool of the World and the Flying Ship*. New York: Collins, 1968.

• Rockwell, Anne. *Planes*. Markham, Ont: Fitzhenry & Whiteside, 1986.

••• Spier, Peter. *Bored — Nothing To Do*. Garden City, NY: Doubleday, 1978.

Books about space travel

•••• Bentley, Roy. *Shuttleburn.* New York: Deutsch, 1984.
•••• Branley, F.M. *Journey into a Black Hole.* Markham Ont: Fitzhenry & Whiteside, 1987.
•••• Ciupik, Larry. *Space Machines.* Milwaukee, WI: Raintree, 1979.
•••• French, Fiona. *Future Story.* New York: Bedrick Books.
•••• Marshall, James. *Merry Christmas Space Case.* New York: Dial Press, Books for Young Readers, 1986.
•••• Marzallo, Jean. *Jed's Junior Space Patrol.* New York: Dial Press, 1982.
••• Sadler, M. *Allistair in Outer Space.* Englewood Cliffs, NJ: Prentice Hall, 1984.
••• Sendak, Maurice. *Where the Wild Things Are.* New York: Harper & Row, 1984.
•• Wildsmith, Brian. *Professor Noah's Spaceship.* Toronto: Oxford University Press, 1980.

Planning for Group Time

NOTE: All music, fingerplays, poems, stories, and games listed here may also be used at other times during the session as appropriate. See Core Library, "Basic Resources," p. 95, for publishers and addresses. Record company addresses can be found on p. 99. In parodies, hyphenated words match the music notes of the tune used.

Music

Songs

From *Musical Games for Children of All Ages,* Nelson
"Two Twin Airplanes," p. 8

From *Piggyback Songs,* Warren
"My Kite," p. 22
"I Wish I Were a Windmill," p. 23
"My Bubble Flew Over the Ocean," p. 34

From *The Goat With the Bright Red Socks,* Birkenshaw and Walden
"The Transportation System," p. 30

From *Singing Bee,* Hart
"Twinkle Twinkle Little Star," p. 64
"Hey Diddle Diddle," p. 67
"Sally Go Round," p. 87

I'M A LITTLE AIRPLANE

(tune: "I'm a Little Teapot")
Adaptation by Bonnie Flemming

I'm a lit-tle air-plane; (RAISE ARMS TO SIDE AT SHOULDER HEIGHT)
I can fly, (TURN RIGHT ARM IN FRONT OF YOU FOR PROPELLER)
Here is my throt-tle; (REACH HAND OUT TO INSTRUMENT PANEL)
Give me a try. (PUSH THROTTLE IN)
When I get all revved up (MAKE ENGINE NOISES)
Then I fly (MOVE FORWARD DOWN RUNWAY)
Off the run-way (KEEP MOVING FORWARD)
To the sky! (GO UP ON TIPTOE RUNNING FORWARD)

Rhythms and singing games

From *Move, Sing, Listen, Play*
"Aeroplane Game," p. 136

Records and cassettes

Anne Murray. *There's a Hippo in My Bathtub.* (Capitol Records)
"Stars Are the Windows of Heaven"

Bob McGrath. *If You're Happy and You Know It Sing Along*, Volume I. (Kids Records)
"Mr. Sun"

Fred Penner. *Special Delivery.* (Troubadour Records)
"Stars"

Sharon, Lois, and Bram. *Sing and Play with Balloons.* (Elephant Records)
"Follow the Clouds"

Fingerplays and Poems

From *Read Aloud Rhymes for the Very Young*, Prelutsky and Brown
"A Kite," p. 33
"Wouldn't You?" p. 33
"Wings," p. 39
"Moon Boat," p. 71
"I See the Moon," p. 71
"Moon-Come-Out," p. 71
"The Star," p. 71

From *A New Treasury of Children's Poetry*, Cole
"I Can Fly," p. 132

From *Where the Sidewalk Ends*, Silverstein
"The Flying Festoon," p. 80

From *Mischief City*, Wynne-Jones
"Invasion From the Planet Pizza," p. 32

From *Don't Eat Spiders*, Heidbreder
"Rockets," p. 44
"Space," p. 45
"Creature from Outer Space," p. 47

Stories

(To read, read–tell, or tell. See Book Centre for complete list.)
Assanthiany and Peletier's *Grandma's Visit* is an excellent story for introducing the subject of air travel.

Games

(See "Learning Games," pp. 50–59, and teacher-made games in this chapter for directions.)
1. Look and see
2. Can you remember?
3. Alike, different, and the same

Routine Times

1. At snack or meal times have children arrange chairs in two double rows. Use trays or paper plates shaped like trays. Have flight attendants put snacks or food on the trays and serve to passengers on the plane. Use finger foods for this snack or meal. Dried fruits can be used instead of fruit juices, and liquids should be omitted with younger children. If liquids are served fill glasses only half full. Try water first.
2. When walking or riding to and from the centre listen for airplanes.
3. At rest time suggest that the children be very quiet and listen for an airplane.

Large Muscle Activities

1. Use a packing box or sturdy carton with a walking board across it for an airplane. Add a steering wheel or dial panel (see illustration, p. 467). A set of stairs pushed up to the packing box can be used for passengers to load. A wagon or wheeled platform can be used for a baggage cart.

   ★ CAUTION: The walking board is placed to represent wings. It is not to be used for walking in this instance.

2. Outdoors is the perfect place for action songs (see Music).
3. Provide the children with a paper pinwheel (see illustration below). Let them run, pretending the pinwheels are propellers and they are the airplanes.

Pinwheel pattern

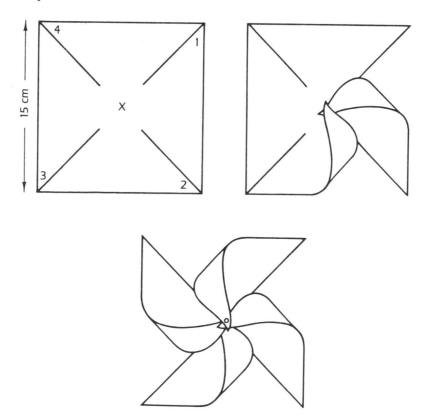

Pinwheel: From each corner, cut three inches toward the centre. Place each A over the X and hold with thumb. When all are in place; fasten pinwheel to a dowel 15 cm to 25 cm long with a large-headed pin. Very young children should not be sent home with pins or large tacks.

4. Paper gliders are fun to hold and run with or fly (see pattern, p. 452).
5. Paper helicopters are fun to drop from the top of the jungle gym, a ladder climber, or a packing box (see illustration below).

Helicopter pattern

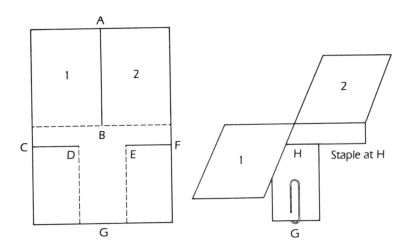

Helicopter: Cut a 21 cm x 28 cm piece of construction paper into quarters. Each quarter sheet will make one helicopter. Following illustration, fold each in half and cut from A to B. Cut C-D and F-E. Fold F to D and C to E. Paper-clip together at G, staple at H. Fold down wings 1 and 2. Hold high, spin, and let go.

Extended Experiences

1. Visit an airport to see airplanes take off and land. For very young children perhaps a first visit to a small private airfield might be best. Jet engines are very noisy and may frighten young children. At a smaller field there would perhaps be a greater opportunity to take a closer look at the airplanes and visit a hangar. Perhaps permission could be obtained for the children to board one of the planes to see what one looks like inside. Older children who have more experience with airplanes may be able to comprehend the various parts that make up a large air terminal.
2. Invite a pilot and/or flight attendant to come to the centre and talk briefly about his/her job. If possible ask that she/he wear the job uniform and bring the seat belt and oxygen mask that is used in the safety demonstration and the earphones for the inflight movie.
3. Show slides of various airplanes and different buildings found at your local airport or one in a nearby larger community. Contact a local flying school or the manager or public relations director of a nearby airport or airline company for slides or names of persons who may have such collections.

Teacher Resources

Pictures and Displays

▷ Display travel posters, airline tickets, baggage claim checks, airline schedules, and models of several kinds of passenger planes.
▷ Display airplanes so they will be out of reach of children, using airplane models built by a hobby enthusiast.

▷ Use sturdy model airplanes as a table centrepiece to encourage discussion about airplanes while children are eating.
▷ Put up pictures from your file of different kinds of airplanes, an airport, a pilot, flight attendants, a control tower, and a windsock.

Books and Periodicals

Chambers, Aidan. *Aidan Chambers' Book of Flyers and Flying.* 1976.
Mondey, David. *Aircraft.* New York: Octopus Books, 1973.
Shepherd, W. *How Airplanes Fly.* 1971.
Tryckare, Tre. *The Lore of Flight.* Gothenberg, Sweden: Cagner & Co., 1970.

Films and Videos

Check with your local library for the list of current materials available from the National Film Board and the CBC

Community Resources and Organizations

▷ Transportation companies
▷ Societies interested in transportation (for example, a model train club, a flying club, a steam train "buffs" club, a car racing club, a hang gliding club, a shipping and ship travel club)
▷ A travel agent
▷ An airlines representative
▷ Hobby centres: For catalogues of model airplanes that could be used to make required materials. Obtain the names of persons who have collections of model airplanes and who may be willing to lend them for display. These people may also have collections of slides that could be borrowed
▷ Flying school: Contact the director about an instructor pilot coming to the centre to talk to the children or about a visit to the flying school for a closeup view of an airplane, with permission to board one
▷ Airline companies: Contact public relations directors for literature
▷ Airport: Contact the manager of your local airport to arrange a visit

Government Agencies

Provincial, territorial, and federal ministries of transportation and/or communication

23 Ground and Road Transportation

★★★★★★★★★★★★★★★★★★★★★★

Basic Understandings

(concepts children can grasp from this subject)

NOTE: The word "car" in the following statements is used to represent all road vehicles. If your group interest at the moment is "trucks" then use only that term in the basic statement instead of car. When car is used it would then refer only to automobiles.

▷ Cars (and trucks, buses, campers) are machines that we drive on roads (or the ground) to get people or things from one place to another.

▷ The person who steers a car is known as the driver and those who ride with him/her are known as passengers.

▷ Cars are made in different shapes, sizes, and colours.

▷ Cars have motors which are run by gasoline, diesel fuel, and batteries.

▷ Many families own a car which they use to go many places, such as to drive to and from work, school, shopping centres, the doctor, the laundry or dry cleaners, to visit friends or relatives, or to take trips to see interesting things.

▷ Cars are usually parked in garages or carports; buses and trucks are parked in larger garages.

▷ Cars get gasoline, oil, water, and air at a service station or self-serve pump. Trucks get diesel fuel or gas at a truck stop.

▷ Cars are repaired in garages, body shops, and some service stations.

▷ Cars can be washed in an automatic car wash.

▷ Cars have safety belts and door locks to help keep us safely inside.

▷ The driver must pay attention to his/her driving and the passengers must be considerate (helpful) by sitting and talking quietly.

▷ A driver has to take special tests to get a driver's licence.

▷ A driver must obey (follow) certain traffic rules or else she/he may get a ticket from a police officer and have to pay a fine (money) or have his/her driver's licence taken away.

▷ Road signs, traffic lights, and police officers help drivers drive safely.

▷ When we travel by car we can eat

    a. By taking a bag lunch and eating it in the car as we ride.
    b. By taking a picnic lunch and stopping at a roadside park.
    c. By stopping at a restaurant (diner, café) and buying a meal (food).

▷ When we travel by car we can sleep

    a. At a roadside rest or campground and sleep in the car, a camper, a house trailer, or pitch a tent.

    b. By stopping and getting a room in a hotel or a motel.

▷ If a car is damaged in an accident it is towed to the garage by a tow truck.

▷ There are different kinds of cars—sedan, convertible, station wagon, sports car, dragster, jeep, racing car, and van.

▷ Some cars are built and equipped to help do special jobs:

    a. Police cars have sirens and two-way radios. They are driven by police officers.

    b. Fire engines are red and carry ladders, hoses, and firefighters to fires.

    c. Ambulances are usually white and have sirens. They are equipped with first-aid equipment and stretchers. They carry people who are sick or hurt to the hospital.

    d. Taxis have meters and two-way radios. People can pay the driver to take them where they wish to go.

▷ Trucks are specially built to carry things, animals, or people, for example, garbage, building supplies, fire equipment, furniture, concrete, milk, mail, livestock, and gasoline.

▷ There are different kinds of buses—school, city, and transcontinental.

▷ Many cars can tow things—trailers, campers, boats, horse van, or other cars.

▷ A ferry carries cars and people across a river.

▷ Tunnels are dug under rivers and through mountains for cars.

▷ Bridges are built so cars can get across rivers and deep valleys.

▷ Sometimes drivers have to pay a toll (money) to cross some bridges or drive through some tunnels.

▷ Other names for a road are street, avenue, boulevard, drive, court, crescent, lane, freeway, thruway, expressway, and highway.

▷ There are two-wheeled vehicles, such as bicycles, scooters, and motorcycles.

▷ Some drivers like to enter car races, such as drag racing, the Molson 500, stock car racing, or the grand prix races in Montreal.

▷ In parts of the country we also use sleighs and snowmobiles as ways of getting people and things from one place to another.

▷ In the north snowmobiles and sleighs run on the snow using skis instead of wheels. Sleighs can be pulled by dogs and horses.

▷ Many people also travel around on bicycles. Some special packages and letters are delivered by people riding on bicycles (courier services).

▷ Tractors, combines, and other farm vehicles are used to plant and harvest crops on farms and ranches.

▷ Some transportation machines run on rails, for example, railway trains, subway trains, streetcars, and monorail trains.

▷ Most trains and streetcars run on two rails called tracks; monorail cars run on one rail.

▷ You may find these rails or tracks in many places:

    a. Railway tracks are laid on top of the ground.

    b. Streetcar tracks are set into city roads.

    c. A monorail is an elevated train which travels on a single rail above or below the vehicle.

▷ Trains take people or things from one location to another.

▷ Streetcars are like city buses; they take people from one part of the city to another part. However, they can move only where tracks are laid.

▷ There are different kinds of trains:

    a. Passenger trains carry people from one location to another.

    b. Commuter trains carry people into and out of cities.

c. Subway trains carry people in tunnels under the ground from one part of the city to another.

d. Freight trains carry things from one location to another. Some things they carry are animals, cars, food, furniture, lumber, and oil.

e. Work trains (maintenance-of-way trains) carry workers and machines to help repair track and trains.

▷ The locomotive or diesel engine pulls the train. Two or more diesel units are needed if the train is very long.

▷ There are different kinds of cars on a passenger train—coach, sleeping car, dining car, vistadome car, lounge or club car, baggage car, and observation car.

▷ There are many different kinds of cars on a freight train—tank car, box car, cattle car, gondola car, hopper car, autoveyor, refrigerator car, and caboose.

▷ Many people work for railway companies—ticket agents, engineers, brakemen, conductors, porters, cooks, waiters, and dispatchers.

▷ The trains stop at various stations so that passengers can get on and off and freight can be loaded and unloaded.

▷ A railway station or terminal is a large building where passengers can buy tickets to ride on the train. Most stations have a snack bar or restaurant, magazine stands, waiting room or lounge, and toilet facilities.

▷ Many of the things you do at home may be done on a train:

a. Sit, talk, read, look out the window, walk, or eat snacks.
b. Eat a meal in the dining car.
c. Sleep in a pullman car in bunk-type beds called "berths" or in a small compartment.
d. Wash your hands and go to a toilet in the lavatory.
e. You may take your pets but they must ride in the baggage car.

▷ There are special signals for drivers on roads to watch for that tell them a train is coming: two flashing red lights, a bell, or sometimes crossing gates are dropped across the road.

▷ The train blows its whistle when it is ready to start, is going to cross a road, or is coming into a station.

Additional Facts the Teacher Should Know

1. Many books, records, songs, fingerplays, and poems still reflect the older titles for the community helpers now called letter carrier, firefighter, and police officer. No need to discard them; simply substitute the correct names as you use the material with the children. You may wish to make edited notes directly in your book. (See the chapter "Families at Work" for complete helper list.)

2. This chapter deals with transportation vehicles which use roads (or the ground) as the surface on which they travel. There are many different kinds of cars, trucks, and buses being designed and manufactured today. They come in varying sizes, shapes, and colours.

3. Two-wheeled vehicles which can be driven on roads are powered both by pedalling and by fuel motor. All bicycles, except those with training wheels, can be ridden in the streets and bikers must follow the same rules as those for automobile drivers. Most communities have a licence requirement for two-wheeled vehicles. In addition, there is a national law requiring all motorcyclists to wear helmets while riding. Most bicycles are referred to as 50 cm, 60 cm, 66 cm, or 71 cm, referring to the diameter of the wheels. Some bikes have hand-powered brakes and special gear mechanisms which allow the driver to pedal at various speeds with less effort. If two-wheeled vehicles are driven at night they must have headlights and rear reflectors.

There are many different kinds of cars

Familiarize yourself with them to identify them correctly for the children.

Cars carry one to six people and may have two or four doors. Most cars have a trunk in the back where a spare tire is stored under the floor and suitcases or other luggage can be stored. Most cars have heaters, radios, clocks, and seat belts. Some seats recline or have head rests.

Convertibles are similar to sedans, or coupes but have roofs which folds back, retract, or can be removed.

Station wagons are similar to sedans, but are longer, with larger floor areas instead of trunks for carrying things. Usually there are luggage racks on the roof.

Racing cars are small one-seat cars which are designed to go very fast for a long period of time.

4-Wheel-drive vehicles have better traction; therefore they are primarily used for driving over open country, rough roads, and on snowy roads.

Vans or *mini-buses* are larger than sedans but smaller than buses. They may have three or four rows of seats and carry up to twelve people. Vans can travel at a maximum speed of 80 to 97 km per hour.

Taxis are sedans with time meters and two-way radios or computers which are used for transporting people for a set fee based on actual kilometres and time spent in the cab.

Ambulances are specially designed to transport sick or injured persons. Stretchers, cots, or rolling tables can be put into the back section. They have emergency medical equipment that varies, depending on the training of the attendant who rides with the patient. A siren and flashing red light warn of their coming.

Limousines are long and comfortable sedans used for transporting up to nine people to and from rail and air terminals. Some businesses provide free limousine service for their customers.

Police cars are sedans with sirens, flashing lights, and two-way radios.

There are many different kinds of trucks

Trucks are used for the transportation of goods and people. The part of the truck that the driver sits in is known as the cab. The cab and the motor are usually mounted over the front wheels of the truck. Smaller trucks are molded onto a single frame like an automobile but most larger trucks are in two or more sections. The part that pulls is called the "tractor" and the section that is being hauled is called the "trailer." A flat bed trailer is a platform on wheels. Containerized freight can be lifted onto it using a crane, while some machines, like tractors and other farm equipment, can be driven up on ramps. Cylindrical or oval-shaped trailers are called tank trailers and rectangular, enclosed trailers are vans. Most trucks are powered by gasoline, propane or diesel fuel. Those burning diesel fuel can be recognized by the vent pipe behind the cab.

Pickup trucks are small trucks with open beds and short sides and are used for carrying small equipment, tools, and other supplies.

Dump trucks are larger than pickups and have higher sides. They are built with hydraulic lifts so the beds can be tilted to allow the contents to be slid out through the hinged tail gates or special openings. They are used to haul dirt, coal, and gravel.

Tank trucks carry liquids, such as milk, chemicals, oil, or fuel.

Moving vans come in various sizes and are large, enclosed rectangular trailers used for moving household goods or office equipment.

Garbage trucks are used to haul garbage to the city dump.

Cement mixers have special round-shaped mixers mounted on the trailers that simultaneously transport and mix sand, gravel, and concrete.

Freight trailers have rectangular vans that are used for carrying food, clothes, equipment, tools, and manufactured goods.

Automobile carriers are designed to carry cars. The cars are driven on and off the trailers on tracks called "skids."

Livestock trucks are rectangular-shaped trailers with air spaces between the slats for transporting cattle, horses, pigs, chickens, and other animals.

Fire trucks carry ladders, hoses, firefighters, and equipment to fight fires.

Canteen trucks are designed like small kitchens and transport prepared foods to job sites for workers.

Delivery trucks are small, enclosed trucks used to deliver commercial products to homes: such trucks are operated by bakeries, florists, diaper services, department stores, and courier services.

Mail trucks are used by Canada Post to transport mail and packages.

Campers are small trailers designed with windows, or with folding tents for camping in parks.

There are many different kinds of buses

School or church buses (usually painted yellow) are rectangular-shaped vehicles that have centre aisles with eighteen to twenty seats, arranged in rows of two on each side. They are used to transport people to and from school or churches or for special outings.

City buses are vehicles that carry people from one part of the city to another. Such buses stop at special places called "bus stops."

Transcontinental buses are sometimes called "scenic cruisers." These buses are air conditioned and frequently have two levels of seats and domed windows for viewing scenery as they travel across the country.

There are many different kinds of trains

1. Diesel or steam engines are called "locomotives." Diesel engines have almost entirely replaced steam engines. Therefore the coal-shoveling job has become obsolete and the diesel engineer is now assisted by a front braker who helps to check the road signals and other safety controls.

2. There are different kinds of trains and different kinds of cars used in making them. It is not appropriate to teach detailed definitions. If children are interested in the type of cars they see in trains, label by their purpose.

3. There are many different jobs involved in operating a train. Again, detail is not really necessary for young children unless they display a specific curiosity. Describe the duties carried by the people in whom they show an interest.

4. Each railway has its own symbol, logo, or herald; for example, VIA Rail has a yellow and blue stripe for its logo.

5. Canadian history is closely tied to the history of railways in our country. Until recently we have had two major rail companies and a few small local rail services. The two companies, Canadian National and Canadian Pacific, provided passenger and freight services across the country. Recently all passenger services were taken over by VIA Rail. The freight industry is flourishing, but there are some problems with the passenger service. Many small towns have lost their passenger services and much of the equipment used by VIA Rail is very old. In contrast we have some very efficient and high speed passenger trains in the very busy Windsor to Montreal corridor. Some large cities also have commuter train services that are comfortable and efficient. Rail service is still considered very important in Canada and it is gradually being improved.

Methods Most Adaptable for Introducing this Subject to Children

1. A child or one of the teachers at the centre relates her or his experience of a trip taken by bus or car.
2. Read a story about cars, trucks, or buses.
3. Put up pictures of cars, trucks, or buses, or make a display of models of all kinds of road transportation vehicles.
4. Visitor: If one of the children's parents drives a taxi, bus, or other vehicle have him or her visit the centre and tell about the job.
5. A child or teacher in your group takes a trip on a train, subway, streetcar, or light rapid transit.
6. There are tracks near your centre and the children show an interest.
7. Read a book about trains.
8. Put up pictures of trains or set out authentic scale models.
9. Have someone who works for the railways visit the centre and talk about his or her job.

Vocabulary

traffic	service station	key	park
light	police officer	drive	parking meter
road sign	firefighter	driver	steer
tow truck	letter carrier	speed	bridge
toll booth	parking lot	ticket	tunnel
attendant	gas	licence	garage
car wash	oil	race	ferry
restaurant	air	haul	taxi
motel, hotel	tow		

kinds of cars, trucks, and buses   parts of cars
names of roads

whistle	subway	berth	switch
freight	locomotive	upper	track
passenger	conductor	lower	tank car
monorail	engineer	coach	flat car
station	streetcar	train	box car
engine	dining car	signal	cattle car
caboose	sleeping car		

Learning Centres

Discovery Centre

1. Set up a display table with toy cars, trucks, trains and buses. Help children understand that each vehicle is specifically designed to do a special job of carrying people or things from one place to another.
2. Show maps of your area, your province, and Canada. Talk about how different maps are used by drivers. Discuss different ways to ride around on the roads in your city, your province, and the country. Talk about how the children got to the centre—by car (kind), taxi, bus, van, truck, subway, or train.
3. If the playground or windows in the centre overlook a busy street which the children can view easily, in safety, talk about the different kinds of vehicles that use the road. If the centre gets special mail or package deliveries, suggest this activity for a time when they are made.
4. Help children discover that every vehicle that drives on the road must have a licence. Trucks that drive in many provinces have several. Start a collection of licence plates from all the provinces and display them so that children can see the similarities and differences. They sometimes have mottos or emblems on them. Talk about the special features of your province's plates.
5. On a table display a driver's licence, licence plate from your province, road maps of your city and province, a model of a car, station wagon, camper, and house trailer, and brochures of parks or well-known landmarks in or near your community. Encourage conversation about how families use their cars for fun and pleasure.
6. Use of brakes: Use several blocks and two boards to make a little hill and a steep hill. Provide cars for the children to roll down the hills. Which car goes faster? Which driver would need to use the brakes the most?
7. Display a VIA Rail train cut-out (contains ten freight cars, a diesel locomotive, and a caboose in colour). One side pictures the exterior of a car and the other side shows the interior of the car. You may wish to mount these on cardboard to help them stand up or insert a double-length unit block beneath to give it additional support. May be used for vocabulary "name it" or "scramble" game.

Discovery centre.
Display various transportation models. Try to use models that are the same scale.

Dramatic Play Centres

Home-living centre

1. Make bus schedules and travel brochures available so a trip by bus or car can be planned. Suitcases and money in purses will increase the amount of travel play.
2. Fill a lunch pail for an auto mechanic, a truck driver, or a bus driver to take to work.
3. A box of toy tools should be available that an auto mechanic might take to work or use to fix the family car. This could be a tricycle if allowed indoors or a ride-on truck or car.
4. Set out hats for the different kinds of helpers who use vehicles.
5. Have several overnight bags available. These may be packed with dress up clothes and doll clothes for taking a trip by train.
6. Put several train schedules on shelves to be used in planning a trip by train.
7. Place play money in purses for use in purchasing tickets.

Block-building centre

1. Unit blocks: Feature road accessories, such as scaled cars, people, and road signs, to encourage building of roads and transportation play. Have cans of small materials, such as buttons, pebbles, and twigs, for children to use as freight.
2. Encourage children with some road-building experience to construct bridges, tunnels, toll booths, garages, or bus stations.
3. Suggest with the aid of pictures and conversation that those with many road-building experiences may wish to make a network of roads, several buildings (restaurants, motels, a bus station, a bus barn, traffic signals, bridges, and tunnels), or a whole city. This kind of activity may last over several days if structures and roads can remain standing from day to day.
4. Occasionally when the children name a structure they have built you may wish to fasten a sign to it: "Martin's Motel" or "Sally's Service Station."
5. Gasoline pumps of the correct scale for use with unit blocks are commercially available or you can make your own with scraps of wood and paint, using plastic clothesline or rope for gas hose.
6. The Road Transportation Flects (Community Playthings) line of toys is excellent.
7. Hollow blocks: Build roads for larger trucks and cars by using blocks and ramps. Encourage the road-builders to make a garage, station, or parking lot. A gasoline pump for use with hollow blocks could be made from wood and garden hose. A less durable pump can be made from the hard cylindrical core around which newsprint is rolled. Two of these cylinders set in a large wooden box or sturdy carton with rope or garden hose attached make very usable gas pumps. Children can help paint them with water base paint. Two tall, corrugated boxes may be weighted by placing rocks in the bottom, painting them, and attaching rope or garden hose to make pumps. These are only sturdy enough for short-term use.
8. Encourage interest in trains by putting up pictures of stations and trains in the block-building centre.
9. Set out an interlocking train set.
10. Miniature traffic signs: 10 signs, 18 cm tall; also traffic signs and symbols, six in each set, 16 cm tall, or models can be made of cardboard.

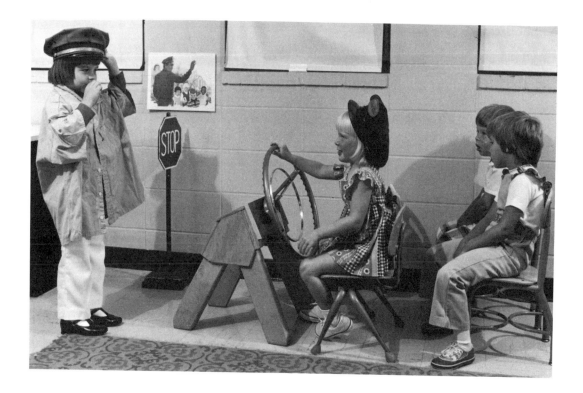

11. To simulate a train station set up a three-way play screen with tables or build a ticket counter with hollow blocks and boards. Use the ride-on type of train or allow the children to build a coach by using two rows of chairs with an aisle between. Provide engineer caps, bandana handkerchiefs to wear around the neck, conductor hats (see pattern, p. 468), paper punches, coloured paper scraps for tickets, and train schedule sheets or folders for this dramatic play centre. A simple lantern (no glass) and a dial panel (see illustration) are other dramatic play accessories children may use. Encourage children to share hats. You may need to get a timer or suggest a defined reasonable time limit for a treasured prop. If not necessary, let children decide and choose.

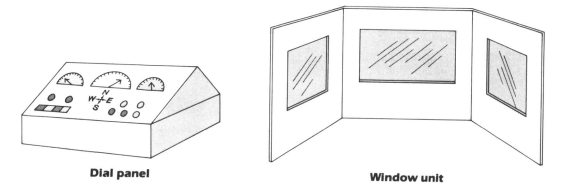

Dial panel   **Window unit**

Cut out "windows" or paste or paint pictures of appropriate scenery for the driver. Place around dial panel or a steering wheel unit. (Contributed by Janice Bailey.)

Other dramatic play centres

1. A bus can be made by lining up two rows of chairs with an aisle between. A commercial or hand-made steering wheel or dial panel (see p. 467) may be added for the driver to use.
2. A car or taxi can be made by putting two rows of three chairs one behind the other. The steering wheel or dial panel should be placed in front of the driver (left front seat). Add traffic signs to this dramatic play.
3. Encourage playing firefighters by providing hats (see pattern, below), ladders, and discarded garden hoses. A bicycle handle grip makes a good nozzle for the hose. A wagon or long, sturdy cardboard box would make a good fire engine. If you have a ladder box or climbing house children could pretend that it is the building that is on fire (the cleated ladders can safely be rested on the runs for climbing).
4. Obtain discarded hats and uniform shirts from police officers, bus, or letter carriers. Less durable hats can be made of construction paper. (See patterns below.)

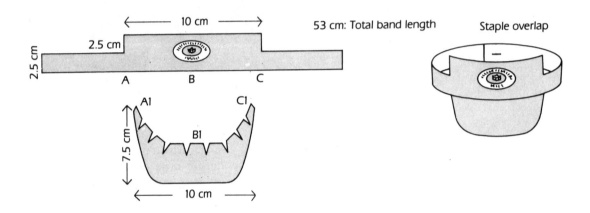

Letter carrier or conductor's hat

Using blue construction paper, cut out a rectangle 53 cm long and 5 cm deep. As shown in diagram, top left, cut away 21.5 x 2.5 cm at each side to leave peak 10 cm x 5 cm at centre of hat. Notch visor as indicated in diagram, bottom left. Staple ends of headband together. Glue visor to band.

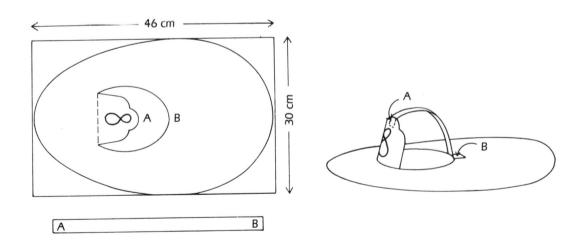

Firefighter's hat

Cut hat shape out of a 30 x 46 cm piece of red construction paper according to illustration. Cut out the unshaded area for child's head. Cut strip A-B to define the crown of the hat. Staple A to the back of the flip-up (marked with the number 8) and B to the middle of the back opening. (See arrows.)

5. In the winter sleighs and toy snowmobiles can provide fun in the snow. Children can volunteer to pull sleighs around the playground.

   NOTE: See Large Muscle Activities for additional ideas.

Learning, Language, and Readiness Materials Centre

Commercially made games and materials

(See "Basic Resources," pp. 79, 100, for manufacturers' addresses.)
1. *Puzzles:* A variety of puzzles with transportation themes. Excellent puzzles are made by Galt, Simplex and Ravensburger.
2. *Construction and manipulative toys:* Wooden steering wheels and wheels that match large wooden blocks encourage the construction of a variety of transportation vehicles.
3. *Small toys for imaginative play:* Vinyl models of various vehicles for younger children. Metal models of various vehicles for older children.
4. *Toys for riding:* A variety of toys for riding both indoors and outdoors. Be sure to choose toys that are replicas of vehicles the children are likely to see, not models of television vehicles. Choose vehicles that are sturdy and that do not have sharp edges. Make sure they are easy to steer and that you have a variety of sizes to fit different children.
5. *Costumes:* Hats and coats that represent various employees of the trucking, mail, bus, railway and transportation industries.

Teacher-made games and materials

NOTE: For a detailed description of "Learning Games," see pp. 50–59.

1. Look and see: Use toy cars, trucks, taxis, buses, and campers.
2. Reach and feel: Use small, sturdy models of a station wagon, tank truck, pick-up truck, and cars.
3. Can you remember? Use car, taxi, and pictures models of various drivers, such as police officer, cab driver, bus driver, and letter carrier.
4. How many?

   a. How many ways can you get to school using machines that drive on the roads?
   b. How many wheels does a bicycle have? A car? A bus? Supply models of these vehicles so children can count rationally.
   c. How many ways can a car get across a river? (bridge, tunnel, ferry)

5. Who am I? Describe drivers of various vehicles, such as: "I drive a truck that carries oil to gas stations, who am I?"
6. Match-them: Make card sets of two each of different kinds of cars, trucks, and buses and two each of the drivers, such as taxi drivers, bus drivers, safety officers, and trash haulers. Mix the pairs up and have children find the two pairs that match.
7. Grouping and sorting by association: Use the cards made in no. 6 and group them as cars, trucks, or drivers. Or have children match a driver with the kind of vehicles she/he drives. Suit the number of pairs offered to the ability of the child or group.
8. Alike, different, and the same: Use the sets of cards made in no. 6.
9. Colour, shape, size, and number: At every opportunity when observing real road transportation vehicles or when using scale models talk about colour, shape, size, and number, for example, "See the big truck." "What colour is the car?" "The cylindrical tank truck carries gas."

Art Centre

•• 1. Pasting: Provide the children with coloured construction paper and precut rectangles, squares, and circles of various sizes and let the children make a design with them. Perhaps some will discover they can make trucks or wagons.

••• 2. At the woodworking bench set out wheels with various-sized discs of wood cut from dowels, bottle caps, or plastic lids and precut shapes of soft wood that children might use to make a transportation machine.

> ★ CAUTION: Do not direct children as to what they should make, but instead offer assistance as needed to help them make what they have in mind. Shapes cut from coloured plastic soap bottles (heat in hot water before cutting with scissors or use an Exacto knife) make colourful bumpers and stripes that are easily punctured by nails.

•• 3. Provide the children with circles and rectangles of various colours and sizes to paste on construction paper. Some may discover these shapes can be put together to resemble a railroad car, streetcar, or subway train.

••• 4. Shoebox train: A usable train with short-term durability can be made from combining two parts of several shoeboxes in various ways, painting them, and tying them together with nylon twine, plastic clothesline, or thin rope.

•• 5. Children could help make a picture book of trains. Those with cutting ability may cut the pictures out of magazines or model catalogues. Others can choose precut pictures they wish to paste onto construction paper and put in a colourful plastic three-ring notebook or contact photo album.

Book Centre

- • Barton, Byron. *Trains*. New York: Thomas Y. Crowell, 1986.
- • _____ . *Trucks*. New York: Thomas Y. Crowell, 1986.
- • Bruna, Dick. *Miffy's Bicycle*. New York: Price Stern, 1984.
- • Burningham, John. *Mr. Grumpy's Motorcar*. London: Cape, 1973.
- ••• Crews, Donald. *Freight Train*. New York: Greenwillow Press, 1978.
- ••• Ehrlich, Amy. *The Everyday Train*. New York: Dial Press, 1977.
- •• Gantschev, Ivan. *The Christmas Train*. Boston: Little, Brown.
- • Gramatky, Hardie. *Hercules*. New York: G.P. Putnam's Sons, 1940.
- • _____ . *Little Toot*. New York: G.P. Putnam's Sons, 1939.
- • _____ . *Sparky*. New York: G.P. Putnam's Sons, 1952.
- ••• Greene, Graham. *The Little Train*. Markham, Ont: Puffin, 1977.
- ••• Harvey. *Gilbert and the Bicycle*. Richmond Hill, Ont: Hippo Paperbacks, Scholastic Books, 1987.
- • Hoban, Tana. *Dig, Drill, Dump, Fill*. New York: Greenwillow Press, 1975.
- •••• Italiano, Carlo. *Sleighs: The Gentle Transportation*. Montreal: Tundra Books, 1974. (Read–Tell)
- •• Kesselman, Wendy. *There's A Train Going By My Window*. Garden City, NY: Doubleday, 1982.
- ••• Kovalski, Maryann. *The Wheels on the Bus*. Toronto: Kids Can Press, 1987.
- • Lenski, Lois. *The Little Auto*. New York: Walck, 1934.
- • Magee, Doug. *Trucks You Can Count On*. New York: Dodd Mead, 1985.
- ••• Morgan, Allen. *Mathew and the Midnight Tow Truck*. Willowdale, Ont: Annick Press, 1984.
- ••• Munsch, Robert. *Jonathan Cleaned Up, Then He Heard a Sound*. Willowdale, Ont: Annick Press, 1981. (subway trains)

- • • O'Young, et al. *Mike and the Bike.* Toronto: James Lorimer, 1986.
- • • Parkin, Rex. *The Red Carpet.* New York: Macmillan, 1967.
- • • • Peet, Bill. *Jennifer and Josephine.* Boston: Houghton Mifflin, 1967.
- • • • Pierce, J. *The Freight Train Book.* Minneapolis, MN: Carolrhoda Books, 1980.
- • • Price, Mathew. *The Working Wheels Series: (Tractors, Special Engines, Diggers, Trucks).* Toronto: Kids Can Press, 1986.
- • Retan, Walter. *The Big Book of Real Trucks.* New York: Grosset & Dunlap, 1986.
- • • Rey, H.A. *Curious Rides a Bike.* New York: Sandpiper, 1973.
- • Rockwell, Anne. *Bikes.* New York: E.P. Dutton, 1986.
- • —————. *Fire Engines.* New York: E.P. Dutton, 1986.
- • —————. *Things That Go.* New York: E.P. Dutton, 1986.
- • • Ross, Diana. *The Little Red Engine and the Rocket.* Albuquerque, NM: Transatlantic Arts, 1978.
- • • —————. *The Little Red Engine Goes to Town.* Albuquerque, NM: Transatlantic Art, 1978.
- • • —————. *The Story of the Little Red Engine.* Albuquerque, NM: Transatlantic Art, 1978.
- • • • Sattler, Helen, R. *Train Whistles.* New York: Lothrop, Lee & Shepard, 1985.
- • • Scarry, Richard. *Cars and Trucks and Things That Go.* New York: Western Publishing, 1974.
- • —————. *The Great Big Car and Truck Book.* New York: Western Publishing, 1951.
- • Siebert, Diane. *Truck Song.* New York: Thomas Y. Crowell, 1984.
- • Slater, Teddy. *The Big Book of Real Fire Trucks and Fire Fighting.* New York: Grosset & Dunlop, 1986.
- • • Stevenson, James. *Are We Almost There!* New York: Greenwillow Press, 1985.
- • *The Train.* Toronto: James Lorimer, 1984.

> **NOTE:** Look in the library for books by Carla Greene about people who want to be drivers of different kinds of cars and trucks.

Planning for Group Time

> **NOTE:** All music, fingerplays, poems, stories, and games listed here may be used at other times during the session as appropriate. See Core Library, "Basic Resources," p. 95, for publishers and addresses. Record company addresses can be found on p. 99. In parodies, hyphenated words match the music notes of the tune used.

Music

Songs

From *The Goat with the Bright Red Socks*, Birkenshaw and Walden
"How Do I Get from Here to There?" p. 6
"Transportation System," p. 30

From *Sally Go Round the Sun*, Fowke
"Going to Chicago," p. 26
"Going to Boston," p. 39

From *Singing Bee*, Hart
"The Bus Song," p. 130

WATCHING TRAFFIC (a parody)

(tune: "Frère Jacques")
Adaptation by Bonnie Flemming (verse 1: Romona Ware)

Watch the cars go, watch the cars go,
Whiz-zing, by, whiz-zing by.
Beep, beep, beep, beep, beep, beep,
Beep, beep, beep, beep, beep, beep,
That's like mine! That's like mine!

Watch the bus go (REPEAT)
Roll-ing by (REPEAT)
Stop for all the peo-ple (REPEAT)
Get on board! (REPEAT)

See the trucks go, see the trucks go
Down the street, down the street.
Gas and oil and milk trucks,
Mail and trash and dump trucks,
On their way, on their way.

THE FIRE FIGHTER (a parody)

(tune: "The More We Get Together")
Adaptation by Bonnie Flemming

Oh, hear the warn-ing si-ren
The si-ren, the si-ren
Oh, hear the warn-ing siren;
Get out of the way!

Oh, see the big red pump-er
The pump-er, the pump-er
Oh, see the big red pump-er
Go off to the fire!

Oh, see the brave fire fighters
Fire fight-ers, fire fight-ers
Oh, see the brave fire fighters
Put out the big fire!

Rhythms and singing games

A very fast chromatic scale (every black and white note) can be played on the piano and children may pretend to be firetrucks racing to the scene of a fire. To simulate a fire alarm, see p. 42.

The rapid repetition of two notes on the piano (C, D, C, D, C, D) simulates the sound of a car motor. This may be played while the children pretend to drive their cars around the room. Cars can run out of gas as the music slows down or get a flat tire when the music stops altogether.

Sand blocks rubbed together can be used with songs or records to accent the rhythm of train wheels.

Trains: Talk about how the children might become a train (each being a car), such as putting their hands on the shoulders of the person in front of them. Let children suggest ways.

Use music about a train on a record or the piano. Play "Goin' Down the Track," p. 480.

NOTE: It is better to let the children imaginatively imitate a train than make rhythm time a structured activity.

A wooden whistle would be another effective sound to accompany either of the other activities. (Needs to be washed between uses if used by more than one person.)

Records and cassettes

Bob Homme. *The Giant Concert of Concerts by the Friendly Giant.* (A & M Records)
"Railroad Concert"

Bob McGrath. *It You're Happy and You Know It Sing Along,* Volume I. (Kids Records)
"She'll Be Comin' Round the Mountain"
"The Wheels on the Bus, a Little Wheel a Turnin'"

Fred Penner. *Special Delivery.* (Troubadour Records)
"Car, Car Song"
"En Roulant"

Raffi. *Baby Beluga.* (Troubadour Records)
"Morningtown Ride"

_____ . *The Corner Grocery Store.* (Troubadour Records)
"Swing Low Sweet Chariot"

Sharon, Lois, and Bram. *Elephant Road.* (Elephant Records)
"Chugga Chugga"
"The Wheels on the Bus"

_____ . *Smorgasbord.* (Elephant Records)
"Rain Is a Comin'"

Fingerplays and Poems

From *Let's Do Fingerplays*, Grayson
"The Train," p. 22
"The Big Train," p. 22
"Choo Choo Train," p. 23
"The Windshield Wipers," p. 24
"Auto, Auto," p. 24
"Driving Down the Street," p. 25
"The Bus," p. 26
"The Steam Shovel," p. 26

From *Where the Sidewalk Ends*, Silverstein
"Bang Clang," p. 120
"Traffic Light," p. 121
"The Little Blue Engine," p. 158

From *A New Treasury of Children's Poetry*, Cole
"Songs of the Train," p. 34
"Steam Shovel," p. 187

From *The New Wind Has Wings*, Downie
"Windshield Wipers," p. 78

From *Read Aloud Rhymes for the Very Young*, Prelutsky and Brown
"The Modern Dragon," p. 35

From *Round and Round the Garden*, Williams and Beck
"Piggy on the Railway," p. 12

From *Sally Go Round the Sun*, Fowke
"Engine Engine Number 9," p. 110

THE ENGINEER

I ride in the engine (POINT TO SELF)
The whistle I blow (PULL CORD)
I do all the things
That will make the train go. (PULL THROTTLE; TURN DIALS)

Whoo! Whoo! Goes the whistle (PUT HANDS TO MOUTH)
Clickety-clack go the wheels (ROLL ARMS IN WHEEL MOTION)
I'm chief engineer (PAT CHEST)
'Til I'm called for my meals! (PRETEND TO EAT)

FREIGHT TRAIN

by Bonnie Flemming

As the big locomotive moves slowly down the track
I wonder where it goes to and when it's coming back.

The engine needs a braker, it needs an engineer
It pulls so many cars of freight that come from far and near.

See the big red box car and there is an orange one too
Now see an autoveyor with cars of green and blue.

Next there are two long flat cars with tractors for the farm
You see, the wind and weather will do them little harm.

Refrigerator, tank, and flat cars go rolling down the track
All these cars have wheels of steel that go clickety-clickety-clack.

Look now at the very end a red caboose I see
And there is the friendly braker waving back at me.

NOTE: Use model railroad cars or pictures to illustrate the poem. If pictures are found they
could be mounted on coloured construction paper and put in a three-ring notebook
to make a picture story.

WINDSHIELD WIPER

I'm a windshield wiper (BEND ARM AT ELBOW WITH FINGERS POINTING UP)
This is how I go (MOVE ARM TO LEFT AND RIGHT, PIVOTING AT ELBOW)
Back and forth, back and forth (CONTINUE BACK AND FORTH MOTION)
In the rain and snow (CONTINUE BACK AND FORTH MOTION)

Stories

(To read, read–tell, or tell. See Book Centre for complete list.)
The choice of stories in this area is simple as there are so many good stories. It is fun to
choose a story that can be enhanced by the addition of sound effects that the children can
imitate, for example Sattler's *Train Whistles* or Burningham's *Mr. Grumpy's Motorcar.*

Games

(See "Learning Games," pp. 50–59, and teacher-made games in this chapter for directions.)
  1. Look and see
  2. Can you remember?
  3. Who am I?
  4. Alike, different, and the same
  5. Grouping and sorting by association
  6. Reach and feel

Routine Times

  1. Use toy cars, trucks, and buses with scale-model people, animals, and road signs as a
     centrepiece at meal time to encourage conversation about road transportation.
  2. During snack or meal time talk about which truck or car brought the food.
  3. At pickup time have children use ride-on trucks, wagons, or castored platforms to carry
     toys back to shelves.
  4. While walking or riding to and from the centre look for cars, trucks, and buses. Talk
     about how to cross a street safely when walking.

5. When riding to and from the centre talk about safety in a car or bus:

    a. Always use seat belts.
    b. Always lock the doors and do not allow children to learn against them.
    c. Talk about being considerate of and not disturbing the driver.
    d. En route talk about traffic signals and rules as you see them on the street.

6. At rest time pretend you have been travelling for a long time and have decided to stop at a motel or hotel for the night.

Large Muscle Activities

1. Encourage use of trikes, wagons, and ride-on cars and trucks as transportation machines. Provide short ropes or commercially available plastic-link chains so that a trike can tow a wagon. Supervize very carefully.
2. Make or buy some traffic signals and road signs. Set up certain traffic patterns. Draw lines on the sidewalk with chalk or use a length of rope for a highway divider. Have a police officer who checks on drivers and issues tickets to those who break rules. Provide the police officer with a hat, whistle, and keys for a jail, if you have one. A driver may need to lose his/her driver's licence for a time.

   ★ **CAUTION:**   Whistles should be washed if shared.

3. Set up a garage or service station next to the pretend highway where drivers can get gas, oil, water, and air. Provide gasoline pumps (see dramatic play), oil can, water and funnel, bicycle tire pump, tool box with rubber or plastic tools (commercially available) for a mechanic, and a pail (can be empty) and rag or chamois cloth to wash windshields.

4. Set up a parking lot where trikes can be parked while driver goes shopping. Provide stiff pieces of paper as checks and money and cash register for an attendant.

5. Set up a restaurant by the highway or a roadside stand where drivers can stop for a snack or meal. Chefs can wear white aprons and hats (Patterns, p. 22) in the kitchen, while those waiting on tables can wear aprons and carry trays. If possible, take tables and chairs outside or use a packing box.

Extended Experiences

1. Take a walk to a nearby mailbox (letter drop) to mail a letter(s) and to watch the mail truck arrive and the letter carrier pick up outgoing mail.

   NOTE: Time your walk to coincide with regular pickup.

2. Visit a post office to see the mail trucks unload and mail to be canceled and sorted and then loaded to go to other cities or to storage boxes in the city.

3. Visit a fire station to see where the firefighters eat, sleep, and care for the fire engines. Find out when they wash the trucks and hoses. If the station has a pole ask for a demonstration or sliding down the pole or jumping into a net. If they have a hook and ladder ask for a demonstration of how the ladder is put up.

   ★ **CAUTION:** One adult for each two children is required on this trip because if an alarm is turned in while you are visiting, the children must be kept out of the way of the firefighters and trucks. Explain to the children in advance that the alarm is very loud so all the fire fighters can hear it.

4. Visit a grocery store to see delivery trucks bringing food to the store. Check with the store manager in advance and find out when deliveries are made in greatest number and find a safe place to stand while watching. Arrange with the store manager to allow the children to go into the storeroom afterward so they can make the association between the delivery and the items on the shelf. Of course, plan to buy something that is needed like milk or bread.

5. If delivery trucks come to the centre allow the children to watch the unloading. Perhaps the driver will allow the children a closer look inside the door of the truck.

6. Take a bus ride or visit a terminal to see arrivals and departures of buses. If you cannot take a trip make arrangements with a bus company for children to board a scenic cruiser that is temporarily idle.

7. Ride a city bus if your city has buses. Allow each child to deposit his/her own fare.

8. Invite a police officer to come to the centre in a patrol car. Have the officer talk about the uniform and what things are carried or worn. Show the children how one talks to the control centre and how the siren and flashing light are activated.

9. If one of the children or a staff member comes to the centre in a taxi, ask if the children might look inside. Ask the driver to show the children the meter, the radio or computer.

10. Invite a letter carrier to come to the centre in uniform and bring a truck so the children may have a closer look inside the door of one. Perhaps they could have a get-well card, invitation to parents, or a Mother's Day card for the letter carrier to take to the post office. The children might send valentines or letters to each other to be delivered to the centre, or the teacher could put a letter, Christmas card, or valentine for each child in a large manila envelope and address it to the centre so that all will arrive together.

11. Invite a firefighter to bring one of the fire trucks to the centre. This is especially good for younger children and for those who show fear of fire engines or fire houses. There is also no worry about an alarm being turned in, and the children are freer to explore the fire

engine and view it more closely. Show the children what is worn to put out a fire and show them where the ax and tools are kept. Listen to the siren. If possible let the children try on fireboots.

12. Take a train ride: Unfortunately most local passenger train service has been discontinued, but if short trips are still available in your area try to take a train trip. Commuter and subway trains are also possibilities.

13. Some steam engine runs and narrow gauge railroads are maintained for recreational or historical purposes. You might also consider these as special excursion opportunities.

14. Ride a miniature train or monorail train in a nearby park or recreational area.

15. Inquire if a roundhouse with turntable is available in your area and if the children could watch it operate.

> ★ **CAUTION:** Locomotives are very noisy when they are running, and very big. Children may become frightened by them. Adult supervision on these trips should be one adult to two children, one for each hand!

16. Take a small group of mature children who show an avid interest in trains to visit the home of a model railroader to see an H-O gauge layout. The model railroader can demonstrate how a freight or passenger train is made up, how a slower train is put on a siding to allow a faster train to pass, and how "Casey Jones's" accident occurred.

17. If parents of some of the children work for a railroad you might invite them to come and talk about their jobs. If possible, they should wear what their job requires and bring something of interest that is related to their job to show the children.

Teacher Resources

Pictures and Displays

▷ Put up road maps of your area, province and Canada.

▷ Pictures of trains, stations, crossings, and train personnel from your own personal file

▷ Most railroad companies put out calendars which are available on request. They usually have large pictures of trains on them.

▷ Make a table display using model railroad trains. If possible have a passenger train, freight train, work train, streetcar, and subway train. Include timetables and brochures with the display. Train crew hat, conductor's hat, rail spike, tickets, and lantern may be obtainable.

Books and Periodicals

Berton, Pierre. *The National Dream.* Toronto: McClelland and Stewart, 1970.

Hollingsworth, Brian. *An Illustrated Guide to Modern Trains.* New York: Simon & Schuster, 1985.

Johnson, Brian D. *Railway Country: Across Canada by Train.* Toronto: Key Porter, 1985.

Swallow, Su. *Cars, Trucks and Trains.* 1974.

The Time Life Book of the Family Car. Chicago: Rand MacNalley, 1975.

Wolfe, Robert. *The Truck Book.* Minneapolis, MN: Carolrhoda Books, 1981.

Films and Videos

Check with your local library for the list of current materials available from the National Film Board and the CBC

Community Resources and Organizations

▷ Transportation companies
▷ Societies interested in transportation (for example a model train club, a flying club, a steam train "buffs" club, a car racing club, a hang gliding club, a shipping and ship travel club)
▷ A travel agent
▷ A VIA Rail representative
▷ Commuter services—rail, bus, subway, streetcar, etc
▷ Cab companies
▷ Department of public safety: An education officer can provide you with information about safety officers and help arrange a visit of one to your centre
▷ Fire department: A safety director or public relations officer can provide you with information about firefighters and help arrange a visit to a fire station or for a firefighter to visit the centre
▷ Post office: A public relations director will help explain the workings of the post office and arrange for a letter carrier to visit your centre or help arrange a visit to the post office. Many post offices do not allow children under six inside the post office working area. New postal boutiques and postal substations are good to visit
▷ Bus company: A public relations director will help arrange a bus trip or tour of a terminal and a bus
▷ Trucking firms in your community may cooperate in letting the children have a closer look at the trucks they use. They may have calendars with pictures of trucks on them
▷ Railroad companies serving your city: Ask for timetables, calendars, brochures
▷ Travel agents: Ask for posters, brochures, and schedules
▷ Hobby centre: train catalogues would be a good source of pictures for readiness materials. The manager may also give you the name of some model railroaders who would be willing to lend or demonstrate model trains

Government Agencies

Provincial, territorial, and federal ministries of transportation and/or communication

Goin' Down the Track
An Accompaniment for Dramatic Play

JoAnne Deal Hicks

24 Water Transportation

★★★★★★★★★★★★★★★★★★★★★★

Basic Understandings

(concepts children can grasp from this subject)

▷ People or things can be carried across (through) the water in a boat or in a ship.
▷ The boat or the ship is made to float on the water.
▷ The boat or the ship moves through the water in different ways:
   a. Wind blowing the sails
   b. People paddling, rowing, or poling
   c. Motors or engines propelling
▷ There are many different kinds of boats—rowboat, canoe, motorboat, lifeboat, sailboat, fishing boat (trawler), ferry, houseboat, tugboat, barge, and steamboat.
▷ There are many different kinds of ships—ocean liners, tankers, cabin cruisers, lakers, freighters, and schooners.
▷ People can travel the oceans in passenger ships (steamships or luxury liners) that have many stores and service personnel:

   a. Each family member has her/his own room as in a hotel or a motel.
   b. The passengers eat in a dining room as in a restaurant.
   c. There are places to buy clothes, food, flowers, shoes, and medicine.
   d. The ship has a doctor, nurse, dentist, and hospital (infirmary).
   e. It has a dry cleaner, laundry, barber shop, and beauty salon.
   f. It has a ballroom, theatre (movies), game rooms, lounges, one or more swimming pools, children's playrooms and gymnasiums.

▷ The captain and the crew manoeuvre the boat or the ship through the water.
▷ A dock or a pier is a platform where people can get on or off a ship.
▷ People get from the dock to the ship by walking up a ramp (gangplank) or steps.
▷ Ships and boats are given names, such as the *Pacific Princess*, the *Queen Mary*, and the *Bluenose*.
▷ The crew of a boat or a ship can talk to or signal the crew of another boat or ship by using whistles, flags, or lights.
▷ Buoys and lighthouses help the crew to know where to safely sail (steer) the ship.
▷ Most boats and ships move on the surface of the water.
▷ Submarines can submerge and move below the surface of the water.
▷ Ferries carry people and cars across rivers, lakes, channels, or bays.
▷ Many people enjoy boating, boat racing, or fishing from boats.
▷ Some people own their own boats; others rent them.

▷ Fishers are people who go out in boats to catch fish, lobsters, and crabs. They then sell their catch to canneries, markets, or the public.

▷ Some people live on houseboats.

▷ Some people own or rent cabin cruisers for vacations on the water. People can eat and sleep in cabin cruisers.

Additional Facts the Teacher Should Know

All boats may be known as ships and all ships may be known as boats. However, the term "boat" is usually used when you are referring to a small craft, and "ship" is used when referring to large craft. A boat floats because of the way it is built. Much of the boat is filled with air which is much lighter than water. Therefore, if the boat is constructed correctly, it will weigh less than the water that would take up the same space even when the boat is loaded with cargo, crew, and passengers.

NOTE: There are many different kinds of boats with which you should be familiar so that you may use the correct term when identifying them for the children.

Boats and ships have many parts with which you should be familiar

Bow is the front of the ship.

Stern is the rear of the ship.

Starboard is the right side of a ship, as you face the bow.

Port is the left side of the ship, as you face the bow.

Deck is the flat surface on the upper part of the ship where the crew and passengers can walk. Passenger ships have several decks.

Hull is the lower part of the ship or boat.

Screw is the propeller that turns, pushing the boat through the water.

Galley is the kitchen on a ship.

Hatch is the door on a ship.

Anchor is the heavy weight at the end of a long rope or steel cable which is dropped or let out when the ship wishes to remain in one place and does not have a dock at which to tie up.

Hold is the large room(s) in a ship where cargo is stowed.

Mast is the slender vertical pole used to hold up the sails on a sailboat.

Boom is the horizontal pole used to hold the sail on a sailboat or is the pole on a cargo ship that sticks up and out and holds the ropes and pulleys used in loading cargo onto the ship.

Wheelhouse is located in the front, top part of the ship. It has windows all around to provide the captain with a view for operating the ship. The wheelhouse is equipped with many instruments which help sail the ship, such as compasses, very accurate clocks, weather instruments, radios, and radar. There is also communication and special equipment to connect the wheelhouse with the chief engineer in the engine rooms down inside the ship.

Many people are needed to run a ship

Captain is in charge of the ship.

First mate or executive officer is the second in command.

Helmsman steers the ship.

Chief engineer is in charge of the engines.

Deckhands look after the ropes, keep the decks clean, and ensure that equipment is in working order. These men or women are also known as sailors or crew.

Dramatic play centre. Children in boat are fishing using cardboard tubes as fishing poles. Other children are "painting" the boat with used paint cans filled with water.

The captain and crew can communicate with other ships and with land in many ways

Telephones can be used and telegraph and radio messages can be sent while at sea.
Flags are used to represent letters and numbers. Messages are spelled out.
Morse code can be used by opening and closing the shutters on a large lamp.

1. Ships have whistles which can be blown in certain patterns of long and short blasts which carry special meanings. One short toot: turning to the right; two short toots: turning to the left; three short toots: backing up; four short toots: danger; one long toot: leaving the pier; three long toots: "hello."
2. On board ship, time is designated by bells. There are six tours of watch duty of four hours each, starting at 8 P.M. Each half hour of the watch is struck by using the bells. One bell: 8:30; two bells: 9:00; three bells: 9:30; and so on, until eight bells are struck at midnight, ending the first watch. At 12:30 one bell is struck and the pattern repeated for each four-hour watch.
3. Smaller craft are moved through the water by use of oars, paddles, sails, or small motors. Larger craft have diesel engines, steam engines, or nuclear reactors to turn the large propellers known as screws. When the propellers turn one way they push the water behind and the ship goes forward. When the propellers turn the other way the water is pushed ahead and the ship goes backward. The rudder can be turned to make the ship turn left or right.

4. Lighthouses and buoys help the captain and crew of a ship avoid shallow water and rocks or other obstructions. They have both lights and bells on them so they can be seen and heard at night or in a fog.

5. Fishing is a very important business, especially for people living by rivers and oceans. Fishermen can be called "fishers." Some commercial fishing is still done by hook and line but trawling and seining have largely replaced this method. Fishers either drag nets through the water (seining) or set out main lines to which shorter lines with baited hooks are attached (trawling). As many as 5000 hooks are sometimes baited and set and the main line may run for miles. The line is marked with buoys or floats so it can be found again. Salmon, tuna, red snapper, and halibut are usually caught this way.

6. Lobsters and crabs are caught in slotted wooden traps called "lobster pots" which are baited with fish. The lobsters and crabs can get in but cannot get out. Lobsters are found in the Maritimes, especially off the shores of Nova Scotia. Shrimp are found primarily in the waters between Vancouver Island and the mainland of British Columbia.

Methods Most Adaptable for Introducing this Subject to Children

1. Display pictures of boats or ships near dramatic play centres and on bulletin boards.
2. Read a story about boats or ships.
3. While on another trip the children may see boats on a river or lake.
4. Invite a parent who may catch fish or work for a shipping company to tell the children about his or her work.

Vocabulary

boat	captain	life preserver	shore
ship	sailor	lifeboat	steer
dock	crew	lighthouse	cargo
oars	cabin	water	row
sails	deck	float	tow
paddles	anchor	sink	rope

Learning Centres

Discovery Centre

1. Obtain authentic, sturdy, toy models of different kinds of ships and boats. Identify them and tell how they are useful and how they move through the water.
2. Some children may wonder how something as big and heavy as a boat can float. You might help their understanding of this by telling them the shape is important. The boat or ship must be made to hold a lot of air, which is lighter than water. The following demonstration might help. Have two pieces of aluminum foil of the same size. Have one of the children wad one of the pieces into a ball. Place it in the water. It should sink. Help the children make a little rowboat out of the other piece by turning up the edges and putting it on the water. It should float.

3. Show the children how sailboats move. Float a toy sailboat in a tub of water. Let children blow on the sails. Ask what would happen if they were sailing and the wind stopped.
4. Submarines submerge see p. 512.
5. Floating boats may lead to an interest in water (see "Water Around Me").

Dramatic Play Centres

Home-living centre

1. Put up pictures of boats and ships used for pleasure and travel. Set out brochures on traveling by ship to encourage the planning and taking of a trip on the water.
2. Have suitcases available for packing.
3. Put money in purses for purchase of tickets.

Block-building centre

1. Make a dock with unit blocks. Set out small model ships and boats for encouraging this kind of play.
2. Have cans or boxes of small materials, such as sticks, stones, buttons, and cloth scraps, to use as cargo.
3. Build a boathouse for boats with unit blocks.
4. Outline a rowboat on the floor with hollow blocks lying on their long edges. Provide sailor hats.

Other dramatic play centres

1. The rocking boat makes a good boat to row or paddle. Sing "Row, Row, Row Your Boat" as children rock. Make paddles or oars out of cardboard if you wish. Provide sailor hats.
2. The rocking boat can also be a fishing boat. Give the children upholstery-roll poles with string tied to a magnet. Stock the lake or river with paper fish which have a paper clip put on for a mouth. Let them fish. Supervise carefully. (See **CAUTION**, p. 515.)
3. Ask your church or florist to save you the heavy waxed cardboard boxes in which flowers are delivered. These make fine boats. Almost any sturdy box will make a boat.
4. Piers for larger floor toy boats can be made from hollow blocks. Piers can also be used for fishing activities.

Learning, Language, and Readiness Materials Centre

Commercially made games and materials

(See "Basic Resources," pp. 79, 100, for manufacturers' addresses.)
1. *Puzzles:* A variety of puzzles with transportation themes. Excellent puzzles are made by Galt, Simplex and Ravensburger.
2. *Small toys for imaginative play:* Vinyl models of various boats for younger children. Plastic models of various boats for older children. Be sure that the toy boats and ships that you choose will float in a water table or small pool.
3. *Costumes:* Hats and coats that represent various employees of the fishing and shipping industries.

Teacher-made games and materials

NOTE: For a detailed description of "Learning Games," see pp. 50–59.

1. Look and see: Use models of different kinds of boats and ships.
2. Can you remember? Use models of boats and ships.
3. Alike, different, and the same: Make sets of two each of the different kinds of boats and ships. Mix them up and let the children find the ones that match. Use a matching pair and one that is different, ask child to point to the one that is not like the others.
4. Grouping and sorting by association: Take one of each of the boats and ships used in no. 3 and mix with one each of trucks, airplanes, and railway cars. Ask the child to find all the ones that go on water, on rails, on roads, or in the sky.
5. What am I? After the children are familiar with some of the boats and ships and their uses, describe one and ask children to identify, such as, "I am thinking of a boat that carries automobiles and people across a river. What am I?"

Art Centre

1. Children could help make a picture book by pasting precut pictures of boats and ships on construction paper. The mounted pictures could then be put in a loose-leaf notebook. Children with cutting experience could help with the cutting.
2. Precut a sailboat stencil. Let children spatter paint it on blue construction paper, choosing the colour they wish. Allow to dry and spatter paint the sails white or paste on triangles cut from cloth or paper.
3. Precut hulls and sails of different sizes and colours from fabric scraps or construction paper and let children paste on blue construction paper.
4. At the woodworking centre provide wooden precut shapes and scraps that would allow children to make boats and ships of their own design. Masts could be made of wooden dowels or plastic straws. Float boats in water.

   NOTE: Hand drills should be provided for drilling mast holes.

5. Styrofoam can be precut to take on the shape of a ship's hull. Provide toothpicks, straws for masts, and smaller styrofoam scraps to be used for a cabin or wheelhouse. Paper or cloth sails can be glued to the masts. Let children float the boats in a tub of water.

Book Centre

- Ardizipone, Edward. *Little Tim and the Brave Sea Captain.* New York: Walck, 1972.
- Bruna, Dick. *Lifeboat.* London: Methuen, 1984.
- Burningham, John. *Mr. Grumpy's Outing.* New York: Penguin, 1984.
- Crews, Donald. *Harbor.* New York: Greenwillow Press, 1982.
- Flack, Marjorie. *Boats on the River.* New York: Viking Press, 1946.
- Graham Margaret Bloy. *Benjy's Boat Trip.* New York: Harper & Row, 1977.
- Gramatky, Hardie. *Little Toot.* New York: G.P. Putnam's Sons, 1964.
- _____. *Little Toot on the Mississippi.* New York: G.P. Putnam's Sons, 1973.
- Haley, Gail. *Noah's Ark.* New York: Atheneum, 1971.
- Krasiloosky, Phyllis. *The Cow Who Fell in the Canal.* Garden City, NY: Doubleday, 1972.
- Lenski, Lois. *The Little Sailboat.* New York: Walck, 1937.
- Maestro, Betsy. *Big City Port.* New York: Macmillan, 1983.
- Morgan, Allen. *Nicole's Boat.* Willowdale, Ont: Annick Press, 1986. (A good book for reading before nap time)

••• Murphy, Shirley R. *Tattie's River Journey*. New York: Dial Press, 1983.
••• Randall, Beverly. *Aboard Lucy Lee*. Richmond Hill, Ont: Scholastic-TAB, 1987.
••• Spier, Peter. *The Erie Canal*. Garden City, NY: Doubleday, 1970.
••• Swift, Hildegarde. *The Little Red Lighthouse and the Great Gray Bridge*. New York: Harcourt Brace Jovanovich, 1974 (paper).
••• Williams, Vera. *Three Press Days on a River in a Red Canoe*. New York: Greenwillow Press, 1981.
••• Wynne-Jones, Tim. *Zoom at Sea*. Vancouver: Douglas & McIntyre, 1983.
••• _____ . *Zoom Away*. Vancouver: Douglas & McIntyre, 1985.
••• Zander, Hans. *My Blue Chair*. Willowdale, Ont: Annick Press, 1985.

Planning for Group Time

NOTE: All music, fingerplays, stories, and games listed here may be used at other times during the session as appropriate. See Core Library, "Basic Resources," p. 95, for publishers and addresses. Record company addresses can be found on p. 99.

Music

Songs

From songs in this book
"Lightly Row," p. 517
"Michael Row the Boat Ashore," p. 518

From *The Best Singing Games for Children of All Ages*, Bloy
"Four in a Boat," p. 22
"Down the River," p. 74

From *Musical Games for Children of All Ages*, Nelson
"A Sailor Went To Sea, Sea, Sea," p. 62

From *Eye Winker, Tom Tinker, Chin Chopper*, Glazer
"Charlie Over the Water," p. 18
"Sailing at High Tide," p. 68
"There's a Hole in the Bottom of the Sea," p. 78

From *Elephant Jam*, Sharon, Lois, and Bram
"Long Legged Sailor," p. 16
"Lots of Fish in Bonvist' Harbour," p. 108

From *Baby Beluga Book*, Raffi
"Baby Beluga," p. 5

From *Musicplay*, Burton and Hughes
"Fish Pole Song," p. 151
"Row, Row, Row Your Boat," p. 89

From *A Treasury of Songs for Children*, Glazer
"Erie Canal," p. 79

From *Piggyback Songs*, Warren
"We Sail a Ship," p. 31
"I'm a Fish," p. 32

From *Singing Bee*, Hart
"Merrily We Roll Along," p. 59
"The Gallant Ship," p. 84
"Lightly Row," p. 138
"I Saw Three Ships," p. 139

From *Sally Go Round the Sun*, Fowke
"The White Ship Sails," p. 37

Rhythms and singing games

"Row, Row, Row Your Boat": Have children sit on floor in pairs facing each other with hands joined and legs spread out in shape of a V, with soles of shoes touching. As you sing the song together have the children pull each other forward on a rotating basis—first one, then the other, in time to the music.

Records and cassettes

Bob Homme. *The Giant Concert of Concerts by the Friendly Giant.* (A & M Records)
"Seafood Concert"

Raffi. *Baby Beluga.* (Troubadour Records)
"Baby Beluga"
"Water Dance" (Good for movement)

Sharon, Lois, and Bram. *Elephant Show.* (Elephant Records)
"Jack Was Every Inch a Sailor"
"Rig a Jig Jig"
_____ . *Smorgasbord.* (Elephant Records)
"Newfoundland Jig Melody"
"Long Legged Sailor"

Fingerplays and Poems

THE BOATS

This is the way, all the day long
The boats go sailing by,
To and fro, in a row,
Under the bridge so high.

(FORM A BRIDGE WITH LEFT ARM AND MOVE RIGHT HAND BACK AND FORTH UNDER IT)

ROW, ROW, ROW YOUR BOAT

Row, row, row your boat
Gently down the stream,
Merrily, merrily, merrily, merrily,
Life is but a dream.

(PUT FISTS TOGETHER IN FRONT OF YOU AND PRETEND TO ROW)

Pittman's two books *Down by Jim Long's Stage* and *One Wonderful Day for a Sculpin Named Sam* are exceptional books of poetry to read for this subject.

From *The New Wind Has Wings*, Downie
"The Ships of Yule," p. 12
"Noah," p. 45

From *A New Treasury of Children's Poetry*, Cole
"Where Go the Boats," p. 130

From *Where the Sidewalk Ends*, Silverstein.
"Homemade Boat," p. 12
"Captain Hook," p. 18
"The Unicorn," p. 76
"Pirate Captain Jim," p. 144

From *Read Aloud Rhymes for the Very Young*, Prelutsky and Brown
"Fish," p. 44
"I'd Like to Be a Lighthouse," p. 78

From *Don't Eat Spiders*, Heidbreder
"The Newfoundland Cod," p. 35

From *Finger Rhymes*, Brown
"Fish Story," p. 12

From *Let's Do Fingerplays*, Grayson
"The Boats," p. 26

Stories

(To read, read–tell, or tell. See Book Centre for complete list.)
There are many interesting stories to read or tell for this theme. Wynne-Jones' books *Zoom at Sea* and *Zoom Away* offer fun and fantasy with a Maritime theme. In contrast Gramatky's classic *Little Toot* stories are diverting, but also contain many interesting facts.

Games

(See "Learning Games," pp. 50–59 and teacher-made games in this chapter for directions.)
 1. Look and see
 2. What am I?
 3. Can you remember?
 4. Alike, different, and the same

Routine Times

 1. At snack or meal times serve chocolate, cocoa, bananas, pineapple, or coconuts. Explain that these foods probably came to our country by freighter. Serve fish, lobster, or crab and talk about how they are caught in nets by fishers in fishing boats.
 2. At snack or meal times have a captain's table. Each day choose one child to be captain who in turn selects those who will dine at the captain's table. Make certain everyone gets included!
 3. At rest time tell the children you will ring the ship's bell four times when it is time to get up. Use a bell with a clapper and ring as follows for four bells: strike bell twice, pause, strike bell twice more.
 4. In busing children to and from the centre or on other trips in the community you may cross rivers, go around lakes, or by the ocean where boats or ships may be seen. Talk about the kinds of boats you see and what they do.

Large Muscle Activities

1. A packing box or other large, sturdy carton could be used for boat play. A cleated walking board could be used as a gangplank to the packing-box ship. Put a real rowboat on the playground (see p. 483). Combine with a steering wheel or dial panel (see illustration, p. 467.) Provide sailor hats.
2. Float boats at a water table or other large container filled with water.
3. Have water available to fill the canals in the sandbox. Provide small boats to encourage water transportation play in this area.
4. See other dramatic play areas for additional suggestions involving large muscles.
5. Slice a tire for a boat canal (see "Water Around Me", p. 521, no. 2).

Extended Experiences

1. Watch boats or ships on a nearby river, lake, or ocean.
2. Take a ferry ride.
3. Ride an excursion boat.
4. Go out in a sailboat, rowboat, or motorboat.

   ★ CAUTION: All children should wear life jackets and one of the adults in the boat should have a current senior lifesaving certificate.

5. Watch a trawler, freighter, or laker unload.
6. Watch a boat race—sculling, a regatta, or a motorboat race.
7. Invite a Chinese parent, university student, or friend to visit your classroom and tell about the Dragon Boat festival in China. Perhaps this person would have, or could find, a picture of one of these boats.
8. Invite a sailor to come in uniform and tell the children about living and sailing at sea.
9. Invite a person who fishes commercially or for a hobby to come to the centre to tell the children about commercial or hobby fishing. (This could be arranged just before the spring return to fishing and could be followed up with a visit to a local fishing dock.)

Teacher Resources

Pictures and Displays

Display pictures from your personal file which might include different kinds of boats, persons who work with boats, buoys, a lighthouse, boat races, docks, fishers, fishing nets, lobster pots.

Books and Periodicals

Blocksma, Mary, and Dewey Blocksma. *Easy to Make Water Toys That Really Work.* Englewood Cliffs, NJ: Prentice-Hall, 1985.

Parry, J.H. *Romance of the Sea.* Washington: National Geographic Society, 1981.

The Sea. New York: Time-Life Books, 1977.

Wall, Robert. *Ocean Liners.* London: Chartwell Books, 1977.

Films and Videos

Check with your local library for the list of current materials available from the National Film Board and the CBC

Community Resources and Organizations

▷ Transportation companies
▷ Societies interested in transportation (for example, a model train club, a flying club, a steam train "buffs" club, a car racing club, a hang gliding club, a shipping and ship travel club)
▷ A travel agent
▷ A fishery
▷ Shipping companies may have calendars or brochures with pictures of ships
▷ Marina for rental of boats
▷ Fishing companies or fishers for permission to watch the unloading of fish
▷ Regatta clubs for schedules of races or names of persons who may be willing to give the children rides in their boats

Government Agencies

▷ Provincial, territorial, and federal ministries of transportation and/or communication
▷ Federal ministry in charge of fishing

Lightly Row
(Alles Neu Macht Der Mai)

Traditional Tune ("Fahrathen")

German Folk Song

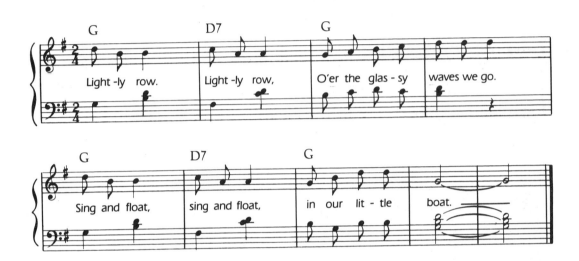

NOTE: Two lines (verses 2 and 3) have been omitted in this adaptation of the original tune to simplify it for use with young children.

Michael Row the Boat Ashore
(Original title: Michael Haul the Boat Ashore)

Traditional Negro Spiritual   Traditional

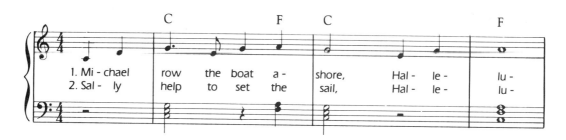

VERSE 3: Pe-ter pad-dle the can-oe, etc.
VERSE 4: Mar—y fly the plane a-round, etc.
VERSE 5: Moth-er drive the car to town, etc.
VERSE 7: Fath-er ride the train to work, etc.

NOTE: The "Hallelujah" is optional. Phrases can be completed by repeating preceding refrain. For example, "row the boat!" "trim the sail!"

Adapted by Bonnie Flemming

PART 7

My World

★★

Contents

25 Day and Night

★★★★★★★★★★★★★★★★★★★★★★★

Basic Understandings

(concepts children can grasp from this subject)

▷ The sun gives off light and heat.

▷ It is lighter and warmer during the day because at that time our part of the earth is turned toward the sun.

▷ At night it is darker and colder because at that time our part of the earth is turned away from the sun.

▷ When it is day in our half of the world, it is night in the other half of the world.

▷ A whole day lasts twenty-four hours and consists of both the day (light) and night (dark).

▷ Sometimes the daylight lasts longer than the darkness (in summer), and at other times the darkness lasts longer than the light (in winter).

▷ Night is nice. (Stress pleasant aspects of night.) It is a good time to sleep and rest.

▷ The sun is a big star. Stars shine (give off light and heat) all the time.

▷ Clouds may hide the sun and stars from our view.

▷ Fog is caused by clouds forming close to the earth. It may hide the sun and stars from our view.

▷ The sun and the stars shine all the time. We do not see the other stars in the daytime because the sunlight is so bright we cannot see them.

▷ Most stars are so far away we see them as tiny dots of light.

▷ Some of the stars appear grouped together. These groups are called constellations.

Additional Facts the Teacher Should Know

1. The earth turns counterclockwise (from west to east) on its imaginary axis, which runs from the north to the south pole as it travels on an elliptical path around our sun. It takes twenty-four hours, or one calendar day, for the earth to turn completely around once on its axis.

2. A moon is a heavenly body that revolves around a planet. We have one moon that is about 149 000 km away. It is 1305 km wide and about 80 times lighter than the earth. Therefore its force of gravity is much less. People weigh less on the moon. The moon's gravity exerts some pressure on our earth and causes large bodies of water to move, resulting in tides. The moon rotates on its axis as it orbits around the earth. It takes the moon 27 days and 8 hours to orbit around the earth and about the same time to turn around once on its axis. Therefore we always see the same side of the moon.

3. The moon gives off no light of its own. What we see is a reflection of the sun's rays off the surface of the moon. One-half of the moon is always lighted by the sun, but when the moon is almost between the earth and the sun, we do not always see the lighted half. The sun's rays are so bright, we do not often see the moon during the day. When we can see all of the lighted half we say we have a full moon. As the moon changes its position, less and less light is reflected off it toward the earth. Accordingly, it becomes less and less visible to humans on the earth. This is why sometimes the moon appears to be only a crescent or half moon shape, although its size does not actually change. The different positions are called phases.

4. An eclipse of the moon is when the earth is between the sun and the moon and the sunlight cannot shine on the moon. The moon gets very dull, and we can barely see it. An eclipse of the sun is when the moon is between the sun and the earth and we cannot see the sunlight.

   ★ CAUTION: It is dangerous to look directly at an eclipse of the sun. Permanent eye damage can result.

5. At certain times of the year, particularly in the autumn, the moon rises early and shines for a long time. This is often called a "harvest moon." It sometimes appears large and orange in colour if there is dust in the air.

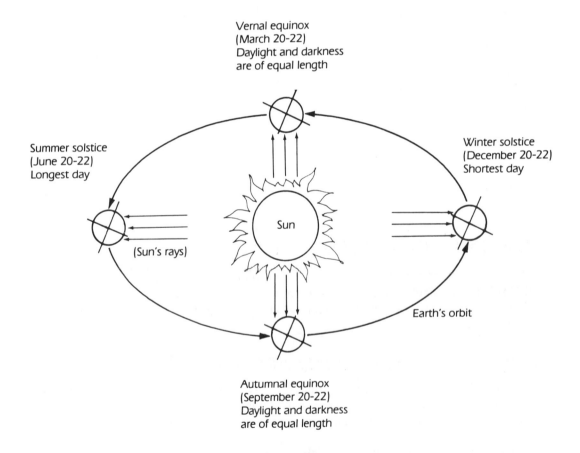

6. Twice during the year in Canada, we have approximately twelve hours each of daylight and darkness. One time is the vernal equinox on March 20, 21, or 22, and the second is the autumnal equinox on September 20, 21, or 22. The exact date is determined officially each year when the sun crosses the equator at noon. During the summer, our part of the earth is tipped toward the sun and we have longer days. In winter, we have the shortest days as our part of the earth is tipped away from the sun. (See illustration, above).

7. Many children are afraid of night time and the dark. Often, at about the age of four and one-half to five, children who have been perfectly willing to go to bed will begin to cry and want a light left on. Children should learn facts about light and dark, but also be encouraged to talk about their fears related to darkness or being away from home at night. They should learn about the beauty, goodness, and necessity of night. Dreams become important to children at about three and one-half years of age. The teacher should be prepared to listen to what the children say about their dreams and offer them reassurance.

Methods Most Adaptable for Introducing this Subject to Children

1. Display pictures showing activities during the day and during the night.
2. Say "good morning" when children arrive and have a "good night" if they leave in late afternoon.
3. Darken room to simulate night at rest time.
4. Put up a mobile of our solar system.
5. Read a story, such as Emberly & Emberly's *Night's Nice* (see Book Centre, p. 504.)

Vocabulary

sun	dark	awake	nightmare
day	light	dream	sun dial
hot	moon	shadows	sunny
fog	cold	prism	cloudy
stars	sleep	sunglasses	shine
earth	rest	flashlight	night

Learning Centres

Discovery Centre

1. Shadows: Call attention to the children's shadows and those of objects on the playground. Discover that shadows are caused by light.

   a. Measure children's shadows in the morning, at noon, and before they leave in the afternoon, all at the same spot.
   b. Have the children put one hand in the sun and one in the shade on a sidewalk. Discuss which is warmer and why.
   c. Pound a long stick (1.5 m) into the ground in an open spot. Measure the length of its shadow from time to time during the day. Discuss.
   d. Indoors, have the children look for their shadows. Use a flashlight as the sun and a stand-up doll as a person. Let each child discover how to make long and short shadows on all sides of the doll. How do you make the shadow disappear?
   e. Use a bright light on a movie screen, sheet, or light coloured wall and let the children make shadow pictures.
   f. Make shadow silhouettes (see Games, no. 3, p. 506).
   g. Display Chinese paper cuts (order from a local import-export store).

2. Make a sun dial and mark the hours. Explain that this is how people told time before clocks were invented. Check an encyclopedia for instructions.

3. Day and night: On a globe, stick a small paper figure to the location of the city where the children live. Stick one on the opposite side also. Darken the room and use a flashlight to represent the sun. Turn the globe slowly. The children will observe what causes day and night. If you have no globe, use a ball instead.

4. Clouds: They can keep us from seeing the sun, stars, and moon. Cut out paper clouds or use a cotton ball to place between child's eyes and the sun (outdoors) or a lamp (indoors) or when looking at constellation boxes.

5. Heat of the sun: Discuss how the sun burns us. Also stand in the sun and then stand in the shade. Which is warmer? Use thermometer to show changes of temperature in sun and shade. The teacher can demonstrate how the sun can burn a hole in a piece of paper with a magnifying glass.

   ★ CAUTION: Watch children closely.

6. Absence of light: Take brightly coloured objects into a closet and slowly close the door. The colours will disappear.

7. Reflected light: Shine a small flashlight on a circle cut out of white material in a dark closet. The object will appear to shine too. That is how the moon shines at night with the sun's reflected light. Our earth is especially bright when the sun shines on it because so many things reflect the sun's light, especially the dust in the air.

8. Light is made up of many colours. Use a prism to demonstrate this (see "Colour", p. 528).

9. Bake cookies: Cut in shape of stars, moon (crescent), and sun (round). Frost yellow or white. Add silver dragées to moon and stars.

Dramatic Play Centres

Home-living centre

1. Darken this area of the room if possible by turning off the lights or partitioning off the area with screens and covering the windows with a dark material.
2. Set out night clothes and blankets for dolls.
3. Bring nightgowns, pajamas, robes, and slippers for dress up.
4. Bring a box big enough for a child to use as a bed or a cot; also provide some cuddly animals and crib blankets.
5. Simulate having the sun rise by lighting the area and removing coverings from windows. Family members get up and get ready for school, breakfast, and work.

Block-building centre

1. Make available sturdy doll house furniture so that children can build a ranch-type house without a roof with the unit blocks and arrange furniture as they wish for eating, sleeping, and so on.
2. Set out commercial or homemade doll houses with open sides or top for children to arrange furniture and family models in various day and night activities.

Learning, Language, and Readiness Materials Centre

Commercially made games and materials

(See "Basic Resources," pp. 79, 100, for manufacturers' addresses.)
1. *Puzzles:* Five-to-ten-piece puzzles showing the sun, moon, bedtime, bath time, clock puzzle, etc. Be sure to have some puzzles with knobs to make them easy to manipulate.

2. *Dolls and puppets:* Dolls' clothes and accessories—night clothes and cribs.
3. *Costumes:* A variety of night clothes for the dramatic play centres.
4. *Miscellaneous:* Clock—A large teaching clock with movable hands and a large digital clock.

   Globe: A large durable globe that show your community well or on which you can mark your community easily.

   Flashlight: A rechargeable flashlight with a handle that young children can hold.

   Prism: A 15 cm prism available in science stores or in educational supply outlets.

Teacher-made games and materials

NOTE: For a detailed description of "Learning Games," see pp. 50–59.

1. Look and see: Use flannelboard figures of sun, moon, and star.
2. I see something, what do you see? I see something round like the moon; black like the night; yellow like the sun; pointed like a star.
3. Who's missing? Change to "Who went to bed?"
4. Match-them: Use sun, stars, and phases of the moon.
5. Alike, different, and the same: Two suns and a star; two stars and a moon.
6. Make a calendar for the month. Each day paste a cut-out of a sun or a cloud on the appropriate square. Count the cloudy and sunny days.

Art Centre

•• 1. Spatter paint: Teacher precuts star and moon stencils. Using a screen, children spatter dark blue or black tempera paint over the stencils and onto white paper.
2. Starry night: Use an old window shade of a dark colour or a night shade.

••   a. Have children use white crayons or chalk on the dark side to draw the sky at night.
•••   b. Have children punch holes in the shade with a bobby pin to form some "constellations." When the window shade is placed in a sunny window, the "stars" will seem to shine.

• 3. Teacher precuts phases of the moon in pale yellow manila construction paper or silver or white gummed-back paper. Children paste these on sheets of black paper. Prepackaged star stickers may be added.
••• 4. Night and day pictures: Join a light and dark piece of construction paper end to end or back to back. Children cut night and day pictures from magazines and paste on appropriate side, or draw pictures with chalk or crayons.
••• 5. Mural: In the centre of a long sheet of brown paper, the teacher or one of the children can make a large yellow or orange ball for the sun. The rest of the children can colour with paint, crayons, or felt pens, a figure (person, house, tree, animal) on one side or the other of this sun. Then they put a black shadow opposite the sun on their figure to show the relationship of light and shadow. Best following Discovery Centre 1(d), p. 501.

Book Centre

••• Asch, F. *Moon Bear.* New York: Charles Scribner's Sons, 1978.
•• Baum, Arline, and Joseph Baum. *One Bright Monday Morning.* New York: Random House, 1962.
• Brown, Margaret W. *Goodnight Moon.* New York: Harper & Row, 1947.
• _____ . *A Child's Goodnight Book.* Reading, MA: Addison-Wesley, 1950.
• deRegniers, Beatrice S., and Isabel Gordon. *The Shadow Book.* New York: Harcourt Brace Jovanovich, 1962.
••• _____ , *and Leona Pierce. Who Likes Sun?* New York: Harcourt Brace Jovanovich, 1961.

•• Dickson, Barry. *Afraid of the Dark*. Toronto: James Lorimer, 1986.
•• Emberley, Barbara, and Ed Emberley. *Night's Nice*. Garden City, N.Y: Doubleday, 1963.
••• Fisher, Aileen. *In the Middle of the Night*. New York: Thomas Y. Crowell, 1965.
•• Hoban, Russell. *Bedtime for Frances*. New York: Harper & Row, 1965.
••• Horwitz, Elinor L. *When the Sky Is Like Lace*. Philadelphia: J.B. Lippincott, 1975.
•• Hurd, Edith T. *The Day the Sun Danced*. New York: Harper & Row, 1965.
•• Leonard, Marcia. *Little Kitten Sleeps Over*. New York: Bantam, 1987.
•• Mayer, Mercer. *There's a Nightmare in My Closet*. New York: Dial Press, 1968.
•• Morgan, Allen. *Nicole's Boat*. Willowdale, Ont: Annick Press, 1986.
••• Munsch, Robert. *The Dark*. Willowdale, Ont: Annick Press, 1986.
••• Rice, E. *Goodnight, Goodnight*. New York: Greenwillow Press, 1980.
• Shaw, Charles G. *It Looked Like Spilt Milk*. New York: Harper & Row, 1947.
••• Shulevitz, Uri. *Dawn*. New York: Farrar, Straus & Giroux, 1974.
•••• _____. *One Monday Morning*. New York: Collier.
•••• Stevenson, J. *We Can't Sleep*. New York: Greenwillow Press, 1982.
••• Tresselt, Alvin. *The Hide and Seek Fog*. New York: Lothrop, Lee & Shepard, 1966.
• Zolotow, Charlotte. *Sleepy Book*. New York: Lothrop, Lee & Shepard, 1966.
• _____. *Wake Up and Good Night*. New York: Harper & Row, 1971.
••• _____. *When the Wind Stops*. New York: E.M. Hale, 1965.

NOTE: Check your library for books on the moon by Franklyn M. Branley.

Planning for Group Time

NOTE: All music, fingerplays, poems, stories, and games listed here may also be used at other times during the session as appropriate. See Core Library, "Basic Resources," p. 95, for publishers and addresses. Record company addresses can be found on p. 99.

Music

Songs

From *Singing Bee*, Hart
"Twinkle Twinkle Little Star," p. 64
"Oh, How Lovely is the Evening," p. 134

From *Sally Go Round the Sun*, Fowke
"Sally Go Round the Sun," p. 11
"No Bears Out Tonight," p. 42

From *A Treasury of Songs for Young Children*, Glazer
"Au Claire de la Lune," p. 23
"Sleep Baby Sleep," p. 55
"Frère Jacques," p. 89
"Go to Sleepy," p. 100
"Hugh Little Baby," p. 124
"Lazy Mary," p. 151
"Oh, How Lovely Is the Evening," p. 174

From *Elephant Jam*, Sharon, Lois, and Bram
"Skinnamarink," p. 58
"Bye 'n' Bye," p. 127

From *What Shall We Do and Allee Galloo*, Winn
"When Ducks Get Up in the Morning," p. 26

Records and cassettes

Anne Murray. *There's a Hippo in my Bathtub.* (Capitol Records)
"Stars Are the Windows of Heaven"
"Sleepytime"
"You Are My Sunshine"
"Lullaby Medley"

Bob Schneider. *When You Dream a Dream.* (Capitol Records)
"In the Morning"
"When You Dream a Dream"

Fred Penner. *Special Delivery.* (Troubadour Records)
"Bon Soir, Mes Amis"

Raffi. *Baby Beluga.* (Troubadour Records)
"Dayo"
"Morningtown Ride"

Sharon, Lois, and Bram. *Elephant Show.* (Elephant Records)
"Go to Sleep Now My Pumpkin"

_____. *Smorgasbord.* (Elephant Records)
"Hobo's Lullaby"

Fingerplays and Poems

Sun, Sun

"Sun, sun overhead,
what's your colour?"

"I am red."

"Sun, sun fiery fellow,
what's your colour?"

"I am yellow."

"Sun, sun in sky of blue,
what's your colour?"

"Orange too."

"I'm golden yellow,
orange and red,
a burning fire above your head."

From *Read Aloud Rhymes for the Very Young*, Prelutsky and Brown
"Swinging Time," p. 3
"Swimming," p. 9
"Before the Bath," p. 26
"Naughty Soap Song," p. 26
"The Way They Scrub," p. 27
"Wish," p. 27
"Happy Winter Steamy Tub," p. 27
"Night Fun," p. 70
"Bedtime," p. 70
"Moon Boat," p. 71

"I See the Moon," p. 71
"Moon Come Out," p. 71
"The Star," p. 71
"Wide Awake," p. 82
"Silvery," p. 87
"Good Night, Good Night," p. 88

From *Finger Rhymes*, Brown
"Sleepy Fingers," p. 30

From *The New Moon Has Wings*, Downie
"After Midnight," p. 71
"The Sun," p. 110

From *Mischief City*, Wynne-Jones
"I Like Drawing Pictures," p. 14
"Don't Drink the Bathwater," p. 18
"They're Having a Party Downstairs," p. 19
"After the Lights Go Down Low," p. 20
"Mrs. Night," p. 21
"The Arrangement," p. 36

From *Let's Do Fingerplays*, Grayson
"Good Morning," p. 80

Stories

(To read, read–tell, or tell. See Book Centre for complete list.)
When choosing stories that are about day and night, remember that some children may be afraid of the dark. Dickson's *Afraid of the Dark* is very helpful to read with children who are anxious. If your children are relaxed in the dark, it can be fun to turn off the lights, close the curtains and tell a story with a flashlight shining on the pictures.

Games

1. World game: To be played after Discovery Centre no. 3, p. 502. Darken the room. Put a lamp or flashlight at one end of the room. Have the children form a circle to represent the earth. Divide into two halves. The half facing the sun (the light) do daytime activities, such as eating, jumping, running. The other half, not facing the sun, pretend to go to sleep. Then the circle re-forms and the earth rotates half way around. Again there are night and day activities but for the opposite half of the earth.
2. Night and day: The teacher tells the children to close their eyes, then calls on a child to tell about one thing that happens at night. Then the teacher tells the children to open their eyes and calls on another child to tell about one thing that happens in the day. Repeat as long as there is interest or every child has participated.
3. Whose shadow? Hang a sheet. Place a light behind it. Have children cover their eyes and put their heads on their knees. Teacher taps one child who goes behind the screen. Others open their eyes and guess whose shadow.

Routine Times

1. At snack or meal times have day and night cookies—stars, moon, sun, baked by the children or a cook.
2. At rest time always darken the room slowly. Pretend night is coming and the sun is going down. Also, brighten the room as slowly as possible at the end of the rest period to simulate the sun coming up.

Large Muscle Activities

1. Play shadow tag or just try to step on each other's shadows outdoors. Show children how you can avoid getting your shadow stepped on by squatting quickly or hiding it in the shadow of a building or a tree.
2. Sally go round the stars (see Circle Games, p. 58).

Extended Experiences

1. Send home with the children notes requesting that their parents take them out at night to see the stars, the moon, and a sunset, or get up early to watch a sunrise.
2. Have a visit from a parent who works at night, and have the parent talk about his or her job, such as police officer, firefighter, security guard, nurse.

Teacher Resources

Pictures and Displays

▷   Use pictures from magazines that show day or night, or activities that go on during the day or night.
▷   Make two dioramas: one could be a day scene, the other a night scene.
▷   Art centre projects could be made entirely by the teacher and used in the room.

Books and Periodicals

Chickadee magazine
Owl magazine
Paten, John. *Astronomy.* New York: Warwick Press, 1982

Films and Videos

Go to your local library to check for useful films and videotapes from the National Film Board and the CBC.

Community Resources Organizations

▷   A planetarium
▷   A university department of astronomy

26 Water Around Me

★★★★★★★★★★★★★★★★★★★★★★

Basic Understandings

(concepts children can grasp from this subject)

NOTE: Most statements below refer to water as a liquid unless identified by another term, such as ice, snow, fog, mist.

▷ Water is necessary to all living things.

▷ Water is all around us, in the air and in the ground. It is in milk, vegetables, fruit, meat, leaves, trunks, roots, and branches of a tree; it is even in stones.

▷ Water is used for many things:

 a. To drink: Toads drink through their skin, birds tip their heads back, horses suck, cats and dogs lap, and other animals drink in their own ways
 b. To wash things—dishes, cars, clothes, ourselves
 c. To cook things in (eggs, vegetables); to use in things we cook (cakes, soup)
 d. To put out fires
 e. To play in—pools, ponds, lakes, oceans; or to play with when using hoses
 f. To water plants, lawns, trees, bushes
 g. To transport cargo and people on ships or boats

▷ Water is wet when it is a liquid. Scientifically it must be stated that it is dry when ice or vapour.

▷ Pure water is colourless. It often appears blue in ice or in a clear lake or green or brown in a river because it contains or reflects other matter.

▷ Water that has mineral salts (calcium and magnesium) is called "hard water." Rainwater is most often soft water. Well water or water from streams flowing over gypsum, limestone, or dolomite is more likely to be hard.

▷ Water is heavier than air.

▷ Ocean water is salty.

▷ More plants and animals live in water than on land (some in saltwater and some in fresh water).

▷ There is much more water than land on the earth's surface.

▷ Water flows: It will run from a higher place to a lower place and seek the lowest possible level.

▷ Water takes three forms:

    a. It is a liquid in lakes, oceans, or when it comes from taps
    b. It is a solid when it is ice or snow
    c. It is a gas when it is steam, clouds, air, fog, mist, or vapour

▷ Water comes to the earth as rain or snow. Most of it goes back into the air. Fog or mist is a cloud on the ground.

▷ Ice is very strong. It holds you up when you skate on it if it is thick enough. Some Inuit used to build temporary winter houses from blocks of snow and ice. If water gets into bottles, iron pipes, or cracks in rocks or pavement it can break them when it turns into ice because it expands when frozen.

▷ Cold water from our taps comes from many sources—surface run-off stored in reservoirs behind dams, deep wells, springs, streams, and rainwater collected in concrete basins.

▷ Hot water from our taps is the same water as the cold but it is heated and stored in a hot-water tank in our homes before we use it.

▷ Water needs to be saved if we are to have enough. We can help by turning off dripping taps and by pouring excess drinking water on plants or in the garden instead of down sink drains.

    ★ **CAUTION:**   Do not overwater plants.

▷ Many things mix with water: sugar, salt, soap. Some things do not, such as sand or oil.

    NOTE: See chapters on animals for uses and needs of water by animals and "Water Transportation" for information about water as a waterway. See "Basic Resources," p. 68, for rainy day ideas.

Additional Facts the Teacher Should Know

1. Pure water is composed of the elements hydrogen and oxygen (two parts of hydrogen to every part of oxygen). When these two invisible gases combine to form a liquid (water) or solid (ice), we can see them. When they remain in a gaseous form, such as steam or vapour, they are not always visible. The earth's surface is about 75 percent water and 25 percent land. The human body is about 70 percent water. Many compounds contain water. Foods hold a lot of water—milk, 87 percent; peaches, 89 percent; eggs, 74 percent; steaks, 60 percent; watermelons, 92 percent.

2. Water is used in great quantities in industrial and power applications, such as electricity and steam. This level of information is usually hard for very young children to understand, so it has not been highlighted in the basic concepts.

3. Water is the most precious material on earth, more than gold, diamonds, or oil. One-quarter of all water is used for industry. It takes 45.5 litres of water to prepare one can of lima beans and 2273 litres to make 4.5 litres of gasoline! One-quarter of the water is used to make electricity with steam power. Two-fifths is used for irrigation, and less than one-tenth for houses and public buildings. We are using so much water that unless we learn to reuse it, there will not be enough for the next generation of people.

4. The four worst sources of water pollution are:

    a. Acid rain
    b. Sewage poured by communities into major streams
    c. Industrial wastes loaded with chemicals dumped back into streams
    d. Agricultural pesticides washed into streams which kill fish and poison birds and animals that prey on them

5. Four ways to stop water pollution:

    a. Build treatment plants for sewage
    b. Have industries build plants to treat their wastes

    c. Control or ban use of dangerous pesticides
    d. Clean-up leaking dump sites like those polluting the Niagara River and Lake Ontario

6. To control erosion by rain and water we can:
    a. Contour farms
    b. Build dams and reservoirs
    c. Build irrigation ditches
    d. Build canals
    e. Reforest logging areas

7. Clouds are water vapour that contains billions of tiny droplets of water. They can be several miles high. Rain occurs when these droplets in a cloud combine and get too heavy to float, so they fall to earth. Water keeps traveling from sky to earth to ocean and back again to sky. This constant movement is called the "water cycle" and has been going on for billions of years. Water gets into the air by evaporation and transpiration from the leaves of plants. An apple tree will lose as much as 182 litres of water from its leaves on a hot day. As raindrops ("soft" or nearly pure water) fall to earth, they pick up tiny particles from the air and the ground to become impure or "hard." Boiled-off frozen water becomes clean again. Water becomes a solid when it is frozen into ice at 0°C. It becomes a gas when it boils into steam at 100°C. Hailstones are frozen raindrops. When water freezes, it expands. Ice floats on water and fish can live below it.

    NOTE: Some children will know about soft and hard water because they have automatic water conditioners in their homes and their parents may require that they drink water only out of a specific faucet (usually a kitchen faucet because of cooking).

8. Water is a natural air conditioner. Water in the thick layer of air around the earth absorbs the hot rays of the sun; if it were not there, it would be too hot on earth for life. At night it is the opposite. The damp air holds in the heat that has been absorbed during the day. Otherwise, the earth would freeze every night. Air is never completely dry; there is always a blanket of moisture around the earth.

9. Water and many other liquids weigh approximately one kilogram per litre. Water is colourless. The deep blue or green colour of lakes or oceans comes from light. The blue of the sky also comes from light rays reflected by water molecules. In space, the sky is black because there is no moisture.

10. All plants and animals began as simple forms in the ocean. The ocean has always been a great source of food. Our ancestors speared fish before they killed land animals. Amphibians, such as frogs and turtles, can get oxygen from the water through their skins and from the air by means of their lungs. Warm-blooded animals and man cannot breathe without mechanical assistance under water. The average adult loses about 2½ litres of water every day through her or his skin, lungs, and body wastes. It is replaced by eating and drinking. The water lost in perspiring cools you off by evaporation.

11. For years, explorers used water routes for transportation, and later added canals for this purpose. See "Water Transportation," "Winter", and "Spring."

Methods Most Adaptable for Introducing this Subject to Children

1. When children notice the weather on a rainy, snowy, or foggy day, relate it to water.
2. On a cold day, the children might notice their breath outdoors; they are making their own clouds but they fade quickly.
3. On the science table have a globe of the earth and two pitchers of water, one salty and one fresh. Point out the oceans on the globe and let the children taste the saltwater. Then point out the lakes and rivers and let them taste the fresh water. Notice how much of the earth's surface is covered with saltwater. Use disposable paper cups or plastic spoons for tasting purposes.

4. Have picture books with children playing in water and books of animals in or near water.
5. Have magazine pictures of lakes, rivers, and oceans around the room. Have an aquarium in a prominent place.

Vocabulary

water	rain	ocean	melt
wet	lake	cloud	drip
pond	stream	mist	damp
swim	river	moist	wash
ice	drops	dew	spray
snow	vapour	freeze	sprinkle
fog			

Learning Centres

Discovery Centre

1. Water is very inexpensive and readily available as a material for play. If you don't have water in the classroom, place a large metal or plastic tub, tank, plastic baby bath, or small wading pool on an old throw rug, blanket, bedspread or towels on the floor. Older children could help to partly fill container by carrying pitchers, buckets, or cups of water from the nearest source. Have lots of wiping-up materials handy, such as mops, sponges, and rags. If plastic aprons are available, use them. When weather permits, use waterplay outdoors. Unadulterated water can be poured on the ground.

2. Pouring and measuring: Start out with plastic or metal measuring cups. Each day add something else, such as squirt bottles, funnels, plastic or rubber tubing, straws, short lengths of hose, sponges, eggbeaters, strainers, wire whips, cooking spoons (metal and wooden), measuring spoons, clothes sprinklers. Be sure all utensils are unbreakable and will not rust. Use plastic eye or medicine droppers of different size and count how many drops they hold. Also do this with a baster. Use measuring spoons and cups to count how many of each in each.

3. Floating and sinking: Use water to try floating and sinking objects, such as nails, rocks, wood, cork, styrofoam, polyethylene objects, spools, cups, and floating and sinking soap. Try a small glass bottle with the lid off; then screw the lid on tightly and try again. Next put some sand in the bottle, cap it, and try again. Keep adding more sand until it sinks. Do the same with water. Explain that when a submarine's air tanks are full of air, it floats; but when filled with water it sinks. As the water is pumped out and replaced with (compressed) air again it will rise to the surface. Air helps things float, such as balloons, corks, wood, and our lungs.

4. Washing: Add detergent or soap to the water and use it to wash toys that are dirty *and* washable, such as cars, trains, tabletops, cupboard shelves, doll furniture and clothes. Experiment to see whether hot or cold water dissolves soap more quickly.

Water play centre. A bathroom with a wall removed allows this area to become a water play centre. It can readily be used with no extra supervision if the area is visible from a classroom area. Note rules on the wall; no 3. is "Wipe up spills on the floor" and no. 4 is "Only teachers turn on the taps."

5. Mixing: Let children mix different things with water, such as soap powder, sand, salt, flour, sugar, oil, baking soda, and cornstarch. Using three jars of water, put sand in one, dirt in one, and salt in one. Shake all three and notice how fast they clear up.

6. Evaporation: Pour water to the same level in two similar jars. Put a rubber band around the outside of both at the water level. Cap one but leave the other uncapped. Observe the change in level from day to day. Notice the residue. Put a salt-and-water mixture in a flat dish. Note the residue after evaporation. Taste it. Iron a damp cloth until dry. To watch evaporation, put some water on a warm sidewalk on a sunny day. Soon the sidewalk will be dry. Indoors, wipe a blackboard with a wet sponge and watch it become dry. Blow on it or turn a fan on it and observe.

7. Hot and cold: Fill one jar with water, one with packed snow, and one with ice cubes or chips. After they have all become water, compare volumes and cleanliness of contents. Use a magnifying glass to see snowflakes. Watch them turn into water in your warm hand. Blow on a cold window to see the water vapour from your breath. Heat a small piece of ice to water and then to steam. Heat water to steam, then turn it back into water on a mirror or a metal pan. Water will take the shape of any container it is put into. Freeze water in a balloon, milk carton, pie pan, or paper cup (cone-shaped, if possible). Notice the shapes when the containers are removed. Spill some water on a flat table and notice the shape it takes. Fill a glass with hot water and another with cold. Measure the temperatures with a thermometer, if you wish. Put a finger in each glass. Put some water from each glass into a third glass. Feel it and measure the temperature. Put some ice cubes into a glass of water. Feel and notice its temperature. Also observe drops of water formed on the outside of the glass.

8. Absorption and displacement: Weigh a dry sponge; soak it with water and weigh it again. Show how water soaks into a paper towel but forms drops or runs off waxed paper. Show how water magnifies by dropping a penny into a glass of water. Suck on a straw in a glassfull of water to show how you can lower the water level. Put your finger on the top end of the straw full of water. Then release your finger. Observe what happens.

9. Put some cut flowers or pussywillows in a jar of water and more in a jar with no water. Observe what happens. Keep a green plant watered, and a similar one unwatered.

10. Observe displacement by partly filling a jar with water. Put a rubber band at the water level. Lower several nails on a thread to the bottom, one at a time, and notice the water level.

11. Fill a glass jar with water. Punch two holes in the lid and screw it on tightly. Put your finger over one hole. Invert. Notice how the water comes from only one hole.

12. Punch holes in a vertical line from top to bottom of a can. Fill with water and observe that the water spurts farther from the bottom holes.

13. Put the top end of a dry towel in a pan of water on a table and the bottom end in a pan on the floor. See what happens.

14. Demonstrate how a siphon works with rubber tubing or a hose.

15. Make small waves by blowing on a flat pan of water.

16. Demonstrate the use of a level. Check to see if tables and shelves are level or not.

17. In the summer, supply a bowl of soapy water (do not use detergent) for each child and wooden spools and plastic straws for each. Let the children blow bubbles. Bubbles will show rainbow colours in the sun and be blown around by the wind, providing real enjoyment.

18. Using five pans, fill one with dirt; one, clay; one, sand; one, coarse sand; and one, pebbles. Slowly pour water on each and notice which pan the water sinks into fastest.

19. Make rainbows in the sun with water from a hose. Notice how waterdrops sparkle on grass.

20. Watch a street sweeper, if possible, to see how water is used in its operation.

21. On a hot day, wear swimming suits and run through a sprinkler or set up a water fight with squirt bottles and hoses, if possible. If no hose is available, use a large water cooler with rubber tubing and a pinch clamp on the spigot.

22. Let each child put out a lighted candle using a spray bottle filled with water.

23. While it is raining, listen for the thunder, watch for lightning, listen for the sounds of cars going by and of rain on the windows or on a metal roof. Use umbrellas and boots. Go outdoors in the rain (if it is not an electrical storm), in raincoats, or if it is warm enough, in swimming suits.

24. In the winter: See Hot and Cold in the chapter on "Winter" for related activities.

25. After a rain: Look for worms, rainbows, how clean the leaves, grass, and street have become. See how dust has settled ... how birds are bathing or drinking from a puddle ... how clouds are blowing away. Look for a deep groove where rainwater came off a roof or washed out from a rainspout. Measure the amount of rain in a transparent tube or gauge. Watch water evaporate from wet sidewalks after rain.

26. Squirt a hose straight up. Also squirt it on the ground, turned on full force to show what water pressure can do. Squirt it on a metal roof or barrel, on the sidewalk, grass, a tree, or a window. Listen to the different sounds and watch the different ways it dissipates.

   NOTE: Draw no conclusions from the above-mentioned activities. Observe and comment only ... *let the children discover.*

Dramatic Play Centres

Home-living centre

1. Let children wash dolls in a plastic tub. Provide soap, powder, and lots of towels.
2. Let children wash and dry play dishes in this centre.
3. Let children wash doll clothes and hang them to dry. This activity can take place outdoors if the weather is nice.
4. Ask the children to do some of the actual cleaning in the classroom (see Discovery Centre), such as mop up spills and clean paintbrushes and other creative art materials. If you have a glass door, a child on each side, washing it at the same time, can be hilarious. Washing a mirror can also be fun.
5. Provide rainy or snowy day dressup clothes, such as rain hats, coats, boots, umbrellas, mittens; also fire-fighting hats, boots, and hoses (see patterns, pp. 20, 468.)
6. Practise pouring: Use real water, coloured with food colouring, if you wish, for tea parties.

   NOTE: Disposable paper cups should be used unless dishes are washed with soap after the party.

Block-building centre

1. Suggest using blocks to build canals, bridges, and dams for toys boats to use.
2. Show how a marina is made.
3. Suggest a car-wash building for toy cars to go through.
4. Suggest building fire stations for fire engines and build houses which have pretend fires to put out.

Other dramatic play centres

1. Sandpile: Use a hose in the summer to make a stream, dams, or a reservoir. Make a channel and let water from the hose flow in it. Sail wooden boats made from scraps at the workbench.
2. Set up a car wash outdoors: Use hose and wash wagons and tricycles. Supply rags and sponges.
3. Use wet sand for cooking with jelly molds, muffin pans, custard cups, and other aluminum or wooden utensils.
4. After a heavy rain, notice how water pushes aside fine sand, and exposes coarse pebbles and leaves trails of dirt.
5. Flood the sandbox and watch the rivers running off, the ponds that are left, and the dirt and sticks that are washed to a pile by the side.
6. Outdoors, arrange packing boxes like a boat or fleet of boats. Add fishing poles with magnets and paper fish with paper clips for fishing.

   ★ **CAUTION:** Careful supervision is needed so that a magnet or pole does not hit anyone.

7. Paint outdoors with water: Provide buckets, large paintbrushes, old paint rollers and trays, and squirt bottles for spray painting. Also supply a painter's hat and overalls. Paint seesaws, boxes, slides, sidewalks, and toys with water. Use water to paint the outside wall of the building if it is one of the play yard boundaries.
8. Use mud dough: Mix dirt and sand with water to correct consistency. Mud dough makes good pancakes and cookies. Sprinkle sand on the products for sugar or add leaves and grass. Let dry and bake in the sun.

Learning, Language, and Readiness Materials Centre

Commercially made games and materials

(See "Basic Resources," p. 79, 100, for manufacturers' addresses.)

1. *Puzzles:* Five-to-ten piece puzzles show a variety boats and water scenes, including some puzzles with knobs.
2. *Construction and manipulative toys:* Water and sand play materials, large indoor water play table, pails and containers in a variety of sizes, scoops, shovels, funnels, flour sifters, etc.
3. *Small toys for imaginative play:* Vinyl and wooden boats in a variety of sizes; be sure that they can float.
4. *Outdoor toys:* Large indoor water play table, pails and containers in a variety of sizes, scoops, shovels, funnels, flour sifters, etc. Provide a variety of blower shapes. Make your own solution (one part liquid soap to twenty parts water) or buy Pustefix for lovely colours.
5. *Posters:* Seaside scenes, scenes of fishers and their catch, posters of rain and rainwear.
6. *Miscellaneous:* Small fishing roads with magnetic bait or plastic hooks. Fish with large loops made of metal.

Teacher-made games and materials

NOTE: For a detailed description of "Learning Games," see pp. 50–59.

Name it: Use objects we use with water, such as a toy boat, a plastic glass, straw, scrub brush, ice cube tray, and hose. VARIATION: Use objects we use with water to get ready for bed, such as soap, washcloth, toothbrush, towel.

Art Centre

- 1. Paint with dry tempera on wet paper, dipping into water, then into dry tempera.
- 2. Let the children mix their own tempera with water. Show how the colour gets lighter with additional water and darker with more paint added.
- 3. Paint with water colours as a change from more opaque tempera.
- 4. Wet a sheet of light-coloured construction paper. Drip paint from a brush or squeeze bottle.
- 5. Drop paint onto a sheet of paper and blow through a straw on each drop.
- 6. Make blotto prints by pressing out a design by blotting paint between two pieces of paper.
- 7. Crayon with bright colours on a large sheet of white construction paper. Then do a wash over the entire paper with thin gray, blue, or purple tempera or water colour.
- 8. Try to crayon on wet paper; then try chalk on wet paper.
- 9. Draw with coloured chalk: Decorate with drops of water from eye dropper or squeeze bottle.
- 10. Use water-soluble felt pens. Show how dry ones can be used again if dipped into water.
- 11. Paint on a blackboard with wet brushes, sponges, or rags.
- 12. Let children mix dry, powdered clay with water to a modeling consistency.
- 13. Make a rain-and-clouds collage: use blue construction paper and paste on absorbent cotton for clouds, gold or silver rick-rack for lightning, Christmas tree icicles for rain, and offer other appropriate collage materials.
- 14. Wet paper for easy tearing in torn paper designs.

•• 15. Make walnut shell boats: Stick a round toothpick through a piece of white paper cut in the shape of a right triangle. Attach the other end of the toothpick to the bottom of the walnut shell at the pointed end with any kind of play dough that dries hard (see p. 27 for recipe). Let dry before using.

•• 16. Make wooden boats at the workbench out of scrap lumber.

••• 17. Make paper boats by paper folding and creating milk carton boats.

Outdoors

• 1. Paint with water on sidewalks and climbing equipment. Use buckets of water, old paintbrushes, and paint rollers.

• 2. Draw in wet sand with sticks.

• 3. If you have a muddy place on the playground after a rain, make mud handprints and footprints. When fairly dry, make plaster casts of them.

• 4. Use mud dough, also try mud and sand mixtures.

•• 5. Draw on dry sidewalk with a squirt bottle of water.

Book Centre

•• Blades, Ann. *By the Sea: An Alphabet Book.* Toronto: Kids Can Press, 1986.

••• Branley, Franklyn. *Floating and Sinking.* New York: Thomas Y. Crowell, 1967.

••• Burningham, J. *Come Away from the Water, Shirley.* New York: Thomas Y. Crowell, 1977.

•• Duvoisin, Roger. *Two Lonely Ducks.* New York: Alfred A. Knopf, 1951.

••• Flack, Marjorie. *The Boats on the River.* New York: Viking Press, 1946.

••• Gramatky, Hardy. *Little Toot.* New York: G.P. Putnam's Sons, 1939.

••• Gantschev, Ivan. *Walk Under the Rainbow.* New York: Silver, 1986.

•• Henkes, K. *Clean Enough.* New York: Greenwillow Press, 1982.

• Hughes, S. *Bathwater's Hot.* New York: Lothrop, Lee & Shepard, 1985.

••• _____. *An Evening at Alfie's.* New York: Lothrop, Lee & Shepard, 1985.

• Keats, Ezra J. *The Snowy Day.* New York: Viking Press, 1962.

••• Larsen, John. *Captain Carp Saves the Sea.* Willowdale, Ont: Annick Press, 1983.

•• Lionni, Leo. *On My Beach There Are Many Pebbles.* New York: Ivan Obelensky, 1961.

• _____. *Swimmy* also *Nageot* (French version) and *Suimi* (Spanish version). New York: Pantheon, 1963.

••• Maestro and Delvecchio. *Big City Port.* Toronto: Methuen Books, 1986.

••• Marzollo, J. *Amy Goes Fishing.* New York: Dial Press, 1980.

••• McCloskey, R. *One Morning in Maine.* New York: Viking Press, 1952.

••• _____. *Time of Wonder.* New York: Viking Press, 1957.

••• Munsch, Robert. *The Mud Puddle,* Willowdale, Ont: Annick Press, 1982.

••• Peacock, David. *The Sea Serpent in Grenadier Pond.* Willowdale, Ont: Hounslow Press, 1986.

• Rockwell, A., and H. Rockwell. *Nice and Clean.* New York: Macmillan, 1984.

••• Rounds, G. *Washday on Noah's Ark.* New York: Holiday, 1985.

• Shaw, Charles. *It Looked Like Spilt Milk.* New York: Harper & Row, 1941.

• Shulevitz, Uri. *Rain, Rain, Rivers.* New York: Farrar, Straus & Giroux, 1969.

• Spier, P. *Peter Spier's Rain.* Garden City, NY: Doubleday, 1982.

••• Staunton, Ted. *Simon's Surprise.* Toronto: Kids Can Press, 1986.

••• Tressalt, Alvin. *The Frog in the Well.* New York: Lothrop, Lee & Shepard, 1958.

••• _____. *Hide Seek Fog.* New York: Lothrop, Lee & Shepard, 1965.

••• _____. *It's Time Now.* New York: Lothrop, Lee & Shepard, 1965.

•• _____. *Rain Drop Splash*. New York: Lothrop, Lee & Shepard, 1964.

•• _____. *White Snow*. New York: Lothrop, Lee & Shepard, 1964.

•• Walter, Marion. *Make a Bigger Puddle, Make a Smaller Worm*. New York: J.P. Lippincott, 1971.

••• Waterton, Betty. *A Salmon for Simon*. Vancouver: Douglas & McIntyre, 1986.

••• Wynne-Jones, Tim. *Zoom at Sea*. Vancouver: Douglas & McIntyre, 1983.

••• Yashima, Taro. *Umbrella*. New York: Viking Press, 1958.

••• Zolotow, Charlotte. *The Storm Book*. New York: Harper & Row, 1952.

•• _____. *Summer Is Here*. New York: Abelard-Schuman, 1967 (all seasons).

NOTE: See book list for the chapter on water transportation for additional books.

Planning for Group Time

NOTE: All music, fingerplays, poems, stories, and games listed here may also be used at other times during the session as appropriate. See Core Library, "Basic Resources," p. 95, for publishers and addresses. Record company addresses can be found on p. 99.

Music

Songs

From originals songs in this book by JoAnne Deal Hicks
"Water Play," p. 581

From *Singing Bee*, Hart
"Merrily We Roll Along," p. 59
"Polly Put the Kettle On," p. 60
"Little Drops of Water," p. 63
"The Gallant Ship," p. 84
"Sur le Pont d'Avignon," p. 108
"Lightly Row," p. 138

From *A Treasury of Songs for Young Children*, Glazer
"The E-RI-E," p. 77
"Erie Canal," p. 79

From *Elephant Jam*, Sharon, Lois and Bram
"Charlie Over the Ocean," p. 36

Rhythms and singing games

Reproduce tone:

a. Add water of varying amounts to a set of eight glasses that are alike. With care you can get a one-octave range of notes when the glasses are tapped with a rhythm stick. Let the children experiment with the pouring also. Simple tunes such as "Mary Has a Little Lamb" can be played.

b. String up a set of various-shaped bottles by their necks, add water to varying depths, and tap with a rhythm stick.

c. Put different amounts of water in stemware. Wet your finger, hold the stem of the glass, run your finger around the rim of the glass, and a clear note can be produced. Close supervision is necessary! If you look closely at the surface of the water, you can actually see tiny ripples that the sound vibrations make. Put different amounts of water in bottles and blow across the tops. Listen to the variations. Dramatize: Wash doll clothes to music. Scrub tables to music. Wash hands to music. Fingerpaint to music.

Records and cassettes

Bob Homme. *The Giant Concert of Concerts by the Friendly Giant.* (A & M Records)
"Seafood Concert"

Raffi. *Baby Beluga.* (Troubadour Records)
"Baby Beluga"
"Water Dance"

Sharon, Lois, and Bram. *Elephant Record.* (Elephant Records)
"London Bridge"
"Noah's Old Ark"
"Jack Was Every Inch a Sailor"

———. *Smorgasbord.* (Elephant Records)
"Long Legged Sailor"
"Newfound Jig Medley"
"Sur le Pont d'Avignon"

Fingerplays and Poems

NOTE: Pittman's *Down by Jim Long's Stage* and *One Wonderful Day for a Sculpin Named Sam* are filled with grand and witty poems for this subject.

From *Mischief City*, Wynne-Jones
"Drink the Bathwater," p. 18

From *Oranges and Lemons*, King
"Noah's Ark," p. 16
"The Big Ship Sails in the Alley, Alley O," p. 44

From *Round and Round the Garden*, Williams and Beck
"Row, Row, Row Your Boat," p. 19
"I Hear Thunder," p. 37

From *Read Aloud Rhymes for the Very Young*, Prelutsky and Brown
"Swimming," p. 9
"Home," p. 30
"Shore," p. 30
"Chums," p. 40
"Fish," (#1) p. 44
"Fish," (#2) p. 44
"Belly and Tubs Went Out in a Boat," p. 45
"Drinking Fountain," p. 85

Stories

(To read, read–tell, or tell. See Book Centre for complete list.)
Stories for this subject should be chosen on the basis of children's experience. For example, Leonard's *Little Racoon Goes to the Beach* would be excellent for children in Manitoba who are more likely to have visited lakes and rivers than oceans. Maestro and Delvecchio's *Big City Port* would be a good option for children living in St. John's, Halifax, Quebec, Montreal, Toronto, or Vancouver.

Games

1. "Mulberry Bush": (using such variations as wash our hands, face, teeth; wash the car; scrub the floor, stairs).
2. "Row Your Boat:" Sit in pairs on the floor with feet together and hold hands; rock back and forth, keeping in rhythm with the tune as you sing.
3. "London Bridge": Sing and play with older children.
4. "Six Little Ducks": Follow the actions suggested in the song. Each child has a feather to hold in his/her hand for a tail.
5. "Musical chairs": Variation, using puddles instead of chairs (see "Learning Games," pp. 50-59).

Routine Times

Snack or lunch

1. Let children mix a powdered drink with water or make their own lemonade.
2. Let children make gelatin, measuring water and powder and stirring.
3. Taste different kinds of water—distilled water, well water, tap water, rainwater, saltwater, and sugar water.
4. Invite children to drink cold, warm, and hot water.
5. Demonstrate what happens when you boil an egg, spaghetti, a carrot. Taste before and after cooking.
6. Try eating some kind of fish at snack time and discuss where it came from.
7. Bake a cake mix for which you add only water, such as gingerbread. See how it changes in cooking.
8. Lick ice cubes.
9. In the summer make popsicles in the refrigerator. Cover and try to make them outdoors in freezing weather. Use juice.
10. Make crushed-ice confections (see "Winter").
11. Float a flower (or candle) in a fairly flat bowl for a centrepiece at snack time.

Toileting

1. Notice how much water is used in the bathroom, where it comes from, and where it goes. Follow the water pipes to their source, if possible.
2. Find the hot water tank.
3. Stress the importance of water for cleanliness and the need not to waste it.

Cleanup

1. Wash tables with a sponge before and after eating. Wash dishes used for snacks a few times.
2. Wash easels and shelves with sponges.
3. Water plants, add water to fish tank, and be sure any small pets such as gerbils have adequate water supply. Talk about exact amount of water needed.
4. Wipe up spills with mops or sponges.

Rest

On hot days, try damp washcloths on foreheads.

Water centre. Children, wearing plastic smocks to protect their clothes, are discovering how water follows channels that have been formed in concrete basin. Child at left is floating boats in the pool formed by the flow of water.

Large Muscle Activities

1. Use a rocking boat both indoors and outdoors as a fishing boat.
2. Sail all the boats made in creative art activities in a play pool or water table, or have a tractor tire split crosswise to form two circular water-filled troughs in which to sail toys and other objects.

3. On hot days set up a play pool.
4. Let a hose trickle for drinks.
5. Play under a sprinkler.
6. Blow bubbles outdoors (see Discovery Centre, no. 17, p. 514.)
7. Plant a garden and water it regularly with a sprinkling can or hose.
8. On a hot day when the children are in swimming suits, run the hose down a slippery slide. Supervize carefully.
9. Fill balloons with water and drop them from a height such as a slide or jungle gym. Discuss how the heavy water broke the balloon.
10. Dig up earth, and turn it over. Notice that it is damper underneath.
11. Set out a chunk of damp earth to dry in the sun. Feel and look at it later.
12. Water the grass.
13. Wash a car.
14. Put out a fake fire with water. Play firefighter (see "Ground and Road Transportation").
15. Make wet footprints on a dry sidewalk.
16. Crawl through or climb over large sewer pipes.
17. Play "jump the brook": Two ropes are laid parallel to jump over. After each child has had a turn, increase the distance between the ropes.
18. Have a digging spot or hole where mud can be made. You will need shovels that really dig, big rocks to push around for stepping-stones, boards for bridges, boxes or tubs for boats and houses, and a handy hose or tap nearby to rinse off with. If children are allowed to go barefoot be sure there are no sharp objects such as glass, tin cans, or pointed rocks in the hole.

Extended Experiences

1. Go for a walk, and find sources of water outdoors, such as hoses, fire hydrants, puddles, drainage canals, and sewers. Notice clothes drying on a clothesline.
2. Take a walk indoors to try to locate water pipes, sewer pipes, and the hot water tank.
3. If possible, visit a house or building under construction to see how the plumbing is installed. Get permission and plan for adequate supervision.
4. Visit a plumbing shop, laundromat, or take a group through a car wash in a car.
5. Visit street construction where underground sewer pipes are exposed or are being laid.
6. Go to see a water tower or water storage tank on the ground.
7. If you visit a farm, notice the water tanks for livestock, the windmills to pump water, and a hand pump, if such is still in use.
8. If there is an aquarium in your area, take the children there.
9. If snorkel or scuba diving is taught in your area, arrange to have the children see a demonstration.
10. Visit an indoor and an outdoor swimming pool.
11. Watch a street sweeper washing and sweeping the street.
12. If you are lucky enough to live near a lake, river, or ocean, take a trip to watch boats of all kinds, water skiing, sailing. Extra supervision will be necessary if the children are allowed to wade or play in the sand or at the water's edge.
13. Visit an area where water is used for beautification, as where there are fountains, waterfalls, swans and ducks, boating, a waterlily pond, fish ponds.
14. Stand on a small bridge and watch the water flow under it on one side; cross to the other side and watch the water flow out from under it. Drop a small floating object (stick, pinecone) over the first side and watch it come out on the other side. Try a nonfloating object, such as a small rock.
15. Visit a small pond on a still day, if possible. Look at reflections in the water. Then disturb it and look again. (This can be done in a play pool in the yard.)
16. Throw pebbles into water and notice how they form concentric circles. On a hot day take off shoes and socks and wade.

17. Encourage children to play in dry and wet sand. Offer them a water source and sand tools.
18. The following activities would not be used every day, but at the teacher's discretion:

    a. Invite the owner of a pet shop to visit and bring a pet turtle or fish and explain its care.
    b. Ask a plumber to visit your school facility.
    c. Invite a scuba diver to visit.
    d. Borrow a globe and maps from a parent for finding water areas and streams.

Teacher Resources

Pictures and Displays

▷ Use posters from travel agencies showing lakes, ski areas, or the seashore.
▷ Some calendars have excellent water pictures.
▷ Make large posters to show clothing which is to be worn for rainy days, for snowy days, or for playing in the water on hot days.
▷ Float a flower (or candle) in a fairly flat bowl.

Books and Periodicals

Blocksma, Mary. *Water Toys That Really Work.* 1985.
Ontario Science Centre. *Scienceworks.* Toronto: Kids Can Press, 1986.
Powledge, F. *Water.* New York: Farrar, Strauss & Giroux, 1982.
Fish. New York: Time-Life Books, 1979.
The Sea. New York: Time-Life Books, 1977.

Films and Videos

Consult your community library for films, filmstrips, and videotapes from the National Film Board, the CBC and their own collection

Community Resources and Organizations

▷ A fishing or anglers club
▷ A sailing club
▷ Harbour Police
▷ A scuba diving club
▷ Canadian Power Squadron
▷ A swimming club
▷ Canadian Red Cross (Lifeguard and Swimming Division)
▷ Royal Lifesaving Society of Canada
▷ Marina or aquarium
▷ Fish hatchery
▷ Plumber
▷ Scuba diving school

Government Agencies

Provincial or territorial ministry of the environment

Going Fishing

JoAnne Deal Hicks

NOTE: Sing during a fishing activity or to recall such an activity.

27 Colour in My World

★★★★★★★★★★★★★★★★★★★★★★★

Basic Understandings

(concepts children can grasp from this subject)

▷ Colour is a word used to describe an object.
▷ Colours are everywhere that we can see—in flowers, clothes, food, cars, and so on.
▷ Colours have names—red, orange, yellow, green, blue, and purple.
▷ We cannot see colours without light (in a dark place). If we cover our eyes we cannot see colours.
▷ Some rocks, minerals, and paints change colour under special lights (fluorescent, ultraviolet, and "black" light) or glow in the dark.
▷ Sunlight (which we see as yellow or white) can be split into a rainbow.
▷ Some colours are used to depict certain things—yellow, sunshine; green, grass; blue, sky. However this does not mean these colours must always be used for these things.
▷ Colours are used for safety symbols that everyone recognizes, such as stop signs, traffic lights, school zones, and railroad crossings.
▷ Some colours (or pigment) can be mixed together to make other colours.

blue + red = purple (violet)
blue + yellow = green
red + yellow = orange

red + yellow + blue = brown
white + colour = tint
colour + black = shade

▷ We cannot make red, yellow, blue, black, or white by mixing paints.
▷ White can be made by spinning a colour wheel but not by mixing paints.
▷ Each person has a skin, hair, and eye colour that is just right for them. Each may differ from ours.
▷ Sometimes we have favourite colours or consider some colours prettier than others and therefore prefer to use these more often than others.
▷ Almost everything has a colour except clear glass, clear plastic, pure air, and pure water.
▷ If we can see through something clearly, it is transparent.
▷ Colours look bright on a sunny day and dull on a cloudy day or when in the shade.
▷ There are paint colours that look like some metals we use—gold, silver, copper, and brass.

▷   Wood comes in different colours and has different names. Wood is usually named for the tree from which the lumber comes: maple, walnut, oak, white or yellow pine, cedar, ebony, and redwood.

Additional Facts the Teacher Should Know

1. Light, the source of all colour, is white when it reaches us from the sun. Each colour wave in the white ray of light has a different wave length, and each wave length, as it passes through a prism, is deflected at a different angle due to its velocity (rate of speed) in passing from one medium to another. Thus the complex white ray of light is dispersed into its many-coloured wave lengths (a rainbow). The longest ray is red; the shortest is violet. The longer wave lengths of light are called warm colours—red, orange, yellow. The shorter wave lengths are called cool colours—blue and violet. Green falls between the warm and cool colours.

2. The primary colours for paint pigment are red, yellow, and blue. Secondary colours of orange, green, and purple are produced by mixing two of the primary colours together. The easiest way for children to get brown is by mixing red, yellow, and blue. Brown can also be obtained by mixing orange and black. Children may discover this method at the art centre when using these paints during Halloween observance.

3. Hue is the name of a colour. Value means the lightness or darkness of a colour. Intensity means the saturation or purity of the colour. A hue may vary in intensity when it is mixed with white to make a tint (be sure to add the colour to the white); mix with black to produce a shade (add black to the colour); mixed with black and white to produce a tone; and mixed with its complement to form gradations of grayed tones.

4. The primary colours of light are red, green, and blue. They are used in stage lighting and window displays. If we take red, green, and blue spotlights into a darkened room and shine them on a white screen we will get the following secondary colours: red light + green light = yellow colour; red light + blue light = magenta or red-violet; and the blue light + green light = cyan blue or blue-green. Red, green, and blue light shining on the screen produces white.

5. Children and adults express their feelings by the use of colour. Colour may transmit an emotion or symbolic meaning to the beholder of an artwork.

6. Many words in the English language have meaning because of colour. For example, we see "red" when we are angry, we are "green" with envy, we are "yellow" when we lack courage, we have the "blues" when we are sad. These concepts are on an adult level and only produce confusing ideas for the preschooler.

7. Some young children seem much more colour-conscious than others. Children tend to be aware of colour distinction and to be able to classify objects by colour before they can attach a name to their groupings. The teacher must understand that children can experience colour activities and enjoy them, but may not be ready for real recognition of the concepts involved. The teacher should avoid forcing these concepts on a child who is not ready.

8. When using colour in art media, begin with the three primary colours. As any two or all three of these are mixed, other good colours are produced. Secondary colours may be added later for variety and for more brilliant hues. Pastel tints are delightful for a change of scene in the spring. Be sure to offer a choice of colours when children might wish to depict skin colour in their art work. Remember that dark colours are as attractive and pleasant to look at and are associated with good things (such as chocolate pudding) just as the brighter, more vivid colours are.

9. The visual disorder of colour blindness could be the cause for persistent colour confusion by a child. There are simple tests to detect this condition. Consult an eye doctor for assistance. More boys show this tendency than do girls.

Methods Most Adaptable for Introducing this Subject to Children

1. Go for a walk and observe colours.
2. Read a simple story about pure colours, such as *My Slippers Are Red.*
3. Explore a colour module (see Discovery Centre, no. 15).
4. Seasonal activity—red, Valentine's Day; orange and black, Halloween; white, winter; and on other such occasions.
5. Daily activity: Colour in food at meal time, discuss colour of skin, hair, eyes at routine times, or colour of cars, trucks, houses, trees, and flowers while in transit.
6. Colour days: A total experience with colour (see Discovery Centre, no. 1.)

Vocabulary

shadow	orange	dark	transparent
silver	red	gold	reflection
maple	blue	white	violet (purple)
brown	yellow	black	shiny
iron	copper	rainbow	glow
sun	walnut	prism	rust
bright	green	pink	ebony
dull	colour		ivory
brass	light		

Learning Centres

Discovery Centre

1. Colour days: Explore a colour for a certain time period. We recommend one week per colour for a beginning experience, three to five days for those with previous experience, and one to three days for those with many colour experiences. The following is an example of a red day:

   On the day preceding the first red day, send each child home with a note explaining the colour days or week with a square of pure red paper pinned to the child's clothing. The child is told to come to school wearing some article of red clothing or to bring an object or a picture showing the colour red. Both parents and children can become very involved in this project. Teachers, of course, should wear the colour of the day. They may add a surprise element at special times during the day by pinning a "colour book" on their smock or jacket. (Fold pages of appropriate coloured paper into a small book 10 cm by 12.7 cm. Paste coloured objects on each page.)

   NOTE: Have scarves, hankies, or coloured yarn loops for children who forget to bring or wear something for the colour day. Display a poster of red objects at the door or in a conspicuous place and put red objects on the discovery table. Feature the red media in the art centre. Use a red fingerplay and read stories or books to the children that emphasize the colour red. Serve red foods at snack or meal times. Sing red songs and use red games and other activities. Feature firefighters in dramatic play. After all the colour days have been presented, all colours are stressed and rainbows are considered. A suggested colour sequence could be— red, yellow, blue, green, orange, and violet. After violet, could be brown, then black and white, and finally rainbow days featuring all the colours.

2. Make a rainbow: A serendipitous event would be a real rainbow after a rain.

    a. A rainbow can be created by placing a small mirror in a glass of water, with the mirror tilted against the glass.

    b. If a prism is held up close to the eyes on a bright day, all objects viewed will be outlined in rainbows.

    c. The sun shining directly through the water in an aquarium makes a rainbow.

    d. Observe how a drop of oil in a puddle produces a rainbow of colours.

    e. Observe how a fine water spray with the sun shining through produces a rainbow.

       NOTE: Always have the sun in back of the child holding the hose. The sun must fall on the water to make a rainbow.

    f. Discover how a prism bends light to make a rainbow. The teacher can find different prisms—beads, chandelier pendants, diamonds, beveled glass.

    g. Commercial soap bubbles have (Rustefix) rainbow colours. (Or make your own, see p. 28.)

3. Observe difference in the brightness of colours in sun and in shade.

4. The children may experiment in making the colour brown by squeezing drops of primary food colours into water in a clear plastic glass.

5. Encourage children to mix primary colours to obtain secondary colours:

    a. Tissue paper of primary colours may be superimposed and held against a window.

    b. Overlay sheets or cut out shapes of coloured plastic or cellophane.

    c. Easel paint or finger paint may be mixed to discover secondary colours.

    d. Water colours brushed and crossed on a large sheet of white paper.

    e. Use commercially made colour paddle, rainbow box, and tri-colour viewer.

6. Try on tinted glasses of different hues to observe same coloured items.

7. Set out kaleidoscopes for examination by the children.

8. Explore a mirror to see how it reflects images.

9. Set out objects you can see through and those you can't—glasses, binoculars, fish bowl, clear plastic tumblers, and magnifying glass, rocks, wood, metal, china, construction paper.

10. Children may explore a coloured flashlight. (Some have two or three colours.)

11. Older children may enjoy dyeing materials and seeing how things of the same colour differ in shade.

12. Dye white eggs that have been hard cooked.

13. Have samples of different kinds of wood and, if possible, pictures of the trees from which they come. Let children sand wood to make it smooth. Notice the different grains.

14. Display rocks and minerals of various colours. Provide hand-held and tripod magnifying glasses. Look at fluorescent minerals under a "black" light if one is available.

15. Colour modules: Furnish a large carton or wooden box (big enough to crawl inside) with nature items, food, upholstery and textured cloth, toys, and equipment to create a Colour Saturation Mini-Room. You could, instead, set up a corner or enclose an area with a three-way play screen. Appeal to all of the child's senses! Invite the child to interact with this special colour environment. Be sure to make the outside intriguing enough to entice the child inside. Prints of good paintings focusing on the colour, windows to peek through, and a rug leading to the door will enhance this area. Equip your room or area in such a way that props can be interchanged to introduce new colours. Use hooks on the walls to hang a roller drop of drapery, wallpaper, plastic, or carpeting. For example: yellow —bananas, daffodils, yellow velvet upholstery, lemon incense, bamboo bug keeper, balloons, yellow cab, sponges, low watt yellow bulb, straw hat, lemon-scented soap, yellow plastic or cellophane on the windows.

Dramatic Play Centres

Home-living centre

1. Make available a full-length mirror and as many brightly coloured objects, toys, and articles of dressup clothes as possible. Reinforce colour awareness in conversation that arises naturally with the children; for example: "The firefighters that we visited had red hats, ours are red too."
2. Dress dolls or paper dolls in variously coloured articles of clothing—use scraps of material or construction paper.
3. Emphasize colour in foods and table service.
4. Talk about metals—copper bottom and aluminum pots and pans, stainless steel utensils, silverware, and iron.

Block-building centre

1. Emphasize colour in cars, trucks, road signs, and other block building accessories.
2. Property lines could be drawn on the floor with coloured chalk.
3. Teachers can identify each child's building with a colourful sign.

Other dramatic play centres

1. Set out traffic signs and signals for use with wheel toys:

   a. Those that are 7.5 cm tall are available in most catalogues.
   b. Make traffic signals using Bulletin Board aids such as Traffic Safety.
   c. Make your own signs and signals. A traffic light can be made by pasting red, green, and yellow circles on an egg carton lid.

2. Go fishing. Cut out paper fish of various colours. Attach paper clip for a mouth. Let children fish with cardboard tube pole and string line with magnet attached. Appropriate during or following this activity would be the song "Going Fishing," p. 524.

   ★ CAUTION: When working with hyperactive children or those with little self-control, do not use magnets. Instead, the child drops a line on the fish he or she wants and an adult, or another child, who is sitting in or near the pond, attaches the line to the paper clip mouth. The child hauls in his or her fish, removes it from the line by sliding the line from under the clip, and drops it in the boat or bucket.

3. Dramatize *Caps for Sale* by Slobodkin, listed in Book Centre. Props needed—red, green, yellow, and blue caps for the monkeys and one brown cap for the peddler.

Learning, Language, and Readiness Materials Centre

Commercially made games and materials

(See "Basic Resources," pp. 79, 100, for manufacturers' addresses.)

   NOTE: Set out puzzles and other cognitive materials featuring the colour of the day.

1. *Puzzles:* Puzzles with large coloured shapes that give children the opportunity to match the shapes and the colours.
2. *Construction and manipulative toys:* Large coloured pegs and coloured peg board. Wooden mosaics that can be formed into a variety of patterns on the floor or on a table.

3. *Miscellaneous:* Montessori colour tablets.

   a. Kaleidoscope with changeable coloured screens.
   b. See-through peel and stick designer: A large plastic stand that can be used with reusable plastic shapes to create unique designs.
   c. Prisms, colour paddles, coloured pyramid.

   ★ CAUTION: Assure that all prisms, paddles and similar equipment are made of unbreakable materials.

   d. Board games: Games for colour matching distributed by Parker, Milton Bradley, and Ravensburger.
   e. Coloured magnetic letter and number sets.
   f. Coloured washable markers; for example Sanford's Mr. Sketch Markers.

Teacher-made games and materials

   NOTE: For a detailed description of "Learning Games," see p. 50–59.

1. Many inexpensive, unbreakable, small coloured objects can be used in interesting colour sorting games. For example: small plastic sports cars (usually red, blue, yellow, and green) can be parked in the matching coloured construction paper parking lots. Cars or airplanes can be sorted into milk carton garages or hangers that have been painted different colours.
2. Spools may be painted pure colours and used as beads to string on long boot strings, or made into a sorting device on graduated lengths of dowel rods.
3. Match-them: Match paint chips, spools of thread, rug samples, or swatches of fabric.
4. Coloured rubber bands of various widths and lengths can be stretched between pegs on a pegboard.
5. Colour lotto game: Make duplicate sets of coloured cardboard squares. Glue one set to lotto boards, making sure the same colour squares are placed in a variety of positions on the various cards.
6. How many? Use coloured-paper geometric shapes, colour chips, or other small coloured objects like teddy bear counters.
7. Play sequence: Make a row of coloured squares or objects.
8. Match-them: Make two or more colour envelopes. Enclose in each a red square, a yellow circle, a green triangle, and a blue rectangle. Ask children to take their envelope and remove matching shapes and match theirs with the teacher's.
9. Alike, different, and the same: Children select the coloured piece that does not belong with a group of like coloured objects or pieces of paper.
10. Match-them: Match coloured paper to pictures or objects in the room.

   NOTE: Any conversation with a child about colour helps to make the child more colour conscious. Always include the name of the object that you are distinguishing by the colour adjective. For example: "Do you want the red paint?" Otherwise, the child may think "red" is the object if you only say "Do you want red?"

Art Centre

   NOTE: In the art suggestions listed below, sometimes only one colour example is given. Substitute other colours as you wish.

• 1. The featured colour is used at the easel. If a secondary colour is being emphasized, also offer the two primaries that produce the secondary.

★ **CAUTION:** To keep paints from getting muddy, use small amounts of paint in unbreakable paint pots (available from Galt). Change as needed. Use one brush for each jar.

•• 2. Red: Blotto pictures or string painting.

•• 3. Blue: Sponge painting on light blue paper.

•• 4. Violet: Fingerpaint. Start with uncoloured fingerpaint. Let children sprinkle dry red tempera and paint with it for awhile. Then sprinkle on blue tempera from a small shaker to discover violet (purple).

•• 5. Brown: Spatterpaint brown animals on pastel paper, or make brown crayon rubbings over pennies.

••• 6. Make a rainbow using either water colours brushed onto a large white sheet of paper with a wide brush or use the long side of peeled crayons.

•• 7. Scribble paintings: Children scribble many colours on a large sheet of white paper pressing hard with wax crayons in bright colours. Then paint over entire paper lightly with either black water colour or thin black tempera.

•• 8. Offer bright tempera paint and brushes to children to paint their woodworking creations. Liquid detergent added to paint makes it stick better.

•• 9. Roller painting: Use small rolling pins or heavy cardboard tubes covered with upholstery, and roll across paint drops on wet surface (see illustration, p. 30).

• 10. Use spool brayers to make stripes and plaids of different colours (see p. 29).

• 11. Sort out crayons for the colour of the day.

• 12. Use big kindergarten chalk for writing on the blackboard.

• 13. Vividly coloured kindergarten chalk may be used on dark papers.

• 14. Orange: Start with uncoloured play dough. Sprinkle yellow dry tempera in a depression in the dough and work in with fingers, then add red tempera. Children will be able to discover orange. Some may make pumpkins or carrots.

• 15. Yellow: Crumple precut yellow tissue circles and paste on green paper to represent yellow flowers in the grass.

••• 16. Multicoloured tissue paper in irregular shapes that children may cut or tear easily can be overlapped and glued on rice paper with thinned white glue and used as transparencies in windows.

• 17. Black and white: Collage made by gluing shavings of white styrofoam (as in packing boxes) on black paper, or make shadow pictures of the children's heads.

18. Multicolour days:

••• a. Decorate eggs dyed in discovery centre.

•• b. Make collage of crushed dyed eggshells by gluing on black paper with thinned white glue.

• c. Sawdust mixed with thick tempera paint and spread to dry may be glued to paper later as a collage tray item.

• d. Rock salt or coarse pickling salt, dyed and sprinkled in glue giving a sparkling effect.

e. Sponge paint/stamp printing allows child to explore overlapping colour.

• 19. Collage from coloured yarns, gift ties, sequins, and glitter. Children can ask for the colours they wish to use.

• 20. Collage of thin wood scraps and shapes glued together. This may be painted.

• 21. Green: Sponges cut in various shapes can be used to make designs. Dip them in dark green paint and press them on light green paper.

••• 22. Fingerprints: Sponges in flat dishes make stamp pads. Use one colour (red, blue, yellow, green) per dish. Children use two fingers on each hand (one for each colour) to print on white paper (requires co-ordination).

••• 23. Make multicoloured wire sculptures from many coloured, covered wires found in short ends of telephone cable (free for the asking!).

Other experiences in this centre using art media

Origami (paper folding): See p. 236 for examples. (Only for older children.)

Book Centre

- Anglund, Joan Walsh. *What Colour Is Love?* New York: Harcourt Brace Jovanovich, 1966.
- ● Cleaver, Elizabeth. *ABC.* Toronto: Oxford University Press, 1984.
- ●● De Paolo, Tomie. *Marianna May and Nursery.* New York: Holiday, 1983.
- ●● Emberley, Ed. *Green Says Go.* Boston: Little, Brown, 1968.
- ● Freeman, D. *The Chalk Box Story.* New York: Harper & Row, 1976.
- ●● _____ . *Mop Top.* New York: Viking Press, 1955.
- ● _____ . *A Rainbow of My Own.* New York: Viking Press, 1966 (paper, 1974).
- ● Gill, Bob. *What Colour Is Your World?* New York: Astor-Honor, 1962.
- ● Johnson, Crocket. *Harold and the Purple Crayon.* New York: Harper & Row, 1955.
- ● Keats, Ezra Jack. *Peter's Chair.* New York: Harper & Row, 1967 (blue and pink).
- ● Lionni, Leo. *Little Blue and Little Yellow.* New York: Astor-Honor, 1959.
- ● Morgan, Nicola. *The Great B.C. Alphabet Book.* Markham, Ont: Fitzhenry & Whiteside, 1985.
- ●● Pinkwater. *The Big Orange Splot.* Toronto: Methuen Books, 1986.
- Shaw, Charles G. *It Looked Like Spilt Milk.* New York: Harper & Row, 1947.
- ● Slobodkin, Esphyr. *Caps for Sale.* Reading, MA: Addison-Wesley, 1947.
- Spier, P. *Oh Were They Ever Happy!* Garden City, NY: Doubleday, 1978.
- ● Stinson, Kathy. *Red Is Best.* Willowdale, Ont: Annick Press, 1982.
- ● _____ . *Those Green Things.* Willowdale, Ont: Annick Press, 1985.
- ● Swift, Hildegard H., and Lynd Ward. *The Little Red Lighthouse and the Great Gray Bridge.* New York: Harcourt Brace Jovanovich, 1942 (paper, 1974).
- Testa, F. *If You Take A Paintbrush: A Book of Colours.* New York: Dial Press, 1976.
- ● Walt Disney Productions. *Colours, Shapes and Sizes.* New York: Bantam, 1985.
- ●● Winik, J.T. *Fun with Colours.* Burlington, Ont: Hayes Publishing, 1985.
- ● Zacharias, Thomas, and Wanda Zacharias. *But Where Is the Green Parrot?* New York: Delacorte Press, 1968.
- ● Zion, Gene. *Harry, the Dirty Dog.* New York: Harper & Row, 1956 (black and white).
- ●● Zolotow, Charlotte. *The Sky Was Blue.* New York: Harper & Row, 1963.

> **NOTE:** Additional books for use in the colour section can be found in the chapter on sight.

Planning for Group Time

> **NOTE:** All music, fingerplays, poems, stories, and games listed here may also be used at other times during the session as appropriate. See Core Library, "Basic Resources," p. 95, for publishers and addresses. Record company addresses can be found on p. 99.

Music

Songs

From *Stepping Along in Music Land*, Murray
"Little Green Man," p. 42
"Rolling Down the Highway," p. 43
"Colour Song," p. 44
"Make a Rainbow," p. 46

From *Elephant Jam*, Sharon, Lois, and Bram
"Jenny Jenkins," p. 122

From *The Colours of My Rainbow*, Wayman
All the songs in this excellent activity book are useful for the colour theme. When choosing songs from this book use the criteria discussed on page 00 to decide if the song is best for singing with or to children.

From *The Goat With the Bright Red Socks*, Birkenshaw and Walden
"Colourfast Song," p. 9
"Goat with the Bright Red Socks," p. 25

Rhythms and singing games

From any record in march tempo
Children could carry brightly coloured flags of solid colours.

NOTE: Balloons, chiffon scarves, felt ribbons and crepe-paper streamers of different colours are good dance props (see p. 33).

Records and cassettes

Bob Homme. *The Giant Concert of Concerts by the Friendly Giant.* (A & M Records)
"Ribbon Concert"

Bob Schneider. *When You Dream a Dream.* (Capitol Records)
"Over the Rainbow"

Raffi. *The Corner Grocery Store.* (Troubadour Records)
"Cluck, Cluck Red Hen"

Sharon, Lois, and Bram. *Elephant Show.* (Elephant Records)
"Five Brown Buns"

———. *Smorgasbord.* (Elephant Records)
"Father Papered the Parlour"

Fingerplays and Poems

From *Read Aloud Rhymes for the Very Young*, Prelutsky and Brown
"Grasshopper Green," p. 63
"Crayons," p. 86
"Silvery," p. 87

From *Colours of My Rainbow*, Wayman
"Urple Purple," p. 41

MY PUSSY WILLOW

I have a little pussy
Her coat is soft and gray;
She lives down in the meadow
And she never runs away.

Although she is a pussy,
She'll never be a cat;
For she's a pussy willow!
Now what do you think of that?

COLOURS IN MY FOOD

by Bonnie Flemming

Colours, colours, what colours do I see
In the food the farmer grows for me?
Orange carrots and ripe, red tomatoes,
Green string beans and nice brown potatoes.
Yellow butter is to spread on my bread,
Cold, white milk and an apple so red,
Yes, these are the foods that are best, I know,
Because they help me to grow and grow!

NOTE: Use flannelboard props of foods. Teacher or children may place foods on flannelboard as poem is read. Use real foods at snack time and allow children to eat them when finished.

Stories

(To read, read–tell, or tell. See Book Centre for complete list.)
The books in the Book Centre list provide a wide range of choices for stories with a colour theme. Any book with colourful illustrations could be used with a story that emphasizes the colours. The illustrations in books of Brian Wildsmith are very good.

Games

(See "Learning Games," p. 50–59, and teacher-made games in this chapter for directions.)
1. Name it or Scramble
2. I see something or I spy
3. Look and see
4. Guess what?
5. What am I? (riddles)
6. Match-them
7. Alike, different, and the same
8. Colour lotto

Routine Times

1. Snack time/meal time: Do have a conference with the school cook and gain his or her imaginative cooperation in providing foods to match your colour days.
   Suggestions:

Yellow days

pineapple juice
lemonade
yellow apple slices
half unpeeled banana
scrambled eggs
custard
lemon gelatin

Red days

cranberry juice
tomatoes
red apple slices
cherry gelatin
strawberry tarts
cherry tarts
bing cherries (pitted)

Purple days

grape juice
purple grapes
purple plums
grape jelly
grape gelatin

Blue days

blue popcorn balls
blue milk (food colouring)
tint cream cheese blue and spread on crackers
blueberries

Green days	**Brown days**
lime gelatin	chocolate pudding
lime drink	peanut butter
lettuce	brown bread
green grapes	hot chocolate
celery	graham crackers
green peppers	gingerbread children
pickles	

Orange days	**Black and white days**
carrot coins	chocolate/vanilla cookies
orange juice	milk
cheese crackers	white bread
orange slices	popcorn
orange gelatin	marshmallows
mandarin oranges	prunes/raisins

    a. Let children colour their milk with drops of food colouring. Use coloured cellophane straws to match colour of the day. Children may choose a favourite colour straw on multicolour days or make fruit based milk shakes to achieve different colours.

    b. Use real or artificial flowers or fruits in appropriate colours to decorate the tables.

    c. Make place mats from shelf paper or paper towels in the colour of the day.

2. When it is time to get up from rest time, write child's name on the blackboard with chalk in the colour of the day.

3. Designate which child should get up from rest time by saying, "Anyone who has on red shoes may get up now."

4. In transit: Look for the featured colour along the way.

Large Muscle Activities

1. Use balls of different colours for ball play.
2. Beanbag toss: Use beanbags of different colours.
3. Blow and chase bubbles: Make wire loop for giant bubbles. Dip loop into a shallow cake or pie pan that has commercial bubble liquid in it. (See bubble recipe, p. 28.)
4. Colour songs: Give each child a small object of red, blue, yellow, or green colour. Child stands up or sits down as the words indicate, or when the colour of child's clothing is called.
5. A tisket, a tasket: Use green and yellow berry baskets; place behind one child instead of a handkerchief.
6. Two little blackbirds: Children sit on the floor in two rows. First pair get up, "fly around," and come back and sit down at the end of the row as song is sung. Repeat until all who wish have had a turn.
7. Hot potato (for brown days): See "Learning Games," p. 58.
8. Fly, little bluebird: See "Learning Games," p. 57.

Extended Experiences

1. Visit a paint store, fabric shop, or carpet mart.
2. Visit a furniture store. Notice different woods, metals, and fabrics.
3. A lapidist or "rock hound" may come and bring colourful rocks and minerals to show, especially those that change colour under black light.

4. An artist might enjoy showing the children how to mix paints on a palette and several ways to use the paint.

5. If you know people who do stage lighting perhaps they would demonstrate how lights and gels are used for different effects.

Teacher Resources

Pictures and Displays

▷ A bulletin board may be sectioned off into a colour area for pictures. Objects that the children bring may be displayed on a colour table.

▷ Pictures illustrating the fingerplays add interest. Be sure to include pictures of rainbows, Easter eggs, and foods.

▷ Grocery stores will often give teachers big pictures of fruits and vegetables that can be displayed.

▷ Large posters can be made from pictures that are all one colour including objects familiar to children. These posters can be used to show the featured colour of the day and are mounted on the classroom door or in a conspicuous place where children may discuss them.

▷ Display creative artwork made during the colour week.

▷ Display clear plastic glasses or vases of water tinted with food colouring on the window sills.

▷ Any pictures from other commercial packets or your personal file on other subjects that depict the colour of the day.

Books and Periodicals

Owl magazine
Chickadee magazine

Films and Videos

Films provide many resources for exploring the subject of colour. Consult your community library for a list of films that may be useful

Community Resources and Organizations

▷ Drapery, upholstery, and rug dealers for colour samples
▷ Paint stores for paint sample cards and formica samples
▷ Grocery stores for colourful display media such as foods, flowers, butterflies
▷ Lapidist in a jewellery store
▷ Rock hound: Collector of rocks and minerals
▷ Geologist in a nearby college or university
▷ A community theatre group
▷ A fabric shop
▷ Some museums have displays on colour and light

28 Tools and Machines to Use in My World

★★★★★★★★★★★★★★★★★★★★★★★★

Basic Understandings

(concepts children can grasp from this subject)

▷ A tool is an instrument held in the hand and used to help do a job easier and faster.

▷ A machine is an object made up of two or more moving or unmoving parts used for doing some kind of work; it may or may not be operated by the hand or hands.

▷ A machine usually makes work easier.

▷ Tools and machines cannot work by themselves; they need people or some kind of power (heat, air, water, chemicals, and electricity) to make them work.

▷ A power tool is a kind of tool that was once operated by hand and is now operated by electricity, batteries, gas, or other sources of energy. We often need to turn a switch or control the tool by hand.

▷ A tool can also be a machine.

▷ Some tools are not machines, for example, pencils, erasers, rulers, drinking straws, cups, bowls, and magnifying glasses.

▷ Some of the tools we use at home are screwdrivers and screws, hammers, saws, pliers, scissors, brooms, hand eggbeaters, can openers, pulleys, ladders, and files.

▷ Tools we may use in the garden are rakes, hoes, spades, and trowels.

▷ Some machines used in our homes are run by electricity, such as vacuum cleaners, food mixers, can openers, washing machines, clothes dryers, and sewing machines.

▷ Some machines used outdoors use chemicals, fuels, or motors to make them run, such as cars, lawn mowers, trains, and airplanes.

▷ Machines which help farmers do their work are known as farm machines—corn shellers, tractors, combines, seeders, cultivators, balers, milking machines, as well as simple tools like shovels and pitchforks.

▷ Machines which help us get from one place to another are transportation machines (see "Transportation").

▷ Tools and machines are used in factories to make cars, furniture, toys, and other products.

▷ Tools and machines are used in offices to help do the work. Office tools often include pens, erasers, rulers, staplers, punches, and pencils. Some office machines used are adding machines, typewriters, telephones, photocopiers and computers.

▷ Machines and tools are used to help build houses and buildings, using tools, such as screwdrivers, saws, hammers, nails, and drills, and machines such as cement mixers, bulldozers, and power saws.

▷ Machines are also used for road building and heavy construction, such as trenchers, steamrollers, road graders, steam shovels, bulldozers, pipe diggers, and cement mixers.

▷ Some tools and machines make loud noises, such as power mowers, electric drills, and hammers.

▷ Some tools and machines are quiet, such as pencils, screwdrivers, clocks, wristwatches, and metal tape measures.

▷ Although machines can help do work, they can also be dangerous if we get in their way or use them the wrong way.

▷ Most musical instruments are a kind of machine.

▷ Computers help bankers, taxi drivers, clerks in stores, librarians, teachers, and many other workers do their work more quickly and easily.

Additional Facts the Teacher Should Know

1. A machine is any device, simple or complex, by which the intensity of an applied force is increased, its direction changed, or one form of motion or energy changed into another form. It usually is made of two or more fixed or movable parts. All complex machines are combinations of six simple machines. These are further divided into

    a. Primary: Lever, pulley, inclined plane, and wedge
    b. Secondary: Wheel and axle, and screw.

2. A tool is a machine which is operated by hand. Complex machines use combinations of simple machines and may be run by various kinds of energy—heat, chemicals, electricity, atomic, oil, gas, and steam. In machines, a small force can be applied to overcome a much larger resistance or load.

3. A screw is actually an inclined plane would around a straight central core. A wedge is another example of inclined plane. It is really two inclined planes joined together at a point. A needle and a nail are examples of a wedge. Tongs, scissors, and a crowbar are simple lever machines.

    NOTE: Other related chapters are transportation, families at work, and animals.

Methods Most Adaptable for Introducing this Subject to Children

1. Display pictures of tools and machines.
2. Read a story about a community helper and his/her tools or machines.
3. Let children prepare soap flakes for soap painting using different tools (see Discovery Centre no. 18, p. 540).
4. Have a display of simple tools and machines on the discovery table.
5. Visit the site of a building or road being repaired or any similar work going on nearby and watch workmen using tools and machines. Talk about the machines being used and how they make work easier.

Learning Centres

Discovery Centre

1. Toss scraps of paper on the floor. Let the children pick up scraps by hand or by using a broom, a hand vacuum, and an electric vacuum cleaner. Talk about the help given in each case by the machine.

Vocabulary

TOOLS

Workbench
nail
screwdriver
pliers
wrench
ruler
tape measure
saw
crowbar
drill
wheel
axle
pulley
screw
wedge
tool
lever
inclined plane
hammer

Household
scissors
brush
can opener
rolling pin
nutcracker
rotary eggbeater
spoon
broom
tongs
needle

Office
stapler
punch
pen
pencil
eraser

Gardening
rake
hoe
shovel
spade
trowel
wheelbarrow

MACHINES

Construction
cement mixer
road grader
pipe digger
truck
bulldozer
trencher
electric motor
gear
switch

Farm
disker (harrow)
baler
combine
milking machine
tractor
seeder
cultivator
mower

Household
grinder
sewing machine
refrigerator
electric saw
vacuum cleaner
electric drill
electric mixer
blender
shaver
dryer
washer
clock
microwave oven
food processor
stove
refrigerator
curling iron
hair dryer
television
VCR
Freezer
iron

Office
typewriter
telephone
computer
photocopier
electric pencil
  sharpener
tape recorder
postage meter

Transportation
bicycle
automobile
train
bus
boat, ship
airplane
wagon

Yard
electric lawn mower
snowblower
electric hedge clippers
fertilizer spreader
sprinkler

2. Make a "feel-it" box (see illustration, p. 52) of simple tools to identify. Include a hammer, screwdriver, pliers, and scissors. Talk about how they help us.

3. Let the children beat an egg with a fork, a rotary beater, or an electric beater. Discuss the work involved.

4. Ask the children to try to pull a nail from a block of wood; then use a claw hammer.

5. Put blocks in a big box. Have the children try to lift it, push it; then put it on a dolly or wagon and move it. Discuss.

6. Use a single pulley fastened to a ceiling or a rope over a tree. Ask a child to lift a tricycle by himself or herself; then tie it on the rope and have him or her pull the other end. Ask, "Which is easier?"

7. Tie a string around a heavy box. Have the children try to lift it. Then fasten the box on a broomstick; put the broomstick across a chair or sawhorses and have children push down the other end. This illustrates the principle of the lever.

8. Have screws started in soft wood. Let children use screwdrivers. Also nails and hammers.

9. Let the children explore and use an old typewriter.

10. Let the children examine an old windup clock to see wheels and gears.

11. Wind a music box and let the children watch the gears move. (See-through music boxes are available from Galt and many gift stores)

12. Provide a science table with tools and machines (old radios, clocks, machines of any kind).

13. Let the children find as many wheels as they can in the room. Help them identify dials and taps as wheels and to note gear wheels in toys and clocks.

14. Identify the number of wheels on various vehicles.

15. Use a magnet to pick up nails.

16. Use a battery and wires to ring a buzzer or light a bulb.

17. Encourage the children to explore instruments. Talk about how they help a person change sound to music.

18. Tell the children you want them to help make whipped soap flakes for fingerpaint. (See recipes, p. 28.) Give some of the children a fork, some a rotary eggbeater, and let some **(with supervision)** help operate an electric mixer. Talk about the time and work needed in each case. Ask the children to think of other machines and tools that help us.

Carpenter's Workshop. See page 542.

19. Use tools and machines when cooking and preparing food. Here are some specific suggestions:

MACHINES

Electric blender:

a. Make milk shakes or eggnog.
b. Make applesauce. Cook apples, beat in blender, and add sugar.

Electric mixer:

a. Whip gelatin.
b. Make meringue or frosting.
c. Make cookies or cupcakes.
d. Make marshmallows. Combine 1 package of gelatin, 150 ml/⅔ cup boiling water, 225 ml/ 1 cup of sugar, and 45 ml/3 tbsp light corn syrup.

   Dissolve gelatin in water, stir in sugar, and blend in corn syrup. Chill until slightly thickened. Beat on highest speed until soft peaks form (15 minutes). Pour into pan lined with wax paper and greased with butter. Refrigerate overnight. Dust pastry board with powdered sugar. Cut into squares and roll in powdered sugar.

HAND TOOLS

Rotary beater:

a. Make meringues.
b. Whip Jell-O.
c. Make scrambled eggs.

Can opener: Open a can of juice or other food.

Hand grinder: Make cranberry relish. Combine 450 ml/2 cups of cranberries and 2 oranges, whole (including rind). Put through a food chopper and add about 450 ml/2 cups of sugar. Serve with crackers for snack.
Use a hand baby food mill to purée fresh fruit.

Dramatic Play Centres

Home-living centre

1. Provide housekeeping tools, such as cleaning brushes, dustpans, dustcloths, brooms, mops, spray bottles. Supervize. Children may also be allowed to clean mirrors, windows, or sinks.
2. Let children beat soap flakes in water.
3. Use play dough, rollers, and cutters with tongue depressors for slicing.
4. Encourage use of doll carriages and strollers or wagons to take dolls on an outing.
5. Talk about tools used in preparing, cooking, and eating foods, such as bowls, rolling pins, spatulas, potato masher, measuring cups, knives, forks, spoons. Discuss how tools make work easier.

Block-building centre

1. Call attention to use of ramps, cranes, pulleys, levers, wheels, gears.
2. Provide rubber or soft plastic tools for use in this area.
3. Have some hard hats, tool aprons, and tool kits.

Other dramatic play centres

1. Carpenter's workshop: Set up workbench and provide nails, screws, hammers, sandpaper blocks, and other tools as well as carpenter hats and tool aprons (see illustration, p. 540.)
2. Painter's workshop: Encourage children to pretend to paint using dry painter's brushes, empty paint buckets, and wearing painter's caps. Caps are often free at a paint store. Supply the painters with sample paint cards or swatches to show to customers. VARIATION: Outdoors, allow water to be used for paint. Invite painters to paint walls and toys.
3. Plumber's centre: Set out real sets of pipes (elbows, nipples, T's, taps with adapter couplings, and a variety of pipelengths) for children to fit together. Include a wrench. Use plastic pipes, which are readily available in building supply stores. Used pipe is often available from plumbing companies but it needs to be cleaned with steel wool and lubricated with Vaseline before using.
   Children will enjoy actually connecting their plumbing pipes to an outdoor faucet. This quickly becomes a discovery experience when water does or does not flow as expected. (See illustration on this page.)

Learning, Language, and Readiness Materials Centre

Commercially made games and materials

(See "Basic Resources," pp. 79, 100, for manufacturers' addresses.)
1. *Puzzles:* Puzzles with tools, machines and musical instruments in the shapes.
2. *Construction and manipulative toys:* Plastic tools for imaginative play, wooden and/or plastic sets with tools, bolts, screws, etc.: child-sized tools that can be used with careful supervision; sheets of styrofoam to be used in place of wood, balsa wood, wood scraps

(available from local lumberyards and contractors); and child-sized washable hard hats (these can be worn in a building centre. They can be used to control the number of children in the centre by establishing a rule that to play in the centre a hard hat must be worn).

Child-sized household tools (for example, brooms, and mops).

Models of simple machines that can be taken apart.

Gear sets: Simple boards with interlocking gears that can be turned by manipulating a variety of knobs. (Available from Brio and Quercetti.)

Imaginative play sets made by Playmates, Fisher-Price and Tonka have examples of levers, cranes and pulleys.

Accessories for block sets made by Duplo, Lasy, Construx, and Lego include levers, cranes, pulleys, etc.

3. *Outdoor toys:* Child-sized gardening tools.
4. *Music boxes.* Be sure the box can be operated by children. See-through music boxes are available and are very interesting for children. (Made by Galt or available from some gift stores.)
5. *Miscellaneous:* Musical instruments; see page 34 for a discussion of choosing suitable instruments.

Teacher-made games and materials

NOTE: For a detailed description of "Learning Games," see pp. 50–59.

1. Name it: Use vocabulary list for suggestions for pictures or objects.
2. Grouping and sorting by association: Sort pictures or plastic models of tools and machines used for various purposes into boxes labeled with pictures relating to farm, house, building, office, transportation, road work.
3. How many? Count the number of wheels on vehicles.
4. Match-them: Pair tools with association picture for its use, such as rake with leaves, eggbeater with eggs or bowl, or hammer with board. VARIATION: pair tools with helpers who use them from flannelboard aids or picture cards.

Art Centre

- 1. Easel paint: Offer different-width brushes.
- •• 2. Gadget printing: Use gears, toy car wheels, nuts and bolts, and other such parts of tools, or items such as sponges, corks, pieces of wood molding, or rolled cardboard.
- 3. Paint with rollers: Use small painting rollers or foam hair rollers.
- 4. Use tools, such as rollers, sticks, or cutters with clay or play dough.
- ••• 5. Use spool brayers to make stripes and plaids (see p. 29).
- 6. Use empty roll-on deodorant dispensers filled with thinned paint as markers.
- 7. Use paste sticks, brushes, or Q-tips to apply paste, and squeeze bottles to apply glue.
- ••• 8. Cut paper with scissors. Children might like to cut and paste a tools-and-machines book.
- •• 9. Let children hammer, saw, sand, and paint to make wood sculpture pieces.

Book Centre

- ••• Alexander, M. *Marty McGee's Space Lab. No Girls Allowed.* New York: Dial Press, 1981.
- ••• Allen, Jeffery. *Mary Alice, Operator, Number Nine.* Markham, Ont: Penguin Books, 1978.
- • Barton, B. *Building a House.* New York: Greenwillow Press, 1981.
- ••• Bell, Bill. *Saxophone Boy.* Montreal: Tundra Books, 1980.
- ••• Branley, Franklyn, and Eleanor Vaughn. *Mickey's Magnet.* New York: Thomas Y. Crowell, 1956.

•• Brown, Margaret Wise. *The Diggers.* New York: Harper & Row, 1960.
•• Brown, M. *The Little Carousel.* New York: Charles Scribner's Sons, 1946.
•• Burton, Virginia Lee. *Katy and the Big Snow.* Boston: Houghton Mifflin, 1959.
•• _____. *Mike Mulligan and His Steam Shovel.* Boston: Houghton Mifflin, 1959.
••• De Paolo, T. *Charlie Needs a Cloak.* Englewood Cliffs, NJ: Prentice-Hall, 1982.
• Domanska, J. *Busy Monday Morning.* New York: Greenwillow Press, 1985.
• Douglass, B. *Good as New.* New York: Lothrop, Lee & Shepard, 1982.
•• Freeman, D. *Corduroy.* New York: Viking Press, 1968.
•• _____. *A Pocket for Coduroy.* New York: Viking Press, 1978.
••• Geringer, Laura. *Molly's New Washing Machine.* New York: Harper & Row, 1986.
•• Gibbons, Gail. *Fill It Up, A Book About Service Stations.* Markham, Ont: Fitzhenry & Whiteside, 1986.
• Haddad, H. *Truck and Loader.* New York: Greenwillow Press, 1982.
• Hoban, T. *Dig, Drill, Dump, Fill.* New York: Greenwillow Press, 1975.
••• Hutchins, H. *Leanna Builds a Genie Trap.* Willowdale, Ont: Annick Press, 1986.
•••• Isadora, Rachel. *Ben's Trumpet.* Toronto: Macmillan, 1979. (A good book to read to children)
••• Kessler, Leonard. *Mr. Pine's Purple House.* New York: Wonder-Treasure Books, 1965.
•••• Krumins, Anita. *Who's Going to Clean Up the Mess!* Toronto: Three Trees Press, 1985. (Read-Tell)
••• Kumin, Maxine. *The Microscope.* New York: Harper & Row, 1987.
•••• Lauber, Patricia. *Get Ready for Robots.* New York: Thomas Y. Crowell, 1986.
• Lenski, Lois. *Davy Goes Places.* New York: Henry Z. Walck, 1961.
••• Morgan, A. *Matthew and the Midnight Tow Truck.* Willowdale, Ont: Annick Press, 1984.
•• Rey, H.A. *Curious George Rides a Bike.* Boston: Houghton Mifflin, 1952.
•• Rockwell, Anne, and Harlow Rockwell. *Machines.* New York: Macmillan, 1972.
• _____. *Tool Box.* New York: Macmillan, 1971 (paper, 1974).
•• Schick, E. *A Piano for Julie.* New York: Greenwillow Press, 1984.
••• Sobol, H. *Pete's House.* New York: Macmillan, 1978.
••• Spier, P. *Bored, Nothing to Do.* Garden City, NY: Doubleday, 1978.
••• Staunton, Ted. *Simon's Surprise.* Toronto: Kids Can Press, 1986.
••• Williams, V. *Music, Music, for Everyone.* New York: Greenwillow Press, 1984.

Planning for Group Time

NOTE: All music, fingerplays, poems, stories, and games listed here may be used at other times during the session as appropriate. See Core Library, "Basic Resources", p. 95, for publishers and addresses. Record company addresses can be found on p. 99.

Music

Songs

From original songs in this book by JoAnne Deal Hicks
"Machine Sounds Around the House," p. 614

From *Elephant Jam*, Sharon, Lois, and Bram
"Monday Night the Banjo," p. 29
"The Very Best Band," p. 120

From *Tunes for Tots*, Warner and Berry
Community helper section can be used to discuss the tools and machines used by various helpers.
"The Brass Band," p. 100
"Making Music," p. 101

From *Eye Winker, Tom Tinker, Chin Chopper*, Glazer
"Peter Hammers," p. 41
"Shoemaker, Shoemaker," p. 38
"When I was a Shoemaker," p. 87

From your own traditional songbook
"Johnny Works with One Hammer"
"I've Been Working on the Railroad"
"Round and Round the Village" (see parody, p. 441)

Fingerplays and Poems

From *Let's Do Fingerplays*, Grayson
"Cobbler, Cobbler," p. 18
"The Steam Shovel," p. 26
"Clocks," p. 27
"I Have A Little Watch," p. 27
"The Windshield Wipers," p. 24
"Driving Down the Street," p. 25
"The Bus," p. 25
"Boats," p. 26
"Row, Row, Row Your Boat," p. 26
"Clocks," p. 27
"The Top," p. 27
"My Garden," p. 46
"Johnny's Hammer," p. 67
"Swinging," p. 77
"The Seesaw," p. 78
"Hammering," p. 88
"Pound Goes the Hammer," p. 89

From *Mischief City*, Wynne-Jones
"The Vacuum Monster," p. 27

From *Don't Eat Spiders*, Heidbreder
"Little Robot," p. 7
"Rockets," p. 44

From *Oranges and Lemons*, King
"Jack in the Box," p. 4
"Oh, We Can Play the Big Brass Drum," p. 10
"The Wheels on the Bus," p. 38

From *Round and Round the Garden*, Williams and Beck
"Peter Works With One Hammer," p. 20
"Grandma's Spectacles," p. 23
"Cobbler, Cobbler," p. 28
"Here's the Lady's Knives and Forks," p. 43

From *Read Aloud Rhymes for the Very Young*, Prelutsky and Brown
"The Toaster," p. 35
"Toaster Time," p. 50

From *Where the Sidewalk Ends*, Silverstein
"Hector the Collector," p. 46
"Bang-Klang," p. 120
"Traffic Light," p. 121

THE DIGGER

I'm a digger, big and strong (PUFF OUT CHEST AND PAT)
Here's my arm, it's very long. (EXTEND BOTH ARMS OUT STRAIGHT)
Here's my scoop, and with a spurt (FORM SCOOP WITH HANDS AND SCOOP ARMS TO FLOOR)
I clutch the ground and bring up dirt. (SCOOP UP DIRT AND RAISE ARMS)
I turn and drop it in the truck (TURN WHOLE BODY AND OPEN HANDS LETTING DIRT FALL)
Then start all over—chuck, chuck, chuck. (SWING BODY BACK TO STARTING POSITION)

THE CLOCK

Tik-tock, tick-tock,
Tick-tock says the clock.
Little boy, little girl,
Time to wash our hands.
      (put the blocks away)
      (go outside)
      (ride the bus)

Stories

(To read, read–tell, or tell. See Book Centre for a complete list.)

Stories for this subject can range from the fanciful (for example, Krumin's *Who's Going to Clean Up This Mess?*), to stories in which children safely and successfully use tools like Staunton's *Simon's Surprise.*

Routine Times

1. Eat food prepared earlier at snack or meal times.
2. Use a rolling cart to bring food to tables at snack or meal times.
3. Call attention to tools and machines as you use them—doorknobs, light switches, levers, stairs, utensils, tops, hand or nail brushes.
4. At pickup time use wagon or rolling platform to return toys to shelves.
5. When out walking or riding watch for use of machines and tools by others.
6. At meal time talk about utensils as tools, including those used to prepare food.

Large Muscle Activities

1. Use wheel toys with ramps.
2. Use wheelbarrows for moving blocks.
3. Use pulleys for lifting pails of sand.
4. Oil the tricycles and wagons.
5. Bring out garden tools (spring).
6. Shovel snow (winter).
7. Rake leaves. Use wagons to collect the leaves (fall).
8. Add a variety of sand tools to the sandbox play area, such as sand combs, sifters, sand wheels, and a scoop and scrape.
9. Water lawn with sprinkler or hose (summer).

Extended Experiences

1. Visit a building construction site if the builder will allow children there.
2. Attend a school band rehearsal.
3. Visit a service station that has a lift and a car wash.
4. Go to a hardware store to show the children where tools and small appliances are sold. Buy some nails or screws, a pulley, a hammer, a screwdriver, some garden tools, or pipe fitting.
5. Invite parent community helpers to come on different days and show children the tools they use, how to use them, and when and why their tools are necessary, such as: person might actually repair a playground vehicle while children watch, a carpenter might build a bird feeder or a simple tote tray to be used at school. Encourage children to help sand, stain, or paint.

   NOTE: If the carpenter has access to a crosscut section from a tree or perhaps a piece of lumber that shows an edge of bark, children can better associate the original source of lumber to trees.

6. Let children watch when a plumber comes to fix the plumbing. VARIATION: Watch the custodian using tools to clean the school building.
7. Children will enjoy attaching their plumbing pipes (see Other Dramatic Play Centres, p. 542) and fittings to an outdoor tap so that they can see what happens. This is an excellent cause-and-effect discovery experience.
8. Some centres may have access to personal computers with programs that are appropriate for use by young children. This is an interesting activity for some children. There are also computers available for young children in local libraries and community centres. For further discussion of the use of computers with young children see the book list under Teacher Resources below.

Teacher Resources

Pictures and Displays

▷ Display mounted pictures of kitchen tools and machines from magazines.
▷ Display mounted pictures of construction machines and tools in the block-building centre.
▷ Set out catalog sections showing gardening or yard tools or other tools and machines to be used around the home. Sale catalogs or advertisements are excellent sources of coloured pictures. These can be cut out to make picture books, games, and puzzles.

Books and Periodicals

Canadian Tire and other hardware catalogues
Chickadee magazine
Farm journals and farm equipment catalogues
Lear, Peter. *Let's Look at Computers.* Burlington, Ont: Hayes Publishing, 1985
———. *Let's Look at Computer Play.* Burlington, Ont: Hayes Publishing, 1985
Mackie, David. *Let's Look at Basic.* Burlington, Ont: Hayes Publishing, 1985
Mail-order catalogues
Marine supplier's catalogue
Office supply company catalogues
Owl magazine

Films and Videos

Consult your community library for up-to-date audio-visual materials from the National Film Board and the CBC

Community Resources and Organizations

▷ A neighbouring building site; make certain it is safe to visit
▷ Parent community helpers, such as a carpenter, a plumber, or a road grader
▷ Implement dealers, automobile dealers, hardware dealers, television and radio dealers, and others who retail tools or machines might give you out-of-date catalogues or illustrative materials to be used for flannelboard aids, games, or sources of pictures for children to cut and paste
▷ A local music school
▷ Community cable television channels will arrange tours
▷ A college or university early childhood education program that offers courses on the use of computers with young children

Government Agencies

▷ Provincial, territorial and federal ministries concerned with labour
▷ Provincial or territorial boards concerned with compensating injured workers have excellent safety posters which would be very useful for this section

Machine Sounds Around the House

JoAnne Deal Hicks

NOTE: Verse 1 is fun to use during a cooking activity—it could be sung during the time the children are waiting their turn to beat the batter.

29 Mathematics in My Everyday World

★★★★★★★★★★★★★★★★★★★★★★★★

Basic Understandings

(concepts children can grasp from this subject)

▷ A group of objects is called a "set," such as a set of blocks or a set of dishes.
▷ We count to find how many objects we have in a set—one to three, one to five, one to ten.
▷ Objects can be grouped in sets in many ways, such as by kind (family), size, colour, use, weight, and shape (*classification*).

    a. Objects that are grouped together because they are similar are alike or are the same.
    b. Objects that are not like the others in some way are not alike or are different.
    c. Two objects that are alike or are used together are known as a pair (socks, mittens, shoes) or twins (girls, boys, lambs, squirrels).

▷ We compare object (*comparison*):

    a. By size—small, large, big, little, tall, short, fat, thin, wide, narrow
    b. By location—near, far, in front of, behind, over, under, in, out, up, down, above, below, inside, outside
    c. By quantity—few, many, a lot, a little, more, less, some, none
    d. By weight—heavy, light

▷ We can arrange objects in order (*seriation*):

    a. By size-smallest to largest, largest to smallest, shortest to tallest, thinnest to thickest
    b. By location—nearest to farthest, farthest to nearest
    c. By position—first, second, third, next to last, last

▷ If we add an object to a set we have more than we did before (*addition*).
▷ If we take an object away from a set we have less than we did before (*subtraction*).
▷ If we remove all the objects in a set we have none left or an empty set.
▷ Objects or sets can be divided into subsets or parts (*division*).

    a. Set are divided into two equal parts or are divided in half.
    b. If we have more chairs or cookies than children we have more than enough or too many.

▷   Objects have different shapes.
  1. Two-dimensional:

      a. Circle: round
      b. Triangle: three sides
      c. Rectangle or square: four corners and four straight sides

  2. Three-dimensional:

      a. Spherical: ball, globe, orange
      b. Triangular: triangular block, rhythm band triangle
      c. Rectangular: rectangular blocks, boxes, books
      d. Conical: funnel, party hat

  3. Other shapes include stars, cylinders, arches, crescents, hearts, and diamonds.

▷   Many things help us measure.

  1. A clock tells us what time it is (the hour of the day).
  2. A thermometer tells us temperature (how hot or cold something is).
  3. A ruler (metre stick, measuring tape) tells us how long, high, or wide something is.
  4. A calendar tells us what day (week, month, year) it is.
  5. Scales tell us how much something weighs.
  6. Measuring cups and spoons help us measure food or other materials.

▷   A numeral represents a number rather than a letter or other symbol or character. Children can learn the correct names for numerals, such as one, 1; two, 2; three, 3. Children who speak other languages have other words for these numerals.

▷   We use numbers in many ways:

  1. On our house so our friends or the letter carrier can find us
  2. On the telephone so we can call someone
  3. On a cash register to find out how much we should pay the store clerk
  4. On money to help us know how much it is worth
  5. On stamps to help tell us how much they are worth
  6. On book pages so we can tell someone where to find a story or picture
  7. On licence plates so we can tell who owns a car

▷   We use money to buy things such as food, clothes, house, car, toys.

  1. We have coins and bills to use as money.
  2. Our coins have names—penny, nickel, dime, quarter and dollar. Many children do not have a clear concept of exact value and are confused by the lack of relationship between size and value.)

▷   We use the word "time" to talk about when things happen. Children begin to understand:

  1. Today or day is the time between when we get up in the morning and the time we go to bed at night.
  2. Night is the time when it is dark and we go to sleep.

  NOTE: See "Day and Night" for additional concepts.

  3. Tomorrow is the time it will be when we wake up after we go to bed tonight.
  4. Yesterday is the day it was before we went to bed last night.
  5. Morning is between breakfast and lunch.
  6. Afternoon is between lunch and dinner (supper).
  7. Evening is between supper and the time you go to bed.
  8. The days have names—Sunday, Friday (children do not always know the correct order).

9. Several days make a week (children do not know how many).
10. The months have names—January, June (children do not always know correct order).
11. A year is a very, very long time. Children do not know how many days or weeks.

Additional Facts the Teacher Should Know

1. Mathematics, which involves concepts about numbers, measuring, money, spatial relationships, time, and problem solving, can be presented to young children in some form that is understandable to them; math, therefore, belongs in the curriculum for young children. The activities and materials suggested in this guide will serve to direct your attention to some of the potentials in the classroom environment for teaching mathematic concepts. You will certainly find many more ways of helping children discover some of the basic understandings.

2. Very young children can discover that we use numbers in many ways, have many ways of measuring, can classify things in many ways, can compare things in many ways; and can begin to understand some of the mathematic skills of counting, adding, subtracting, and dividing. However, very young children have difficulty realizing that objects can have more than one property and can belong to several classes—a red pencil can be grouped with red things, hard things, long things, and wooden things. This realization is acquired by grouping and regrouping according to different traits. At first the young child may need to group by traits suggested by the teacher, but the child with more experience should be encouraged to decide for herself or himself the traits that make certain things go together. Grouping in different ways encourages flexible thinking.

3. The very young child's concepts of money are mainly confined to the knowledge that we earn it by working and then use it to buy the things we need or want (see "Families at Work"). They are beginning to know the names of some of the coins but do not know their exact value. A very young child will most likely think a nickel is worth more than a dime because it is bigger in size.

4. Time is one of the most difficult understandings for young children. They can learn that a clock tells us what time it is but they will be much older before they can tell the actual time for themselves. In the meantime it is helpful if the teacher verbalizes the use of the clock to familiarize the child with telling time. For example, she/he can point to the clock on the wall and say, "It is ten o'clock, time for juice," or looking at a wristwatch, can say, "My wristwatch says it is eleven thirty, time to go outside." The understanding of the passage of time from one day to the next, one week to the next, and one year to the next develops slowly. Through conversation and the use of the calendar in the classroom children can come to understand that days of the week have names, that several days (one line of numbers on most calendars) make a week, several weeks (several lines or one page of the calendar) is a month, that the months have names, and that a year is a very long time. Children become most aware of the concept of a year when they hear much discussion about this around New Year's Day and on their birthdays. Children are usually five before they realize that holidays and birthdays recur on a regular basis. Some calendars read vertically and some have put Monday in the first space. It is best to use those which read horizontally.

5. Many different approaches to teaching math to very young children are being used today and many commercial materials are now available. This chapter represents a potpourri, or a little bit of everything. A brief explanation of some of the methods follows to aid you in understanding their inclusion.

6. The math being taught in most public schools today emphasizes understanding of how and why the mathematical processes work rather than demanding rote learning or acceptance on faith for many of the steps in problem solving. This basic philosophy of seeing, doing, and understanding has long been used on the preschool level. This method,

however, has a new vocabulary with "set" (a group of one or more) as its basic unit. It is appropriate to use this term with young children as they are already familiar with a set of dishes or set of blocks. However, use the term when referring to other things not normally referred to as sets, such as a "set of hats."

7. The extensive study done by Piaget of children's understanding of mathematical concepts is being given renewed attention in many early childhood centres. While his labels of "equivalence," "conservation," and "seriation" are not widely used, the activities basic to understanding the concepts are appropriate. It is imperative that you review Piaget's materials in his texts or in child development texts (see p. 567).

8. Montessori's major contribution to the teaching of math to young children is her ingenious self-teaching materials. They are all designed on the metric system and are self-teaching in that they vary in only one dimension at a time. Thus, if children order

Mathematics centre. Child is counting puppies on an apron flannelboard before choosing the corresponding numeral at the bottom of the flannelboard.

them incorrectly, the errors will be obvious and can be corrected. Montessori's sets of graded cylinders which vary in only one dimension (length, diameter) are excellent materials for teaching Piaget's concept of seriation. Thus, in these statements, we are suggesting the blending of many different approaches to the teaching of math to young children.

9. Canada uses the metric measuring system. The metric system uses centimetres, metres, and kilometres as units of length, and and grams and litres as units of volume. The following table shows metric/Imperial equivalents

Metric		Imperial	Metric	Imperial
25.4	millimetres	= 1 inch	1 millimetre	= 0.039 inch
2.54	centimetres	= 1 inch	1 centimetre	= 0.394 inch
0.914	metre	= 1 yard	1 metre	= 1.094 yards
1.6	kilometres	= 1 mile	1 kilometre	= 0.621 mile
28.35	grams	= 1 ounce	1 gram	= 0.035 ounce
453.6	grams	= 1 pound	1 kilogram	= 2.2 pounds
0.94	litre	= 1 quart	1 litre	= 1.06 quarts

NOTE: Other chapters related to mathematics are "Families at Work," "Colour," "Ground and Road Transportation," and "Day and Night."

Methods Most Adaptable for Introducing this Subject to Children

1. Cooking activities involving the measuring of ingredients and the use of various-sized utensils and pans.
2. Dramatic play: A grocery store where children can talk about and handle different-sized containers, bags, and money.
3. Flannelboard story emphasizing quantity and size, such as *The Three Bears* (great big daddy bear, middle-sized mother bear, wee little baby bear; various-sized bowls, chairs, and beds). (See illustration opposite.)
4. Number readiness materials: Commercially or teacher-made (see Learning, Language, and Readiness Materials Centre).

Vocabulary

numbers	thermometer	less	set
count	metre stick	more	pair
measure	calendar	enough	twin
shape	birthday	none	both
scales	same	add	circle
ruler	alike	divide	square
clock	different	half	triangle
time	match	empty	star

Learning Centres

Discovery Centre

1. Make cookies, pudding, no-cook candy, gelatin, or other dishes that require the use of measuring spoons and cups and various sizes of pans, bowls, utensils. Talk about full, half full, and empty; big, little, in, out, and measuring.

2. Measure and weigh children: If done at beginning of year repeat at a later time or end of year to tell them how much they have grown—who is shorter, taller, heavier, lighter, the same? Tape plain paper, a tree, or giraffe picture chart to the wall and mark off in inches. Write children's names by the marks for their height.

3. Balance scales: Let children experiment with how many beans will balance a bolt or how many acorns (in terms of many or few) will balance a pebble. Talk about heavy and light.

4. Thermometers: Have a large, accurate one in the room and on the playground. Talk about the weather and if it is hot or cold. Help children to see that as the weather gets warmer the mercury goes up, and as it gets colder, the mercury goes down. An indoor–outdoor thermometer is nice so the children can see the similarity or difference between the two.

5. Make a large cardboard thermometer with markings from -40°C to 50°C. Make two horizontal slots 12.7 mm long at the highest and lowest markings. Cut a length of 9.5 mm wide elastic that is twice the distance between the slots, plus 6.3 mm for overlap. Thread the elastic through the slots from the front and overlap elastic 6.3 mm on the back and sew securely. Run the overlap down to the bottom slot. Colour all the elastic that is showing on the front of the thermometer with a red felt tip marker. To lower mercury, pull the elastic down. To raise the mercury, pull it up. The elastic can be moved up or down by the child or teacher to help the child understand the concept of temperatures rising and falling.

6. At a water or sand table or in a large pan provide measuring cups, containers of various sizes and shapes, measuring spoons, pitchers, and funnels. Let children experiment with pouring water or sand into the various containers and making comparisons. Watch for opportunities to help children who are ready for it to discover that objects or liquids do not change in amount (number and quantity) when they are put in a smaller or larger container (conservation). Have child fill a 250 ml measuring cup (with handle and spout) to the 250 ml mark. Then have the child pour the contents into a tall narrow container. Notice the contents go higher. Ask if there is more in the new container than in the old one. Let child pour the contents back to check the answer.

7. Count body parts on animals: "How many feet?" "Ears?" "Tails?"

8. Count trees, leaves, flowers, petals, and seeds.

9. Count pebbles, pieces of coal, or seashells.

10. Classifying: Children can group items of various kinds as to type, colour, shape, weight, or texture. Use real objects from nature or pictures. Beginning experiences should include two or three different types of items with three to five in each group. Increase number and type as children gain skill. Let children decide on the groupings and explain their reasons for doing so.

11. Look for and identify shapes, indoors and out.

Dramatic Play Centres

Home-living centre

1. Talk about sets of dishes and flatware and their sizes; sort by size and shape—saucers, cups, plates, glasses, knives, forks, and spoons.

2. Include plastic or metal measuring cups, spoons, mixing bowls, and beaters to bake with. Sometimes allow water or sand for measuring.
3. Talk about equivalence or one-to-one correspondence: "Are there enough cups and saucers for everyone? Too many? Too few? How many do we need?"
4. Put a discarded telephone book by the toy telephone to encourage looking up a number and calling someone. Underline the names of families in your centre. Remind children that they need parental permission to use the phone at home.
5. Put a bathroom and/or kitchen scale in this centre so children can weigh food, themselves, or their dolls. If possible, obtain a baby metric scale.
6. Put up a calendar on the wall in this centre.
7. Put out a toy clock with movable hands or an old alarm clock.
8. Talk about portions of food being served. Talk about more or less. Have child put food in two dishes. "Your doll is very hungry; will you give him/her more?"

Block-building centre

1. Call attention to taller or shorter buildings, long or short roads. If a metre stick is handy you could help children measure their buildings or roads. "Who has more blocks?" "Do you need more blocks to make yours as tall as Joan's?" Count blocks used to make a road or bridge. Many and few: "Jimmy used many blocks to build a tower."
2. Call attention to shapes used—rectangular, triangular, or square. Help children see spatial relationships—up, down, above, below, under, beside. Help children discover that two triangles can make a square, two squares together make a rectangle, two rectangles equal one longer rectangle. Use good set of unit blocks and ask for a specific number of blocks by name. "Please give me one square block." "Give me two arches."
3. Encourage older children to build a parking lot. Have one child park the cars and another collect the fees.
4. Encourage older children, who are familiar with them, to add bridges and tunnels to their block building.

Other dramatic play centres

Set up a grocery store. Emphasis should be on pricing (putting up signs with prices displayed, such as "2/50¢"). Scales for weighing produce, size and shapes of containers, a dozen is twelve, use of cash register (or divided box for coins), paying for food, and making change should be emphasized.

Learning, Language, and Readiness Materials Centre

Commercially made games and materials

(See "Basic Resources," pp. 79, 100, for manufacturers' addresses.)
1. *Puzzles:* All puzzles are useful, but shape and number puzzles are particularly relevant.
2. *Construction and manipulative toys:* Montessori materials—cylinder blocks, shapes and templates, tower, long stair, broad stair, number rods.

Weaving mats: To teach over and under.

Sorting boxes: Boxes for sorting by shape and size.

Scales: Simple balance beam scales with containers that can hold a variety of media, liquids, solids etc. Simple spring balance scales with a large dial that is easily read, sturdy simple bathroom scale with the readout in kilos.

Plastic containers: A variety of plastic (both clear and coloured) containers that can be used to pour and compare liquids, cornmeal, sand etc. Include measuring containers that are clearly marked with metric measures.

3. *Outdoor toys:* Thermometers—large outdoor thermometer to place in the playground.

Plastic containers for sand and water play: A variety of plastic (both clear and coloured) containers that can be used to pour and compare liquids, sand, etc. Include measuring containers that are clearly marked with metric measures.

4. *Games:* Beginning board games with spinner dials that will teach the children how to count and move objects to a corresponding number of spaces.

Dominoes—traditional and picture dominoes.

Pegboards.

An abacus.

5. *Miscellaneous:* Clocks: A large easily read clock, a large teaching clock with both analog and digital readout, simple wind up egg timer.

Play money: Be sure it is a facsimile of Canadian money. A play cash register. Be sure to choose a register that is sturdy and that will work when the children push the keys. (Fisher Price makes a cash register.)

A teaching thermometer with sliding colour for mercury.

Teacher-made games and materials

NOTE: For a detailed description of "Learning Games," see pp. 50–59.

1. Counting: Rational counting of any objects the child is using during free choice period, such as blocks, beads, feathers, pegs, or scissors.
2. Classification: Children can be given objects to group or classify, such as beads, cubes, buttons, and plastic lids of various sizes.

   • Children are asked to put those together that are alike.
   •• Let children decide how objects should be grouped, such as colour, size, texture.
   ••• After the first groupings by children ask if they can group objects another way. This encourages flexible thinking and the concept that there is more than one way to do things.

3. Number stair: Collect fifteen or fifty-five spools of identical size. Find doweling that will allow the spool to slide down easily. The spindles should be of graded height so that the first one holds one spool, the second holds two, and so on. Paint the spools that represent each number a different colour with nontoxic paint. Fifteen spools will make a 1 to 5 number stair and 55 spools will make a 1 to 10 number stair. Let the children discover there are different pattern arrangements possible with this number stair.
4. Talk about shape, size, weight, and location of objects that children are working with during their free choice activity (as appropriate).
5. Use flannelboard with geometric or animal shapes allowing child to group things by shape which may be different in size or colour. Later children can regroup by colour or size, illustrating that objects can belong to different groups.
6. To establish one-to-one correspondence or equivalence (just enough for everyone); use spools to represent people and pop bottle caps for hats; let children pick out enough hats for all of them. Discover the meaning of just enough, not enough, too many, too few.
7. Use of numbers: Look for meaningful ways to use the calendar, clocks, scales, thermometer, telephone, money, stamps, and measuring sticks.
8. Look and see:

   a. Use different coins and bills.
   b. Use different stamps.
   c. Use thermometers, alarm clocks, metre rulers, measuring cups, desk calendars, and measuring tape.

9. Reach and feel: Use items in (c) above.
10. Match-them: Match objects by shape, size, weight, location.

11. Cover-ups (variation of match-them).
12. Alike, different, and the same: Use geometric shapes, coins, stamps.
13. Which comes first? Use items of current interest.
14. How many? Set out varying numbers of objects.
15. Block form board: On a large piece of cardboard trace around one of each of the shapes in your set of unit blocks. Let children match blocks with the shapes on the form board.
16. Object form board: Trace around familiar objects and let children find the matching objects and place on the form board.
17. Make sand paper, felt, or flocked number cards.

Art Centre

•   1. When painting give children a choice of one or two colours. Talk about the paint pots being empty or half full.
•   2. When molding and sculpting talk about the size of the ball of clay or dough being worked with. A large ball can be divided into two small balls.
•• 3. Paste geometric shapes of various sizes on coloured construction paper to make different designs. VARIATION: Use gummed paper or pieces of fabric.

Art centre. *Geometric forms on the display shelf, as well as colour cones, give children an opportunity to explore the concept of geometric forms as solids. Pictures on the display board show shapes from children's everyday experiences. Child at right is arranging a shape picture from geometric forms.*

•• 4. Cut geometric shapes out of sponges. Let children use them to print designs on coloured construction paper.

••• 5. At the woodworking table provide a ruler for measuring the boards to be cut. Provide nails of different lengths. Show children how to measure and how to decide the right-length nail to use.

Other experiences in this centre using art media

••• 1. Cutting: Show children with cutting skills how to cut a valentine (heart shape). Fold a square of paper in half. (This paper could be one of their fingerpaintings or easel paintings.) Teacher would, starting at fold, draw half of a valentine on the paper with a magic marker. Children should be instructed to start cutting at the bottom point on the fold and cut up and around and back to the centrefold top point.

Book Centre

NOTE: The Book Centre list has been divided into subgroups for convenience.

Numbers

•• Anno, M. *Anno's Counting Book.* New York: Thomas Y. Crowell, 1977.

• Baum, Arline, and Joseph Baum. *One Bright Monday Morning.* New York: Random House, 1962 (paper).

• Bruna, Dick. *I Can Count.* Toronto: Methuen, 1986.

• _____ . *I Know About Numbers.* Toronto: Methuen, 1986.

• _____ . *I Know More About Numbers.* Toronto: Methuen, 1986.

• Children of la Roche and Friends. *Bryan and His Balloon: An English Chipewyan Counting Book.* Edmonton: Tree Frog Press, 1984.

•• Cowther, Robert. *The Most Amazing Hide and Seek Counting Book.* Markham, Ont: Penguin Books, 1986.

••• Crews, D. *Ten Black Dots.* New York: Greenwillow Press, 1986.

••• Elkin, Benjamin. *Six Foolish Fishermen.* Chicago: Childrens Press, 1957 (paper).

••• Françoise. *Jeanne-Marie Counts Her Sheep.* New York: Charles Scribner's Sons, 1963.

• Friskey, Margaret. *Chicken Little Counts to Ten.* Chicago: Childrens Press, 1946.

• Gretz, S. *Teddy Bears 1 - 10.* New York: Macmillan, 1986.

••• Hoban, Tana. *Count and See.* New York: Macmillan, 1972.

••• Langstaff, John. *Over in the Meadow.* New York: Harcourt Brace Jovanovich, 1956 (paper, 1973).

•• Lewin, B. *Cat Count.* New York: Dodd Mead, 1981.

••• Lottridge, Celia. *One Watermelon Seed.* Toronto: Oxford University Press, 1986.

••• Mack. *Belmont the Bat Catcher and Other Nutty Number Stories.* Toronto: Methuen, 1986.

• Magee, D. *Trucks You Can Count On.* New York: Dodd Mead, 1985.

•• O'Halloran, Tim. *Know Your Numbers.* Burlington, Ont: Hayes Publishing, 1986.

• Peppe, Rodney. *Circus Numbers: A Counting Book.* New York: Delacorte, 1986.

• Pienkowski, J. *Numbers.* New York: Simon & Shuster, 1981.

•••• Sendak, M. *Chicken Soup With Rice.* New York: Harper & Row, 1962.

•• Sherman, Diane. *My Counting Book.* Chicago: Rand McNally, 1963.

••• Slobodkin, Louis. *Millions, Millions, Millions.* New York: Vanguard Press, 1955.

•••• Viorst, J. *Alexander. Who Used to Be Rich Last Sunday.* New York: Macmillan, 1978. (Read-Tell)

••• Wadsworth. *Over in the Meadow.* Toronto: Methuen, 1986.

• Wildsmith, Brian. *Brian Wildsmith's 1, 2, 3's.* New York: Franklin Watts, 1965.

• Winik, J.T. *Fun With Numbers.* Burlington, Ont: Hayes Publishing, 1985.

•• Wood, A. *Kids Can Count,* Toronto: Kids Can Press, 1976.

• Zolotow, Charlotte. *One Step Two.* New York: Lothrop, Lee & Shepard, 1955.

NOTE: Look in your library for the *Twins* book series by Helen Wing, New York: E.M. Hale, 1960-1966, and *The Sesame Street* books on numbers.

Time

•• Barrett, Judith. *Benjamin's 365 Birthdays.* New York: Atheneum, 1974.
••• Françoise. *What Time Is It Jeanne-Marie?* New York: Charles Scribner's Sons, 1963.
•• Hoban, Russell. *A Birthday for Frances.* New York: Harper & Row, 1968.
••• Hutchins, Pat. *Changes, Changes.* New York: Macmillan, 1971 (paper, 1973).
• Krasilowsky, Phillis. *The Very Little Boy.* Garden City, NY: Doubleday, 1962 (paper).
• _____. *The Very Little Girl.* Garden City, NY: Doubleday, 1958 (paper).
••• Slobodkin, Louis. *Dinny and Danny.* New York: Macmillan, 1951.
••• Spier, Peter. *Fast-Slow, High-Low.* Garden City, NY: Doubleday, 1972.
••• Watson, Nancy Dingman. *When Is Tomorrow?* New York: Alfred A. Knopf, 1955.
•• Zolotow, Charlotte. *Over and Over.* New York: Harper & Row, 1957

Space, shape, and size

••• Allen, Pamela. *Who Sank the Boat?* New York: Coward, 1983.
•• Bruna, D. *I Know About Shapes.* New York: Price Stern, 1984.
••• Fisher, L.E. *Look Around! A Book About Shapes.* Markham, Ont: Penguin Books, 1986.
••• Galloway, P. *When You Were Little and I was Big.* Willowdale, Ont: Annick Press, 1984.
•• Hoban, T. *Circles, Triangles and Squares.* New York: Macmillan, 1974.
• Pienkowski, J. *Shapes.* New York: Simon & Shuster, 1981.
• _____. *Sizes.* New York: Simon & Shuster, 1983.
••• Stinson, K. *Big or Little.* Willowdale, Ont: Annick Press, 1985.
•••• Walter, Marion. *Make a Bigger Puddle, Make a Smaller Worm.* Philadelphia: J.B. Lippincott, 1971 (discovering the concepts of big and little with a mirror).

Planning for Group Time

NOTE: All music, fingerplays, poems, stories, and games listed here may also be used at other times during the session as appropriate. See Core Library, Basic Resources, p. 95, for publishers and addresses. Record company addresses can be found on p. 99.

Music

Songs

MEASURING

(tune: "Pussy Cat, Pussy Cat")
Adaptation by JoAnne Deal Hicks

Meas-ure your hand, and then meas-ure your nose,
Meas-ure your feet and then meas-ure your toes,
Meas-ure your head, then your ears, and your chin,
You're smil-ing, you're hap-py! Let's meas-ure your grin!

(Teacher may supply tape measure; children love to see how big they are. Children might also enjoy measuring the body parts of toy animals.)

From *Stepping Along in Music Land*, Murray
"Coloured Sticks," p. 33
"Shapes," p. 34
"Five Toes," p. 35
"Incubator," p. 36
"Hop Little Bunny," p. 37

From *Elephant Jam*, Sharon, Lois, and Bram
"One Elephant, Deux Elephants," p. 34
"Five Little Monkeys," p. 48
"Three Little Monkeys," p. 49
"One Finger, One Thumb," p. 50

From *The Goat With the Bright Red Socks*, Birkenshaw and Walden
"Echo Clock," p. 5
"I Can Count," p. 8
"Let's Do the Numbers Rumba," p. 10

From *Tunes for Tots*, Warner and Berry
"Counting Songs," pp. 89–97

From *What Shall We Do and Allee Galloo*, Winn
"The Clock Song," p. 36
"My Hat it Has Three Corners," p. 54

Record and cassettes

Anne Murray. *There's a Hippo in My Tub.* (Capitol Records)
"Inchworm"

Bob McGrath. *If You're Happy and You Know It Sing Along*, Volume I. (Kids Records)
"Five Little Ducks"
"Six Little Monkeys:

Bob Schneider. *When You Dream a Dream.* (Capitol Records)
"Computer Man"

Fred Penner. *Special Delivery.* (Troubadour Records)
"My Grandfather's Clock"

Sharon, Lois, and Bram. *Elephant Show.* (Elephant Records)
"One Elephant Went Out to Play"
"Five Plump Peas"
"Noah's Old Ark"
"Ten in the Bed"

Fingerplays and Poems

NOTE: Many fingerplays in the other sections of this book involve number concepts. Select those that are of current interest to your group.

From *Don't Eat Spiders*, Heidbreder
"Count on Me," p. 15
"Counting's Easy," p. 17

From *Read Aloud Rhymes for the Very Young*, Prelutsky and Brown
"Ten to One," p. 37
"Just Three," p. 54
"Three Tickles," p. 79
"It's Eleven O'Clock," p. 80
"Ten Fingers," p. 82

From *Hand Rhymes*, Brown
"Five Little Babies," p. 6
"Two Little Monkeys," p. 9
"Five Little Goblins," p. 12

From *Finger Rhymes*, Brown
"Five Little Pigs," p. 8
"Five Little Mice," p. 16
"Two Blackbirds," p. 19
"Ten Little Candles," p. 26

From *Round and Round the Garden*, Williams and Beck
"Five Fat Sausages," p. 8
"Ten Little Men," p. 16
"Ten Little Fingers," p. 18
"Two Fat Gentlemen," p. 22
"Five Fat Peas," p. 29
"Five Little Soldiers," p. 42

From *Oranges and Lemons*, King
"Five Brown Teddies," p. 6
"Noah's Ark," p. 16
"Five Little Speckled Frogs," p. 32
"The Wheels on the Bus," p. 38

From *Let's Do Fingerplays*, Grayson
The section on counting and counting out, pp. 60–74, is very useful.
"Ten Fingers," p. 3
"Right Hand, Left Hand," p. 9
"Point to the Right," p. 11
"Five Fingers," p. 11
"Two Little Hands," p. 12
"Five Little Girls," p. 20
"Clocks," p. 27
"I Have a Little Watch," p. 27
"The Metronome Song," p. 28
"People," p. 50
"The Stilt Man," p. 50
"Counting and Counting Out," pp. 59, 60, 62–68, 70–74
"Five Years Old," p. 101

GREAT BIG BALL

A great big ball (ARMS MAKE CIRCLE OVER HEAD)
A middle-sized ball, (MAKE BALL WITH BOTH HANDS IN FRONT)
A little ball I see. (MAKE BALL WITH THUMB AND FOREFINGER)
Now let's count the balls we've made; 1—2—3 (MAKE EACH BALL AGAIN AS YOU COUNT)

HICKORY, DICKORY, DOCK

Hickory, dickory, dock, (STAND, SWING ARM LIKE PENDULUM)
The mouse ran up the clock. (BEND OVER; RUN HAND UP BODY)
The clock struck one, (CLAP HANDS OVER HEAD ONCE)
The mouse ran down, (RUN HAND DOWN TO FEET)
Hickory, dickory, dock. (STAND; SWING ARM LIKE PENDULUM)

TWO LITTLE BLACKBIRDS

Two little blackbirds sitting on a hill, (PLACE A FIST ON EACH KNEE)
One named Jack and one named Jill. (MOVE EACH FIST A LITTLE)
Fly away Jack, fly away Jill, (FLING EACH HAND OVER YOUR SHOULDER)
Come back Jack, come back Jill. (BRING EACH HAND BACK TO KNEE)

Stories

(To read, read-tell, or tell. See Book Centre for complete list.)
Care should be exercised when choosing stories to read aloud or tell in this area as many books that children enjoy on their own become repetitive when read aloud. Books with a story and characters are well suited to use in this area such as Wadsworth's *Over in the Meadow* or Mack's *Belmont the Bat Catcher and Other Nutty Number Stories.* Many books in this area have simple vocabulary, but are conceptually beyond the young child. Be sure to assess stories for conceptual as well as linguistic suitability.

Games

(See "Learning Games," pp. 50–59, and teacher-made games in this chapter for directions.)
  1. Look and see: Use thermometer, clock, timer, measuring cup, and ruler.
  2. How many? Count objects.

Routine Times

  1. At snack or meal times talk about whether there are enough napkins, cups, plates, or spoons for each child.
  2. At snack or meal times talk about the size of a serving. Would you like a big serving or a small serving? Tell children a specific number of crackers or snacks to eat. "Today you may have two square crackers."
  3. At snack or meal times what happens to the level of juice or milk as it is poured from a pitcher into individual cups? (See-through containers are best for this.) What can you say about all the plates, the cups, and the pitcher when the food or juice is gone? "They are empty!"
  4. At snack or meal times serve sandwiches cut in half; fill juice or milk glasses each half full; serve bananas or apples cut in half.
  5. Use an alarm clock, timer, or clock-radio to signify the end of rest time.
  6. At the end of rest time you could say, "I am going to slowly count to ten and then I want you to get up slowly and walk slowly over to _____."
  7. As you walk or ride call attention to the use of numbers on houses, stories, road signs, clocks, and thermometers. "Here we are at 215 Chestnut Street, Johnny's house."
  8. Talk about tall and short buildings; things that are near and far; big trucks and small cars, while walking, or busing.
  9. Count familiar objects while in transit.
  10. Call attention to basic concepts involved while dressing, for example, we need a pair of mittens, socks, shoes (one for each hand or foot), or count how many children have blue coats, brown shoes, red mittens.
  11. At pickup time ask for a specific number of objects. "Please give me two blocks to put on this shelf."
  12. Comment on child's ability at pickup time: "You put many books on the shelf."

Large Muscle Activities

1. Walking, running, or hopping can be done fast or slow. Call attention to how long each method takes.
2. Throwing or rolling a ball can be done fast or slow. Did the ball go a long or a short way with each method?
3. Taking turns on the equipment requires that the children understand that there are not enough trikes, swings, or teeter-totters for everyone and they must wait. If a piece of equipment is in big demand you could use a timer, a clock, or counting as a means of regulating length of turns.
4. Use of outdoor equipment offers opportunities to use basic concepts. Swings—swinging high or low, swinging fast or slow. Jungle gym—"Peter reached the top of the jungle gym first." (This is made as a statement of fact, not the result of a teacher-inspired race.) Sandbox—"I see Mary and Edith sitting beside each other in the sandbox." Teeter—up and down; balancing each other's weight, heavy and light.

Utilizing wall space: This display of numbers from 1 to 10 with the equivalent number of objects next to each one is on a well-travelled stairway. As the children use the stairs to go from one area to another, they can pause to study the relationship between the numbers and the objects.

5. "Two Little Blackbirds" (see variation under Fingerplays and Poems, p. 564.)
6. When playing circle games talk about who is in the middle; who is beside or next to someone else; between, behind, in front of, as appropriate.
7. Skill games (see "Basic Resources"):

   a. Beanbag toss: Use five beanbags. Talk about the results: "The first one got in; the second one didn't go far enough; the third one was close"; "You have two more to throw"; "Count how many you got in."
   b. Johnny can you jump over the puddle: Use measuring stick to see how far each child jumps.
   c. Bowling: Count how many are knocked down and how many are left standing.
   d. Balls: Use different-sized balls; talk about shape and texture.

Extended Experiences

1. Take a ride on a bus and let each child deposit his/her own fare in the box. Look for uses of numbers as you ride around your community.
2. Take a trip to a store to buy something needed for the classroom or a special activity. Notice use of numbers to mark prices of items and the use of scales, cash register, and money.
3. Take a trip to the post office to buy stamps or to mail letters or invitations.
4. Take a walk and look for uses of numbers on houses, stores, street signs. Talk about things that are far and near, tall and short, high and low. Talk about directions: "turn right," "turn left." Count objects you see or find.

Teacher Resources

Pictures and Displays

▷ Clock display: Set out different kinds of clocks on a low table, windup, alarm clock, electric alarm, clock radio, cuckoo clock, cooking timer, egg timer (sandglass), kitchen wall clock, and a clock that strikes on the quarter hour. On wall above table put pictures of clocks that you are not able to obtain, such as grandfather's clock, a sunburst or other decorative clock, or a clock in a church or tower.
▷ Display of scales: Set out metric scales, postal scales, bathroom scales, balance scales, kitchen scales, baby scales. Pictures of those you cannot obtain like health and produce scales could be put up.
▷ Thermometer display: Different kinds of thermometers, indoor–outdoor, deep fat, candy, meat, fever. Pictures of hot and cold objects could be put on the wall behind the table.
▷ Display various kinds of measuring devices—metric ruler, measuring stick, folding rule, metal roll-up tape, measuring tape.
▷ Display a stamp collection: Talk about the shape, size, colour, or subjects. Find the numbers telling how much they are worth. Have different sizes of envelopes and different shapes—square, rectangular, large, medium, and small. Show postal cards with and without pictures and post cards and envelopes with stamp printed on and with stamps glued on.
▷ Display your coins and bills: Talk about shape and size and identify by name.
▷ Talk about the fact that there are pictures on the money. Use only with older or experienced children.

▷ Make a calendar to mount on the wall near your group time area. Use one sheet of construction paper for each month. Make squares at least 4 cm x 4 cm for each day. Dennison or Hallmark stickers can be used to mark special days and birthdays. You can also put on appropriate pictures or symbols to show trips or other special group discoveries that were made or will be made.

▷ Rearrange your room so that a post office or grocery store can be set up between the home-living centre and the block-building centre to encourage interaction between these two groups.

▷ Show pictures of subjects that can be counted or will lead to discoveries about some of the basic concepts in this guide, such as a bridge over water, an empty vase and one filled with flowers, a picture that shows things close up and at a distance.

Books and Periodicals

Evans, Richard. *Piaget: The Man and His Ideas* New York: E.P. Dutton, 1973

Ginsberg, H., and S. Opper. *Piaget's Theory of Intelectual Development.* Englewood Cliffs, NJ: Prentice-Hall, 1979

Lavatelli, Celia. *Piaget's Theory Applied to an Early Childhood Curriculum.* Boston: Boston American Science and Engineering Inc., 1970

Piaget, Jean. *The Child's Conception of Number.* London: Routledge and Kegal Paul, 1952. (If you are fluent in French the original *La Genese du Nombre chez l'Enfant.* Geneva: 1941 is much clearer.)

Skemp, Richard. *The Psychology of Learning Mathematics.* Markham, Ont: Penguin, 1971

The following journals often have useful articles to support the teaching of mathematics

The Journal of the Canadian Association for Young Children

The Canadian Journal of Early Childhood Education

The Ontario Journal of the Association for Early Childhood Education

The Journal of the National Association for the Education of Young Children

Films and Videos

Consult your local library for up to date films and videotapes that are available from the National Film Board and the CBC

Community Resources

▷ Bell Telephone teaching kit

▷ Post office for stamps and posters of stamps

▷ Stamp collectors